COLLEGE OF MARIN LIBRARY
KENTFIELD, CALIFORNIA

WITHDRAWN

The Bantu-speaking Peoples
of Southern Africa

FRONTISPIECE

Zulu diviner (*isangoma*)

The Bantu-speaking Peoples of Southern Africa

Edited by

W. D. Hammond-Tooke

GN
656
H35
1974

Routledge & Kegan Paul
London and Boston

The Bantu-Speaking Tribes of South Africa
was first published in 1937
Sixth impression 1959
This second edition was published in 1974
by Routledge & Kegan Paul Ltd
Broadway House, 68–74 Carter Lane,
London EC4V 5EL and
9 Park Street,
Boston, Mass. 02108, USA
Printed in Great Britain by
W & J Mackay Limited, Chatham
© Routledge & Kegan Paul Ltd 1974
© chapter 9 A. C. Myburgh 1974
© chapter 14 B. A. Pauw 1974
No part of this book may be reproduced in
any form without permission from the
publisher, except for the quotation of brief
passages in criticism

ISBN 0 7100 7748 3

Library of Congress Catalog Card No. 74-75855

Contents

Preface to the First Edition	xii
Preface to the Second Edition	xv
Notes on Contributors	xxi

I The People and their Environment

1 The Biology of the Southern African Negro
        Phillip V. Tobias   3
   I Introductory Thoughts   3
   II Human Biological Parameters   5
   III Affinities and Origins   30

2 The Ecological Setting
        J. P. Jessop   46
   Topography and Climate   46
   Vegetation   49
   Recent Changes in the Vegetation   54
   Pests and Diseases   55
   Game   55

3 The Classification of Cultural Groups
        N. J. van Warmelo   56
   Introduction   56
   Numerical Strength of Groups   59
   Nguni Group   60
   Tsonga Group   68
   Sotho Group   71
   Venda Group   78
   Lemba   81

4 Material Culture
        Margaret Shaw   85
   Settlement   85
   Transport   90
   The Bases of Subsistence   90
   Dress and Ornament   101
   Ritual Life   104
   Music   106
   Dancing   111

CONTENTS

Toys and Games	111
Smoking and Snuff-taking	112
War and Weapons	113
Crafts and Tools	113
Exchange and Trade	126

II The Traditional Societies

5 Traditional Economic Systems
  Basil Sansom

The Traditional Economy	135
	136
Boundaries	137
Economic Regulation and Ecology: A Thesis	138
Adaptations: Type A and Type B	139
The Apparatus for Regulation	145
Cattle as Capital	149
Capital, Interest and Work	152
Grain: Equality of Production	153
Other Products	157
Division of Labour	158
The Management of Familial Production	159
The Dual Economy	167
Subsistence Production Today	168
Draught Animals and the Plough	169
Crops	170
Trading Stores	170
Three Phases of Development	171
Variation and Adjustment	175
Conclusion: The Dual Economy	175

6 Kinship and Marriage
  Eleanor Preston-Whyte

I Broad Characteristics of the Systems of Kinship and Residence among South African Bantu-speaking Peoples	177
II The Nature of Marriage	187
III Unilineal Descent Groups: Clans and Lineages	194
IV The Implications of Marriage Differences	203

7 Growing Up in Traditional Society
  Virginia van der Vliet

The Birth of a Child	212
Infancy	217
Weaning and Early Childhood	219
From Six Years Old to Puberty	220

	Puberty	225
	Initiation Schools	227
	Circumcision	228
	Boys' Initiation Schools	229
	'Supplementary' Schools	231
	Girls' Initiation Schools	232
	The Function of Initiation Schools and Rituals	234
8	Traditional Rulers and their Realms	
	Basil Sansom	246
	I The Types of Bantu State	247
	II Political Themes and Processes	251
	III Case-studies in the Expansion of Polity	267
9	Law and Justice	
	A. C. Myburgh	284
	Introduction	284
	Public Law	287
	Private Law	301
10	World-view I: A System of Beliefs	
	W. D. Hammond-Tooke	318
	Creation, Impersonal Nature and High-Gods	319
	Local and Nature Spirits	321
	The Ancestral Spirits	324
	Extra-Descent Group Ancestors	333
	Witchcraft, Sorcery and the Problem of Evil	335
	Witch Beliefs	337
	Magic of Protection and Cure: The Herbalist	339
11	World-view II: A System of Action	
	W. D. Hammond-Tooke	344
	World-view and Social Roles	345
	The Occasions for Ritual Action	351
	Divination and the Interpretation of Misfortune	356
	World-view and Morality	359

III Incorporation in the Wider Society

12	The Process of Political Incorporation	
	J. A. Benyon	367
	I The Southern Nguni and the Moving Frontier:	
	First Stage	367
	II Natal and Zululand	375
	III The Genesis of the High Commission Territories	378
	IV The Boer Republics	385

CONTENTS

    V The Southern Nguni and the Moving Frontier: Second Stage ... 386
    VI Union and After: 'Homelands' and Heartland ... 390

13 **The Process of Economic Incorporation**
    D. Hobart Houghton ... 397
    Two Centuries of Farming ... 398
    The Mining Revolution ... 401
    The Growth of Manufacturing Industry ... 404
    The Migratory Labour System ... 405
    Vertical Labour Mobility of Africans ... 408
    Earnings and Standard of Living ... 410
    Population Growth and Economic Development ... 412

14 **The Influence of Christianity**
    B. A. Pauw
    I Historical Outline of Missions and Churches ... 415
    II Patterns of Acceptance and Growth of Christianity ... 420
    III The Local Church Group ... 423
    IV Christians in Tribal Society ... 427
    V Belief and Ritual: Christianity and Bantu Tradition ... 430
    VI Christianity among Urban Bantu ... 438

15 **The Impact of the City**
    Allie A. Dubb ... 441
    Introduction ... 441
    African Settlement in Town ... 441
    Why Africans Come to Town ... 444
    The Urban Milieu ... 446
    Urbanization: Some Important Concepts ... 447
    Aspects of Town Life ... 456
    Conclusion ... 468

Bibliographical Index ... 473
Subject Index ... 511
Tribal Index ... 521

Illustrations

Plates

    Zulu diviner (*isangoma*) (M. West)   *Frontispiece*

Facing page

1 Territorial organization   74
  a Swazi homesteads (S.A.R. and H.)
  b Tswana village, Mochudi (I. Schapera)

2 Territorial organization   75
  a Natal Nguni (S.A.R. and H.)
  b Transvaal Sotho (N. J. van Warmelo)

3 Aerial photo of part of Serowe, Botswana. Note horseshoe-shaped sub-wards occupied by lineage segments (Botswana Survey Department)   106

4 Material culture   107
  a Stretching of thong, Gaberone, Botswana, 1962. Note ox licking salt (South African Museum)
  b South Sotho boys with clay oxen, Leribe, Lesotho, 1958 (South African Museum)

5 Material culture   138
  a Ngwane hut with several enclosures, Bergville, Natal, 1969 (South African Museum)
  b Venda man making a twilled basket out of slivers of wood, Sinthumule, Louis Trichardt, 1962 (South African Museum)

6 Agriculture   139
  a Kgatla fields (threshing floors can be seen in the foreground on the right (I. Schapera)
  b Threshing corn (Kgatla) (I. Schapera)

7 Agriculture   170
  a Milking (Kgatla) (I. Schapera)
  b Tlôkwa woman potter, Gaberone, Botswana, 1962 (South African Museum)

ILLUSTRATIONS

8   Interior of a Zulu hut (S.A.R. and H.)   171

9   Initiation   202
    a *Vhusha* rite of the Venda (N. J. van Warmelo)
    b Kgatla *magwane* (male novices) about to be whipped in the *kgotla* (I. Schapera)

10   Dance of the *abakhwetha* (Xhosa) (S.A.R. and H.)   203

11   Zulu wedding dance (S.A.R. and H.)   234

12   Initiation   235
    a and b Scenes from the Venda *domba* (initiation) dance (N. J. van Warmelo)

13   Political life   266
    a Morning gossip at a *kgotla*, Mochudi, Botswana (I. Schapera)
    b Hearing a lawsuit, Kgatla (I. Schapera)

14   World-view   267
    a Divining cause of patient's illness (Venda) (N. J. van Warmelo)
    b Rainmaker performing his magic (Kgatla) (I. Schapera)

15   World-view   298
    a Sacrifice of beer on black calf which symbolizes the shades of the chief's clan (Venda) (N. J. van Warmelo)
    b Sacrificing beer to the spirits of the ancestors (represented by spears). Venda *thevhula* (first-fruits rite) (N. J. van Warmelo)

16   Blessing a newly-ordained minister and his wife in a Zionist church, Soweto, Johannesburg (M. West)   299

17   Independent church ritual   330
    a Healing rite in river near Soweto, Johannesburg (M. West)
    b Zionist healing rite. The exorcism of an evil spirit (M. West)

18   Independent church ritual   331
    a Apostolic bishop blesses a sheep before slaughtering for a feast (M. West)
    b Prophet-healer, Soweto. Note healing aids including candles, stick, Bible, water, vinegar and soap (M. West)

19 Municipal housing in Soweto, Johannesburg, 1972 (M. West) — 362
20 Urban life — 363
    a Single men's hostels, Soweto, Johannesburg, 1972 (M. West)
    b A wealthy man's home in Soweto (M. West)
21 Urban life — 394
    a Sunday afternoon in a Soweto side-street, 1970 (M. West)
    b Selling grilled maize cobs, Soweto (M. West)
22 Urban life — 395
    a Municipal beer hall in Soweto, with municipal police (M. West)
    b A 'Red' migrant in town. Transvaal Ndebele woman selling groundnuts near Orlando station, Soweto (M. West)

Figures

1.1 Sexual dimorphism of stature among Southern African Bantu-speaking Negroes — 6
1.2 Relative sexual dimorphism of stature among Southern African Bantu-speaking Negroes — 7
1.3 Percentual sexual dimorphism of stature — 7
1.4 Skin reflectance in Southern African Negroes and Bushmen — 19
1.5 The spectrum of skin colours in sub-Saharan Africa — 20
1.6 Percentage distribution of A, B and O blood-group phenotypes among 122 Southern African Negro populations — 25
1.7 Estimated percentage of San admixture in 23 populations — 26
5.1 Hierarchies of estates in land — 146
5.2 The house-property complex — 161

Maps

Distribution of principal groups of Bantu-speaking peoples in the Republic of South Africa and surrounding territories — xx
5.1 Bhaca settlement 1949 (after Hammond-Tooke 1962) — 142
5.2 Kgatla settlement at Mochudi c. 1930 (after Schapera 1943c) — 143
5.3 Veld cover in Southern Africa (after J. P. H. Acocks 1953) — 149
5.4 Zones associated with 'Eastern' and 'Western' modes of ecological adaptation — 150
8.1 Lobedu country and settlement pattern (after J. D. and E. J. Krige 1943) — 277

Preface to the First Edition

This book is the outcome of a resolution adopted by the (South African) Inter-University Committee for African Studies in July, 1934, to 'sponsor the preparation and publication of a handbook of South African tribes'. The need for such a book has long been felt, not only by teachers and students of anthropology in the South African Universities, but also by others interested in the racial problems of the country. There exist some large monographs about individual groups or tribes, and many useful short accounts, of a more general nature, published either as articles in scientific journals or as sections of works dealing with the continent as a whole. But there has hitherto been no single comparative survey sufficiently detailed, and sufficiently catholic in scope and content, to form a satisfactory manual of South African ethnography. It is our hope that this work will be found to fulfil reasonably adequately the purpose for which it was written. Increasing specialization in study has made large-scale collaboration not only desirable but essential, and although the book may in consequence perhaps have suffered some loss of unity it has certainly gained in authoritativeness. The contributors have all had considerable first-hand experience of field investigation among the peoples dealt with, and almost all of them are or have been engaged in teaching anthropology, Bantu languages, or allied subjects in South Africa.

The present state of South African ethnography has to some extent dictated the limitations in the range of this book. Certain areas and ethnic stocks have already been dealt with sufficiently fully in standard works to make it unnecessary to include them here as well. The information relating to the Bushmen and Hottentots is summarized in Schapera's *Khoisan Peoples* (1930); the Bergdama of South-West Africa are treated exhaustively in Vedder's great work, *Die Bergdama* (1923); while the small handbook, *The Native Tribes of South-West Africa*, issued in 1928 by the South-West Africa Administration, covers the Ambo and Herero tribes of that Territory, as well as its Bushman, Hottentot, and Bergdama inhabitants. The present work is therefore restricted in the main to the Bantu-speaking peoples of the Union of South Africa and the adjoining British Protectorates, although reference has occasionally been made by some of the writers to other groups for comparative purposes. Our aim all along has been essentially to summarize existing knowledge rather than to present merely the results of individual investigations; but most of the writers have utilized in their contributions original work whose final results have not yet been published.

The greater part of the book is devoted to an account of the Bantu as they were before affected by the intrusion of Western Civilization. The four final Chapters will, however, indicate how considerably their traditional life has already been altered by this overwhelming new influence—a theme more fully treated in another collective work, *Western Civilization and the Natives of South Africa* (edited by I. Schapera, Routledge, 1934). It has rightly become the fashion in modern ethnography to study 'the changing Native', and not to concentrate merely upon his traditional culture. But the understanding of present-day Native life must rest largely upon a knowledge of the former culture, and the time is rapidly approaching when such knowledge will no longer be obtainable in the field. It is highly desirable, therefore, that more intensive fieldwork should be done in this country before too much of the old culture has been obliterated; and if this book succeeds in stimulating any of its readers to inquire more fully into some of the topics or peoples dealt with, it will, for that reason alone, have been worth compiling.

Some reference should be made to the forms used here in writing the names of Bantu tribes and languages. These forms have been chosen in conformity with the principles laid down by the International Institute of African Languages and Cultures, and adopted by the Inter-University Committee for African Studies. All names are used in their root form, without prefixes, as nouns and as adjectives, in the singular and in the plural, e.g. *a Zulu, two Zulu, Zulu customs, Zulu* (the language), not *an umZulu, two amaZulu, isiZulu customs*, and *isiZulu* respectively. The spelling of the forms is that used in the languages themselves, e.g. *Sotho*, not *Suto*; but diacritic signs have been omitted in the commoner names, e.g. *Venda*, not *Venḓa*. The designations applied to the larger cultural groups are those now in common use in South Africa, e.g. *Nguni*, not *Zulu-Xhosa*; *Sotho*, not *Sotho-Tswana*. The only one calling for special comment is that of *Shangana-Tonga*, for the group hitherto known as *Thonga* (more correctly *Tonga*). Since there are at least three other tribal groups in Africa bearing the name *Tonga*, the form *Shangana-Tonga* has been chosen as an identifying designation, in conformity with the principle that when two or more tribes have the same name they should be distinguished from each other by some appropriate geographical or other label.*

The task of editing the book was originally entrusted by the Committee to Professor W. M. Eiselen, of the University of Stellenbosch, and Professor I. Schapera, of the University of Cape Town. Soon after its commencement, however, Professor Eiselen was appointed Chief Inspector of Native Education for the Transvaal Province, and owing to the pressure of his new duties he felt obliged to relinquish any further share in the work. He was also unfortunately unable to contribute the various Chapters originally allotted to him, apart from his section of the Chapter on 'Religious Beliefs and Practices'. The Committee thereupon invited Professor Schapera to carry on as sole Editor.

The Editor wishes here to thank his collaborators for the generous assistance they have given him, not only in the preparation of their own articles, but also in advice regarding the book as a whole. He would also mention

PREFACE TO THE FIRST EDITION

Professor R. F. A. Hoernlé and Mr J. D. Rheinallt Jones who, although not contributors to the book, have been of much help in various matters relating to its preparation. He is further indebted to Mr V. Ellenberger for the photograph forming the Frontispiece; to Dr N. J. van Warmelo for Plates II, III, IV, VI*b*, VIII*a*, XIX*a*, XX, and XXI, and for the map showing the location of the principal tribes dealt with; to the Publicity Department of the South African Railways and Harbours Administration for Plates V*a*, VI*a*, IX, X, and XVI; to the Rev. J. Reyneke for Plates VIII*b* and XXII*a*; to Mrs E. P. Hellmann for Plate XXIII*a*; to Mr A. J. H. Goodwin for Plate XXIII*b*; and to Mr H. V. Meyerowitz for Plate XXIV.

* Since the above was written, and after most of the proofs had already been corrected, the Inter-University Committee for African Studies, at a meeting held in November, 1936, adopted a recommendation that the form *Shangana-Tonga* should be employed when writing of Africa generally, but that when reference is clearly being restricted to South Africa the shorter form *Tonga* is sufficiently accurate to stand alone. The occurrence of both forms in the text is due to the fact that the recommendation came too late to allow of uniform changes being made throughout the proofs.

Preface to the Second Edition

While on a visit to the London School of Economics in the autumn of 1968 I renewed acquaintance with my former teacher, Professor I. Schapera. He suggested to me that the time was ripe for a new edition of *The Bantu-speaking Tribes of South Africa*, a completely revised, authoritative version that would incorporate new knowledge achieved since the volume was first published in 1937 and make use of new interpretative insights. Professor Schapera felt that the burden of this revision should be shouldered by a younger generation of South African scholars and asked me to undertake the task of editing the work. This I agreed to do, not without some hesitation as to the responsibility of producing a worthy successor to the original book, which has been an indispensable handbook to a generation of students of anthropology in South African universities. The result is the present volume.

Those familiar with the original book will notice two changes. The one is in the title. We have called our volume *The Bantu-speaking Peoples of Southern Africa*.* The reason for this is the vagueness and ambiguity of the word 'tribe' as currently used by both anthropologists and laymen. Technical definitions range from the 'group the members of which claim unity on the grounds of their conception of a specific common culture' (Nadel 1942: 17), through Gluckman's formulation of 'tribal society' as one with simple technology, an egalitarian standard of living, lack of socio-economic classes, and dominated by status based on kinship and multiplex relations (Gluckman 1965: 4ff.), to Evans-Pritchard's explicit use of political criteria. For him, the tribe is the largest group of people 'who, besides recognizing themselves as a distinct local community, affirm their obligation to combine in warfare against outsiders and acknowledge the right of their members to compensation for injury' (Evans–Pritchard 1940: 5).[1]

Although all Southern Bantu have state-type societies, unlike, for instance, the position among some East African peoples, the problem is not resolved thereby. The Xhosa, for example, are a congeries of peoples of diverse provenance, but practising a common culture and with a strong sense of historical unity, divided into nine chiefdoms whose heads (with one exception) all belong to a common royal lineage. Each chiefdom was autonomous, except in ritual matters when deference was paid to the genealogically senior chief, often termed a 'paramount' (Hammond-Tooke 1965a). Does one call this whole cluster of chiefdoms a tribe or should the term (as is usually the case) be reserved for the chiefdom itself? And what of smaller cultural groups which lead a fairly autonomous existence without chiefs? I have asked my colleagues to use, where possible, the term *chiefdom* for the political units under chiefs and *people* for the larger (and vaguer) cultural-regional groups, but it has been impossible to avoid completely the term 'tribal' as a synonym for 'traditional'. Where it occurs it means just that: there are no pejorative overtones of 'primitive', 'backward' or 'inferior'.

The same goes for 'tribesman'. Where used it refers to Africans who are, in Mayer's phrase, country-rooted, and who belong to rural communities which are under the immediate control of chiefs and headmen. Their value system tends to be strongly traditionalist and conservative, but not all country folk are tribesmen in this sense. There are, for instance, the country-rooted 'School people' whose reference group is white South Africa and who are western in their orientation and way of life. Structurally they are tribesmen in that they live in 'tribal' society: culturally they are not traditionalists, though many still have a lively respect for chiefs. Another important class, the farm people, are more difficult to classify. While not living under chiefs, they tend to be strongly conservative. Little work has been done on their social life since the publication of the original volume (apart from Loudon 1970), and reference is made to Professor Wilson's chapter there and to *Reaction to Conquest* (Hunter 1936 and 1937).[2]

Gulliver (1969b: 24), who still finds the term indispensable, defines a tribe as 'any group of people which is distinguished, by its members and by others, on the basis of cultural-regional criteria'. Members of such a group, when confronted by alien tribesmen in the town situation, tend to categorize them on an ethnic basis and to behave towards them in broadly stereotyped ways. This phenomenon, familiar from the Copperbelt (Mitchell 1956b), has not been documented for South Africa, but no doubt exists in the emerging African urban society on the Witwatersrand and elsewhere where Nguni, Sotho, Venda and Tsonga intermingle. Mayer's work in East London (Mayer 1961) showed that the main clash there was not between members of chiefdoms or of what I have called elsewhere 'tribal clusters' (more correctly *chiefdom clusters*), but between two groups, Xhosa and Mfengu, who have a history of conflict extending over a century. It is relevant that the African population of Eastern Cape towns is predominantly Cape Nguni. Research urgently needs to be done on the role of *tribalism*, in this sense, in situations of competition for jobs in urban labour centres or, in the Transkei and other areas with limited self-government, for political power. Tribalism in town is a relative term reflecting social distance—and a useful category for defining sectional interests.

The other main departure from the original book is in approach and content. The present volume concentrates on general ethnography and on social change, among the African peoples of the Republic of South Africa, Mozambique and the former High Commission Territories of Botswana, Lesotho and Swaziland. Apart from Professor Tobias's valuable chapter on human biology and Dr Jessop's survey of physical regions, the approach is confined to what Schapera called in his *Select Bibliography* (1941) 'general ethnography' and 'modern status and conditions'. The sections on language and music have been omitted. The main reason for this is that the increase of data has involved great pressure on space: in any event development of Bantu linguistic studies has been such as to deserve a volume on its own. It is hoped that the narrower coverage is amply compensated for by the attainment of depth.

Despite the lapse of thirty-seven years since the appearance of the original volume it cannot be said that our knowledge of the Bantu-speaking peoples of Southern Africa has made spectacular progress, especially with regard to their social life (advances on the biological front have been much more impressive). There have been a few outstanding monographs on specific groups, notably the Kriges' elegant account of the fascinating *Realm of a Rain-Queen* (1943), Hilda Kuper's brilliant analysis of rank among the Swazi (1947a), and Schapera's extensive documentation of the Tswana, but the quantity and quality of research papers on specific aspects of social life is not particularly impressive. There has been enough to make a new synthesis imperative, but there are still large gaps in our knowledge. This becomes glaringly evident when comparative surveys, such as underpin most of the chapters in this book, are undertaken. Apart from sheer lack of information on certain societies there is the problem of quite patent inaccuracies and misunderstandings in the sources, particularly those deriving from earlier writers. The problem most contributors have faced is whether to take these at their face value or to enter into a lengthy exegesis, for which space was not always available. Most of us have reached a compromise.

To return to the plan of the book. It is divided into three sections—dealing respectively with the people and their environment, the traditional social and cultural systems and the processes of incorporation into the wider (plural) society.

The first four chapters are introductory. Professor Tobias discusses the present state of our knowledge of the African peoples from the biological point of view, and this is followed by a botanist's account of the environmental background, the stage on which the people play out their social life. In chapter 3 Dr N. J. van Warmelo has brought his unrivalled knowledge to bear in a greatly-expanded exposition of traditional groupings (he has also wise words to say on the pitfalls of historical reconstruction), and Miss E. M. Shaw deals with the close relationship between the resources of the Southern African eco-system and material culture.

Section II discusses, from the point of view of comparative institutions, the nature of traditional Southern Bantu societies. This emphasis on 'timeless ethnography' was an important focus of the original book, and the intrinsic importance of these societies for our understanding of the wide diversity of human culture needs no justification, or apology. The difficulties and dangers of reconstructing the past have been stressed too many times to need recapitulation here. What is perhaps necessary, in a study emanating from South Africa, is to state unequivocally that the contributors, in making

PREFACE TO THE SECOND EDITION

their analyses, are all aware that what they are describing is undergoing (and has undergone) extensive change. This is often quite explicit in their chapters. The material handled in Section II is important, not only because it presents pictures of what Marwick has called 'Nature's experiments in human living' (Marwick 1958: 193) and, as such, is a contribution to our collection of models of social forms, but also because large numbers of our fellow countrymen still live in societies (or part-societies) in which traditional values and forms of behaviour are part of the warp and weft of existence. This fact is part of the reality of the South African situation.

If a realization of the presence of change is implicit in much of Section II, it becomes explicit in Section III. For over three centuries an incorporative process has taken place that has drawn the traditional societies of the southern part of the continent into a wider society, breaking down the exclusiveness of the chiefdoms, creating new values and goals and, for some, exchanging the particularism of traditionalists for the universalistic norms of Western-oriented townsmen and rural School people. It is doubtful whether the traditional societies were ever entirely closed—there was always movement of peoples between chiefdoms, trade, 'diplomatic' royal marriages and cultural borrowing; after the various annexations (extending from the early years of the moving frontier to the accelerated take-overs during the 1870s)[3] and, particularly after the development of mining enterprises after 1870, they ceased forever to be so. Today the traditional societies form pockets of relatively intense interaction within a total social structure in which Africans are inextricably involved in economic relations with all other groups and in which membership of common organizations, such as the church, and an overall political system, bring all within a common social field, although perhaps to a lesser extent now than in the immediate past.

The four final chapters seek to document this process of change, both political and economic, and the reaction of tribesmen to the challenges of Christianity and urbanization. Involvement in political and economic change concerns all, however indirectly; the challenge of the other two depends still on a voluntary commitment, which may be withheld.

We have not considered it necessary, in a book of this nature, to discuss in detail the South African system in general, or the official policy of 'separate development' in particular. This has been discussed in numerous studies and is well known. Reference has been made to the position of Africans in the total society, especially in Section III, but the reader should always be aware of the nature of the wider South African plural society. The same is true for the ex-High Commission Territories which have seen dramatic changes since independence.

It remains for me to express my gratitude to the contributors to this volume for agreeing to collaborate and for producing their manuscripts (more or less) on time, to Mrs D. du Toit of Rhodes University and Mrs Arlene Guslandi of the University of the Witwatersrand, who uncomplainingly coped with the typing, to Dr Martin West and the South African Museum

PREFACE TO THE SECOND EDITION

for permission to reproduce new photographs of urban and ethnographic interest, and especially to Professor Schapera for graciously allowing the mantle of editorship to be placed ritually on my shoulders. I should like to retain continuity with the past by quoting from his original Preface: 'if this book succeeds in stimulating any of its readers to inquire more fully into some of the topics or peoples dealt with, it will, for that reason alone, have been worth compiling'.

W. D. H.-T.

Department of Social Anthropology,
University of the Witwatersrand,
Johannesburg

Notes

* Although we have tried to avoid the term 'Bantu', the use of which has political overtones in the Republic of South Africa, it has not always been possible to do so. In any event the term (originally a linguistic one) is a useful, if not indispensable, shorthand for the more cumbersome 'Bantu speaking-peoples', especially in adjectival form, and has a long history in the scientific literature.

1. For a full discussion of the problem of definition see Gulliver (1969b), Argyle (1969), and the essays in Gulliver (1969a). Also, for an American viewpoint, Helm (1968).

2. See also Roberts (1959) for a discussion of the economic conditions of farm labourers, and SABRA (1954); du Toit (1959); South Africa (1939).

3. See chapter 12, Wilson and Thompson (1969) and Thompson (1969). For a discussion of the relative 'openness' of Xhosa society see Raum (1969).

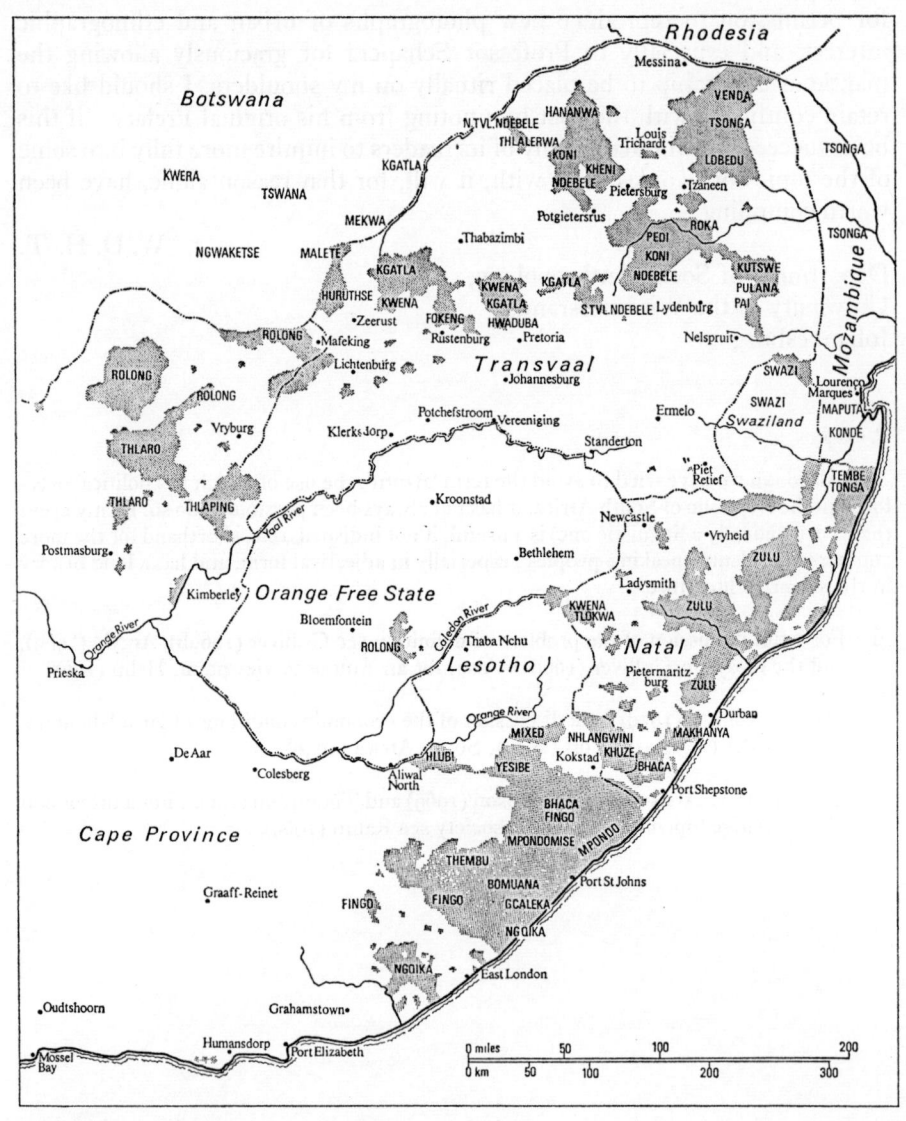

Distribution of principal groups of Bantu-speaking peoples in the Republic of South Africa and surrounding territories

Notes on Contributors

Phillip V. Tobias, Ph.D., D.Sc., M.B., B.Ch., F.R.A.I., F.R.S.S. Afr., is Professor of Anatomy in the University of the Witwatersrand, Johannesburg.

J. P. Jessop, M.Sc. (Cape Town), Ph.D. (Rhodes), is Chief Botanist, Botanic Gardens, Adelaide, South Australia.

N. J. van Warmelo, M.A., Ph.D., now in semi-retirement, was formerly Chief Ethnologist, Department of Bantu Administration and Development, Republic of South Africa.

Margaret Shaw, B.A. (Cape Town), is Ethnologist and Deputy Director of the South African Museum, Cape Town.

Basil Sansom, B.A. (Hons) (Rand), Ph.D. (Manchester), is Lecturer in Social Anthropology in the University of Manchester.

Eleanor Preston-Whyte, B.Soc.Sc. (Hons), Ph.D. (Natal), is Senior Lecturer in Social Anthropology in the University of Natal.

Virginia van der Vliet, B.A. (Hons) (Rand), is Lecturer in Social Anthropology at Rhodes University, Grahamstown.

A. C. Myburgh, B.A., LLB (Stell.), D.Phil. (Pret.), is Professor of Anthropology in the University of South Africa, Pretoria.

W. D. Hammond-Tooke, M.A., Ph.D. (Cape Town), is Professor of Social Anthropology in the University of the Witwatersrand, Johannesburg. He was formerly Professor of Social Anthropology at Rhodes University, Grahamstown.

J. A. Benyon, B.A. (Hons) (Rhodes), M.A., D.Phil. (Oxon), is Senior Lecturer in History at Rhodes University, Grahamstown.

D. Hobart Houghton, B.A. (S.A.), M.A. (Oxon), was Director of the Institute of Social and Economic Research, Rhodes University. He

NOTES ON CONTRIBUTORS

was also formerly Professor of Economics and Economic History at that University.

B. A. Pauw, M.A., B.D. (Stell.), Ph.D. (Cape Town), is Professor of Anthropology in the University of South Africa, Pretoria.

Allie A. Dubb, M.A., Ph.D (Rhodes), is Senior Lecturer in Social Anthropology in the University of the Witwatersrand, Johannesburg.

I
The People and their Environment

1
The People and
their Environment

Chapter 1
The Biology of the Southern African Negro*
Phillip V. Tobias

I Introductory Thoughts

Africa is the second largest of the world's land-masses. Its surface area of some 30 million square kilometres comprises no less than 22·4 per cent of the inhabited parts of the globe (excluding Antarctica). Yet its peoples constitute less than 10 per cent of the total world population. Of an estimated 3,600 million people on earth at mid-1970, about 350 million inhabited the African continent.

Approximately one-third of the population, or some 115 million, dwell in North Africa including the Sahara; the remaining two-thirds, or about 235 million people, live in sub-Saharan Africa. Fifty million of these 235 million people occupy the ten territories of Southern Africa, with which we are mainly concerned here.[1] About 85 per cent of the 50 million—or some 42·25 million —are classified linguistically as belonging to one or other of the family of Bantu language groups. The remaining 7·75 million people in Southern Africa comprise whites, coloureds, Asians, and non-Bantu African groups such as the San (Bushmen), Khoikhoi (Hottentots), Griqua and Twa.

The peoples of sub-Saharan Africa are divided by language, culture, economic systems, social structure, tribal or chiefdom limits, political boundaries and geographical barriers, into myriad populations. These populations, in turn, have been classified on a variety of criteria, such as language and mode of subsistence. The units vary in size from several millions (e.g. the Xhosa and Zulu peoples) to a few hundred or even fewer (e.g. certain San groups and the surviving Kora Khoikhoi).

The picture is complicated because the definition of a population by one set of criteria like language frequently does not coincide with the limits set by other criteria such as chiefdom, mode of subsistence or political boundaries. For example, the pastoral and hoe-cultural Swazi people are located, in approximately equal numbers, both in Swaziland and in the Eastern Transvaal (Republic of South Africa). Second, the San (Bushmen) are to be found in Botswana, South-West Africa, Angola, South Africa, Rhodesia and Zambia —and some of those who speak one or other of the Bushman languages are hunters and gatherers, whilst others are pastoralists.

If it is hard to find accord on population limits by such social, cultural, political and economic criteria, it is doubly so when one brings biological variables into the picture. For the physical anthropologist, too, studies populations. Only his conception of a population is different again from those of the demographer, the social anthropologist and the linguist.

The modern approach to the study of human biological diversity starts out by seeking to identify breeding populations, their genetic composition (or gene-pool) and limits of variability. Once we have some idea of the genetic make-up of populations, we may, if we choose, use such information for purposes of classification, which has long been a goal of classical physical anthropology. Today, classification is seen to be less biologically meaningful as an object of study. The new approach stresses rather the environmental or selective pressures which have led populations to diverge in genetic composition. It is concerned with the adaptive benefits, the usefulness, the survival value, the selective advantage or disadvantage, of a particular gene or set of genes. Thus, it sees man in his environment, physical, biotic, social. It demands a closer look at that environment—and at past environments which operated when the distinctive features of a population evolved.

In Africa, the speed of social and political changes, with massive population movements, has created special difficulties. Numbers of populations are no longer living in the areas where their gene-pool came into being; and many of these have not been in the new areas long enough for the new niche to have effected any serious change in genetic composition. A recent immigrant population may have come to live cheek by jowl with an ancient population, long-established in the same area. Thus, two populations may be neighbours, but may evince marked differences in genetic make-up from each other.

Such problems make a micro-taxonomy of sub-Saharan peoples most difficult, if not impossible. Hiernaux (1968a: 106–17) abandoned all the old classifications and simply analysed data, anthropometrical and genetical, for some hundreds of African populations. By applying a variety of measures of biological distance from population to population, he sought meaningful or suggestive clusters of samples upon which to base a classification—and, using his set of parameters, he sought in vain.

Taxonomy at this fine level of population analysis is a risky business. We do not pretend to be able to offer a meaningful biological taxonomy of the Bantu-speaking peoples of Southern Africa. The most we can hope to do at present is to characterize the traits of sub-Saharan peoples in general; and within the broad spectrum to delineate the biologically most distinct groups, such as the San, from other sub-Saharan Africans, such as the family of Bantu-speakers.

Demographic note

With its 350 million people inhabiting 30 million square kilometres, Africa has an average population density of fewer than twelve people per square kilometre. In contrast, the world average is twenty-seven per square kilometre. These figures speak tellingly of the sparseness of Africa's populace by world standards.

Within the ten territories of Southern Africa, 50 million people occupy 5·9 million square kilometres. Hence, the population density of Southern Africa is roughly 8·5 people per square kilometre, or scarcely three-quarters of the density for the whole of Africa.

At the same time, it is a population which is growing rapidly. Its estimated annual increase of 2·4 per cent is exceeded only by that of Asia with an average annual increase of some 2·9 per cent.

These demographic data are important, because the genetic effects of rapid growth in a relatively small population may be expected to differ somewhat from those of slow growth in a large, relatively stable population.

Within Southern Africa, the rate of population growth varies considerably. Thus, Cappieri was able to adduce figures to show that the Tswana population of Botswana was increasing more than twice as rapidly as the Sotho of Lesotho, while the Bantu-speakers of Rhodesia were multiplying more than one-and-a-half times as rapidly as the Swazi (Cappieri 1950: 1–18).

Moreover, as mentioned previously, the population at risk varies considerably from one chiefdom to another.

These demographic differences, coupled with variations in the degree to which exogamy and endogamy are practised, affect the intensity and direction of gene-flow within and between populations. Thus, socio-cultural practices may have important repercussions on the genetic structure of a population and on gene-diffusion between populations.

Migration and genetic structure

The present geographical location of many populations is a relatively recent development. Historical and prehistorical records reveal great population movements up and down Africa in the past 2,000 years and, especially, the last few centuries. Thus, the great southward march of Bantu-speaking Africans (Dart 1937: 1–31) and the northward reverse migrations of Nguni-speaking peoples in the nineteenth century, and of Khoikhoi and Basters in the eighteenth and nineteenth centuries, have blurred the distribution patterns of phenotypes and of marker genes. In consequence, only the most rapidly selected or eco-sensitive systems of genes may be expected to provide any clear-cut evidence for presently or recently operating selective agencies, since few populations would seem to have been subject to their present conditions for very long (Tobias 1969: 4–21).

II Human Biological Parameters

(1) Stature (body height)

Southern African Negroes are of medium height, that is, the average stature falls in the range 1600 to 1700 mm (about 63 to 67 inches). Of 89 populations surveyed, no fewer than 76 of the averages lie between these limits. Of the rest, one sample—that of the Nyasa Maravi of Northern Mozambique—has a mean (1590 mm) in the short category; whilst twelve samples fall in the lower part of the tall category. The main focus of these moderately taller populations lies in Angola, Zambia, South West Africa and Botswana; a secondary focus occurs among the Nguni-speaking peoples of the Eastern Cape, Natal, Swaziland and Mozambique.

Data for Southern African Negro women are available for only nine samples. These show that, on the average, female stature is 93·2 per cent of male stature, although the values range widely among these populations—from 88·2 to 95·0 per cent (Figures 1.1 and 1.2). If these data are added to those of Hiernaux (1968b: 42–50) for 35 other sub-Saharan populations, the overall average for 42 sub-Saharan African groups is 93·7 per cent (Tobias 1972a). In contrast, the corresponding figure in 41 European samples is 93·2 per cent (Hiernaux, 1968a). This confirms Hiernaux's conclusion that sexual dimorphism in sub-Saharan Africa is on the average less than it is in Europe. The trend is maintained if data for a further 6 San (Bushman) series are added, making 48 African samples in all (Figure 1.3). The histogram for African samples shows a clear shift to the left compared with that for European populations.

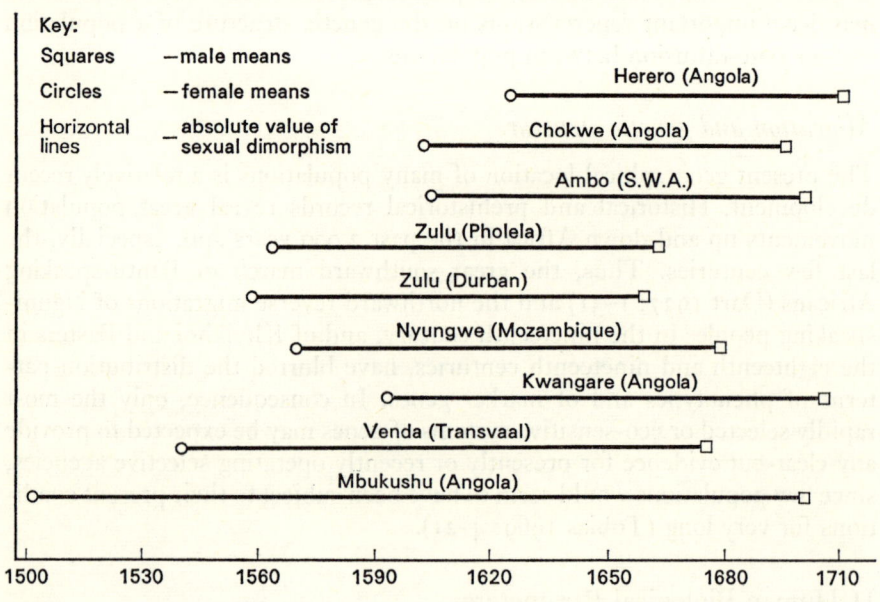

FIGURE 1.1 *Sexual dimorphism of stature among Southern African Bantu-speaking Negroes*

The figure shows mean stature (in mm) for male and female samples of nine Southern African Negro populations from Angola, Mozambique, South Africa and South-West Africa.

THE BIOLOGY OF THE SOUTHERN AFRICAN NEGRO

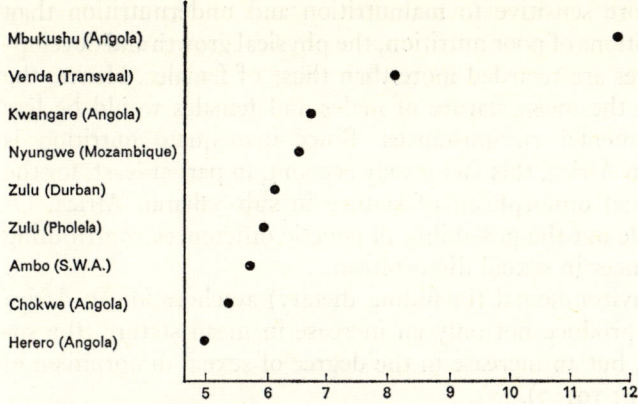

FIGURE 1.2 *Relative sexual dimorphism of stature among Southern African Bantu-speaking Negroes* $\left(\dfrac{\male\bar{x} - \female\bar{x}}{\male\bar{x}} \times 100\right)$

The figure shows relative sexual dimorphism of stature among nine Southern African Negro populations: the difference between the adult male mean and the adult female mean is expressed as a percentage of the adult male mean. Values range from 5·0 to 11·8 per cent, the average being 6·8 per cent. Thus, on the average, female stature is 93·2 per cent of male stature in Southern African Negroes.

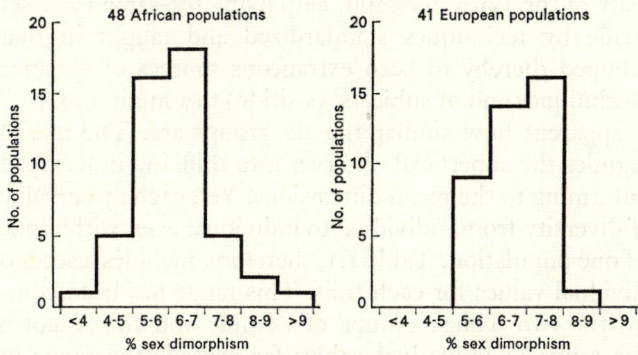

FIGURE 1.3 *Percentual sexual dimorphism of stature*

The figure shows the relative or percentual sexual dimorphism of stature in 48 African and 41 European populations. The lower the value, the less the degree of sexual dimorphism. The histogram for the African samples shows a clear shift to the left, compared with that for the European samples; that is, there is somewhat less sexual dimorphism of stature in Africa than in Europe.

The explanation for the different degrees of sexual dimorphism of stature in Africa and Europe, as Hiernaux points out, may be genetic, environmental or both. While no clear evidence is presently available for genetic differences being responsible, a possible environmental explanation suggests itself: males are known to be more sensitive to malnutrition and undernutrition than females. Under conditions of poor nutrition, the physical growth and development of male juveniles are retarded more than those of females. Hence, the discrepancy between the mean stature of males and females would be less under poor environmental circumstances. Since inadequate nutrition is widely encountered in Africa, this factor may account, in part at least, for the somewhat lower sexual dimorphism of stature in sub-Saharan Africa. Of course, we cannot rule out the possibility of genetic differences contributing as well to the differences in sexual dimorphism.

As a corollary, environmental (including dietary) amelioration in Africa may be expected to produce not only an increase in mean stature (the so-called secular trend), but an increase in the degree of sexual dimorphism of stature (Tobias 1970b: 101–7).

(2) *Other bodily measurements and indices*

In Table 1.1, ranges of mean values are given for a selection of bodily measurements and indices for adult male samples of six Southern Bantu populations, two in Zambia, one in Angola, one in Malawi and two in South Africa. These six populations are, of course, not the only ones for which data are available. They have been selected partly to give a good geographical spread, and partly because all six groups have been measured by workers from the Anatomy Department, University of the Witwatersrand, employing the same basic set of measurements, made by techniques standardized and taught in that Department. It was hoped thereby to keep extraneous sources of variance (such as diversity of techniques and of subjects' position) to a minimum.

It is immediately apparent how similar the six groups are. The use of means alone often beguiles the superficial observer into thinking in terms of *typical individuals* conforming to the mean dimensions. Yet, each mean value covers a multitude of diversity from individual to individual even within one sex- and age-group of one population. Table 1.1, therefore, includes a second range, namely of individual values for each trait. This range has been compiled from data from the two Tonga groups of Zambia and the Angolan group. Obviously, the range of individual values far exceeds the range of sample means.

Most of the Southern African groups have a relatively light body weight, of the order of 56–8 kg. Two somewhat heavier groups are the Plateau Tonga (62·9 kg) and the urban Venda (64·1 kg). Both groups are apparently exposed to more favourable living conditions, especially nutritional, than the other closely related groups; the weights seem to reflect this difference more strikingly than do the stature and other bodily dimensions.

The striking bodily characteristics of the Southern African Bantu Negro are medium stature; slender build reflected in the relatively light weight for any given height, in the moderate breadth measurements of the trunk and in the small thoracic circumference; relatively long upper limbs and especially

TABLE 1.1 *Selected bodily measurements and indices of Southern African Bantu-speaking Negroes (adult males): ranges of sample means and of individual values from six populations*[1]

Trait	Range of sample means	Range of individual values
Weight (kg)	56·0–64·0	36·7–86·2
Stature	1657·0–1686·1	1507·5–1839·5
Sitting height	836·1–847·0	742·5–916·0
Cristal height (height of iliac crest)	984·1–1033·0	858·0–1203·0
Bi-acromial diameter (shoulder breadth)	358·8–387·7	304·0–420·5
Bicristal (bi-iliac) diameter	248·5–259·2	219·0–298·5
Thoracic circumference	825·2–873·8	731·0–970·0
Span	1766·8–1788·1	1479·0–2007·5
Length of upper limb (acromial height—dactylion height)	769·5–778·4	632·0–939·5
Arm circumference	240·7–270·2	200·0–328·0
Fore-arm circumference	196·8–223·6	—
Humeral bi-epicondylar diameter	66·6–67·9	—
Hand length	183·8–189·3	137·5–211·0
Hand breadth	81·3–86·3	54·5–96·0
Length of lower limb (stature—sitting height)	817·7–837·9	719·5–988·5
Thigh circumference	454·0–491·3	—
Leg circumference	277·9–349·9	—
Femoral bicondylar diameter	91·3–92·8	—
Relative sitting height (sitting height/stature)	50·2–51·2	46·1–60·8
Relative shoulder breadth (bi-acromial diameter/stature)	21·3–23·2	18·2–25·2
Relative span (span/stature)	105·9–107·2	93·8–115·2
Relative upper limb length (upper limb length/stature)	46·1–46·7	39·1–56·4
Relative fore-arm length (fore-arm length/stature)	15·3–15·7	12·9–18·9
Brachial index (fore-arm length/upper arm length)	77·9–81·9	58·2–117·4
Relative lower limb length (lower limb length/stature)	49·1–49·9	45·4–54·8

[1] The populations comprise Valley Tonga and Plateau Tonga (Zambia), Angolans, Nyasa Maravi (Malawi), urban Venda and rural Venda (South Africa).

forearms; relatively short trunk and long lower limbs. In fact, the mean relative lower limb lengths for two populations (Angolans 49·9, Plateau Tonga 49·8) are greater than any recorded by Martin-Saller (1959: 964) for adult male samples of nineteen populations from all parts of the world.

The groups which are somewhat more favourably situated (Plateau Tonga in relation to Valley Tonga, urban Venda in comparison with rural Venda) show an increase in *absolute* body weight and stature, length of lower limb, chest circumference, limb circumferences, and hand dimensions, but most *relative* measurements (except the relative lower limb length) show a drop, presumably because of the increase in stature.

(3) *Head measurements and indices*

Table 1.2 lists a selection of head measurements and indices for the same series of populations. The Table brings out the relatively narrow limits within which the sample means vary. As before, ranges of individual values have been included.

In absolute terms, the mean maximum head lengths fall partly into the long (186–93 mm) and partly into the very long (194–X mm) classes, whilst the mean maximum cephalic breadths lie entirely in the narrow category (140–7 mm). As a result, the average cephalic index, that time-honoured analytical tool of physical anthropologists, lies in the dolichocephalic category (71·0–75·9 per cent). Individuals in our populations range from hyperdolichocephalic (X–70·9 per cent), to the upper end of the brachycephalic category (81·0–85·4 per cent).

The head is of medium height in five of our six samples, the mean head height/length index falling into the orthocephalic category (58·0–62·9 per cent). One sample, the Angolan, is relatively high-headed: it has a mean (63·8 per cent) in the hypsicephalic category (63·0–X per cent).

The mean breadth of the forehead (minimum frontal breadth) is medium to just above medium, in comparison with Martin-Saller's (1959: 1277) list of means for populations. Despite the long, narrow braincases, the faces tend to be of medium length in relation to their breadth. Thus, the mean total facial indices of five out of six of our populations fall into the mesoprosopic category (84·0–87·9 per cent), while that of the Plateau Tonga (83·1 per cent) lies in the broad-faced or euryprosopic category (79·0–83·9 per cent). Galloway's (1937: 351–64) mean index for fifty male adult Ambo of South West Africa was 83·8 per cent, which, too, lies in the euryprosopic class.

In her study on skulls of South African Negroes (Natal and Cape Nguni, Sotho and Shangana-Tsonga), de Villiers (1968: 218–19) found that, while the mean for a pooled sample of 454 adult crania lay in the mesoprosopic category (85·0–89·9 per cent on dried skulls), there was, too, a strong tendency towards the long, thin (leptoprosopic) face. No fewer than 47·9 per cent of her sample fell into the leptoprosopic category, as compared with 48·9 per cent in the mesoprosopic and 3·2 per cent in the euryprosopic categories. Her

TABLE 1.2 *Selected head measurements and indices of Southern African Bantu-speaking Negroes (adult males): ranges of sample means and of individual values from six populations*

Trait	Range of sample means	Range of individual values
Head length	191·3–196·4	171·0–212·0
Head breadth	141·9–145·8	129·0–161·0
Cephalic index	73·1–74·8	66·8–85·2
Head circumference	547·9–558·9	510·0–591·0
Head height	119·5–122·1	98·7–137·5
Head height/length index	61·3–63·8	50·1–70·9
Minimum frontal breadth	105·0–108·7	94·0–123·0
Frontoparietal breadth index	73·3–76·2	65·7–85·9
Total facial height	115·7–120·4	96·0–137·5
Upper facial height	69·8–71·9	51·0–85·5
Bizygomatic breadth	132·4–139·3	119·0–152·0
Bigonial breadth	99·2–104·9	80·5–119·0
Facial index	83·1–87·3	72·1–103·0
Upper facial index	50·8–53·7	40·8–66·3
Binocular breadth	91·3–100·2	77·5–112·5
Interocular breadth	35·4–36·8	27·5–49·0
Interocular/Binocular breadth index	36·6–38·8	27·6–51·1
Ear length	54·1–59·3	44·9–70·5
Ear breadth	32·8–36·5	26·0–44·0
Ear index	58·4–61·3	46·9–86·7
Nasal length	50·5–53·2	38·0–62·0
Nasal breadth	43·4–46·9	32·1–54·0
Nasal index	81·6–92·9	62·0–144·9
Transverse nasofacial index	31·4–33·7	25·7–40·1
Mouth height	22·1–27·2	10·5–34·5
Mouth breadth	54·7–57·9	44·0–65·5
Mouth height index	18·6–22·8	10·0–29·5

data for skulls suggest some variation among different groups of South African Negroes.

The tendency of the upper part of the face (i.e. excluding the lower jaw) is to be medium to long in relation to the facial (bizygomatic) breadth. On the other hand, the total face (which includes the lower jaw) on the average tends from medium to less than medium height. The inference is that the lower jaw in our six samples is not overly deep. In de Villiers's four samples of skulls, the mandible is appreciably deep in the chin region, thus reversing the distribution of the upper and total facial indices. For the inclusion of a deep chin obviously lengthens the face as a whole.

The characteristic broadening of the Negro nose produces in our six populations mean nasal indices ranging from 81·6 to 92·9 per cent, that is, from the mesorrhine to the chamaerrhine classes. Variability, however, is considerable and individual noses among 520 living South African Negroes have indices ranging from 62·0 per cent to 144·9 per cent, that is, through all categories from the narrow-nosed (leptorrhine) to the very broad-nosed (hyperchamaerrhine). Such a spectrum of noses is to be found in virtually all our samples, underlying once more the wealth of variability in individual human populations, as well as the danger of 'typing' any single person on one or more of his facial features.

The eyes are fairly well spaced apart, as is shown by the interocular-binocular index. In absolute dimensions, the ears are small, especially in length (or ear-height): short, squat ears are a widespread and striking characteristic of Africans. The mouth height, which reflects the thickness and degree of eversion of the lips, is large: the means of six adult male series range from 22·1 to 27·2 mm. Isolated individuals, however, may have a mouth height as low as 10·5 mm or, on the other hand, as high as 34·5 mm.

(4) Skeletal features

(a) The skull

A definitive study on the skulls of Southern African Negroes has been made by Dr Hertha de Villiers (1968). She analysed in considerable detail 745 crania and 648 mandibles from the following sub-groups: Natal Nguni, Cape Nguni, and Sotho; in addition, there are male samples of Shangana-Tsonga and a variety of smaller sub-samples (e.g. Venda, Kalanga, Malawi, Transvaal Ndebele etc.). These groups were all analysed separately, but it became strikingly clear that there were no major intergroup differences. As de Villiers stated, 'For practical craniological purposes, the tribal series may be regarded as samples of a single South African Negro population' (1968: 201). The following account is based largely upon the work of de Villiers.

The brain-case of the South African Negro is both absolutely long (male mean 186·3 mm, female mean 180·8 mm) and relatively long or dolichocranial (males 72·1 per cent, females 73·2 per cent). It is moderate in height or orthocranial, the mean ratio of height to length being 71·5 per cent in males and 71·1 per cent in females. In shape, most of the crania are ovoid, as viewed from above. The forehead region is smoothly and evenly curved in all directions. The brow is only slightly to moderately salient and the forehead recedes in an even, uninterrupted convexity to the highest point of the brain-case, vertically above the ear-holes.

The eye-sockets are relatively high and fairly widely spaced. The upper part of the face is of medium height. When the lower jaw is added, the total facial height and index prove to be relatively higher, the females falling into the long-faced or leptoprosopic category. The difference is caused by the deep chin region of the lower jaw-bone.

Protrusion of the jaws—or prognathism—has long been regarded as a hallmark of the Negro. In these Southern African Negroes, however, such projection is on the average only moderate—the faces are described as mesognathous. The opening of the nasal cavity is broad and the nasal bridge low. The upper teeth are arranged in a divergently U-shaped arcade.

The shape of the bony nasal aperture has long been correlated with climatic factors. The evidence is based largely on a geographical association between nasal index and climate, especially the vapour pressure of the air: the correlation coefficient between nasal index and vapour pressure is 0·82 according to Weiner (1954: 1–4). The hypothesis of a climatic influence upon the distribution of nasal form has been corroborated for nasal breadth in Eskimo crania from Alaska and in Aboriginal crania from Australia (Wolpoff 1968: 405–24). Thus, climatic factors may have acted as a selective mechanism contributing to the variability of nasal shape.

Moreover, nasal shape is strongly correlated with other facial features, for example the upper facial index, the orbital index and one of the facial profile angles which is used as a measure of prognathism (Pearson and Davin 1924: 328–63; Morant 1927: 318–81). Glanville (1969: 29–38) has shown that prognathism tends to be accompanied by an increasingly broad and short nose. He found, too, that particularly high correlations exist between nasal height and the length of the cranial base, and between nasal breadth and the distance between the upper canine teeth. Hence selective agencies acting on nasal shape (e.g., climate) may produce as side effects some variance in the prognathism-upper tooth arch complex; conversely any selective agencies primarily influencing the jaw-tooth complex may as a by-product contribute to the variance of nasal shape. It may be difficult, therefore, to identify the factor or factors *primarily* responsible for the broad, flat nose of the Negro.

The mandible has a prominent chin region which is pointed in just over half the jaws in de Villiers's series. The jaw is wide but low, while the ramus or ascending branch is fairly broad compared with that of caucasiform mandibles, though generally not as broad as in San (Bushmen).

This is a general description to satisfy the curiosity of those who wish to know what a Negro skull looks like: the account is not used here in an attempt to read into the dried bones a long history of tribal and racial wanderings and genetic misdeeds.

The only slight evidence of historical racial movements and minglings which de Villiers's study generated was the presence in the Southern African Negro skull of an array of features known to characterize the skulls of Khoisans and, to a lesser extent, of Eastern Hamites and caucasiforms. Since there is ample collateral evidence in both proto-historic and historic times of Negro-Khoisan and Negro-Hamitic intermixture, it seemed reasonable to de Villiers to attribute the presence of these features to early hybridization, rather than to natural selection, genetic drift or mutation. For example, great cranial length provides the main difference between Southern African and other African Negro series: since great cranial length characterizes some

13

populations of the Khoisans, de Villiers suggested that the source of increased cranial length in the Southern African Negro is probably one or more of the long-headed groups of Khoisans.

Rightmire (1970: 169–96) found it possible to discriminate between skulls of South African Bantu Negroes, on the one hand, and those of San (Bushmen) and Khoikhoi (Hottentots) on the other. He measured well documented crania representative of these three groups in several South African museums and universities. The measurements were then examined by the multivariate statistical techniques of generalized distance and discriminant function analysis. Although his samples were small, compared with those of de Villiers, his results show that the generalized distance of Negro-San and Negro-Khoikhoi series is moderately large, achieving statistical significance at the 5 per cent level; whereas the San-Khoikhoi generalized distance appears small and non-significant. In other words, the analysis suggested that San and Khoikhoi were very similar in cranial form, as they are in blood group and serum protein distributions. Rightmire comments, 'That these people [Bushmen and Hottentots] should be "lumped" in a Negro category[2] appears doubtful on the evidence available' (1970: 169). Applying vector analysis to his data, Rightmire concluded that various aspects of skull *form* are the most efficient discriminators among the three populations, although measurements of overall vault *size* are generally important in distinguishing between the sexes.

This inference on the importance of shape differences confirms with greater precision the earlier work of J. H. Gear on cranial form in the indigenous peoples of South Africa (1929: 684–97), summarized by Dart (1937: 15–19). Using a system of classifying crania devised by S. Sergi (1912) and modified by Frassetto (1909–18), Gear had shown that the modal cranial form among South African Negroes was *ortho-ovoid* and among San *chamae-pentagonoid*.[3]

(b) The teeth, jaws and palate

Until recently, there had been only two major studies on the size and the form of the teeth of living man in Southern Africa, that of Drennan (1929: 61–87) on San (Bushmen) and that of Shaw (1931) on Southern Bantu-speaking Negroes.

Both of the earlier systematic works by the late Professor J. C. Middleton Shaw and the late Professor M. R. Drennan are now superseded by larger and more comprehensive studies, involving bigger samples and a wider range of observational, metrical and analytical techniques. That on San teeth —which does not concern us here—is by Professor J. F. van Reenen and that on South African Negro teeth is by Dr A. Jacobson (1967).

Jacobson's large study is on a comparable scale to that of de Villiers on the skull. He studied the dental traits of 460 adult skulls, 356 male and 104 female, most of which fell into three large sub-groups, Natal Nguni, Cape Nguni and Sotho. Although he found some intergroup differences, they were minimal, and, like de Villiers on the skull (1968) and Washburn on the pelvis (1949: 425–32), Jacobson concluded that, for practical purposes, the sub-sets could be considered as samples of a single South African Negro population. Most of the following account is based on the work of Jacobson.

The Southern African Negroes possess large, well-developed jaws and the dental arches are longer and broader than those of most modern human populations. Malocclusion between the upper and lower teeth is minimal. In about 75 per cent of the dentitions, all the teeth are well accommodated; in some 10 per cent of upper jaws and 25 per cent of lower jaws, crowding of teeth is evident, while in 12·5 per cent of all dentitions, both male and female, spacing of teeth is evident.

Corresponding figures for the Tonga of Zambia show fewer well accommodated dentitions, more crowding in the lower jaw, though less crowding in the upper jaw, and more spacing in both upper and lower jaws (Tobias 1957–8: unpublished data).

Jacobson confirmed that projection of the *jaws* is not marked, though the front *teeth* (incisors) project often to a marked degree. This feature (prodontism), causes some protrusion and rolling out of the lips, thus often giving a spurious impression of the amount of prognathism present in the living. Skeletal studies serve to correct this misconception: prodontism is a much more striking feature than prognathism. In 347 Tonga adult males, 46·1 per cent showed prodontism of variable degree (Tobias 1957–8: unpublished data). The wear or attrition on the surfaces of the teeth is only moderate and certainly less than that of the San and other peoples on a coarse and often gritty diet.

Males have larger teeth than females. In a study of sexual dimorphism of tooth-size, Jacobson (1967: 407–25) showed that it varies in degree from tooth to tooth. In the upper jaw, the canine and third molar (wisdom tooth) and, in the lower jaw, the canine, reveal the greatest degree of sexual dimorphism of size and shape.

The incisors and wisdom teeth tend to be most highly variable in size within the South African Negro population. In general, the mean dimensions of South African Negro teeth are close to the middle of the range of population means for living man. The molar teeth tend to depart somewhat from this mid-range position in the direction of shortening and broadening; indeed, the lower second and third molars are relatively the broadest teeth of all modern populations studied.

(c) The pelvis
The Southern African Negro pelvis is absolutely smaller than that of whites and the pelvic brim is narrower transversely. In a study of fifty Ronga and Shangana women of Mozambique, Barreto (1955: 21–2) found somewhat larger dimensions of the pelvis, though he confirmed the tendency for the pelvis to be transversely flattened. Since the true pelvis constitutes the birth canal, he has drawn attention to the correlation between the long and narrow

(dolichocephalic) heads of Africans and the similarly-shaped pelvic brims in Southern African Negroes.

Among the Ganda of East Africa, the average head-size of newborn babies is scarcely any smaller than the average cross-sectional area of the pelvis, whereas in other populations neonatal heads are, on the average, appreciably smaller than the bony canal they traverse during the process of birth. This probably accounts for the high incidence of obstetrical difficulties among Ganda women. However, pelvic diameters and the adequacy of pelvic shape generally increase with a rise in socio-economic level in any community. Hence, the shape and size of the pelvis in African peoples will probably improve with environmental betterment, as it seems to have done over the past half century in Great Britain (Allbrook 1962: 102–14).

Washburn (1949: 425–32) studied the degree of sexual dimorphism among Southern African Negro and San (Bushman) pelves. As de Villiers did on the skull, and Jacobson on the teeth, he found that on pelvic features the Southern African Negro formed a single population. He showed that sexual differences in the pelvis of Southern African Negro and San were pronounced and of the usual kind he had previously described in American whites and blacks.

The degree of sexual dimorphism is virtually identical in all four populations studied by Washburn (Southern African Negro, San, American Negro and American White). It follows that, contrary to commonly held beliefs,[4] it is no more difficult to assign the correct sex to a Southern African Negro or San skeleton than to skeletons drawn from other populations.

(5) *Pigmentation*
One of the phenotypic traits which readily throws light on the genetic make-up of a population is pigmentation—of skin, hair and eyes.

(a) Skin colour
Formerly a comparator chart or blocks, such as the von Luschan Tablet, was used for recording skin colour. By this means, the skin colour of 392 Tonga, read on the face and on the relatively little exposed inner and upper part of the arm, matched up mainly with Tablets 26 to 34. The face was naturally darker—it is often not appreciated how much potential for tanning a dark-skinned person possesses. Over the face, the modal match was with Tablet 30, no fewer than 53.8 per cent of subjects having skin of this colour, while as many as 86.6 per cent of faces matched up with the five darkest Tablets, numbered 30–4. Lighter colours were met on the arm, where exposure to sunshine was less on the average: the modal match was with Tablet 29 (32.1 per cent) followed closely by Tablet 28 (28.4 per cent). No fewer than 92 per cent of subjects had an arm colour matching up with the five Tablets 26 to 30. The difference between the medium browns to reddish-browns of the arm and the medium to deeper browns and chocolate hues of the face may be taken as a measure of the differential exposure and degree of tanning of the two areas.

THE BIOLOGY OF THE SOUTHERN AFRICAN NEGRO

This method of colour determination is very subjective and imprecise. Since the early nineteen fifties, the employment of colour tablets, tops and charts has given way to a more accurate method, the use of portable reflectance spectrophotometers. This technique is based upon the precise measurement of the reflectance of the skin surface, when an incident beam of light is played upon it at each of nine different wavelengths over the range of the visible spectrum. The skin reflectance is expressed as a percentage of the reflectance of a pure white standard (Weiner 1952: 152–3). The reflectance is usually measured on maximally exposed skin (the forehead) and minimally exposed skin (the arm). The nine filters interposed between the light source and the skin transmit maximally at wavelengths of 426, 470, 490, 520, 550, 580, 600, 660 and 685 mμ.

The reflectance of light at different parts of the spectrum depends upon a variety of chemical substances in or immediately beneath the skin, such as melanin, melanoid, haemoglobin and carotene, as well as on the thickness of the skin and the scattering of incident light from the skin. However, it is mainly variations in the amount of melanin that influence skin colour (Edwards and Duntley 1939: 1–33; Harrison and Owen 1956: 481–4; Harrison 1957: 73–6). On a waveband at the red end of the spectrum, a linear relationship between the reciprocal of the reflectance and the concentration of melanin holds good *for a wide range of concentrations*. Filter 609 (685 mμ) is therefore recommended for determining the concentration of melanin.

Since 1959, readings have been made with the reflectance spectrophotometer on a variety of Southern African populations, San (Bushmen) from Botswana and South West Africa, Coloureds, Bantu-speaking Negroes from Malawi, South West Africa and South Africa, whites from South Africa, as well as on South African black and white psychotics (Tobias 1961b: 461–71; Weiner and Tobias, unpublished; Weiner *et al.* 1964: 294–307; Wassermann and Heyl 1968: 98–101). Some of the available data for Southern African Negroes together with readings on male and female San, are summarized graphically in Figure 1.4. It will be noted that females reflect more light than males at all wavelengths, since their skin colour is lighter than that of males. This is true of Southern African Negroes, as well as of Kalahari San (Tobias 1961b: 461–71, and unpublished data), Coloureds and South African whites (Wassermann and Heyl 1968: 98–101).

The variability of the reflectances in Southern African Negroes is for the most part comparable with that of the white group, whereas in the coloureds it is greater for all measurements in males and females (Wassermann and Heyl 1968: 98–101). These workers also drew attention to a slight tendency of the variability to decrease towards longer wavelengths: this probably indicates that non-melanin factors are playing a lesser role and melanin a greater role at the red end of the spectrum.

Table 1.3 gives the mean reflectances at 685 mμ for a variety of populations. The African Negro peoples have the most melanin of the populations surveyed, the values over the arm ranging (at 685 mμ) from 22·47 to 41·3 per

TABLE 1.3 *Mean reflectance of forehead, arm and forearm skin at 685 mµ, in Southern African Negroes and other Populations*

Population	Males				Females				Reference
	n	Forehead	Arm	Forearm	n	Forehead	Arm	Forearm	
S.A. Negroes (Malawi mainly Cewa)	38	—	27·04	23·25	—	—	—	—	Weiner and Tobias (1959–68, unpublished data)
S.A. Negroes (Kwangare of South West Africa)	65	20·31	23·68	20·02	94	23·54	25·38	23·34	Weiner et al. (1964)
S.A. Negroes (Mbukushu of South West Africa)	36	—	22·47	—	42	—	23·69	—	After Weiner et al. (1964)
S.A. Negroes (S. African mainly Xhosa)	104	—	32·11	—	100	—	38·90	—	Wassermann and Heyl (1968)
S.A. Negroes (mainly urban Sotho)	21	—	41·3	38·3[1]	33	—	44·7	41·4[1]	Robins (1970)
W. African Negro	24	—	31·19	—	—	—	—	—	Harrison and Owen (1956)
Ghana and Nigeria Negroes	65	—	35·54	—	—	—	—	—	Harrison and Owen (1956)
Yoruba (Nigeria)	100	—	—	23·6	74	—	—	26·1	Barnicot (1958)
Ibo (Nigeria)	52	—	—	28·2	—	—	—	—	Barnicot (1958)
'Black San' (Angola)	27	—	28·07	—	39	—	30·46	—	After Weiner et al. (1964)
San (Botswana)	57–142	39·93 (n=57)	42·46 (n=142)	37·38 (n=86)	60–117	40·16 (n=60)	43·68 (n=117)	38·73 (n=60)	Tobias (1961a and unpublished data) and Weiner et al. (1964)
San–White Hybrids	7	49·93	52·35	—	3	50·33	52·17	—	Tobias (1961a)
Khoikhoi (Hottentots) (Namaqualand, South West Africa)	25	—	45·45	38·72	34	—	48·13	41·27	Weiner et al. (1964)
Khoikhoi (Hottentots) (Warmbad, South West Africa)	25	—	41·86	36·22	50	—	37·67	37·69	Weiner et al. (1964)
Cape Coloured (South Africa)	187	—	50·14	—	112	—	51·29	—	Weiner et al. (1964)
Cape Coloured (South Africa)	103	—	49·18	—	107	—	52·11	—	Wassermann and Heyl (1968)
Griqua or Baster (Rehoboth, South West Africa)	10	—	47·90	41·75	21	—	51·93	44·93	Weiner et al. (1964)
Mexican (Parachoan)	41	39·78	44·68	—	46	42·00	44·13	—	Lasker (1954)
Whites (South Africa)	108	—	63·49	—	109	—	64·41	—	Wassermann and Heyl (1968)
Whites (South Africa)	40	—	65·8	58·7[1]	40	—	65·9	63·7[1]	Robins (1970)
Whites (Belgium)	143	62·5	67·3	—	177	65·7	65·9	—	Leguebe (1961)
Whites (Europe)	50	—	—	61·5	50	—	—	63·5	Barnicot (1958)

[1] Measured on the hand, not the forearm.

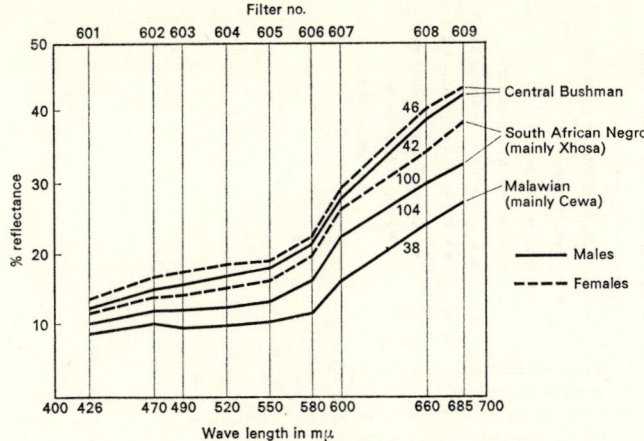

FIGURE 1.4 *Skin reflectance in Southern African Negroes and Bushmen*

The figure indicates skin reflectance of the upper and inner part of the arm (relatively unexposed skin) in males and females of Southern African Negro and Bushman samples. The lighter the skin, the higher the percentage reflectance. The graphs show that (i) Bushmen are lighter than Southern African Negroes; and (ii) females are lighter than males in both populations.

cent in males. The darkest skin is that of a group of seventeen Kwangare adult males from Mazua Kraal, northern South West Africa, with a mean reflectance of 20·29 per cent (Weiner *et al.* 1964—not shown in Table 4). Yellow San have a similar quantity of melanin to Khoikhoi (Hottentots) and to Mexicans (male means: 42·46 to 45·45 per cent). The next step down in quantity of melanin is to the Griqua, Cape Coloured and San-White hybrid groups, which have relatively little melanin (male means: 47·90 to 52·35 per cent). The white populations reviewed have least melanin with mean reflectances of 63·49 to 67·30 per cent. Although more scanty, the female data fall into the same pattern. The virtually stepwise retrogression of melanin through these four groups of populations probably depends upon a variable number of melanizing alleles of skin-colour genes present from group to group. Figure 1.5 summarizes the spectrum of skin colours in sub-Saharan Africa.

Of the few Southern Negro populations studied, the Malawian and South West African samples seemingly have the most melanin, with very low reflectances of 20·29 to 27·04 per cent. The Xhosa (making up the bulk of the Southern African Negro sample of Wassermann and Heyl) are somewhat lighter, as are the small urban group of Southern African Negroes studied by Robins (1970). Our studies on San and Malawians and those of Weiner *et al.* (1964: 294–307) have shown that foreheads and forearms are appreciably darker—and reflect correspondingly less—than the inner and upper part of the arm.

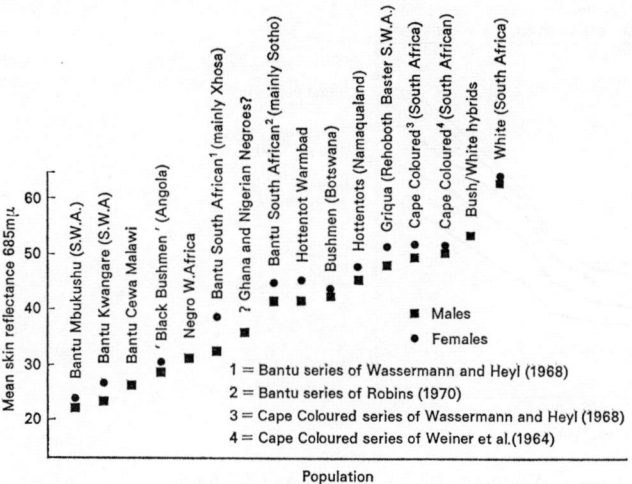

FIGURE 1.5 *The spectrum of skin colours in sub-Saharan Africa*

The figure shows the mean reflectances of little-exposed arm skin at a wave-length of 685 mμ for males (squares) and females (circles) of 16 sub-Saharan African populations (data from various sources).

Among the possible selective advantages of deep pigmentation which have been suggested are protection against sunburn, skin cancer, hypervitaminosis D, tropical diseases and heat absorption; and the possibility of camouflage and of social selection (reviewed by Harrison 1961: 99–115 and by Livingstone 1969: 480–93). Genetic models have been constructed to meet the facts of skin-colour variations in human populations and hybrids. Several attempts concur in suggesting that at least four, or even five or six, different genes are involved, for each of which two alleles would normally be present (Stern 1953: 281–98; Livingstone 1969: 480–93). Populations might then differ in the average number of heavily melanizing alleles and of lightly or non-melanizing alleles possessed by each person; such a model allows a wide range of intermediate shades from very dark to very light.

(b) The congenital blue spot

The well-known *congenital blue spot* (formerly called the Mongolian spot) occurs in a very high frequency of newborn African babies. Sarmento's figures in Angolan Negroes (quoted by Alberto and Barreto 1952: 1–6) showed an overall incidence of 90·5 per cent (males 89·2, females 91·9), while in Mozambique Africans, Alberto and Barreto found a slightly lower frequency, namely 79·5 per cent (males 78·8, females 80·3). The spot is most commonly localized over the sacral region or buttocks, but may be present in a variety of other positions (Alberto and Barreto 1952: 1–6).

(c) Eye colour

Negro peoples, in general—and that includes Southern Bantu-speaking

Africans—have brown to very dark brown eyes. Thus, in 402 adult male Tonga of Zambia, the following eye-colours were recorded (Tobias 1957-8, unpublished):

	%
Black	2 (0·5)
Dark brown	215 (53·5)
Medium brown	171 (42·5)
Light brown	14 (3·5)

In a classification using only three categories, brown-black, intermediate, and blue, Wassermann and Heyl (1968: 100–1) recorded 100 per cent of 204 Southern African Negroes as having eye-colours in the brown-black category.

Light eyes and even blue eyes do occur occasionally in Negro peoples. These may be unaccompanied by any other unusual or abnormal feature, or they may be associated with other manifestations such as the hereditary Klein-Waardenburg syndrome—a well-recognized complex featuring anomalies of the eyes, of skin, hair and eye-coloration, and deafness (Soussi 1968). In subjects in whom blue eyes are the only departure, this form of light iris is inherited as a *dominant* trait, in contrast with the pattern of *recessive* inheritance usually shown by the blue-eyed trait in white people (Tobias 1961a: 161; Soussi 1968).

(d) Hair colour
Hair colour is generally dark brown or black. Thus, in 405 adult male Tonga, aside from 90 men (22·2 per cent) with white or greying hair, 309 (76·3 per cent) had black hair, 5 (1·2 per cent) dark brown, and 1 (0·25 per cent) medium brown hair. A reddish tinge of the hair is occasionally encountered, but here, as elsewhere in Africa, it is commonly associated with indications of malnutrition, of which reddening of the hair may be a sign. But genetically red hair does occur now and again in negriform peoples.

(6) *Some soft tissue features*

(a) Hair-form
The *hair* of the Negroes is implanted rather shallowly and obliquely in the skin. The hair-shaft itself is oval and sometimes even flat-oval to ribbon-shaped in cross-section. Commonly, in Negroes, the medulla—the central, strengthening core of the hair-shaft—is not a continuous rod, but interrupted or segmented, and sometimes it is completely missing. These anatomical features lead Negro hair to be coiled and even spiralled. The net effect is a head of tightly curled and helical hair, different degrees of which are commonly spoken of as 'woolly', 'frizzy' or 'frizzly', or even 'matted' hair. Such hair is almost universal in sub-Saharan Africa and it reaches its tightest spiralling in the 'peppercorn' hair of Kalahari San (Bushmen) and of some central African Pygmies. The hair of 394 adult male Tonga of Zambia was

classified into the following descriptive classes (Tobias 1957–8, unpublished):

		%
Peppercorn	38	(9·6)
Peppercorn and woolly	92	(23·4)[5]
Woolly	248	(62·9)
Frizzy	16	(4·1)

Helical hair occurs on the body, too, though body-hair and, for that matter, facial hair is sparse in Negroes generally and in most Southern Bantu Negroes in particular.

Like dark skin colour, spiral hair has its focus at the Equator and in tropical and subtropical regions flanking it. This suggests some selective value in this form of hair (Coon, Garn and Birdsell 1950: 63). However, although speculations have been made about its protective value 'like a pith helmet' against the sun, no convincing hypothesis on the adaptive or selective value of hair form has so far emerged.

(b) External genitalia

The *external genitals* show some distinctive features in Africans. Whereas in male San (Bushmen) the horizontal phallus (*penis rectus*) is frequently encountered, among Southern Bantu-speaking Negroes a pendulous phallus is commonest.

The phenomenon of *macronympha* or *macronymphia*, *longinymph* or *tablier*, often miscalled 'Hottentot apron', is widespread in Africa. Although commonly believed to characterize Khoisans (Khoikhoi or Hottentots, and San or Bushmen), this enlargement of the labia minora occurs in many other African populations, including Southern Bantu-speaking Negroes (Schapera 1930a: 59 and 62; 1940a: 47; Stayt 1931a: 108; Lagercrantz 1937: 145–74; de Almeida 1956: 131–50; de Villiers 1969: 48–51). Observations on the tablier of several Southern African populations are summarized in Table 1.4.

TABLE 1.4 *Percentage incidence of macronympha in various Southern African populations*[1]

Population	n	Tablier present	Tablier absent
Southern African Negro (mainly Nguni and Sotho)	97	42·3	57·7
Griqua (Khoikhoi-Caucasiform Hybrid)	36	52·8	47·2
Kalahari San (Bushmen)	103	99·0	1·0

[1] From de Villiers 1969, 48–51, based on observations by H. de Villiers, T. Jenkins, C. J. Orkin, M. Stumke and P. V. Tobias.

According to de Villiers, there were no significant differences in either the incidence or the length of the tablier between the two main Southern African

Negro sub-sets, the 46 Nguni and 40 Sotho women. The mean length of the tablier was smaller in the Negro women than in San women at all ages; the maximum value in an adult San woman (90 mm. below the labia majora) was almost double the greatest length in a Bantu-speaking Negro adult (47 mm.).

Several workers (e.g. Stayt 1931a: 108; Schapera 1940a: 47; Lagercrantz 1937: 145–74; de Almeida 1956: 131–50) have concluded that, in Southern African Negroes, the tablier is a culturally acquired ethnic mutilation. Schapera gives a fairly detailed description of how young Kgatla girls stretch the labia minora from puberty or a little later (1940a: 47) and of the role of the tablier in sex-play (1940a: 188). Stayt describes how old Venda women may show 'quite tiny girls' how to stretch the labia minora and adds that, often, a stone is tied to the parts to hasten the process (Stayt 1931a: 108). In the Khoisan peoples, most workers have failed to find evidence that the tablier is produced artificially and they regard it as a genetically-determined trait.[6] This view is supported by the differential incidence and length of the tablier among various populations, paralleling similar differences (polymorphisms) in many well-known gene-determined traits.

(c) Eyefolds

A variety of eyefolds has been described in Southern African peoples. For example, a medial epicanthic fold is common among Khoisans, as well as a thick transverse fold which has been regarded by some as a 'Mongoloid' feature. The latter interpretation has been questioned by Tobias (1955d: 439–43; 1957: 33–40), who suggests rather that parallel evolution has occurred—a view supported later by the serum protein findings of Jenkins and Steinberg (1966: 405). In Southern African Negroes, three forms of eyefold have been recognized: an external epicanthic, an internal epicanthic and a palpebral fold. The occurrence of the three kinds in adult male Zambian Tonga is as follows (Tobias 1957–8, unpublished data):

		%
External epicanthic fold	slight	3·4
(n = 404)	moderate	2·1
	absent	94·5
Internal epicanthic fold	slight	22·3
(n = 400)	moderate	3·0
	marked	1·2
	absent	73·5
Palpebral fold	slight	15·8
(n = 405)	moderate	5·4
	marked	2·7
	absent	76·0

(d) Ear-lobes

The smallness of ear length in Africans is often exaggerated by the absence of an ear-lobe, or the presence of an ear-lobe which is attached to the skin of the side of the neck. Free-hanging ear-lobes do not seem to be as common as among whites. Among 402 Zambian Tonga, the following patterns were encountered:

	%
Ear-lobe absent	14·3
Ear-lobe attached	37·3
Ear-lobe free	48·4

In over half of the total number of subjects studied, the size of the ear-lobe was rated as small, and in only 3 per cent as large.

(e) Overrolling of the helix
Another striking characteristic of the ears of Africans is the tendency for the helix or outer rim of the ear to be rolled over on itself, to a marked degree. We have been impressed by the frequency and degree of this feature in Kalahari San, but the trait is present, too, in Southern African Negroes. In 404 Zambesi Tonga, the helix was not at all overrolled in only 19·2 per cent of subjects; overrolling was slight in 38·4 per cent, moderate in 33·9 per cent, and marked in 8·5 per cent.

(7) The genotype of the Southern African Negro
With few exceptions, the biological variables considered up to now—whether metrical or non-metrical traits—have been of uncertain genetic foundation, or based upon polygenic determination.[7] We may now turn our attention to a series of traits, which with few exceptions are of simpler genetic determination. Most of them, such as the blood-groups, are monogenic (one gene determines one trait); a few, like fingerprint and palmar print patterns, are certainly genetic but the pattern of inheritance is more complicated. It is because of their generally simpler genetic determination that this series of traits has enabled human biologists to make great strides in defining the genetic constitution of various populations and, so, the interrelationships among populations and ethnic groups.

The traits in this category are many and diverse: they include about a dozen blood group systems; variants of haemoglobin; of proteins in the blood serum; of enzyme polymorphisms and deficiencies in red blood cells and blood plasma; of antigens in body cells with nuclei, especially the white blood cells; and a group of traits such as colour blindness, taste 'blindness' (inability to taste a chemical substance called phenylthiocarbamide and related compounds), and dermatoglyphs (finger- and palmar-prints). The newer data on these aspects are too voluminous and too technical to be reviewed in any detail here. It can, however, be mentioned that sufficient data are on record to enable one to piece together a tentative overall picture of the African genotype, south of the Sahara (Tobias 1966: 111–200; 1972b). As the gene frequency data have proved most valuable in elucidating the biological relationships of Southern African populations, three examples will be selected to

THE BIOLOGY OF THE SOUTHERN AFRICAN NEGRO

illustrate the kind of information and historical reconstructions they have made possible.

First, Figure 1.6 shows the distributions of blood groups A, B and O among 122 Southern African Negro samples. Despite great variation, it can be said that the modal frequency of the blood group O phenotype lies in the range of 50 to 60 per cent; the mode for A lies in the 20 to 30 per cent class; that

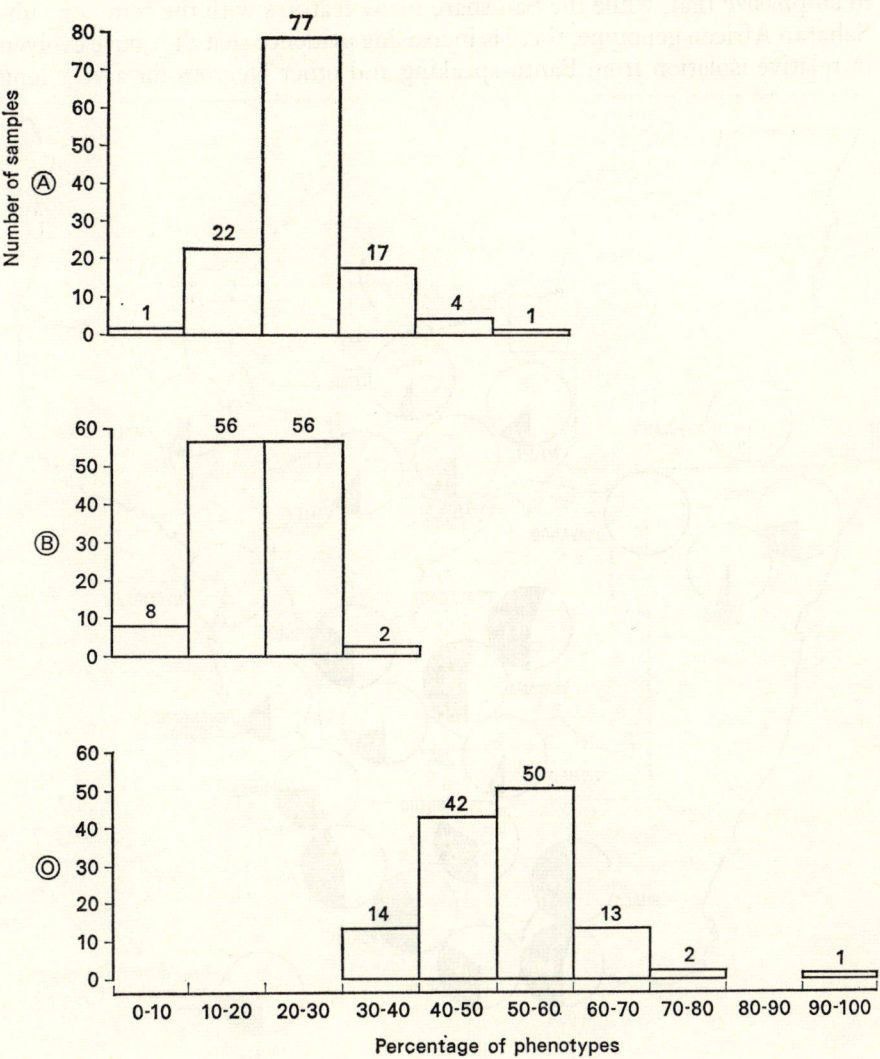

FIGURE 1.6 *Percentage distribution of A, B and O blood-group phenotypes among 122 Southern African Negro populations*

The data for this figure were collated by Tobias 1966: 111–200.

for B close to 20 per cent; and that for AB between 3 and 4 per cent. Compared with the Southern African Negro, in the San A is high and B low, whereas in Khoikhoi B is higher, occasionally exceeding the frequency of A.

A second example centres on the so-called Gm group of serum proteins. Certain variants are present in fairly high frequency among the San, whereas they are almost or totally lacking among other Africans, including Southern African Negroes (Jenkins and Steinberg 1966: 399–407). These data serve to emphasize that, while the San share many features with the common sub-Saharan African genotype, there is increasing evidence that they have evolved in relative isolation from Bantu-speaking and other Negroes for a very long

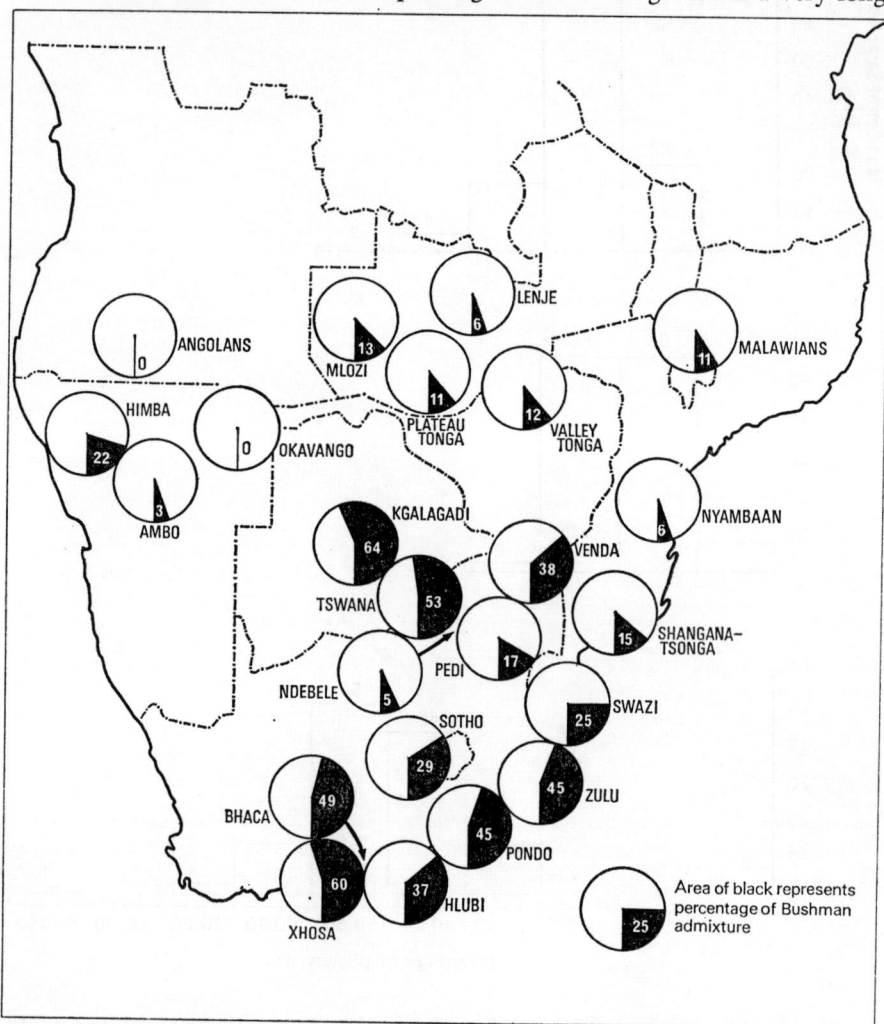

FIGURE 1.7 *Estimated percentage of San admixture in 23 populations*

Estimates are based upon the frequency of the serum protein allele $Gm^{1,13}$ (after Jenkins, Zoutendyk and Steinberg 1970: 198).

time. In a later study, Jenkins, Zoutendyk and Steinberg (1970: 197–218) have developed the use of the Gm types for determining the amount of San admixture in a number of South African populations: their approach is based on the premise that a particular form of Gm ($Gm^{1,13}$) was widely distributed among the earliest San and Khoikhoi inhabitants of the sub-continent and that its presence in Bantu-speaking Negroes can be ascribed to hybridization with these early indigenes. Given these assumptions, they have been able to classify some twenty-three Bantu-speaking Negro chiefdoms according to the percentage of San admixture in them (Figure 1.7). The composite picture ranges from 64 per cent of admixture in the Kgalagadi and 60 per cent in the Xhosa to 5 per cent in the Kuanyama Ambo and 0 per cent in the Mbukushu and mixed Angolans. A more general picture of Southern African population affinities will be discussed in the concluding section of this chapter.

A third example, of evolutionary importance, is the frequency of an abnormal kind of haemoglobin (the red colouring matter in the red blood cells). This variant, haemoglobin S, is genetically determined. The mutant gene responsible is widespread in Africa and reaches high frequencies in populations living between the Tropics. It causes the red blood cells to form sickle shapes under some conditions: hence, the trait is generally called the sickle-cell trait. In the homozygous state, that is, if one has inherited the mutant gene from both parents, it causes a severe anaemia. In the heterozygous state, that is, if a subject has inherited the gene for haemoglobin S from one parent and that for ordinary haemoglobin from the other, the severe anaemia is absent. On the contrary, there is evidence to suggest that heterozygotes are at a biological advantage and are favoured by natural selection over homozygotes. This advantageous tendency helps to maintain the gene for haemoglobin S in a high percentage of persons, despite the loss of genes through selection against those who are homozygous for haemoglobin S. This is an example of Haldane's concept of *balanced polymorphism*.

How does the selective advantage of the heterozygotes come about? The distribution of haemoglobin S coincides very closely with the area of Africa within which malaria is endemic. It is suggested that heterozygous 'carriers' of haemoglobin S offer greater resistance to the malarial parasite than do homozygotes. This may be because of differential mortality, operating primarily on children; or because of increased fertility among heterozygous females, or among heterozygous males (Eaton and Mucha 1971). The hypothesis has some evidence to support it, though it has not been without its critics. At present it seems reasonable to conclude that 'severity of malaria is a very important factor in determining the frequency of the sickle-cell trait' (Allison 1954: 312–18).

The frequencies of African carriers of HbS rise as high as 45 per cent among the Amba of Uganda and 44 per cent among the Mbangala in Angola. South of the Kunene and the Zambesi Rivers, however, the frequency of sicklers is extremely low, the trait being virtually absent in South African Negroes, San and Khoikhoi. It is high in Angola, largely absent in Mozambique, save for two extraordinarily high frequencies of carriers, 38 per cent in a Makua sample and 40 per cent in a Makonde sample at Porto Amelia (Foy et al. 1952: 247–51).

According to Jenkins (1969: 1–7), the Tonga people on the north and south banks of the Zambesi, as well as on the Plateau to the north, have the *lowest* frequencies—'less than 5 per cent'—of all Africans living in a hyperendemic malarious area. At the same time, they have one of the world's *highest* rates for the hereditary deficiency of an enzyme, glucose-6-phosphate dehydrogenase. Jenkins suggests that 'This could be because the Tonga (and the Bantu-speaking tribes further south) were settled in their present location before the sickle-cell gene was introduced' (Jenkins 1969: 2). The possibility that the sickle-cell gene was introduced to Africa from Asia has been mooted: for sickling occurs to a high frequency among Veddoids of southern India and among the Achdam of southern Arabia (Lehmann and Cutbush 1952a: 404–5; 1952b: 380–3; Lehmann 1954: 1–23). The possibility has been supported by implication by Brain, who has drawn attention to the fact that the distribution in Africa of the sickle-cell trait closely parallels that of the shorthorn zebu variety of Indian cattle: 'Is it possible,' he asks, 'that the sickle-cell gene was distributed in Africa by the custodians of the shorthorn zebu?' (Brain 1953: no. 233).

(Whilst discussing this with the late Dr J. C. Trevor, then Director of the Duckworth Laboratory at Cambridge, in 1955, I recall his telling me that he vividly remembered Professor A. C. Haddon on more than one occasion, many years earlier, wishing he could find a research student willing to undertake a project designed to prove 'the Indian origin of the Negro'!)

Hiernaux (1955: 455–72) and Neel (1956: 24) feel that there is no good evidence of substantial gene flow in either direction, between India and Africa. However they both draw attention to the fact that, given the selective advantage attributed to the heterozygotes for haemoglobin S under the theory of balanced polymorphism, a very few immigrants carrying this trait into a foreign group could serve as a nidus of dissemination—and this would be true for migrants in either direction. Given the same conditions of intensive selection as exist today in tropical Africa, the frequency of the sickle-cell gene could increase from 0·1 per cent to a near-equilibrium value of 20 per cent in 35 generations (Smith 1954: 51–7). The same reasoning would apply to the views of those who have sought to localize the origin of the sickle-cell gene within Africa; for example, R. Singer located it in the region of the Ruwenzori Mountains, where a small patch of very high frequencies is surrounded by much lower ones (Singer 1953: 634–48). This idea remains a possibility, but just as good a case could be made out for the Mozambique origin of the sickle-cell trait, since Foy, Kondi, Rebello and Martins (1952: 247–51) found a patch of high frequencies (average 39 per cent) among the Makonde-Makua. Similarly, we cannot rule out Lehmann's theory, though a case could be made out for the African origin of the sickle-cell trait of India.

Whatever the origin, we certainly can agree with Hiernaux (1955: 455–72) that the sickle-cell trait appeared somewhere in the ancestral stock of the living Negro, *after* the forking of the Bushman and Negro branches, and, we may add, after the separation and southward migration of the Southern African Negroes (see page 35). Because of the intensity of the selective pressures operating on the trait, the frequency of the gene could have risen to very high levels in a relatively short time, so that the centre of origin of the gene, or the ethnic group in which it originated, cannot safely be determined from the trait's present distribution. Hiernaux counsels that 'physical anthropologists should be very cautious when working with a highly adaptive character, and should keep constantly in mind the implications of its value in natural selection' (1955: 470–1).

(8) The role of nutrition

Many students have addressed themselves to the problem of the diet of blacks under both rural and urban conditions.[8] Several schools of investigators have been occupied with different aspects of the problem of malnutrition and undernutrition in Southern Africa for decades.[9] The literature is enormous and it would be impossible to review and appraise it here. This problem is primarily one for the sociologist, the economist and the social anthropologist; the human biologist's interest is with the consequences of the diet on living human subjects.

During this survey, we have had occasion to note some of the effects of poor nutrition on the bodily structure and functioning of Southern African Negroes.

Perhaps the prime question for the human biologist is to see how and to what extent dietary factors are inhibiting, modifying or even challenging the genetic endowment with which each man enters the world; to what extent they are or have been acting as selective agencies during the recent evolution of man in Africa; and to what extent they have so modified the pattern of living and dying as to have influenced the demographic structure of the population and even its socio-economic systems. We hear a great deal about Africa's diseases, such as malaria, acting as selective agencies; we have heard precious little about whether Africa's greatest scourge, malnutrition, has acted likewise as a tool of the evolutionary process, selecting some genomes for a relatively light impact, and others for a heavy onslaught. We are told about the influence of climate, geography, ecology, on the development of man's cultures: but has his debility, his kwashiorkor, his sub-optimal functioning on an inadequate diet, played no role in moulding his way of life?

These are among the many problems before which the human biologist stands perplexed—and which he wishes to pose for the consideration of social anthropologists and ethnologists.

Before leaving this topic, I should refer to one especially insidious by-product of malnutrition, its effect on the brain.

Evidence has accumulated in recent years that undernutrition at critical stages during the development of experimental animals may lead to permanent impairment of the brain. The effect occurs provided the period of undernutrition begins before the cerebral cortex has reached its adult state, or at least, during the period of maximum vulnerability of the brain to stress. If the nutritional insults are administered within this critical post-natal period, or even if it is the pregnant mother who is undernourished, the impairment to the size, structure and chemistry of the brain is *not* reversed by any subsequent restoration of normal nutrition. For man, too, an increasing body of evidence is showing that functional impairments of the human brain follow early undernutrition.[10] There is already some evidence suggesting that the electro-encephalographic changes outlast the acute stage of the nutritional insult, though further follow-ups are necessary to confirm the hypothesis that malnutrition at a critical age results in permanent brain damage, with permanent impairment of intellect and emotions, and of brain rhythms.

The results of an International Conference on Malnutrition, Learning and Behaviour have been summarized as follows:

> Children reared in poverty tend to do poorly on tests of intelligence. In part this is due to psychological and cultural factors. To an important extent it is a result of malnutrition early in childhood. . . . It seems likely that millions of young children in developing countries are experiencing some degree of retardation in learning because of inadequate nutrition (Abelson 1969: 17).

Hence, the effects of malnutrition during the sensitive developing years are apparent not only in bodily structure and functioning years later, but probably also in the psychological realm. Here, too, there may be an impact on the cultural and social patterns assumed by a population following many generations of exposure to such conditions.

III Affinities and Origins

(1) *When 'the Bantu' were considered a separate race*

In the decades which have elapsed since the publication of Schapera's *The Bantu-speaking Tribes of South Africa*, a great change has come about in our knowledge of Southern African Negroes. At the date of the earlier book (1937a), there was little precise information bearing on the relationship between Bantu-speakers and other sub-Saharan Africans. It was obvious that they shared some phenotypic features—such as a dark skin, prognathism, woolly hair, thick lips, and a rather low nasal bridge. But there was a definite feeling (in the absence of secure knowledge) that the Bantu-speakers were physically different from the 'forest Negro' and other negriform peoples north of the 'Bantu line', who were said to show Negro features 'to an extreme degree'. Then, too, their supposed physical distinctness was supplemented by their speaking a Bantu tongue, considered then to differ markedly from all other African languages. It was easy to slip into the error of confusing the biological population with the language group.

So the peoples who form the topic of this book came to be known by the name 'Bantu' as a racial epithet. There were those who spoke of 'the Bantu race' with the same assurance with which they might speak of one of the well-attested human subspecies such as Neandertal Man (*Homo sapiens neanderthalensis*). Numerous research reports appeared describing the qualities and features of 'the Bantu'—as a glance at the Bibliography of this book will confirm.

(2) *The Southern Africans as Negroes*

The study of genetic markers effected an important change. Instead of concentrating attention on features the genetic basis of which was not known or at best ill-understood, or on those difficult polygenic traits, like stature or head-shape, which were so difficult to analyse genetically and were so subject to the whims of the environment, the new physical anthropologists focussed on monogenic traits. They were easy to identify and to analyse, not subject to much environmental modification during an individual's life, and believed to yield ultimately more precise information on the genetic affinities of populations.

It was this new approach that re-united the Bantu-speakers to the rest of the sub-Saharan continent. For the gene frequencies showed that all the sub-Saharan negriform peoples were broadly alike in genetic constitution: at least, the variations among them were relatively minor compared with the differences which separated sub-Saharan African man from other major racial constellations, like the caucasiform and the mongoliform.

As more and more genetic markers were discovered, so abundant confirmation came to light on the essential genetic unity of sub-Saharan Africa. It was this which enabled me earlier to limn a tentative overall picture of the sub-Saharan African genotype (Tobias 1966: 117–21). Even some of the 'newest' of the genetic markers, the Gm groups of serum proteins, have confirmed that 'the Bantu-speaking Negroes have obvious strong genetic affinities with the Negro peoples of West and Central Africa' (Jenkins, Zoutendyk and Steinberg 1970: 212).

The same is true whether we consider the Rh blood-group system, or the fingerprint and palmar patterns, or the incidence of colour-blindness—or virtually any of the identified polymorphisms, save the most *eco-sensitive* ones. By eco-sensitive traits, we mean, for example, the sickle-cell trait and glucose-6-phosphate dehydrogenase deficiency; both of these seem to be highly vulnerable to selective pressures operating from some environmental factor, like malaria, and both show widely fluctuating frequencies *which do not necessarily reflect population affinities.*

It has thus become clear that there is no 'Bantu race' and that it is biologically unjustified to continue speaking of 'the Bantu' as a biological entity. From a study of the generalized 'distance' in body measurements and where possible gene frequencies between all pairs of 101 sub-Saharan African populations, Hiernaux has reached exactly the same conclusion: 'it makes no sense to group all Bantu-speaking populations into a race: many of them are biologically much nearer to some non-Bantu-speaking ethnic groups than to some Bantu-speaking ones' (Hiernaux 1968c: 508). The people about whom this book has been written are Negroes, like the men of Congo, Gabon or Ghana. If we wish for convenience to limit them geographically—and this book has a geographical limit—by all means let us use the term *Southern African Negro*: the epithet is purely geographical, not a racial qualification.

(3) *Genetic and historic relationships with Khoisan peoples*

The bodily distinctness of the San (Bushmen), as compared with Southern African Negroes, is manifest in their light yellowish-brown skin, short stature (although their average stature has increased by about 3 cm in males and 1·5 cm in females in the last three generations—Tobias 1962: 801–10; 1972a, pending), 'peppercorn' hair, very small ears with overrolled helices or rims and commonly lobeless, palpebral and medial epicanthic eyefolds, broad flat noses, small flattish faces, many other distinctive features of skull and head, macronympha (enlargement of the labia minora), steatopygia and steatomeria (accumulation of fat over buttocks and thighs respectively), *penis rectus* in males, sparse facial and bodily hair (Tobias 1957: 33–40; 1964: 67–86). In many of these anatomical features, the San is closest to the Khoikhoi, both differing in a number of respects from the Negro. Archaeological skeletal evidence supports the belief that the San have been distinct for a long time. For these reasons, they had initially come to be recognized by some as the remnant of one of the world's four or five major racial constellations known as the khoisanoid or khoisaniform: they were even placed on a level of distinctness with the caucasiform, mongoliform, negriform and australiform racial clusters, as for instance in Trevor's (1955) classification of mankind.

However, genetical studies subsequently showed the general sub-Saharan African affinities of the Khoisans, just as they did with South African Bantu-speaking Negroes. It is now known that San share a number of allelic frequency patterns with South African Negroes and with other sub-Saharan Africans. In general, San agree with other African populations in blood group frequencies and especially resemble or surpass them in many respects in which Africans generally differ from non-Africans (Tobias 1966: 124, after Zoutendyk *et al*. 1953: 361–8 and Weiner and Zoutendyk 1959: 843–4).

Soon after this was first realized, Singer and Weiner (1963: 168–76), on the basis of a limited number of genetic polymorphisms, actually proposed that the definition of the Negro should be extended to include these lighter-skinned peoples, namely the San and Khoikhoi. Their suggestion seemed to be supported by somatic evidence, too, for closer examination showed that a number of bodily features previously regarded as distinctive of the Khoisans occur as well in Southern African Negroes, though not as frequently nor to as marked a degree. This is true, for instance, of macronympha and steatopygia, which our studies have shown to occur in Southern African Negroes, though less commonly and to a lesser degree than in San.

As numbers of 'new' genetic polymorphisms have been discovered and tested for in Southern African Negroes and Khoisans, it has been confirmed that, in general, San and Khoikhoi share a common sub-Saharan African pool of genic alleles: the Khoisans have more in common genetically with Negroes than either group has with any non-African peoples.[11] As Rightmire summed up: 'one may reasonably conclude that both Bushmen and Hottentots are generally African and Negroid serologically' (Rightmire 1970: 173).

Then came a third phase in which it was appreciated that the sub-Saharan picture is far from homogeneous. Many facts have accumulated to confirm what the somatic evidence formerly indicated, namely that in numerous characteristics San and Khoikhoi are more like one another than either group is like Southern African Negroes. This is true, for example, of many serological differences,[12] and of many of the morphological or anthroposcopic differences traditionally recognized by physical anthropologists as distinguishing Khoisans from Negroes. Similarly, too, the result of Rightmire's multivariate analysis of Southern African Negro, Khoikhoi and San cranial series 'suggests Bushmen and Hottentots to be fully as similar in cranial form as in blood group and serum protein distributions. That these people should be "lumped" in a Negro category appears doubtful on the evidence available' (Rightmire 1970: 169).

The differences led me to suggest that, although San and Khoikhoi belong to the same major genic constellation as other sub-Saharan Africans, the morphological and genetic markers point to a lengthy period of differentiation in relative isolation (Tobias 1966: 132–3). 'Isolation' here means *reproductive* and hence genetic isolation: although many isolating mechanisms are known, in recent phases of human evolution a common mechanism is likely to have been *geographical* isolation.

It is a striking fact that for a number of genetic markers, the Khoisans show extreme values (e.g. Rh_0 and Henshaw). This holds, too, for some somatic traits, the genetic basis of which is less certain. For example macronympha occurs in virtually 100 per cent of San females, but in only 42 per cent of Southern African Negro females (de Villiers 1969). The same kind of relationship is true of steatopygia and steatomeria, peppercorn hair, lobeless ears with markedly overrolled helices, vertical or nearly vertical (orthognathous) faces, very flat noses, and many other presumably genetical features, in which San have close to 100 per cent frequencies, whilst Southern African Negroes show much smaller percentages. On the other hand, in a few respects Negroes show a higher incidence of genetic traits than Khoisans, for example, skin pigmenting alleles, a gap (median diastema) between the upper central incisor teeth, whorls on fingertips, haemoglobin S, and a haptoglobin allele

Hp[1]. What is the implication of the fact that, in San, a number of polymorphisms (and phenotypic traits) show extreme frequencies of certain alleles?

One possible line of thinking is that the gene-pattern of present day sub-Saharan Negroes—especially of certain West-Central African populations which Hiernaux (1968a; 1968c: 505–15) has shown to be probably somatically little changed descendants of an early African stock—resembles most closely the gene pattern of the earlier sub-Saharan proto-negriforms. If the San gene-pattern had developed originally from such a proto-negriform pattern, then to explain the extreme frequencies of certain alleles we should need to postulate that in the subsequent micro-evolution of San, selective agencies operated on a number of widely different polymorphisms—including the Rh_0 and Henshaw blood-group genotypes, haptoglobins and dermatoglyphic patterns—selecting each of these to a maximum (or minimum) frequency. Similarly, selection would have had to operate on the genotype for skin colour, steatopygia, macronympha, and many other somatic features, carrying each to an extreme value in the spectrum of sub-Saharan variation. Though unlikely, this is not impossible, when one considers the variety of potential selective agencies operating in Africa. But the other possibility is more likely, namely that the San genome represents, at least in part, an approximation to the ancestral proto-negriform genome, being a relatively little changed derivative of it. From such a genome, the somewhat 'watered down' version possessed by Negroes could have been produced by mutation, changing selection pressures (including relaxation of selection), genetic drift, and hybridization, for example with Erythriotes from north-east Africa or with other genetically different ethnic groups (after Tobias 1966: 133–4).

It is postulated then that, from a basically Khoisan-like genome, proto-negriform Africans split into two major branches, the Khoisans and the Negroes. The separation must have begun a long time ago: certainly, on the archaeological evidence, it must have been upwards of 6,000 years ago. Indeed, it is likely that the divergence had begun by the onset of the Later Stone Age, perhaps ten to fifteen thousand years ago. In the long history of human evolution, this still means a fairly recent common origin. The subsequent micro-evolution of the two sub-groups has not led them to diverge so far from each other as to obliterate their basically similar genetic make-up. Hence, we infer that the Khoisans and the Negroes both belong to the same major racial constellation, the negriforms, sometimes regarded as a subspecies of modern man, *Homo sapiens afer*.[13]

Once the dichotomy was established, there followed a fairly lengthy period of reproductive and, hence, genetic isolation between the Khoisans—who seem to have gravitated mainly to eastern and southern Africa—and the Negroes, whose further development took place mainly in Equatorial and Tropical Africa. During the period of isolation, certain genetic divergences arose: 'new' alleles took root in both populations. Thus, from the work of Jenkins, Zoutendyk and Steinberg (1970: 197–218), the $Gm^{1,13}$ allele must have entered into the Khoisan genome *after* the original split of Khoisan and Negroes into two stocks; it came to attain a high value among the Khoisans, though we do not know whether this was by selection or genetic drift. Similarly, we must assume that the gene for the sickling trait (haemoglobin S) and, probably, that for glucose-6-phosphate-dehydrogenase deficiency entered into the Negro population *after* the original split of Khoisans and Negroes; and perhaps even after the Southern African Negroes had moved to the south-east and south, away from the rest of the Negroes, as was suggested for the gene for haemoglobin S by Budtz-Olsen and Burgers (1955: 109-10).[14]

On the whole, it would seem that the Khoisans departed relatively little from the inferred ancestral genotype, whereas the Negroes, by selection, genetic drift and/or hybridization, departed fairly appreciably from the presumed ancient genetic picture: extreme gene frequencies became 'watered down' to high or even only moderate values.

The adoption of a new way of life—agriculture—may itself have expedited biological changes among some Negroes. Thus the clearing of large tracts of tropical rain forest for agricultural purposes multiplied the number of breeding places for the mosquitoes which carry malaria, especially the *Anopheles gambiae* species complex: it is suggested that this man-made change in the biotope led to malaria becoming hyperendemic in West Africa (Livingstone 1958: 533-62). Malaria is believed to be the selective agent producing high frequencies of the sickle-cell trait, possibly also of G6PD deficiency, and even perhaps of the lower levels of adenosine triphosphate (ATP) found in the red blood cells of Negroes (Brewer 1967: 25-34; Eaton and Brewer 1969: 389-90). Since, under these new intensely malarious situations, the viability of the 'normal' individual is reduced and there is selection for individuals with the sickle-cell trait, we can see how the nature of the population's gene pool will change with time. Thus man's cultural changes have catalysed genome changes (Wiesenfeld 1967: 1134-40). Since the adoption of agriculture occurred among certain Negro populations, this would provide an additional factor making for genetic divergence of agriculture-dependent Negroes from non-agricultural negriform peoples, including the Khoisans.

The later numerical and geographical expansion of the Negroes brought some of them, especially the Southern African Bantu-speaking Negroes, once more into contact with the Khoisans. The breakdown of geographical isolation led to a breakdown of genetic isolation. Hybridization now brought some of the 'new San alleles' into the genetic constitution of these Southern African Negroes. To some extent, gene-flow occurred in the reverse direction, but the cultural predominance of the Southern African Negroes ensured a greater flow of Khoisan genes into *them*, than of Negro genes into the Khoisans. The consequences are apparent in the lighter skin colour of many Southern African Negro groups, in their cranial form and in many other somatic features. What happened during this phase is well illustrated by the story of the *Gm* types of serum proteins (see pages 26f). Once Jenkins and Steinberg (1966: 399-407) discovered that San possessed two alleles of the *Gm* gene ($Gm^{1,13}$ and Gm^1), which had not previously been found in indigenous African peoples, and moreover possessed these alleles to a considerably higher frequency than the 'classical Negro alleles' also found to be present, they were prompted to speculate on the usefulness of these alleles in studying San admixture in the Bantu-speaking Negro tribes of Southern Africa:

> The Bantu-speaking Negroes have obvious strong genetic affinities with the Negro peoples of West and Central Africa, possessing as their commonest allele $Gm^{1,5,13,14}$. . . . However, a marked divergence from their northern relatives becomes apparent when the $Gm^{1,13}$ . . . allele is considered. In most of the Southern African populations $Gm^{1,13}$ is seen to be fairly common and its frequency increases as one proceeds from north to south. . . . This cline is particularly evident along the eastern seaboard and the virtual absence of the $Gm^{1,13}$ allele amongst the inhabitants of southern Angola and northern South West Africa is striking . . . it seems likely that there were larger concentrations of [the Bushman and Hottentot indigenes] in the more southerly parts of the area compared with the north or else that they repeatedly retreated in the face of the migrating tribes until, reaching the southern tip of the continent, further retreat became impossible and assimilation became total.
>
> Since the Angolans and the northern inhabitants of South West Africa are also classified with other Southern African tribes as Bantu-speaking Negroes, the marked difference in $Gm^{1,13}$ frequency between them and the eastern and southern Bantu-speakers needs to be explained. The early origins of these people must have been in closely situated geographical regions (traditionally thought to have been in the vicinity of the Congo watershed) and the divergence of their Gm allele frequencies might well be explained by the fact that those who moved to the east and south hybridized with the Khoisans, whilst those whose routes took them to the west did not do so to any appreciable extent. The Khoisans might well have been restricted in their distribution to these eastern areas . . . and there is anthropological and archaeological evidence to support this view (Tobias, '55; Wilcox, '56). There may have been no comparable southern migrations on the west side of the sub-continent so that contact between the Bantu-speakers like the Angolans, Ovambos and Okavangoans with Bushmen and Hottentots would have been minimal (Jenkins, Zoutendyk and Steinberg 1970: 197–218).

Thus, the genome of various Southern African Negro groups came to be altered by the inclusion of 'Khoisan alleles', varying in proportion as the populations had genetic contact with the Khoisans.

This tentative reconstruction of events would account for most of the known genetic facts on the relationships between Negroes and Khoisans.

(4) *The origins and expansion of the Bantu-speaking Negroes*

It has been suggested that Upper Pleistocene man of sub-Saharan Africa underwent a dichotomy, probably late in the Pleistocene rather than early in the Holocene, into Negroes and Khoisans. There is support for the view that the Khoisans were geographically stratified, the Khoikhoi (or Hottentots) living in the eastern to south-eastern parts of Africa and the San in the south (Wenner-Gren Conference on Bantu Origins 1968: 2). The archaeological evidence would suggest that all of these populations go back to Later Stone Age times.[15]

Amongst the sub-Saharan Negro population (that is, excluding the Khoisans), a complex of cultural features seems to have accompanied what is commonly spoken of in the literature as 'Bantu origins', 'Bantu genesis' and 'Bantu expansion'. These features comprise (a) the origin and spread of the Bantu subfamily of languages: (b) the spread of iron-working in and from Central Africa; (c) the expansion of an Early Iron Age industrial complex or complexes, with which are associated at least two pottery traditions, that of Dimple-based wares and that of Channelled wares; (d) the progressive adoption of, and dependence upon, agricultural pursuits.

It should be stressed that 'Bantu origins' and 'Bantu expansion' refer, essentially, to the adoption and spread of some or all of these *cultural* features: that is, to a changed way of life, a new technology, a new subfamily of languages. They do *not* refer to a process of race formation, to which the biological principles of race formation and of racial taxonomies apply.[16] As Clark put it, 'The fundamental change is not so much in the population as in the economy' (Clark 1964: 182). Notwithstanding, it cannot be denied that biological changes may have and probably did follow in the wake of the cultural changes, though to varying degrees in different parts of the geographical dispersal of the Bantu-speakers. For one thing, the new way of life seems to have been of enormous survival value and the population must have increased proportionately (Posnansky 1961: 86–93). Again, the widespread migrations which followed the new cultural advantages and the augmenting population pressure brought Bantu-speakers into new biotopes, in which they were exposed to diverse ecological circumstances. Since, as we have seen, ecological diversity is a potent factor in modifying gene frequencies, variations in the population genotype must have followed, at least in respect of eco-sensitive parts of the gene set. A further consequence of the movements of Bantu-speakers was to bring some of the populations into contact with other Africans, such as the Erythriotes and the Khoisans: hybridization must have followed inevitably, with consequential modifications of gene frequencies. Hence, it is easy to appreciate that the cultural changes accompanying 'Bantu genesis' had biological consequences. However, the basic changes are cultural. It would therefore be of value to examine briefly what evidence and views exist on the origins of this cultural revolution.

(a) Linguistic approach
There is general agreement that 'The striking fact about the Bantu languages is their fairly close similarity over a wide area' (Posnansky 1961: 86). This

would imply, as Greenberg (1955, 1963), Oliver (1966: 361–76), Hiernaux (1968c: 505–15) and others have stressed, that 'the Bantu (linguistic) family or subfamily must be regarded as a distinctly new subfamily, the speakers of which must have expanded very rapidly indeed in order to have achieved such a wide geographic dispersion along with such a small degree of linguistic divergence' (Oliver 1966: 361). Apart from some disagreement with the bases of Greenberg's classification (e.g. Westermann 1952: 250–6; Fodor 1966)—the pros and cons of which cannot be entered into here—there has been some difference—or change—of opinion on the amount of time necessary to bring about the diversification noted. The similarities between the present Bantu languages originally suggested to Greenberg (1955) that they are probably not older than two to three thousand years. More recently, at the Chicago Wenner-Gren Conference on Bantu Origins (1968: 1), 'The linguists postulated that the degree of differentiation existing between Bantu languages could not have come to pass within such a brief period as 2,000 years, the conventionally accepted limit of the African Iron Age'. If this view is correct, the origin of the Bantu subfamily of languages must be older than the Iron Age expansion of Bantu-speakers across large parts of Africa. Indeed, there is no intrinsic reason why the adoption of the Bantu languages should have triggered off the movement of Bantu-speaking peoples. It would seem that economic, rather than linguistic, aspects of the culture would have provided the stimulus to 'Bantu expansion'.

There is more general agreement as to the area in which the Bantu languages arose. Attention is focussed on the West African forest area (Wenner-Gren Conference 1968: 2), or on an area immediately north of the forest, possibly the central Cameroon or Ubangi-Shari (Guthrie 1962: 273–82). Greenberg (1963) reached the conclusion that Bantu belongs to the Niger-Congo language family, 'and that the Bantu languages, for all their vast extension, do not even form a single subgroup within the family, but that, taken all together, they merely form part of a subgroup which includes also most of the languages spoken in the central Cameroons and East-Central Nigeria' (after Hiernaux 1968c: 505–15).

> The historical inference for (Guthrie) was that, at the period when the speakers of the Niger-Congo languages had moved southwards from the savanna to occupy the forest belt as well, those of them who started from the eastern Nigerian end of the line, and who were not therefore brought to a halt by the Atlantic coast, simply moved straight on southwards and eastwards into the Congo basin, and from there fanned out to occupy the whole of what is now Bantu Africa (Hiernaux 1968c: 505–6, after Oliver 1966: 365).

According to Guthrie (1962: 273–82), a first migration might have carried a few dozen or hundred Bantu-speakers from a region north of the forest (possibly the central Cameroon or Ubangi-Shari) to an elliptical area with its main axis running east and west, roughly from the mouth of the Congo on the

Atlantic coast to the mouth of the Rovuma on the Indian Ocean, with its centre in the Luba country of northern Katanga. There, he suggests, the descendants multiplied, and from there they progressively dispersed over the rest of Bantu Africa.

Further support for the West African origins of Bantu-speakers comes from other lines of cultural evidence. Thus, such features as matrilineal inheritance, anthropomorphic art, secret societies and spirit possession cults all support the inference that the affinities of the central Bantu were with the Negroes of the West African forest and related fringe areas.

(b) Archaeological approach

The archaeologist is able to provide evidence bearing on the origins of the staples of African agriculture, the distribution of Channelled and Dimple-based pottery wares, the introduction and dispersion of iron metallurgy. Food production and domestication first made their appearance in Africa in the latter half of the sixth or early fifth millennium B.C. in Egypt. Since this is later than the beginnings of cultivation of wheat and barley and of animal domestication in the Near East, it seems that in the first instance Africa derived its knowledge of these things from immigrants into the Nile Valley (Clark 1962: 211–28; 1964: 161–83). The new economy spread rapidly across North Africa: it was in Cyrenaica by 5,000 B.C. and throughout much of the Sahara by 3,500–3,000 B.C. (Clark 1964: 180). There followed a pause: the new way of life did not immediately spread southwards, primarily because

> Cereal crops and domestic stock in the rich environment of tropical Africa were not the necessities for permanent village life that they were in the arid and semi-arid regions in which they were first developed . . . .The abundant vegetable and animal resources of the tropical savannah and forests provided all that was needed to maintain the Mesolithic populations at much the same level of subsistence as did the crops and stock of the Neolithic farmers, and probably with less expenditure of labour (Clark 1964: 180).

Only when the Sahara began to dry up after 2,500 B.C., the consequent over-grazing forced some of its Neolithic populations to move southwards into what is now the Sudan belt. Sub-Saharan African farming may then have arisen as a serious pursuit, although vegecultural practices around the forest margins had probably been in use for some considerable time before that (Clark 1964: 180–1). Neolithic cultivators are known from northern Nigeria, Ethiopia and the Kenya Rift about 2,000 B.C. Africa further south remained at the collecting stage of economy. Although it is possible that agriculture was introduced into this area during Later Stone Age times, Stone Age cereal agriculturalists have not as yet been identified in most of sub-Saharan Africa (Clark 1964: 181; Wenner-Gren Conference 1968: 2).

Finally, it was not until the population explosion that precipitated the Bantu movements around the beginning of the Christian era that the fundamental change in the economy of the sub-continent came under way, no doubt facilitated, probably indeed made possible, by the development of iron-working (Clark 1964: 181).

Inadequate as is the archaeological evidence on the spread of cereals into the sub-continent, that bearing on the spread of Iron Age cultures associated with the two characteristic forms of pottery, Dimple-based and Channelled, is more substantial and convincing. The earliest dates for such wares and/or Iron Age remains in Central and East Africa are A.D. 96 ± 220 at Machili in the Zambezi Valley; A.D. 205 ± 170 and A.D. 295 ± 95 at Phopo Hill in Malawi; A.D. 360 ± 120 at Nkope Bay at the south end of Lake Malawi; A.D. 345 ± 40 at Kalambo Falls in Northern Zambia; A.D. 250 ± 100 at Ndora in Rwanda; A.D. 270 ± 115, A.D. 260 ± 115, at Kwale in south-eastern Kenya (summarized by Hiernaux 1968c; 505–15 and Tobias 1972c). Thus, apart from isolated instances of early metal usage (Tobias 1949: 2–13; Dart and Beaumont 1967: 407–8; 1968: 241–6), systematic metal working entered south-central Africa about the beginning of the Christian era and by the fourth century A.D. was well-established over an extensive area including Rhodesia (Fagan 1965: 107–16; Wenner-Gren Conference 1968: 1–4).

Hence, the archaeological evidence supports the linguistic evidence, in testifying to the widespread expansion, in an area and at a time compatible with those indicated by the linguistic evidence, of a group of industries similar enough to be considered as parts of one industrial complex, or two related industrial complexes, embracing the Channelled wares and the Dimple-based wares (Hiernaux 1968c: 506).

(c) Anthropobiological evidence

Hiernaux (1968a; 1968c: 505–15) has determined the degree of biological similarity between all pairs of 101 sub-Saharan populations. His method is based on 'a number of the most commonly measured anthropometric characters', with the addition of blood traits when data were available. Using these parameters, he has compiled a matrix of all 'distances' between pairs of populations. These 101 populations, he points out, make up some 10 per cent of the total number of ethnic groups in Africa, which is roughly estimated at 1,000; unfortunately, however, he had relatively few sets of data for Bantu-speaking populations in southern Africa, so that their biological position could not be determined. The 'distances' for all pairs of these 101 populations range from 7 to 2,871. Although only provisional, as the sets of variables are not uniform and the geographical coverage of populations is uneven, Hiernaux has nevertheless found that an analysis of certain aspects of the matrix throws some light on the biological problems of the origin and expansion of Bantu-speaking groups.

The first point is that the clustering of the population scores on the matrix forms a quasi-continuum.

Any partitioning of the total set into clusters of populations, either the classical races or new taxons, is unjustified; it would group together some populations which are more dissimilar to each other than to populations belonging to other clusters. In particular, it makes no sense to group all Bantu-speaking populations into a race: many of them are biologically much nearer to some non-Bantu-speaking ethnic groups than to some Bantu-speaking ones (Hiernaux 1968c: 508).

The second point is that if one computes the *mean* distance of each population from all other populations, the twelve populations with the lowest mean distances include six Bantu-speaking and six non-Bantu-speaking ethnic groups. The six Bantu-speaking series are the Ewondo and Basa of southern Cameroon, the Nyoro of Uganda, the Haya and Nyamwezi of western Tanzania, and the Swahili on the east coast. The six non-Bantu-speaking ethnic groups are the Dyola of southern Senegal, the Koniagi and Badyaranke at the Senegal-Guinea border, the Kasena on the Haute Volta-Ghana border, the Mayogo in northern Congo, and the Logo in north-eastern Congo. All but one (the Logo, who speak an eastern Sudanic language) speak languages of the Niger-Congo family to which Bantu is said to belong. Hiernaux suggests that the central anthropobiological position of these populations implies that they are relatively little modified descendants of an old African stock. All six non-Bantu-speaking populations live north of the moist forest, in a north-west/south-east belt extending in latitude from 13° to 3°N and in longitude from the west coast to 29°E. Their habitat is savannah, woodland, or a forest-savannah mosaic. A number of Bantu-speaking populations share an important part of their gene pool with them.

This seems to imply that a large component of the ancestry of these Bantu-speaking ethnic groups comes from an area north of the wet forest, where many populations akin to them live. From a completely independent body of data, physical anthropology thus supports the views of the linguists about the earliest phase of Bantu expansion (Hiernaux 1968c: 508).

Another approach to the data on anthropobiological distances is to take a central Bantu-speaking population as a reference and to relate all the other populations to it. Hiernaux did this for several reference populations (the Ewondo, Bushong, Duala and Basa), and obtained the same general results from all of them. Analysing those populations with a distance of under 100 from the reference population, he found that most of them are located in a ring which encircles the equatorial forest and includes the forest-savannah border.

Such a low distance between populations requires, it seems, three conditions: (1) a relatively recent common origin, (2) the populations concerned remaining in a not too different biotope, and (3) the absence of any important admixture with genetically largely different populations (Hiernaux, 1968c: 509). With the exception of one population, the Kuanyama Ambo, all of the populations with low distances from the reference population have a similar biotope; it is patent that they have had a recent common origin and there is little indication of mixture with other genetically diverse populations. Hiernaux's data permit him to infer the following reconstruction of events:

> From a nuclear population or group of closely related populations living north of the moist forest, not far from its border, migration and expansion took place in a relatively recent past. The resulting populations remained little differentiated between themselves and from the nuclear population in areas where they were not submitted to a strongly different biotope, and where they did not assimilate a large number of individuals belonging to physically contrasting populations. They still keep a strong biological similarity with some non-Bantu-speaking populations, which like them are relatively little modified descendants of the old West-Central African stock (Hiernaux 1968c: 510).

Where, however, the populations wandered further afield from the ring around the forest, they were more liable to diverge somatically from the physical structure of the nuclear populations still living near the source of the expansion. Such change in the make-up of some of the migrants is likely to have occurred as a result of at least three possible sets of factors: (1) a move into a different biotope (e.g. from moist savannah into a more arid zone; or from a malarial to a non-malarial region), which would subject the population to a new or enhanced or diminished set of selective pressures; (2) hybridization with populations which had already long lived within the area now penetrated by the Bantu-speaking migrants, for example the Mbuti Pygmies of the Ituri forest, or the Khoisans of east, south-east and southern Africa, and which had, over a long period of reproductive isolation from the ancestors of the newcomers, evolved appreciable changes in genetic structure; or (3) a combination in varying degrees of both of the previous factors.

For instance, Hiernaux's distance statistics show that the physique of the Bantu forest agriculturalists diverges from that of the Bantu grassland dwellers in the direction of that of the forest dwelling Mbuti Pygmies (who are hunter-gatherers but have come to speak a Bantu language). This change of physique could be the result of exposure of the recently-arrived Bantu agriculturalists to a similar forest biotope, or to hybridization with the Mbuti (who have seemingly lived in the forest far longer than have the agriculturalists), or to both factors. In point of fact, a comparison of the blood-group frequencies makes it likely that this convergence to the Pygmy physique has resulted more from the influence of the forest biotope than from genetic admixture with the Pygmies (Hiernaux 1968c: 512).

Some of the Bantu-speakers moved south-eastwards and southwards into the territories of Southern Africa. They moved from moister equatorial and tropical conditions, to more temperate and drier tropical, sub-tropical and semi-desert conditions. Hence, they moved into a markedly different biotope. The length of time for which they have been exposed to the new biotope varies from close on 2,000 years—for example, in Zambia, Malawi, Rhodesia and, perhaps, Angola—to about 1,000 years in the Transvaal and less in the most southerly parts of the sub-continent. The effect a particular biotope would exert on an immigrant population would depend (in the absence of hybridization) on at least four factors: (a) the time of exposure of the immigrants to the new biotope; (b) the contrast between the new biotope and the old one in which the population originated; (c) the rigours of the new environment, its biological stresses, and its challenge to human adaptability, that is, the selective pressures of the new biotope; and (d) the degree of advancement of the immigrants' culture, that is, the ability of the culture to buffer the people against too blatant an exposure to the environment.

That the southern drier biotope has not exerted much effect as yet on at least the Kuanyama Ambo of southern Angola and northern South West Africa is shown by their possessing a bio-statistical distance of only seventy-eight from the Ewondo of southern Cameroon (Hiernaux 1968c: 509–11). The Kuanyama's close affinity with West African Negroes in the source area finds an echo in the inferences drawn from the pattern of *Gm* alleles of these and other Angolan and South West African Bantu-speakers.

Some Bantu-speaking migrants to the south and south-east encountered not only new biotopes, but genetically well differentiated, Khoisan populations. There is little doubt from skeletal, serological, anthropometric and anthroposcopic evidence that hybridization occurred in varying degrees between the Southern African Negroes and the Khoisans. So the immigrant populations were subjected to twofold processes of change: those engendered by exposure to selective forces in the environment, and those resulting from hybridization.

The distinctive gene frequencies of the Khoisans might be due to a combination of selection (or relaxation of selection) and of random genetic drift, if we may assume a long period of autochthonous development in the biotope under consideration. To the extent that the gene-pool of the Khoisans was based on selection, to that extent we may be led to infer that the absorption of Khoisan genes by Bantu-speaking migrants provided the new arrivals with a short-cut towards selective adaptation to their new biotope. In this sense, hybridization may provide a mechanism facilitating and expediting the attainment by a migrant population of a gene-pool better adapted to success in the new environment.

To what extent Southern African Negroes have acquired San admixture is suggested by the figures of Jenkins, Zoutendyk and Steinberg (1970: 210), based upon the key allele, $Gm^{1,13}$. Assuming that the Bantu-speaking populations, prior to their great southward migrations, did not possess the allele $Gm^{1,13}$ and that those who possess it to-day acquired it from the San, these investigators used the frequency of the allele in each Bantu-speaking ethnic group and the frequency in present-day San to assess the proportion of admixture in various Bantu-speaking chiefdoms. Their results in order of magnitude are Kgalagadi 64 per cent admixture, Xhosa 60, Tswana 53,

Bhaca 49, Zulu 45, Pondo 45, Venda 38, Hlubi 37, Sotho 29, Swazi 25, Himba 22, Pedi 17, Shangana-Tsonga 15, Kuangari 13, Mlozi 13, Valley Tonga 12, Plateau Tonga 11, Malawi (mixed) 11, Bunja 7, Nyambaan 6, Lenje 6, Ndebele (Transvaal) 5, Kuanyama 5, Angola (mixed) 0, Diriko 0, Ila 0, Kuambi 0, Mbukushu 0, Sambio 0 (Figure 1.7).

These figures are interesting and suggestive, though of course they need to be corroborated by other independent gene markers, for it is dangerous to rely exclusively on one particular allele as a marker of population admixture. A similar analysis of phenotypic traits such as skin-colour and macronympha would undoubtedly provide valuable source-data on this question, supplementing the information which may be garnered from monogenic polymorphisms.

Finally, by a combination of biotopic influences and hybridization, perhaps tempered by genetic drift, we see that the features which characterize the various and varied Southern African Negroes have come into being. Where the two or three sets of influences have been minimal, departure in physique and genotype from the nuclear populations of Central and West Africa will be slightest; where these effects have been maximal, a moderate degree of divergence will be apparent. However, even in those of the Bantu-speaking Negroes who have diverged most from the nuclear populations, this degree of modification has not been such as to mask the overall physical and genetic affinities of the Southern African Negroes with other sub-Saharan African Negroes. Neither the lapse of time nor cultural and ecological diversification has been sufficient to generate a new race of man: the Bantu-speakers of Africa remain a part of Africa's Negro population.

Notes

* I thank the Medical Research Council of South Africa and the Research Committee of the Witwatersrand University; Dr T. Jenkins, Dr Hertha de Villiers, Dr A. Zoutendyk, Dr H. Gordon, Dr A. G. Steinberg, Mr H. Harpending, Mr M. M. Keraan, Miss Sheila Johnston; Miss Carole J. Orkin, Mr C. S. Block, Mrs June P. Asch and Miss Jeanne Walker.

1 Angola, Botswana, Lesotho, Malawi, Mozambique, Rhodesia, South Africa, South West Africa, Swaziland and Zambia.

2 As had been suggested by Singer and Weiner (1963: 168–76).

3 *Ortho-ovoid* means that the cranium is of moderate height (orthocephalic) and has moderately curved parietal bones, so that when viewed from above, the vault looks ovoid or egg-shaped.
Chamae-pentagonoid means that the vault of the skull is low (chamaecephalic) and, when seen from above, is pentagonal or coffin-shaped in outline owing to strongly-bossed or conical parietal bones.

4 In East Africans, for instance, Allbrook has claimed that 'blurring of skeletal sexual differences is the rule' (Allbrook 1956: 607).

5 Tobias's 'peppercorn and woolly' category corresponds to Gates's (1957: 1–4) 'tufted' class and, probably, to Santos Junior's 'dictiulotrichous' (J) category (1959: 25–33).

6 For example, Drury and Drennan 1926: 113–17; Schultze-Jena 1928: 147–228; Dart 1937: 175–246; Schapera 1930: 59; Fischer 1955: 58–66; Tobias 1957: 33–40; 1964: 67–86; de Villiers 1961: 223–7; 1969: 48–51.

7 Polygenic inheritance refers to the mode of inheritance of a trait when it is governed by many genes, which are called *polygenes* or *multiple factors*. Each of these genes acts independently, and their total effect is generally cumulative. Height and weight and other dimensions of the body are determined by polygenic inheritance. Traits governed by this form of inheritance are often difficult to analyse, especially when the trait is strongly liable to environmental modification.

8 Examples of such studies are those of Ashton (1939: 147–214) on the Sotho diet, Beemer (1939: 199–236) and Jones (1963) on the Swazi diet, Quin (1959) on the foods and feeding habits of the Pedi, and Thompson (1954: 1–57) on a rural community in the Serenje District and an urban community at Lusaka, Zambia.

9 For example, Fox (1936: 25–36), the Gillman brothers (1951), Walker (1958: 989–1008; 1966: 814–52), Brock (1961), and many others.

10 See, for example, Engel 1956: 489–500; Nelson 1959: 73–84; 1963: 777–87; Stoch and Smythe 1963: 546–52; 1967: 1027–31; Cravioto and Robles 1965: 449–64; Brown 1966: 512–22; Eichenwald and Fry 1969: 644–8; Baraitser and Evans 1969: 56–8.

11 Zoutendyk, Kopec and Mourant 1953: 361–8; Weiner and Zoutendyk 1959: 843–4; Singer and Weiner 1963: 168–76; Tobias 1966: 124–7; Rightmire 1970: 172–3.

12 Most San (Bushman) groups tested differ from most other African groups in possessing high A and low B, highest *Rho* frequency, virtual absence of *rh*, high M and low N, high He^+ (Henshaw), rising in two population groups to the highest on record, high K^+ (Kell), absence of Lu^a (Lutheran), high Fy^a (Duffy), relatively low P^+, fairly low V^+ (Tobias, 1966, 125–6). More recently, Jenkins *et al.* (1971: 513–31) have shown that Khoisans have significantly fewer alleles for the A^+ and A^- variants of G6PD, and for PGD^c, but a much higher frequency of AK^2, than Southern African Negroes.

13 For those who would place all living man in a single subspecies, *Homo sapiens sapiens*, to distinguish living man from such extinct subspecies as *Homo sapiens neanderthalensis* and *Homo sapiens rhodesiensis*, the taxonomic appellation of this negriform racial cluster would require the quadrinomial nomen, *Homo sapiens sapiens afer*.

14 'The sickle-cell trait is therefore virtually absent in the Union of South Africa. . . . The best explanation is undoubtedly that the South African Bantu arrived south of the Zambezi before the haemoglobin S gene was introduced into Africa.' (Budtz-Olsen and Burgers 1955: 109–10).

15 Clark 1950: 80–5; 1964: 161–83; Hiernaux 1959: 26–30; 1968c: 505–15; Posnansky 1961: 86–93; Fagan 1961: 199–210; 1963: 157–77; Clark and Fagan 1965: 354–71; Robinson and Sandelowsky 1969: 1–40; Sandelowsky 1971.

16 As defined for instance by Garn (1961), Coon (1962), Hulse (1962: 929–45), Montagu (1962: 919–28), Livingstone (1962: 279), Washburn (1963: 521–31), Johnston (1964: 822–7), Boyd (1964: 119–69) and Neel (1969: 389–403).

Chapter 2

The Ecological Setting
J. P. Jessop

This account of the natural environment of man in southern Africa deals with South West Africa, Botswana, the southern half of Mozambique, Swaziland, Lesotho and the Republic of South Africa. That part of the Cape Province west of the 25° line of longitude has been largely excluded as the Bantu-speaking peoples did not settle in this area. In all Africa the distribution of the Bantu-speaking peoples coincides broadly with the December–February rainfall area. Particularly in the south, the Bantu have confined themselves to the region of high summer rainfall.

Topography and Climate

The physical structure of the Republic of South Africa resembles an amphitheatre with the stage, which is the Orange River Basin, to the north-west. To the south-east, the theatre rises slowly to 2,000 metres (6,500 ft) or more, before dropping rather abruptly to the sea. This shape is of the greatest importance in the formation of man's physical environment. On the one hand, it has formed an extensive, undulating interior, mainly over 1,000 metres (3,300 ft) above sea-level, but, on the other, it has ensured that much of the moisture in the winds blowing in off the Indian Ocean is deposited in the narrow and often steep belt to the east and south-east of the escarpment.

This seaward belt includes a narrow coastal plain which is as little as 16 km (10 miles) broad along most of the South African coast, but is more extensive in Mozambique, where virtually all of the country south of 20° latitude is under 400 metres (1,300 ft) above sea-level but up to 320 km (200 or more miles) wide. From the west coast there is, in parts, also a distinct rise to the escarpment, but this is not as steep as along the southern and eastern coast of the Cape and Natal. In northern South West Africa and around the Orange River mouth the plateau is not cut off from the sea by a rim of mountain ranges as it is elsewhere. The wettest parts of southern Africa lie to the east of the escarpment in both the eastern coastal belt and along the mountain ranges bordering the great central plateau. Not only do these regions—especially in Natal—enjoy up to 1,000 mm (39 in) or more of rain each year, but both the mountains and the coastal regions receive considerable moisture from mists. Except in the extreme south and west very little rain falls in winter and the mists, therefore, play a very important role during this time of the year. The coastal regions have a further advantage to man in that they are almost entirely frost- and snow-free.

Most of Mozambique falls within a rainfall range of 750–1,000 mm (*c.* 30–39 in) per annum, while the coast of South West Africa receives an extremely low rainfall, fairly extensive areas having no more than 100 mm (4 in) a year.

The mountains of the escarpment do not form a continuous, uninterrupted range. From the north-eastern Transvaal the Drakensberg range runs south to the Lesotho-Natal border (where it rises over 3,000 metres (10,000 ft) above sea level) and into the eastern Cape. Lesser ranges, such as the Stormberg, the Amatolas and the Nieuwveld Mountains, form the main southern border of the plateau with other ranges, such as the Swartberg, parallel to them towards the coast. In the west the escarpment is less well-defined but does exceed 2,000 metres (6,500 ft) at, for example, the Tsaris Mountains in the southern half of South West Africa and the Auas Mountains near Windhoek. At Tsumeb is a great copper deposit originally worked by both Bergdama and Herero smiths. From the mountains of the escarpment numerous, relatively short, and often temporary, rivers run through deep valleys to the sea. In their lower reaches these valleys tend to be hotter than the intervening ridges and to receive rather lower rainfalls.

The great central plateau makes up the southern part of what has been described as the largest plateau in the world. It is broken by hills and undulations, but by few mountain ranges. In the Transvaal, ranges, such as the Soutpansberg in the north and the Waterberg in the west, rise to 500 metres (1,600 ft) or more above the general level of the surrounding country. Otherwise the altitudinal variation is provided by the slope from the heights of the surrounding escarpment down into the largest rivers—the Orange between the Cape and South West Africa and the Limpopo forming the northern boundary of the Transvaal. The extent to which the Limpopo has cut into the plateau is shown by the fact that it rises less than 900 metres (3,000 ft) in over 1,000 km (600 miles) from the sea: by comparison, the Umtamvuna River, one of the rivers draining the escarpment to the south-east, reaches a similar height in 65–80 km. A third considerable river is the Kunene, forming part of the northern boundary of South West Africa, but its valley is nothing like the extent of that of the Limpopo and Orange. The Okavango river flows eastward and, with the Kwango, 'spreads like a trellis' over Lake Ngami.

> This Ngami region, though of tremendous interest anthropologically, is the home of such a welter of tribes and mixed races and cultures that little direct comparison between people and environment is possible. Tswana cattle-keepers, Masarwa hunters, Herero refugees . . . and Mpukushu tribes all form a varied population, largely the scrapings of the Zambesi and the Kalahari (Goodwin 1937: 40–1).

The Orange River and its main tributary, the Vaal, drain the western slopes of the eastern escarpment. From the south-eastern Transvaal and Lesotho it runs more than 1,300 km (800 miles), as the crow flies. The Limpopo is not much shorter, rising in the western Transvaal and receiving tributaries from Botswana, Rhodesia and Mozambique. The plateau obtains most of its rain during summer or, especially in the west, autumn, but the amount varies considerably. Most of South West Africa and Botswana, except in the north of these territories, receive 150 mm (6 in) or less per annum. The annual rainfall increases to the east, reaching 500 mm (20 in) or more over most of the Transvaal.

There were significant fluctuations in the climate of South Africa during the Pleistocene. There is also a widely held belief that there has been a decrease in rainfall over the past three centuries, but one investigator came to the conclusion that 'whilst the rainfall in some areas seems to have diminished in others it appears to have increased' (Kokot 1948: 136). With longer series of records it may be possible to determine trends in rainfall, but it is unlikely that changes have greatly affected man's environment over the past few centuries.

In Southern Africa, where the rainfall tends to be strongly seasonal, rather low and in many areas erratic, permanent waters, where they occur, are of considerable ecological importance. There are a few freshwater lakes, such as Lake Sibayi in Zululand. The Okavango Swamps in northern Botswana, although permanent, are brackish. Perennial rivers arise in the mountains of the escarpment, but in most of South West Africa, Botswana and the plateau of the Republic of South Africa water is to be found in rivers only for a short period after rain. Undoubtedly water has been at a premium in Southern Africa throughout historical times, and agricultural practices, veld burning and grazing, by encouraging rapid drainage, have aggravated the position.

Temperatures do not appear to have influenced man's activities in Southern Africa directly, but rather through their influence on vegetation and on diseases both of stock, such as nagana, and of man, such as malaria. On the higher parts of the Drakensberg, frost can occur throughout the year and is of fairly frequent occurrence during winter over most of the plateau. The coastal belt is mainly frost-free. Snow can be expected from time to time, especially in areas above 1,500 metres (5,000 ft) altitude.

The soils of Southern Africa are poor. In many areas they are shallow and several of the elements necessary for plant growth are not present in sufficient quantities or are present only in forms in which the plant cannot use them. This deficiency has been greatly aggravated by man's activities. Veld fires must have occurred in Southern Africa even before the appearance of man. Man has, however, increased their frequency. A fire just before the advent of spring growth may actually stimulate the new shoots and an occasional fire at this time may not be harmful, but if the grass is burnt as soon as the year's growth has died down, the ground is left exposed for several months. Under these conditions part of the top-soil may be blown away and the resulting sheet erosion seriously impoverishes the soil. Cattle and sheep may also reduce the ground cover to the same effect. Destruction of natural cover for agricultural purposes and the removal of stubble has also added to the deteriora-

THE ECOLOGICAL SETTING

tion of the soil. In many areas, particularly where there is rapid run-off, water erosion has created very considerable gulleys. When it is realized that it may take 1,000 years for 25 mm (1 in) of soil to form (according to one estimate), the significance of these factors on an already not particularly rich soil can be imagined.

Vegetation

Southern Africa, for the purposes of this chapter, can be divided into five broad vegetational regions. Of these, the three major ones, in descending order of extent, are savannah, grassveld, and desert and semi-desert. The remaining two types, forest and Cape macchia, occur as isolated patches.

(1) Savannah

Savannah and grassveld types of vegetation are related to one another. In much of the former and all of the latter the ground is more or less covered by a low plant growth which is usually dominated by grasses. Above this there are larger bushes, trees, or, in the savannahs, clumps of bushes and trees. In areas where these larger plants are well separated from one another, or where they are altogether absent, the vegetation may be called grassveld. Botanists do not always agree on exactly where to draw the line between these types of vegetation.

(a) *Brachystegia*-woodland

Savannah covers extensive areas of both Central and Southern Africa. A large part of Rhodesia and most of the territories as far north as Tanzania, are covered by a type of savannah often referred to as *Brachystegia*-woodlands. This region is dominated by deciduous trees belonging to the genera *Brachystegia* and *Julbernardia*. They are not, however, the only trees. In some habitats, as along the edges of river valleys, species of *Monotes*, *Terminalia*, *Combretum* and *Acacia* may replace them. Although *Brachystegia*-woodlands are normally found nearer to the Equator, they do enter Mozambique, both in the north and across from the Rhodesian border. Along the Mozambique coast they extend in a belt less than 160 km (100 miles) broad as far south as the 25° line of latitude, just north of Lourenco Marques. In the west they reach the northern border of South West Africa at the Caprivi Strip but there is no *Brachystegia*-woodland in either South West Africa or Botswana.

(b) Mopane-veld

To the south of the *Brachystegia*-woodland belt are two regions of savannah occupying a rather drier environment. Here the rainfall tends to be lower than 750 mm (30 in) a year; too low for the *Brachystegia*-woodland. These

49

regions are also characterized by the poorly-drained hot valleys of large rivers—the Kunene and Okavango in the west and the Limpopo in the east. These two blocks are dominated by another deciduous tree—the mopane (*Colophospermum mopane*). The baobab (*Adamsonia digitate*) is a well-known tree often associated with mopane in both areas, but is relatively infrequent elsewhere. It supplies bark for cordage and string-making.

The western block covers a 640 to 800 km (400–500 miles) wide area in the north-western corner of South West Africa, including most of Ovamboland, the Etosha Pan Game Reserve and a small part of the Caprivi Strip. It also extends north into Angola. The eastern block, in which the rainfall is still lower—down to 400 mm (16 in) per annum—includes the flat country north of the Soutpansberg, the Kruger National Park north of the Olifants River, a fairly large part of Mozambique adjoining the Transvaal, a small part of eastern Botswana and part of Rhodesia.

The mopane in these areas is often, particularly in the eastern block, virtually the only type of tree. In other areas other trees, such as *Terminalia* (vaalboom), are associated with it. In the western block it usually produces a well-formed tree, but in the eastern part of its range it tends to be low-growing and shrubby.

The mopane is of the greatest importance to a rural community. The leaves are edible to game and stock, both when still growing and when shed in winter. Certain caterpillars, 'mopane worms', which feed on the mopane leaves, are often the richest source of protein available to man in the mopane-veld. The mopane also provides firewood and can be so used even when still green. Its timber is difficult to work, but has been found suitable for building huts.

(c) Bushveld
A third type of savannah for which the best available term seems to be the rather vague name 'bushveld', occurs to the south and east of the mopane-veld. It occupies a block in north-eastern South West Africa, adjoining the two main mopane-veld regions. The vegetation of the larger part of the Transvaal, from the Soutpansberg to just south of Pretoria, as well as part of eastern Botswana, is bushveld. From the eastern Transvaal it descends from the escarpment into the coastal belt of Mozambique, where it forms a belt between the mopane-veld and the *Brachystegia*-woodland towards the coast. It also extends south, covering most of Swaziland and a belt of relatively low-altitude country through Zululand, Natal, the Transkei and the eastern Cape to just north-west of Port Elizabeth.

Within the bushveld region there is a wide range of savannah types, as well as zones of transition to other kinds of vegetation. This is associated with differences in climate and topography. By and large, the bushveld is not an easy type of savannah to describe as, in addition to variation under different environmental conditions, there is generally no tree which can be regarded as typical. Of the 70 'veld types' recognized by Acocks in South Africa, at least

THE ECOLOGICAL SETTING

sixteen can be entirely or partly included under the heading of bushveld. Only three main variants will be discussed here.

(i) The *plateau bushveld* is the form of bushveld occurring on the great central plateau, as its name indicates. It generally occurs where there is an annual rainfall of about 500 mm (20 in), or a little more. It is by no means a uniform type. Between areas there are changes in the types of trees, their size and density. Over much of the plateau the trees are far enough apart for their crowns not to touch, and there are all stages of transition through parklands to grassveld. At the other end of the range there are areas, as in parts of northeastern South West Africa, where the crowns of the trees are entwined to form a dense thicket. The trees are deciduous and often only 5–7 m (15–20 ft) high. Among the commoner trees are several species of *Acacia*. One of the most useful of these is *Acacia karroo* (sweet-thorn), which is a useful fodder plant. The leaves appear in early spring, before grass has become plentiful, and both the pods and the old flowers are eaten by cattle. Among the other useful characteristics of the sweet-thorn is the edible gum exuded from the woody parts. In some areas acacias make up the entire tree layer, but usually there are other trees as well. *Peltophorum africanum* (African wattle) is a common species which is used for carving. *Combretum apiculatum* (bushwillow) and *Terminalia sericea* (Transvaal silverleaf) are also widespread and, in certain areas, dominant. The leaves of both of these trees are browsed by cattle. *Baikiaea plurijuga* (Rhodesian teak) is an important element of the South West African and Botswana bushveld, not occurring in the Transvaal lowveld, and is a valued timber tree. Other trees in the South West African bushveld show similarities with the Transvaal lowveld rather than with the Transvaal plateau bushveld. Among these are *Pterocarpus angolensis* (kiaat) which, in the Transvaal, occurs on the slopes of the escarpment rather than on the plains of the lowveld proper. Smaller bushes may be scattered amongst the trees, but in many areas little growth disturbs the rather uniform level of the trees and grass. The grass layer is made up mainly of more or less tufted species of grass including the rooigras (*Themeda triandra*). Cattle thrive, but because of the long dry winters and the associated dormancy of the grasses, large concentrations of stock may be difficult to maintain in a small area throughout the year.

(ii) The *lowveld*. In Mozambique and in areas of the Transvaal, Swaziland and Zululand below about 1,000 metres (3,300 ft), the temperature and rainfall is higher than elsewhere in the savannahs. There is generally more than 750 mm (30 in) of rain a year. The lowveld is characterized by deciduous trees of a wide range of species forming a number of very different communities. The trees are, on the average, closer together than on the plateau and as tall as 10–12 metres (30–35 ft) in parts. Among the most conspicuous trees—especially frequent in temporarily wet areas—is the well-known fever tree (*Acacia xanthophloea*). Other species of *Acacia*, for example *A. nigrescens* (knob-thorn), which is regarded as an indicator of good ranching country, are common. *Sclerocarya caffra* (marula) is an important source of valuable wood and fruits among the Tsonga. Because of its value, the marula is often preserved even in cultivated lands. Below the trees there may be shrubs and the grass layer is taller than in the plateau bushveld.

In the Transvaal the lowveld and plateau bushveld are separated by the Drakensberg. The savannah along the lower slopes of the escarpment differs from either of the main blocks. Here *Parinari curatellifolia* (mobola plum), with its edible fruit, is especially common.

(iii) *Temperate thornveld.* The savannah to the south of the lowveld, through Natal to the southern Cape, is dominated by *Acacia karroo*. In being characterized by a single type of tree it differs from the other bushveld types, with their rich tree floras. The terrain is undulating and the rainfall usually about 600–900 mm (24–35 in) a year. Other trees or bushes which occur are species of *Maytenus* (mainly pendorings) and *Rhus* (karee). These sometimes occur singly, but often form small clumps made up of several trees and climbers. The commonest grass is again the rooigras, which is also the principal species grazed by livestock. However, much of the temperate thornveld falls within the sour grassveld in which the grasses lose their palatability as they mature.

In the numerous river valleys there are often denser types of vegetation. Characterizing the hot dry depressions are succulent plants, such as species of *Aloe* and *Euphorbia*, and an entangled growth of often spiny bushes. Replacing these thickets there are patches of true forests in parts where there is more moisture.

(d) Kalahari thornveld

Like the temperate thornveld, the savannah of the Kalahari is dominated by species of *Acacia*, *A. giraffae* (camel-thorn) and *A. mellifera* (swarthaakdoring) being among the commonest. The pods of both these trees are eaten by stock. In some parts these trees, which tend to be rather scattered but often grow up to 10 metres (30 ft) high, are replaced by lower-growing bushes. For example, in the south-east, in the Griqualand West region, a very common low bush is *Tarchonanthus camphoratus* (camphor bush). The vegetation of most of the Kalahari is dominated by acacias which flourish in an area of low rainfall, below about 500 mm (20 in) a year, on loose sand. Cultivation of crops is not possible in this area, but it can support a sparse cattle population where there are springs. The ground cover is largely grass, especially species of *Aristida* and *Eragrostis*, but the grass plants are rather far apart. Under grazing the ground cover tends to disappear, especially in the drier south, leaving wastes of shifting sand dunes. Several plants store water underground or, as with the tsama melon (*Citrullus vulgaris*), in their fruits. This is the only source of water available to animals and man over large tracts.

The northern and eastern parts of the Kalahari thornveld are inhabited by Tswana peoples who, because of the scarcity of surface water, are forced to live in large settlements or towns, unlike the Nguni, whose environment allows them to adopt a scattered homestead pattern.

(2) Grassveld

The grassveld is neither as extensive nor as varied as the savannahs. To some extent there are regional variations in the species of grass, although *Themeda triandra* is common in most areas. The general absence of trees is ascribed to the very dry winters with frequent frosts, but in protected places, such as river beds and rocky outcrops, trees and bushes do occur. An important distinction is made between sour grassveld and sweet grassveld. Sour grassveld usually occurs in areas of high rainfall where its growth is vigorous. At first, grasses in sour grassveld are highly palatable but, as they mature, they develop a high fibre content making them unpalatable and indigestible. Sweet grassveld provides good grazing all the year round. An intermediate 'mixed' type is also recognized. To some extent these differences are associated with different species of grass in these areas, but some grasses, like *Themeda triandra*, which occur in all types, exist in different forms in the sweet and sour grassveld. Heavy grazing of sour grassveld during the early stages of growth prevents a very rank growth forming and increases palatability during the rest of the year.

(3) Desert and semi-desert

The Namib Desert, a belt which rarely exceeds 160 km (100 miles) in breadth, extends along most of the South West African coast. Much of this area is without vegetation of any kind. A few scattered perennials do however occur along the water courses, and there are annuals, mainly grasses, which appear after rains. Of the few plants that grow in the deserts the best known are probably *Welwitschia bainesii* (tumboa), in the north, and *Acanthosicyos horrida* (naras), a widespread spiny bush with edible fruits. Towards the interior, the Namib Desert is bordered by a belt of semi-desert vegetation which broadens out further south to form the Karoo. Grasses occur, although in parts these are almost exclusively annual species. Low perennial bushes, of which many have succulent stems or leaves in some parts (succulent Karoo), and other annuals, make up most of the semi-desert vegetation. In the east of the Karoo, the western Orange Free State and adjoining parts of the Cape almost as far south as Port Elizabeth, there tend to be more grasses. This is associated with a transition to grassveld vegetation. It was probably only in this eastern area that the Bantu regularly found sufficient pasturage in the form of grass for their cattle. Even here, with a rainfall between 250 and 500 mm (10 and 20 in) per annum, intensive cultivation would have been hardly practical.

(4) Forest

Small patches of forest occur both along the coast and on the damper eastern and southern slopes of the escarpment. Their greatest development is in areas where there is water available all the year round and where temperatures are uniformly warm. Under ideal conditions, such as in parts of Zululand and Mozambique, they regenerate quickly. In other areas, as in most of the eastern Cape, savannah or other vegetation types virtually replace forest that has been cleared.

Over most of South Africa there is some uniformity in the structure of the forests. The trees are evergreen, with rather small leaves, usually forming several strata of which one forms a dense canopy. Widespread species include yellow-woods (*Podocarpus* spp.), white stinkwood (*Celtis africana*, a species not confined to forests), and the black ironwood (*Olea capensis*). In the more tropical forest areas of Zululand and Mozambique there tend to be more climbers and the trees have larger leaves. In parts of Mozambique the forest species are largely deciduous, providing a link between savannah and forest types of vegetation.

Except as a source of timber the forests have not been used to any extent. Once the trees are felled, however, the soil is very fertile.

(5) *Cape Macchia*

The Cape macchia, or *fynbos*, is the dominant vegetation of the south-western Cape, but it also extends into tropical Africa as isolated patches along the mountains. Its characteristically wiry, hard-leafed shrubs do not provide very satisfactory grazing, but its extent is so restricted that it does not play an important role outside its main centre in the Cape.

Recent Changes in the Vegetation

Before the advent of pastoral man, antelope formed large herds, especially on the plateau, and many of these moved from place to place as the food plants were grazed down. These heavily-grazed areas were then rested naturally for fairly long periods. Man tends to remain in the same area for longer periods with his livestock. New shoots of palatable species are eaten down as they appear, while less palatable species are left to grow and propagate themselves. Associated with a marked, and more or less permanent, reduction in ground cover is soil erosion which in its turn leads to impoverishment of the soil and further changes in the vegetation. These, and other factors, have brought about very significant changes in the vegetation of Southern Africa. Acocks, whose knowledge of the vegetation of South Africa is unsurpassed, estimated in 1952 that the Karoo had, in parts, spread 150 miles (240 km) into sweet grassveld. Another considerable change which has taken place is the reduction of forest area. Acocks considers that most of the slopes of the eastern and southern escarpment were at one time more or less covered by forest and scrub-forest (Acocks 1953). All but a few small fragments of this forest have disappeared. This reduction of forest area has probably been to the advantage of agriculture, although with the disappearance of vegetation in catchment areas there has been a serious reduction in the availability of water.

Pests and Diseases

Although there have always been serious human diseases in Southern Africa, none of these is known to have prevented the spread of the Bantu-speaking peoples into areas they would otherwise have occupied.

White settlers in Southern Africa encountered malaria in virtually the entire savannah region, including not only the hot wet parts of the lowveld but also the central Transvaal and the Kalahari.

The tsetse fly (*Glossina* spp.) was prevalent in the lowveld, but acted as the vector only of nagana in stock and not of sleeping-sickness in man. It is possible that sleeping-sickness was introduced into parts of Mozambique after the advent of European exploration in central Africa.

Tick-born diseases of stock occurred and must always have been a significant cause of stock losses everywhere.

Termites occur throughout southern Africa and wood-eating species are present over all the areas occupied by the Bantu-speaking peoples. Locust swarms have also been reported in all these areas and would from time to time have destroyed crops and grazing.

Game

Antelope were numerous throughout Southern Africa at the time of the arrival of the white settlers. In the open plains there were large herds of springbuck, but their migratory movements would probably have limited their value to a largely agricultural community.

Other buck, however, existed in smaller herds and probably moved around less. Of these, gemsbok and black wildebeest in the drier areas, blesbok over most of the plateau of South Africa, impala in the lowveld and blue buck in the Cape would always have been among the most numerous and economically important.

Predators, such as lion, cheetah and leopard, as well as hyaena and the smaller species of carnivores, were widespread, as were elephant and hippopotamus. The utilization of the products of hunting and trapping will be discussed more fully in chapter 4.

Chapter 3

The Classification of Cultural Groups
N. J. van Warmelo

Introduction

Information concerning the history of the South African Bantu tribes comes from two sources, European and African. The personal observations of the earliest European explorers and navigators, and of shipwrecked seamen, such as Perestrello (1554), the pilot of the *Santo Alberto* (1593), and the men of the *Stavenisse* (1686), establish beyond doubt not only that the Bantu were already dwelling in South-Eastern Africa at that time, but also that in part at least they were the identical tribes found in the same localities at the present day.[1] Much beyond that these early sources do not go. On the other hand the European writers who witnessed the subsequent phases of traditional history in this country can tell us only about events of comparatively recent date, much too recent in any case to be of use in an attempt to classify the tribes. Of course, the narratives of the few men who were actually on the scene in the early days are of inestimable value; but they contain little about the distribution and names of tribes, their customs and languages, as they were before the great upheaval of the early nineteenth century.

The African sources of history consist of the traditions, legends, and tales handed down orally from generation to generation in each tribe. Of these only that small portion is available which has been recorded, mostly by Europeans, and then only too often in a European language, without the original vernacular version. This latter circumstance has reduced the usefulness of many of the records in question to an extent unsuspected by the collectors. It is not out of place here to stress that a scrupulous regard for the actual letter and phraseology of oral tradition is essential in the collection and editing of such material. But even were everything still extant to be rescued from oblivion, it is well to remember that this also would represent but a fraction of the wealth of traditional lore which existed up to say 1810-20, before wars and famine laid waste to Bantu culture, and caused the premature death of the aged, who were the repositories of tradition.

And here two further points require mention. First, what this history is. The oral tradition is history in a sense totally unrelated to the search for truth or an understanding of the past. In South Africa, tribal histories are mostly rather brief, consisting of a genealogy of the royal family and sundry details about origins, migrations and important events. They are selectively distorted.

Why certain things should be remembered is often not clear, but the main function is clear enough, viz. to explain the status quo and validate claims to power, land, privileges, etc., in other words to remind oneself and others *who is who*. Control of history is a part of power, especially in non-literate societies lacking written records. Power not only makes history, it also dictates the official version of it. Rival versions, like political opponents, are hunted down and destroyed. The oral tradition *may* therefore contain much truth, but not necessarily. Yet it contains, in many cases, the weightiest evidence available. Always the main question will be not what it says, but what it means.

So we get the second point, that of *method* in the use of material. It must be said that much of South African reconstructed indigenous history consists of uncritical theory-building. Genealogies, for example, must of necessity taper off into the past. They should not mislead us too easily into the construction of precise time-tables of distant events. Then there is the reckless equating, on the grounds of resemblance, of names and words from different languages, areas and periods. Names may recur independently. Similarity is not identity. Errors due to careless listening, peculiar spelling, even bad handwriting, lurk everywhere.[2] Owing to sound-shift, etymologically related words in different languages are likely to appear *dissimilar* rather than similar. It is the borrowed words, due to contact, that tend to look similar. Thus it can be shown that words so different-looking as, say, Zulu *izwi*, Tsonga *rito*, Venda *ipfi*, Sotho *lentšu* ('word') all derive from a common root according to rules of sound shift. On the other hand one cannot (as has been done) equate Zulu *umfana* with Latin *infans*, or *Bathokwa* (= Zulu *abaNtungwa*) with *Baṯôkwa* (= *Batlôkwa*) without throwing all sound method to the winds.

The oral tradition is only a part of all the facts. There also is other evidence of different kinds, ethnographical, linguistic, and physical (such as bloodgroups)[3] to be taken into account. The difficulty with archaeological evidence is the tie-up with living people and known existing cultures. There is nothing wrong with calling a type of pre-historic pottery 'Sotho' instead of a code number, except that this suggests certainty where only surmise exists.

In a *Preliminary Survey of the Bantu Tribes of South Africa* (1935) a classification was made as follows:

1. Nguni   Cape Nguni
                Later immigrants
                Zulu-speaking
                Swazi
                Transvaal Ndebele
                Recent Nguni offshoots
2. Tsonga
3. Sotho   South Sotho
                Tswana
                North Sotho
4. Venda
5. Lemba

The last two are numerically insignificant but of considerable scientific interest. This classification was based on a blending of all sorts of criteria. Whilst it has a certain practical usefulness, it also has the defect that it creates a false impression of clarity where actually there is nothing but problems. It is a misleading over-simplification. It also leaves unexplained the provenance and affiliations of many small enclaves which do not fit into the above scheme. However, nothing better suggests itself, and problems are not solved by re-arranging them in different boxes.

Whether we may postulate a single South-Eastern culture province to include the groups named above, but excluding those of Rhodesia, is also debatable. Certainly one may point to common features, as that of pure patrilineal descent, word-roots, as those for 'chief' (*inkosi, hosi, kgosi*) and 'bovine' (*inkomo, homu, kgomo*) and sounds, as the unusual laterals (*dl, hl, tl*) which only give way to interdentals in the extreme North.

But it is the anomalies, that is, the conflicting correlations, which arrest attention and defy explanation. For example, grainpits are found amongst the Cape Nguni in the extreme South and the Venda in the extreme North; but against that it is the Zulu speakers[4] and Venda who do not circumcise. The possessive first person singular ('mine') *-anga, -aka* is shared by Venda, North and South Sotho, but Nguni and Tswana have *-ami, -ame*. And only Tswana correlates with Nguni in respect of *-azi, -itse* ('know'), in contrast with *-tiva, -tseba, -divha* of Tsonga, North and South Sotho, and Venda. Yet South Sotho is invariably declared to be the language of immigrant Tswana people. The argument hinges on the fact that *-anga* and *-ami* are not derivable the one from the other; both are old forms, of equal status. The correlation cuts right across the accepted grouping. So does the first person singular *ndi-*, which is common to Venda, Tsonga and, remarkably enough, Xhosa, whilst Zulu and the Sotho-Tswana group have *ngi-, ke-*. These anomalies run counter to some of our basic assumptions, and make it appear doubtful whether we really have any idea as to how the present situation in Southern Africa came about.

It will be seen that the grouping largely coincides with geographical distribution, and also that the groups are almost a picture of the language groups of South Africa. This could hardly be otherwise. Roads, travel and communications were restricted in the olden days, and so geographical units inevitably became the seat of a particular dialect and form of culture if it was left undisturbed, but with gradual transitions in all directions. Clear contrasts on the other hand signal abrupt movements and happenings in the past.

We are here concerned with the ancestors of the Bantu we know today. However, a question of some interest is that of continuity with earlier populations. Southern Africa has, we know, been inhabited from early times, probably without a break. Besides the findings of archaeology, interest also attaches to the evidence of very early mining;[5] stone hut settlements;[6] pottery, old and contemporary;[7] and many other disconnected signs of foreign influence, such as traditions like the story of Esau and Jacob,[8] the ark of the covenant and a chosen people on the move under the aegis of a god to protect it.[9] Indian hemp is called *mbangi* (Tsonga) and *mbanzhe*[10] (Venda) from its Indian name *bhang*. Nguni *imali* and Hottentot *marib* ('money') are from Arabic *māl*. There is, in the Northern Transvaal, the complex associated with the terms *Thobela, she, Ralebepe/Raluvhimba, Pedi/Mbedzi*.[11] The Basotho are the 'black people' (called that by whom? in contra-distinction to whom?).[12] There is pyre-burning of the dead (an Indian custom) in Swaziland[13] and in Venda.[14] The xylophone (*mbila*) is an Asian instrument, and the big Venda *ngoma* drums with their 'frog-knee' handles closely resemble the 'bronze drums' of Tonkin and China, which always have four frogs on their sides.[15] Clearly, earlier populations and contacts about which we know nothing have left their mark on the Bantu of this country.

Numerical Strength of Groups

The numerical strength of the ethnic groups was, in the past, a matter of conjecture within fairly wide limits, for several reasons: the procrustean nature of any classification, the futility of asking the people themselves, labour migration, the presence of so many alien workers, and our ignorance of the masculinity ratio.

However, the census for 1946 incorporated in the census form certain questions designed to produce figures for the Bantu language groups. To make use of those figures as published would be misleading, for reasons explained in my *Language Map of South Africa* (1952), and that also applies to results of later census. They have to be adjusted in the light of internal evidence (e.g. the masculinity ratio, one of the most valuable by-products of the census) and of what else we know. Taking now the most recent (1960) totals for the Republic of South Africa and adjusting these in proportion, plus estimated annual increment, we get the figures given below. The

TABLE 3.1 *Republic of South Africa, Bantu languages as home languages*

	Estimated total of speakers for 1970 (aliens excluded)		
	Persons	%	
Xhosa	3,780,000	31·5	
Zulu	3,480,000	29·0	
Swazi	360,000	3·0	
Southern Ndebele	230,000	1·9	
Northern Ndebele	70,000	0·6	66·0
Tsonga	408,000	3·4	3·4
South Sotho	1,212,000	10·1	
Tswana	960,000	8·0	
North Sotho	1,200,000	10·0	28·1
Venda	300,000	2·5	2·5
Total	12,000,000	100·0	

hundreds of thousands of aliens working in the Republic are excluded. Most of them are from the former Protectorates, Mozambique, Rhodesia and Malawi. To give any but rounded-off figures would create an impression of accuracy incompatible with the fictional aspect of the classification itself.

This fictional aspect must at no time be lost sight of. These are not languages but clusters of dialects, some so marginal that they are classifiable as intermediary between clusters or as *sui generis*. The further fictional assumption, unavoidable at this stage, is that of equating language with culture or what is left of it.

From this there emerge some very significant facts: the Nguni together add up to no less than 66 per cent of the whole population, though the Northern Ndebele are better excluded because in language and sympathies they are Sotho. The Tsonga are 3·4 per cent, the whole Sotho complex 28·1 per cent, the Venda 2·5 per cent.

Nguni Group

The people themselves have no collective term for this group. *Abenguni*, *Abanguni* is used with varying meaning in different places. 'Nguni' is therefore a term chosen for ethnographical convenience.

The tribes belonging to this group live mainly below the high plateau of the interior, between the escarpment of the Drakensberg and the sea, and stretch, in a long broad belt of hundreds of tribes, from Swaziland right through Natal far down into the Cape Province.

The Nguni were wealthy in cattle. Their beehive huts, descendants of the pastoralists' (e.g. Hottentots') movable dwellings, bespeak a former nomadic pastoral mode of life, which became unnecessary in the rich grazing grounds of South-Eastern Africa. The presence of 'click' sounds in all the Nguni languages seems an argument for their common origin, but there are difficulties. Clicks are found in greatest variety and profusion in the South (Cape Nguni), becoming fewer and less carefully distinguished as one proceeds northwards. Moreover, each language has largely its own vocabulary of click words. But whereas in Xhosa they have been shown[16] to derive from contact with that purely pastoral people, the Khoikhoi (Hottentots), further north a Bush origin becomes more and more probable. Clicks are common in *hlonipha* terms, as one would expect if these sounds were introduced into Nguni by Hottentot and Bush wives. The Nguni have such a characteristic culture and language that one must assume a markedly isolated focus of development. But where can this have lain? For click words must have become part of the language at this stage, and yet the process of absorbing click words was only completed much later, after diffusion. We do not know the answer.

Interesting questions are posed by the presence, inside the Nguni area, of the Lala enclave, which used to occupy parts of the present central and southern Natal. The Lala tribes were apparently largely dispersed or destroyed in the Shakan period, and little study has been devoted to what remains of their culture and language, except the dialect of Kranskop.[17] There are sound-shifts in Lala far in advance of Nguni, consonant fading similar to that of Shona and Tsonga. About Lala culture and differences from neighbours little or nothing is known.

Having regard to the widespread loss of tradition and culture of the Nguni before they could be recorded, we have reason to be grateful to the diligence of Bryant and Soga. Especially in the case of the former, we would probably have been happier with the actual statements of his informants than we are with his synthesis of them, for actually the early history of the Nguni group is still a field wide open for enquiry, not a subject to be dogmatic about. In fact, the massive volumes of Bryant (*Olden Times in Zululand and Natal*) and of Soga (*The South-Eastern Bantu*) have not only laid a groundwork that can neither be done over again nor undone nor ignored, but have also achieved something else not intended. By coming to conclusions impossible to reconcile, they have shown that as regards Nguni origins we are up against a fundamental and intractable problem. The theories hitherto put forward appear to me not even worth repeating here. They are fanciful and do not meet the case. Nothing would be gained by putting forward other, equally uncritical, theories. Those further details of history which do require mention are given below for each separate sub-group.

The rise of Zulu power and the attendant movements of tribes gave the Nguni group an entirely new appearance, with profound effects; to mention a few: the creation of a Fingo (Mfengu) block in the Cape, on the west or far side of the Cape Nguni; the creation of a Zulu-speaking entity which, despite lack of internal cohesion, possesses the unifying bond of a common language; the lasting effects of Ngoni power in Mozambique; and the birth of the Ndebele nation in Matabeleland.

Cape tribes proper

These are the southernmost Nguni tribes. They had already been in occupation of the present Transkei and Ciskei for centuries by the time the influx took place of the immigrant Fingo and other refugee tribes mentioned under the next sub-group. The Cape tribes speak the same language with but small variations, but, while a common descent is traceable for a number of tribes, this is not the case with most of the others, between whom no sort of genealogical relationship, as far as tradition goes, can be said to exist.

An example of a group of related tribes is found in the Xhosa, represented by the Gcaleka of Willowvale, the Ngqika of the Ciskei, and smaller tribes like the Ndlambe, Dushane, Qhayi, Ntinde, and Gqunukhwebe. The last-named are of mixed Hottentot Khoikhoi descent. Tradition regarding the genealogical ramifications of the Xhosa royal lineage and its offshoots has been well preserved, and is of value as being virtually a synopsis of the relations of the Xhosa tribes to one another. This Xhosa tradition, according to

Soga, says that some centuries ago the tribe dwelt along the upper reaches of the St Johns River, far to the north-east of their present home. History before that is pure conjecture, while their subsequent history, which is well described by Soga, is too recent to interest us here.

Farther east and north-east of the related Xhosa tribes are the Thembu and their offshoots, such as the Hala, Jumba, and Ndungwana. With them may be classed the Bomvana, Qwathi, Nqabe, and Mpondomise, which although not related are nearest to them in culture. All these tribes also have traditions to the effect that they immigrated from the direction of Natal. Otherwise their recorded history is meagre, containing few indications of value.

Still farther east are the numerous tribes and clans of the Mpondo, ruled over by several independent chiefs. The Mpondo are again distinct, in some respects, from the tribes mentioned above. They are divided into a great many clans, of which the largest though not necessarily the most important in rank are, amongst others, the Bhala, Kwalo, Gingqi, Kwetshube, Nyawuza, Khonjwayo, Nci, and Ngutyana. There are, further, amongst them some tribes not of true Mpondo descent, but now looked upon as being practically their equals. Besides these we find many descendants of the refugees from Natal, whom Chief Faku took under his protection. While some of these managed to maintain their identity intact, others simply merged in the Mpondo population. There are for instance sections of Tolo, Tshangase, Tshwawu, Zizi, Hlubi, Bhele, Ngwane, and similar names commonly encountered amongst the immigrant Fingo. The earliest known history of the Mpondo also shows them already settled, several centuries ago, not very far to the north-east of their present country. Of their relationship to other tribes nothing definite is known.

Mfengu and other recent immigrants into the Cape

When Shaka embarked upon his career of empire building in Natal, numerous tribes were dislodged either directly or indirectly as a result of the ensuing state of war. Early in the nineteenth century many thousands of refugees from Natal began to cross over the Umzimkulu, seeking a new home among the Cape tribes, especially the Xhosa, and among the white colonists. They came both as solid tribes, and in large and small bodies of homogeneous or of composite character. Their numbers were further augmented from another direction by the fugitive Hlubi of Mpangazitha, who had been driven out of Basutoland, whither he had first fled, by Matiwane and his Ngwane, who were themselves also fugitives from Natal. The latter chief also came down into the present Transkei where, in August 1828, his tribe was defeated and broken at Mbholompo in an encounter with colonial and indigenous forces.

Many refugees returned to Natal when peace was restored there, but many others remained behind. The real 'Fingo' (Mfengu) were subsequently led out of Xhosaland, but when at a later date part of the Western Transkei became vacant they were settled there and still form the bulk of the population. There are today many thousands of detribalized Fingo. Of those still bearing tribal names, whether they still recognize chiefs or not, the majority belong to the big Hlubi, Zizi and Bhele tribes. Smaller units include the Kunene, Maduna, Gubevu, Tolo, Miya, Khuze, Mbuthweni and Zotsho. The question as to how far the Mfengu still form a cultural unit in the face of strong Cape Nguni levelling influences would require wide-ranging study of this continuing process. It was hard for chieftainships to survive amongst people who were all refugees alike, yet they did so, though some are but a shadow. Many of the Mfengu of course live in areas of the Transkei where they fall under the control of non-Mfengu chiefs.

The same applies to a large proportion of those immigrants into the Eastern Transkei who are not called Fingo. To these belong the Bhaca and sections of the Wushe, and clans related to the Bhaca. Others again are independent, such as the two Bhaca tribes of Mount Frere. Two others are in Southern Natal, in Bulwer and Ixopo districts. In the same category as the Bhaca we may place the Nhlangwini tribes of Griqualand East and Southern Natal (Harding and Ixopo districts), and a number of small clans said to be related to them, together with the Xesibe (chiefly in Mount Ayliff) and the Xolo and Nzimakwe of Port Shepstone. Of some of these tribes we know more or less how they came to be where they are now. But of what they were before they migrated, and where they lived, as of their present distinctive traits (if any) little is recorded.

Zulu-speaking Nguni

Here again we have a term adopted for ethnographic convenience. *Zulu* is the clan-name (*isibongo*) of only one clan. The people themselves call their language *isiNtu* ('human speech'). Before Shaka's time they could not have called it *isiZulu*, since it was only through him that his clan became well known.

Today, the use of 'Zulu' for the language, though not African practice, is practical and justifiable inasmuch as such a sufficiently uniform language exists.

But it is also common nowadays to speak of 'the Zulus', meaning all the speakers of the language and, in addition, implying that they are one people or, going still further, one political entity. This they have never been. One might distinguish: (a) the 'Zulu' nucleus of tribes closely bound to and loyal to the royal house, though split by the Usuthu-Mandlakazi factions; (b) those whose ancestors held out against the Zulu might and neither fled nor subjected themselves; (c) those whose ancestors never were willing subjects of the Zulu kings, who fled when opportunity offered, and who were ready to take the field against the Zulus too; (d) those who fled in time and never came under Zulu rule, and have no desire to be ruled by the house of Zulu to this day.

These distinctions are historical and cannot serve as criteria for ethnographic categories.

Prior to 1816 a classification might, it seems, have been made into (a) true Nguni or Ntungwa, with perhaps a subdivision for (b) the *Mbo*; and (c) *Lala* tribes. What their distinguishing characteristics were would be difficult to say now.

However, in 1816 (according to Bryant) Shaka became the head of his small Zulu clan, and began attacking and subjecting his neighbours. Even allowing for exaggeration in traditional accounts of fights, raids and massacres on an unprecedented scale, it is clear from the effects that a mighty upheaval took place.[18] Many large tribes and newly-formed hordes of displaced persons took to flight in all directions, never to return. Many smaller were utterly destroyed. An uninhabited buffer zone was created around Zululand, where only refugees still hid in caves and forests. Later, when Zulu power waned, these people and many others returned from exile to settle wherever they could. Many, dispersed 'like the children of the guinea-fowl that call one another together', even managed to re-assemble as tribes and rescue their political identity. Numberless others were not so fortunate.

We now find the Zulu-speakers subdivided into well over 300 tribes, including some dozens of the so-called *amaKholwa* (converts, mostly on Mission reserves) and other artificially created tribes, besides a nondescript population on farms and in rural towns in the Orange Free State and the S.E. Transvaal. To classify these into subgroups is at present beyond us. The rule of the Zulu kings promoted the uniformity of custom and language we see today over large areas. European rule and education, first by missions and then by the state, favoured this trend. Only studies in depth will uncover such differing traits as may still make a classification possible.

The tribes of the Zulu-speaking Nguni are mostly known by the family or clan names (*izibongo*) of their chiefs. A few exceptions occur, e.g. abaThembu, amaHlubi, amaNgwane; these embrace the whole tribe. Tribal names consisting of *izibongo* do not reflect the actual composition of tribes. Though a tribe be known for instance as *abakwaMkhize* ('Mkhize's people' or 'Mkhize's descendants') there may be twenty or fifty different clan names (*izibongo*) represented within that tribe. Some of these, though of commoners here, may be royalty elsewhere.

As there are these hundreds of tribes (ranging, incidentally, from some hundreds of persons to *c.* 50,000), we may confine ourselves to naming some of the more important. In the southern and south-western districts of Natal there are a number of Nyuswa tribes, the Dumisa, Cele, Khuze, several tribes of Dlamini, the Nxamalala and many others. They are flanked, farther north, by the tribes living under the Drakensberg, the Ngwane and Ngwe (or Ngweni) and others. More towards the centre are the Mabaso and the powerful and still very raw tribes of Msinga district, the Bomvini, Cunu, and Qanyini. Proceeding farther towards the coast, we find numerous sections of Mkhize and Mafunze, the Gcumisa, two large Zondi tribes, the Makhanya,

Ximba, several tribes of Thulini all near to the coast from Umzinto to Stanger, the Qadini in Ndwedwe and adjacent districts, the Khabeleni, the Ntuli, Buthelezi, Qwabe, and Mpukunyoni. Farther to the west, in Msinga and neighbouring districts, are the Sithole tribes, the Thenjini or Thembu, and, in the northernmost districts, the Hlutshini Hlubi, Nkosi, Khumalo, and Mdlalose. Turning thence towards the east we encounter amongst others the Mbatheni, Ntombela, Gazini, Mthethwa, and in Nongoma and thereabouts the Zulu. To the extreme north-east are the tribes of Ubombo and Ingwavuma divisions: the Nxumalo, Zikhali, Myeni, Nibele, and others, and the Mngomezulu, Nyawo, and Mathenjwa, whose next-door neighbours are the southernmost Tsonga, viz. the Tembe.

Swazi

This sub-group is of recent origin. Before Shaka's time the present Swaziland was partly occupied by various Sotho tribes about which we know virtually nothing, but who are best represented today in the Pai and Pulana referred to in the Sotho group. The southern part of Swaziland was occupied by clans of Nguni origin, mostly of the variety characterized by the *tekeza* way of speaking, and by the customs commonly associated therewith. Commencing with the increasing power of the Ngwane Chief Sobhuza (*c.* 1820), the 'Swazi' people gradually began to come into being, especially through the conquests of Sobhuza's descendant Mswazi (*c.* 1840–75), after whom they are named. The latter subjected the Sotho clans of Swaziland, or drove them out, and by extensive raiding increased his wealth and power. The Swazi, having never been subdued by force of arms, remained a nation in spite of the imposition of European control, and are intensely proud and conscious of the fact. The circumstance, however, that the many thousands of Swazi living outside the borders of Swaziland were freed from the control of the Paramount Chief has weakened tribal cohesion among them. Nevertheless several Swazi tribes near the border may be considered almost integral parts of the Swazi nation.

In Swaziland itself the old Sotho population seems to have disappeared, except in name. The descendants of the Sotho clans are collectively known as abeSuthu or amaKhandzambili. Another non-Swazi element are the clans from Zululand, no distinction being made between true Ntungwa and Mbo stock. Thirdly there are the Swazi proper. To outline areas or to define groups in which these elements of the Swazi culture-unit preponderate is impossible. The difficulty lies both in the lack of attention paid to this problem, and in the comparative uselessness of tribal names as a guide. According to Nguni custom the tribes are known by the clan name (*isibongo*) of their chiefs. But since in a tribe any number of clans may be represented, the chief's *isibongo* is but a weak clue to the origin and composition of his following. There is for instance a considerable preponderance of chiefs with the *isibongo* Nkosi, but this is explained by the fact that Nkosi is the clan-name of the paramount house. One infers from this that a large proportion of the followers of these men are not true Swazi, for the latter would be ruled by their own hereditary chiefs who have other clan names. On the other hand it is likely that, where non-Swazi are in control of tribes, these latter are tribes also largely of non-Swazi origin. All we can do for the present is to give some indications based on the clan-names of the ruling families. About the elements that form the tribes mentioned below it is not possible to say anything more definite.

Taking first the Swazi proper, there are fifty-odd tribes ruled over by chiefs with the royal *isibongo* Nkosi. Their following, as noted above, is likely to be partly non-Swazi, but on the other hand the influence of the chief and his entourage is not negligible. Other true Swazi tribes are likely to be those under, e.g., Malangatonke and Siboshwa (both Fakudze), and chiefs with such *izibongo* as Hlophe, Hlatjwako, Mamba, Katse, Madvosela, Motsa, Mndzebele, Shiba, Shongwe, and Tsabetse.

Amongst the clans of 'Zulu' origin one finds such *izibongo* as Biyela, Mkhatshwa, Mtsetfwa (Mthethwa), and Zwane.

The original Sotho population of Swaziland is represented by the 'Khandzambili' clans, some of which, however, are said to be not of Sotho origin. It is natural that when the Sotho turned Swazi in language and custom, their clan names should also have assumed a Swazi garb, and that they should now all be provided with the *izinanatelo* (a sort of complement to the *isibongo*) demanded by Nguni usage. Amongst the Khandzambili there are such clan names as Bhembe, Gama, Gamedze, Magagula, Maseko, Nkambule, and Sukati. These are not tribal names as commonly found amongst the Sotho, but clan names. It is accordingly difficult to identify Sotho elements, if there are such. The Pulana (Eastern Sotho) have the tradition that they were the original inhabitants of northern Swaziland until Swazi pressure forced them out. Under such circumstances, it remains a matter for conjecture how many fled and how many stayed behind to be absorbed in course of time.

The Swazi living outside Swaziland in the adjacent districts of the Republic of South Africa were in the past mostly subject to the Swazi regime, though in the south some were subject to Zulu power. Since the establishment of Swaziland as a separate entity they have tended to go their own way. Family ties between the chiefs and the royal house in Swaziland have been maintained. Fairly large and important Swazi tribes, under chiefs of some genealogical standing are to be found in Barberton, Nelspruit (Nkosi, Shongwe, Khumalo), Carolina (Maquba), and other units such as Hlatjwako, Dlamini, Magagula, Sukati, Shongwe, in other Highveld districts and Piet Retief. In the south, Zulu influence is strong. Smaller stray groups are found farther afield. They are in part small sections that lived on the periphery of happenings in Swaziland and were only too glad to be left unmolested at the price of submission to the Swazi kings; in part they represented outposts of empire deliberately placed there; and some are the descendants of people who left Swaziland for the sake of their health after being accused of witchcraft or worsted in politics. For instance, Somquba, the son of the king Somhlolo, lived in the Transvaal but was attacked and killed, the survivors of the group seeking asylum in Sekukuniland, where they still are today.

Transvaal Ndebele

AmaNdebele or Matebele may be a term originally used for the Nguni by the tribes of the interior. The Transvaal Ndebele must not be confused with the Ndebele of Matabeleland, Rhodesia. The latter left Zululand in *c.* 1816 under their leader Mzilikazi, whereas the former had by that time already been settled in the Transvaal for centuries. Surrounded as they were by various Sotho tribes, they could not avoid being influenced considerably by Sotho culture and language. Where they formed ruling elites with Sotho accretions, their tribes have become in most respects, not surprisingly, very like neighbouring Sotho tribes.

The Transvaal Ndebele fall into two sections, Southern and Northern. They are divided by a considerable stretch of country, which has only of late been bridged by movements of small groups. They are also distinct in point of language, for each of the two dialects is characterized by a number of features peculiar to it alone. The Ndebele dialects of the south are better preserved than those of the north, which have been largely superseded by Sotho. The same may be said of custom and possibly also physical characteristics.

The Southern group today comprises a single senior tribe, the Manala, and a junior tribe, the Ndzundza (popularly known as Mapoch or Mapôrs, after their chief Mabhogo), which was broken up in 1883 and is now represented by several sections. These two tribes have retained Ndebele custom and language with astonishing tenacity. This is not the case with the Hwaduba of Hammanskraal district, who, though said to be descended from the same parent tribe, are now to all intents and purposes an Eastern Tswana tribe. The Southern Ndebele trace their descent from the tribe of their first chief Msi or Musi, who long ago lived near Pretoria, where the Manala still lived until recently. A rather vague but plausible tradition has it that before Msi's time the Ndebele had come from the south-east, the direction of Natal. The Northern tribes have the same origin.

The Northern group is composed of the Ndebele of Langa (in Sotho pronunciation, Laka), represented by several sections, mostly in Potgietersrus; and of the Maune or Letwaba, likewise represented by several sections. The Seleka living on the border with Botswana are originally of Ndebele stock but are now Tswana in language and culture. Finally, this group includes the Moletlane or Sebitiela, who, according to tradition, left the parent tribe of the Southern Ndebele and migrated northwards very many years ago, and settled near the great bend of the Lepelle river. An earlier offshoot of Moletlane is the Mokôpane (Magwambane) just outside Potgietersrus. There is also a more recent offshoot under Johannes Kekana, now settled very near the ancient home of the Ndebele in Hammanskraal district.

Recent Nguni offshoots

Early last century three outstanding men led bodies of Zulu-speaking people in flight from Zululand to escape impending destruction at the hands of Shaka. They marched north and north-west, living by rapine and murder and incorporating recruits from local populations to make good their losses. After many vicissitudes, all three eventually founded empires, where they perpetuated their race, customs and language amongst the alien Bantu tribes they had subjected to their rule. Of these, parts have survived to greatly varying degrees.

When Mzilikazi (*isibongo*: Khumalo) and his followers left Zululand they trekked over the Highveld of the Transvaal and settled for a while near Pretoria, then later near Zeerust, harrying the Sotho tribes and raiding as far south as Basutoland (1831). When he turned his attention to the emigrant farmers the latter retaliated (1837), and finding things getting too hot for his liking, he led his people over the Limpopo into the present Matabeleland. The Ndebele kingdom founded there collapsed before the advance of white colonization, but the language and culture of the invaders has survived to this day though in diluted form.

The 'Ngoni' (vátua = abaThwa of the Portuguese) left Zululand in 1820-1, led by Soshangane also called Manukuza or Manukosi. They went north and founded the empire of Kwa-Gasa (after an ancestor of Soshangane's) in Gasaland, Mozambique. They were not very numerous, yet strong enough to take the forts at Delagoa Bay and Inhambane, and to conquer all the lands of the Tsonga, introducing their own language and customs to such an extent that the Tsonga have come to be known as 'Shangaans'. Most Tsonga readily call themselves *vaTsonga*, but where the old Ngoni influence is strong this term is rejected as derogatory (which indeed it is in Zulu usage) and *MaChangana* is preferred. Soshangane died in 1856 and the struggle between his sons Mawewe and Mzila caused many people to seek safety in the North-Eastern Transvaal. Ngoni power came to an end with the overthrow in 1895 of Ngungunyana, son of Mzila, by the Portuguese. Some of his family found sanctuary in the Transvaal, where their descendants still enjoy considerable status, especially in Bushbuckridge.

The third body of Zulu-speaking emigrants was led north by Zwangendaba. There was no room in Gasaland for both him and Soshangane, and so Zwangendaba after being worsted moved further north. After an astonishing career these Ngoni made themselves a home and a state of their own in the neighbourhood of Lake Nyasa. Their descendants, who still speak a Zulu of sorts, may be found on both sides of the Lake, in groups now widely separated from one another.

Tsonga Group

The Tsonga form a populous group, almost wholly located in Mozambique. The northern limits are ill-defined, but it is clear that the Chopi and Tonga of Inhambane should be excluded. In the south the Tsonga have had the Nguni as neighbours for a long time. The differences between them are, however, profound: cylindrical conical-roof huts, few if any cattle (the cattle terminology is all Zulu), no right and left in hut-status, no clicks in the language, cl. 8 *swi-* retained, and *ndi-* for 'I'. From the Sotho the Tsonga differ, amongst other things, in not having totems. In this they are, of course, on the Nguni side. Closer contacts with the Sotho and Venda of the interior were made only in recent times, since 1835, when numbers of Tsonga moved from Mozambique to the North-Eastern Transvaal. The main reason for the previously limited contact was probably geographical. The Lowveld was tsetse-infested and subject to severe droughts, and therefore thinly populated, if at all. An old trade route did, however, run from *Ka-Mpfumo* (Delagoa Bay) to the ancient mining centre of *Phalaborwa* (*Palaote* of early sources) and on to *Bvesha* (Tsonga equivalent of *Venḍa*, i.e. the Zoutpansberg; the *Beja* of the Portuguese), where the ivory came from. In the extreme north-east there was another much-travelled route: that taken by the parties on their way to consult famous Tsonga diviners like Phafula on accusations of witchcraft.

A classification is given by Junod in his *Life of a South African Tribe*. Generally speaking, it may be said that the original Tsonga group falls into three tolerably well-defined sections: Southern, Central, and Northern. To the first belong the clans of Maputa, Tembe, Mpfumo, and others, classed together by Junod under the name Ronga. This is, of course, derived from the same root as Tsonga. Junod uses Thonga (the Zulu pronunciation) for the whole group, which is a bit confusing. The Sotho equivalent, *baRôka*, is used by the Sotho to designate, not the Tsonga, but the Sotho tribes of the Lowveld. And a *moRôka* is also a rain-maker, even in South Sotho.

To the Central Tsonga belong the clans of Khosa, Nkuna, Mavunda, Valoyi, Maluleke, Nhlanganu, and others, classified by Junod into the subgroups of Nwalungu, Bila, Hlanganu, and Djonga. To the northern section belong the Hlengwe, Tswa, and others, extending far to the north and north-east.

About the early history of the Tsonga group little has been recorded and perhaps there has been little to remember. According to Junod the traditions as to the direction of immigration differ from clan to clan, some having come from the north, others from the west, still others from the south. This, one infers, must have happened a long time ago, in view of the present homogeneity of the group. From early Portuguese sources Junod cites the account of Perestrello (1554) as proof that 'four or five hundred years ago at least, the chiefs Tembe, Mpfumu, Manhisa, Libombo, all of whom still have descendants, were already in the country round Delagoa Bay'.[19]

After having thus lived undisturbed, as a mainly agricultural people possessing few if any cattle, which would account for the weakness of the chieftainship as an institution, the Tsonga were suddenly overwhelmed by the displaced Nguni from Zululand. These were led by Soshangane, already referred to. These Zulu-speakers were few in number but nevertheless succeeded in establishing the new kingdom of Gasa over the Tsonga tribes (except around the Bay), exacting tribute and drafting the young men into the ranks as Mabulundlela, 'Road openers', a euphemism for 'Front-line expendables', bestowed as an honour. Soshangane reigned until his death in 1856, when six years of unrest began, caused by the rival claims of his sons Muzila and Mawewe. The latter won the day, but proved a despot. Muzila then emerged from exile in the Northern Transvaal and in 1862 defeated Mawewe with help from the south. Muzila was succeeded by his son Ngungunyane, the last of the independent Ngoni monarchs. By this time there were, according to Junod, not more than a few hundred Ngoni left in the whole country. In 1895 the Ngoni power was broken by the Portuguese.

Although the Ngoni invasion was nothing like the calamity of the other Zulu migrations elsewhere in Southern Africa in terms of massacre and starvation, many Tsonga were unwilling to submit, and fled to the Eastern and North-Eastern Transvaal in the years 1835–40; again later during the wars of succession (1856–62); in the Portuguese war against Ngungunyane (1895) and at various other times whenever things seemed to be going badly. The refugees mostly headed westwards, over the Lebombo range, and kept going until they found a suitable place. Accordingly, Hlengwe and other Northerners preponderate in the north (Sibasa, Louis Trichardt), Nhlanganu in the south, and people from the centre in between, corresponding to the areas from which they fled.

Upon arriving in the Transvaal, they soon discovered that they were on somebody's land, either occupied or hunting ground, and as disorganized refugees they sought permission from the local chiefs to settle. They never used force of arms, and were in no position to do so.

The natural leaders came to the fore. Immigration of the Tsonga was encouraged by Albasini, who himself appointed ndunas and helped them to settle the people. The Tsonga got involved in the politics of the times. They served as levies and were rewarded for loyal service. In the conspicuous absence of royalty, all manner of men became what was later termed 'independent headmen', not only aristocrats but also doughty fighters, policemen of Albasini's, even faithful batmen and other protégés of white men with influence.

Like all displaced people, the Tsonga found it easier to move on again and again. Over the years, therefore, they have moved out of the Lowveld to the interior plateau, to Louis Trichardt, Pietersburg, Potgietersrus, Nylstroom and Warmbad, until today pockets of them are found on farms and under North Ndebele, North Sotho and Tswana chiefs, well into Rustenburg district.

As representative of the southern group of Tsonga there is but one tribe living within the borders of the Republic of South Africa, viz. chief Mhlupheki's tribe of Tembe or (in Zulu) Mabhudu, north-west of Kosi Bay in Ingwavuma district, Zululand.

Going north, we find in the first Tsonga tribes we meet, in Barberton district, the three branches of the Ngomane, an interesting case of present-day Tsonga claiming to have been Highveld Sotho originally. The next subgroup are the Nhlanganu of the Lowveld of Bushbuckridge. There are many Shangaans amongst them. The Shangaans proper (maChangana), however, form another sub-group. As mentioned under the Nguni, these are the descendants of Zulu-speakers led by Soshangane, people who formed an élite in the Ngoni kingdom until its collapse in 1896. With them are Tsonga who threw in their lot with these Ngoni, whose menfolk aped their masters and spoke only Zulu, even to their Tsonga-speaking mothers and wives, an interesting form of bilingualism. Their acknowledged leader was Thulilamahashe, a son of Ngungunyane. A further subgroup is composed of the tribes living in the great bend of the escarpment (Leydsdorp-Tzaneen-Duiwelskloof). By far the largest and most important tribe here is the Nkuna of the late chief Muhlava. But again, interestingly, these are not original Tsonga, but Zulu-speaking people from Ngome in Zululand, who trekked to Lydenburg on the interior plateau before moving down into the Lowveld and into Mozambique where they presumably turned into Tsonga, later becoming vassals of Soshangane but eventually settling in Sotho territory (of Maake's Kgaga tribe).[20] However, most of the Tsonga who drifted into these parts over the years recognized and became the subjects of the rain-queen Modjadji when they settled on her extensive hunting grounds in the malarious tsetse-infested bush country of the Eastern Lowveld.

Finally a fifth subgroup may be recognized for those further north and north-east, as far as the Limpopo. Here we find the descendants of some of the earliest immigrants from Mozambique. Maswanganyi, of no account now, is said to have been the pioneer. Fair-sized tribes such as those of Xikundu, Mhinga, Xigalo, got their permission to settle from the Venda chief Mphaphuli but later were given locations and became independent. In this area, as elsewhere further south, there also are scores of small units under the so-called 'independent headmen', a contradiction in terms indicative of their independence (under the government) on the one hand and their lack of hereditary status on the other.

As poverty-stricken refugees living on sufferance on the land of others, the Tsonga were for many years accorded very unequal status. In the olden days the Tsonga, like the outcastes of India, were supposed to walk not on footpaths but alongside. They were not allowed to enter the villages of chiefs. As late as 1936 the Native Commissioner (as he was then called) and I had an audience with the Lobedu chieftainess Modjadji. Our constable thought he ought to accompany his master, and tried to follow us. But whilst the others merely took their shoes off and went in, he, because he was a Shangaan, was ordered back outside. And he a government servant in uniform!

Sotho Group

With the exception of some Tswana, all the members of this group call themselves *baSotho*, an old word which has been shown to mean 'Black people'.[21] This insight raises new problems, such as, by whom coined and why, in contra-distinction to whom? The Sotho are the inhabitants of the great interior plateau, and differ from all their neighbours in numerous important respects, linguistical as well as social and technological. The Sotho seem to fall naturally into three major divisions, viz. (1) South Sotho in Lesotho and adjacent areas; (2) Western Sotho or Tswana, and (3) the remainder in the north-east, formerly called *maAwa* (from their word for 'no') by those in the south, and Transvaal Sotho or North Sotho (to contrast with South Sotho) by European writers. The Voortrekkers called all the tribes of the interior '*Maketese*' (from 'Mantatees') and noted their distinctive male dress as differing from that of the Nguni. In respect of pottery 'South Sotho, Tswana and Transvaal Sotho appear as three distinct groups with no obvious relationship to each other' (Lawton 1967: 314).[22] Still, the division into three is an over-simplification inasmuch as it leaves out some very atypical elements along the periphery, and others inside the Sotho area, notably the Kgalagadi of the desert and the Pai in the extreme east.

Within these divisions there are gradual transitions. The South Sotho subgroup as a whole is clearly defined by its relative isolation from the others, but the boundary between Tswana and North Sotho is less precise. The North Sotho cluster contains sufficient diversity to raise doubts, at times, about its essential unity, but, in wider perspective, this unity is perceived readily enough. It derives, however, not from a single origin, but from convergence of culture traits of different components.

The early history of the Sotho group is a matter for conjecture. The essential unity it exhibits is, I think, remarkable; it indicates a rapid expansion over the vastness of the South African interior. There are traditions of an origin in the distant north, in a land of lakes and mountains, but this must lie far back in the past, as few tribes have such traditions. There is no clue as to where their ancestors dwelt in that isolation which must have been necessary to produce the distinctive Sotho form of Bantu speech, to mention but one criterion. The Sotho language must be mentioned here. It is one of the most remarkable of Bantu languages, not for its consonantal sound shifts, though these are unusual, but for its retention in the vowel system of the original distinction between 'closed' and 'open' *i* and *u*, of fundamental importance in Bantu philology. By what route the ancient Sotho came south, how long ago, and whether even a majority of all Sotho tribes are descended from one parent tribe, these are matters some writers have guessed at, but, I think, unconvincingly. Even assertions that have practically become articles of faith, such as that the South Sotho are just a branch or offshoot of the Tswana, appear open to doubt. How is it that the homogeneous Sotho language group is split in two in respect of *-ame*, *-aka* ('mine') and *-itse*, *-tseba* ('know'), the first-mentioned in Tswana (and remarkably enough, also in Nguni), the second in South and North Sotho? These are amongst the oldest words in the language. The split is not on a par with e.g. *-tsamaya/-sepela* or *kgotla/kgôrô*, though again *kgotla* is the same as Nguni *inkundla*. Is there a special connection between Tswana and Nguni? As with the relative *-ng/-go*, these are basic differences, forms not derivable the one from the other, and therefore dating back to early stages of the language, and posing baffling problems.

The Sotho group contains foreign elements that have been assimilated. Tribal names such as *baPô* (= *abaMbo*, a branch of the Nguni), *baMatlhako* (= *Mahlangu*, a section of the Ndebele), *baKoni* (= *abeNguni*), *baPedi* (= *vhaMbedzi*, of the Venda), *Nkwane* (= *Ngwane*, i.e. the Swazi) may afford clues to distant origins, though we must recall our earlier caution against mere playing with words and names.

South Sotho

Prior to the troubled times that followed the rise of Zulu power, the inhabitable western part of Basutoland (Lesotho) and the adjoining country were occupied by divers tribes, such as the Fokeng, Tlokwa, Taung, Kwena, Kgwakgwa, Kgolokwe, Sia, and numerous others. These were all South Sotho, as we term them, but the people themselves used the term *baSotho* without further qualification. There were culture and language differences between the tribes but we know very little about these. The history of the South Sotho has been described in great detail by Ellenberger (*History of the Basuto*, 1912). This monumental and splendid work is, of course, a synthesis, not a collection of source material; the credentials of the informants cannot be checked and their actual statements are not available.

The earliest inhabitants of the country were Bushmen, now practically extinct. The South Sotho have some Bush blood and the clicks in South Sotho are partly of Bush origin. According to Ellenberger the first Bantu to enter the country were not Sotho but three small Nguni tribes from the east, the maPhetla, maPolane and baPhuthi, the earliest of whom 'traversed the mountains during or about the year 1600' (p. 21, a remarkable statement). After them there came the tribes of Sotho stock, Phuthing, Kgolokwe, Sia, Tlokwa, Fokeng, Kwena, Hlakwana, Digoja, Taung and others. Their geographical distribution is given by Ellenberger on pp. 120-1. They were, he says, of Tswana origin, but he does not mention several problems posed by culture and language differences between Tswana and South Sotho if this proposition is accepted.

All these tribes lived, it appears, comparatively peacefully and undisturbed until 1822, when the first fugitive Nguni tribe, the Hlubi under Mpangazitha (Pakalita), fleeing from Natal, broke over the Drakensberg into Tlokwa territory, and a new era was ushered in. The Ngwane of Matiwane followed. As elsewhere, tribes were dislodged from their homes and, destitute and hungry, fell upon others, setting up a chain reaction of attack and flight. Chaos and famine became general. Some tribes, more powerful and better led, e.g. the Tlokwa and Taung, moved far afield in their wanderings and inspired a special terror. The Tlokwa under their queen Manthatisi even got a new name (Mantatees), which the Voortrekkers corrupted to *Maketese* and used for all the interior tribes that wore the breechcloth, to distinguish them from the Nguni whom they, like the North Sotho, called the 'Naked Men' (Kaalkaffers, Sotho *maPono*).

One other leader at least also went far afield. This was Sebetwane, who led his followers north through Bechuanaland and the Kalahari until they reached the upper Zambesi. Here they founded the so-called Kololo kingdom of Barotseland, in which South Sotho language and culture still survive to some extent.

Meanwhile, in Basutoland the Kwena chief Moshesh (*Moshweshwe, Moshoeshoe*) followed another course. With great political wisdom he accepted all stray people who came to him for protection, first at Butha Buthe, then at his stronghold Thaba Bosiu. He warded off all attacks of Tlokwa and Mzilikazi's Ndebele and became the acknowledged leader of all the South Sotho tribes excepting the Tlokwa in the west and some others in the south. In 1853 the Tlokwa stronghold Jwala Boholo also fell, and thus arose what we know today as the 'Basuto Nation' of Basutoland or Lesotho. Those South Sotho dwelling outside Lesotho on the south side are still organized in tribes under chiefs of their own, and so are the small number in the reserve at Witzieshoek. In the rest of the Orange Free State many South Sotho live on the farms. A small pocket is to be found in Nqutu in Natal.

The policy of Moshesh and his successors was to place their kinsmen as governors in charge of areas all over the country, and to break up the tribes. This favoured the general trend towards uniformity in custom and language. In respect of the latter, the early start of mission work (1833) and printing by the Paris Mission was a factor of great importance. Yet the South Sotho are not a homogeneous people, and may never be.

Of the old tribes there are a few survivals, e.g. Tlokwa and Kgwakgwa, but concentrations of tribesmen are to be found in many places. A large number of Kwena are found in Butha Buthe, Berea and Maseru, as well as in Matatiele and Mount Fletcher in the Transkei. There, in Matatiele, we also find the large Hlakwana tribe of Sibi. The Fokeng live mostly in the north, in Berea and Mafeteng districts. Kgwakgwa and Kgolokwe live in Butha Buthe, Sia and Taung especially in Mafeteng. The mountainous parts of eastern Lesotho (Mokhotlong district) were first occupied by the Tlokwa shortly after 1880, followed by mixed groups that settled between them and the border. Another branch of Tlokwa lives in Mount Fletcher. The Phuthi are represented by a large tribe in Mohale's Hoek, by some smaller ones in Quthing and by some groups living in the Transkei, where they are subject to chiefs not of their own tribe.

In the northern districts of Lesotho there also are unassimilated pockets of Nguni whom the Sotho call *maTêbêlê*, besides others in the south lumped together as *baThepu* (= Thembu), and that singular case, the old Fokeng tribe that became Cape Nguni in the Transkei and later returned to the fold as amaVundla. There are many South Sotho in Thabanchu, which is actually a

PLATE I
Territorial organization

1 Swazi homesteads
2 Tswana village, Mochudi

PLATE 2
Territorial organization

a Natal Nguni
b Transvaal Sotho

Tswana (Rolong) stronghold, and numbers of Zulu and Xhosa speakers respectively live in the north-east and southern parts of the Orange Free State. A shadow of tribal cohesion has survived on the farms in districts where the uninformed might presume only detribalized farm labour. And so also in Lesotho, there are cultural and historical associations the existence of which is not revealed by an enumeration of the chiefs or even of the smaller fry. Here detailed studies will have to be made.

Western Sotho or Tswana

beTswana or *baTswana* is a group term used by the people themselves, especially in the west and south-west, where some say, 'We are Tswana, not Sotho,' whilst further east some say, 'We are Tswana and also Sotho,' and still others hardly know the term and do not apply it to themselves. It is a convenient classificatory term and of ancient origin, about which, despite sterile speculation, we know nothing.

A number of independent tribes bear the same names and still possess the historical and genealogical knowledge to explain their relationships and relative seniority. In the extreme west, along the fringe of the Kalahari, there are Tlhaping, Tlharo, Rolong, represented by four sections, viz. Ratlou, Ratshidi, Seleka (at Thabanchu in the Orange Free State), and Rapulane, the largest being the Ratshidi Rolong of Mafeking district; the Hurutshe in Zeerust and Rustenburg districts; some small sections like the Kubung, Nogeng and Kolobeng; and the large tribes farther north in Botswana, viz. Ngwaketse at Kanye, Kwena at Molepolole, Mangwato at Serowe, and an offshoot of the latter, the Tawana, at Lake Ngami. The Ngwato tribe incorporates many small alien tribes inhabiting the country from early times, such as Kaa and Phaleng, Khurutshe, Matswapong and an appreciable number of 'Shona' not of Sotho or Tswana stock.

Amongst those tribes that exhibit transitions towards the east we mention the Kgatla tribes, which live widely dispersed, from the Kgafela of Mochudi and Pilansberg in the west, the Mmakau and Mosetlha in the centre (near Pretoria), the Motšha on the Springbuck Flats, and some smaller sections; the Fokeng or Kwena of Rustenburg, and several other Kwena tribes in the same district (Mmanamela, Modimosana, Mmatau, etc.); the Malete at Ramoutsa and in Zeerust district; the Phalane or Tlase; Phiring; Taung; Matlhako (of Ndebele origin); baPô (Zulu); Tlôkwa in Rustenburg and Gaberones. The Hwaduba of Hammanskraal belong in origin to the Transvaal Ndebele, but have changed into Tswana. On the other hand the Kôpa and Ntwane near the Olifants river, though of Tswana origin, are in my opinion better classed with the North Sotho.

From Tswana traditions concerning their origins and history one gathers that their ancestors arrived from the north in several migrations separated in time. This latter point would make it seem probable that these successive waves of immigrants were of different stocks. They were all cattle people and remained in the grazing areas skirting the Kalahari. They found a Bush population already in occupation and, judging from physical indications, absorbed some of their blood. In the extreme south there was extensive contact with Korana. These were themselves a pastoral people, and some inferences may perhaps be legitimately drawn from the fact that they called the Tswana (Tlhaping, to be exact) 'goat people'. The ancestors of the Kgalagadi may have been early Tswana immigrants who lost their stock and had to modify their way of life to survive. We don't know. There is no contradiction between this view and the discovery that their language is not so much Tswana as a separate type of Sotho. A somewhat mysterious people, the Digôja (Lihoya, mis-spelt Leghoya) seem to have been of some importance until their decline and incorporation in the Taung shortly after 1800. Perhaps they would have excited less interest if more information had been available about them. There is agreement that the Rolong and Tlhaping came in before those important peoples, the Hurutshe and Kwena. From the beginning all these tribes showed a tendency to split after quarrels over the chieftainship. But the country was large and there was room for everybody and on the whole the Tswana seem to have multiplied and prospered until in 1825 Mzilikazi appeared on the scene and began slaughtering them wholesale.

North Sotho

In addition to using their tribal names, all the people under this heading also call themselves *baSotho* without further qualification. The term 'Transvaal Sotho', current at one time, has yielded to 'North Sotho' which probably suggested itself as counterpart to 'South Sotho'. Though there is considerable diversity within this cluster, there is also a unity. Without searching far we note that they all say '*awa!*' (no! cf. South Sotho *che!* Tswana *nyaa!*), they *sepela* (walk), they *bolela* (talk), they *nyaka* (search) and they *hwetša* (find), and 'one' is *tee*. Contrast this with the South Sotho and Tswana who *tsamaya*, *bua*, *batla* and *fumana*, and 'one' is *-ngwe*. Against this background of uniformity it is well to emphasize the above-mentioned diversity and, more important, the absence of any dialect strong enough to serve as standard, though there are many dialects so weak as to be rejected out of hand as certainly not standard. To this extent, then, the North Sotho language is a fiction.

As with language, so culturally, this cluster consists of a large main body felt to be, despite variations, typical, and many others, some big, some small, departing from that norm in various ways (see below). The bulk consists of the tribes of the centre, viz. of Sekukuniland, Nebo and parts of neighbouring districts which once were under the power or influence of the Pedi rulers. These baPedi or Maroteng, a small offshoot of the Kgatla, made their appearance in Sekukuniland around 1650–80[23] and gradually subjected all the tribes there. This rise to power culminated in the reign of the famous Thulare, who ruled over a large empire of subject and satellite tribes, skilfully kept together by political marriages, diplomacy, force, and other devices such as *kôma* (circumcision lodges) and an elaborate *motseta* (agent) system. The Pedi remained a small ruling caste. The older elements of the population they had subjected were Tau (of Swazi origin), Koni (i.e. Nguni), offshoots of Matlala's (Pietersburg) Koni, and numerous other groups with totems *tlou*, *phiri*, *phuthi*, *nare*, *kwena*, *nkwe*, *tau*, *tšhwene* of diverse origins. Inhabitants of northern Sekukuniland, originally from further north and north-east and collectively called *Rôka*, were regarded as inferior. The Pedi empire collapsed shortly after 1826 under the onslaught of Mzilikazi's Ndebele, but was re-established by Thulare's son Sekwati, who, however, had to accommodate himself to the immigrant farmers. He died in 1861 and was succeeded by his son Sekhukhune. Independent Pedi power ended with his defeat and capture in 1879.

North of the Olifants and the range of mountains ringing the plain of Pietersburg we begin to meet those tribes whom the Southerners like to call *baKgalaka*, that is, Karanga (of Rhodesia). Linguistically and culturally things begin to shade into the South Rhodesian culture complex. The tribes of Mphatlhele, Tšhwene, Mathabatha, Matlala and Dikgale are still Koni or Kgaga from the east, who scaled the escarpment around Haenertsburg and settled on the plains beyond. But then we meet other people. The Tlôkwa north of Pietersburg are, one must presume, in origin the same as their namesakes amongst the South Sotho and Tswana, but here they tend towards the Venda. The large Hananwa tribe of the Blauwberg in the north-west is of Tswana origin, but this is merely a historical fact. Under its suzerainty there are, or were, numerous small diverse units, insufficiently investigated. North of the Hananwa the country is arid and sparsely inhabited, but it leads to the famous archaeological site of Mapungubwe and deserves attention. There are some people here connected with the *Ngwale* (*Nwali*, *Mwali*) cult.

Here we find the Birwa, with branches in the south-western tip of Rhodesia and in nearby Botswana. They are *nare* (buffalo) people originally from far-away Letswalo (Tzaneen) but are now well adjusted to their hot dry environment. The remarkable thing is their language, for Birwa, an unusual form of Sotho, has retained the prefix cl. 8 *vi-* (bilabial), a rare feature shared with the Matswapong dialect near Palapye, and the *hiPai* dialect of Pilgrimsrest, at the other end of the Sotho area. No less remarkable is *te* (= *ndi*) both for the first person singular (*te re* = Sotho *ke re*, 'I say') and as copula (*te motho*, 'it is a person'). This is shared with Xhosa and Tsonga (not for copula, of course) and Venda, in contrast with all other North Sotho, the South Sotho, Tswana and Nguni, which have *ke*, *ngi*. This is another example of that gradual transition from group to group to which earlier reference has been made.

Turning now to the north-east, below the escarpment we find as major culture and power centre the Lobedu tribe of the rain queen Modjadji. Tribute and gifts, to get her to make rain, used to come in regularly from all quarters, from near and far, and a corresponding Lobedu influence emanated outwards. The Lobedu at one time, according to Venda tradition, lived in

Venda in the Nzhelele valley at Tshavhalovhedzi hill which is called after them, and they were Venda themselves. They moved south many generations ago and are today more like the North Sotho though in many respects still very unlike them. We class with them the other Lobedu sections and Mamabolo, all of them having as totem *kolobe* (wild boar). Venda influence persists to the south of the Lobedu. Here we find a number of tribes now similar to one another but of diverse origins, viz. those with totem *nare* (buffalo), the Narene of Letswalo and Sekôrôrô, who believe they came from the south-east though others deny this. Further east there are the Koni or Kgaga (Maake) and Koni of Mametša, with totem *phuthi*, also the Tlhabine or Beli (Pedi) of Mogobôya (totem *noko*), evidently of Pedi origin as they say, and the people of Phalaborwa, an ancient mining and smelting centre. These Lowveld tribes, except Mametša, somewhat contemptuously and loosely called *Rôka* by other Sotho, speak dialects showing Lobedu and Venda affinities, the Letswalo actually using the Lobedu *khe* (= *se*) whilst the rest use interdental *ṭhe*, e.g. *khelô khe*, *ṭhelô ṭhe* for *selô se*, 'this thing'.

At the edge of the escarpment in the extreme east, there is a further subdivision of peripheral North Sotho, namely the Eastern Sotho: *Pulana*, *Kutswe* and *Pai*. The Pulana are under some dozen minor chieftains; the Kutswe under one, and much in with the Tsonga; the Pai are dispersed and being absorbed into the Swazi of these parts. Linguistically, Pulana and Kutswe belong closer together, but traditions show they are not related. The Pai, before being subjugated by the Swazi, were living in the Lowveld north of Swaziland. The Kutswe are Kwena from the interior plateau in the west. The Pulana have the tradition that they were the original inhabitants of northern Swaziland until forced out by the rising Swazi power. In their mountains they have resisted Swazi and Tsonga influences. Of Pai culture and their distinctive language (*hiPai*) very little is left. All three peoples are marginal to North Sotho. What has been rescued from oblivion (Ziervogel, *The Eastern Sotho*, 1954) is of more than ordinary interest, and opens intriguing vistas on the diversity of Sotho and its origins.

Venda Group

This group is distinguished by a language peculiar to it, suggesting in many ways a fusion of North Sotho and Karanga forms of speech, and by a culture sufficiently characteristic to separate it clearly from the other Southern Bantu. The major part of the Venda appear to have been concentrated in the mountains of the Zoutpansberg for a long time, as is still the case. The mountain area is well watered and in the olden days was covered with dense forest which offered a safe retreat for those prepared to accept the conditions: much fever and other disease, little scope for large stock. The Venda were shielded from foreign influences in several quarters by natural isolation. The flat country to the south-east was almost unpopulated and tsetse-ridden until Tsonga refugees from Mozambique began moving in during the last century.

The extensive flat country north of the mountains to the Limpopo was lacking in open water and carried a handful of people. The contacts were therefore with the south and south-west.

To the south the Venda appear to have penetrated a considerable distance, beyond the Lobedu (who, according to tradition at one time lived in the Nzhelele valley) to the edge of the escarpment along the Letlhabine (Thabina) river. Tribes of Venda origin, like the Kolobe (wild boar) of Mamabolo, extended into the Woodbush. In the course of the previous century all of the smaller chieftains living outside the mountain area found themselves inundated by a rising flood (gradual, it is true) of immigrants, Sotho from the west and south-west, Tsonga from the east. All came in peacefully, prepared to accept the ruling chiefs, but swamping them with their numbers nevertheless. In the south-west, Venda contact with the Sotho (mainly Tlôkwa) is of much longer standing.

The Venda themselves distinguish many groups and areas, with names, some descriptive, whimsical or faintly opprobrious for each. For our purpose we may distinguish three culture regions, which however shade into one another, viz. Western, strongly coloured by contact with the Sotho of the interior plateau; Southern, with contacts with the Sotho below the escarpment and more recently with the Tsonga; and the Eastern or Central, depending on how one looks at it, least influenced by any foreign contacts, and having in the extreme north-east (*Niani*) a fringe of population somewhat oriented towards the Karanga across the Limpopo.

To the newcomer, who comes to the Venda with experience of tribal set-ups elsewhere in South Africa, the scene appears familiar. He sees a number of chiefs, each with his own territory and people. He concludes that what he sees is a number of tribes in the sense he is familiar with, something akin to the queen bee and her swarm. They may nest here or there, but remain a swarm. Queen and swarm are one. Not so here. In Venda, it is royalty and the land that are one. The people, the commoners, are dwellers on that land. They do not and would not dare say, 'This is our land'. This notion would not occur to commoners, for only royalty exercises dominion over land. Royalty chased off its land becomes like the rest of the populace, landless and subject to the local rulers. Of course, the rulers were always trying to enlarge their domains at the expense of their neighbours. But all a disgruntled commoner could do was to move to another chief's country. He could not change the management where he was living because he was only a tenant paying his dues.

The whole of Venda at one time consisted of these mutually independent kingdoms, polarized around a few powerful dynasties. The smaller kingdoms were to varying degree satellites or vassal-states, but hardly subjects. Now, for kingdoms to exist they must first be won, but given the fact that for commoners this only meant a change of rulers, it is not surprising that conquest often was remarkably easy. A few determined men might seize a country, for the commoners often would not lift a finger to defend their chief for fear of the consequences if he lost. Thus Venda history turns out to be family or clan history. When tradition relates that the people X or Y came in and occupied the country, we must visualize this in terms of small groups rather than large migrations. It says nothing about the populations already in occupation.

The personal names of rulers are not used to distinguish tribes. Dynastic names which remain unchanged, or the names of areas, are used for this purpose. Thus Vha ha Mphaphuli, 'the people of Mphaphuli', each successive chief bearing this name; or Vha Lwamondo, 'the people of Lwamondo', which is the name of the country, the chief being Ne-Lwamondo, 'Lord or Owner of Lwamondo'.

All tradition agrees that there was at one time an aboriginal population called the *VhaNgona*, a name which can be shown to be an equivalent of the *Kwena* of the Sotho. If they had chiefs or tribal cohesion it is not recorded in history. Rare is the person today prepared to admit he is descended from this formerly despised race. A few other very old groups are also remembered. Approaching the question from another angle, viz. by taking the existing dynasties and tracing them back into the past, we find that without exception their genealogies are extremely brief, five to seven names from the turn of the century, and all start with the founder who first came into the country. Among those of whom there is early mention in tradition and whom we can still identify today there are the people of *Tshivhula* (*Sebola*) now in the extreme west at the Salt Pan, *Ndou* (elephant) people, *Dau*, *Tavhatsindi*, *Ndalamo*, *Mbedzi*, *Laudzi*, *Singo*, and those of *Tshivhase* and *Mphaphuli*. Some traditionally came from the north, others from other directions, as the *Laudzi* who came from the south-east (Pulana Sotho) area of what is now Pilgrimsrest and Bushbuckridge. Some trace their line to a *makhadzi*, a female of a royal line, others to a founder who was not of royal blood but held high office at court. The Mbedzi for example were not rulers but rain-makers. The Mphaphuli clan has several versions, each giving a different direction of origin, suggesting a fusion of elements, whilst the Singo, the latest arrivals from Rhodesia, have legends into which are blended tales of *Ngoma-lungundu*, the sacred drum[24] which was borne along on their wanderings like the Ark of the Covenant, with much else equally mystifying to the enquiring historian.

Western Venda, showing strongest Sotho influence, was in pre-European times the single domain of the Singo, whose early ancestors built *Dzata* (now in ruins), in the Nzhelele valley. The first Voortrekker, Louis Trichardt, took a hand in the succession trouble between Ramavhoya and Ramabulana. The latter's grandson Mphephu defied the government and since his brothers Sinthumule and Kutame had taken sides against him, they got locations of their own. Mphephu was reinstated after the Anglo-Boer War and his descendants have a location in the Nzhelele valley. It is an *idée fixe* with many Europeans that the Venda have a paramount chief, and that it is Mphephu. Neither has ever been the case. In the west and south-west there are other smaller units, as of Mashau, Mashamba, Masakona and Nthabalala (both of the Nzhelele Singo), much Sotho-ized, whilst Mulima is even more so. Sotho groups also acknowledge the Singo house, as for example Matshavha (Matshaba), who are dissident Tlôkwa long separated from the parent tribe.

The Southern Venda I consider to be those of the plains, formerly linked with their kin much further south (e.g. Lobedu). They have been in contact with Sotho for a long time and more recently with Tsonga, who tendered homage and were accepted as subjects by the chiefs ruling the land. Such were *Ne-Tshimbupfe, Masia, Ne-Nngwekhulu, Magoro, Muila, Mashau.* Their Venda language and tradition were swamped by numbers. All their children grew up bi- and tri-lingual. But recent events have shown how resistant language and culture can be. With government recognition of the Tsonga right to existence as a separate ethnic group and to land (which as refugees they formerly did not have), there came a notable resurgence of Tsonga feeling of identity, and in response to this, a similar reaction on the other side.

The Venda heartland is where there has been least influence from outside. This is the area of the two major tribes of Ha-Tshivhasa and Mphaphuli, Thengwe, Rambuḑa and Khakhu, and the slightly more south-oriented tribes of Lwamondo, Mugivhi and Tsianḑa, and Tshakhuma. In the extreme north-east there are Makuya and the Lembethu of Mutele. In the olden days only Lwamondo on his mountain fastness maintained his complete independence from the big two: Tshivhase and Mphaphuli. All the others were drawn into the orbit of one or other of these. This meant that defectors had nowhere to go except over to the 'enemy', Tshivhase and Mphaphuli being of course jealously watchful of one another most of the time. But this, as stated at the beginning, meant little to the commoners, many of whom had relatives on the other side. The result of the situation was that remarkable uniformity in language and culture exhibited by this area.

Lemba

The Lemba are not a group of the South African Bantu like the others, but a small handful of people of alien origin. However, they require mention because they are an important part of the scene.

The Lemba at no time formed a political entity; they never had a country or chiefs of their own. They have always lived widely dispersed in small groups, often no larger than a family, amongst their host tribes in the south of Rhodesia and the Northern Transvaal. They were not, however, despised refugees. As masters of the magic art of smelting and working iron, copper and gold, and as skilled potters, they were everywhere highly regarded.

But this alone would not have set them so much apart. Let us enumerate the differences. Physically, many Lemba have a distinctive appearance: angular features with prominent hooked nose. The men used to wear a long cotton upper garment (*khanzu*) as found along the East Coast. Amongst themselves they spoke a language not understood by their hosts in the Transvaal. We now know Tshilemba to be a form of Karanga. Only a few speakers survive today.

The Lemba did not give their daughters in marriage to any but their own people, and avoided marriage with Bantu women. This strict endogamy was the secret of their survival as a distinct people. It was based on the dogma of the 'uncleanness' of non-Lemba, who ate what the Lemba had been taught was forbidden, viz. pork, certain other animals and the flesh of cattle not kosher-killed according to their law.

The Lemba practised circumcision. Their boys were initiated after puberty in secret closed lodges. The Sotho thought this natural, but amongst the Venda, who did not circumcise, this custom set the Lemba apart as aliens. On the other hand, family organization was much the same, and it was the ancestor cult with its annual (July) rites that held it together. Ancestors were addressed by name (genealogies were therefore important) and age-old prayers, now meaningless, were recited and responded to by all present. No strangers were allowed to attend.

There were about thirteen clans, each named after its founding ancestor. Linked to each of these there was the 'hill' or place of origin, a set of taboos, the oath of men and the oath of women. Most clans consist of a number of branches. Amongst the names of the founding ancestors we find some of Arab origin: *Bakali* (Ar. *Bakr*), *Haji* (Ar. *hajj*), *Hamisi* (Ar. *hamis*), *Hasane* (Ar. *hasan*), *Sadiki* (Ar. *sadih*), *Salifo* (Ar. *sharif*).

The Lemba do not particularly like this name. They are honoured in Venda as *Vhashavhi, Mushavhi*. Other names are *Vhasoni, Vha Mwenye* (the Lord's or Master's people) and *Vha Sena* (from Sena on the Zambesi). On ceremonial occasions they like to call themselves *Vhalungu* or *Vhalumbi*, and especially *Vhalungu-na-nguvho*. In many Bantu languages further north *Lungu* and *Lumbi* mean 'non-Negro, European, (respected) foreigner'. All non-Lemba they call, rather disparagingly, *Vhasenzi*, cf. Swahili *washenzi*, 'wild interior dwellers, savages'.

The Lemba smelted and worked metals and their womenfolk made fine pottery. In places they had the monopoly in these crafts. To sell their wares they did not just wait for customers, but made long journeys to find them. In the absence of currency they had to accept grain, livestock and anything else they could use or resell. They were thus wholly a producing and trading people, with an outlook very different from that of their stock-keeping and grain-growing hosts. It was natural for their shrewdness, acquired in trading, and knowledge, acquired on their travels, to be often employed at the court of chiefs. So they were frequently found to be confidants and advisers of chiefs, within limits of course, due to their depressed status as outsiders.

All these facts point to the conclusion that the Lemba are the descendants of Semitic traders from the East Coast, in other words, of Arabs. This is supported by the texts of prayers which have more recently come to light.[25] They are unintelligible and look unlike Bantu, but suggest some mangled suras from the Koran. The words *Saidi sangu* or *Zaidi zangu* are constantly repeated and are said to mean 'my master' (cf. Ar. *seyyid* 'lord'). In the family name *Hadzhi* (*Haji*) and the oath *Seremane* (Ar. *Sulaiman*) we see a link with what is mentioned from the Arab side further down.

A tradition about early origins has lately come to light. According to this, the ancestors of the Lemba came from a huge town somewhere across the seas, where dwelt many craftsmen in metalwork, pottery, textiles and ship-building. They came to this country to trade their goods, especially for gold. They began leaving some of their men behind with unsold cargo and thus established posts. They moved further and further inland and became well known to the natives, but did not mix with them as they deemed themselves superior. Then one day came shattering news: the city had been taken by the enemy, they could never go back home. So they began taking native wives, chiefly Rozwi, Karanga, Zezuru, and Govera. By this time they were already organized in the clans as we know them today.

Now, starting from the other end, it is well known that in the year 696 the two princes of 'Omân, Sulaimân and Sa'îd were attacked by the forces of the Khalif 'Abd al-Malik ibn Marwan of Damascus, and forced to flee to the land of Zanj (East Africa). There we also find the tradition of the coming of the Arabs who settled along the coast, and the name of their chief, who was Haji Sa'îd.

Notes

1 Cf. also M. Wilson, 'The early history of the Transkei and Ciskei', *African Studies*, 18,4 (1959), 167–79; H. Wilson and L. Thompson, *The Oxford History of Southern Africa*.

2 Mis-spellings and misprints are not a small matter. For example, in periodical articles alone, up to 1950, we find the comparatively easy name *Ndlambe* rendered as *Chlambe, Chlambi, Dhlambe, Dhlambi, Hlambi, Hlambie, Illambi, Isambi, Islambi, Islambie, Ndhlambe, Ndhlambi, Ndhlambie, Sambie, Slambi, Slambie, Tchlambe, T'Slambie, Tzlambi, Umhlambe, Unchlambe, Undhlambe, Un Thlambe*; and *Nqeno* spelt *Enno, Eno, Queno, Un Queno, U'Queno*. Yet conclusions and hypotheses have been based on comparison of words and names no less likely to have been mis-heard, mis-spelt or misprinted.

3 R. Elsdon-Dew, 'The blood-groups of the Bantu of Southern Africa', *S.A. Inst. Med. Res.*, Johannesburg, 39,7 (1936), 217–300; R. A. Dart, 'African serological patterns and human migration', *S.A. Archaeol. Bull.*, 6 (1951), 1–39. Elsdon-Dew's findings are most instructive. Cf. also G. C. Cook, 'Lactase deficiency: a probable ethnological marker in East Africa', *Man*, 4,2 (1969), 265–7; and J. Jersky and R. H. Kinsley, 'Lactase deficiency in the S.A. Bantu', *S.A. Med. J.*, 41 (1967), 1194–6.

4 Shaka and Mswazi are said to have abolished the custom, but can we believe this? Their power did not extend to those who fought them off or fled. More probably, some tribes observed the custom, others did not, so that these dictators confirmed a trend rather than made an innovation.

5 A. K. Boshier, 'Mining genesis', *Mining Survey*, 64 (1969), 21–8.

6 P.-L. Breutz, 'Stone kraal settlements in South Africa', *African Studies*, 15,4 (1956), 157–175.

7   A. C. Lawton, 'Bantu Pottery of Southern Africa', *Ann. S.A. Mus.*, Cape Town, 49,1, (1967).

8   H. C. M. Fourie, *Amandebele van Fene Mahlangu*, Zwolle, 1931, p. 33; N. J. van Warmelo, *Transvaal Ndebele Texts*, Pretoria, 1930, p. 61; E. F. Potgieter, *Enkele volksverhale van die Ndzundza van Transvaal*, Pretoria, 1958, p. 11.

9   H. von Sicard, 'Ngoma Lungundu, eine afrikanische Bundeslade', *Studia Ethnogr. Upsal.*, 5, Uppsala, 1952; E. Mudau, 'Ngoma Lungundu' in van Warmelo, *The copper miners of Musina and the early history of the Zoutpansberg*, Pretoria, 1940, 109–32.

10 *mbanzhe* is regularly derived from *mbange*, cf. *mulenzhe* ('leg') from root *-lenge*. North Sotho has *patšē*.

11 C. V. Bothma, 'Pedi origins' in *Ethnol. Publ.*, 52, 1969, 187–98 of Bantu Administration Dept., Pretoria.

12 N. J. van Warmelo, 'Wer sind die Basotho', pp. 1–7, in *Afrikanistische Studien*, 1955, Veröff. Nr. 26 Inst. f. Orientforschung, Dtsche Akad. d. Wissensch., Berlin.

13 H. J. E. Dumbrell, 'Pyre burning in Swaziland', *African Studies*, 11,4 (1952), 190–1.

14 N. J. van Warmelo, *Contributions towards Venda history*, . . ., Pretoria, 1932, p. 135.

15 Kirby quoting von Hornbostel in P. R. Kirby, 'South African native drums', *S. Afr. Museum Assoc. Bull.*, 3,2, 1943, 48.

16 C. Meinhof, 'Hottentottische Laute und Lehnworte im Kafir', *Z. d. Dtsch. Morgenl. Ges.*, 58 & 59, 1905, 727–69, 36–89; W. Bourquin, 'Click-words which Xhosa, Zulu and Sotho have in common', *African Studies*, 10,2 (1951), 59–81.

17 P. R. van Dyk, *'n Studie van Lala, sy fonologie, morfologie en sintaksis*, Ph.D. thesis, Stellenbosch, December 1960, 1–157 roneo'd folio.

18 See J. Omer-Cooper, *The Zulu Aftermath* (1966) and W. Lye (1967 and 1969b) for further details.

19 H. A. Junod, *The life of a South African tribe*, London, 1927, 1,27; H. A. Junod, 'The condition of the Natives of South East Africa in the 16th century according to the early Portuguese documents' *S.Afr.J. Sci.*, 10 (1914), 137–61.

20 P. M. Shilubana, and H. E. Ntsanwisi, *Muhlaba, hosi ya va ka Nkuna*, Nkuna tribe of N. E. Transvaal at Morija Press, 1958, pp. 25, 49.

21 See note 12 above, 'Wer sind die Basotho', p. 7.

22 Lawton 1967, see 7 above, p. 314.

23 Estimates of Hunt and Schwellnus respectively. D. R. Hunt, 'An account of the Bapedi', *Bantu Studies*, 5,4 (1931), 281.

24 *Ngoma Lungundu*, see 9 above.

25 N. J. van Warmelo, 'Zur Sprache und Herkunft der Lemba', *Dtsches Inst. f. Afrika-Forschung*, Hamburger Beiträge zur Afrika-Kunde Bd.5, 1966, 273–83.

Chapter 4
Material Culture
Margaret Shaw

The material culture of a people is perhaps more than any other aspect of culture dependent on the environment in which they live. It is not surprising, therefore, that the material culture of the South African Bantu-speaking peoples reflects both the ecological regions which they occupy and their modes of subsistence, especially their reliance on cattle and hoe-culture. It is also sensitive to the changes brought about by contact with other cultures. The emphasis in this chapter is on the traditional material culture, while some indication of the changes that are taking place is also given.

Settlement[1]

There are three types of domestic settlement among the Bantu-speaking people in South Africa: the individual homestead situated at a distance from its neighbour; the village, essentially a group of homesteads; and the town, which differs from the village in size and complexity of organization, being often divided into sections known as wards.

The individual homestead, all of whose members tend to be related to its head, is characteristic of the Nguni and the Tsonga (see Plates 1a and 2b). It is the type of dwelling found throughout the Transkei, Natal and Zululand, Swaziland and the areas of the Transvaal where Ndebele and Tsonga live. It is occupied by a man and his wife or wives and children, perhaps a married son or sons and unmarried daughters. Traditionally the huts were arranged in a definite pattern, their doors facing the cattle kraal, which had the central position, with a kraal for small stock against its side. The central hut was that of the chief wife, and the others were ranged on either side, according to the status of their owners. Each wife was entitled to two or three huts—a living room, a store room and sometimes a kitchen—and one or more granaries. Separate huts were usually provided for the older boys and girls, and there used always to be one set aside for guests.

Among the Cape Nguni and Swazi, huts were arranged in a semi-circle, but among the Natal Nguni and the Tsonga they made a full circle round the cattle kraal. In the larger establishments of former days among the Zulu, two or three concentric circles of huts might be necessary to accommodate all the members of the homestead. The Ndebele retained this arrangement in Rhodesia. The Cape Nguni and some of the Swazi did not fence their homesteads, but all the others of this group did so with brushwood. There seems to be no record of the early settlements of the Ndebele of the Transvaal, before they adopted the walled enclosure of the neighbouring Sotho.

The village, composed of a number of homesteads, whose heads might or might not be related to the head of the village, is characteristic of the Sotho generally, and of the Venda. In Lesotho neither the individual homesteads nor the villages are fenced, but, among the Transvaal Sotho and the Venda, individual homesteads are generally fenced or walled. Traditionally among the South Sotho the circular form prevailed, and a sloping site, or, latterly, a terrace, was preferred. At the highest point was the homestead of the chief of the village, with the hut of his chief wife at the centre. The homesteads of the important men of the village lay on either side, and those of commoners completed the lower part of the circle. The open central space was divided between the cattle kraals, in the centre, and a general gathering place and a fenced courtyard, next to the chief's huts, where the men of the village gathered to discuss affairs. Among the Transvaal Sotho and Venda the huts and open spaces of each homestead are clearly separated and enclosed as a whole by a series of fences or, especially latterly, walls, which make courtyards, the floors of which are plastered hard. The outer fences or walls of all the homesteads join up so that the village is enclosed. Among the Pedi each homestead is wedge-shaped, so that several adjacent homesteads make a segment of a circle. It is characteristic of the Transvaal Sotho and Venda that each individual homestead has two courtyards, front and back, separated by the main hut and, formerly, a reed fence (but nowadays a wall). Visitors are received in the front courtyard, but the back one is private. Venda villages used to be very large and strongly enclosed for defence, but now in more peaceful times it is only the chiefs who have this type of village. Commoners tend to live in smaller villages or even individual homesteads.

The above description would fit the smaller settlements of the Tswana, but this group is unique in Southern Africa in that the majority live in permanent settlements large enough to be called towns (see Plates 1b and 3). Serowe for example is several miles across. Each of the Tswana chiefdoms has its main town with, usually, a number of smaller satellite villages. The towns are divided into ranked wards. Formerly, and to a certain extent today, each family homestead was fenced with reeds or brushwood, and a common kraal served the group of families or the village. There is an increasing tendency, however, for each homestead to have its own kraal, and for the large encircling fence to disappear. But whether the whole is fenced or not, the dwelling huts, kitchen and store huts of each wife are surrounded by a six-foot wall or fence, which forms an enclosed yard in front of and behind the dwelling huts. The general appearance is of streets between walls or fences, with only the tops of the huts visible behind them.

Where walls are used to enclose the homestead and the courtyard is plastered, as among the eastern Tswana and the Sotho, Venda and Ndebele of the Transvaal, styles of decoration, both in moulding and in colour, have been developed, the most remarkable and the best known to the public being those of the Transvaal Ndebele, especially of the Ndzundza in the south.

Among the Nguni and South Sotho, and others who inhabit hilly country, a sloping position is chosen for the settlement, and everywhere the tendency is for the homestead to face the rising sun, with the chief hut at the highest point. Among the Nguni the meeting place of the men, the *inkundla*, is the space between the gate of the kraal and the main hut (women of child-bearing age are not supposed to walk across it). In the villages and towns of the Sotho and Venda, the men's meeting place, the *kgotla*, or *kgôrô*, serves the whole settlement, but at various places in the larger settlements there are often small 'squares' with screen and fireplace, which serve the men of a family or related group of families. Kraals for cattle and small stock generally serve one family, but in larger settlements one kraal may serve several families or the whole village.

In many areas the traditional fencing material for kraals was brushwood, or closely packed stakes, but in certain areas, particularly where wood is scarce and stone plentiful, stone walls are built. Originally these were circular, but nowadays they are very often square. The kraal for calves and small stock is built against the fence or wall of the main kraal, but sometimes small stock sleep in one of the huts. Among the Nguni the gateway has special ritual significance. In the Cape it faces the door of the chief hut, but among Zulu and Swazi it faces away from the homestead. Among the Venda and Sotho of the Transvaal, where the stock kraal of the village serves all its homesteads, it is situated alongside the men's meeting place and not in the central position as in the Nguni settlements.

Granaries and storage differ markedly in form. Among the Cape and Natal Nguni, the Swazi, Venda and Lobedu, the main grain store is a pit under the cattle kraal. The Xhosa used, in addition, to have a large wicker cylinder for grain still on the ear and for other crops, and so did the Venda and the Lobedu. The Swazi used platforms for unthreshed grain. In addition the Natal Nguni stored grain and other crops in large, loosely woven baskets, some very large, which might be kept in the open or in a storage hut behind the others. The Ndebele of the Transvaal, some of the western Tswana and the South Sotho, made similarly sized sewn baskets. The former buried them in a pit, the latter stood them on a platform of stones in the store-hut or outside under a roof. The principal Tswana method was to build large clay granaries in the courtyard or in a hut, while the Pedi and other Sotho of the Transvaal stored cereals in basket bins of greatly varying sizes and lesser crops in large clay pots. The Tsonga used grain bins for corn and small, roofed granaries for other crops.

In addition to the main settlements, individual families in many groups have cattle posts where some members of the family go at certain times of the year, or where the cattle are kept in special circumstances—for grazing, or to avoid East Coast fever for example. The permanence of these posts varies from group to group. The important factor is grazing for the cattle. In the Cape the tendency was, and is, to move them in winter from the central areas to the coast or to the mountains: in the Transvaal the bulk of the cattle are always kept at cattle stations, consisting of a hut and a large kraal, often situated some distance away from the village. In Botswana the near desert conditions force the cattle to be moved from place to place following the grazing, and they seldom if ever are brought back to town. In addition, because of the shortage of arable land, the Tswana spend much of the agricultural year in homesteads near the lands, so that, in fact, town life is enjoyed for the shorter part of the year only. The more outlying cattle posts consist of byres for the stock and a few huts for the young men who are the herds.

Small hen-coops and pigsties are dotted about the homesteads of some groups. Others do not house the poultry and pigs at all.

Today the circular, clay-walled hut, with a thatched conical roof, has been adopted so widely throughout the country that it gives the impression of being the indigenous form for all tribal groups. This is not the case. The Nguni form, which the Cape Nguni perpetuate in the huts used by initiates during their seclusion and which the Natal Nguni and Swazi still use, was the beehive-shaped hut, with a withy framework, roughly semi-circular in section and thatched with grass, although sometimes covered with mats as well. The Cape Nguni framework, especially that of the Xhosa and Thembu, was very simple and easily constructed. That of the Natal Nguni and especially the Zulu had a much firmer frame in which many more withies were used and interlaced at right angles. The Natal Nguni and the Swazi built a tall reed fence in front of the door of each hut to give shelter from the wind and some privacy. These fences were often very ornamental and they may still be seen among the Ngwane of Natal and Swaziland (see Plate 5a). Among the Cape Nguni the beehive hut evolved into a low-walled plastered cylindrical framework with rounded roof, a half-way stage to the later rondavel.

The early form of hut among the South Sotho was also a thatched beehive shape on a withy framework, with a long porch projecting at the front. The inside surface was plastered. Later a wall of clay or stone was built round the framework, and only the apex thatched.

In all other groups the cylindrical walled hut with separately made conical roof appears to have been the indigenous type, but the entire wall was not always plastered. Tsonga and Venda walls were made of stakes planted close together in a circle and secured by pairs of horizontal lattices, one inside and one outside the wall of uprights on to which they are fixed, by wrapping or twining with a continuous strand. The roof-frame was made separately and lifted on to the top of the wall before it was thatched. Extra strong supporting poles were placed at intervals, either as part of the wall or two or three feet outside it, to support the roof and, in the latter case, to make a small verandah round the hut. Tsonga and Venda still retain their stake-walled huts, but Venda hut walls are now plastered.

Transvaal Sotho hut walls have a number of poles embedded in a clay wall to about five feet. The conical roof rests on the tops of these poles and on another outer and lower ring of poles, making a verandah.

The Tswana used to build two concentric walls of stone or clay, the outer walls being lower than the inner. The main rafters of the roof rested on the tops of the walls. In this case the space between the two walls was used for storage. Today it is usual to have only one wall, with the eaves overhanging.

Today, throughout the Transkei, Botswana and among the South and Transvaal Sotho, plastered rondavel huts are the rule. They may be made of box-bricks, of plaster over a withy frame, or, very commonly among the South Sotho, of dressed stone. In Natal and Swaziland they occur side by side with the traditional beehive huts. In all groups a more modern method of thatching has been adopted.

In all groups hut floors were made of a mixture of clay and cow-dung, smeared and stamped to a hard surface. (Archaeological excavations have shown that some groups that built their walls of stone also used stone for flooring, but this, too, may have been smeared.) Among the Venda, Transvaal Sotho and some Tswana the smearing of the hut floor is extended to include the floor and walls of the courtyard in front of the hut. Doors used formerly to be of some form of wicker work, except among the Venda and Lobedu among whom carved wooden doors were used for the main hut. Nowadays almost all use wooden doors, either of wooden planks nailed together or ready-made and bought at the store.

In addition to these permanent dwellings most groups erect temporary huts from time to time for a variety of purposes, especially initiation or crop-watching.

The furnishings of huts and courtyards are very simple. In the centre of the Nguni hut is the hearth, which is circular and bounded by a raised rim (see Plate 8). All except Tswana use sleeping mats of sedge fastened by sewing or twining. These are rolled neatly against the wall in the daytime. Similar mats are spread indoors or outdoors for sitting on, and a mat is frequently carried by travellers. The Tswana use animal skins, which are hung on lines in the hut during the day, instead of mats. Most people in former times used a wooden pillow or head-rest, which varied from a simple block or log to elaborately carved rests: the Zulu and Tsonga particularly developed the carving of these rests to an art form. Stools for the head of the house or for visitors were not much in evidence. It was reported of the Zulu king that on formal occasions he sat on a thick roll of matting. Very early, however, Western-type chairs were copied, sometimes carved out of the solid block. The Tswana used stools, but later copied the folding chair with thong seats. Inside the rondavel type of hut among the Nguni, and in the courtyards of the Transvaal Sotho, Venda and Tswana, clay seats are often built out from the walls. In the huts, shelves built into the walls, wooden racks, ropes or thong loops hung from the rafters, serve to store odds and ends.

While it is evident from the differences in style that the type of settlement follows the tradition of the group that uses it, nevertheless the influence of the physical conditions of the area into which the people have moved, and the condition of the group itself at any given period, are discernible. For example, the Nguni have for long lived in hospitable country, where it was easy enough for each family to live at a distance from others. The Tswana, on the other hand, live in largely inhospitable country and it is understandable that settlement should be close. Again, the South Sotho, who for many years lived at a cross roads for migrating or warring peoples, liked to place their villages on the slope of a hill or on mountains, so that they could see who was approaching.

Transport[2]

The main means of personal movement was on foot, and the tribal areas are criss-crossed with narrow paths made by travellers.

Many of the tribes formerly rode oxen, but the practice declined after the introduction of horses in the early nineteenth century in the south, from where they gradually spread northward. Particularly in mountainous Lesotho horses, introduced in the time of Moshesh, have become a tradition, and the classic picture of a Mosotho man is now a man on horseback. In some parts of the country, however, where horse-sickness keeps the numbers down, donkeys have been adopted as riding animals.

For the transport of goods, again the most important means was by human carrier. Considerable loads were and still are carried on the heads of women.

In former times, and especially among the Nguni, oxen were used as pack animals. When a move had to be made the household goods were strapped on the back of an ox and women or children might be given a ride as well. Since the early nineteenth century in the south, and somewhat later elsewhere, triangular sledges, some with high wicker or wattled walls, and drawn by oxen, have been used for bringing in the harvest, to the great detriment of the countryside, so much so that they are now forbidden in certain areas. In the northwestern Transvaal and Botswana ox-drawn wagons are much in evidence.

Donkeys are increasingly being used as pack animals.

Boats and rafts were not normally part of material culture, but both were used in certain areas. The Zulu and Xhosa made rafts of a bundle of reeds on which a man could lie or packages be carried on sticks stuck into the bundle, while a man held on to it and swam it across the river. Other groups used logs in a similar way. Zulu and Tsonga both crossed the Maputa River on boats made of planks lashed together with cords made of rushes. Further inland Tsonga used bark canoes or rafts made of branches of palm. The Venda made bark and wooden canoes, which were propelled with a pole, on the Levubu river.

The Bases of Subsistence

Agriculture[3]

Among the Southern Bantu women are the agriculturalists. This does not mean that the men do no agricultural work at all. In all groups they perform the heavy work of clearing virgin ground and help to break the soil. Among the central tribes, too, the men generally have a small garden of their own. The Swazi, Tsonga, South Sotho and Venda, especially, make much use of the system of work parties where neighbours are invited to help in an arduous task. Beer is provided and the work party can be a gay and enjoyable affair. But on the whole, and particularly among the southern groups, any work other than actual clearing is regarded as a favour to the women whose province it is. Small boys, however, help their mothers by scaring away birds when the grain is first sprouting and when the crops are ripening.

The type of soil to be cultivated differs in different parts of the country, as does the climate which affects it. The Bantu-speakers in Southern Africa are distributed over the summer rainfall area. The northern areas fall within the tropics and hence have tropical vegetation. South of this the most fertile and well watered and wooded land is in the south-east and it becomes drier with scantier vegetation towards the west (see chapter 2). In hilly country the uplands are generally used for grazing and the valleys for cultivation, but in some mountain areas every available patch of ground between the rocks is used. When the rainfall is good the land is fertile, but often a cycle of dry years sets in and hardship is caused. The Tswana are settled on the edge of the Kalahari, only parts of which, mainly in the north and east, are suitable for agriculture and cattle-raising.

Bantu agriculturalists are well aware of which soil is best suited to which crops (the Pedi recognize seven types of soil). It is recognized that river silt is the most fertile and, after that, virgin bush because of the leaf-mould, so that bush was often cleared even when open land was available. It was not always possible, however, to pick and choose as there are areas where good agricultural land is very scarce.

Traditionally there is no individual ownership of land. The land belongs to the tribe as a whole, but is administered by the chief through his sub-chiefs and headmen, who allocate it to private individuals. Thereafter, it is, to all intents and purposes, the individual's private property in that he owns rights over it to the exclusion of others. Land not allocated to individuals is common property for grazing, hunting, gathering and water rights. The household head divides his land among his dependants. Each wife is entitled to at least one field for her own special use.

Lands are generally situated a little distance away from the homesteads, except that tobacco, occasionally gourds, and some vegetables are often grown in gardens next to the huts. In the fertile regions, lands may be only five or ten minutes' walk from the homestead of the owner, but those people who live in the more arid parts of the country have a good distance to go to their garden plots. Lands are irregular in shape and marked off by grass strips, or, today, fenced to keep off animals.

The main indigenous agricultural implement was the hoe. It consisted of an iron blade with a pointed tang at the back, by which it was inserted through the head of a wooden haft and held there by exactness of fit or wedged by a small wooden wedge. With the exception of the Nguni tribes, this iron-headed hoe seems to have been universal, but the size and shape of the blade and the length of the handle varied from group to group. The Tsonga used a medium-sized, roughly diamond-shaped hoe-blade with a haft about two feet long. The Venda and other Transvaal tribes had large heavy diamond-shaped hoe-heads, again with a fairly short handle. The South Sotho and Tswana used large oval hoe-heads with a horizontal curve, hafted in a long handle about one to one and a half metres long. Hoe-heads were formerly made by smiths from locally-mined iron and were of such value that, among the Venda who had few cattle, they frequently took the place of cattle as bride-wealth. The Nguni, at least up to the early nineteenth century and probably considerably later, used a digging stick, or wooden hoe, made of very hard wood. It consisted of either a straight shaft, pointed and hardened in the fire at each end, or had a flat blade, in the same plane, at one or both ends. Iron-headed hoes are said to have been used by the Nguni before contact with whites, but there were very few of them, and it was not until the introduction of the European iron hoe, and later of the plough, that the old wooden hoe disappeared. The plough has very nearly ousted the hoe in most places and has caused a great many changes in Bantu agriculture (see chapter 5).

Another implement used in agriculture is the axe, with which trees and bushes are chopped down in clearing the land. Nowadays axes are bought at the stores.

Originally the most important and widespread of the crops grown was sorghum (kaffir-corn, *Andropogon sorghum* Brot. and other species). It has been practically replaced by maize, introduced comparatively recently and now the most important crop. Two other crops which are cultivated by all groups are pumpkins and a variety of gourds, which are both eaten when young and green, or allowed to ripen, when the shells are converted into vessels for holding milk, water, snuff, oils and fats. Other crops vary according to area. Several varieties of bean are grown in most parts, sweet potatoes in the east, groundnuts in the northern Transvaal and (occasionally) in Zululand, and tobacco and Indian hemp in most parts, although the latter is now prohibited.

Most people try to cultivate a little new ground each year. After the trees have been cut down the branches are piled against the stumps, allowed to dry, and then burned. The fire burns down into the roots of the stump below the ground. Grass that is too rank to burn green is cut and allowed to dry and then burned, the ash enriching the soil. This is done at the end of winter or in the spring. Sometimes a man and his family work alone, but generally everyone helps and work parties of neighbours are frequently arranged.

Some rotation of crops is practised and when a plot is worked out it is left to lie fallow for a year or two.

The Sotho, Tswana and Tsonga generally hoe the ground after it has been cleared and before planting, but the Nguni sow first and hoe afterwards. Sowing takes place between October and January as soon as the first rains have come. The Nguni method is to scatter the seed over the ground and then hoe, or nowadays plough, it in. Mpondo women when hoeing took a mouthful of seed which they spat out as they worked. All but the Tsonga followed this method of scattering the seed and generally mixed two or three crops together in the same field. The Tsonga make little holes as they go along and put a few grains in each and, though they may alternate crops in the same field, do not mix the seed before sowing. When the seedlings appear above ground they are thinned out and, after about six weeks, the laborious process of weeding is commenced. Women are assisted in the weeding by the children, whose main work, however, is to scare the birds away as soon as the grain crops begin to seed. Raised platforms for this purpose are made in the fields and the children spend the whole day there shouting, banging tins, throwing stones, or flicking lumps of clay from the end of long sticks, to keep the birds away.

The agricultural year ends with the harvesting of the grain crops, by which time the vegetable crops have generally been harvested. The heads of corn are broken off and carried home in baskets, sledges or bags, and stored on racks or temporary granaries until dry, when some are set aside for the next year's seed. Most, however, are threshed with flails (which may be straight sticks or clubs), winnowed, and stored in permanent granaries (see Plates 6a and 6b). Maize is frequently shelled by hand. In most groups this work is done near, if not in, the homestead or village, but in Botswana and Lesotho it may be completed at the lands and the grain then carried back to the village.

The success of a season is not expected to depend solely on empirical techniques. A considerable amount of magic and ceremony is included as part of the process. In most agricultural rituals the chief plays a very important part. Rain-making ceremonies are widespread. In some cases the power is vested in the chief himself; in others he has his professional rain-makers. In the well-watered regions of the south-east these ceremonies take place usually only in times of drought, but in the more arid regions of the west they are performed every year. In addition to the rain-making ceremonies various means are used to further the growth of crops. In many groups the chief formally opens the hoeing, planting and reaping season with a ceremony in which the ancestors are invoked and no-one may begin before he has done so. The chief may also distribute doctored seeds or these may be bought from a herbalist. Medicines may be scattered over the fields or burned near them so that the smoke blows across. Some of these measures are intended to prevent harm from coming to the crops by pests or other natural or supernatural causes; others are intended to secure abundant crops. Among all tribes there was some ritualization of the first fruits. No one could taste the new crop until the chief had first done so and made an offering to his ancestors.

Modern times and contact with other people have brought about changes in agricultural methods and in the crops grown. Most important has been the introduction of the plough which, besides ensuring better preparation of the ground and bigger plots, has caused men to take more direct part in agricultural work, particularly as ploughs are drawn by cattle. Government agricultural officers have in some instances been able to bring about an improvement in method. In South Africa Government Acts have also decreed that on the death of the cultivator the land reverts to the state, though his heirs may apply for its re-allocation. In recent years, after surveys of arable land and grazing, people in some areas have been persuaded to live in clusters on the least fertile land, and to reserve the most suitable agricultural and grazing land for those purposes.

Animal husbandry [4]

Agriculture may be the principal source of subsistence, but the Bantu themselves attach more importance to their cattle. Animal husbandry is perhaps most strongly developed among the Nguni, who inhabit the most favoured parts of the country; whereas among the Tsonga and Venda disease, warfare, and other factors have greatly reduced the size of the herds, and the presence of the tsetse-fly in many parts has been an insuperable obstacle to stockfarming. But cattle are kept wherever it is at all possible. They are not merely a source of food, in the form of milk and, occasionally, meat. Their skins provide material for clothing, shields, bags, and other useful objects; their horns are made into receptacles; and their dung is used both as fuel and in the cement plastered on walls and floors. The oxen in many tribes serve as beasts of burden and as a means of transport. Often, too, they are trained specially to race without riders, contests between them being one of the most favoured sports; and such racing cattle are sometimes commemorated in tradition long after their death.

Cattle are further[5]

> the principal medium of exchange, and the medium in which court fines are levied. . . . [They] are the means of keeping on good terms with the ancestral spirits, and so of securing health and prosperity, because the maintenance of good relations with the ancestor spirits depends upon making the proper ritual killings of cattle at various stages in the life of the individual, and in sickness.

Cattle are also the means of obtaining sexual satisfaction, since a legal marriage cannot take place without the passage of cattle . . .[6] The possession of cattle gives social importance for they are the means of securing many wives and adherents, and of dispensing hospitality and showing generosity, on which virtues status largely depends.[7]

Cattle therefore loom largely in a man's thoughts. They are his principal form of wealth, his most treasured possession; and anything concerning them and their welfare focuses his attention. The Bantu languages abound in terms minutely differentiating cattle according to sex, age, colour, and shape of horns, and reflecting the intense interest taken by the people in their beasts. A man often knows his cattle by name; and his bull, the pride of his herd, is hailed in laudatory phrases as it comes out of the kraal. The slaughter of an animal is normally reserved for ceremonial occasions, whose importance is heightened by the magnitude of the sacrifice. Some Cape Nguni tribes, especially the Bomvana, even have sacred herds of cattle, held inalienably by the chief in trust for the tribe, and sacrificed to his ancestors in times of national importance. Cattle raids were among the most frequent causes of warfare, and cattle theft one of the most serious offences. *Kgomo modimo wa mogae, modimo wa nkô e meetse; kgomo leotlanya dithšaba, o bolaile banna ba le bantsi*, says a Tswana song: 'Cow god of the home, god with the moist nose; cow that makes the tribes fight, you have killed many men'—an apt summary of both the religious and political importance of cattle.

The cattle kraal, a circular enclosure of stout poles in which the cattle are kept at night, is not only the central feature of most village settlements, but also the centre of village life. [It is not unknown for a kraal to be built for its ritual significance only, by people who do not possess cattle.] Inside it the cattle are killed for sacrifices; here men meet for secret discussions; women may not enter unless they belong to the family, and even then not when they are menstruating; and here, too, the family head is often buried, wrapped in the skin of a newly-slaughtered ox. Adjoining it is the meeting-place of the men, where they sit daily to eat and gossip round the fire and sometimes to feast, where justice is administered, and where strangers are received. Women may not come there except when bringing food, and must in other ways *hlonipha* (respect) it.

But despite this intense preoccupation with cattle, the Bantu pay little attention to quality. For most social purposes one fullgrown beast is as good as another; and, if anything, preference is shown for animals of a particular colour or with horns of a certain shape rather than for well-developed oxen or good milch cows. The cows give little milk, and then only after calving, so that this important source of food fluctuates considerably in yield. And since it is every man's ambition to have as many cattle as possible, no matter how poor they may be, there is little attempt to prevent the propagation of inferior stock. Most bulls are castrated, only one or two being kept in each herd for breeding purposes; but they are not castrated early enough, and as bulls always run freely with the herd, mating is indiscriminate, although the widespread custom of lending out cattle mitigates to some extent the dangers of constant inbreeding.[8]

No fodder of any kind is grown for the cattle. They feed solely upon the available pastures, except after harvest, when they graze on the stalks in the fields; but the practice is widespread of burning parts of the veld to provide early spring grazing. All land not actually under cultivation is common pasturage. 'There are no clearly defined areas to which particular individuals have prescriptive grazing rights.'[9] But among the Mpondo, and probably other Nguni tribes also, people living in the same locality regard the area surrounding their villages as their special grazing ground, and try to exclude others, even to the extent of driving away their herds; while among the

Tswana each ward similarly has its own special area, where no other cattle may graze without permission.

In the rainy season cattle graze near to the villages, but during the dry winter grass must often be sought many miles from home. On the well-watered eastern side of South Africa the uplands form summer grazing, while in the winter the cattle are taken down to the deep, sheltered valleys, where grass is lush and abundant. In the more arid regions to the west, where as among the Tswana the people are settled in large villages, the cattle are kept all the year round at special grazing posts, often a day's journey or more from home. These cattleposts are during the dry season located close to river beds, where pits are dug to water the cattle; in the rainy season they are moved away to fresh pastures. No cows at all are kept at the villages. Milk is sent there from time to time in the milksacks, but appears less frequently in the daily diet than it does farther east.

By day the cattle are let out to graze in the vicinity of their kraal, to which they return at sunset. In autumn, when there is plenty of grass and water after the summer rains, they may be unattended. But during the rest of the year they are always herded, especially during the dry season, when they must be taken to water. At such times, in the more arid regions, they are often watered only every two or three days. The cows are in some tribes milked in the morning before they go out and in the evening after they come back; but in others they are brought back in the forenoon to be milked for the only time, and then taken out again to graze (see Plate 7a). The calf sucks first, but is soon driven off; the milker, sitting on his haunches to one side of the cow, then fills his wooden pail, after which the calf is allowed to suck again. The calves are always separately herded near the kraal, the very young ones being kept in it all day.

The Bantu know from practical experience where to find good grazing and water for their herds, how to protect them from wild animals, and what remedies to apply for such common ailments as liver disease, ophthalmia, and protracted delivery. But, as Stayt remarks, they really understand little about cattle diseases, 'and epidemics are quite beyond their control'.[10] In these and such other aspects of stock-raising where experience alone cannot afford them safe guidance, they fall back once again upon magic. They bury 'doctored' sticks in the kraal to protect the cattle from witchcraft and disease; they sprinkle their cows and inoculate their bulls with certain 'medicines' to stimulate fertility; they burn other 'medicines' to promote the general well-being of the cattle; and as an additional safeguard forbid newly-widowed and other ritually impure persons to approach the animals closely. Women generally are prohibited from handling the cattle in any way, or even from walking through a herd, particularly when menstruating, newly pregnant, or in some other way 'impure'.[11] But there do not appear to be any tribal ceremonies relating to cattle similar to these noticed above in regard to horticulture.

Goats and sheep are kraaled and herded separately from the cattle. Sheep are not numerous, but even the poorest people have goats, which among them fulfil the same uses as cattle. They provide milk and meat; their skins are made into clothing; and they also serve as mediums of exchange, *lobola* payments, and sacrifices. 'The distinguishing terms applied to cattle are applied also to goats, and they are supposed to suffer from contact with *umlaza* [ritual impurity of women]. But no one ever makes praises of goats.'[12] Fowls, the only domesticated bird, are very common. They are occasionally fed with grain, but are otherwise left to fend for themselves. They generally roost on trees or on specially erected perches in the household enclosure. They are often killed for eating or sacrificed to the spirits, and are also used as mediums of exchange. Dogs, the only other indigenous domestic animal, are used principally in hunting. They are never eaten or sacrificed, and are often half-starved and brutally treated; but good hunting dogs are much valued and sometimes well cared for. Pigs were introduced comparatively recently from European sources.

Hunting[13]

Hunting is essentially an occupation of men. Formerly the country abounded in all types of game, and hunting was the most important source of meat and the most popular sport and occupation. As a result of the wholesale destruction of game there is very little scope for hunting nowadays. Game was hunted principally for food and used as such even if it were hunted for some other reason. For example it was necessary to hunt destructive animals that might harm the crops, herds and gardens. Skins and horns were useful, too, for many purposes—clothing, drum-heads, blankets, milksacks—and the sinew provided string for bows and thread for sewing. These were particularly needed by the northern tribes, who were not so rich in cattle.

Hunting methods were very much the same throughout the area. The most effective method was the digging of pit-falls of which there were two types. Deep, straight pits were dug at gaps in fences of stakes that were placed across a narrow valley, or, in open country, arranged in a V-shape with the pit at the apex. The hunters gathered in a group and chased the game towards the fence, and the animals, making for the gaps, fell into the pits. They were then despatched with axe or spear. The second type of pit was intended to catch animals singly. The bottom was set with sharply-pointed wooden stakes, pointing upwards, and the whole covered lightly with branches and grass. Rope snares were set for large and small game and birds. A rope with a noose was attached to a sapling which sprang back and tightened the noose round the leg of the animal that had released the trigger. A variety of other traps was used, particularly for dangerous game. The Venda alone stretched nets across valleys; they were loosely fixed so that they collapsed on the animals that walked into them.

In addition to traps, weapons were used both by a hunting party and in individual effort. Boys still practise with throwing sticks from their earliest childhood and develop sufficiently good aim to hit and stun small animals on the run or birds on the wing. Axes were used for finishing off animals caught in traps, but their most spectacular use was in elephant hunting. Elephant would be stalked by a group of hunters and efforts made to separate one from the herd. Then the main party would attack the animal with spears or arrows while one of their number would approach from behind and hamstring it. Bows and arrows were used mostly by boys for hunting birds and small animals, but Venda men used also to use them for larger game and for war. A special type of blunt wooden arrow was used for shooting birds so as to stun them without damaging the flesh. The most important weapon used in hunting, however, was the spear. Men might go out singly or in groups with dogs, and stalk game until it was exhausted. In a large combined hunt, when all the men of the district gathered, some acted as beaters to chase the game towards those who were ready with spears to tackle it as it came on. The Zulu method of advancing on the game in a line from behind, encircling it by bringing the two ends of the line together and then moving inwards, was the model for Shaka's army tactics.

Dogs were the indispensable allies of the hunters. They were used particularly for tracking game and pursuing it until exhausted. Special dogs were kept and trained to attack.

In former times several villages might join together under the organization of one of the men who was reckoned master of the hunt. Large public hunts used to be called by the district or paramount chief, either for sport or for some special reason; for example, the Mpondo had an organized hunt as part of the treatment of the army.

Various medicines were prescribed and various ceremonies performed for the safety of the hunter and the success of the hunt, and dogs as well as hunters were treated. Today hunting has become practically entirely an individual matter, since the game laws have put an end to large-scale hunting.

Fishing[14]

Fishing was not generally practised, being practically confined to the Tsonga. It was not regarded as a sport like hunting, but merely as a means of adding to the food supply.

The Tsonga relish fish and it is also eaten occasionally by the coastal Mpondo, but elsewhere there is not much enthusiasm for it except among boys. The Cape Nguni (with the exception of the Mpondo at the coast), the Zulu and the Pedi did not eat it at all in former times, regarding fish as akin to snakes.

Mpondo men used to spear fish in shallow pools while the women occasionally caught them by hand in the rock pools. Tsonga women use a conical basket trap, with a hole in the top. The trap is pushed down in shallow river water or pools, and any fish trapped removed by hand through the top. Tsonga men at the coast build a weir across the mouth of a river or an arm of the sea, with gaps in which a valved basket trap is placed with the mouth against the receding tide. Venda boys use the same type of trap in rivers, and they also shoot fish with bows and specially slender arrows.

Modern changes have affected fishing methods very little, except by adding angling with rod and line to the fishing methods.

Gathering[15]

In addition to the production of food and to hunting and fishing, great reliance is placed in all groups on the gathering of wild foods—wild plants, fruits, honey, and insects and, by the coastal Mpondo, shellfish. This is the work of women, helped by children, and is mostly done while going to and returning from the lands.

In most places these foods form a high proportion of the general food supply. Krige and Krige (1943) list over a hundred edible wild fruits and berries that are gathered by the Lobedu. Similar lists have been made for the Pedi (Quin 1959) and could no doubt be duplicated for most groups.

Preparation and serving of food and drink[16]

The staple diet nowadays is ground maize, or more rarely sorghum and, in the Transvaal, a little millet. To this are added relishes of meat, if available, cultivated vegetables and a great variety of wild foods. Two centuries ago the staple diet of the Cape Nguni was said to be meat and milk, the latter taken sour, but grain has gained in importance.

Bulk supplies of grain and other crops are stored in the granaries and store-houses mentioned above, but food for immediate use is kept in pots, baskets, or, nowadays, enamel or galvanized containers in the store or kitchen hut. Much of the vegetables and wild foods is collected daily. Some food, for example pumpkin, may be dried and stored for the off-season.

There are two ways of preparing grain. It may be stamped to different degrees of fineness, according to the dish for which it is to be used, in a wooden, or occasionally stone, or (among the Tsonga) pottery, mortar, with a wooden, or, nowadays in the south-east, an iron, pestle; or it may be ground between two stones to a meal of varying fineness. Either of these methods involves a heavy daily task for the women and older girls. In many places today both methods are used, stamping for the coarser and grinding for the finer product, but it may be that these are two separate traditions which through contact have been assimilated. Ground meal is caught at the front of the lower grinding stone on a closely woven mat, or in a shallow basket. Stamped meal may be sifted in a shallow basket to separate the fine from the coarse.

Cooking takes place on an open fire and, if weather permits, most of it is done out of doors, otherwise in the centre of the kitchen hut. In former times fire was made with fire-sticks, by the rapid twirling between the hands of a hard stick in a depression in a soft stick, and this method is still used for kindling ritual fires. This early gave way to flint and steel and then to matches. In some tribes the pot is placed in the ashes, but more usually three or more round stones are used as a support. By far the most common cooking pot, however, is the three-legged cast-iron pot which was introduced in the Cape by traders over a hundred years ago. It is an excellent utensil and has displaced local pottery in most areas. Fuel is predominantly wood, but, where this is scarce, dried cow dung is used. This is criticized by agricultural officers on account of the loss of the fertilizing manure. Most cooking is by boiling or simmering, but strips of meat may be laid on the coals or spitted and roasted over the fire. Wooden spoons are used for stirring, but for meal porridge a stirrer in the shape of a straight wooden shaft with four or more projections at an angle to it, at one end, is twirled between the hands to make it smooth.

Food is served in different utensils in different areas. The Nguni and some Sotho usually serve porridge on small closely woven mats, and meat either on wooden dishes, in the north, or on wicker trays, in the south. Among the Venda, Lobedu, Pedi and some other Sotho in the Transvaal, wooden plates or bowls are used, and, when serving men, the Venda and Lobedu place these plates in a lidded basket which is characteristic of these groups only. In some groups shallow pottery bowls or half calabashes were used. Today, store-bought utensils of various kinds are found everywhere, but not to the exclusion of the older types. Wooden spoons are used for serving, but individuals help themselves with their fingers, though meat may be eaten with the aid of small sticks or skewers.

In addition to water and milk, which is drunk sour except by the very young and the very old, beer (from grain), palm wine and ciders from various fruits are drunk. Beer is by far the most important beverage, and is universally made. It is made traditionally from sorghum (which makes the best clear beer), but maize is increasingly used, especially for the type that is so thick as to be virtually a fermented porridge. Malt is obtained by adding sprouted grain to the required amount of unsprouted grain, grinding them together, and fermenting the resultant meal in water. Very large pots were, and in most places still are, used for the preparation of beer, but in former times among the Cape Nguni, and even today among some Tsonga, large baskets were used for the fermentation. When fermented, the mixture may in addition be boiled; it is finally strained for use through loosely woven tubular strainers. When ready, the beer is poured into smaller, often decorated, pots, and served in individual small pots or basketwork (Mpondo) or calabash drinking vessels. The Natal Nguni and their offshoots made a basket-work spoon for skimming off the froth and flies. In addition to its food and narcotic value, beer is of tremendous social significance, and often has a part in ritual. Those Zulu and Tsonga who live in the *lala* palm belt, tap the sap of the palm and ferment it to a wine. Some Tswana brew a potent honey mead. In the Transvaal the fruit of the marula and the 'Kaffir plum' (*Harpephyllum caffrum*,

Bernh.) is fermented to a highly intoxicating drink. These are all seasonal drinks, however, and do not have the importance of beer.

Dress and Ornament[17]

Clothing

All clothing was originally made of animal skin, but cotton cloth and blanketing and woollen blankets were adopted very early after contact with the whites. Some skin clothing is still worn today, however.

The basic garments for women were one or more small aprons (which might or might not be covered by a skirt), a wrap or cloak, and, in some groups, a breast-covering. Among the Cape Nguni and South Sotho the apron was short and fringed. When beads became more easily available among the former people the fringe was made of strings of beads and this garment may still be worn under Western-style dresses. The South Sotho still make the fringe from cords rolled from the leaf of a species of *gazania*. Elsewhere the apron was of skin, later replaced by cloth. The shape of the skirt differed. It was sometimes nothing more than a large apron covering the buttocks and allowing the small apron to show in front (Xesibe, Bhaca, South Sotho); sometimes it was a full skirt (Zulu and Tsonga); sometimes two separate skin panels, straight or cut to shape, hanging down back and front (Transvaal Sotho). The breast-covering was mostly confined to the Nguni and may have been an early concession to Western convention. It consisted of a wrap, worn tucked in under the arms and hanging down straight, but Nguni women also wore a small piece of skin, with a fringe of beads attached. The cloak of the Cape Nguni woman was a voluminous affair, with triangular gussets let into the main skin to make it flare. In some other groups the cloak was shorter and less voluminous.

Ordinary dress for men was less elaborate. Cape Nguni and Tsonga men wore a penis-sheath only. The westernmost Cape Nguni, however, added an apron of skin—possibly due to Hottentot influence. Natal Nguni wore, in addition to a prepuce covering (they did not circumcise), an apron of skin in front and, at the back, a kilt of animal tails or twisted strips of furred animal skin. Swazi men wore two aprons, front and back. Sotho and Venda did not wear the penis-sheath, but a triangular skin loin cloth, with one point taken through the legs and tied to the others at the back. For warmth a cloak of skin was worn by all groups.

The style of garment varied, not only from tribal group to tribal group, but according to age and social status within the group, for example between initiated and uninitiated, married and unmarried. Neither sex wore sandals habitually, but might do so on a journey.

In most groups the head was not covered, but the hair was dressed by both men and women in a variety of styles, some very elaborate. Xhosa and Thembu women, however, covered their heads with dressed skin caps, sometimes heavily beaded. Tswana men often wore skin caps with the fur left on. When Burchell visited them early in the nineteenth century some Tswana were wearing basketry hats of shallow conical shape, and the South Sotho wore (and still wear) both brimmed and unbrimmed sharply conical hats. The origin of these is obscure.

The availability of western manufactured goods has influenced clothing perhaps more than any other aspect of material culture. At first, and, except in towns, until quite recently, the tendency was to reproduce traditional styles in cloth instead of skin, but new styles have developed, especially where missionary or school influence has been strong. The blend of materials and styles is admirably shown in the drawings of Barbara Tyrrell (1968).

These new styles have become just as characteristic as the old. Cape Nguni men early adopted woollen blankets as cloaks while the women favoured a plain coarse weave of sheeting or cotton-blanketing which they dyed with ochre to different shades of red and orange or, latterly among the Mpondo, pale blue. This was made into skirts—short for girls, and ankle-length for married women. In the late nineteenth century Xhosa, Mfengu, Thembu and Mpondomise followed the widely flaring European style. Breast-cloths, wraps and cloaks of the same material were added and the whole topped with a complicated turban of fine black cloth. The latest fashion for women in the Transkei is to make similar-shaped garments of a variety of materials and colours, with all sorts of fantasies in the turban. Among the easternmost Cape Nguni and the Natal Nguni, a smoother cloth was made up in the same style as the skin garments it replaced, and dyed black or brown. The Venda, Tsonga and Transvaal Sotho favoured striped salempore cloth. South Sotho women adopted the very full, ankle-length, gathered skirts, supported by several petticoats and with blouses and cloth shawls, of the nineteenth-century European fashion. South Sotho men developed such a taste in woollen blankets that for some time these have been specially woven for them. Whether affecting blankets or not, most men today wear shirts and trousers.

Costume

In addition to clothing for everyday and best wear, certain professions or occasions demanded a special costume for the main participants. Perhaps the most striking in their difference from everyday wear were those of initiates, especially boys, worn for the dances at the end of their term of seclusion after circumcision. One of the objects was to hide the identity of the wearer. Elaborate costumes of palm-leaf or reed were made by the Cape Nguni, and even more elaborate ones by Tsonga and North Sotho.

Warriors, too, were splendidly dressed, generally in a more elaborate form of the everyday dress, with the addition of a special head-dress of crane's feather (Cape Nguni), colourful feathers (Zulu), ostrich and other feathers (Rhodesian Ndebele), ostrich feathers (South Sotho) and so on.

Diviners and herbalists wore elaborate costumes which included certain characteristic touches such as a cap of baboon skin. Nguni diviners typically wear white clothing and white beadwork, since white is the colour that symbolizes a special relationship with the ancestral spirits (see frontispiece).

Chiefs, when in formal dress, were distinguished in most groups by a cloak of leopard skin, reserved for royalty, and their capitals, among the Cape Nguni, were distinguished by the royal insignia of an elephant's tail on a pole.

Ornament

Today beadwork ornaments are so characteristic of the Southern Bantu that it is hard to think of them as other than indigenous. Before the introduction of glass beads, however, many other objects were used—pieces of reed, wood, shell or root, claws and teeth of animals were strung for necklaces; whole shells, especially cowrie and nerita, were strung for arm-bands and headbands; and, in some areas, arm-bands and other ornaments were carved from ivory. Necklaces and bangles for arm and leg were woven of shiny yellow grass, such as appears every autumn when the grass is ripe. Metal, too, was much used for ornaments, especially arm- and leg-bands. Iron and copper were both mined in various places, but more important for ornamental purposes were the brass and the brass wire of varying thicknesses that were imported from the east coast and, later, from the Cape. It was wound round a core to make bangles and girdles, which were worn in quantity. For a long time before European settlement at the Cape glass beads had been coming into the country in small quantities by way of the Arab and (later) Portuguese trade on the east coast of Africa. Because of the source they were more common in the north than in the south. When they became available from the Cape Colony traders their use for ornaments and decoration of clothing became widespread. Particularly amongst the Nguni of the Cape, Natal and the Transvaal, and the South Sotho, beads were strung into elaborate ornaments, woven into a beadwork fabric, embroidered on clothing, or strung into articles of clothing themselves. Elsewhere they tended to be used more simply in single strands.

A more ancient and durable form of ornament was tattooing and cicatrization, which was widely practised in traditional patterns by Nguni and Tsonga.

Cosmetics

Cosmetic practices vary considerably and have not been much studied except for the Xhosa (de Lange, 1963, and sporadic mention by early writers).

The most commonly used cosmetic is fat (today sometimes butter fat) to anoint the skin and give it a shining, dark, healthy appearance. Powdered red ochre is mixed with the fat by Xhosa and Thembu girls and women and, to a lesser extent, by other Cape Nguni for ordinary beautification and ritually by newly-initiated young men. It is also used by Sotho, Tsonga and Venda who are in a ritually important state—e.g. newly initiated girls, brides and nursing mothers. The Tswana formerly used yellow ochre on the face.

Various styles of hair-dressing utilize fat (or sour milk) and red ochre (e.g. Pedi girls, Zulu and Bhaca married women, Venda girl initiates, Tsonga nursing mothers), soot (Pedi women), powdered iron ore and fat (Tswana), charcoal (Venda and Tsonga young women), antimony (Tsonga young women), graphite (Pedi girls); while young Swazi men use fat and aloe leaf ash, or more recently soap, to bleach the hair.

Cosmetics are used by young people of both sexes, especially those of marriageable age, but also by older women.

The Xhosa have developed patterns of facial decoration with ochres of various colours, many of which can now be bought at stores, whereas previously they might have to be fetched from a suitable deposit a long way away. Kaolin clay, soot, washing blue, and certain plants, mixed with butter or animal fat, are used.

Certain ritual conditions demand the use of cosmetics, for example Cape Nguni boy initiates and South Sotho girls are painted all over with white clay.

Ritual Life[18]

Religion and ceremonial

The most important part of traditional religious belief is the ancestor cult—the belief in the immortality of the soul and that it is the ancestors who hold in their hands the destinies of their descendants. To influence them favourably, therefore, worship in the form of propitiatory practices is directed. There is little special paraphernalia connected with the cult, no carved figures to represent the ancestors for example. Its practices concern the disposal or offering of ordinary things. Among the Nguni the place for the offerings to be made is in the cattle byre or at the grave of the ancestor concerned, but some groups, such as Tsonga and Venda, have shrines. The Venda, for example, place a spear in a special place in the homestead to represent its owner who has died, and the offering will be made there.

Propitiatory offerings may be daily routine offerings of a little food or drink at meals, or at least whenever a new brew of beer is made or an animal slaughtered. There may be regular offerings at all the important occasions in the life of an individual—birth, initiation, marriage and death—or at important communal occasions such as the opening of the agricultural season, or the harvest. There are also special occasions such as, in former days, the start of a hunting expedition or a war, or rain-making ceremonies. All these are generally accompanied by sacrificial offerings, be it fowl, sheep, goat or ox. Offerings may also be made in thanksgiving.

The daily offerings of food and drink are made as a matter of course and without ceremony, but the other occasions mentioned are all accompanied by a lesser or greater degree of ceremonial.

The ceremonies at a birth are small family ceremonies aimed chiefly at the safety of the new infant. They always include some form of medication of the child and its mother. Charms may be given to both. When the two emerge from the hut after a period of seclusion, a goat is usually slaughtered as a thank-offering and to provide a skin in which to carry the child.

The period of initiation for boys and in some groups for girls also involves seclusion in a specially erected hut, the wearing of special clothing throughout the period, of special costumes for the dancing, and the provision of new clothing for the newly initiated. The articles used in these schools tend to be of traditional pattern—for example the Xhosa beehive hut and a spear blade for circumcision—and most of them are burned at the end of the period. Almost the only instance of ritual art is the use by the Venda, and some Sotho, of carved wooden figures of people and animals, which are used as puppets in the enactment of moral plays or tales to teach correct ways of behaviour and conduct. The marriage ceremony is an occasion for special dress, for the exchange of gifts, for the handing over by the bridegroom to the bride's family of cattle, or hoes as bride-wealth. At death the corpse was buried as soon as possible, wrapped in a mat or a cloak, or preferably, if it was an important person, in the skin of a black ox slaughtered for the occasion. His personal belongings were buried with him, but the Cape Nguni excluded metal objects. The correct place for burial of the head of the homestead was at the gate of the cattle kraal. Others were buried in or near to the hut in which they died and which was burnt or abandoned. In some groups in former days the whole homestead was abandoned—hence the custom of the Cape Nguni of leaving the dying person out in the veld to die. Mourning rites differ but include shaving of the head, removal of ornaments, wearing of undyed clothing and, for the widow or widower, the destruction of clothing at the end of the mourning period and the provision of a new set.

For communal occasions, such as the opening of the planting season and the feast of the first fruits, some heirloom or sacred ancestral object was often used as for example the Venda sacred axe and symbolic hoe onto which a libation was poured during the ceremonies of the first sowing. Special medicines might be prepared, and a sacred fire lit with fire-sticks.

When misfortune struck two methods were used to diagnose the cause. Among the Cape and Natal Nguni the diviner might induce a trance or divine with the aid of a wand, a forked stick or a calabash full of water. Elsewhere divining tablets or 'bones' were used. The diviner had his own set, which consisted of four main bones or carved tablets and a variety of other bones, claws of animals and other objects. These were thrown onto a mat, with special intention for the case in hand, and according to the way in which they fell the message was read. The Venda had, in addition, another form of divination in which seeds were floated in water in a wooden bowl that was decorated with carved symbolic patterns. The Tsonga had a second divining set—four fruit shells (*hakata*)—while the Pedi divine with a set of four calabashes, or a wand, or, in cases of illness, through the medium of a goat.

Music[19]

All the South African Bantu are vocalists and instrumentalists. Their musical instruments have been fully described by Kirby (1934), and their music has been recorded by the International African Music Society and discussed in the journal of the African Music Society.

There is a great predominance of solo instruments, especially numerous varieties of the musical bow. Whistles are used by herd-boys, and horns for signalling on special occasions. In the north, Tsonga and North Sotho have the small 'hand-piano' (*bira* or *sansa*).

The percussion instruments are rattles, drums, xylophones and the *mbira*; the wind instruments a variety of horns, whistles and reed flutes; and the stringed instruments the musical bows and the *gora*.

[20]All the Bantu peoples of South Africa use dancing-rattles, either worn on the ankles or shaken in the hand. The Sotho make their ankle-rattles from cocoons, scores of which are filled with small stones or hard seeds, threaded on [a thong] and wound round the ankles of the dancers. In [Lesotho], however, tiny bags of goatskin are used as substitutes for the cocoons which cannot readily be obtained there. The Nguni likewise use the cocoons, but in clusters and not in long strings, and, in addition, some tribes make similar instruments from woven palm-leaf. Among the [Tsonga] rattles of woven palm-leaf are also used, but the Venda ankle-rattles are made from small hollow fruits filled with stones, and fitted on reeds in rows, giving an appearance somewhat like cricket pads. Hand-rattles, made from calabashes filled with stones and mounted on sticks, are used by Venda, [Tsonga], and to some extent by Swazi and Zulu. The latter peoples seem to have derived them from the former.

Among the Sotho, we find conical wooden drums, with single heads of skin pegged in position, in regular use; they are beaten by the women, who use the hand as a beater, and are called *moropa*. They are still made and played by Transvaal Sotho and Tswana, though in Lesotho they are now made from clay, owing to the lack of suitable wood. Such drums are used chiefly for ceremonial purposes, though they are sometimes used at ordinary dances. The Nguni peoples apparently did not originally have drums in the strict sense. The hide shield served the Zulu as a drum, being hit with knobkerrie or assegai, or itself being struck flat on the ground. The use of a stiff ox-hide (*ingqongqo*) as a temporary drum was, however, common at Zulu and Xhosa [divining seances], and among the latter it was also used [by mothers at boys' initiation]. . . . The Zulu, however, had a temporary drum, made by securing a goatskin over a clay beer-pot. This drum, the *ingungu*, was not struck, but was sounded by the friction produced by the wetted hands of the player being slid down a reed held vertically upon the centre of the skin. The instru-

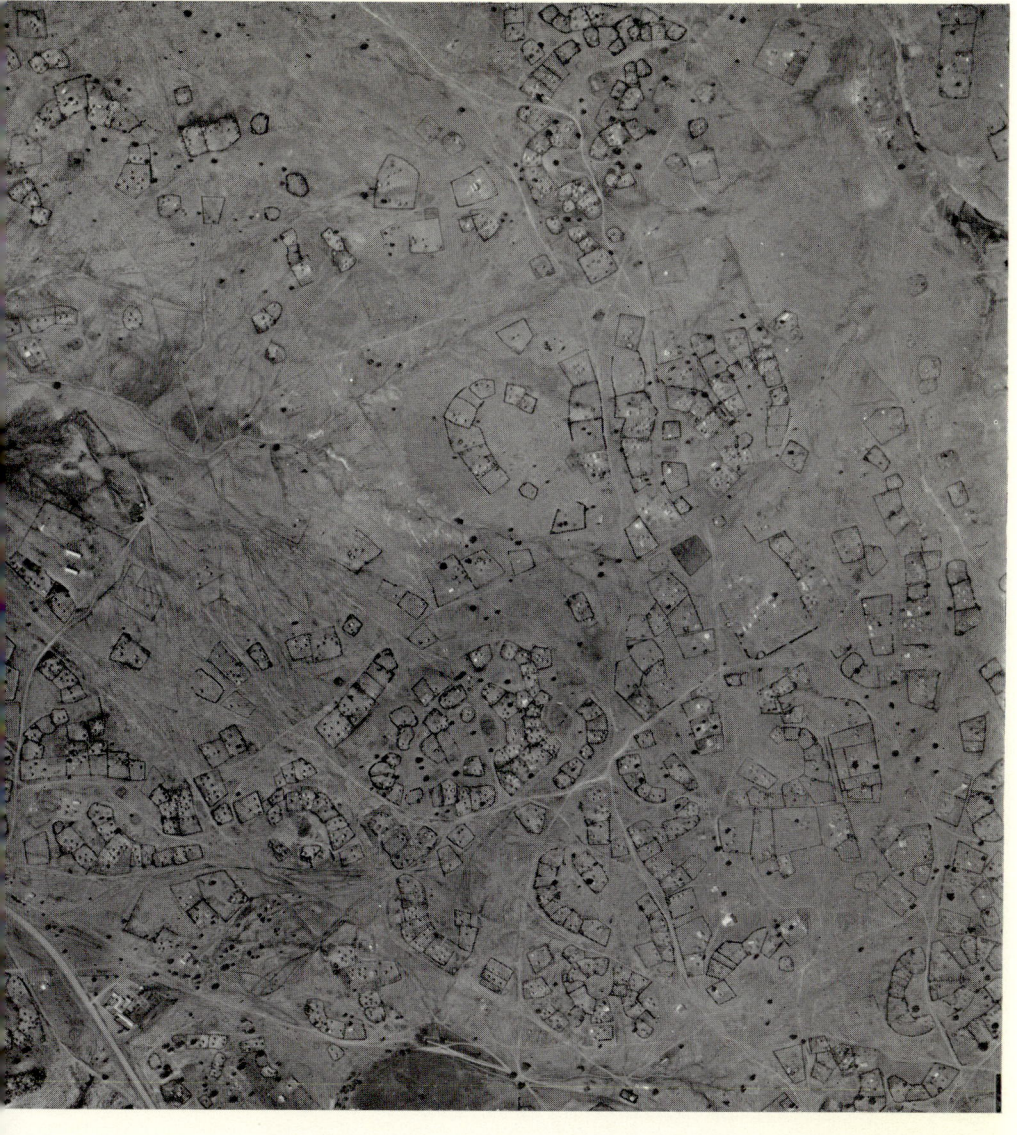

PLATE 3
Aerial photo of part of Serowe, Botswana. Note horseshoe-shaped sub-wards occupied by lineage fragments

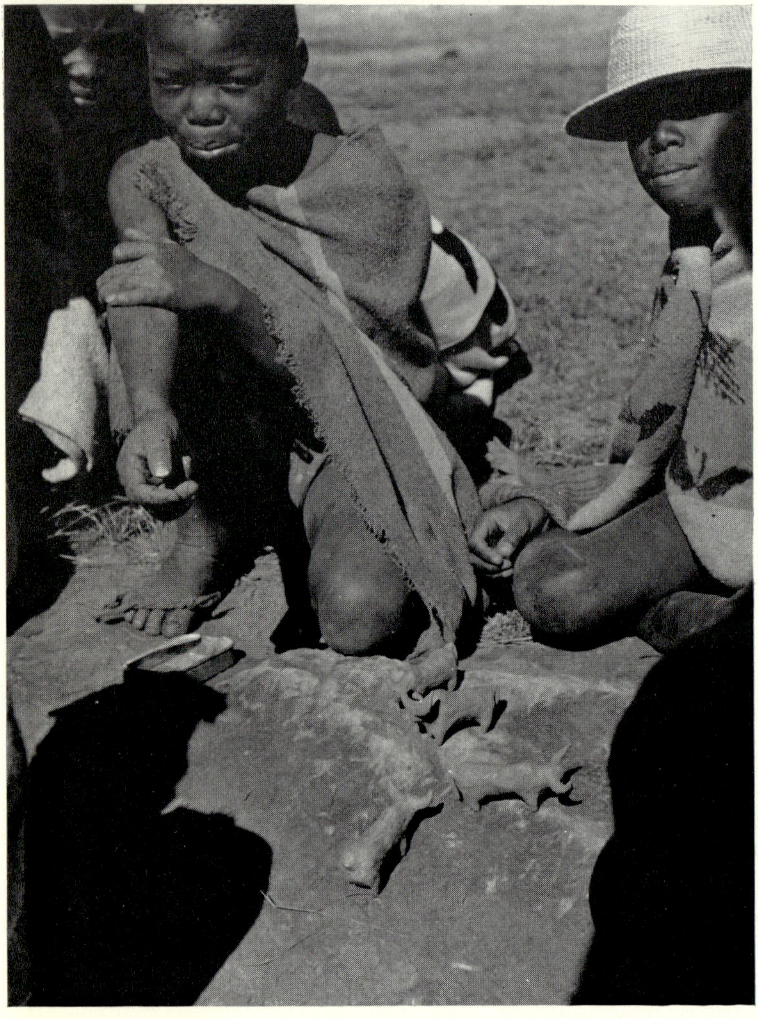

PLATE 4
Material culture

a Stretching of thong, Gaberone, Botswana, 1962. Note ox licking salt
b South Sotho boys with clay oxen, Leribe, Lesotho, 1958

ment was only used at the ceremonies held on the occasion of the first menstruation of a Zulu girl.

The modern *isigubu* of Zulu and Xhosa is merely a reproduction of the bass drum of the European regimental bands. Like that instrument, it has a wooden resonator (made from a tree trunk), two skin heads laced in position by thongs, and two padded beaters. The method of playing is identical with that of the European type. It was unknown in early times.

The Swazi have a temporary drum made from a clay beer-pot, with a goatskin held over it by one man while another beats the instrument with a stick. It is used in the exorcism of spirits, as is the [Tsonga] drum. The latter (the *mantshomane*) is made in the form of a tambourine with a single head of skin pegged in position and struck with a stick. It is played by both men and women, and is used mainly in the *gongondjela*, or exorcism of spirits, although also used in ordinary dances. [Diviners] throughout the northern areas of the country use the *mantshomane* and it has been taken over to a slight extent by the Swazi. None of the other tribes have it.

The drums of the Venda are of two types, a conical wooden drum with a single head of skin pegged in position (*murumbu*) and beaten with the palms of the hands by women who straddle the instrument, and the *ngoma*, a large hemispherical drum with a single head also pegged in place, which is beaten by men or women with a stick. The former type is analogous to the *moropa* of the Sotho; the latter is peculiar to the Venda and is used for all sorts of ritual purposes. Both types are played with the Venda reed-flute ensembles.

Resonated xylophones (*mbila*), consisting of a number of tuned slabs of hardwood fitted on insulated frames over similarly tuned resonators of calabash, and struck with rubber-headed beaters, are found alone among the Venda. They are played by men, in pairs, the music being polyphonic.

The so-called *sansa* (also called *mbila*, though more commonly *deze* by the Venda), which consists of tuned tongues of tempered iron fixed to a wooden base and placed inside a large calabash resonator, is characteristic of the Lemba of Vendaland, formerly noted for their skill in working metals. Both these instruments came from the north, the former having been originally acquired from Malaya where it is still in use. The xylophone was seen among the Karanga on the Zambesi in 1586.

All the Bantu use animal horns as signal trumpets, antelope horns (especially those of the sable antelope) being the oldest variety and giving their names to the instruments. The *phalaphala* of the Venda is typical. The interior of the horn is removed and an opening made in the side, immediately below the solid tip. By blowing as a trumpet is blown, two sounds can be readily elicited, the fundamental tone and the first harmonic, which may or may not be in tune. Among the Nguni an ox-horn (*uphondo*) is now used as a substitute, although the instrument still retains the name of the buck, *mpalampala*.

The Venda also use miniature horns made in the same way from the horns of the smaller antelopes. They are used by boys for signalling.

Whistles made as simple stopped pipes of reed, bone, or horn are used by all the Bantu of South Africa. They are blown key-wise usually by boys although [diviners] have their own varieties. A more developed form is also in use. Originally a buck horn having an opening drilled through the extreme tip, it was later made from wood, the conically shaped piece of wood being split and, after having been hollowed, put together again, covered with skin and bound with fibre or wire to render it airtight once more. Several sounds could be produced, both when the lower hole was left open and when it was stopped by the finger. It was used by men for signalling in hunting or in war, and also by [diviners].

The Tswana about the beginning of the nineteenth century acquired the reed-flute ensemble, previously described, from the Korana Hottentots, and with it also the Hottentot method of tuning the flutes. The only other Bantu people in South Africa who have a similar ensemble are the Venda, from whom some of the neighbouring Sotho have imitated it. The Venda, however, accompany their flutes with ankle-rattles and drums. The flutes, too, are of fixed intonation, being stopped by a natural knot in the bamboo from which they are made, and tuned by cutting sections off the open end. Further, they are tuned to a seven-note scale, but the Sotho who have adopted them retain their own scale of five notes. These reed-flute ensembles are tribal, and are used for ceremonial purposes. Men alone are the flute-players, who dance while they play, though women may beat the drums.

Flutes used as solo instruments by individual performers vary in type. . . . A transverse flute, played in similar fashion to the European flute, is made from reed and is played by Venda, [Tsonga] and, to a lesser extent, by Swazi who borrowed it from their neighbours. It is usually closed at both ends by natural knots and has three finger holes. Elaborate melodies may be played upon it, although its scale is largely accidental. The Swazi, Zulu, and Xhosa use an end-blown flute of reed, about three feet in length, with the mouth end cut obliquely, the lower opening being used as a finger-hole. This instrument yields the harmonic series, upon which melodies played upon it must be based. The Zulu alone make a peculiar flute from two pieces of reed, one pushed into the end of the other, and the top of the thicker being cut obliquely, the lower opening, as in the previously described instrument, being used as finger-hole. This type is used in pairs by two male performers, the music played being antiphonal. Both types were made and used by the Zulu immediately after the feast of the first fruits.

A rudimentary 'ocarina' made from the Kaffir orange, with mouth-hole and two finger-holes, is made and played by the [Tsonga]. It is a curious fact that, with the exception of a secret instrument played by the Venda *nonyana*, an official who participates in the initiation ceremonies of girls, no wind instrument with a vibrating reed as the medium of sound production is found in South Africa.

The Hottentot *gora* has been adopted by practically all the Bantu peoples of South Africa. Its gradual spread from the south-west to the north and east can be readily traced. The last to adopt it were the Venda, who appear to have acquired it from the Zulu of Mzilikazi as he passed through their territory towards the north . . . [and] they called . . . it by its Zulu name, *ugwala*. In Bantu hands it received slight improvements, but the music performed upon it was, in the nature of the case, similar to that played on it by the Hottentots. Among the Bantu it is always played by men. . . .

Eight types of stringed instrument are in use among the Bantu of South Africa. All have been evolved from the shooting-bow, and it would therefore appear that those peoples who did not use the bow as a weapon derived the instruments from peoples who did. The music played upon all these instruments involves either the unconscious or deliberate use of harmonics. . . . These harmonics are either (1) sounded together as a chord, (2) isolated for melodic purposes, or (3) used in conjunction with their fundamentals in order to produce elementary polyphony. In all cases a resonator is employed in order to amplify the sound produced by the string, and such resonator is sometimes the mouth of the performer and sometimes a calabash or other hollow object, which may or may not be permanently attached to the instrument.

The first group includes two varieties, commonly, though erroneously, regarded as one and the same. The first of these, undoubtedly the older type, consists of a well curved bow-stave of wood, fitted with a string of thin brass wire, but formerly of sinew or twisted hair from a cow's tail. Attached near the lower end of the stave is a calabash, with an opening on the side away from the stave. The calabash is insulated from the stave by a pad of bark, grass, or coarse cloth. The instrument, after the string has been tuned to a pitch suitable for accompanying the performer's voice, is held upright, the opening of the calabash being held close to the left breast, the second, third, and fourth fingers of the left hand grasping the lower end of the stave so as to leave the first finger and thumb free to pinch the string, and so raise its pitch. The string is struck, staccato, by a thin grass or reed held in the right hand. When so struck the string gives forth its fundamental note, together with several of its harmonics, the result being, to the performer, a clear chord. Two such chords, a tone apart, are generally used. This instrument is found among Nguni and Sotho. It is mainly, though not exclusively, a man's instrument, except among the Xhosa where women are the chief performers.

The second type is similarly constructed, except that the calabash resonator is secured near the middle of the bow-stave, and the string is tied back towards the stave at that point by means of a loop of sinew. The technique is similar to that of the first type, but each portion of the string produces its own fundamental and harmonics. By pinching the string a third chord is obtained. This type is used by Venda, [Tsonga], Transvaal Sotho, Swazi, and Zulu, but not by Tswana, South Sotho, and Xhosa. The second type appears to be of northern, and comparatively recent, origin. It was not used by the Zulu in the time of Shaka, so far as I can discover. The larger sizes are played by men, the smaller by women. Among the Venda it is only played by males.

The second group contains two types. The first of these is a simple shooting bow, with the string stretched more tightly than usual. It is held by the performer against the left shoulder, the right foot steadying the lower end. The string is then tapped with a light reed, when it gives forth its fundamental tone. By touching the string at the appropriate "nodes" the lower harmonies can be elicited. It is only used by the Tswana, who unquestionably acquired it from the Korana. It is played chiefly by men, although women may also use it. The second type is of relatively recent origin, and may possibly owe its origin to European or other outside influence. It consists of a hollow tube of wood or bamboo, fitted with a wire string and tuning peg. The string is set in vibration by means of a miniature friction bow of wood strung with hair from a cow's tail, resin being applied to the hair. The mouth was originally used as a resonator, and is still so used by the Venda; more recently a one-gallon paraffin tin has been attached to the instrument, which is then held on the left shoulder, and in this form it is used by Sotho, Zulu, and Xhosa. By bowing the string with a kind of circular motion its harmonics may be elicited, and simple tunes played. By pinching the string near its lower end the harmonics of one or two other fundamentals may also be sounded. The fundamentals, however, are not normally used.

The third group contains four varieties. The first is a bow of hollow river reed, fitted with a string of sinew or fibre, which is plucked by the forefinger of the right hand. The pitch may be altered by pressure upon the string by the fingers of the left hand. The mouth acts as a resonator of variable size, which serves to isolate certain harmonics of the string. These, together with the fundamentals, produce a simple two-part polyphony, the intervals of which are governed by natural laws. This type of instrument is found among all the Bantu of South Africa without exception. It is generally played by women and girls and, occasionally, by young boys.

The second type in this group is a bow of special construction, being either of solid wood, thinned towards the tips, or with a thick central portion into the ends of which thin tips of wood are fitted. The string is of wire, looped back with sinew or thread near the centre, and plucked with the finger or with a plectrum of thorn or other substance. The mouth serves to resonate the harmonics, and the pitch of the string can be altered by pressure and pinching. On this instrument, as on the first type of this group, simple two-part polyphony is performed. It is found among Transvaal and South Sotho, Swazi, Zulu, [Tsonga] and Venda, and is played only by males.

The third type is a short bow of solid wood, thinned towards the ends, which are bent up sharply. The central portion of the bow is notched along one side. From tip to tip of the bow a flat 'string' of palm leaf or broad grass is tightly stretched. The instrument is sounded by rubbing the stick which forms the handle of a rattle, made from a dry seed-box containing small stones, across the notches, thus causing the string to vibrate. The mouth is used as a resonator, and selects and amplifies certain harmonics from the fundamentals of the open string and from two fingered notes. The resulting music is in two parts as in the case of the two previous instruments. The instrument is used only by the Tsonga and the Venda. It is a man's instrument.

The fourth and last instrument in this group is made from a length of hollow river-reed, or hollow piece of wood from the *umsenge*, or cabbage-tree, into one end of which a thin, pliable rod is inserted. A string of vegetable fibre or twisted rush is fixed to the lower end of the reed, and to the tip of the thin rod, which is thereby made to curve. The string, after being rubbed with the juice of a leaf, is 'bowed' by a piece of thin mealie stalk held beneath it. The mouth acts as a resonator to the harmonics of the string, the pitch of which can be altered by stopping with the first finger of the left hand. The musical result is simple two-part polyphony as before. This instrument is found only among the Swazi, Zulu and Xhosa, and, in a simplified form, among the Mpondo. It is usually played by males (Kirby 1937: 274–81).

Dancing[21]

Dancing usually accompanies any special ceremony—initiation, weddings, the feast of the first fruits and (formerly) mobilization for war or preparation for a communal hunt. But it is often performed for pure recreation. Apart from party clothing, or the special dress of initiates or warriors, there are few appurtenances. Sticks are carried by girl dancers and these are often beaded. Natal Nguni men may carry a small replica of the fighting shield. Young people often wear some form of rattle round the legs and ankles to enhance the noise of the stamped rhythm.

Toys and Games[22]

Toys are made by children rather than for them. The most universal are oxen and other figures modelled in clay, by young boys especially (see Plate 4b). It is interesting that throughout the country the style of ox is the same, with the wide horns and humped back of Zebu cattle. People and other domestic animals, especially horses, are modelled, the latter typically in Basutoland. Latterly motor-cars and aeroplanes have begun to be made.

Little girls make dolls, often of maize cobs, and dress them in scraps of cloth or skin.

Like children all over the world Bantu children make models in miniature of the weapons, implements and utensils used by their parents. Little boys cut sticks, make bows and arrows, and, latterly, 'motor cars' with perhaps small calabashes for wheels. Little girls may be allowed to add a small pot to their mother's batch of pots to be fired.

A widespread game for older boys is that of the 'rolling target', in which a large bulb or other round object is rolled down a hill and the boys try to hit it with sharpened sticks, or shoot at it with bow and arrow.

A game similar to draughts is played by Tsonga, North Sotho and Venda men. This game is known over a wide area from West Africa to Indonesia. Each of two players has two rows of holes, which may be scooped out of the ground or chipped out of a rock, in which he places a certain number of stones or seeds to represent 'men'. The game involves capturing the opponent's men by a series of moves within stipulated rules.

Smoking and Snuff-taking[23]

Much use is made of tobacco, either smoked or snuffed, and hemp (*Cannabis sativa*, dagga, marijuana), which latter is now illegal. There are a number of aromatic herbs which have been used as substitutes for both in times of scarcity.

Dagga was introduced on the east coast, presumably by the Arabs, and grown in small gardens next to the homestead. It was smoked through water in a horn container into which a reed stem was inserted, the bowl placed on top of the stem. Early Nguni pipe-bowls were made of earthenware and were very small; later, bowls became progressively larger and might be of earthenware, carved stone, converted ink-bottles or anything suitable! Zulu dagga-smoking equipment also included hollow tubes of a thin stem, and the water and saliva were spat out to make patterns in the sand. Dagga-smoking was a communal activity, and the pipe was passed from one to another of a group. Today the practice is illegal and its use is not generally admitted.

Tobacco was probably introduced on both the west and the east coast. It had found its way down to the south by the time of the white settlement along the coast, which gave it a great boost as tobacco was found to be a good trading article. It is grown in the gardens near the homesteads and the leaves are dried and made up (in the south and east) into a roll wrapped in matting and, among the Transvaal Sotho and Venda, into a shaped block or a ball. These rolls or balls were standard quantities in exchange. Tobacco is still more frequently used as snuff than it is smoked—the Xhosa and Thembu, both men and women, are the greatest smokers—but smoking is gaining ground.

Snuff-boxes have been a great stimulus to artistic effort. Small calabashes or hard fruit shells were covered with beadwork, especially by the Cape Nguni, or embroidered with brass or copper wire by the Zulu. Among the South Sotho and Tswana particularly, the open end of a horn was filled in and a hole made in the side, and sometimes the horn was carved to the shape of a figure; or the container was carved out of hard wood and decorated with conventional patterns. Failing this an empty cartridge case, or a piece of reed with the ends stopped, did duty. To take snuff the Nguni and South Sotho used a small ivory, bone or horn spoon with which to convey it to the nose. Other groups simply shook the snuff into the hand.

The pipes used for smoking were, and still are, carved out of wood, originally patterned on the seventeenth- or eighteenth-century clay pipe. Many modifications were made however. The Xhosa and South Sotho, particularly, carve very decorative pipes or ornament them with beadwork, or, in the

Cape, with patterns inlaid in lead. Characteristic of the pipes is a flanging end to the stem, into which a separate mouthpiece is inserted.

War and Weapons[24]

In all groups it was the duty of every man from the age of about sixteen to fight if called on to do so.

Among the Cape Nguni the only addition to normal dress was the warrior's head-dress of a wing of the blue crane above each ear. Elsewhere a more elaborate version of everyday dress was worn, with special ornaments, and, especially among the Zulu, an elaborate head-dress. The Zulu regiments were distinguished by their ornaments, their head-dresses and the colour of their shields.

Mobilization was effected by the sending of messengers from the chief to the homesteads and villages. In Vendaland they were re-inforced by the beating of the drums. Tsonga messengers blew a special note on an antelope horn; Xhosa messengers carried ox-tails as an indication of their office. Once mobilized, the army was treated with medicines.

The principal weapon used by all South African groups, except the Venda, was the spear. A bundle of several was carried, and the Xhosa particularly were adept at spear-throwing. Shaka introduced a somewhat shorter-hafted and broader-bladed spear for stabbing. Clubs were carried as a secondary, but very effective, weapon. To deflect the spears all groups carried oxhide shields. Those of the Nguni were oval in shape, some wider, some narrower, and those of the Zulu were the largest. Sotho shields were smaller, the Tswana hourglass-shaped, the Pedi apron-shaped and the South Sotho winged. The Venda shield was round and, while they carried spears and clubs, they placed more reliance on bows and arrows. Axes with crescentic blades were included among the weapons of the Sotho, Venda and Tsonga, but there is little record of their use as a fighting weapon. Although they have been reported from the Nguni, axes were not a true part of the fighting equipment.

Intertribal warfare no longer takes place, but there is still a good deal of sporadic fighting between factions. The weapons used are mainly modern versions of club and axe, said to be obtained by young men when working on the mines of the Witwatersrand and Orange Free State.

Crafts and Tools

The material objects previously mentioned depended on the existence of a body of craftsmen and craftswomen for their manufacture. With one exception, metal-working, people tended to make for their own family use, though there would always be those individuals known for their particular skill or specializing in a particular branch. Latterly, however, crafts have become more and more confined to specialists. Metal-working was always a specialist craft and in some places a secret one.

Metal-working[25]

Iron, copper and gold were mined, smelted and worked, and tin was mined and smelted. The most important of these was *iron*, which was used for weapons, implements and ornaments. The main deposits were in the Transvaal and adjacent areas of Botswana and it was the Sotho, Lemba and Venda people who became the great iron-workers of southern Africa and supplied, amongst others, the Tsonga of Delagoa Bay. The people of Swaziland and northern Natal also had fair desposits at their disposal and the latter probably supplied the Transkei and Eastern Cape, where there are no major deposits but a good deal of lateritic ironstone. Early authors differ in their accounts of whether or not the Xhosa and Thembu mined and smelted the ore before the arrival of the Mfengu, who had been iron-workers in Natal. From the fact that a single iron bangle was considered a worthy ornament for a chief, that wooden spades were used instead of iron hoes, and that the first commodity ship-wrecked sailors were asked for was metal, it would seem that iron was not easily obtained locally in the Eastern Cape.

The next most important metal was *copper*, which was, however, used almost entirely for ornaments or ornamentation of utensils. Again the major deposits, and hence the most important workings, were in the Transvaal, especially near Messina and Phalaborwa, but small deposits are found in many parts of the country, including the Transkei and Natal. In neither of these areas, however, is there any definite record of its having been mined.

In the Leeuwport, Blauwbank and Rooiberg areas of the Transvaal traces remain of the mining of considerable quantities of *tin*, and from metal found in old workings, and from reports by Moffat, it would seem that the Northern Sotho and some Tswana mixed tin with copper to produce a bronze alloy, but again the only use appears to have been for ornament.

Alluvial gold was gathered and gold-bearing rock quarried and mined in the eastern Transvaal and probably in Swaziland, but the only traces of its use are the thin plating of certain core-covered objects, and the small tacks with which it is secured. These have been found only in an archaeological deposit (Mapungubwe) in the Zoutpansberg, and there is no certainty that the workers were Bantu. It is certain, however, that there was an extensive market for gold on the east coast of Africa and people in the Transvaal may have joined in this trade. It has been estimated that very considerable amounts of metal were mined in the Transvaal, especially copper and tin, more than could easily have been used by the local people. An interesting feature of the old workings is that the shafts appear to have been filled in after abandonment.

Iron was mostly found above ground, but sometimes the iron-bearing reef would be followed for some distance underground. Stones were used as hammers, and iron gads served to split the rock.

Copper was also found on the surface, sometimes in a native state, but incline shafts to a depth of 25 metres (80 ft), and even vertical shafts, have been found in the Transvaal. The method of splitting the rock to obtain the ore was to heat the rock surface by building fires in front of it, throwing cold water onto the face to split it and then inserting iron gads into the cracks to break it off. After being carried to the surface it was hammered into small pieces to get rid of as much waste rock as possible before being taken to the furnace.

The tin mines were often shallow, but at least one has been found that reached 40 metres (120 ft). From artefacts found in them, including iron gads, hammer stones, piles of firewood, and grinding-stones, it would seem that the method of detaching the ore was by means of gads, or fire-setting, or a combination of both, and that the ore was ground fine and the waste washed away before smelting.

There is no record of the method of mining gold.

The recorded methods of smelting iron and copper were roughly the same throughout the country, with perhaps individual patterns in the design of the furnace. An earthen mound of up to a metre high was built, with the inside hollowed out (the Swazi used two mounds). At the base were one or more holes into which the nozzle of a pair of bellows could be inserted. The nozzle, or tuyere, was generally of clay. The bellows was made of two skins of a small animal. A horn or wooden tube was inserted into the neck or one of the hind legs of each skin and bound fast, and all the other apertures were sewn up, except a slit in the stomach or the neck. This opening was strengthened with a strip of wood. The two skins formed a pair of bellows, and the ends of the horns were inserted into the tuyere. The bags were grasped at the open end and raised and depressed alternately to keep up a steady draught.

For the smelting of iron ore charcoal was prepared first, then a fire was made in the bottom of the furnace, with a layer of ore on top and then alternate layers of ore and charcoal. Some tribes let the ore run out into moulds down channels leading from the bottom of the furnace. Others waited till a block of roughly smelted metal had been formed, then took it to the forge for further treatment—hammering and re-heating until the dross was removed.

The smelting oven for copper was similar but smaller. The Lemba, who were the main copper miners and smelters of the Transvaal, built a cylindrical kiln of clay about 45 cms high, with the base lined with clay. In this alternating layers of charcoal and ore were laid down and when the copper was melted the wall of the kiln was broken down and the molten copper left to cool in the base.

The forge was an open fire, again with charcoal as fuel, and the fire was kept going with bellows. When the metal was clean it was run off into moulds in the sand, roughly in the shape of the object to be made, or into rods for turning into smaller objects.

The Lemba copper smelters broke the lump of copper from the first smelting into small pieces and re-smelted them in a potsherd crucible from which the molten copper could be poured into moulds in the ground. The copper smelters of Blaauwbank used earthenware crucibles.

A piece of bark or wood served as tongs, though sometimes iron tongs were made. The anvil was a flat hard stone, or latterly a piece of scrap iron. The hammers were stones of various weights or a heavy piece of iron.

Wire too was drawn by the Venda and Lemba. Holes of different sizes were bored in a thick oval iron plate. A rod of the required metal was beaten thin and pointed sharply at one end. The point was heated and forced through the largest hole in the plate, and clamped into a vice that had been firmly wedged in the fork of a tree. With the aid of a stick as a lever the plate was then pulled away from the tree, so that the wire was drawn out. This was repeated through each hole in the plate until the required thinness was obtained.

The profession of smith was an exclusive one, sometimes passed on from father to son, or to an apprentice who had to pay a high fee. The learner had to serve for a number of years.

Mining and smelting no longer take place and there is very little smithing. Scrap iron is used for making spear heads and some other objects.

Pottery[26]

Pottery making was and is the domain of women. It is probable that originally the women of each family kept the family supplied, but the tendency to specialize has grown. In some areas pottery is no longer made at all, the Xhosa and Thembu having lost the art a long time ago—but in most areas it is still valued for its slightly porous quality, which keep liquids fresh and cool, and it is often imported from considerable distances.

In most parts of the country there is clay suitable for pottery, though the potter may have to fetch it from some distance. The banks of rivers or streams, swamps and anthills are favourite sources. If the clay does not prove suitable in its natural state a filler of crushed sherds, sand, or other material is added. For colour decoration various ochres and graphite are used and there is an active trade where these are not readily accessible. The potter's wheel is not used; instead the pot may be started on an old sherd, or a flat stone or, latterly, on a metal dish or lid, on which it can be revolved, but for very large pots the maker has to walk round the pot. Tools are simple—a piece of wood, calabash, fruit rind, or a bone to scrape and smooth the walls of the pot; a grass stem, or a shell or a knife to impress or incise the decoration.

Four main techniques of building up a pot have been recorded from Southern Africa: moulding from the lump, with the base completed at the beginning or the end (some Natal Nguni, Tsonga, some South Sotho, Hananwa and Venda (Lemba)); building from the base with the addition of lumps or rings (some Cape Nguni, some Natal Nguni and some South Sotho); building from the base by continuous coiling (Mpondo, Swazi, Lobedu); and building upwards from the widest diameter or below it with the addition of flat pieces, after which the work is turned upside down and the base built on (Tswana, Transvaal Sotho). The work might be done indoors or out, according to personal preference or the state of the weather, the criterion being that the drying should be even. Firing takes place out of doors and for the most part in open fires in a hollow which may vary from a slight depression to a deep hole, but some South Sotho build a stone kiln round the pots (see Plate 7b).

There is considerable variety in the shape and size of pots and in the colour used for decoration. Each major tribal group has its characteristic style and colour.

It is likely that in former times a much wider variety of pots was made in each group and that potters were more numerous than is the case now. Nevertheless, despite the increasing availability of cheap alternatives, pottery, if diminishing, is still very much a live craft, especially among the Venda, Lemba and Transvaal Sotho.

Skin working[27]

Working in skin is a man's craft which before the introduction of woven cloth was a very important one. Skins were used for clothing, baby-slings, bedding, sandals, shields, quivers and a variety of bags for holding liquids, tobacco, or small personal belongings. The skins of cattle, oxen, sheep and wild animals were used, including the tails for ornament. The skin of the leopard was reserved exclusively for the chief and the members of his family.

A man was expected to make the clothing for his family and himself, but he would call on family and friends to help with the softening of the skin and might call in an expert to cut out garments. Sandals and shields were, however, always made by specialists.

Skins were chosen according to the purpose to which they were to be put, and the preparation varied accordingly. For some purposes the skin had to dry hard, for others it had to be worked soft. As far as possible the skin was removed whole from the animal, by cutting round the head, down the stomach and down the centre of the legs, but when the skin of a small animal was to be used as a bag it was cut either at the neck or at the back and peeled off. It was then scraped clean, and worked at once by rubbing between the hands until dry and soft. For garments and blankets, skins were first pegged out to dry and scraped and cleaned with an adze on the inside. (An interesting by-product of this among the Cape Nguni was the making of a paste with the scrapings and some clay; the paste was then spread over a clay model, shaped like a calabash, or an animal figure, and allowed to dry, when the model would be removed through a hole cut in the dry paste and which latter served as an opening for the container.) If the hair was to be removed it was shaved off at this stage. There was then a protracted course of rubbing between the hands, wetting, rubbing again and braying with sharp metal points or aloe thorns until the skin was quite soft and a fairly thick nap had been raised. In this work friends were called in to help. Fat or sour milk might be rubbed in, and some workers buried the skin in the manure of the kraal for twenty-four hours. Different dyes were used in the various areas.

The Xhosa used ash from touchwood to colour their skins black; the Zulu, a mixture of charcoal and fat. Some tanning of skins has been recorded. The Zulu used the bark of *Sclerocarya caffra* and the Venda a mixture of antelope fat and the fruit of *Ximenia caffra*.

The skins were now ready to be made up. The first task was to mend with a matching patch any holes, and the garment was then cut out with a knife or spear blade. The pieces were sewn together with sinew thread, which was pushed through a series of small holes made with an iron awl, and tied, each stitch separately. The hairy side was generally worn inwards and the plain outer side was often decorated. Men's cloaks among the Xhosa, and blankets (especially among the Tswana), were often made of small skins sewn together and selected for their colour.

If the skin was to be used for sandals or shields and needed to be hard it was scraped only to clean it and was then pounded with stones to toughen it before it was pegged out to dry. After it had been cut to shape it might be buried in the kraal overnight.

Skin-working was one of the first crafts to decline with contact with whites. Woven cloth appealed, not only for its novelty and colour, but for its comfort. In the north-east, adoption of Western cloth took place very early, through trade with Delagoa Bay. There is still skin clothing to be found, sometimes in regular use (some Zulu and some Transvaal Sotho), sometimes for special occasions (Cape Nguni), and shields and small skin bags are still made in some places, but the craft is now confined to specialists.

Basketry[28]

Basketry was, and still is, a very widely used technique for many things besides containers and utensils, for example, mats for serving food or for sleep or roofing, strainers, traps, hut-doors, hut walls, fences, sledges, hats and personal ornaments. Certain types of basket-work have disappeared, but it is probably the least affected of crafts, probably due to its qualities of lightness, durability and flexibility and even, in some types, impermeability. Basketry is practised by both men and women—in each tribal group custom fixes who makes what—but this division of labour does not correspond throughout the country.

There are two major techniques of basketry—weaving and sewing. In woven work two sets of elements are interlaced by crossing over and under each other to make a fabric. In sewn work one set of elements is sewn together by the other. In South Africa each of these has a number of variations, which are not only used for the fabric, but exploited for decoration. Very few tools are needed—a spear blade or knife to cut and trim the material for use, and to cut off loose ends, and an awl or needle for sewn work. The more fragile materials are generally dampened for use, and a container of water is then placed at hand.

A great variety of materials is used, depending upon availability, though in some cases materials are imported. Grass stems are used for delicate work, such as ornaments, and whole grass for the foundation elements of much coiled sewn work. Sedge stems are probably the most used material. They may be used whole for weaving, as in the Cape Nguni garden baskets, or as the warp or foundation element in woven or sewn sleeping mats which are made by all the groups, or they may be split, and perhaps have the pith removed, and be used straight or twisted for the foundation or sewing element of sewn basketry, as in the garden baskets of the South Sotho and Tswana. Rush stems are used for the rougher type of sleeping mat in Natal. Palm leaf is as important as sedge in the areas where it grows, mainly near the coast. Strips of the leaf are used for weaving the flat pouches made in Natal and one type of beer-strainer. Thinner strips of the leaf are used for both the foundation and sewing of the fine coiled baskets of the Zulu. In the northern and eastern Transvaal creeper stems and thin root stems are used, whole for the foundation and split for the sewing of coiled garden basket, and make a hard and beautiful fabric. Trimmed slivers of wood are used for weaving the Transvaal Sotho and Tsonga winnowing baskets and for the characteristic lidded basket of the Venda and Lobedu (see Plate 5b). Bark is greatly used for oversewing of edges, and for decoration, but also for the sewing strand of much Tswana coiled work. Dyes, originally obtained from local materials, mainly plants, have been supplemented latterly with bought chemical dyes.

Specialization occurs in basketry as in other crafts, but many women still provide for their own families, and especially is this the case with sleeping mats. Men basketworkers tend very much more to be specialists. For a long time baskets and mats competed well with introduced goods, but the introduction of cheap plastic containers in very recent years has made a marked difference.

Wood-carving[29]

The art of wood-carving was not nearly as well developed in South Africa as north of the Zambesi. There are none of the works of art that are found in the Congo and West Africa. Nevertheless decorative work on utensils reached a fair standard among the Zulu, some Sotho groups, and the Venda.

Wood-carving was for the most part a specialized craft and confined to men. Some people specialized in only one branch, for example stools, or pipes. Traditionally there was no joinery—each object was cut out of the solid. For small and precious articles the dark heart wood of the log was used. The tools used were an axe for felling the tree, or cutting off a branch or piece of root wood, and for rough-hewing larger objects; an adze to finish the outside and as much of the inside as could be reached by this means; a gouge, consisting of a bent blade, used to hollow out larger objects; and a knife to do the finer work on small objects. To aid the cutting of large trees a fire might be made round the trunk. Pipe-makers have a variety of chisels and gouges. Wood, unless cut from a dead and dry tree, was allowed to season, and might be rubbed with fat during the making to keep it from splitting. Decoration was of two kinds—carved or branded. Carved decoration on utensils consisted of conventional designs in a series of grooves and ridges. Sticks, clubs, and pipes, however, might have naturalistic decoration—the head of a stick, for example, might be carved to the shape of a human or animal head.

Branding with a hot iron was used both to make conventional designs on woodwork, or to blacken the whole surface, after which it was greased and polished to a hard finish.

The objects made were troughs for feeding animals, mortars, pestles, drums, doors (Venda and Lobedu doors were elaborately carved), bowls and dishes, milk-pails, ladles, spoons, snuff-boxes, pipes, knife-sheaths, head-rests, shafts for spears, hafts of axes and adzes, staffs, sticks and clubs, and in the Transkei, in former times, spades. The Sotho and Venda used to carve figures of wood as puppets for use in initiation schools.

A certain amount of wood-carving is still done for local use or, more usually, for sale to the curio trade, where spoons and wooden bowls are popular.

Gourds or calabashes[30]

The dried shells of various sorts and sizes of gourd are used practically everywhere for utensils of one sort or another. The largest of all, with a large bowl at the bottom and a smaller one on top, are used particularly for sour milk and generally have a plugged hole in the bottom through which the whey can be let out. Large specimens may also be used for beer or water, or cut in half and used as dishes. Those with a long thin neck and a smallish bowl have a hole cut in the side for use as ladles or drinking vessels. Small specimens of the same shape may be cut in half, lengthways, to make spoons. Medium-sized gourds act as resonators for musical instruments. The smallest are used for snuff-boxes, medicine flasks or containers for grease, or for milk for a baby.

Gourds are grown in all suitable areas. They are gathered when ripe and then treated to toughen the skin. The Xhosa are said to have buried them for a while, but the Mpondo simply let them dry. The Ngwane of Natal boil them, or put them in boiling water.

A hole is cut in the required place through which the seeds and flesh are emptied out, and water and small stones are put in to clean the inside. The gourd may then be rubbed with fat, ornamented by branding, or, especially in the case of the small containers, covering with beadwork. The preparation of gourds is women's work and generally each provides them for her own family. They are still widely used.

Horn-, bone- and ivory-carving[31]

This is an unimportant craft that was practised by men. Few specimens have survived, and there is little record of the techniques of making. Horns were, and are still, used for whistles and musical horns, and for snuff-boxes, and the solid horn was carved into spoons, snuff-spoons, small snuff-boxes and the mouthpieces of pipes. Bone was similarly carved to make snuff-spoons, small snuff-boxes and awls. Ivory was used for more ornamental purposes—ornaments, the carved fronts of Tswana knife sheaths, snuff-spoons, and the plain heavy arm-rings worn by distinguished Cape Nguni warriors and other persons as a gift from the chief. Ivory was a royal perquisite and could only be disposed of by the chief. In the early period of contact huge quantities of ivory were traded, until the elephants became extinct in most tribal areas. There is still some carving of horn spoons and snuff-spoons and mouthpieces for pipes. There is also some ornamental carving of horn for the curio trade.

Beadwork[32]

This craft, which is practised by women, has a different history to the others in that it grew and flourished through contact with other peoples, from whom the beads were obtained. Originally beads of unbaked clay and of metal were made, and worn strung singly or in chains. Glass beads were later obtained by trade with the Arabs and, from the sixteenth to the eighteenth centuries, from the Portuguese on the east coast. They reached the Transvaal in greater quantities than they reached the Cape, where a single string of red glass beads was in the early days royal insignia. Sufficient quantities of small beads to make ornaments of beadwork fabric came later, from the white settlers in the south. The beads were strung on a fine two-ply thread of shredded sinew. At first the ornaments themselves were not very large—a 2 cm wide headband, or a wider anklet—but beads were sewn onto clothing. For example Xhosa and Thembu women's caps had the whole of one surface covered in beads. Bead ornamentation of clothing has been extended to include personal belongings, especially snuff-boxes, but greater emphasis has come to be placed on elaborate necklets (perhaps 20 cm wide), waist and shoulder bands, girdles, a series of thick neckrings and so on. The craft continues to flourish. A young unmarried Xhosa man visited in 1969 possessed a small trunk full of beadwork finery, contributed by three girl admirers. In Zululand a 'language of colours' in beadwork was developed.

Most women make beadwork and particular colours and styles are favoured by certain groups or in certain areas. Children wear a little beadwork but beadwork ornaments are worn mainly by young men and women of marriageable age. Women continue to wear them after marriage, but men less so.

Stonework[33]

Stone was not much used except in building, where Sotho and Venda used it for building the foundation or the walls of huts and the walls of kraals and enclosures. The South Sotho still use stone for hut walls, and the Nguni build kraal walls of stone in areas where wood is scarce. A good deal of South Sotho stonework is of dressed stone.

In former days pipe bowls for dagga pipes were carved out of stone by South Sotho and Nguni. Some of them were highly decorated.

Stone bangles have been found in iron-age deposits.

Calendar of work[34]

The activities outlined above are not all carried on simultaneously and continuously throughout the year. The Bantu, like most primitive peoples, depend essentially upon the rotation of the seasons for their food supply, and their activities are accordingly determined. This is most clearly seen among the Tswana, whose life falls every year into two clearly-distinguished phases. Their villages are fully inhabited during the winter months only, when there is much bustle and activity. As soon as the first rains fall, about November, the people go out to their fields, remaining there right through the agricultural season until the harvest is reaped in June. During this time village life is almost at a standstill. In the other tribes, whose fields are within easy distance of their homes, there is not the same sharp division; but here too agricultural work determines the time for most other occupations.

The periods of most intense agricultural activity are at planting (late November, December, and early January in Botswana), weeding (January, February, and March), scaring away the birds (May), reaping and threshing (June and early July). Most other occupations are carried on at suitable moments in between.[33] The clearing of new fields is generally done during the two months preceding planting. Basketwork and woodwork are done mostly in the months between harvest and planting, but also between weeding and reaping; (pottery is made mainly in the autumn and winter months, but specialist potters may work at any time); while hut-building is in Botswana done only after the harvest, but in other tribes between weeding and harvesting as well. Cattle-herding, too, as we have seen, is affected by the seasons, the cattle having separate winter and summer grazing; while hunting, especially of big game, is carried on most actively in the dry winter months, when the movements of the animals are restricted by the scarcity of surface water.

Running parallel to this seasonal activity is the food consumption. The first fruits of the new year become available in the latter half of the rainy season. For the next three months or so the people revel in the green maize, pumpkins, melons, and sweet cane supplementing the staple cereals, while milk is abundant. With the gathering-in of the harvest, grain, and therefore beer, is plentiful; and as the people now have more leisure, this is the great festive season. Weddings, initiations and other ceremonies of a similar nature are most often celebrated; tribal meetings, lawsuits, and other public business are most actively pursued; and there is much informal visiting and entertaining. The green foods, however, are more and more replaced by the standard diet of boiled or roasted [maize grains and maize and sorghum meal porridge]; while the milk supply gradually diminishes as grazing becomes poorer and the cattle are taken further away. [In former days the] spring and early summer months saw the people reduced almost entirely to the standard cereal foods and such wild plants as can be gathered after the first rains have fallen. (Today the food supply may be supplemented by food bought from the store, but it is still a thin time. Grain is stored in bulk, and pumpkin, beans and some of the wild spinaches may be dried for use in the unfruitful months, but for the most part the cultivated and wild foods are not suitable for storage without refrigeration.)

Division of labour[35]

In many forms of production the only division of labour is between the sexes. Everywhere among the Bantu different occupations are traditionally assigned to men and to women; and despite occasional variations, the lines of division are fundamentally the same throughout. In agriculture, the men clear the new fields of bush and grass, except among the [Tsonga], where this is women's work. The actual tilling of the soil, from the initial planting to the final reaping and threshing, is very largely done by women and the older girls, although younger children of both sexes assist in driving away birds, and men occasionally take part in planting, weeding and reaping. The women also look after the fowls. But all work connected with cattle, goats, and sheep—herding, milking, making thick milk, washing the milking utensils, and slaughtering—is essentially within the province of the men, women, as we have seen, being prohibited by taboo from handling these animals. Adult men really do not often herd or milk, unless poverty compels them to adopt this as a means of livelihood. The younger boys go out with the small stock and calves, while the older boys and youths look after the cattle; but the men closely supervise their activities. Hunting is done by the men and youths. Women gather edible wild plants, but men may also gather wild fruits and berries when out in the veld.

Both sexes take part in hut-building, each having special tasks to perform. Among the Nguni and Sotho the men cut wood and do all timberwork, while the women cut grass, thatch, and make the floor. Where necessary, women also plaster the wall of the hut or, as among the Tswana, themselves make the earthen wall. Among the Venda and [Tsonga] the men not only do all timberwork but also thatch. The women merely make the floor and plaster the wall. Cattle-kraals, grain pits, fences and wooden palisades are all made by the men, but the earthen walls surrounding many Sotho courtyards are built by the women, who also do all the decorating. [Either sex may make the earthen box bricks with which walls tend increasingly to be built, but men do the building.]

Housework is almost entirely done by women and girls. They stamp and grind corn, prepare food and make beer, wash the cooking and eating utensils, smear the walls and floors of the huts and courtyards, clean the huts and keep them in good repair. Men, however, occasionally cook meat, particularly at feasts or when by themselves, while boys at the cattleposts prepare and cook their own food. The women also fetch water and collect firewood, and do most other carrying work, such as transporting grain home from the fields, or bringing in the poles cut by the men for building.

The occupations just dealt with are in no way specialized. Every man is expected to be able to herd cattle, hunt, and do all the work normally performed by men; and so too every woman is expected to be able to till the soil, cook, make beer, and do all the other work normally done by women. The necessary knowledge is acquired mainly through increasing participation in the work of the household. Children are required and taught from a fairly early age to be of assistance to their parents. Girls are made to help in fetching water and firewood, stamping or grinding corn, cooking, and smearing and cleaning the huts. They start by imitating these activities in their play, and are gradually drawn into actual domestic work under the instruction of their mothers and older sisters. As they grow older, they begin to take part in agriculture. Young boys are put to herding small stock and calves. Older boys herd and milk the cattle, learn to handle weapons, hunt for themselves or accompany the men, help build the cattle-kraals, and do other work of a similar nature. At the initiation ceremonies marking the transition from childhood to manhood they are emphatically reminded that cattle-herding and warfare are the two dominant spheres of masculine activity, while girls are similarly exhorted in regard to agriculture and housework.

To a considerable extent, too, all such work is carried on by every household for itself. Each has its own fields, cultivated by its women, and generally also its own livestock, looked after by men and boys; every man used to hunt, and every woman gathers edible plants. It is thus able to produce directly the food it consumes. Every household further builds its own huts as required, and all the necessary cooking, cleaning and other housework is done by its women and girls.

Household tasks are as often done collectively as individually. Even in such simple activities as fetching water, collecting firewood and stamping corn, the women and girls prefer to work in company, the presence of others affording a welcome relief from the monotony or burden of the task. The boys herding cattle spend much of their time playing together while their animals graze; and, while individual men hunted, hunting was for the most part undertaken by groups of men. The major activities, like clearing a new garden, planting, weeding, reaping and threshing, building the framework or wall of a hut, thatching, putting on the roof, fencing a field or cutting timber, are almost invariably done by several people working in co-operation to save time and energy. Each married woman has her own fields, but usually the fields of the same household are worked collectively, each being planted, weeded and reaped in turn by all the women and girls.

Sometimes the members of a household are sufficient for the purpose. More generally the assistance of outsiders is invited. Often enough help is given by near relatives, who are indeed expected to assist. But in all tribes there is also found the institution of the work-party (Nguni, *ilima*; Sotho, *letsema*). Anybody with a big task on hand with which he and his household alone cannot cope, or which he wishes to complete reasonably soon, will invite his neighbours and friends to help him. He brews a large quantity of beer, or slaughters an animal, and makes it known that with this he will entertain all those coming to work with him on a certain day. Anybody wishing to do so can take part and receive his share in the feast. Payment is sometimes also made in milk, porridge, salt or tobacco. The work is lightened by rhythmical songs of various kinds and by the presence of so many other people, while the feast awaiting them is a stimulus to eager activity. But it is not only this material reward that makes people lend a hand. Poor people have no other method of getting sufficient labour to carry out big tasks and, as they are therefore all dependent upon one another for assistance, it is good policy to help others and thus ensure their willing co-operation when required for one's own work. And people notoriously slack in attending work-parties often find their neighbours equally reluctant to help them in turn.

It is only in regard to the making of household utensils and implements that some degree of specialization is found. Here there is also a primary division of labour between the sexes, determined mainly by the material employed. All work in wood, leather, bone and metals is done by men; pot-making and beadwork by women; both sexes do basketwork, although in each group each makes a different type of object or uses a different technique for similar objects—for example, women make sewn beer-strainers and men make woven ones, yet the shape and the purpose are the same—but the techniques and the objects made by each sex differ in different groups. Some crafts are known only to a small number of people of the sex concerned. The outstanding examples of such specialization are metalwork (men), and pottery (women), the craft in both cases being largely confined to certain families, within which it is handed down from parent to child, although in fact anyone can learn. In former times most families were between them able to make enough utensils to supply their own needs. This is not always the case now, but then as now a few people were noted for the superiority of their products, or because they made certain objects which others could not, since there is considerable variation in skill which here is of greater significance than in food-producing or building.

No specialist, however, ever devotes himself exclusively to one particular occupation as a means of livelihood. They all herd and hunt, cultivate their fields, build their huts, and carry out the ordinary domestic work like the rest of the tribe; the special craft they also practise is merely a subsidiary source of income. This is as true of the smith and the magician as of the potter or worker in wood. Nor is there any special craft which cannot also be learned by outsiders. Any person wishing and able to do so may become a magician or smith, a kaross-maker, woodworker, or potter, although the first two occupations require an apprenticeship for which a fee must be paid to a practising professional. Perhaps the only major instance where any particular occupation is confined to a special caste is with the Lemba, until quite recently the only coppersmiths and potters of the Venda and neighbouring tribes (Schapera and Goodwin 1937: 151–3).

Exchange and Trade[36]

Internal

The general self-sufficiency of the household in regard to food, shelter and many other products, the fact that everybody was a herdsman or cultivator, builder or housewife, and the relatively slight development of specialization in other occupations, were reflected in the marked absence of systematic trade. There was little production for exchange, except with pots, baskets, iron goods and similar utensils and implements; and no markets, periodical or otherwise.

A certain amount of irregular trade is nevertheless carried on. A man requiring metal goods, pots, baskets, wooden utensils, skin cloaks or similar objects which he does not himself make will procure them from an expert craftsman. He goes directly to the latter, and either buys the object he wants, if it is already available, or, as is frequently necessary, orders it to be made. Such articles may also be acquired by exchange from other people possessing more than they need at the moment. Livestock, too, are fairly often obtained in this way; while in time of food shortage grain is sought from more fortunate neighbours. There was no standardized medium of exchange until the present money standard was introduced. Grain, meat, cattle, small stock, fowls, hoes, and spears are still exchanged for one another and for other objects, or used as payment to magicians and herdsmen [but payment may also be made in money]. Where it is made in kind there are, however, certain stabilized relative values. Pots and baskets are almost universally exchanged for their content in grain. Among the Tswana, again, two goats were given for a sheep or a bag of corn, and ten goats or five bags of corn for a heifer; among the Mpondo ten spears are given for a young beast and ten goats for a full-grown beast; while among the Venda two hoes are given for a goat.

Barter of this description, always on a small scale, takes place not only within the tribe, but also between members of different tribes. In Botswana, e.g., people were in times of famine often compelled to purchase corn in some neighbouring tribe less sorely afflicted. The [Tsonga], who do very little work in iron, obtain most of their metal goods from the Venda; the Tswana buy skins from Bushmen and Kgalagadi for spears, knives, tobacco and dogs; the Mpondo get copper rings from the tribes farther east, in exchange for corn; and the South Sotho formerly traded 'otter skins, panther skins, ostrich feathers and the wings of cranes' to the Zulu, as ornaments for warriors, in exchange for cattle, hoes, spearheads, necklaces and copper rings. Permission to trade must in such cases be obtained from the chief, who usually expected and received a present in return.

Commodities are not only used in this way to acquire goods which people cannot produce for themselves. They may also be given in exchange for labour. We have already seen that people helping in work parties are paid with beer, meat or other foodstuffs. So, too, the magician is paid for his special services, generally in livestock, sometimes in grain or metal goods. It is fairly common also for a man with no sons or young male relatives to look after his cattle to employ some other man or boy to do so. The herdsman is paid a heifer, which with its offspring then belongs to him. This form of wage-labour must be distinguished from the widespread custom of *ukusisa* (Nguni) or *ho fisa* (Sotho), by which the wealthy man places one or more of his cattle in the keeping of another. The herdsman is entitled to use their milk for his own purposes, and may be given some of the meat when an animal dies, but he may not sell or slaughter them. It is also usual, if the cattle flourish under his care, to reward him with a heifer from time to time.

Serving another man like this was perhaps the principal way in which a poor man can acquire cattle. And the man lending out his cattle not only has the task of herding them simplified. It serves partly to insure against total loss from disease, witchcraft or some other agency which might annihilate them should they all be concentrated in one kraal; and is also a means of disguising the full extent of his riches and so of escaping the jealousy and evil designs of less fortunate neighbours. Above all, perhaps, it is a means of acquiring prestige; the greater the number of retainers thus attached to a man, the higher his status and the more considerable his influence in the tribe generally.

Barter and payment for special services are only two of the mechanisms by which goods are circulated and thus made more widely accessible. Lobola payments, the fines and compensations levied at the courts, the various gifts made by relatives to one another, and the various forms of tribute paid to the chief, all serve the same end (Schapera and Goodwin 1937: 153–5).

External

External trade, both intertribal and with Arabs and Europeans, first on the coast and then as settlers, has been going on for a very long time. The exception in South Africa were the Lobedu who are said to have despised it (Krige and Krige 1943: 68). Intertribal trade was more in the nature of exchange—where commodities that were scarce in one tribe would be obtained from another. But real trade with first the Arabs, then the Portuguese and some others on the east coast, and especially at Delagoa Bay flourished for some centuries. The goods offered were ivory, copper, gold, horns, skins, which were exchanged for cloth, beads, brass and copper rings, and even iron hoes. Enterprising individuals might go from the interior to the coast, but bands of carriers under a leader were sent off from the coast to the interior as well.

In the nineteenth century trading depots were established in the interior by Europeans from the south, especially for ivory. The Fort Wiltshire weekly fair on the Cape Border had a short but colourful existence. Finally trade was taken over by the stores that were soon established all over the country where business was carried on at first by Europeans, or in some places Indians, and latterly increasingly by the Bantu themselves.

Great changes have taken place in the material culture of the Bantu-speaking people in South Africa during the last two hundred years, at first slowly, but at an increasing tempo as their environment has changed around them, partly by their own influence upon it and partly by the influence of other peoples. One of the main and earliest factors has been the availability of new objects and materials—ploughs are more practical than hoes for the initial turning of the soil, coloured glass beads are more eye-catching than seeds, shells or grass for ornaments, woven fabrics are easier to wear than skins. The availability of mechanical transport has brought ease of movement and, with the increasing need and opportunity to earn money to pay new taxes, there has developed a knowledge of and taste for many more new things which could be bought with money earned. A large proportion of the people has in fact changed its environment by going to work and live permanently in a new environment. At least as many have done so temporarily. At the same time there has been an increasing scarcity in the tribal areas of certain things that were used before—animals to hunt for their meat and skins, ivory to carve. Christian missionary influence on clothing and dwellings and the teaching of new crafts and skills has brought about many changes and, as an offshoot, there have come into being a great number of separatist sects each with its own special dress and paraphernalia. Overall there has been the new government, with laws against fighting, mining, and hunting of what was left of the game, with control of the agricultural land, reduction in numbers of cattle to save the land, and, latterly, re-settlement and rehabilitation schemes which make fundamental changes in the pattern of living.

Notes

Material for this chapter has been provided by the published sources listed and by the author's field and museum observations and those of colleagues, especially Mrs A. C. Lawton. Use has been made of an unpublished manuscript by Shaw and van Warmelo on the Cape Nguni. The sections on animal husbandry, music, calendar of work, division of labour and exchange have been reprinted in whole or in part from the first edition, with modifications.

1 Alberti 1810: 111–14, 129, 144, 188–9, 204; E. J. Krige 1936a: 39–54, 213; Kay 1833: 117–18, 143, 146; Marwick 1940: Chap.II; Hunter 1936: 15–17, 86, 97–9; Krige and Krige 1943: 20–2; Mönnig 1967: 172–3, 208–14, 218–25; Shaw 1860: 410–11; Stayt 1931a: Chap. IV; Winkelman 1788: 75–6; Schapera 1953: 26, 35–6; Hammond-Tooke 1962: 26–7, 33, 36, 147–9; Casalis 1861: 129–37; Ashton 1946; Ashton 1952: 136–7; Walton 1956a: 127–60; Cook 1931: 158–9; van der Kemp 1804: 437; Bryant 1949: *1*: 200.

MATERIAL CULTURE

2 Alberti 1810: 109; Campbell 1815: 367, 370; Kropf 1889: 109; Hunter 1936: 373 note; Krige 1936a: 214–16; Isaacs 1836: *1*: 224; Junod 1927: *2*: 127; Schapera 1953: 23; Mönnig 1967: 172; Ashton 1952: 134; Hoffman 1952: 23–8; Berglund 1968: 29–30; Walton 1954: 24–33; Lindblom 1931: 54–9; Shaw and van Warmelo n.d.

3 Winkelman 1788: 72; van der Kemp 1804: 438; Alberti 1810: 113; Bonatz 1834: 279; Döhne 1843: 72; Hammond-Tooke 1962: 147; Krige 1936a: 189–203; Marwick 1940: 60–1, 165–72, 192, 195–207; Junod 1927: *2*: 1–32; Ashton 1952: 120–33; Casalis 1861: 161–4, 171–8; Schapera 1953: 21–2; Mönnig 1967: 147–63; Krige and Krige 1943: 34–51; Quin 1959: 14–22; Stayt 1931a: 34–7.

4 With one or two additions and emendations, e.g. in nomenclature, this section is unchanged from the first edition of this book (Schapera and Goodwin 1937: 137–41).

5 Schapera and Goodwin 1937: 137.

6 Mönnig 1967: 53.

7 Hunter 1936: 69.

8 Stayt 1931a: 38.

9 Hunter 1936: 115.

10 Stayt 1931a: 40.

11 Schapera 1934b: 561–84.

12 Hunter 1936: 71. Also Casalis 1861: 161–4; Mönnig 1967: 163–74; Ashton 1952: 134–43; Krige and Krige 1943: 43; Schapera 1953: 21–4.

13 Winkelman 1788: 76–7; Alberti 1810: 153–8; Hunter 1936: 96; Krige 1936a: 203–7; Marwick 1940: 81, 174; Junod 1927: *2*: 52–84; Ashton 1952: 158; Schapera 1953: 24; Mönnig 1967: 174–7; Krige and Krige 1943: 45; Stayt 1931a: 76–80; Casalis 1860: 179–86; Shaw and van Warmelo n.d.

14 Stavenisse 1686: 62; Campbell 1815: 367; Krige 1936a: 388; Junod 1927: *2*: 84–9; Ashton 1952: 158; Casalis 1861: 223; Schapera 1953: 24; Stayt 1931a: 80; Quin 1959: 128; MacLaren 1958.

15 Krige 1936a: 385–6; Krige and Krige 1943: 46; Quin 1959: 61–92, 108–21.

16 Van der Kemp 1804: 438–9; Alberti 1810: 37 note; Shaw 1860: 368–9, 413, 471; Kropf 1889: 99–105; Junod 1927: *2*: 36–46; Stayt 1931a: 46–50, 154; Marwick 1940: 77–80, 166–7; Quin 1959: 132–45, 261; Schapera 1953: 25; Ashton 1952: 88, 89, 93; Krige 1936a: 53–60; Mönnig 1967: 188–91; Krige and Krige 1943: 23–4; Ashton 1940: 147–214; Shaw and van Warmelo n.d.

17 Sparrman 1785: *2*: 7; Carter 1927: 37–8; Winkelman 1788: 64–71, 85–91; Hallbeck and Fritsch 1826: 303–4, 309; Kay 1833: 111–15, 194, 200, 373–4; Döhne 1843: 23–41; Hunter 1936: 101; Hammond-Tooke 1962: 9–11; Krige 1932: 370–82; Hughes and van Velsen 1955: 74, 95; Junod 1927: *1*: 178, 195, *2*: 91–104, 146; Casalis 1861: 143, fn. 150; Marwick 1940: 40, 84–6; Angas 1849: *passim*; Summers and Pagden 1970: 24–29; Burchell 1822–4: vol. 2: 182–3, 228, 357–9; Schapera 1953:

25; Mönnig 1967: 107, 128; Krige and Krige 1943: 135–40, 243; Plates 9 and 10; Stayt 1931a: 22–8, 109, 141, 148; de Lange 1963: 85–95; Tyrrell 1968: 42–198; Shaw and van Warmelo n.d.

18 Tyrell 1968: 46–55, 135–7, 153, 156, 172–4; Krige 1936a: 64–9, 87–117, 138–54, 159–75, 243, 249, 280–96; Hughes and van Velsen 1955: 103–9; Junod 1927: *2*: 71–96, 371–427, 409–10, 536–72; Marwick 1940: 182–95, 222–34; Ashton 1952: 27–30, 48–52, 66–70, 102, 104, 112–19; Stayt 1931a: 85–9, 101–52, 161–2, 165, 230–61, 309; Mönnig 1967: 43–70, 85, 99–142; Krige and Krige 1943: 102–40, 271–81.

19 Kirby 1934: issues of *Journal of the African Music Society*; de Lange 1967: *passim*.

20 This section is taken from part of P. R. Kirby's chapter in the first edition (Schapera 1937a). The names of the former High Commission Territories have been brought up to date, and there are slight stylistic changes, with modifications indicated by square brackets.

21 Krige 1936a: 340–4, 408–9; Junod 1927: *1*: 110, 374, 463; *2*: 202; Stayt 1931a: 320–4; Burchell 1822–4: vol. 2: 292.

22 Krige 1936a: 77; Junod 1927, *1*: 174–5; Ashton 1952: 98–9; Stayt 1931a: 364–6.

23 Shaw 1935: 141–62; Shaw 1938: 221–52; Junod 1927: *1*: 342–50; *2*: 14–15, 103; Krige 1936a: 50, 60; Mönnig 1967: 191; Stayt 1927: 50.

24 Winkelman 1788: 69–72; Soga 1932: 312–13; Alberti 1810: 186–8; Shaw and van Warmelo 1972; Döhne 1843: 36–7; Krige 1936a: 243, 257–9, 261–79; Summers and Pagden 1970: *passim*; Junod 1927: *1*: 450–81; Schapera 1953: 29; Stayt 1931a: 69–70, 72.

25 Lavanha 1593: 294; Sparrman 1785: *2*: 158; Winkelman 1788: 70, 85–6; Alberti 1810: 149–52; Angas 1849: Pl. 23; Morgan 1833: 43–4; Poto Ndamase 1925: 118; Casalis 1861: 137; Wagner and Gordon 1929: 563–74; Krige 1936a: 209–12; Marwick 1940: 175–7; Hughes and van Velsen 1955: 61; Junod 1927: *2*: 138–40; Ashton 1952: 158–9; Giesekke 1930: 5–9; Hamilton 1935: 582–6; Campbell 1815: 225, 393; van Warmelo 1940: 81–6; Stayt 1931a: 59–68; Baumann 1919: *19*: 120–32, 209–14, 282–91; *20*: 32–4; Mönnig 1967: 146; Trevor 1912: 267–75, 370–2, 414–15; Moffat 1842: 467; Lichtenstein 1812: 2: 537. For comparison see Summers, R. 1969.

26 Schofield 1940: 125–62, 177–201; Lawton 1967: *passim*.

27 Winkelman 1788: 66; Alberti 1810: 53–60; Kay 1833: 132, 342; Hunter 1936: 101; Krige 1936a: 211, 399–400, 402–3; Junod 1927: *2*: 94, 145; Casalis 1861: 140–3; Ashton 1952: 159; Stayt 1931a: 59.

28 Lichtenstein 1812: 440, 449, 463, 464; Döhne 1883: 29, 41, 42; Junod 1927: *2*: 119–27, 132; Krige 1936a: 207–8, 395; Mayr 1906–7: *1*: 453–71; *2*: 392–8, 633–45; Müller 1917–18: *12–13*: 852–8; Quin 1959: 136, 137, Plates 15, 114, 117, 125; Stayt 1931a: 46, 56, 80, Plates 17, 18; Mönnig 1967: 146.

29 Thompson 1827: 361; Krige 1936a: 209, 398; Hughes and van Velsen 1955: 61; Junod 1927: *2*: 127–37; Ashton 1952: 161; Casalis 1861: 146–9; Krige and Krige 1943: Pl. 3; Mönnig 1967: 146; Stayt 1931a: 53–6; Tyrrell 1968: 45, 47, 64, 113.

30 Junod 1927: *1*: 50; *2*: 101, 130–3; Krige 1936a: 55, 209, 397–8; Quin 1959: 134; Stayt 1931a: 53.

31 Winkelman 1788: 86; Krige 1936a: 398; Stayt 1931a: 59.

32 Mayr 1907: 159–65; van der Sleen 1967: 76–91; Schoeman 1968: *passim*; Krige 1936a: 378–82; Junod 1927: *1*: 275; *2*: 102–4, 146.

33 Walton 1956: Pls 21, 25, 54, 57, 72, 87, 112; Stayt 1931a: 6–8.

34 This section is taken from the first edition with some modifications.

35 This section is taken from the first edition with some modifications, indicated by square brackets (Schapera and Goodwin 1937: 149–53).

36 This section is taken from the first edition, with modifications.

II
The Traditional Societies

Chapter 5
Traditional Economic Systems
Basil Sansom

This chapter is about the ways that people of the Southern Bantu areas, both past and present, have gone about the business of making a living. It is written around two themes. One is that the traditional economies of Bantu tribes in Southern Africa were of two kinds, produced as adaptations to the contrasting ecologies of East and West. To the east of the sub-continent, between the escarpment of the Drakensberg and the sea, people concentrated their investments in small localities and in corporate economic groups. This policy made the Eastern economy an economy of contained investment. Western peoples, in contrast, had less in the way of capital to invest. Situated on the other side of the Drakensberg divide, mainly on hinterland plateaux, Westerners adopted a contrary policy, spreading their assets and activities. The Western mode produced an economy of distributed investment. I begin with an account of East versus West in traditional times, relating economic practices to regional differences in the natural environment. In dealing with the past, I am able to discuss subsistence economics pure and simple.

While the first theme is about regional variation, the second relates to differences that are the product of historical development. The unitary subsistence economy of traditional times has been superseded and a dual economy has emerged to replace it. In the dual economy, subsistence activities survive to provide one sector. The other component is a market sector introduced by white initiative. My second theme is that modern developments in the tribal areas are best understood as a progress towards interpenetration of subsistence and market sectors in a dual economy (see also chapter 13).

The era of the dual economy began with effective economic contact between black and white. As soon as money began to feature regularly in transactions to which tribesmen were party, they employed a new standard of value which could be set against traditional standards and compared with them. They were faced, too, with the problems of bridging the gulf that separated one mode of economic thinking and action from another. My account of modern developments charts successive ways of managing the interchange between market and subsistence sectors.

Duality has pervaded economics in the tribal areas of Southern Africa for a period that has been artificially prolonged. First as a Union and then as a Republic, South Africa has imposed peculiar restrictions on the employment of African labour and on the ability of Africans to own property, especially land. The inhabitants of what are now Lesotho, Botswana and Swaziland are not exempt from these restrictions when they enter South Africa. And, because the centres of industrial development are within South Africa, the peoples of these rural territories are affected by the labour restrictions imposed on African workers by the South African government. Effectively, all tribesmen of Southern Africa are men of two worlds because the income of tribal territories is supplied, in part, by the wages of tribal migrants who work in the white areas of South Africa. Hence economic dualism, in which tribespeople combine subsistence agriculture and wage labour, persists.

In the context of this chapter, the persistence of dualism gives added importance to my account of the traditional economy. It is not merely the account of a finished era. Trends in the old tribal economy have been projected into modern times with the maintenance of tribal populations whose members still exploit the land under customary rules of tenure. A picture of the Bantu past is particularly useful to the outsider who must come to understand the present economic situation as a development in which elements of tradition have been consciously preserved. Whenever Africans behave in what seems, by Western standards, to be an 'uneconomic' manner, they are either acting in terms of cultural values that derive from their heritage, or battling to reconcile competing demands of market and subsistence sectors in the dual economy.

The Traditional Economy

Before the advent of the whites, Southern Bantu were hoe-cultivators and pastoralists who supplemented the products of herds and fields by hunting and by gathering wild foods. Their subsistence activities were conducted within tribal units governed by independent rulers. There was little incentive to inter-tribal trade as, in Southern Africa, there was hardly any variation between areas in the types of commodity produced. Further, there was hardly any specialization of economic importance. The stimulus to trade was therefore in unevenness in production between groups and not in specialization of production. In one year, a group might experience a shortfall in grain but have cattle to spare. Cattle would be bartered for grain even though the second party to the transaction was also a pastoralist and farmer. A further stimulus to exchange was that the rewards of status and prestige could accrue to wealthy individuals who invested surpluses in relationships with others, gaining wives, alliance, and henchmen.

All in all, the tribal economy was redistributive and redistribution was largely limited to the bounds of a politically defined tribal area. The general trend implied in the notion of a subsistence economy is towards an identity between producer and consumer. The products, too, were basic essentials and there were few luxury goods. Hence, even when a surplus was produced, it was normally a surplus of food. The worker, whether he gained a surplus or not, 'produced for provisioning' (cf. Sahlins 1968: 75). A subsistence economy that is locally confined is highly dependent on its region, and variations between regions in Southern Africa produced the contrasting economic styles of East and West. There were no significant inter-tribal differences in technology, nor was knowledge of techniques unevenly distributed. The major domesticated plants of the East were also those of the West. Hence the separate adaptations in the two regions were to immutables—to altitude, climate, soil and associated plant cover. Easterners and Westerners were peoples with similar knowledge and techniques who differed in the ways in which they deployed labour and assets in contrasting environments.

The subsistence activities of the individual tribesman were carried out within limitations which derived from the natural environment and from regulations imposed by men in authority. He could use only the resources available in the tribal area, and his access to them was controlled by chiefly regulation. My description of the traditional economy proceeds in two stages. The administrative and ecological background is set out and then I discuss the economic tribesman's activities against it.

Boundaries

In Southern Africa, the chief regulated public access to the means of production. If people drove cattle wherever they liked or burned veld indiscriminately to promote spring growth or tramped over the fields of others, economic anarchy would prevail. Against feckless and selfish use of resources the chief set boundaries in both time and space, using his authority to enforce them. The chief defined areas for pasture and lands for fields. He declared open and closed seasons. By doing so he imposed a pattern of work and a patterned use of resources on his tribespeople.

A chief's regulation of the economy through maintenance of boundaries is obvious in his administration of land tenure. Acting through ranked officials he—in the Swazi phrase—'served out' land to the people (Kuper 1965: 493). The idea that chiefs managed boundaries in time as well as in space is, perhaps, more subtle. In Sotho regions, no one was allowed to cut thatching grass before an official declaration that the grass was ready (Schapera 1956: 71). This is an example of the setting of temporal boundaries and it is worth considering for its general implications.

During my own fieldwork (among present-day Pedi, a North Sotho people), I walked the veld with a chief as thatching-time approached. The chief explained his purpose. Vagaries of rain and climate result in maturation of grass at a different time each year. If left too long, the grass dries out to become a hazard to veld fires. Dry grass is also brittle and the thatchers find it difficult to work. Yet, premature cutting by people anxious to roof houses would reduce the total yield of thatch in the tribal territory. The chief thus inspected the veld with his aides to judge the propitious moment when nothing would be gained by further delay. Thatching grass is a communal resource to which every tribesman has a right. By insisting that people waited for an order to start, the chief served public interests, ensuring that no one gained an unfair advantage and that the whole yield was increased to the optimum. As a privilege of chiefship and a return for his services to the community, the chief is presented with bundles of the first thatch cut to use in building and repairing houses in his ward.

A combined logic of parsimony and concerted activity underlies the declaration of open and closed seasons. Thus, when a chief opens the tilling season he, in effect, creates a division between exclusive areas of arable and grazing land. Between harvest and the commencement of tilling, the lands are given over to cattle and they eat the stubble. The fields become commonage as any man's cattle graze on any man's fields. Months later, when cultivation is due to start, cattle are removed from the unfenced fields and are kept away by conscientious herding. The logic of concerted activity is that people should not compete to use the same land at the same time for different purposes. The definition of fields is not simply 'land under crops' but 'arable land segregated by official order for the season of cultivation'.

In imposing patterns of work and use, the chief orchestrates subsistence activities. His control is over access to the means of production and, in exercising it, he sets the bounds to individual action. As rights held by one man are held against others, the chief both limits individuals and creates the privileged rights that they enjoy.[1]

Economic Regulation and Ecology: A Thesis

Boundaries in space and time are set in both East and West. However, there is greater delegation of this administrative function in the East, where the chief's subordinates put control of boundaries into effect. Eastern decentralization of control is part of a more general adaptation. The ecology of the East is suited to local regulation of resources, while central control is an imperative in the West.

The ecologies of East and West require different adaptations on the part of people who intend to exploit them in the Bantu way—by combining pastoralism with cultivation, hunting and gathering. Thus I distinguish two adaptive modes, Type A in the East and Type B in the West.

Adaptation of Type A is common to Nguni people with few exceptions. Adaptation of Type B, while associated with Westerners, varies in the intensity with which its trends are pursued. It is most developed among the Tswana tribes whose westward extension ends only as the drought and desert lands of the Kalahari begin. They reach the limit of the distribution of Southern Bantu peoples which coincides with an isohyet that separates regions that receive less than ten inches of rainfall from better watered grasslands (Goodwin 1937: 35). In arid lands, the Bantu combination of cattle-keeping and cultivation is not viable and San (Bushman) hunters and gatherers, who live and move in nomadic bands, represent the appropriate adaptation to the desert rigours of the Kalahari.

The Bantu East is characterized by dispersed settlement of its inhabitants, whose homes dot the landscape. Residentially scattered, the Easterners confine their subsistence activities to small and exclusive areas near their homes. Western people concentrate their dwellings and disperse their economic activities over a wide zone of exploitation. These contrasts are associated with trends in the regulation of access to resources. Western regulation proceeds from a centre; in the East decentralization is the norm. These clusters of characteristics are not fortuitous, but combine as two integrated patterns of adaptation in which administration is geared to ecological conditions. In the East it is reasonable to expect fair returns if investments are concentrated on a small patch of country. In the West, to secure adequate returns from investment, individuals must range over, and commingle in, a wider territory.

The key to all this is in the notion of risk. Southern Bantu practised mixed subsistence activities and men had to decide how to distribute investment among the possibilities open to them. They faced the uncertainty inherent in subsistence production—crop failure, cattle disease, drought, blight, locusts, shortage of game, etc. They met the situation by calculating risk and hedging one investment with another. In the East, an individual could diversify investment and spread risk within a small physical area. In the Western region, distributed risk demanded distribution of activity over territory and involved distributed relationships between persons.

The range of differences between Eastern and Western peoples can be related to two distinct strategies for exploiting rights of access to resources and to people. Westerners adopted a ranging, open strategy; Easterners concentrated investment within both a compact territory and a narrow span of social and economic relationships. For clarity, features of the distinctive Eastern and Western modes of adaptation are presented in Table 5.1.

Though in this chapter I am concerned with economics, it is worth noting that the strategic mode adopted by a particular people had pervasive effects on their social life.

Adaptations: Type A and Type B

The ecological preconditions for the dispersed settlements characteristic of Type A are those that allow a chiefdom to be divided into districts that are economically self-sufficient. Ideally, such districts should offer their inhabitants access to the full range of natural resources that they wish to exploit. The area that contains this range of resources is, for the individual, his *unit for exploitation*.

In practice, the Nguni district did not need to contain every type of resource desired by its inhabitants. Clay for potters, wood for local carvers and iron for smiths, for instance, are subsidiary resources that can be imported. However, the basic demands for water, arable land of specific types and aspects, and an area of wild for hunting and gathering, should be met within its bounds. The *unit for exploitation* is, further, an area that contains

TABLE 5.1 *Modes of adaptation*

Characteristic	Type A	Type B
Location and tribal groups	Eastern region, Nguni peoples. Some exceptional Western areas e.g. those of Lobedu and Venda of Northern Transvaal	Western region. Sotho peoples
Settlement pattern	Dispersed kraal settlement	Concentrated residence in large villages and towns
Unit of exploitation	Mainly the local district or ward under a headman	Entire tribal territory under chief
Regulation of access to resources	Decentralized: headman prominent	Centralized in person of the chief
Modal strategy	Territorial confinement of investments. Concentrated economic relationships. Emphasis on herding corporation	Dispersal of investments over tribal area. Dispersed economic relationships

people in their seasonal movements. Thus the Nguni district should provide year-round grazing, perennial water, etc.

These requirements demand a specific type of terrain. The tribal territory must contain a number of areas, each offering a similar combination of natural resources in similar quantity. Such areas, whose boundaries are natural features in the landscape, can then be defined as administrative districts and put in charge of headmen. In general, this is the basis on which the Nguni of the Eastern seaboard divided tribal lands. The country they occupied allowed them to do so. It was a *country of small-scale repetitive configurations that contained a variety of natural resources.*

Among Nguni, it was possible to take the allocation of natural areas a step further. Repetitive configurations allowed definition of tiny areas associated with neighbourhood groups or kraals within a district. Gluckman provides this description of pre-conquest Zululand:

> Each homestead had its own fields and cattle-fold. A demographic survey would show the homesteads scattered at some distance apart (a few hundred yards to a mile or two) along the hills which, intersected by deep bush-filled valleys, characterized the interior of Zululand. The fields were mostly along the ridges and the banks of streams; the low valleys, uninhabited because of fever, were winter-grazing and hunting grounds. The coastal tribes lived, similarly distributed, on the

malarial sandy plain between the hills and the sea (Gluckman 1940: 28–9).

The Zululand coast and interior yielded two regions in each of which the notion of repetitive configurations applied.

People were held to their district and to the smaller areas within districts. Holleman has shown how Zulu apply a criterion of proximity in granting grazing rights. When a district headman has to decide whether a man should be allowed to use a particular pasture, the headman judges whether the man's kraal is near enough to (*eduze*), or too far (*ekudeni*) from, the coveted grazing land. The Nguni tribesman is forced to pursue his subsistence activities within a zone centred on his kraal (Holleman 1941: 255).

Working in the south of the Nguni region, Hammond-Tooke (1962) has reported the continuing adherence of contemporary Bhaca to the Nguni pattern. In East Griqualand, the Bhaca are fronted by tribes of the coastal strip and by tribes that occupy land similar to the thornveld of the Zululand interior. Bhaca live on the higher sourveld (see Map 5.1).* Here the fertile valleys are used for cultivation and kraals are sited on high ground. In describing neighbourhood groups, the people 'speak of *ummango*, a ridge, and, indeed, the typical situation for such a grouping is on a ridge overlooking the fields of its members, situated in the valley below' (Hammond-Tooke 1962: 54–5). Map 5.1, which I reproduce from Hammond-Tooke, shows the integrity of a district as a relatively self-sufficient ecological area.

Mpondo, who front the Bhaca towards the coast, cultivate fields on hill slopes. But, again, district and neighbourhood are clearly defined and tend towards self-sufficiency. Though Bhaca and Mpondo do make some use of cattle posts removed from the vicinity of the herd-owner's kraal, these are used only for a fraction of the year and are not too far removed from the home area (Hunter 1936; Hammond-Tooke 1962). Typically in Nguni cattle-keeping there is a diurnal round in which cattle are taken from the home kraal in the morning and returned to it in the evening.

While the territories occupied by Nguni tribes differ in particulars, they all allow concentrated exploitation. What the Nguni areas have in common are repetitive configurations of terrain within each tribal territory. To provide a further example, in the tribal territory of the Makhanya of the Natal South coast, 'the terrain undulates in a sequence of lozenge-like formations, bounded by brooks, streams or rivers' (Reader 1966: 30). People need not travel far to gain access to basic resources. A further point is that adaptation of Type A is limited to relatively well-watered and productive lands. As I shall show, it is unsuited to the highland and arid zones of Southern Africa.

Nearly all territories that were inhabited by Sotho-speakers contrast markedly with those occupied by Nguni. Sotho-speakers are Western people and they represent adaptation of Type B.

The Bantu West was characterized by concentration of people into large villages and towns. Typically, whole tribes were grouped in single settlements.

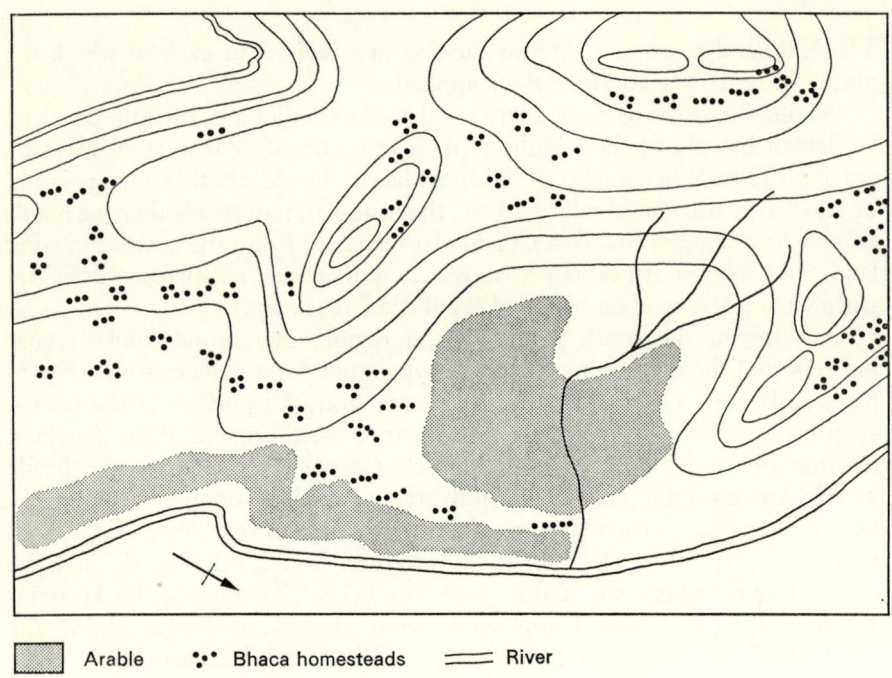

MAP 5.1 *Bhaca settlement 1949 (after Hammond-Tooke 1962)*

This concentration was, and is, complemented by a seasonal movement of the population between town and countryside. Among the Westerners, the Tswana had the largest towns and ranged more extensively over tribal territories (see Plate 3). Van Warmelo, without elaborating, notes that the Tswana mode 'is merely an adaptation of the Sotho economic system to the exceptional conditions imposed by the country in which they live' (1935: 103). In short, the Tswana adaptation is the culmination of Type B.

In the West, several factors militate against concentration of subsistence activities within small areas. The first is the nature of the terrain: a variety of resources is less frequently contained in small configurations such as those provided by the convolutions of Zulu hill country. On the inland plateaux one is often confronted with large expanses of relatively uniform country. To move from one type of plant cover to another, or to find different soil types, one must travel over larger distances. There is a general problem of finding a constant water supply and water sources are often far apart. Because people need to exploit variations of terrain, they must range over an extensive area. To accommodate a ranging and open strategy, the tribal territory replaces the district in supplying the self-contained area in which the variety of its inhabit-

TRADITIONAL ECONOMIC SYSTEMS

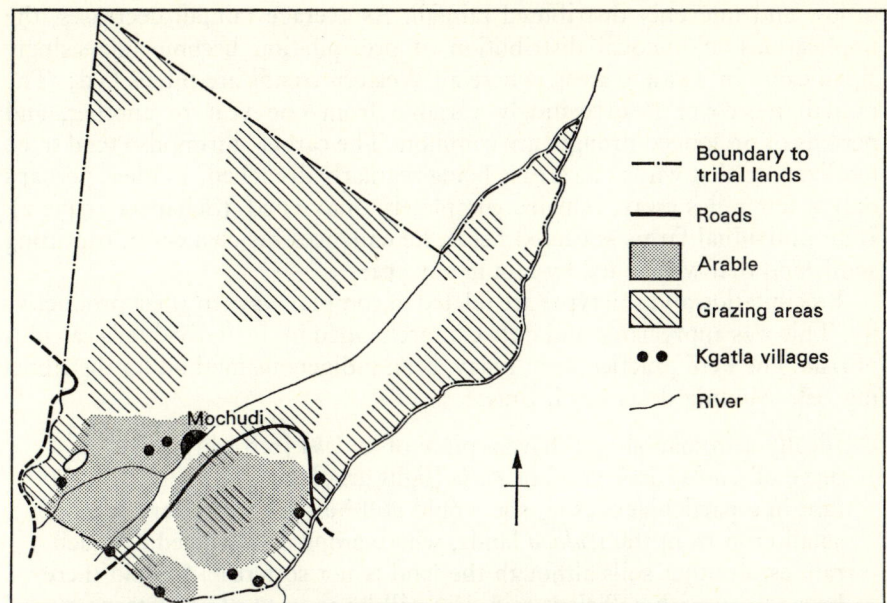

MAP 5.2 *Kgatla settlement at Mochudi c. 1930 (after Schapera 1943c)*

ants' requirements will be satisfied. In the West there are also large tracts eschewed by the Bantu, who found them unendowed with the appropriate combination of resources which are necessary as a base for mixed subsistence exploitation. Thus 'the somewhat bleak and sparsely wooded "High Veld" has never been much favoured by them' (van Warmelo 1935: 96). As one progresses westwards, the pattern of inclusive districts and neighbourhoods is increasingly less viable. At the limits of Bantu settlement, where grasslands merge into Kalahari, attempts to concentrate subsistence activities in confined spaces would be economic suicide. The Western tribal territory is the tribesman's unit of exploitation.

Natural separation of zones on a larger scale is one stimulus to the distribution of activity over terrain. But distribution is further stimulated by human consideration of risk and possibilities for investment. Nguni could usually distribute fields within a single district. They might consider further separation, but tended to be deterred: 'scattered fields entail much travelling to and fro between them and the farmer must decide between caution and convenience' (Hammond-Tooke 1962: 17). This scatter referred to in Bhaca country involves but a few miles. Western tribesmen could not afford the luxury of considering convenience in their calculations. Spreading risk was integral to their activities, an essential to ensure returns. In the territory of the Khuruthse of Botswana, distances of over twenty-five miles could separate the fields worked by one cultivator. Werbner (1970: 12), who reports this, stresses that such separation of fields was a feature of the traditional system.[2]

The wider scatter of fields in the West was, among other things, a response to low and unevenly distributed rainfall. As average rainfall decreases, the implications of unequal distribution of precipitation become increasingly significant. In Tswana areas, where all Western trends are intensified: 'The rainfall moreover is exceedingly variable from one year to another, and periods of prolonged drought are common. The earlier storms also tend to be localized, so that while one area is being regularly drenched, another, perhaps only a few miles away, remains completely untouched' (Schapera 1947: 2). If an individual farms scattered fields, he enhances his chances of capturing some land that will be fed by rain in any year.

Precipitation and soil types are related in complex ways to affect productivity. This was appreciated and duly comprehended in the individual's calculus of risk. The Pedi practice, seen today, is an indigenous method for distributing risk. Mönnig describes it thus:[3]

> Ideally a woman should have a piece of *sehlaba* [red soil] as well as a piece of *seloko* [dark grey] or *mašu* [light grey]. Should there be little rain in a particular season, she would still be reasonably sure of a small crop from the *sehlaba* lands, where crops do not need as much rain as on other soils although the land is not so fertile. Should there be a season with sufficient rain, she will be assured of good crops from the *mašu* or *seloko* lands (Mönnig, 1967, 153).

In other words, there is a choice between investing more or less labour in soils that will yield bumper crops under optimum conditions or sowing drought soils that always produce, but do not produce in quantity. The calculation can be even more complicated. Of the two major traditional grain crops, sorghum and millet, millet was a drought crop while sorghum gave greater yields. But, central to this argument, seeking out various soil types promotes greater scatter of the fields worked by one family.

On the grazing lands, both Eastern and Western peoples experienced an annual lean period when grass cover on pastures was sparse and dry. In consequence the condition of stock reached a yearly low. Nowhere was fodder stored and cattle were wholly dependent on standing grass or stubble. The Eastern dry season does not present annual privation equal to that experienced by cattle on the hinterland plateau. In the West, there was need for sheer space on the veld. Measured in our terms, the acreage required to support a beast increases spectacularly as one moves westward. In the ranching country cattle are shifted across the grassland in search of areas where late rains or loamy soils, retentive of moisture, give pastures an extra lease into the dry season. Zulu grazed cattle on pastures near to their kraals. Among Sotho, herding centres were permanent cattle posts situated appreciable distances from the tribal settlement.

The map of Mochudi illustrates separation between residential, arable and grazing land on a tribe-wide basis in modern times. Headmen of wards into which the town was divided were allocated blocks of land, and each ward was associated with particular cattle posts. However, both ward holdings and the holdings of individuals could be distributed. Nguni insisted that a man farmed and herded within district and neighbourhood confines, thus maintaining an identity between residential locale and area for exploitation. If an Nguni moved his house for any distance, he shifted from one area of exploitation to another. Sotho and Tswana could hold fields in the ward holdings of different headmen. If a man changed his allegiance, he moved from one ward to another within the town. He did not have to relinquish land that he had cultivated as a member of his original ward.

Thus Sotho grew up in an environment where separation of resources and distribution of holdings was regarded as an advantage. Individuals could make compacts with one another, giving others access to their fields. One could thus distribute investment by borrowing and lending land. In these dealings, dispersal of holdings is achieved by entering into more ranging and distributed economic relationships. The Sotho economy turned men outward. Each man surveyed the tribal territory from the town, seeing in it a wide ambit for personal opportunity. There were sections of territory to which he—as a ward member—held privileged rights of access. But he could gain secondary rights in other areas through his relationships with others. Tswana pastures were controlled by special officials from whom individuals sought permission to graze their animals (Schapera 1938a; 206). Ward-heads tended also to hold the office of pasture-controller (*modisa*), but the articulation between headmanship and control of pastures was not precise. This contrasts with the inwardness of the Nguni whose complement of resources comes in a neat package. The Nguni overlooks a neighbourhood from his family kraal, and that neighbourhood contains, if not the sum, the best part of the resources to which he has access.

One device for spreading risk was exploited by Eastern and Western peoples alike. This was the set of arrangements for herding cattle whereby cattle owned by one man would be placed in the herd of another. The herdsman took any milk and could share in the increase of cows. One man's cattle could thus share the fortunes of a number of herds, their luck in finding good grazing, and in escaping raids, disease, and predators.

The Apparatus for Regulation

A similar apparatus for the delegation of authority to administer rights in land is found in all Southern Bantu tribes. My concern is with contrasting emphases in the use of this machinery for control.

Very briefly, the tribal territory was administered as a set of estates ranged in a hierarchy. The supreme independent authority, a chief or paramount, controlled a primary estate of administration that included the entire tribal territory. The primary estate was divided into estates of lower orders. The echelon of subordinates immediately below the ruler had secondary estates of administration. In smaller tribes, this is as far as sub-division of administrative estates went. In more complicated polities, there was a third level, tertiary estates of administration. Tribes with paramount chiefs had at least three levels (see Figure 5.1). In large polities, headmen of districts or wards held tertiary estates of administration while headmen in smaller tribes were officers of the second echelon. As I intend to compare Western chiefs with Nguni headmen, I shall avoid ambiguity by writing about the district estate as opposed to the primary estate of administration.

FIGURE 5.1 *Hierarchies of estates in land*

Hierarchy with four tiers		Hierarchy with three tiers	
Official	*Grade of estate*	*Official*	*Grade of estate*
Paramount/ King	Primary estate of administration	Chief	Primary estate of administration
Sub-chiefs	Secondary estates of administration	Ward/ District head	Secondary estates of administration
Ward or District heads	Tertiary estates of administration		
Householder	Estates of production	Householder	Estates of production

As the terminology (derived from the work of Gluckman 1943, 1965) suggests, administrators did not—unlike feudal lords—own their estates. The estate 'belonged' to the official only in this limited sense: within the estate he controlled access to resources, concerting the work pattern of his followers and protecting individual and communal rights. Political officers were rewarded according to their status with donations of produce and by the tribute labour of their followers.

The hierarchy of estates corresponded in a general way with devolution of political authority. Each officer, a paramount, a lesser chief, or a headman, presided over a court. In it he upheld the rights of individuals within his jurisdiction. He also punished those who infringed the boundaries that he sought to maintain. There was right of appeal from lower to higher courts.

Headmen of wards and districts granted rights to estates of a different kind. These were *estates of production* and grants in them were for the use of resources, not for regulation of access to them. Productive activity and its regulation is what land tenure is all about. The administrative apparatus

TRADITIONAL ECONOMIC SYSTEMS

existed to subserve the granting of rights to individuals so that they could work local resources. What I have to demonstrate is that there was more delegation in the East: ward heads, officials of the lowest echelon, performed tasks that were reserved to chiefly controllers of primary estates in the West.

Now, everywhere headmen did most of the work entailed in granting estates of production, which they carved out of their estates of administration. The shift of emphasis is visible when the regulation of consequences of collision between working tribesmen are considered. Such collisions must either be avoided by regulations that anticipate them or resolved when they happen.

The first point is the most obvious. The total tribal territory in the West looks like an integral unit made up of three sections—residential, arable and grazing lands (Map 5.2, see page 143). It must, therefore, be administered as a unit. A Western headman did not have an estate of administration in a single locality. He had control of access to several locales, blocks of fields or grazing areas, which were separated by intervening spaces in the charge of others. The chief was overseer of the entire unit. In contrast, Nguni wards are contained and compact. They are units that embrace much of the economic life of their inhabitants. Therefore they could be, and were, individually controlled by their headmen.

The two great temporal divides—harvest and the beginning of the new tilling season—were ritually celebrated in Southern Africa. First fruit ceremonies after harvest and rain-making before planting were ritual occasions: no one could eat the harvest nor could anyone plant before those in authority had performed the appropriate ritual. The secular consequences of these rituals have been dealt with—they divided time to segregate seasonal work patterns. Among Sotho, the chief was unique and central in these ritual performances. He effected a tribal synchronization and established central time. Among Nguni, 'district time' was permitted. After the chief had given them permission, Nguni headmen were able to hold local ceremonies. The inauguration of the seasons did not occur at the same moment in each district. The celebration of the goddess Nomkhubulwana, a spring rite confined to Nguni and associated with hoeing, was similarly organized on a district and not on a chiefdom basis (Holleman 1941).

The lack of a developed law of trespass is a second index of Nguni devolution. Trespass among Nguni was an affair to be settled among neighbours. People likely to come into collision, especially through careless herding of cattle (which could ravage standing crops), were likely to be people of a district involved in day-to-day economic co-operation. Hence Krige notes that it is difficult to decide whether Zulu enforced the law of trespass in the courts (Krige 1936a: 229). Errant herdboys were thrashed, and there the matter was left to rest. Harries recorded the Pedi law of trespass at the turn of the century (Harries 1906 and 1929). Schapera's (1938a: 269f.) description of Tswana procedures confirms that Westerners treated trespass on a formal legalistic basis. In the Western context it is obvious that relative strangers were likely to collide. They must appeal to the chief if they could not settle the damage themselves.

Finally, Nguni headmen were more like chiefs and enjoyed more privileges than did their Western counterparts. Some Nguni headmen had 'fields of office' cultivated by people of their district (Holleman 1941: 252); tribute went to Nguni headmen of district and wards but not to the Sotho ward heads (Holleman 1941: 255).

Comparing East and West, Krige remarks that 'among the Zulus it is not the custom for corn and beer to be sent from every kraal to the king at harvest time, as is the case in some of the Sotho tribes' (Krige 1936a: 202). The logic of tribute is that it is sent as 'thanks' to an administrator for doing work to make production of the commodity represented by the tribute possible. I argue that the contrasting emphases between East and West are reflected in the identity of the recipient of tribute. The Western chief, who concerts activity in the tribe, is thanked, while in the East it is the district head who is given a reward for his services. Nguni chiefs did, of course, receive both tribute labour and tribute in produce, but they received these donations from people in the immediate locality of their kraals (Holleman 1941; Krige 1936a). Regular agricultural tribute to Nguni chiefs came from locals because estates of administration nest within one another. A chief who controls a primary estate is also the headman of his home district and, in it, the controller of a secondary or tertiary estate. It is in his role as a district official that the Nguni chief receives these regular contributions.

Adaptations of Type A and Type B are thus Eastern and Western modes of adjusting human activities to the environment. What remains is to relate these adaptations more precisely to the geographical distribution of tribes. Adaptation of Type B is pre-eminently an adaptation to the plateaux of the middleveld. It is unambiguously associated with Tswana and North Sotho tribes, excluding the Lobedu. The South Sotho, inhabiting what is now Lesotho, represent a variant of Type B. In the Basuto highlands, the sectional relief reveals a sequence of stepped peneplanes. Grassland succeeds grassland at increasing altitude. Use of the pastures is conditioned by their altitude and thus winter and summer pastures may be distinguished (Sheddick 1954: 34–50). Again, separation provides the basis for a ranging strategy. Among South Sotho there was some specialization: people who used lower lands could produce more grain than the cattle-herders of the highest pastures.

Adaptation of Type A is the mode of the Nguni of the South East. In addition, it is encountered amongst the Venda and the Lobedu of the Transvaal. The Lobedu are a lowveld people who do not live in concentrated settlements. Description of their terrain, a specialized and exceptional Transvaal region, reveals the repetitive configurations necessary for adaptation of Type A. Venda and Lobedu regions are seen as two 'islands' of unusual character in Maps 5.3 and 5.4 (pp. 149–50). Venda occupy a particularly fertile Transvaal area and are capable of raising two crops a year on their lands. Here I cannot do justice to some of the intriguing variants of the main types, but the general and pervasive differentiation between West and East on ecological grounds is tellingly illustrated in Map 5.3 which shows the distribution of veld cover in Southern Africa. The companion Map 5.4 shows the distribution of adaptations of Type A and Type B. Lobedu and Venda areas appear as Eastern 'islands' in a Western sea.

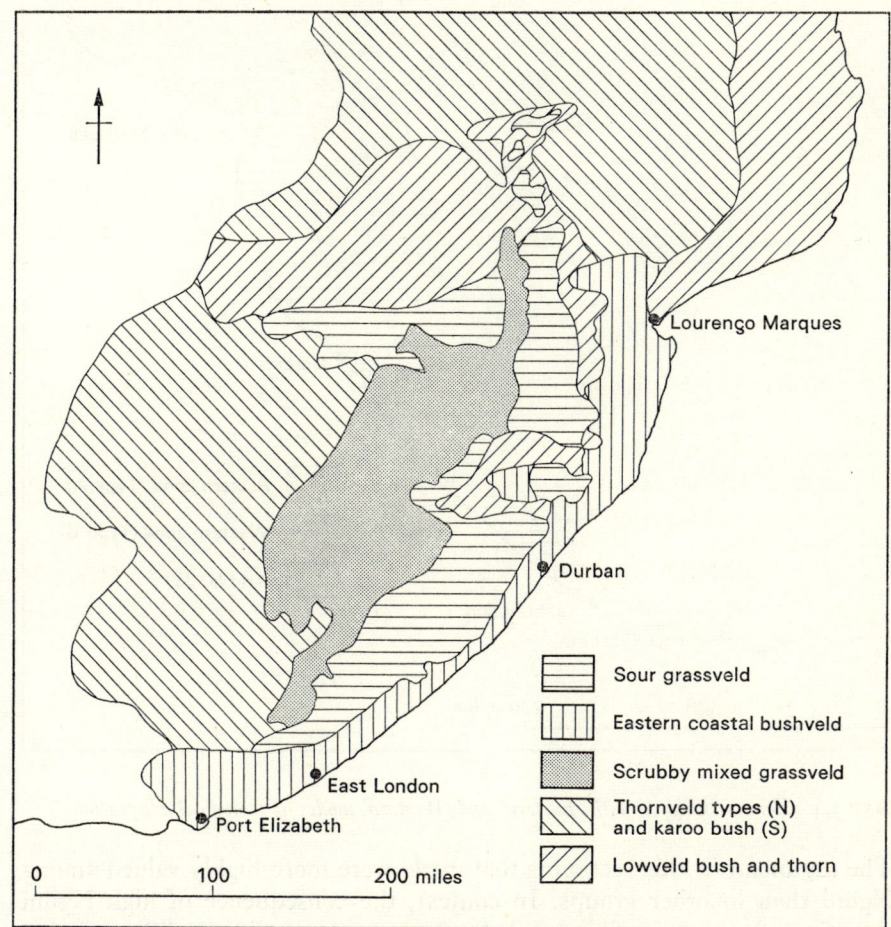

MAP 5.3 *Veld cover in Southern Africa (after J. P. H. Acocks 1953)*

Cattle as Capital

I have, so far, distinguished two modes of adaptation. Translated into investment policy, Types A and B entail respective emphasis on concentrated and dispersed investment over territory. But the major variants of Type A and B are characterized by a further difference. This time it is a difference in the relative value and significance of two major items of diet—grain and milk.

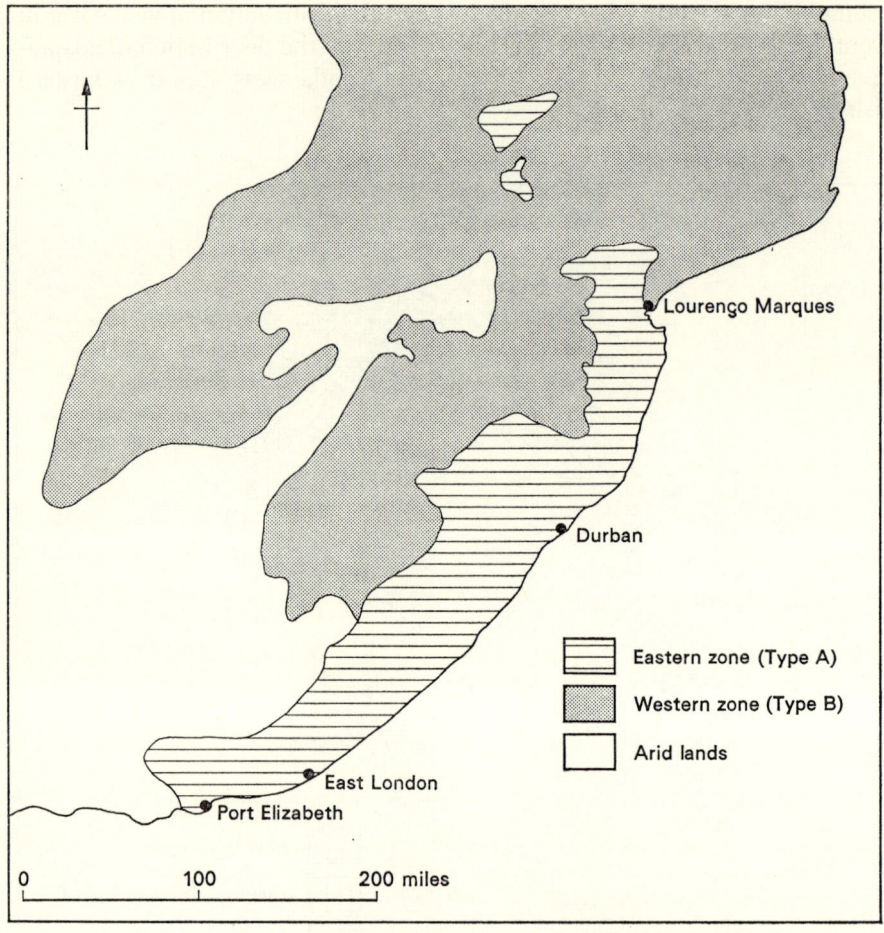

MAP 5.4 *Zones associated with 'Eastern' and 'Western' modes of ecological adaptation*

The argument in this section is that cattle were more highly valued among Nguni than in other groups. In context, the consequence of high Nguni valuation of cattle is profound. It led to greater opportunity for differentiation on the basis of ownership, greater discrepancies between rich and poor. The Nguni economy contrasts with that of other tribes as one in which there is greater opportunity for capital investment.

As well as allowing concentration, the Eastern ecology permitted a closer integration of cattle into the tribal economy than could be achieved in the West. For Nguni, milk vied with grain to provide the people with their staple food. 'The mainstay of the Zulu diet is *amasi* or curds of milk and most of their dishes are a mixture of this *amasi* with different vegetables' (Krige 1936a: 55). Milking was part of the daily round in every kraal and men tried to get sufficient cattle to provide milk throughout the year. Zulu herds were dairy herds, and the Nguni managed to monopolize the one great region of Southern Africa in which they could combine perennial milk production with other subsistence activities. The East can support a dense cattle population. The Swazi (an Nguni people) provide an interesting test case that shows that milk can only continue to function as a staple within the proper confines of the Eastern area.

In the north of Nguni country, some Swazi spill over westwards to occupy middleveld—country of tall grass and parkland that I have associated with adaptation of Type B. In Swaziland, 'the middleveld merges with the bush and sweet grass of the lowveld' (Kuper 1965: 482). Kuper observes that the sweet grass area of the lowveld is where 'cattle thrive'. In 1936 she also noticed that:

> In the Bushveld where milk is plentiful, grown men also eat *emasi*, but in the middle and highveld, one seldom finds any but children taking *emasi*. They often say that their stomachs are not used to *emasi* since it is only available in summer in these parts of the country (Kuper [née Beemer], 1939: 220).

Thus Swazi, despite the milk-drinking proclivities of their Nguni culture, cannot sustain this dietary emphasis when they inhabit the middleveld pastures. Using milk as a staple is not just a cultural pattern. It demands grazing conditions that permit maintenance of dairy herds. Perennial bovine lactation is impossible in the West without stores of fodder and no Bantu provided these.

Among Cape Nguni in 1931, Hunter observed that, although milk consumption fell during the winter months, families well endowed with cattle could sustain milk production the year round (Hunter 1936: 68-9). Though the observations of both Hunter and Kuper were made in modern times, they relate cattle to veld and climate, establishing the features of a relationship that has not changed drastically over the years.

To the extent that milk 'rivals grain' as an Nguni staple, it releases people from agricultural work. It is well established that pastoral activities generally require less input of labour than does agriculture. Bantu cattle-herding was not demanding of manpower because herding was generally the task of boys and younger men. The evidence is scanty, but it seems that the hoed house fields of the Nguni were not large (Hunter 1936: 73). Early observers noted that men among Sotho seemed to work more often with women in the fields than did Nguni males (Wangemann 1957: 35). Logic and sparse observations combine to suggest that, because they were more reliant on crops, non-Nguni peoples had to ensure a greater yield of grain per head to provide food. It therefore seems likely that, by adopting milk as a staple food, Nguni released labour from agriculture. But the most significant consequence of the closer integration of cattle into the Nguni economy was that the economy was more highly capitalized.

Capital, Interest and Work

For the Southern Bantu generally, the amount of cultivation done was limited only by the extent to which the manager of a holding had access to labour. A married household head had the right to demand an estate of production from his headman, a right he gained through membership of the headman's following. Fields could be extended or new fields established by tribesmen as long as they did not infringe on fields already allocated to others. Land was not scarce though, of course, choice land in any district would be recognized and be in demand. Thus, in so far as agricultural production is in the control of man, the amount of the harvest brought in by members of a production unit was a function of the amount and quality of their work. Investment in agriculture was investment in work. Cleared fields, recovered from the bush, were a capital asset. But cleared fields were exhausted after a number of seasons and, in any case, newly cleared land, fertilized with the ash of its natural cover which had been burned upon it, was more fertile. The best policy was to clear a little land each year (Hunter 1936: 72). Fields themselves were gained by expenditure of effort. In Bantu agriculture, therefore, there is a fairly direct relationship between the amount of labour invested and the amount of grain that accrues to the producer.

Cattle, however, are unlike fields because rights to cattle and their increase vest in individuals and in production units. While returns from land were a function of labour, returns from cattle were returns on capital investment. Cattle, as capital individually held, provide the means for spectacular discrepancies in wealth.

In his analysis of the place of cattle in the tribal economics of Eastern Africa, Schneider has distinguished between three economic roles that cattle play. Cattle serve as *real capital*, *money* and *consumption goods* (Schneider 1968: 427). For all Southern Bantu, cattle are the tribal equivalent of money. They are stores of value, standards of value and media of exchange. They provide what Schneider calls the 'big notes' rather than the 'small change' in tribal transactions.

As consumption goods, cattle are eaten. They also provide hides which Southern Bantu turned into cloaks, war shields, thongs etc. Cattle were slaughtered on occasion, usually a ritual occasion, and observers consistently report a reluctance to kill beasts 'merely for meat'. Further, in consumption of beef, there are rules of distribution based on criteria of kinship and residential association (Hammond-Tooke 1963). These hinder the use of meat as a commodity to be marketed. While all Southern Bantu celebrated marriages, gave funeral feasts and sacrificed to the ancestors, slaughtering beasts with each celebration, there are some indications that Nguni ate more meat than the Western tribesmen. Again the balance in diet between cattle-products and other foods seems to shift towards a greater emphasis on cattle in the East. Meat-eating is eating capital and a fine example of conspicuous consumption, something the richer Eastern economy could support.

In East and West cattle breed cattle and offer a return measured as the net reproduction rate of herds. The regional difference in this was that herds were exposed to less risk of drought in the East although, with concentration of cattle, risk of disease sweeping through the herds increases. Cattle manure lands incidentally as herds graze on stubble, and dung has uses in house building and can provide fuel. Sites of old byres can be cultivated to give high yields. In these ways cattle yield interest throughout Southern Africa.

Only Nguni, however, are able to make full use of milk as interest on capital. The Sotho herdboys who work at cattle posts drink milk. Milk from the cattle posts was also sent in skin bags to Sotho homes and milch cattle could be kept in the villages and towns. Milk was not wasted but, in relatively short supply, it was not a staple of Sotho-Tswana diet. In contrast, a well-managed Nguni herd yielded its owner a daily ration. If he produced milk surplus to the requirements of his household, a man could share it among members of his kraal, becoming a local provider and notable.

What one must recognize is that *all* transactions involving cattle are affected by their greater usefulness to Nguni. The contrast can be expressed this way: a Sotho cattle unit is a productive asset that yields an annual return which we can represent as X. A Nguni cattle unit yields an annual return that can be $X+M_s$, where M_s is the extra value ascribed to cattle that form part of a dairy herd in a region where milk is a staple. Nguni cattle are not the same economic good as cattle among Sotho. On moving from East to West we find that the nature of the beast has changed.

Grain: Equality of Production

Among Southern Bantu, discrepancies of wealth were expressed in cattle. Grain (the traditional crops were sorghum and millet) was a staple of diet and the commodity of equality. To place grain in the traditional economy, I show how production factors and related social values conspire to prevent the cultivation and accumulation of significant surpluses of grain among commoners.

Like cattle, grain served disparate ends. It was food with intrinsic worth. It was also money. Divisible down to single pellets, it provided 'small change' in the economy. It functioned as store and standard of wealth and as a medium of exchange, and grain could be converted into small stock and cattle. However, this apparent versatility was devalued.

In the first place, grain was not an efficient store of wealth. Southern Bantu stored their crops in large grain baskets or (especially among the Nguni) in grain pits. Grain stored in either pit or basket grows musty and there is risk of loss to rot and pests. Typically, part of the store from each crop was lost. Lack of adequate storage was a disincentive to surplus production (Beemer 1939: 215).

Among commoners there was an overall trend towards an equal per capita production of grain for disposal by the producer. This trend maintained the position of grain as the commodity of equality and was based on the principle of equal access to arable land. As unequal production could not be based on unequal access to land, any designed inequality would be produced by unequal access to labour.

In the first instance, field labour was recruited on a familial basis. Thus a manager who controlled a family unit in which the ratio of field-workers to non-workers was high, had an undeniable advantage. This yields the principle: build up a family in order to gain workers.

Familial recruitment apart, people worked in each other's fields in response to invitations to join work parties. A host provided beer or meat and then issued a general invitation to locals to attend a work party on his fields. Those attending a work party were expected to form a work gang and help to complete a set task. There was a general assumption of reciprocity in these arrangements: if I attend your work party, I expect you to attend mine. While the work party ensures concerted input of labour on an individual's field, expectation of reciprocity equalizes access to labour. The question is, to what extent did work parties give men the opportunity to employ extra hands for a beer or meat 'wage'? I argue that such opportunity was extremely limited.

Traditional cultivation was effected with digging-stick or hoe. Metal hoes were in short supply as the Pedi valuation equating a hoe with a beast indicates (Quin 1959: 19). Using a digging-stick, 'the cultivator squatted on her heels, held the stick in both hands, and dug with the sharpened point' (Hunter 1936: 74). With hoe and digging-stick there is a limit to the amount of land that can be turned by a labourer in a given time-span (cf. Kuper 1952: 27).

Available tools and the agricultural cycle created a peak demand for labour, a yearly period of full employment. In the cycle of work, the crucial period was the tilling and sowing season. Tilling and sowing are activities sandwiched between rains that fall sometime between October and December. The duration of the tilling season varies from year to year with the periodicity of rainfall. Hence the rains produced an annual race to complete the tilling of fields.

The dilemma of the man who wanted to produce grain in excess of the amount that he could sow through reliance on family labour, is that he must find additional labour at the peak period when everyone is busy on their own holdings. Rewards offered to non-familial workers must compensate them for investing labour in employers' fields rather than in their own. Beer and meat are a paltry reward, insufficient to induce people to invest labour in the tilling of the fields of others, when their own crops are at stake. The opportunity cost is too great. At the beginning of the season people would be willing to work for others on a reciprocal basis, but not for food alone. When tilling is completed and the work of weeding begins, there is more slack in the labour market. At this time some people could, if they wished, attend work parties given by a greater number of people than attended their own. Others could buy release from field labour by expenditure of beer or meat. In weeding and harvesting there is less urgency and less insistence on reciprocity of labour input.

I argue that the period of high employment was universal in Southern Africa and that a tightening of the conditions governing contributions of outside work was a general response to full employment. This period was succeeded by a time of greater flexibility when adjustments were possible. The Lobedu of the North Transvaal explicitly recognized this divide by organizing two types of work party, the *khilebe* and the *lejema*. Close neighbours and kin participated in the former, proceeding from the field of one member to that of the next in order. 'The great distinction between the *khilebe* and the *lejema* was and still is that no beer is provided' (E. J. and J. D. Krige 1943: 55). The *khilebe* was based on direct reciprocity of work. The *khilebe* was most important at time of tilling and this is evidenced by modern developments. In Lobedu country, the plough 'was perhaps the most potent agent of destruction of the old *khilebe*' (E. J. and J. D. Krige 1943: 55). The *lejema* still survives. The Lobedu *khilebe* was thus an institution that encapsulated the factors of production and technology that lead to an insistence on the strict application of the principle of reciprocity of work at the beginning of the annual cycle of production. In tribes without the *khilebe/lejema* distinction, the laws of supply and demand would ensure strict reciprocity in the work parties at tilling time.

A Tswana seasonal regulation enforced by the chief also falls into this perspective. In the 1930s Schapera noted that tilling was banned throughout the tribe once shoots appeared in the pace-setting field of the chief in which each of the distinct agricultural operations, beginning with tilling and ending with the harvest, was initiated year after year. Schapera could see no sense in this ban which, he comments, acted as a brake on production by limiting the total area brought under the plough. (Schapera 1943c: 186).

I argue that there was once a logic to this ban. While the chiefly termination of the ploughing season has become an anachronism, it served to abet the chief in his regulation of tribal production in the days when the Tswana tilled with digging-stick or hoe. In the days of hand implements a strict divide between the period of tilling and the period of weeding was required. The latter period was more relaxed. People competed freely for labour, enticing the needy or industrious to work on their fields for a reward of meat or beer. However, they could only improve the already cultivated area by working around standing crops. The area under cultivation could not be extended but was fixed, being made up of the arable established during the tilling season. There is thus a qualitative difference between the work of subsequent cultivation and the work of initial tilling. The first establishes the extent of the year's arable, the second improves the chances of a good harvest—weeding can be done once, twice or even three times within a growing season. If there was no regulation of the length of the tilling season, the poor and politically subordinate would suffer from unfair competition on two scores. First, it would be more difficult for them to arrange weeding parties on their own account when rich cattle-owners offered rewards of meat to vie with the poorer man's offering of beer. Then, the poor or the improvident or the politically susceptible might be tempted to neglect their own fields to till for an immediate return of provender or because they feared the power of a demanding tribal official. The limitation of the period of tilling thus worked to check the powers of a chief's vassals and to encourage a more even distribution of wealth measured in grain. The chief could only lose by relinquishing this aspect of his control. The overall result was that people generally reaped a harvest on lands whose size was directly related to the number of workers in a familial labour force.

Temporal control of tilling was a control of the total area put under crops. Through it, an overall limitation on the demand for labour was imposed.

To conclude, work parties did not provide an obvious opportunity for the mobilization of extra labour at the most critical time of the year. People generally reaped a harvest on lands whose size was determined by the number of workers in the familial labour force.

Anthropologists who study the Southern Bantu unanimously emphasize two cultural elements that affect farming by discouraging production of surpluses. The first of these is the principle of reciprocity in exchange, the second is fear of accusation of witchcraft. These disincentives, I contend, express values that emerge directly out of the mode of production. They are not, as some authors imply, things of a non-economic order that happen to affect economic life.

Reciprocity is the means by which Southern Bantu effect 'a system of social insurance' (Beemer 1939: 212). It means giving in response to another's need without expectation of direct or specific return: 'we give because one day we, too, will suffer the same need'. This is precisely the answer that Holleman's Zulu informants gave him when he asked them to explain their behaviour. He had noted that if a man was short of seed he would ask for some at the kraal of people unrelated to him without offering any payment (Holleman 1941: 248).

Reciprocity works to counter misfortune that strikes individuals. There are manifold reasons why one producer can experience need. In face of shortage, the unfortunate and needy seek help in the community. The prospect of a measure of help—provided disaster has not been general—lessens the need to keep and produce large reserves of grain to consume in bad years. Acts of apparently unstinting giving are the premiums in social insurance, contributions to a fund of goodwill.

Fear of accusation of witchcraft is a related disincentive to production of surpluses. Wealth incites envy and the envious accuse the wealthy of witchcraft, setting them down and detracting from their position in the community if the accusation is generally accepted. But there is an intervening step that links accusations of witchcraft to the primary value of reciprocity. It is not just wealth that causes resentment. Malice, and then accusation, is incited by hoarding and selfish use of wealth, by failure to share one's fortune with the less fortunate, rather than by wealth alone.

Martin (1903a: 34) described how South Sotho who harvested a bumper crop would store their surplus grain in secret hoards. They dug pits away from their homes in quiet places which they visited surreptitiously by night. The hoarder, wrote Martin, secreted grain 'to avoid unpleasantness'. The hoarder kept his surplus in selfish secrecy so that he and his own could consume it. He feared the needy who would beg grain if they knew he had it and whose frustration would burgeon as accusations of witchcraft if he did not answer their need. Sharing grain is more like sharing fortune than sharing goods. If everyone has worked in the fields, everyone should have a similar return. Spectacular success is thus attributed to magical practice rather than being regarded as the result of superior management.

Rights to land, labour relations, technical limitation, and the pattern of work thus act in concert to give grain its character as the commodity of equality rather than the capital of unequal ownership. The strictures on recruitment of field hands applied only to commoners. Political officers set the tilling season by having the first sod turned in their own fields. Followers gave service labour to chiefs and headmen before tilling for themselves. Privileged access to field labour and, hence, the right to keep and produce a surplus, was made an attribute of political office. Commoners could become wealthy in cattle: it was difficult for them to become wealthy in grain.

The contrast between Nguni and other peoples can be supplemented in terms of this argument. The greater Nguni emphasis on cattle was a stress on capital individually owned. For other people, whose grain is the main staple and milk merely a supplementary item of diet, there is less room in subsistence economies for expression of differences in wealth unless a system is devised to grant some men privileged access to labour. In the West there were *fewer* officials who could command followers to work their land. Fields of office were vested in chiefs, not headmen. The Nguni thus score twice, their economic organization placing greater surpluses in individual control on two counts.

Other Products

I deal summarily with other products in the traditional economy, not because they were unimportant, but because they fitted into the system of production and into the flow of exchange in ways that have been covered in discussion of cattle and grain. Other products fall into three categories: small stock, crops and veld products.

In addition to cattle, Southern Bantu kept sheep and goats. Small stock functioned like cattle: sheep and goats were individually owned. As consumption goods they provided meat and they were more readily slaughtered. As money, sheep and goat units stood between 'small change' and 'big notes' to facilitate exchange. Cattle could be broken down into goat units or goats converted into cattle. In the economy of the West, sheep and goats were an additional means by which the model strategy of diversity of investment could be pursued. The role of small stock, however, should not be overemphasized. Southern Bantu were primarily cattle-keepers.

Apart from grain, vegetable crops such as cucurbits, sweet reed, melons and calabashes were grown in fields or in small gardens. Tobacco was also cultivated. Crops other than grain were, for the most part, seasonal and perishable, defying storage. They supplemented and added variety to diet. Produced on arable land to which people enjoyed tribal rights, such crops were raised by family labour. Because they are perishable, these crops do not, like grain, offer a ready medium of exchange.

Veld products are of two kinds, game and the rest. Hunting was a male pursuit and the tribal hunter's weapons were the spear and the axe. Traps offered another means of securing game. Hunting larger game was seasonal, though smaller animals were available the year round.

The remaining products of the veld include a variety of vegetable foods that were cooked to make side-dishes and relishes. These have great significance in diet. In addition, raw materials were gleaned from the veld for a variety of purposes. Indigenous fruit-bearing trees were further sources of nutriment. Especially in the Transvaal region, the *morula* was fruit used in preparing a potent drink. Southern Bantu diet included exotic items such as caterpillars, flying ants and locusts. Chiefs maintained the right of general access to wild products. Thus the fruit of trees that grew on ploughed fields belonged to the person who picked them. No one could claim a tree simply because he ploughed around it. I have already described how a Pedi chief dealt with thatching grass. In the different regions, the local varieties of veld products were brought under similar régimes of administrative control.

Veld and garden products can be classified with grain for this reason: there is general access to the means of production and commoners acquire these products by expenditure of effort. The able-bodied and the skilful enjoy advantages over the unhealthy and the inept, but products of garden and veld present little opportunity to gain spectacular wealth, or to break free of the constraints of familial production. Again, political officers benefit as they receive specified portions of game killed and fractions of other products gained by their followers from the veld.

Division of Labour

Women performed domestic tasks. They prepared food, grinding grain, brewing beer and cooking. They kept house and made a variety of domestic artefacts and utensils. Women cared for children unless they could delegate this responsibility to girls. In the female sphere, girls grew into women's work as they became old enough to perform various tasks. Together, women and girls performed the daily chore of bringing water and firewood to their homes. A married woman cooked every day at her own hearth, providing food for inmates of her house. Women thus established the identity and unity of their houses as commensual units. Fowls, a source of food not yet mentioned, were a woman's concern.

Outside the home, the major brunt of agricultural work was a woman's lot. She was responsible for weeding fields, for harvesting, threshing, winnowing and for bringing the harvest home from the fields. Though men could help with these tasks, they were primarily a female responsibility. Women were the main collectors of veld foods.

Traditionally men did some of the heavier work in agriculture—clearing new fields, helping with tilling and sowing. We have already noted that Nguni men seem to spend less time in the fields than did men of other tribes.

In housebuilding, tasks were divided between the sexes, the allocation of these tasks varying slightly between tribes. Among Tswana, men fashioned the wooden parts of the house, making and fitting the rafters and doors. The work of packing soil for walls, and of plastering and applying decorative motifs was the woman's part. Using the technique they employed in laying courtyards at home, women made threshing floors in the fields.

Care and management of stock was exclusively a male preserve. Indeed, notions about ritual impurity effectively kept women away from cattle which in Bantu belief are subject to mystical contamination by females. The main work of herding and milking was done by boys and youths under adult supervision. The Zulu *amasi* is made by men, who are also responsible for the care of the milking vessels. The butchering of animals is also male work. Cattle byres, fenced with poles or with brushwood, are set up by men.

Artefacts were manufactured by men and women who made objects deemed appropriate to their sex. Men were carvers and did all work in leather and bone. Women did beadwork and were potters. Many sorts of basket were woven, some types being made by men and others by women.

Hunting was a male activity. Chiefs organized the most rewarding hunts when men of the chiefdom beat the bush, moving in formation reminiscent of the line of battle. On collective hunts, the man whose spear first struck an animal claimed it, though he surrendered a portion to the chief. Independent hunting was also done. The weapons used—axe, spear and (unique to the Venda) the bow and arrow—were made by men.

There were trends towards specialization in the making of pots and the working of iron. These activities tended to be associated with particular families. The ritual specialist or doctor was probably the only man—important chiefs apart—who could hope to be released from the common run of subsistence activities. Lack of specialization implies lack of trading opportunity. The unspecialized economy was essentially redistributive, a major incentive to exchange being the need to even out differential surpluses between production units.

The Management of Familial Production

In regulating the tribal economy, officials provided a setting in which the main work of familial production could be carried out. I now briefly sketch a model that comprehends management of the family estate.

Men became managers of production units as they married wives and established them in houses. Figure 5.2 depicts the elementary unit of production and management. Its members are a married couple and their children. The assets tied to it are family holdings in fields and cattle. Working from their home, the family members also had access to the resources of veld and pasture. They carried out tasks appropriate to their age and sex.

While a husband managed the estate, he was required to respect the rights of his wife and children. Family assets were segregated into *house property* and *men's property*, a divide represented by the line XY in Figure 5.2. A wife was identified with the house set up for her and the notion of 'a house' comprehended its inmates (a woman and her children) plus property assigned to them. A wife was supplied with a house field, a house granary, a hearth and domestic goods. These were hers by right, and she could sue for their provision if her husband denied them. The produce of the house field was stored in the house granary controlled by the housewife. In Tswana tribes, wifely control over house grain was made patent as women often stored their grain in their mother's homes where a husband could not purloin it (Schapera 1943c: 200). Men needed grain to provide the beer of hospitality and for use in barter. Such grain was the product of men's fields set aside to provide it. Men's grain was separately stored.

Cattle, tended exclusively by men, could also be assigned to houses, and rights in the family herd were apportioned between the house and a man's holding. Thus the line XY cuts through the cattle byre. Cattle assigned to a house were used to further the interests of its inmates. Like the grain of the house granary, house cattle could be disposed of by a husband only in consultation with his wife. The demands of bridewealth occasioned spectacular fluctuation in the size of the family herd. For each daughter married out of a house, there was compensation in marriage cattle supplied by her husband. Marriage cattle were attached to a bride's natal house to become part of its holding. There was a presumption that incoming marriage cattle would be used again as bridewealth to enable a son of the house to marry. Brothers and sisters were often paired and 'cattle-linked', the sister being regarded as the enabler of her brother's marriage. In this, one can see an attempt to make exchange of bridewealth self-sustaining and autonomous, a system bound to function imperfectly for obvious reasons. First, it would demand an equal number of sons and daughters to be born into each house. Second, demand for cattle was not a unitary demand for cattle as bridewealth and cattle could not be perpetually reserved to finance marriage. Bridewealth demands had, from time to time, to be made subordinate to other more immediate requirements for cattle as consumption goods or as the medium of exchange in other transactions. The effects of bridewealth exchange on the size of the family herd are well illustrated by the situation among Lobedu in modern times. Owning few cattle on the restricted pastures of their reserve, bridewealth exchange absorbs almost all Lobedu cattle. The result is that today, 'most Lovedu families do not possess cattle except for short periods of time' (Krige 1964: 160). The number of cattle involved in traditional bridewealth exchange

TRADITIONAL ECONOMIC SYSTEMS

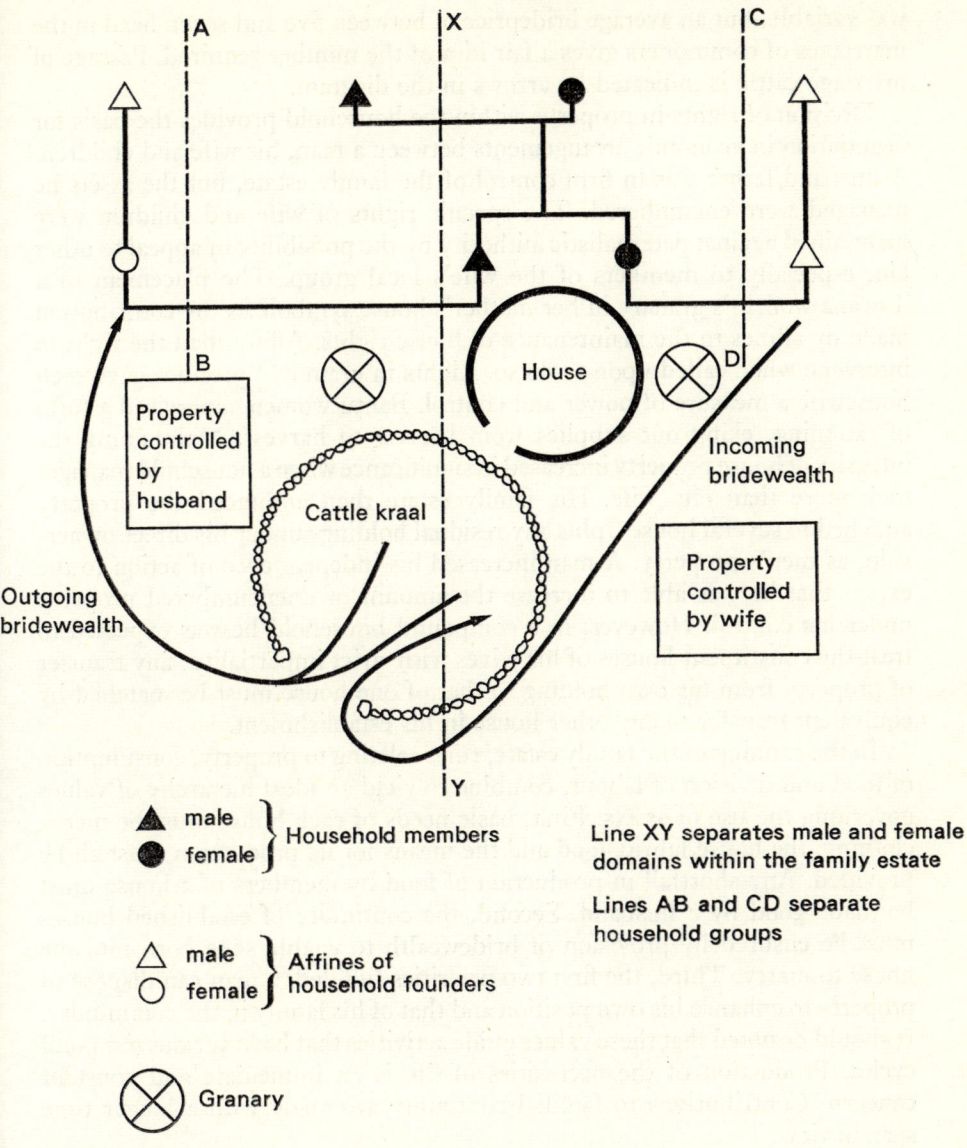

FIGURE 5.2 *The house-property complex*

was variable, but an average brideprice of between five and seven head in the marriages of commoners gives a fair idea of the number required. Passage of marriage cattle is indicated by arrows in the diagram.

Division of rights in property within the household provides the basis for negotiation in economic arrangements between a man, his wife and children. A husband/father was in firm control of the family estate, but the assets he managed were encumbered. The specific rights of wife and children were maintained against paternalistic authority by the possibility of appeal to other kin, especially to members of the wife's local group. The placement of a Tswana woman's granary in her mother's house symbolizes the contribution made by affines to the maintenance of house rights. Affines had the right to intervene when called upon to do so. Rights in grain and produce gave each housewife a measure of power and control. Bantu women supervised a form of rationing, eking out supplies from harvest to harvest. Maintaining the integrity of house property increased in significance when a household manager took more than one wife. His family estate then embraced the property attached to several houses, plus any residual holdings under his direct ownership, as men's property. A man increased his independence of action to the extent that he was able to increase the amount of unencumbered property under his control. However, in a compound household he was expected to treat the constituent houses of his wives with strict impartiality: any transfer of property from his own holding to that of one house must be matched by equivalent transfer to any other house in his establishment.

In the running of the family estate, rules relating to property, consumption of food and division of labour, combine to yield an ideal hierarchy of values governing the use of assets. First, basic needs of each house must be met—clothing, the house fabric, food and the means for its production must all be provided. Any shortfall in production of food by members of a house must be made good by a husband. Second, the continuity of established houses must be ensured by provision of bridewealth to enable sons born into the house to marry. Third, the first two priorities fulfilled, a man can dispose of property to enhance his own position and that of his family in the community. It should be noted that these values guide activities that have various temporal cycles. Production of the necessities of life is an immediate and constant concern. Contributions to familial continuity are made with a longer time span in view.

This descriptive model shows disposition of property in the elementary family. But elementary families were always integrated into larger local groups. Neither elementary families nor the plural families of polygynists could stand alone. Local groups in which household heads joined were recruited on agnatic principles, and there were two major economic bases for combination. First, in the organization of work, the local group was a unit in which there was co-operation across divides that separate familial estates, each with its complement of family labour. It is obvious that the ratio of family workers to non-producing consumers and the ratio of male to female workers within each elementary family alters with family development. Work-capability and the demand for food etc. varies over time for each house and household. The local group of kinsmen was a context in which these differences could be evened out. In equalizing the amount of grain available per family member, the emphasis was on shared labour rather than on shared produce. The ethic of the Lobedu *khilebe*, discussed above, exemplifies this. To satisfy their requirements, large households cultivated bigger fields with the help of kinsmen. Exchange of harvested produce created specific debt between houses in the local group.

Fields allow greater individuation of control than do cattle which must be managed as herds. The herd was associated with the local group and the management of group herding facilitated adjustment to the ebb and flow of cattle-holdings due to exchange of cattle in marriage transactions. In herd-management, the reproduction of cattle could be correlated with human increase and the social control of human mating. Marriage promised children just as ownership of a heifer promised a calf. Thus expectations of human and cattle increase could be balanced against one another to create complicated debt relationships. If a man needed to finance a marriage and cattle were not immediately available, he could contract debts, pledging future income in bridewealth against the immediate acquisition of a bride. Thus the indication of the flow of cattle in the diagram is over-simple. Cattle are not always provided from the family estate and income from the marriage of daughters may accrue to outsiders to whom it has been pledged. Gluckman, writing about Zulu, indicates the ensuing complications.

> In a simple legal family, if a man gave the cattle himself he or his sons are entitled to all the cattle of his daughters. But if he borrowed the cattle and has not repaid the loan, the lender can claim the cattle of his elder daughter. If the lender is the father's chief, the father would not offer to return them, because it is an honour for his eldest daughter to 'belong' to the chief. If the husband did not deliver the marriage-cattle to his affines they claim the eldest daughter's cattle; and a poor man can marry a wife by pledging his eldest daughter thus. If he has no daughter, there is no liability (Gluckman 1950: 194–5).

This implies a chain of bridewealth transactions that can span generations. People who give daughters on promise of bridewealth, or those who invest cattle in the marriage of their kin, invest at risk yet receive no interest. Indeed, they lose the natural increase of cattle disposed in this way. However, their investment of cattle does yield a return. Men are bound to others through cattle, owing them special loyalty. Cattle are converted into fealty and political support.

The following economic consequences can be adduced from the integration of cattle into marriage arrangements:

(1) Because every man can reasonably press his claim to a wife, local ethics

demand that wealthy kinsmen or chiefs contribute towards the marriage of sons of houses that are poor in cattle. This establishes a trend towards redistribution of large holdings in cattle.

(2) The linking of cattle to family development produces an ebb and flow in family holdings of cattle and each manager of a family estate must calculate in terms of it.

(3) Modification of the composition of the family estate of one man through addition of wives entailed modification of the cattle-holding of the estate. With each polygynous marriage, the ratio between family members and cattle held alters unfavourably.

(4) These consequences imply a criterion for wealth measured as number of cattle owned. The wealthy man has sufficient cattle to make him independent of inescapable familial and kinship demands in the disposition of his investments.

Cattle can be invested in several ways, each with differing implications. They may be used to enable the marriages of (a) kinsmen or (b) non-kin. They may be herded out, a practice which reduces their visibility. They may be given to others who, in return, become political supporters, followers or clients of the donor.

Cattle are inherited and the rules of inheritance maintain continuity of local groups and, at the same time, create authority within them. The main heir of a family estate—the first son of a first wife—takes his father's unencumbered property. In addition, he is heir to the property of his mother's house, controlling the cattle associated with it. Sons of lesser houses inherit house cattle in their respective houses, there being a main heir to each house. Fathers may also assign property to particular sons before they die. In general, the economic consequences of inheritance are to create viable household units and to distribute both cattle and authority in a manner that gives continuity to the pattern of economic life within local groups. Because significant numbers of cattle pass from one owner to another as bridewealth and portions of inheritance, fortune plays a large part in determining individual success. Sex, birth-order, and the health of children are deemed. As a man can inherit debts as well as goods, his heritage plays a large part in determining his economic status after marriage.

Finally, the effects of the different valuation of cattle in East and West may be related to the nature of local groups as economic units.

The Nguni kraal is pre-eminently a cattle herding and milk producing corporation that cannot be conceived apart from cattle. The corporateness of kraals and their unity is manifest in practices that relate to the management of herds and in the rules that govern the consumption of milk. For Nguni, the cattle byre is itself the architectural centre of kraal life, an exclusive structure private to kraal members. Nguni belief made the herd of a kraal distinctive, decreeing that it was mystically dangerous for cattle held by one kraal to approach the byre of another local group (Krige 1936a: 188). Each Zulu kraal owned its own small pasture (*idlelwana*) near the byre. Here some cattle could be left to stand while others were being tended in the byre (J. F. Holleman 1941: 255). These small pastures had no Western parallel. But, most emphatic of all, taboos on the drinking of milk dictated that only kinsmen who shared the same patronym (*isibongo*) and a few of their blood kin could drink milk from the kraal herd (Krige 1936a: 34). Rules of exogamy corresponded with rules governing consumption of milk for they specified the same kin: Nguni can drink the milk of those whose daughters they cannot marry. The kraal herd fed the men for whom it supplied bridewealth. Commensality of milk could be extended to outsiders only if they accepted brotherhood with kraal members (Krige 1936a: 34). When adopted into a kraal, a man shared the marriage restrictions of its members. Adopted men were normally dependants. Thus joint management of a herd and the sharing of its milk was a corporate affair.

The demand for cattle among Nguni was qualitatively different from that among Western tribes. Western peoples ran breeding herds, their main concern being to secure increase for bridewealth, loans, or for consumption as meat. Nguni herds had to provide increase for these purposes but they were dairy herds as well. In management of a dairy herd, continuity of milk production is the aim. Southern Bantu exercised no control over mating of cattle and, hence, the most important method of ensuring a steady milk supply was to combine cattle in sufficient numbers. One man's holding was insufficient unless he was very wealthy. Thus the kraal herd was treated as a unit that produced milk for kraal members. While individual rights in cattle and the milk they yielded were explicit, there was a daily distribution of milk among the inhabitants of the kraal. The ban on drinking milk produced in the kraals of non-kinsmen was not an impediment to herding-out arrangements. Cattle placed in other kraals were held by them and milked in that kraal's byre. The Nguni kraal was, therefore, a corporation whose members showed their ability to gain and hold sufficient cattle to keep members supplied with milk.

In the West, the main herds were kept out at cattle posts. There herdboys drank milk regularly and, while the wet season lasted, sent some milk to families in the town, the milk being transported in skin bags. To get milk a youth did not have to belong to a group that held cattle. Rather, milk was the return for herding service and, naturally, a herdboy would probably work with family cattle if there were any. But the separation of cattle post and home, plus the absence of any restrictions on the consumption of milk, enabled Westerners to treat herdboys as labourers who should be employed where there were cattle to herd. This is another instance of greater Western flexibility in the ties that bind people to each other in economic co-operation. Herd management did not emphasize the unity of the local group to the extent achieved among Nguni.

Individuals in the West were better able to cope with fluctuations in herd size occasioned by bridewealth demands. Thus a Tswana, W., has eight cattle, and wishes to take a second wife. The marriage requirements will take six of his cattle, leaving him with two. These two are cows and one cow is in calf. W. is complacent that the next time demands are made on his herd, he will have increase. In addition, W.'s eldest daughter by his first wife will marry within the next few years. He calculates that he can afford the second wife. Comparable calculations by a Nguni would have been complicated by the need of the individual to be associated with a milk-producing herd. His marital arrangements affect the interests of fellow kraal members more closely, for any man's marriage can diminish the kraal holding in cattle and, hence, affect the production of milk. This points up the greater emphasis on cattle as a focus of corporate life in the East.

Property in cattle and property in grain can again be contrasted to make this point. Cattle were not so much consumption goods as productive assets. By herding-out arrangements, a man surrendered the milk of his cattle while retaining ownership. He might also surrender part of the increase. The difference between cattle held (though owned by others) and cattle owned is that the former cannot be slaughtered or used in transactions by the holder. By lending cattle, at least part of their productive value is distributed, even though ownership is maintained. Further, ownership was rendered less visible by herding out arrangements. Remember that men herd out cattle, not only because they are surplus to their requirements, but also to spread risk. A man with a small herd may put out some cattle, and being the owner of an animal thus disposed does not necessarily indicate wealth. A man's wealth can be measured only if the total number of cattle lent out by him is known. In herding out arrangements there was the constant possibility that the owner could recall his stock. This is an obvious sanction that can be used to ensure a debtor's compliance to a lender's wishes.

A circle in the argument about exchange can now be completed. If a man is poor in cattle and wishes to acquire a herd, his best recourse is not to build up a surplus in other commodities to be exchanged for beasts. Instead, he should use ties of social obligation. First, kinsmen may be willing to help him. If kinsmen fail, or if indebtedness towards them is unattractive, non-relatives may be sought. Among Nguni, a man could (a) become a milk-drinking dependant and lowly member of an unrelated kraal, (b) seek cattle under the herding-out system to provide milk, (c) try to gain cattle as an outright gift from chief, headman or wealthy herd-owner. In all of these alternatives, fealty is offered against cattle. Similarly, in marriage alliance, the bond between contracting parties can be given a special character if full payment of bridewealth is deferred. What should be eminently clear is that Nguni peoples were overly concerned with cattle, their economy was more highly capitalized, the drive to own cattle was intense, the people more acquisitive.

The Western manager of a local group held cattle, but they were not the overweening cause of his prominence. Sotho peoples are notable for their readiness to resign membership of one group to join another (Schapera

1956: 28). This is partly a reflection of their policy of dispersed investment. The members of a local group managed fewer of their assets jointly than did Nguni. Groups were more flexible, able to reform and less incorporative. The manager of a local group tried to hold a number of people together by treating his group as a holding that should include people whose various assets combined together so that one man's deficits would be complemented by another's surplus. The best manager was able to secure rights of access for his group to a variety of resources that, inevitably, were distributed over the tribal territory. If he was unable to do this, he would have to resign himself to the knowledge that his followers would dilute his authority over them by multiplying their arrangements with people outside the group in order to satisfy their striving to spread investments. A paradox in the organization of Sotho groups is that the more that members extend links that give them access to resources outside the group, the better group members are able to complement one another's activities. A group whose members' assets are well distributed through outside involvement—a counter to group unity—can be better able to redistribute a variety of products among members and this gives the group a *raison d'être*. Headmen and those who sought prominence had to contend perpetually with such countervailing tendencies in economic arrangements.

The Dual Economy

My analysis of the traditional economy has exhibited its inherent limitations. One by one these could be modified as Africans began to earn cash. But, in Southern Africa, a new set of limitations is imposed to inhibit the free play of economic factors in effecting the transformation of the economic activity of Africans. Most importantly, restrictive labour policies and the support of conservative administrations by tribal authorities, preserve the backwardness of the tribal areas. Because opportunities for urban employment exist almost wholly within the Republic of South Africa, the territories of Lesotho, Botswana and Swaziland, though politically independent, resemble the tribal areas of that state. People of the three territories must, like tribesmen of South African Reserves, submit to a regimen of control of influx of Africans into towns. This is a control of the rural man's access to alternative opportunities for employment. A large population of Africans are restricted to the role of migrant labourer, travelling to and fro between country and town. Tribesmen combine work for wages in town with rural production. The stubborn persistence of a dual economy in the Southern Bantu areas is a product of the consistent policy of successive South African governments.

This general background to modern economic life in a tribal area is presented in a later chapter. My task here is to trace the development of a dual economy in the tribal areas, but the delineating features of the overall situation must be re-stated. The African areas are now geographically delimited and, within them, there is an ever-increasing population, both human and bovine, that exceeds the capacity of local resources to support it. In most areas, with over-use of land, a cycle of degradation of rural resources is under way. Everywhere, manufactured items replace those made by local craftsmen, and demand for an increasing range of consumer goods has been created. Failing permanent migration of the population to work-centres, the general trend is for an increase in the rate of labour migration measured as the number of males temporarily absent from tribal homes. The tribal area is increasingly dependent on export of labour, and wages provide for basic needs of the rural population. For many, ultimate security in sickness and old age lies in ownership of scanty rural assets. This binds Africans, especially the uneducated, to the rural areas.

Since its inception, the dual economy has moved through three stages of development. The first step was the initial creation of dualism by the addition of a novelty cash economy to subsistence activities. In the second phase, the market economy increased in importance: it co-existed with subsistence production but the cash sector and the subsistence sector were maintained as separate spheres. The final phase is that of interpenetration, when two sources of income—wages and agricultural products—can be recognized, but when the distinction based on source of income no longer provides the basis for the separation of two seemingly autonomous systems for organizing labour and exchange. Preparatory to a description of these developments, I outline the substantive changes in subsistence production that the opening of African areas to outside influences has produced.

Subsistence Production Today

The most dramatic changes in subsistence production have been occasioned by a general shortage of land, due both to population increase among Africans and their restriction to defined areas. Next, technological innovations have altered the work of production. Finally, changes in values and in organization result from the absence of migrants and from the extent to which people of particular areas live on wages rather than on rural produce.

In attempts to reform tribal agriculture, whites have been most successful in the introduction of a few simple items of technology. But there has been an overall failure to convert tribesmen to Western techniques of farm management, a failure predetermined by the poverty of the tribal areas. With the partial exception of Botswana, where the cattle trade assumes importance (Landell-Mills 1970: 81), the tribal areas present no real opportunities for production of crops or animals for sale. Cash-cropping demands land, and tribal lands are insufficient. Nor, given shortage of resources, are there significant possibilities for rural investment. Modern farming techniques are geared to production of cash returns, a proportion of which can be re-invested to expand or improve the farmer's assets. With acute shortage of land, the conditions for modern farm management are subverted.

The scarce land of the tribal areas is apportioned to individuals on traditional lines. Tribal authorities have had to adapt customary land tenure to meet new conditions of shortage. Gluckman summarizes the general trend:

> The first step by the chief was to take power to commandeer land allocated to a subject which he was not using, for distribution to the landless. Then —in a developmental series—the chief took power to take over for the landless, land which had lain fallow for a certain period: the cycle of soil degradation has here begun. The final step was to restrict each family to a limited area of garden land. People get around these laws by various devices, but the trend of development in the view of both the leaders and the mass of tribesmen is clear. Every man who is a member of the tribe has a right to live and support his family on the tribal land (Gluckman 1961: 78).

While this is a statement of ideal policy that the best chiefs maintain, scarcity of land and the general demand for it provide opportunity for bribery and other malversation in particular chiefdoms and districts (e.g. Hammond-Tooke 1962: 147; 1964: 520–1; Jaspan 1953).

With the preservation of rules that allow general access to field and pastures, the shortage of land becomes pervasive and leads to insecurity of ownership for all. Lands used by a family are subject to progressive attrition in order to satisfy the demands of landless people. The insecure situation favours short-term exploitation of local resources and does not encourage producers to think in terms of investing to improve them.

Draught Animals and the Plough

Introduction of the plough caused cattle, previously unused as draught animals, to be inspanned and, because cattle management is men's work, brought male labour onto the fields at ploughing time. More extensive cultivation is now possible and tillage is no longer the critical business described for the time when primitive implements were used. In addition, cattle are used to draw sledges and wagons. Donkeys, another innovation, serve as substitutes for cattle as draught animals and enter the tribal economy.

Apart from making work in the fields less onerous, the plough has brought other changes. A plough is capital equipment and, similarly, the plough team represents capital. The role of cattle as draught animals adds a further dimension to herd management. In addition to controlling the composition of herds to provide milk, meat and beasts for exchange, oxen are appropriately included if a man is to exhaust the productive potential of herd-ownership.

Plough teams alter the traditional conception of work in agriculture which can now be regarded in terms of wages. First, the ploughman may stay in the tribal area to till instead of going to town to work. Thus the cost of ploughing for an individual who owns the equipment can be the cost of wages foregone. Returning home for ploughing has been reported for several areas (e.g. Schapera 1947; Houghton and Walton 1952: 145). Secondly, absentee migrants or people without ploughs can employ a ploughman to till their fields either for cash payment or on a crop-sharing basis (Houghton and Walton 1952: 142f; Sansom 1970). In the 1930s among the Lobedu, the Kriges identified a new type of work-group that centred on men who owned ploughs (E. J. and J. D. Krige 1943: 42). At that time the plough-owning leader of the Lobedu group did not benefit financially from the arrangement. Rather, he was paid in the coin of prestige. Later accounts of other areas (cited above) show that remuneration for ploughing is now accepted. By paying money for this service, absent migrants can find country surrogates who play the absentee's part in rural production. Supplying plough service becomes one of the few rural enterprises that yield cash. The poor in the tribal area stand at a marked disadvantage: every year they must somehow find the means to make an annual cash investment in tilling the land.

Crops

Maize has, in many areas, ousted the traditional sorghum and millet as a staple crop. Non-indigenous vegetables provide new gardening possibilities and crops such as beans open up the way for rotation of crops. However, gardens are generally small, partly due to irrigation problems, and the possibility of rotation has been little exploited. Cereal monoculture remains the dominant mode.

Trading Stores

Trading stores were established early on in all African areas. Today traders, both white and African, make manufactured goods available and import food into the tribal area. Everywhere traders also conduct a brisk trade in locally produced grain. However, they serve mainly to redistribute grain among the local population, evening out unequal production as they buy from some families and sell to others. Only in years of bumper harvests do the traders sell grain on outside markets. It seems that every observer who reports on the part traders play in the rural economy, has commented on what I refer to as the trader's practice of holding grain in pawn. At the time of harvest, when the price of grain is low, tribespeople—especially women—sell grain to a trader to realize cash which they spend in his store. Later in the year, with their granaries empty, many women find it necessary to recoup grain, and buy it back from the trader at a higher price than they received. In their comments, authors generally note this practice as rural improvidence. This important activity is better understood as a system for lending cash at interest with grain as security. The motivation that drives women to use it inheres in the organization of the household economy and I shall discuss it presently.

Finally, I note that, countering the introduction of new elements into subsistence production, the significance of the veld as a source of food has generally declined. Game has been killed out in most of the reserves in the

PLATE 7
Agriculture

Milking (Kgatla)
Tlôkwa woman
potter, Gaberone,
Botswana, 1962

PLATE 8
Interior of a Zulu hut

South African Republic although hunting is still of great importance to some of the peoples of Botswana, notably the Kgalagadi (von Richter 1970). Denudation of forest cover and progressive conversion of veld to pasture and arable has decreased the area available for collecting wild foods.

Three Phases of Development

1867 is a climactic year in the economic history of Southern African peoples. In Kimberley, the diamond diggings were opened and a demand for African labour was created around mining operations in a part of the Cape with a sparse African population. The Tsonga, hundreds of miles away towards Mozambique, call 1867 'Diamond', the year of the diamonds (Junod 1927). Centralized mining enterprise initiated the fact that continues to dominate tribal areas. Outside tribal territory there is a regional demand for migrant labour.

Watson (1958) and others have noted that patrilineal peoples in Africa seem better able to adapt the tribal economy to migrant labour than those with matrilineal kinship. The matrilineal Bemba of Rhodesia provide an example of the rapid deterioration of a rural economy based on agriculture once migrant labour is introduced (Richard 1939). In discussing the traditional economy, a distinction emerged between domestic production for household surplus and the household manager's participation in prestige economics. This division has been projected into modern economic organization. In a sense, males are detachable from the household economy. A wife's rights to house, house field and associated property remain intact, as does the house as an economic sub-unit. Over-simply but tellingly put, men could remove the locus of their activities and, where traditionally cattle had provided a focus for their efforts, cash could be assimilated to cattle and treated like them in financing a man's endeavours to place himself and his family within the wider society. To a degree, these features of traditional organization have minimized the impact of male absenteeism.

In the initial phase of the dual economy, cash earned as wages was used to satisfy new demands for manufactured goods. Thus Aylward, a Fenian who espoused the Boer cause, saw, during his campaigning in the Transvaal, tribesmen who were 'well acquainted with both breeches and breech-loaders' which they bought at the diamond fields (Aylward 1878: 188). His description confirms Morton's observation of the habits of early labour migrants on the diamond fields. He noted that, typically, workers stayed for a three-month stint 'remaining just long enough to supply each worker with a gun and ammunition' (Morton, in van der Horst 1942: 15). As the tribal areas were brought under white control, imposition of taxes, to be paid in cash, created a demand. Taxes were seen by officials as an incentive to provision of labour for industrialization. This is a period in which subsistence production continues in the traditional way while cash is obtained to satisfy novel demands.

The second phase is initiated when cash is used to buy essential household items. What is essential to households is also redefined to include goods such as imported cloth, utensils and blankets. Money and subsistence sectors become irreversibly engaged when cash is used to buy clothes, food or the implements used in its production.

However, in the second phase, the relationship between subsistence sector and cash sector is one of separation and co-existence. Although bound together, both sections retain a high degree of autonomy. For tribespeople there are now two ways of dealing: one may either conduct exchanges in the traditional manner or one can conduct what Lobedu in the 1930s called *bizmus* (E. J. and J. D. Krige 1943). The remarkable feature of the economy of the tribal areas is the protracted length of the phase of co-existence. In some tribal areas, even the latest reports indicate that the notion of co-existence is still applicable. The general trend during this period is the progressive enlargement of the market sector—*bizmus*—at the expense of the modes germane to the traditional relationships between subsistence producers.

The significance of co-existence is best exemplified with reference to the media of exchange and exchange rates. In the Pedi Reserve today, there are two possible ways of purchasing a pot. One may give the potter a standard price of fifteen cents for a cooking pot called *pitsa*. Alternatively, the traditional rule of the Southern Bantu areas that pots are priced at their own volume of grain may be invoked. There is an anomaly in this. Grain is a commodity with a fluctuating market price: the worth of a volume of grain, in money terms, varies from month to month. One could calculate which gave the better bargain at a particular time—payment in cash or in grain. This example illustrates a general feature in the phase of co-existence. Traditional products and commodities which have a fluctuating value in the outside money market are, in the tribal area, given fixed value. Parity in local rates that equate grain, cattle, money and other items is maintained by chiefs.

The effects of fixed prices are most spectacular when livestock is considered. In the tribal areas, relatively constant equivalences between items was maintained. This is illustrated in Table 5.2 which shows exchange rates reported in various areas.

Fixed equivalents in dealings between tribesmen was a solution adopted in solving the problem raised when people wanted to conduct exchanges across the divide separating subsistence and market sectors. For a long time, fixed equivalents were maintained despite knowledge of and access to prevailing values in the outside market. Grain was bought by traders and a limited trade in importing and exporting of stock occurred across the boundaries between tribal and white domains. A tribesman was in the position to note that his favourite cow was worth a fixed £5 in the tribal area while, outside, it would fetch, perhaps, £12. In 1962, in the Pedi area, cows in fair condition fetched about £30 when sold to white farmers. The local fixed price was £5. In Pondoland during the depression the discrepancy worked in the reverse direction: the tribal price was £5 while the merchant price was £3.

TABLE 5.2 *Livestock and money equivalents*

People	Date of observation	Rates	Source
Tswana	1930s	£5 = 1 heifer = 5 sheep = 10 goats	Schapera (1938a: 242)
Keiskammahoek Reserve	1949	£5 = 1 head cattle	Houghton and Walton (1952: 170)
Bhaca	1949	£5 = 1 head cattle = 1 horse = 10 sheep/goats	Hammond-Tooke (1962: 134)
Pedi	1961	£5 = 1 head cattle = 10 goats	Sansom (1970: 157)
Mpondo	1933	£5 = 1 beast = 10 sheep/goats	Hunter (1936: 140)

Schapera sums up the Tswana situation in the 1930s. 'The introduction of European currency has provided a standard medium of exchange, but in many cases, the old relative values still persist. Among the Kgatla and Ngwato, e.g., a heifer is generally sold for £5, a sheep for £1' (Schapera 1938a: 242). Schapera posits the existence of two independent markets, internal and external economy. In this exposition I follow his lead.

The choice between two types of transaction in the periods of co-existence is largely based on the role-relations between the transacting parties: it is not a choice about conventions of sale between the same contracting parties, but a choice one man makes about the identity of the other partner to a contemplated exchange. You may have cash dealings with the trader on a market basis, or you may transact with a fellow-tribesman on the basis of fixed tribal equivalents. As the period of co-existence comes to an end, fellow-tribesmen appear in the role of men doing *bizmus*. As *bizmus* relations become more pervasive, the market and subsistence sectors of the economy no longer co-exist. They interpenetrate.

During the phase of co-existence, market values become increasingly relevant in agricultural production. The presence of the trading stores is significant for here women, in particular, sell fractions of their crop at market prices. Food, the agricultural product, is related to cash, not as a cash crop, but because shortfalls must be made good through purchase and because introduced foods are also bought. The capitalization of ploughing with its commitment of work for wages, introduces market calculation into rural production.

Given the division of labour in which women weed, harvest, thresh and then control consumption of grain stored in their own granaries, female production in the tribal area is increasingly related to cash, which thus invades the subsistence sector.

Cattle management, in contrast, is the last stronghold of traditional modes. Cattle are managed by men, who are able to adjust the size of their herds by working in town for wages. Herds are not managed to produce consumption goods. They are relevant in bridewealth transactions and as stores of value—the only long-term investment the tribesman is likely to make. Thus in their analysis of Kieskammahoek, Houghton and Walton use a model in which cattle are a source of investment, to be sold only to meet direct family needs. In Keiskammahoek, cattle were a wasting asset often killed off by drought. Thus men invested at high risk in stock that held little prospect of economic return. In the district, 80 per cent of bridewealth was paid in cattle. Although a standard cattle equivalent of £5 was recognized, fathers insisted on cattle bridewealth for their daughters with the consequence that commutation of cattle payments into cash payments was inhibited (Houghton and Walton 1952: 170). Similarly, among the Lobedu, the Kriges (reporting in the 1930s) noted that nearly every transaction in which cattle were exchanged between tribesmen was a transaction involving payment of bridewealth (E. J. and J. D. Krige 1943: 66). The last stage in the phase of co-existence is reached with breakdown of the relative autonomy of cattle exchange.

In co-existence, people stationed in the rural area are producers of agricultural products and consumers of food. Men earn wages and have to supplement the income of their wives with contributions of cash. But men, generally, wish to invest in the prestige economy and buy cattle. There is thus an opposition in male and female responsibilities and ambitions. Women are more concerned with the immediate needs of the family than with a husband's long-term plans. This division is basic to adjustment to labour migration. The traditional kinship system with its patrilineal emphasis and definition of a woman's rights in her house, makes it possible. Pawning grain, a female activity, falls into this perspective. Women pawn grain at harvest time in order to raise sums for purchase of supplementary items of diet, new clothes and a few luxury consumer goods. They expect husbands to make good any shortfall they experience later in the year. During my own research, I found that women, when in want, would also borrow from other tribespeople during the absence of migrant husbands or sons. Thus a woman can accumulate debt and have pawned grain to redeem on her husband's return. In this way, women can bring pressure to bear on men to increase cash contributions to the household budget. Pawning and debt also function to ensure the upkeep of a woman's household during extended periods of absence of the wage-earner. Even if he sends regular remittances, these are not calculated to take care of contingencies that demand expenditure.

The final phase of interpenetration is reached when economic transactions are generally calculated in market terms. The economy remains a dual economy only in the sense that the participants have two sources of income and must divide their time between town and country. Reader, describing petty trade items among Makhanya, shows how fixed equivalents no longer apply. 'The new rule in barter is to equalize each commodity of the exchange in terms of its cash value. If a paraffin tin of madumbes is worth 5s. at current rates, and a calabash is priced at 2s. 6d., then it will exchange for half a tin of madumbes' (Reader 1966: 41). In contemporary Sekhukhuneland, marriage negotiations are commercial transactions. Although £5 is called 'a cow' and 50p 'a goat', these sums are not regarded as equivalent in value to animals. The bride's father determines a cash amount that he would like to receive and the groom must make it up in stock and/or money. If he offers three cows, two goats and £20, the value of the animals is discreetly calculated in cash terms. Here cattle exchanges are exchanges of the market place.

Variation and Adjustment

The successive phases presented here represent a general trend throughout Southern Africa. But they permit detailed and complicated forms of local adjustment. Variation is between small, local chiefdoms rather than between regions. My last comment on modern developments is to note that, in the face of intractable economic circumstances, there is room for flexibility through modification of social arrangements.

Mitchell has distinguished between the rate and the incidence of labour migration. Rate of migration refers to the number of male absentees expressed as a percentage of males in a rural population. Incidence of migration refers to the social identity of migrants. While rate tells us how many migrate, incidence provides information about the difference between people who migrate and people who stay (Mitchell 1959: 42). The Kriges provide a neat example of the relevance of this distinction. They compare the contrasting labour migration patterns of Christian and non-Christian tribesmen in two Lobedu chiefdoms. The populations were characterized by similar migration rates. In one chiefdom, tribesmen start migrating at an early age. In the other, Christian youths have a higher absentee rate than tribal youths. What the Kriges discovered was a differential age-specific division of labour between the two populations rather than any gross difference of rate between them (E. J. and J. D. Krige 1943: 58–60).

Mitchell posits that rate of migration is determined by economic factors while incidence is a product of social conditions. The point here is that similarities in rates of migration do not imply similarities of social and economic organization between tribal areas. Local systems develop in which the incidence of migration is related to different modes of investing economic goods in social relationships. For the uneducated tribesman, the greatest scope for altering his situation is by altering his position in the webs of social relationships in the tribal area.

Conclusion: The Dual Economy

In this discussion of the dual economy I have presented a developmental sequence in which the relationships between market and subsistence sectors is progressively changed. First there is a relationship of tradition to novelty, then one of co-existence and, finally, a relationship of interpenetration. The first phase was of relatively short duration and has long been superseded. The period of co-existence, however, has continued for at least fifty years in this century. Only investigators who report research done in the last two decades discuss the final interpenetration of market and subsistence economies in selected areas. It requires minute study of small units in order to determine where the economy of a particular locality fits into the developmental sequence outlined. Today there is no single or even regional tribal economy. Generalizations can only be made about overall trends which should be given specific referents by study of particular communities.

Notes

* I would like to thank Mr T. P. Baxter who drew the maps for this chapter and the map in chapter 8.

1 This argument owes much to the work of Barth (1960) who shows that the development of the state among pastoralists in South-West Asia was contingent on chiefly control of boundaries in time and space. Homans's (1960) analysis of English villagers in the thirteenth century is also instructive.

2 Schapera (1943c: *passim*) consistently argues that dispersal and distribution of the holdings of individuals between wards is a modern development. This is contrary to the argument presented here. Werbner's data (1970) is important in this regard. Further, there is an 'explanation' of Schapera's view. Wardheads and chiefs would like to see the holdings of their subjects concentrated under distinct areas of command. The headmen thus idealize the past as a time when their predecessors had firm control over followers. They credit the traditional ward headman with the power to hold his following to limited areas of land.

3 Schapera (1943c: 138f.) describes Tswana appreciation of the potential of soil types and details the Tswana classification of soils.

Chapter 6
Kinship and Marriage
Eleanor Preston-Whyte

I Broad Characteristics of the Systems of Kinship and Residence among South African Bantu-speaking Peoples

The recognition of kinship relations and the assumptions made about them, as well as the nature and implications of marriage, are essentially the same in all Bantu-speaking societies in South Africa. Family and domestic arrangements are likewise similar. Striking local variations do occur, however, in the details of the different systems. These are noticeable, in particular, in the rules defining incest and exogamy, in marriage preferences, in the nature of unilineal descent groupings and in the systems of kinship terminology. It is possible, on the basis of the marriage differences, to distinguish two major sub-groups within the wider Bantu-speaking complex. The most clearly defined cluster consists of the Nguni-speaking peoples, who generally prohibit marriage and sex relations between all kin. In the remainder of the Bantu-speaking area, in contrast, marriage within certain kin categories is not only allowed but preferred.

All these differences have striking repercussions on wider social organization and tend to mask the more basic similarities. It is largely to the common features of the systems that attention will be directed in the first two sections of this chapter: the variations and their repercussions, both in terms of kinship and wider social relations, will be considered in the following sections.[1]

The importance of kinship

In these societies ties of kinship traced either through blood (consanguinity) or established by marriage (affinity) are recognized and are of fundamental importance to the individual since they have a moral, religious, and often a jural, content which cannot be lightly ignored. The social recognition of these linkages provides the individual with major criteria upon which to categorize his fellows and with a corresponding set of rules to guide interaction with them. Thus kin and non-kin are distinguished and treated differently, while various categories of kin are recognized, and behaviour towards individuals falling into them organized, according to a blueprint of kinship expectation. Residence may be influenced by kinship affiliation and, where this is the case, the individual's major domestic, social and economic relations are typically kinship relations ordered by kinship principles. The kinship system, however, provides not only a blueprint of interaction, but a potent tool for the manipulation of fellows in the attainment of both legitimate and unorthodox

177

goals. The individual's success in many ventures may depend, therefore, on his or her position in the kinship structure and upon accepted patterns of consanguineous and affinal interaction. In order to understand the full implications of this situation it is necessary to consider the rules which govern and determine interaction between these categories.

Patrilineal descent and descent groupings

In all these societies descent through males is recognized for jural purposes and forms a vital basis for co-operation. Inheritance of property and succession to office follow the patriline along clearly defined paths of genealogical seniority, based generally on primogeniture. Individuals descended from a common male forbear (agnates) recognize a fundamental bond which is particularly binding in the case of males. Clans, consisting of descendants in the male line of a named but distant and often mythical ancestor, are found in all Nguni societies. These descent groups are exagomous and thus of paramount importance in interpersonal relations. Amongst the Sotho totems or praise-names are inherited patrilineally, but, since these provide no bar to inter-marriage, they are of lesser importance than clanship amongst the Nguni. Neither clansmen nor totem brothers can trace their exact genealogical connections to each other. In contrast, lineages consisting of the descendants of a known ancestor some three to six generations removed in the male line are recognized in both Nguni and Sotho societies. The exact genealogical relationships of members is known and can be demonstrated. The functional importance of these structures varies and will be considered in detail later. Suffice it to point out here that minimal lineage segments may form the basis for residential clustering. Where this is the case the agnatic tie is of vital importance in day-to-day interaction at the local level.

Patrilineal descent does not mean that kin on the mother's side are not important to the individual in these societies. The 'warmth' of the relationship with the mother's brother is well established (E. J. Krige 1936a: 26; Kuper 1950: 102-3; Hammond-Tooke 1962: 51-2; Stayt 1931a: 174, 185) and the joking relationship between the *malume* and his sister's son in Tsonga society has led to much comment (Junod 1927 I: 229-37; Radcliffe-Brown 1924). In Sotho societies there is frequent contact with the mother's kin. Visiting of a temporary and long-term nature appears common, and maternal relatives may form part of the permanent membership of local residential units (Schapera 1935; Krige and Krige 1943). There is, in addition, a preference in these groups for marriage with the matrilateral cross-cousin and a man regularly seeks his spouse from amongst the ranks of his mother's descent group (Schapera 1950; Krige and Krige 1943: 142). It is, therefore, not surprising that interaction should be frequent and close, particularly in cases where marriage alliances have linked two agnatic groups over a number of generations. Amongst the Nguni, where kin marriages are forbidden, one basis for intimacy is absent, and it does not appear that non-agnates are

KINSHIP AND MARRIAGE

regularly included in local groupings (E. J. Krige 1936a: 39; Hammond-Tooke 1962: 38).

Basic rules underlying marriage

Yet another set of vital social relations is established by marriage. The broad similarities in the manner in which marriage is brought about in the societies under discussion arise from the common acceptance of three basic marriage rules. First, while a woman may have only one spouse, a man may have more than one wife at a time if he so wishes. Second, a woman should join her husband after marriage, either at his own homestead or at that of his father or brothers. These two rules, the one allowing for polygyny and the other ensuring patri-virilocal residence after marriage, have important repercussions on the composition and development of the family and upon domestic arrangements within the family. A third rule, which is accepted by all Southern Bantu, is that marriage is brought about only by the transfer of bridewealth, in the form of cattle, from the agnatic group of the groom to that of the bride. The structural implications of this transfer are far-reaching since it decides the filiation of children. It is an important influence also on interpersonal relations within the family between husband and wife, between each spouse and his or her affines, and between affinal groups linked by marriage. Let us consider the nature and composition of the family established by marriage before dealing in detail with the implications of the marriage transfer itself.

Polygyny and the 'house' systems

The possibility of polygyny means that the internal development in the family may be complicated by the husband taking more than one wife. If he remains a monogamist, the family remains elementary in form and is of what Gluckman (1950: 183) has termed the 'simple legal' variety. Should the husband, however, take subsequent wives during the lifetime of any one spouse, the family takes on a compound nature. In this case it is composed of two or more constituent units each of which centres on one of the co-wives and her children. In many respects it is this unit composed of a woman and her offspring, rather than the family consisting of a man, wife and child, which should be considered the basic structural feature of the kinship systems of many African societies. Certainly in the majority of these societies the independence of the so-called 'house' (Nguni: *indlu*; Sotho: *lapa*), formed around a wife and her children, is basic, not only to social and domestic arrangements within the wider family, but also to the development and internal differentiation of the lineage and lineage segment for which the family provides the growth point.

Whether the family has a simple legal or a compound form, each new marriage is seen as establishing the house of the woman concerned. She must be provided eventually with dwellings for herself and her children and with fields, a kitchen and a granary for the provision of food for the unit. Livestock, in particular cattle in the case of the Nguni, may be attached to the house and their issue remains as house property. It is the duty of a polygynist to treat each of his wives with utmost fairness and to allocate property to their houses equally. Once allocated, house property is inviolable and should be used only for the benefit of the children born to that house: it can be inherited by them alone. The Lobedu express this principle in the saying 'houses do not eat one another' (E. J. Krige 1964: 175). Among both Nguni and Sotho bridewealth cattle coming into the family from the marriage of a daughter belong to the house of her mother and may be used to provide, in turn, the bridewealth to enable a son of that house to marry. The brother and sister concerned are said to be 'cattle-linked' and this establishes a particularly close relationship between them (J. D. Krige 1934; Hammond-Tooke 1962: 133; Krige and Krige 1943: 142; Schapera 1953: 45). Should the father wish to use the cattle to gain a wife for a son of another house, or for himself, he must first get the consent of the wife of the house concerned. If she agrees, the new wife may be subordinate to her and to her house (Gluckman 1950: 195; E. J. Krige 1964: 175). The woman and her children, particularly the daughters, work in the house fields and thus support the house. Grain from this source may not, as with cattle, be used for the benefit of another house without the consent of the wife concerned.

A wife may add to the property and general prosperity of her house by practising as a diviner or making craft articles. Among Lobedu if a woman has not enough fields for her family's needs, and her husband's family have no more to give her, it is possible for her to be given additional fields to cultivate by her own people. These cannot however be inherited by her children as is the case with fields allocated by her husband's family (E. J. Krige 1964: 176). A house, once it is established, sees its fulfilment and continuation in the birth of children, and eventually grandchildren, to it. Should a woman be barren or die, various arrangements may be made to continue the house (see below).

The principle of the independence of the house and the woman's control over its property puts a wife in an extremely strong position within the domestic group (E. J. Krige 1964: 172, 175). Although the husband has the final say in any dispute, it is his duty to respect the wishes of his wives and not to impair their house property in any way. In this respect a wife in a compound family is probably in a stronger position than is a wife in a simple legal family where there may not be the same clear division and allocation of property (E. J. Krige 1964: 173).

The relationship of the constituent houses within the compound family is always formalized. Each wife and her accompanying house is ranked or graded with respect to her co-wives and their houses. The principles underlying the grading of houses vary slightly from society to society and may differ in the case of commoners and aristocrats. Order of marriage is one important factor in deciding a wife's status. Today, among Nguni commoners, it is the first wife married who takes the position of chief or great wife and it is her son who is the main heir and his father's successor in office. She has important ritual duties within the family and homestead and it is in her house that meat from sacrifices may be laid aside for the ancestors. Subsequent wives are ranked in order of their marriages. Traditionally among the Zulu, it appears that the great wife might have been married only late in life (Gluckman 1950: 183). Certainly, in the case of a chief in many Nguni societies, the great wife is married only after he has assumed office. Theoretically her position and that of her first born son, his heir, are publicly proclaimed by the fact that the bridewealth is collected from the political group as a whole. In the case of the Bhaca, for instance, each area is asked to contribute a certain number of cattle to the bridewealth of the chief's great wife, and headmen and wealthy tribesmen are expected to give liberally (Hammond-Tooke 1962: 36).

Ranking of wives may sometimes be affected by the social position of the woman herself. Should a Zulu man marry a woman of an aristocratic lineage she immediately takes precedence over any other wives he may have. Among the Pedi, a woman who is chosen from among the range of kinswomen preferred as mates should be elevated to the position of the great or ritual wife who bears the heir. Among the Lobedu and some other Sotho groups the uterine mother's brother's daughter is always the chief wife and, failing such a marriage, it is the woman acquired with the man's sister's cattle or by cattle provided by the father who assumes this position (E. J. Krige 1964: 173; Mönnig 1967: 212). Tswana rank wives in order of betrothal rather than on order of actual marriage (Schapera 1953: 40) and in most cases a wife married to replace another assumes the rank of her predecessor.

The grading of co-wives within large Nguni compound families is more complex than in the other Bantu-speaking groups. Wives are not only ranked but are linked together to form definite subsections within the overall family and homestead unit. These divisions are given expression in the physical layout of living quarters. With the exception of the Bhaca, who distinguish merely a great wife (Hammond-Tooke 1962: 36), all Cape Nguni divide co-wives into two sections, each occupying its own side of the homestead. In the one are found the dwellings and kitchens of the 'great wife'—usually the first wife to have been married by the polygynist. The other side of the homestead is the preserve of the 'right-hand' wife, who is usually the second woman to be married. Any further wives are affiliated as 'rafters' (Xhosa: *amaqadi*) to the sections of either of these principal wives and their houses are established on the side of the homestead controlled by their principal (Hoernlé 1937a: 75). Though subordinate to one of the main wives, the houses of women married after them are completely independent as far as house property is concerned. It is possible for a son in a subordinate house to inherit in the house of the main wife should she bear no heir but, unless this crisis occurs, the children of subordinate houses inherit only within their own unit.

Among the Natal Nguni the grading and organization of houses in the compound family are similar to the above except that, in the case of a very large family, three, instead of two, houses may be differentiated. At the top of the homestead opposite the main entrance is the principal dwelling, the *indlunkulu*. The mistress of this and its subsidiary wives and surrounding area is the chief wife. To the right of the *indlunkulu* section (as one looks towards the main entrance of the homesteads) is situated the section of the left-hand (*ikhohlo*) wife and the third section, the *inqadi*, may be situated on the other side of the *indlunkulu*. Traditionally the first wife married was eventually settled in the *ikhohlo* section, when the man took his great wife and established her in the *indlunkulu* (E. J. Krige 1936a: 39–41). It is to one of these sections that any subsequent wives are attached. The *inqadi* section is really subordinate to the *indlunkulu* and may provide the heir should the great house fail to do so. Among the Nguni the *ikhohlo* section appears to be largely independent and can in fact move out of the main homestead as soon as a son is married and able to take responsibility for a separate unit. The pattern sketched above is seldom achieved today. Reader writing of the Makhanya of southern Natal states that the practice of establishing an *inqadi* section had fallen into disuse. The Makhanya spoke of only two houses, 'the *indlunkulu* as the right, and strong arm; the *ikhohlo* as the left and weak one', and any further wives were affiliated to one of these houses. As Reader comments: 'the *inqadi* . . . is an institution which rested upon the economics of times of plenty which are gone, and political power which is no more' (1966:61).

The position of great wife and the general order of marriage does not necessarily involve a corresponding hierarchy in terms of authority, although it may do so. E. J. Krige points out that amongst the Lobedu a chief wife, although she has important ritual and other duties, exercises no control over other wives. If the preferred wife of a man is one of his younger wives and one whom he has married only late in his life after marriage to other wives, she may be completely overshadowed by the more established women (E. J. Krige 1964: 174). A similar situation obtains amongst the Pedi (Mönnig 1967: 217). In the case of the Nguni there appears to be more likelihood that senior wives will wield authority over junior wives. Among the Lobedu a wife married with cattle belonging to the house of another wife will be subordinate to her and will cook for her 'like a daughter-in-law' (Krige: personal communication).

The grading of wives within the polygynous family is of great importance since it indicates unambiguously the rights and social position of the children of co-wives. The status of a man in the wider agnatic group may be contingent, furthermore, not only upon the place of his father in this descent group, but also, if his father is a polygynist, upon the status of his mother within the compound family.

The development cycle of the family

The family undergoes changes in response to the birth, social maturation, marriage and death of its members. At two points in time any one family may have a completely different composition so that it may appear that the family takes a number of different forms. As Fortes (1949; 1958: 4–5) points out, however, there is a typical cycle of family development in any society, and what may appear to be different family forms are merely stages in this overall process.

Using Fortes's paradigm of expansion, dispersion and replacement, we may trace the cycle of development in family and domestic groups in Bantu-speaking societies. The first stage in the cycle is brought about with the public validation of marriage by the passing of bridewealth and the subsequent birth of children to the union. During this phase, in which the family may be either of the elementary or compound type, the offspring are economically, emotionally and jurally dependent upon their parents. A second phase in the stage of expansion is initiated when the children of the marriage union or unions reach adulthood and marry. Though the daughters leave the domestic unit to join their husbands, the bridewealth from their marriages facilitates the marriage of the males in the family and the sons bring their wives to join their father's homestead. This gives rise to the *extended family* which may grow to a considerable size, particularly if the grandsons of the founder, in their turn, bring their wives to join the unit. It is a major characteristic of the extended family that it spans generations and may also link together constituent units composed of simple legal and/or compound families. In fact traditionally it was relatively seldom that either the simple legal family or the compound family were found living as independent spatial units. Today the situation is changing. There is pressure in some societies, particularly amongst Christians, for fission either at, or soon after, marriage (Wilson *et al.* 1952: 46, 59). This is made possible by the relative independence of the men who can earn money in towns and so free themselves from dependence upon kinsmen. In certain areas pressure on land militates against the development of large extended families. Nevertheless, in many rural areas, and particularly amongst traditionalists and non-Christians who stress the value of the agnatic tie and who practise the ancestor cult, the extended family is still the prevalent form of family and residential grouping (see, for instance, E. J. Krige 1964: 185). It is during the phase of expansion that the seeds of the future dispersion and replacement of the family are sown. As sons marry and establish their own families they create the basis for future independent domestic units.

The domestic arrangements within the extended family are determined by an interplay of the principles of seniority, based on generation and marriage order, and upon the acceptance of the fact that each house established by marriage should eventually receive its independence. A bride, when she first joins her husband's family, is subordinate to his mother or to some other senior woman. While in certain societies, such as the Bhaca (Hammond-Tooke 1962: 115), she may be allocated her own dwellings, and thus some modicum of independence immediately after marriage, in the majority a bride is only granted her own establishment and fields after some time, usually after the birth of her first child. In any case it is expected that a bride should cook for her mother-in-law, help her in the household and work in her fields. It is often only the arrival of another bride that frees her from these tasks. Even when she has had dwellings and fields allocated to her, and her house has grown in stature with the birth of children and the allocation of property to it, she is still nominally under the control of her mother-in-law and may have to feed her aging in-laws (E. J. Krige 1964: 178). This control is lifted fully only after the death of the senior woman, when the younger woman herself assumes a senior and independent position in the family. It is this position which is the aim of every woman, as it brings with it both tangible and emotional rewards for the years spent as a dutiful daughter-in-law under the strict control of the husband's mother.

The second stage of the domestic cycle, that of dispersion, is usually initiated by the demise of the patriarch or founding male, since this foreshadows the segmentation of the original family into its constituent units. Either soon after the death and mourning period, or later, possibly after the death of the homestead head's chief wife (should she have survived him), some or all of the sons may move out of the extended homestead to establish their own homesteads as independent units. In compound families this segmentation is often on 'house' lines, the various sons of each wife moving with her to a new homestead. Even if their mother is no longer alive two or more uterine brothers may choose to live together under the headship of the senior. This is particularly common among the Lobedu (E. J. Krige 1964: 185). Amongst the Nguni this type of extended family usually arises when one of the brothers is a minor, or at least unmarried at the time of the death of his father, and is thus dependent upon his older brother. He may later leave his brother's homestead and so set up his own individual or compound establishment. Among the Tembe-Tsonga dispersion usually occurs before the death of the patriarch as sons establish their own homesteads at or soon after marriage (E. J. Krige 1969b: 31).

The segmentation or dispersion of the extended family heralds the stage of its replacement by the independent homesteads of the various sons. The developmental cycle of the original family is completed with the establishment of these new homesteads and the developmental cycle is initiated anew in each new unit.

Kinship and residence

We have seen that the elementary family, consisting of a man, his wife and children, or the compound family, made up of a polygynist, his wives and their children, was, and even today in some areas is seldom found living as an independent domestic unit. As a rule the family is extended to include certain of the family head's male agnates and their wives and children. In many cases, particularly in Sotho-speaking groups, other kin, cognates or affines of the head, may be included either permanently or temporarily in this unit. Though managing its own internal affairs, even the extended family living in a single homestead (Zulu: *umuzi*; Sotho: *lapa*) cannot always be considered as completely independent. It forms, in many cases, merely a segment of a wider grouping consisting of a cluster of homesteads, the majority of whose heads may be, in turn, linked by the ties of kinship and of agnation in particular. We may now consider the use of kinship in the recruitment to and control of local residential groupings.

Among the Nguni and certain of the North-Eastern Transvaal Sotho such as the Lobedu and Kgaga, the individual homesteads are dispersed over the hillsides and each is separated from its neighbours by fields and adjacent grazing land (see Plates 1a and 2a). Despite this scattered appearance, the homesteads of agnates tend to be clustered in the vicinity of each other and those belonging to the sons of one man tend to be situated closer to each other than to the homes of the sons of his brothers. Similarly the homesteads of uterine brothers tend to be closer to each other than to the homesteads of the sons of their mother's co-wives.

In the case of the Nguni the members of these agnatic clusters form clearly defined local lineages or local lineage segments in that the homestead heads are the descendants of a common grandfather or great-grandfather and can trace their genealogical relationship to each other. They consult in matters of common interest and may accept the arbitration of the segment head in quarrels. The Zulu term this lineage segment the *umndeni* or *umzalo* (H. Sibisi, personal communication) and refer to its head as the *umnumzane* (Reader 1966; Vilakazi 1962: 15–20). Mpondomise refer to the head as the *inkulu* (Hammond-Tooke 1968a: 38) and both societies recognize that members of the lineage segment have common rights in land and stock. These units are clearly corporate in nature. In cases where non-agnates live adjacent to an agnatic cluster of this nature, they may fall under the control of the lineage head in neighbourhood matters, may recognize his authority and may be represented by him much in the nature of dependants. They are, however, clearly distinguished from the agnatic core and this is the case even if they are related to lineage members by ties of affinity. In contrast among the North-Eastern Transvaal Sotho, though agnates live near each other, affines and non-kin are also settled in the near vicinity. Agnates living in the neighbourhood of each other do not appear to act as an exclusive unit and members of agnatic clusters do not distinguish themselves from surrounding cognates and affines in the same manner as do members of Nguni lineages (E. J. Krige 1964: 157–9). This is in keeping with the situation amongst other Sotho-speaking groups (Mönnig 1967: 218–34; Sheddick 1948: 32–40) where, while the homesteads of a number of the male descendants of a common grandfather or great-grandfather cluster together, this 'family group', as Schapera terms it in the case of the Tswana, regularly includes also the families of female relatives, and in composition is a 'group . . . closely united by blood or *by marriage*' (Schapera 1938a: 16; italics added). The family group among the Tswana and South Sotho may also include the homesteads of unrelated persons who may eventually marry into it. The Tswana family group is referred to as *bana ba motho*—'children of the same man'—and if large enough has its own court which is presided over by the senior male descendent of the ancestor from whom the 'family group' takes its name. The head is referred to as the *mogolwane* (Schapera 1935: 16) and, though he gains his position by virtue of being the head of an agnatic descent group, he has control also over the non-agnates attached to the 'family group'.

Residential distribution in most South Sotho and Pedi groups is characterized by contiguous settlement (see Plate 2b). The homesteads of 'family groups' are gathered close together in villages which range in size from some twenty to five hundred inhabitants (Hoernlé 1937a: 90; Sheddick 1953: 26) all of whom recognize the political leadership of an hereditary headman, to whom most but not all are related by blood or marriage. In the case of the Tswana the general Sotho tendency towards closer settlement is accentuated and, possibly due to scarcity of water supplies, local groups may consist of over a thousand persons living together at a favourable site (see Plates 1b and 3). At one time most of the members of a tribe lived in a central town and a number of surrounding villages (Schapera 1934a: 7). Within Tswana towns and villages there are territorial and administrative divisions which Schapera terms 'wards' (*kgôrô, kgotla*). These consist of three hundred to six hundred members and may in themselves be over a thousand strong (Schapera 1953: 46–7). Each ward is made up of a number of 'family groups' under the control of the ward head (*kgosana* or *mong wa kgotla*) whose position is hereditary in the male line and to whom many but not all ward members are related. While the agnatic group of the head tends to dominate within the ward, this unit, as in the case of South Sotho and Pedi villages, is not exclusively agnatic in character. It merely has a patrilineal bias and includes maternal and affinal kin of the head and their families. Though children normally belong to the ward of their fathers, it is possible to change one's affiliation and completely unrelated individuals and family groups may be adopted into the *kgôrô* (Schapera 1935: 20–2). The members of wards not only live together but interact closely. There is a ward court which is under the control of the headman who, with the help of the heads of the various 'family groups' in the ward, deals with lawsuits and other local business. Though some wards may have grown out of a lineage (Schapera 1935: 20) the fact that the ward court deals with problems relating to the members of different agnatic groups indicates that it is by no means ordinarily or necessarily a purely agnatic or even cognatic unit. Yet the Tswana *kgôrô* is more than merely a territorial and administrative division. Members form a social group (also referred to as *kgôrô*) which is held together by multiplex ties of agnation, wider kinship, neighbourhood and historical association. Members regard themselves as a body of related people and refer to each other as *ba ga etsho*—'the people of my home'—whether they are related or not (Schapera 1938a: 22). Tswana do, however, distinguish between ward matters and issues such as marriage which concern only the 'family group' and which are dealt with in this unit under the leadership of the *mogolwane*. The ward headman's control over ward members is one stemming from the wider political system of the tribe and not one which derives from the kinship and patrilineal system alone. At any time the chief may create a new ward and place it under a head of his choice, for instance one of his sons. Ties of wider kinship and of agnation are thus secondary to, or at least not distinguished from ward affiliation in terms of neighbourhood interaction and control.

It is in the emphasis given to agnation as a basis for residence and social control at the local level that one of the chief differences between the Tswana and other Sotho-speaking groups on the one hand, and the Nguni on the other, lies. Among the Zulu and Mpondomise there is a lineage court presided over by the lineage head. This deals *exclusively* with matters affecting agnates and their families. Cases involving non-agnates must be taken to the court of the headman of the administrative district or ward. It is this unit which is probably equivalent to the Tswana ward. Its head (Zulu: *induna*) is not regularly an hereditary officer. Since the homesteads within the district are widely dispersed the members do not, of necessity, interact as closely as do members of a Tswana ward or Sotho village. In their case the closest association is within the lineage or lineage segment and with neighbouring groups of this nature (Mbatha 1960: 37–9; Vilakazi 1962: 82; H. Sibisi—personal communication).

II The Nature of Marriage

Bridewealth and the rights it transfers

It is the passing of bridewealth in the form of cattle from the agnatic group of the man to that of the woman which is the essential act in legalizing a new marriage union. By this transfer certain vital rights over the woman, and consequently over any children she may bear, are transferred from her father or guardian, as representative of her family, to her husband and his family. The stress in marriage is upon the linking of two groups of kin rather than merely upon the union of a man and a woman standing alone and independent of their kin. From these facts stem many of the unique features and implications of traditional marriage and of the long-lasting linkage and exchange relationships established between affines.

The rights over a woman which are transferred to her husband and his agnatic group include rights in her both as a wife (rights *in uxorem*) and as a mother (rights *in genetricem*). Into the first category fall rights of sexual access and to her labour, both domestic and in the fields. Her husband can claim reparation for adultery or any other injury which impairs the fulfilment of these duties. Rights *in uxorem* are, of course, matched by the duties on the part of the groom and his agnates to provide the woman with a 'house'— living quarters, fields and lifelong security. The second set of rights transferred on marriage relates to the procreative powers of the woman. Rights *in genetricem* acquire for the husband and his lineage legal control over all children born to a woman unless and until the marriage is dissolved by divorce, which may entail the return of bridewealth. The importance of this aspect of marriage is expressed in the saying found in many of these societies: 'Cattle beget children' (Gluckman 1950: 184; Jeffreys 1951). So complete is the transfer of the childbearing capacities of the woman to her husband and his lineage that, whoever actually fathers her children (their *genitor*), it is the woman's husband who is regarded as their *pater* (social father). It is the facts of the bridewealth transfer that fix a child's social position in society. An impotent man may ask one of his kinsmen to have intercourse with his wife and so give him children and, most important, an heir (Gluckman 1950: 184). Similarly, children of an adulterous union entered into by a married woman belong to the family of her husband. The *genitor* may have to pay a fine for adultery but he cannot, among most Southern Bantu, claim guardianship over his children. In the prolonged absence of a husband, possibly as a migrant labourer, the birth of adulterine children may be welcomed by the husband and lineage as fulfilling one of the major aims of marriage (H. Kuper 1950: 92).

Safeguards for the continuation of the 'house' established by marriage

The passing of bridewealth does more than merely transfer the childbearing capacities of the woman from one agnatic group to another. It gives the man and his family the *right* to children and, in addition, lays the foundations of a new house within the family. It is a basic precept of all Southern Bantu societies that, once established, a house should not be allowed to die out. The greatest internal threats to the continuation of the house lie in barrenness on the part of the woman, in her failing to bear a male heir and in the premature death of either spouse. These vicissitudes are to some extent ensured against by the sororate and levirate as secondary unions and by the possibility of woman-to-woman marriage.

(a) The sororate
The sororate is initiated in the event of a wife proving to be barren or dying without issue. In the case of barrenness, a sister of the woman may be sent, as the Swazi say, 'to put children in the womb' of the barren woman. It is argued that, in failing to bear children, the wife and, by extension, her agnatic group, have not fulfilled one of the major purposes for which the marriage was initiated. Thus, at least amongst the Zulu and Swazi, no bridewealth is passed for the second woman. The obligation to replace a wife is so strong in these societies that, if no substitute is sent, the bridewealth of the barren woman should be returned in order to allow the husband to acquire another wife to bear children. The barren woman is not usually sent home but the second wife is placed in her house to bear children for her (Gluckman 1950: 185). In both cases maternity is fictitious but the house established by the

original marriage is continued and fulfilled. This form of the sororate is found also among the Tswana (Schapera 1950: 152), although they do not appear to enforce it as strictly as the Swazi and Zulu. In the case of the Lobedu and South Sotho, while a substitute may be sent to bear children for a barren wife, this is done at the instigation of the woman's people. Full bridewealth is due for the second union, though the amount may be less than in the case of the first marriage (Krige and Krige 1943: 159–60).

In the case of the death of the wife without progeny, the family of the dead woman may send a substitute 'to set up the house that has fallen' (Krige and Krige 1943: 159). Among the Zulu and Swazi, should no children have been born of a union, sending a substitute is a definite affinal obligation and no bridewealth need be passed (Gluckman 1950: 185, 188; H. Kuper 1963: 23). The alternative is to return the bridewealth cattle so that the man may initiate a new marriage. Among the Zulu some cattle may be returned also if the wife bore up to two children, but if she bore three or more before her death, she is regarded as having fulfilled her duty and her family are absolved of the obligation to provide a substitute or to return the cattle (Gluckman 1950: 188). The position is slightly different amongst the South Sotho and Lobedu where, even in the case of a death before the birth of any children, the widower has no absolute right to a substitute. As in the case of barrenness, it is usually his affines who initiate the sororate if they so wish. They can expect full bridewealth, though may demand less or only half the amount of the first transaction if the man has proved a co-operative son-in-law and good father (Krige and Krige 1943: 159–60; Sheddick 1953: 38). The Kriges suggest that this form of the sororate is motivated among the Lobedu mainly by the decision on the part of the dead woman's people to keep alive the links with the group of her husband and the fact that a woman has the right to a daughter of a union established with her bridewealth cattle (Krige and Krige 1943: 159).

It must be remembered that the sororate occurs against a social background in which under normal conditions the wives of a polygynist are often sisters or classificatory sisters. Among the Zulu sororal polygyny is believed to be advantageous as less friction is thought to occur between sisters than between unrelated co-wives (Gluckman 1950: 182). In this case the sisters are completely independent of each other and each establishes her own house, the relationship between these houses being subject to the normal rules of ranking. In this connection it may be noted that among the Tsonga there is a definite preference for a secondary marriage with the wife's younger sister or even the wife's brother's daughter (Junod 1927 I: 260–2) and this appears also amongst the Venda (Stayt 1931b: 179–80).

(b) The levirate
In all the groups with the exception of Xhosa, Thembu and, possibly, the South Sotho (Sheddick 1953: 39), should a married man die, an approved relative may assume responsibility for the widow and children. While in some

cases the levir undertakes full domestic and marital duties in relation to the woman, in others he visits and provides some economic support for the widow, who remains in the homestead of her deceased husband. He may also help with the bridewealth needed by the sons of the dead man. The most important duty of the levir is to beget children for the deceased. No bridewealth is paid and the issue of the leviratic union refer to the deceased man as 'father' (*pater*). Clearly this type of union is, like the sororate, viewed as a continuation of the original marriage. The levir is usually a younger brother or some other junior agnate of the dead man. He may be a son of the deceased, but not a son by the woman concerned. He is fulfilling an agnatic duty in ensuring the continuance of the house established by the marriage.

The levirate may have other important consequences. It serves to keep the woman, and hence her children, particularly if they are still young, under the effective control of her deceased husband's agnatic kin. Their position in the family and in the homestead remains virtually unchanged, and the security offered by legal marriage is ensured, even beyond the death of the husband and father. The Kriges report that among the Lobedu the main duty of a younger brother who takes his elder brother's widow is seen, not primarily in terms of 'raising seed' to the dead man, but rather as of caring for the widow and her children and also, as in the case of the sororate, of *maintaining* intact the vital linkages created by marriage and the passing of marriage cattle (Krige and Krige 1943: 160–1).

The levirate in its most developed form derives from the assumption that marriage is an exchange in which rights in the woman, both *in uxorem* and *in genetricem*, are transferred to the lineage of the man in return for the cattle which go to the group of the bride. Since it is the two groups which are important, rather than the individual bride and groom, it is logical that (as was the case until the reign of Mpande) a Zulu widow could not go and live with a man not related to her husband without being prosecuted. It must not be thought, however, that a leviratic union is inevitable for all widows. The Zulu chief, Mpande, ruled that a widow be permitted to go to the man of her choice but that the children should be retained by the agnatic group of her deceased husband (Gluckman 1950: 183). Certainly, if a woman is beyond childbearing age when her husband dies, the levirate need not be enforced. She may merely remain on in her husband's homestead. It is usual, if fission of the family follows the death of a homestead head, for the widow to move with her eldest son to his new homestead, where she has a place of security and honour. Among the Cape Nguni she lives with her youngest son, who may take over his father's homestead.

Under certain circumstances, notably when there is property or position at stake, a form of marriage superficially similar to Nuer ghost marriage (Evans-Pritchard 1951: 109–12) may occur in some Bantu-speaking societies. E. J. Krige discusses the practice of *ukuvusa* which occurs amongst the Zulu when a man of property dies without leaving a son. His natural heir, usually a full or half brother, instead of appropriating the property, may 'from affection or fear of his spirit marry a woman to the dead man's name, and thus produce an heir' (1936a: 182). A house of this nature ranks as a minor or subordinate house in the homestead of the surviving brother. Gluckman mentions similar unions in which a brother marries a woman betrothed by a man before his death, or else 'wakens' a dead kinsman by marrying and bearing children to his name (1950: 184). Mönnig (1967: 206), writing of the Pedi, reports that a marriage which is arranged on his behalf by the relatives of a man who has died without issue, is termed *tsoša leina la mohu*—to raise the name of the deceased—and is contracted particularly among nobles and chiefs where succession is important and the death has occurred before the man could marry the woman designated as the bearer of his heir. This type of marriage occurs for specific purposes and is probably relatively rare. It is not mentioned in the literature on most other Bantu-speaking groups.

(c) Woman-to-woman marriage

Yet another means of ensuring the continuity of a house in the absence of sons is through raising an heir to property or position by woman-to-woman marriage. In these cases the 'wife' bears children for her 'husband' either by an appointed lover or by a suitor of her own choice.

Woman-to-woman marriage may be undertaken among the South Sotho and Pedi by a childless widow in order to provide a son for her husband and an heir to his property (Sheddick 1953: 38; Mönnig 1967: 206). Among the Lobedu a widow who has no sons may use the cattle coming into her house from the marriage of a daughter in order to marry a wife and provide an heir to her house (E. J. Krige 1964: 165). Alternatively, if there are other daughters in the house, one of them may use the cattle and so provide the heir to her own line (E. J. Krige 1964: 165). A similar situation is possible among the Zulu (Gluckman 1950: 148). Van Warmelo points out that a Venda man may allot property to a house which has only daughters just as he does to one with sons. One of the daughters then marries a wife in order to raise an heir to the house (1948a: 391). The South Sotho use the term *lefielo* (broom) for a girl whose bridewealth has been paid by a wealthy man on behalf of his daughter (Jones 1966: 70).

Among the Lobedu, Venda and Pedi woman marriages appear to be rather more frequent than in the other societies mentioned above. In the case of Lobedu and Venda a woman who has earned wealth from divining or trade may use this to marry a wife in her own right (E. J. Krige 1964: 165; Stayt 1931a: 143–5; van Warmelo 1948a: 33). The children of such a union, though they may take the name of the wealthy woman's husband, belong essentially with their mother to the house of the principal woman and are under her control. In both Lobedu and Pedi groups another striking variant of woman marriage occurs. A woman is regarded as having a moral right to a daughter from the house which was established for her cattle-linked brother with the bridewealth obtained from her own marriage. Even if she has no son, and especially if her husband is dead, she 'marries' the girl herself, using the bridewealth received from a daughter's marriage (E. J. Krige 1964: 165; Mönnig 1967: 206).

Although undertaken primarily in order to raise an heir woman marriage may serve other purposes. The Lobedu Queen is sent wives by headmen and individuals of high birth who desire her favour. Some of these women remain at the royal court, but others are sent as wives to men elsewhere in the kingdom and some who are particularly favoured are placed as headmen of districts. In this way affinal ties centring on the queen are spread widely throughout the Kingdom and the network created by the institution of the queen's wives has important political connotations (Krige and Krige 1943: 173-7). This kind of arrangement is, however, unusual and not found in other Bantu-speaking groups.

Marriage rules and preferences

In all Bantu-speaking societies incest prohibitions forbid sex relations within the elementary family. Infraction of this rule (Xhosa—*imbulu*) is a heinous offence and can only be 'washed away' by rituals directed towards the ancestors who have been offended by this grievous breach of custom. Incest is a family matter and sanctions are supernatural.

The Nguni generally extend these prohibitions beyond the family in rules of exogamy which proscribe marriage with a woman from the clans of all four grandparents. In some groups marriage is, however, allowed with a woman from the mother's mother's clan and the Swazi may permit a man to marry into the clan of his maternal grandparent of either sex or even that of his paternal grandmother (H. Kuper 1952: 18). The effect of far-flung rules of clan exogamy is to draw a clear distinction between consanguines and affines. The two categories of relative can never be confounded. Affinal ties are, in addition, spread widely throughout society, and particularly where there is a tendency for members of descent groups to be settled in the same area, marriage links are created over considerable distances and between distant groups. There is an emphasis also on the exclusiveness of the agnatic unit, and, while marriage creates a desired alliance between two separate descent groups, it is, at the same time something of an attack on the cohesion and unity of each consanguineal unit.

In Sotho-speaking societies a man is allowed to marry into the groups proscribed among the Nguni and his choice of spouse may be affected by various forms of preferential marriage. We have seen that there is a general liking for marriage with the wife's sister in most Bantu-speaking societies and with the wife's brother's daughter in some cases. The Swazi approve of all the kin marriages mentioned above and particularly that with a woman of the man's father's mother's clan (H. Kuper 1947b: 97-8). In a number of Sotho-speaking groups and among the Tsonga there is also approval for marriages with any women from the mother's side of the family. More specifically among the South Sotho, Tswana, Lobedu and Venda preferred unions occur with a cousin and with the mother's brother's daughter in particular. The Lobedu allow only this form of cousin marriage, but in the other groups marriage with the father's sister's daughter is also approved (Schapera 1950: 15; Mönnig 1967: 198; Sheddick 1953: 34; van Warmelo 1948a: 29). Among the Venda, in fact, if a man marries his patrilateral cross-cousin she will be the mother of his heir and will rank higher than the daughter of the mother's brother because she sacrifices to the same ancestors as her husband. This type of marriage occurs very largely in chiefly families (van Warmelo 1948a: 29). Marriage with the father's brother's daughter is also allowed and liked in many Sotho-speaking societies although it is forbidden among the Rolong and Kgatla and occurs only rarely among the Lobedu. In certain South Sotho groups marriage with the father's eldest brother's daughter is regarded as verging on the incestuous (Sheddick 1953: 35). In other groups marriage with the father's brother's daughter is the first preference amongst nobles. Ashton (1952: 327-71) reports this trend among Tlokwa nobles and among the Tswana, while commoners marry their mother's brother's daughters most frequently, Schapera gives evidence that agnatic marriages predominate amongst nobles and are made for political ends (Schapera 1957: 140-2). The Pedi reverse this order (Mönnig 1967: 201).

It is impossible with the evidence at present available to explain either the variations in the type of cousin marriage allowed and preferred in the different Sotho-speaking groups, or the specific differences between the Tswana and Pedi in the type of cousin married most frequently by commoners and nobles respectively. The general effect of all these unions is, however, to merge affines with both patrilineal and matrilineal kin. If a man's cross-cousin is his wife, his mother's brother is also his father-in-law. Similarly where a man marries the daughter of his father's brother, the latter, an important agnate, becomes also a major affine. These situations would be unthinkable among the Nguni, where agnates and affines are not only vigorously separated but each category is treated according to a different pattern. In Sotho groups no such sharp behavioural distinctions appear and a complex range of interaction develops between individuals united both as agnates and affines. Cousin marriages tend also to blur the boundaries between descent groups and, as will be seen, these structures do not, in fact, stand out as clearly among Sotho as among the Nguni. Similarly residential groups among the former are, as already noted, not as exclusively agnatic in character as among the latter.

The importance and stability of marriage

In concluding this discussion of the nature of marriage in Bantu-speaking societies it must be stressed that by the act of marrying, both bride and groom move towards social maturity. Though it is in the birth of children that their final fulfilment as adult male and female will lie, it is recognized that it is marriage alone which makes this possible. Marriage must be viewed as a vital rite of passage. In Hoernlé's terms 'the man and woman are transferred from the group of the unmarried to the group of the married, the whole transfer involving an important change of status in society' (1925: 483). Marriage is regarded as the appropriate, and indeed the only acceptable, state for both male and female adults in all these groups. It is rare to find individuals who have never married and the few who do exist are usually either mentally or physically disabled. Such persons may be ridiculed and called by derogatory names (Mönnig 1967: 130). In keeping with this, traditional marriage in these societies appears to have been stable. The various forms of secondary union ensured that the full reproductive potential of the marriage was realized and that the union itself extended beyond the death or incapacity of one of the spouses. Sheddick, writing of the South Sotho, stresses that marriage was a lifelong contract terminated only by the death of *both* partners (1953: 39; italics added). Gluckman notes that Zulu 'marriage constitutes a long and enduring union between the spouses, which extends to their kin, above all their agnatic lineages' (1950: 185). Though the legal machinery for divorce existed in all these societies, the various authorities indicate that it was uncommon (Gluckman 1950: 182; E. J. Krige 1964: 171; H. Kuper 1950: 92; Mönnig 1967: 334-6; Sheddick 1953: 39).

The infrequency of divorce was not due to the amount of bridewealth, nor to the difficulty of achieving its return. As Gluckman has suggested for the Zulu, sound structural reasons existed for the infrequency of marriage failures. He points to the strength of Zulu patrilineal and patrilocal groupings as being basic to marriage stability and argues that the large bridewealth transferred at marriage must be seen as the symbol, and not the cause of, marriage stability in this society (1950: 191–2). In other Southern Bantu societies it is possible that different factors are involved in ensuring the traditional stability of marriage. E. J. Krige notes for the Lobedu that 'The use of a woman's brideprice by her brother and the interest which his cattle-linked sister has in maintaining this "house" in which her son will find a wife, made divorce difficult in the old days' (1964: 171). Mönnig describes how, amongst the Pedi, both groups of relatives will do their utmost to dissuade any applicant from a divorce; they even 'endeavour to remove the cause of the complaint and . . . reconcile the partners' (1967: 334). Clearly marriage in all these societies is the alliance of two bodies of kin rather than merely of two individuals. Marriage continuity and stability (as indeed the total functioning of marriage) must be viewed in this context if it is to be fully understood.

III Unilineal Descent Groups: Clans and Lineages

Just as striking differences occur in regard to the rules and preferences governing the choice of spouse in Southern Bantu societies, so significant variations appear to exist also in the strength and functional importance of unilineal descent groupings. These two areas of contrast are not unrelated. Among the majority of Nguni groups where exogamy forbids marriage, not only within a clan, but also between a man and a woman from the clan of his mother or either of his grandmothers, clans and lineages are well developed. In contrast, amongst Sotho-speaking peoples, where it is possible and indeed preferred for a man to marry an affine or even an agnate, it is debatable if clans, as usually defined in anthropological literature, exist. Lineages are not only shallow in depth but, in at least the case of the Lobedu, do not appear distinguishable from a wider cognatic kinship grouping based on descent traced through both parents. The nature of both types of unilineal descent group will now be considered and, following this, the structural implications of affinal alliances between and within descent groups will be discussed.

The nature, functional importance and areas of social interaction in which lineage groupings operate

Attention has been drawn to the extension of the patrilineal principle to form the basis of lineages in many of the Bantu-speaking societies. These structures as far as one can tell from available literature are generally prominent and clearly defined among the Cape and Natal Nguni where, in the case of commoners, an average lineage depth of five to six generations has been recorded (Hammond-Tooke 1962: 58; 1968: 30; Vilakazi 1962: 16; Reader 1966: 82; H. Kuper 1952: 20; Wilson *et al.* 1952: 63). Lineages among Sotho appear to be shallower, although exact information on this score is unfortunately vague. Both Ashton (1952: 16) and Sheddick (1948: 40-2) place South Sotho lineages at between three and five generations, and the latter states in another context that these groups are often restricted to three to four generations (1948: 28). E. J. Krige reports that effective lineage depth among Lobedu commoners is extremely shallow, and indeed it even seems doubtful if the Lobedu have lineages in the true sense of the word. Although a group of kinsmen related to a common ancestor some four or five generations back may reside near each other and meet informally to discuss marriage and litigation, they do not emerge as a distinct group in everyday activities. Instead the lineage (if indeed such a term can be used in this connection) 'tends to pale into insignificance beside the marriage or the bilateral kin groups' (Krige and Krige 1943: 86). Though the Lobedu use the term *leloko* to describe a group of agnates this term may refer also to a wider grouping consisting of both agnates and relatives on the mother's side of the family. Similarly, while the descendants of a common grandfather in the male line may share a major shrine and meet occasionally at harvest festivals, on most religious occasions they are joined by the descendants of the group's daughters and their children (E. J. Krige 1964: 159). The position amongst the Venda is also somewhat atypical and there may even be the elements of a dual descent system in this society. Stayt (1931a: 185) notes that each individual is closely linked, not only with the members of an agnatic lineage, but also with a parallel lineage on the mother's side. Recent work among the Tsonga (D. J. Webster—personal communication) suggests that among them, too, lineage depth is shallow, usually averaging three generations. In some Tembe-Tsonga areas, lineages do not appear to exist at all (E. J. Krige 1969b: 102; 113).

In those societies in which lineage groupings are clearly identifiable, they are conceptualized by members as consisting of both the living and the dead descendants of the founding ancestor. Although all members do not live together, the unity of the lineage is expressed in the recognition of the genealogically senior male who acts as lineage head. There is a belief also that all members should be notified of important events affecting the group and should attend, or at least be informed of, all rituals held to placate the spirits or to celebrate important stages in the life cycle of living members. Lineage groups are thus ritual units, particularly among the Nguni, and are also corporate property-owning units in the sense that members are at least potentially heirs to its cattle through the operation of the inheritance rules (Hammond-Tooke 1962: 60). Lineage members recognize binding obligations to each other and these are particularly strong between members of minimal segments who live adjacent to each other.

The social functions of lineage groups appear to differ considerably in the various groups of Bantu-speaking peoples.[2] It must be stressed, however, that in all these societies their overall significance is limited by the centralized nature of the political systems which result in the state assuming most of the organizational functions which, in uncentralized societies such as the Nuer (Evans-Pritchard: 1940) and the Tallensi (Fortes: 1945) are associated with deep and prominent lineage structures.[3] It is only in royal or aristocratic descent groups, where lineage depths of eight and ten generations are recorded, that lineage membership may confer both prestige and political office (Gluckman 1950: 159; Mönnig 1967: 231–2; Hammond-Tooke 1968a: 32–3; E. J. Krige 1969b: 113). In everyday social life there appear to be four areas of social interaction in which descent groups operate, or in which lineage membership may have relevance for the individual, viz. in the recruitment to, and the organization of, residential and local groups, in the organization and distribution of certain scarce resources, in the settlement of disputes between lineage members and in the rituals of the ancestor cult. The first three will be considered here and the last in chapter 10. In all cases lineage functions appear most pronounced amongst the Cape and Natal Nguni and the greater depth and development of their commoner lineages may be related to this fact. In these societies lineages are clearly corporate groups the members of which acknowledge their unity and, in certain circumstances, act as a single unit under the lineage head.

(a) The lineage as core of the local group

We have already noticed that the practice of patrilocal marriage and the typical pattern of growth and segmentation of domestic groups leads in these societies to a clustering of the homesteads of agnatically related males. Settlements are frequently built up around a core provided by a localized

KINSHIP AND MARRIAGE

lineage segment which comes to dominate a neighbourhood or village, both numerically and socially. Where this occurs the genealogically senior male of the descent group acts not only as the head of his lineage segment, but also as the official head or informal spokesman of the wider residential cluster (Schapera 1953: 40; Sheddick 1953: 26-7; Bothma 1962: 14; Mönnig 1967: 218-34; Reader 1966: 93-4). Amongst the Sotho the local group regularly includes, besides agnates and their families, the head's affines, maternal kin and also unrelated family units. Schapera, who calls this unit amongst the Tswana a 'family group' (1953: 40), notes that it may take up either the whole of, or a section of, the basic territorial division of the society which he terms a ward (*motse, kgotla, kgôrô*).[4] The ward in its turn is under the control of an hereditary headman and also has a strong patrilineal bias (Schapera 1953: 43). A similar situation exists in other Sotho local territorial units (Sheddick 1953: 26-7; Bothma 1962: 14; Mönnig 1967: 218-34). Local organization amongst the Zulu, as described by both Reader and Vilakazi, is even more formally tied to lineage and lineage segment scatter. 'The territorial kinship pattern of the tribe is . . . primarily one of dominant descent groups, each in occupation by right of birth or as members of the subwards (formal territorial units) which jointly exhaust the tribal territory' (Reader 1966: 93-4). The lineage head has important organizational functions and appears also to be a force for social control within the area of his descent group. Where non-agnates live within his area, they too fall under his informal jurisdiction (Vilakazi 1962: 19; Mbatha 1960: 41-2).

The correspondence of the principles of locality and lineage affiliations in these societies create multiplex ties between neighbours and so add to social and political integration at the local level. The internal organization of the descent group, centering on the segment head, provides also a convenient base for wide neighbourhood co-operation. In these respects the lineage proves of importance in local organization.

(b) *The lineage and the organization and distribution of scarce resources*
In some Nguni groups the corporate lineage is reported to have specialized functions apparently absent in the case of the Sotho. There appears, however, to be no uniformity in this respect within the whole Nguni complex, but this may be the result of unique historical factors or perhaps of inadequate research. Among the Natal Nguni the descent group, through its head acting in agreement with his other adult male agnates, has an important say in the allocation of land. Among the Mpondomise the lineage or lineage segment forms the core of, and provides the structural framework for, hospitality groups (*izithebe*) which are concerned with the distribution of beer and meat at feasts and which may also provide the basis for the local organization of communal labour and even the raising of levies within the chiefdom.

(i) *The Zulu descent group and land allocation*
Among the Makhanya, Nyuswa and Qadi, all Zulu groups who have been

established in their present territory for some four or five generations only, large tracts of arable and residential land have come to be controlled by the agnatic descendants of the men who first entered the area and to whom land rights were allocated by the early chiefs. Although the descendants of these founders are by no means the only people living in these areas, they do dominate both numerically and socially and have come, in particular, to have a predominant (if informal) say in the allocation of land, both to kinsmen wishing to establish new homesteads, and to newcomers wishing to settle on what is referred to as 'lineage land' amongst the Nyuswa and Qadi (Reader 1966: 65; Vilakazi 1962: 19; Mbatha 1960: 69).

In the case of the Nyuswa, Vilakazi reports that, although land is theoretically allocated by the headman as official representative of the king, in fact it is more usual for a man wanting land in an area to approach the dominant lineage head first. If the lineage head, in consultation with all other adult members of his descent group, agrees, he carries the plea to the headman. Alternatively, should the headman, or even the chief, wish to allocate a portion of lineage land to a newcomer he must gain consent of the lineage. Without this the life of the settler would be made unbearable by lack of co-operation and even active opposition from the members of the lineage concerned. It is thus only on land not specifically claimed by a long-settled lineage that newcomers can be settled directly by the political authorities.

Land apportionment among the Makhanya is even more clearly under lineage control. The whole Makhanya territory is divided into areas controlled by dominant lineages. It is to the heads of these descent groups, the *abanumzane*, that prospective settlers make their applications, for it is they who apportion land at the chief's pleasure. Reader states that the descent-group system 'can be seen as a political system in a kinship idiom' (1966: 65, 93).

It must be stressed that this lineage control over land allocation is by no means typical of all Nguni, at least today. Among Cape Nguni land allocation is in the hands of the ward[5] headmen alone (Hammond-Tooke 1962: 60; 1969a: 39; Wilson *et al.* 1950: 4–5). While it is possible that this is due to the imposition of a white-controlled administrative system and to land shortage in the Transkei, there is at present no direct evidence that lineages in these societies were ever land-holding or land-allocating units. The pastoral traditions of the Xhosa may explain this, or it is possible that the controlling position of lineages and lineage heads in respect of land amongst the Nyuswa, Qadi and Makhanya is the result of particular historical and social conditions not found among other Nguni, or it may reflect a form of organization from which the Cape Nguni have since changed. Among the Tswana and Sotho neither the lineage group as a whole nor lineage segments appear to have any definite control over land. Land is allocated directly to the heads of homesteads by the local political authority (Sheddick 1953: 57–9; Schapera 1953: 20–1). Although an application for land may be made through a genealogically senior male or through a clansman this is merely by way of introduction and guarantees good behaviour and acceptance by the local community.

(ii) *Mpondomise lineages and lineage segments as the core of hospitality groups*
When attending feasts Mpondomise sit together in recognized groups—*izithebe* (sing. *isithebe*)—and are allocated beer and meat as members of these groups. The word *isithebe* means a grass tray or eating mat upon which the meat is served, hence its use for the groups through which the distribution of food and drink at social gatherings is organized. Hammond-Tooke (1963) refers to the *izithebe* units as 'hospitality groups' and has shown that they are usually formed around a core consisting of a lineage or lineage segment and that they are controlled by the head of such groups. *Izithebe* are, however, not restricted to unilineal kin and include non-kin who have applied for membership. Though Mpondomise do differentiate terminologically between non-kin and core members this distinction is not emphasized and informants stressed that status rivalry among members would destroy *esprit de corps*, and 'quarrels are to be avoided as much as possible' (1963: 308).

Mpondomise clearly conceptualize *izithebe* in kinship, and particularly in lineage, terms (1963: 316), but Hammond-Tooke stresses that these groups are essentially associational in nature. Their membership is heterogeneous and they provide the basis for co-operation between a group of kinsmen and non-kin. He points out that the lineage proper and the *izithebe* can be differentiated in terms of their respective interests and fields of influence. '*Izithebe* groups are oriented almost exclusively toward the socio-economic ends of food distribution and cooperation in contexts of hospitality. The lineage enjoys a different sphere of relevance, notably the regulation of livestock inheritance, succession and ritual matters' (Hammond-Tooke 1963: 311). Though the membership of these two groups may overlap, the contexts in which each operates are clearly distinguished.

The vital point about Mpondomise *izithebe* is that the lineage or lineage segment operates as a basis for their organization in much the same manner that it provides a basis for residential units. *Izithebe* are, in a sense, quasi-kinship groups in that for some of their members (non-kin of the lineage core) recruitment is voluntary or semi-voluntary but for others (members of the lineage) recruitment is closed since they are 'born into' the group. Similarly, in residential groups, while most men remain in the area of their birth, others leave and are replaced by non-kin or by individuals sharing maternal or affinal ties with the dominant lineage segment. In both cases the descent group thus provides stability and a central core around which non-kin congregate. Mpondomise hospitality groups are thus necessarily of a segmentary nature. These groups among other Cape Nguni differ from those found among the Mpondomise in that they are formed upon a purely territorial basis.

Finally, *izithebe* link not only kin and non-kin together but also 'stand structurally between, and unite, the local territorial groups, on the one hand,

and the lineage segments on the other' (Hammond-Tooke 1963: 316). Membership crosses the boundaries of administrative areas. It provides an important basis for co-operation between lineage groupings and territorial units and, in so doing, reinforces 'the indigenous political system by providing cross-cutting alliances which divide people in certain contexts and unite them in others' (1963: 316).

(c) *The settlement of internal disputes within the lineage*
From the above it would seem that Nguni lineages are of considerably more significance than those of the Sotho and possibly the Tswana also. The Nguni lineage plays also a greater role in the settlement of disputes between its members than among the Sotho, where the group of agnates may not be so clearly differentiated from the wider 'family group'.

Both Reader (1966: Makhanya) and Hammond-Tooke (1962: Bhaca; 1968a: Cape Nguni) stress the importance of the lineage in arbitrating quarrels between members. Whereas the head of the Tswana or Sotho family group has patriarchal authority over all living in his unit, it appears that the Nguni lineage head has a more specific kinship authority. Hammond-Tooke (1968a: 38) writes of a lineage 'court' amongst the Mpondomise which consists of all the adult males of the lineage and is held under the 'chairmanship' of the lineage head, often at his homestead. It regularly deals with disputes between lineage members over such matters as the inheritance of land and property, the obligations of heirs to their father's dependants and deals, in particular, with the plight of widows. While this court has no authority to punish, there is evidence that the lineage head may end a dispute by threatening to curse recalcitrant members, and great pressure is brought to bear upon them to reach a settlement. Although dissatisfied litigants may eventually take their case from the lineage court to that of the headman or subheadman, at these courts they are always asked, 'What did your own people say about it?' The higher court may even refuse to proceed with a case before it has been discussed by the lineage group. The position among the Makhanya, Nyuswa and Qadi is essentially similar, and Reader (1966: 314) stresses that nearly all disputes within the lineage are taken immediately to the lineage head.

The lineage thus stands out in these Nguni societies as a clearly defined unit separate from other residential and territorial groupings. Whether this is the case among other Bantu-speaking groups, especially the Sotho, is uncertain. It is at least not so in the case of the Lobedu among whom, as we saw earlier, the lineage is subsumed within a wider cognatic or bilateral local groupings. The question as to why there should be this difference is a fascinating one. It may be connected with the Nguni-Sotho differences in marriage rules which lead to a clear distinction being made between patrilineal descent groups, on the one hand, and maternal and affinal kin, on the other, among the Nguni, and a merging of agnatic, matrilateral and affinal kin among the Sotho-speakers.

The nature of clan-groupings

Clans and clan-like groupings exist in all Southern Bantu societies. Among the Nguni and Tsonga common clan membership is signalled by the possession of an eponymous clan name (Zulu and Swazi: *isibongo*; Cape Nguni: *isiduko*; Tsonga: *sibongo*) and among the Sotho by the name of a totemic species or object of praise (Lobedu: *motupo*; S. Sotho: *seboko*; Pedi: *moane* or *seano*; Tswana: *seboko*). Both clan and totem names are inherited patrilineally but persons sharing them do not form, or even think of themselves as forming, a group of any kind. Clanship is rather a category concept and is brought into play situationally when individuals meet. Among the Nguni, clans are the basic exogamous unit; the Sotho totem group and Tsonga clan, however, have no connections with exogamy and, at least today, are of minimal social importance. The situation among Nguni on the one hand, and Sotho and Tsonga on the other, may therefore be discussed separately.

Clans consist of the descendants in the male line of a distant and possibly mythical ancestor. Clansmen cannot, and need not be able to, trace their exact genealogical connections to each other and there is, as the Mpondomise data indicate, a complete break, particularly in the case of commoner clans, between lineage and clan genealogies (Hammond-Tooke 1968a: 35). The rule of clan exogamy is strictly adhered to in all these societies and a breach must be compounded by a ritual to wash away the 'incest'. There is evidence to suggest that some Nguni clans may have once adhered to distinctive customs such as the burial rituals described by Marwick (1940: 55) and Nguni clansmen observe an injunction against drinking milk in the homestead of a non-clansman. The milk taboo is consciously connected with exogamy rules, and Hunter quotes Mpondo informants as saying, 'You do not drink milk at a strange *umzi* (homestead) because you might see a girl there whom later you may want to marry' (1936: 52).

Fellow clansmen recognize certain obligations of hospitality and mutual aid towards each other, mainly the offering of food, drink and shelter to clansmen when travelling (E. J. Krige 1936a: 34; Hammond-Tooke 1962: 61; Hunter 1936: 52). Mbatha (1960: 61) reports that still today clansmen amongst the Nyuswa should support one another in quarrels, and may be expected to offer economic help to each other in times of crisis. Reader (1966: 86), on the other hand, reports that present-day Makhanya lay little stress on clanship (as opposed to membership of the lineage) and do not regard it as obligatory for an individual to help a fellow clansman. Taken all in all it would appear that, today, common clanship amongst the Nguni provides an initial facilitating link between individuals, especially useful to the stranger coming to town. Of course clanship may be used as a basis for a more demanding relationship should there be the need and should both partners be agreeable. In this connection Mbatha (1960: 20) has suggested that, where clans are dispersed over chiefdom boundaries, the tie of clanship may operate to mitigate hostility between adjacent tribes.

Sometimes clans have special functions. The members of certain Mpondomise clans have particular duties to perform in tribal ritual (Hammond-Tooke 1968a: 34). In all Nguni groups membership of the royal clan carries some prestige and is the basis for conferring political office (Gluckman 1940: 34). The correspondence of clanship, social status and political authority is seen most clearly in the case of the Swazi (H. Kuper 1947a: 59), among whom clanship appears rather more important than in other Nguni chiefdoms. The royal Dlamini clan has spread throughout Swazi territory and all other clans are graded roughly according to the relationship they have with the kingship. This affects the general standing of clan members. Political authority is delegated first and foremost to royal relatives, who are sent as chiefs to many outlying districts. These princes are expected to report on public opinion to the King and to enhance his prestige. Within each district relatives of the chief also enjoy significant authority and power and the interplay of aristocrat and commoner clans in the political process is one of the most fascinating aspects of Swazi politics.

Among Sotho-speakers, in contrast to the Nguni, only the most tenuous of links exist between individuals bearing the same praise-name or totem. Marriage is not affected in any way and certainly today membership of a totem group does not normally demand any meaningful and lasting co-operation. Thus, while certain Sotho totem groups are reported to have once adhered to distinctive birth, initiation and burial customs, and also may have kept common food taboos (Sheddick 1953: 28; Stayt 1931a: 186; Ellenberger and MacGregor 1912: 40–5), this is no longer the case. Both the Sotho and the Tswana may formerly have refrained from touching, killing and eating their totem on pain of supernatural retribution. Schapera (1953: 35), in fact, suggests that Tswana at one time performed cleansing rituals after the accidental violation of their totem. Stayt (1931a: 186) claims that Venda totems were associated with one or more 'honorific praises'. Mönnig (1967: 235) and the Kriges note that both Pedi and Lobedu may swear by their totems, but the latter state that this has no more meaning than 'when we swear by Jupiter' (Krige and Krige 1943: 88).

There is some evidence to suggest that under special circumstances the sharing of a common totem may provide a basis for limited hospitality and companionship in some Sotho groups. Sheddick (1953: 28–9) mentions that totemic affiliation among the South Sotho may, in the absence of near kin, provide a basis upon which an individual is introduced into an alien community. Mönnig (1967: 235) suggests that similar help is given to members of a Pedi totem group and notes that strangers travelling together, if they find they have the same totem, immediately join one another and share their food.

Of such minor importance is clanship among Sotho-speakers that a number of authorities hesitate even to use the word 'clan' in this connection, particularly as the group is not exogamous. They prefer the terms 'totem group' or 'totemic grouping' (E. J. Krige 1964: 157; Mönnig 1967: 234;

PLATE 9
Initiation

Vhusha rite of the Venda

Kgatla *magwane* (male novices) about to be whipped in the *kgotla*

PLATE 10
Dance of the *abakhwetha* (Xhosa)

Sheddick 1953: 28–9). In Krige's words, 'The totemic name is useful only as a distinguishing mark' (E. J. Krige 1964: 157) and beyond this has little of the implications usually associated with clans and clanship.

The use of the totem as a 'distinguishing mark' may, however, have importance in certain circumstances. It has been suggested (Ellenberger and MacGregor 1912; Mönnig 1967: 235) that Sotho totems may serve to isolate political groups and to map their movements and integration into other political communities. Thus the Pedi proper, when entering their new country, changed their totem from the monkey to the porcupine and this served to distinguish them as a distinct tribe. A common totem may, of course, also foster nationhood. Tribes who were originally separate but who came under Pedi hegemony adopted the Pedi totem, thus symbolizing their new unity. The adoption of a new totem does not displace the old one, which still remains as a pointer to past history and origin (Mönnig 1967: 235).

The question of why Sotho developed totemic groupings (absent from the Nguni) is one which cannot be fully answered at this stage. Wilson has, however, suggested that this may be linked to differences in the economy and mode of subsistence of these two groups in the early days of their development. Her thesis is that the economy of the Sotho peoples was one based upon hunting, cultivation and iron-smelting, and that herding was always of secondary importance (Wilson and Thompson 1969: 142–53; also chapter 5 above). This emphasis was reflected in their rituals through which wild animals and, in one case, iron, became associated with various descent groups. Totemic associations of this nature did not develop amongst the Nguni, whose economy was based upon cattle-keeping and for whom hunting was of minor importance. Instead, in keeping with their emphasis on unilineal descent and on the agnatic tie, Nguni clans came to be associated with the individuals who founded them, their clans being eponymous. As a corollary of this thesis, Wilson suggests that the present-day attenuation of totemic observances among the Sotho is related to the disappearance of iron-smelting and the lessening in importance of hunting in their economies.

IV The Implications of Marriage Differences

Whatever their historical background, the differences in clanship and totemic observances in Nguni and Sotho groups do have certain repercussions on the social arrangements of the societies concerned. Clan exogamy and the strength of the lineage among the Nguni appear to be associated with certain striking features and emphases which characterize the social relations created between a bride and her husband's group and between the two families brought together by marriage in these societies. In the case of the Sotho it is not only the absence of clan exogamy and the lesser stress laid on the lineage as an exclusive group, but the possibility of and preference for kin marriages which is significant and which, it may be suggested, affects the social structure.

Among the Nguni, while each new marriage union is welcomed and celebrated, the exclusiveness of the agnatic groups of the bride and groom is nevertheless suggested at every turn. The haggling over the bridewealth, the reluctance of the bride to enter the groom's home, the insulting songs and the competitive dancing so characteristic of Zulu wedding ceremonies all draw attention to the separate identity of the groups involved and to the clash of interests as one group loses a valued member and the other is forced to admit an outsider to its ranks (Kuper 1952: 18; Hammond-Tooke 1962: 102–11; E. J. Krige 1936a: 138–48; Reader 1966: 200). The gifts which pass between the bride's and groom's families before and after the marriage serve, in truth, to bring groups of strangers together and build a relationship of friendship and amity between them (E. J. Krige 1936a: 120–1).

In Sotho societies the same elements of distance and the slow building of a firm social relationship are present, but the extreme competition of the groups is absent. In marrying, a Sotho-speaking man is often seeking a bride from a group to whom he is already related and whom he knows well, and the union may be merely the consummation of a match which has been planned and anticipated for years—possibly since his early childhood. Cross-cousins are said to be 'born for each other' in Lobedu society, and infant betrothals are common among the Tswana (Schapera 1953: 41). This obviates the necessity for the slow introduction of stranger groups to each other. Bargaining over bridewealth is frowned upon (Mönnig 1967: 133; Krige and Krige 1943: 149) and among the Lobedu competitive dancing and singing are absent from wedding ceremonials which symbolize not the potential antagonism between the families involved but the completion of an expected union and the continuation and reinforcement of existing and valued alliances. The use of love magic is regarded as witchcraft in this society, since to involve the affections of a girl may be to distract her from a preferred match (Krige and Krige 1943: 258). In the case of the Nguni, love magic is not only a legitimate strategy but an art and an expected part of youthful courting activity. In Sotho groups, even in cases where marriage is not with kin and not with a preferred mate, the overall emphasis is upon the union itself and not upon the exclusiveness of the agnatic groups involved.

Wide-flung clan exogamy among the Nguni means that the bride is an outsider in the home of her affines (Hammond-Tooke 1962: 113–14). This is symbolized in various ways. She may not eat of the meat or drink of the milk of the homestead until publicly permitted to do so by an aggregation ritual in which she touches the gall of an animal sacrificed to the groom's ancestors (Reader 1966: 209–10; Hunter 1936: 36–9). Before this she consumes meat brought with her from her own home and drinks the milk of an animal which her father has provided for this purpose. She must observe stringent rules of etiquette (*hlonipha*) which involve the linguistic avoidance of words which contain syllables occurring in the names of her husband's father and senior agnates (Hammond-Tooke 1962: 117; E. J. Krige 1936a: 30). Her shoulders and breasts must always be covered in their presence and she must wear a headcloth bound low over her forehead 'out of respect' for them (Hammond-Tooke 1962: 117). In addition, no new bride may enter certain areas of the homestead, notably those associated with cattle or with men. It is only slowly that these restrictions are eased, and it is usually only after long years spent in her husband's home, and the birth of sons to his name, that they are completely erased (Reader 1966: 210-11; Hammond-Tooke 1962: 120).

The preference for cousin marriages among the Sotho has the effect of changing the whole emphasis of the relationship between a wife and her affines and makes the interaction experienced by the bride during the early years of her marriage far less strained than is the case among the Nguni. Her position in her husband's home is relatively free of the restrictions imposed upon a Nguni wife. Though a Lobedu bride may have to be acknowledged by each member of her husband's homestead with a small gift before she may speak to them (E. J. Krige 1964: 161) and, like most Sotho brides, abides by linguistic avoidances involving the name of her husband's father (Ashton 1952: 76-7), she is not treated as a rank outsider to the group. Indeed it is seldom that she has not visited her affinal homestead before, and it is usual that she has been an accepted and loved visitor to it for years in her role as the daughter of the sister of its head or even as an agnate. Among the Tswana and Pedi the major marriage ceremonies and the early months of marriage may be spent not at the home of the husband but in the bride's own homestead (Mönnig 1967: 136-7; Schapera 1953: 41). Whatever the exact arrangements, there is seldom the necessity of introducing the bride slowly to a completely new and unknown group of people. Above all she is known to her husband's ancestors and indeed shares and sacrifices to many of them with him (van Warmelo 1948a: 31; E. J. Krige 1964: 187). This overlap between agnatic and affinal shades expresses a basic structural feature of Sotho society and lays bare the nub of the differences between them and Nguni groups.

If rules of incest and exogamy are seen as serving to force women out of one set of restricted descent groups into similar units and so to lay the foundation for alliances leading to overall solidarity (Lévi-Strauss 1969), Nguni and Sotho marriage conventions operate in a contrasting manner. Among the former, marriage ties are spread widely, and different descent groups come to be linked in each generation. The majority of unions create new affinal ties and each descent group thus has numerous, individually contrasted, alliances, spread widely throughout the society. D. J. Webster (personal communication) reports that in an Inharrime Chopi headman's district he found that male members of the eleven resident clan groups had married women from sixty-two different clans, spread throughout Chopiland. The functional importance of this spread is great since affinal ties are strong and binding. Among the Zulu a man refers to his daughter's husband as *umphini wekhuba*—the handle of the hoe—(E. J. Krige 1936a: 121) and looks to him for support in times of crises and dissension. Affines may be called upon for support in quarrels with outsiders, and this has definite social and political advantages, both for a man who has married into a powerful affinal group, and also for his sons, whose maternal kin they will be. Among the Swazi it is a man's mother's group who support him in gaining and maintaining political office (H. Kuper 1947a: 59; 1950: 102–3; 1963: 32). The gifts which pass between affines both before and after marriage may serve to distribute local products, and affines who live in different districts can be expected to provide help for each other in times of drought or crop failure.

In Sotho societies preferential cousin marriages have the effect of perpetuating alliances over generations and so renewing and reinforcing already existing affinal and maternal ties. A man's affines are his life-long intimates and can be trusted absolutely. As in the case of Nguni, Sotho-speakers may rely upon affines living in other districts for help in times of crises and crop failure, eventualities only too likely to occur in the harsh environment in which Sotho groups live. Marriage may give a family access to fields in different areas and ecological zones. Sotho women are lent fields by their cognates, and crop failure in the district of a woman's husband may thus be offset by produce from the area of her cognatic kin. Sansom has suggested (chapter 5) that Sotho distribute their fields widely and so guard against complete crop loss in times of drought and pestilence. One way in which this may be done is through establishing affinal ties in districts which are far from and economically different from a man's own district.

Unlike the Nguni, in some Sotho-speaking groups families do not count cattle as a permanent economic asset. In the case of the Lobedu, families possess cattle for short periods immediately after the marriage of a daughter. A woman's bridewealth should be used to establish a new 'house' in her agnatic home, and ideally to facilitate the marriage of her cattle-linked brother. Cattle and marriage are thus intimately and inextricably united in the social organization of these people. A woman looks to the house established with her cattle for a bride for her son, and in making this demand she is said to 'follow the tracks of her cattle' (E. J. Krige 1964: 161–2). In this manner marriage alliances between two families made in one generation inevitably lead to others in the next. Marriages and their accompanying marriage gifts are consciously used to cement and continue existing alliances. Krige cites an example of an unusual brother-sister exchange which was designed to unite two families whose heads felt that they were 'growing apart' as no marriage had linked them in the current generation (1964: 186–7). As a rule Lobedu matrilateral cross-cousin marriages serve this purpose and indeed the repetition of this type of union gives rise to a situation where kin groups come to stand in a permanent relationship of wife-givers (*vamakhulu*) and wife-receivers (*vadakhulu*) to each other. They do not, however, form a 'chain' which is 'joined back on itself' as is suggested in the classical model of asymmetrical matrilateral cross-cousin marriage discussed by Lévi-Strauss. Each family may be the focus of more than one set of marriage alliances and, in any case, other types of marriage, many of them with non-relatives, do occur. In other Sotho-speaking groups the chain-like effects of a 'pure' form of matrilateral cross-cousin marriage does not exist either, because preferred

KINSHIP AND MARRIAGE

unions occur also with the father's sister's daughter and with the father's brother's daughter.

In all these societies the various forms of cousin marriage have important, though apparently differing, social consequences. In by no means all cases have these been investigated or analysed fully as yet. Interesting material on the political implications is however available. Among the Lobedu the pattern of cross-cousin marriages centring on the queen provides one of the mechanisms by which the county is united. As the queen's wives 'follow her cattle' in each generation, so dispersed and far-flung groups are united in a kinship network (Krige and Krige 1943: 173–8). Among the Tswana, marriages are used in rather a different manner to provide solidarity. Although agnates belong to the same lineage, they do not necessarily live within the same ward or political subdivision of the tribe. In fact royal lineages tend to become dispersed over many wards (Schapera 1957: 156) and, furthermore, the headship of different wards come to be vested in minor or major branches of the royal lineage. Each important noble becomes the focus of a personal following of his own and, when in the past disputes over chieftainships were common, the rival factions were often made up of wards headed by half-brothers or other first kin of a late, or even a ruling, chief. The consequence of this system, and of these rivalries, was that secession of dissident wards under their own political leader was fairly common. Schapera suggests that one of the results of agnatic marriage amongst Tswana nobles is to 'counterbalance' the tendency of wards to split by the establishment of new affinal ties between agnatic groups which have become, or who are showing signs of becoming, politically distinct (1957: 157). In addition, there are certain advantages for the children of such a union, since this type of marriage converts distant agnates into closer maternal kin, and at least one set of potential rivals are converted into allies. It is usual amongst Tswana for the maternal kin of a contender for office to support him, and it is to the maternal uncle above all others that a man looks for disinterested advice and staunch support in times of crises and political manoeuvre. Should the marriage of a man's father be with a distant agnate of another ward, his son reaps the benefit in terms of a close affinal alliance with this ward and thus the likelihood of unstinted support rather than rivalry in a competition for authority. Finally, as Schapera has suggested in a later study of kinship and politics in Tswana history (1963a: 167), a man can rely more upon agnates who are also his maternal kin or affines than he can upon other distant agnates, who may be also related by similar ties to his competitor for office.

In similar vein, Jones (1966: 59), writing of chiefly succession in Lesotho, notes that the marriage of parallel cousins may be used by a chief as a means of linking together rival or potentially rival chiefly dynasties. He gives one clear example. The most serious potential rival of the Paramount Chief Letsie I was his brother Molapo, the chief of the largest ward in Lesotho. Malapo's two sons, the one his heir and the other a full brother of the first who later acted as regent for him, both married parallel cousins, the daughters of their father's brother, the Paramount. After the death of Letsie and Molapo, the new chief, Lerotholi, was able to intervene effectively in the internal politics of the Molapo ward since his sisters were married to its ward chief and to its regent and were the mothers of their respective heirs.

Conclusions

In summary, then, it is clear that despite basic similarities the Bantu-speaking peoples of South Africa fall into clearly-marked categories from the standpoint of the various differences in their systems of kinship and marriage. On the one hand the Nguni present a picture of strongly patrilineal societies with well-developed lineages, strict descent group exogamy, a clear distinction between consanguines and affines and, in general, a highly-structured social system. On the other hand among the Sotho, cousin marriages make for a marked cognatic tendency, and although descent groups are present, they appear less formalized than in the case of the Nguni. In turn residential arrangements are affected and are less exclusively agnatic in character. Husband and wife may share some of the same ancestors and in fact among the Lobedu a shrine to the wife's shades may be found in her husband's village. The absence of wide-flung rules of exogamy and the preferred unions which lead to a tendency to overlapping between agnates and affines means that there is no mechanism for extending marriage links widely throughout the society in each generation, and this may be speculatively associated with the preference of Sotho for village life rather than the dispersed and scattered settlement characteristic of most Nguni.

It would be a mistake, however, to suggest that the Sotho-speaking societies enjoy anything like the similarities which characterize Nguni-speakers. The Tswana chiefdoms of Botswana and the Western Transvaal must be distinguished from the cluster of groups living in the Eastern Transvaal which are dominated by the Venda and include Lobedu. While the former show the cognatic tendencies mentioned above, they are closer to the Nguni pattern of patrilineal emphasis than are the latter, where separate lineages are difficult to distinguish and the importance of the father's line is matched by that of the mother's people.

Yet another sub-group may be distinguished within the Southern Bantu complex, this time largely on the basis of the type of kinship terminology used by the people concerned. This is a topic too complex to deal with in this chapter. Suffice it to point out that most Southern Bantu groups have variations of the so-called Iroquois system, in which the father's brother is equated with father, the mother's sister with mother, and parallel cousins are called 'brother' and 'sister', while cross-cousins are distinguished by separate terms. Among the Tsonga and the Chopi of Mozambique, in contrast, we find the Omaha system. This classifies all men of the mother's lineage as 'mother's brothers', including the mother's brothers' sons, and all women as 'mothers', including the mother's brothers' daughters. Cross-cousins on the mother's side are thus 'raised' to the father's generation. Conversely, fathers' sisters' sons and daughters are called 'son' and 'daughter' respectively by Ego: they are thus 'lowered' genealogically in relation to him. This means that all affinal alliances made by a man immediately preclude the possibility of his son marrying into that clan. The general effect of this is that not only are alliances widely dispersed throughout the country as described above, but there is also a wide flexibility in choice of marriage partner. This contrasts with the position among the Sotho, and though it links these peoples with the rest of the Nguni complex, most of whom also prohibit marriage into the clan of the mother, another factor distinguishes them from the Nguni. Both the Tsonga and Chopi actively practise preferential secondary marriage unions. This may be linked with the fact that a man has the right to marry his wife's younger sister and also his wife's brother's daughter (and wife's brother's son's daughter—all women of the same descent group) calling them *lamu* (a joking term for wife), while his son calls them *mame* (i.e. 'mother') (D. J. Webster—personal communication). It is clear that the Tsonga and Chopi have a large degree of choice in their marriages, which reflects the marked individuality and 'flexibility' of their societies, especially when compared with Nguni and Lobedu. This is reflected in shallow lineages and in a much more 'open' system, which allows individual options to a much greater extent than in all other Southern Bantu societies.

Notes

1 I would like to express my gratitude to Professor E. J. Krige for her help in the writing of this chapter. She read and commented upon many of the drafts of the work, and some of the major ideas and emphases, particularly those dealing with marriage and the structure and importance of lineage groupings, are due to her assistance. Professor W. D. Hammond-Tooke and Dr B. Sansom also helped me in the formulation of ideas.

2 The literature is particularly confused and lacking on this topic. What follows is an attempt to bring some order to it and must be regarded as tentative.

3 I acknowledge my debt to Professor Krige and Dr H. Sibisi for help in this section, and for drawing my attention to this important emphasis in particular.

4 The close correspondence of lineage segments and local residential units has led to a confusion both in terminology and in conceptualization which bedevils this field, and which is particularly marked in writings on the Sotho. The term *kgôrô* (or *kgotla*) appears to be used by most of these peoples for both the physical assemblage of closely settled homesteads which form a segment in the overall territorial and political system, and also for the group of people who live in this unit and who are related as described above—patrilineal kin plus affines, maternal kin and also non-kin attached to the dominant cluster. Schapera, by using the term 'ward' as the translation for *kgôrô* is stressing its territorial nature; Mönnig, following Bothma, is dubious of his rendering, as he sees the Pedi *kgôrô* as essentially a social group of individuals linked by various kinship and local ties. In that this unit is not a purely agnatic group, the terms lineage or lineage segment cannot be used. On the other hand, as Hammond-Tooke points out (personal communication), Schapera's 'family group' is not specific

enough either, as it ignores the strong patrilineal bias and does not allow for the inclusion of non-kin. It does not, furthermore, indicate whether a functional separation is made between the interests of the lineage or lineage segment in purely internal affairs and the 'family group' which is concerned in wider political and territorial matters. This would appear to be the case amongst the Nguni where the lineage or lineage segment (consisting of agnates only) forms a strong and cohesive unit (Hammond-Tooke 1968a: 38–40; Reader 1966: 91–109). This patrilineal descent group emphasis may, however, be related to the fact mentioned in the text that in Nguni societies these groupings appear to be the important basis of co-operation in a number of spheres in which, in non-Nguni societies, there is no evidence that they operate.

5 The word *ward* is used here to refer to a territorial unit in the white-controlled political and administrative system.

Chapter 7
Growing Up in Traditional Society
Virginia van der Vliet

In essence, the problems of socializing the human infant are universal—the child must be taught to accept, value and reproduce the behaviour and sentiments of the society into which he is born. The specific aims and methods of the process, however, will vary considerably depending on the nature and needs of that society. Socialization in heterogeneous, technologically complex and constantly changing Western society, for instance, is likely to differ fundamentally from socialization in one which is more stable and static. Since traditional Southern Bantu societies were homogeneous, conservative and technologically unprogressive, we must expect to find that child-rearing and socialization took very different forms from those found in the West.

The stated aim of modern Western educationalists is the uncovering and development of the potential aptitudes and qualities of each individual—the careful cultivation of his individuality and uniqueness—a goal no doubt essential in a society with a complex role structure and a belief in the desirability of change and progress. The traditional system, by contrast, was an education in conservatism and conformity, in acceptance of and loyalty to a traditional way of life.

Not only the aims, but also the methods, show fundamental differences. Western socialization is characterized by an extended period spent in formal educational institutions, with the emphasis increasingly on vocational training and the development of skills, rather than training for social relationships. By contrast, technical training in Southern Bantu society was acquired informally by imitation of the limited range of skills the child witnessed around him and, where it existed, the short period of formal education was concerned with training in social, rather than vocational, behaviour.

The socialization process in traditional society was simplified by the fact that status was ascribed rather than achieved. Each individual could be labelled at birth in terms of the status and roles he was likely to fill by virtue of his sex, position in the family, and parents' rank; the socialization to which the individual was subsequently exposed was goal-oriented in terms of these predicted roles.

Traditional society was also relieved of the problem of different socializing agents pursuing conflicting goals. In Western society, home, school, church and peer group may all have very different ideas about what constitutes suitable behaviour; in Southern Bantu society all the institutions and individuals concerned with socialization worked together within a homogeneous framework to produce the ideal community member. The child was not handed over to the specially trained few; rather his models for behaviour were all around him, and, with not only his immediate family, but usually the whole community interested in his progress (and likely to praise or punish his efforts), he learned by emulating their behaviour. Presented with a single set of beliefs, values and behaviour patterns, the acceptance of which ensured the advantages of recognition and status in the adult community, there were few problems of choice or rebellion. The individual generally conformed without question.

Much of the success of traditional methods of socialization rested on the homogeneity and relatively static nature of the society. With the accelerating rate of change in these societies today, child-rearing techniques have undergone many changes. The influence of the missionaries has brought many old customs and beliefs about socializing the young into question, often to the point where rituals such as those of initiation at puberty, once essential to adult status in many groups, have lapsed or been drastically curtailed. Schooling, too, takes the child out of his home environment and teaches him facts and values often in direct contradiction to tradition. Employment in the Western industrial sector means that traditional training for economic roles is totally inadequate, and the absence of a large percentage of men from the rural areas for long periods at a time has caused a marked increase of unruly, even delinquent, behaviour in the youth, who openly flout the authority of the women and the elderly who remain the main source of discipline in the rural areas. All these factors, and many others, have broken down the old, homogeneous patterns of Bantu society, and with them the smooth functioning of the traditional socialization process.

What follows presents a picture of the traditional pattern of individual development from birth to adolescence, the threshold of adulthood. It must be remembered that this account of socialization, although using the conventional ethnographic present, depicts in many cases an ideal no longer realized in rapidly changing societies.

The Birth of a Child

No Bantu marriage is considered complete until the woman has borne her husband at least one child. A young wife will anxiously await her first pregnancy, for a child ratifies the bridewealth contract between her family and that of her husband and completes her status as an adult woman. The child is seen as a valuable acquisition, not only because it provides emotional satisfactions, but also because it is an economic asset from an early age. The little girl becomes a nursemaid for younger siblings or kin and takes many minor household chores off her mother's hands; the boy will herd cattle, sheep and goats and later, as a grown man, provide security for his parents in their old age. A son, too, will ensure the continuity of the father's lineage and his immortality as an ancestor.

With children so important to the family, it is not surprising that barrenness in a woman is dreaded and most of the tribes have medicines and formulae which attempt to cure the condition. Special dolls to promote fertility are used among Nguni and South Sotho (De Lange 1961). Since the role of the man in conception is also recognized, he too may be treated if the condition persists. If the woman still fails to fall pregnant, steps are taken to ensure that the man is not left without an heir. A common practice, as for instance among the Swazi, is the giving of the barren woman's younger sister (or some other female relative) as a co-wife 'to put (children) into her womb' (the sororate). In such a case the man need not give a full bridewealth for the second wife, though it is customary to give the parents between one and three head of cattle to thank them (H. Kuper 1963: 23).

During pregnancy the wife continues with her normal activities, although she may discontinue heavier work in the later months. Many taboos and avoidances must be observed by pregnant women, usually to protect the child, but sometimes, also, to ease pregnancy and labour. South Sotho women, for instance, must not go out of their compounds lest they walk on 'bad paths' of malevolent persons who might harm the child; Bhaca and Pedi women must not see corpses, nor should Pedi women have contact with other pregnant or ritually impure women or look at people with physical disabilities. Many tribes impose food restrictions on pregnant women. Venda women must avoid hot food, lest it scald the growing child, and abstain from sweet foods and vegetables; beer is not restricted until the last few months, when the woman is supposed to eat very little and drink only water, lest the baby grow too big and cause difficulties in delivery. Among the Zulu even an unmarried girl must avoid certain foods lest, when she becomes pregnant, these interfere with her baby's development. Eating guinea-fowl, for instance, will cause children to have long, flat heads, hare will cause long ears, rock rabbit long front teeth, and eating swallows will produce children unable to make a decent nest (i.e. hut) for themselves (Krige 1936a: 63).

Women are often given medicines during pregnancy to relieve the pains and sickness, to facilitate birth or to protect the foetus against harm. Bhaca and Mpondo women, for instance, are given a plant (usually some variety of agapanthus) from which an infusion is made, or water drunk from the pot in which the plant is growing. The mother is made to confess any bad dreams or adultery to the plant; if she does not do so, neither the plant nor the foetus will grow.

In the last months of pregnancy, the mother-to-be in some tribes (e.g. Bhaca, South Sotho, Venda, Pedi, Tswana, Hlubi) returns to her parents' home for the birth. This custom often applies only to the first child, the woman remaining in her husband's kraal for subsequent confinements. Wherever the child is born, the birth is strictly a women's affair. A male herbalist is called in only if it presents exceptional difficulties. Normally delivery takes place in the woman's living hut under the supervision of the older women of the household, preferably past child-bearing age and therefore ritually 'pure', free from the ritual pollution associated with menstruation called, by the Cape Nguni, *mlaza* (Hunter 1936: 46–7; Hammond-Tooke 1962: 69–70). A midwife is not always present, but will be called in, as among Mpondo and South Sotho, if there are any complications. Difficulties during birth are usually interpreted as being due to the wrath of the ancestors or to sorcery; suitable appeasement is made or counter-magic used to facilitate normal delivery.

The cord is cut at birth, and the afterbirth is buried secretly to prevent strangers or witches from tampering with it and causing harm to the child. The infant is washed and often given a little soft porridge, gruel or medicinal infusion soon after being born. For some time after birth, it is believed to be very weak (e.g. the Tsonga contend that the child is 'not yet firm; it is only water' (Junod 1927 I: 43)) and most tribes have rituals aimed at strengthening and protecting it. Venda, Pedi and Zulu, for instance, make numerous cuts on different parts of the child's body and medicine is rubbed into the incisions, while Xhosa, Bomvana, Bhaca, Mpondo, Pedi and South Sotho hold the baby in the smoke of a fire containing burning medicines or charms. The Zulu, in a similar rite, include in the ingredients for the fire scrapings of the father's body dirt which, besides strengthening the child, 'was the recognized way of imparting a portion of the *iThongo* or ancestral spirit to the child, the means by which the new member was linked on to the past and the whole corporate life of the sib' (Krige 1936a: 67).

Mother and infant remain secluded in the hut for a period varying between six and ten days, usually depending on the time it takes for the cord to drop off. During this period the mother must continue to observe food taboos, and visitors are limited to certain categories, e.g. the ritually 'pure' old women. Men, especially the husband, are almost always excluded lest they harm the child or are themselves polluted by the impurities which surround childbirth.

Usually before the mother is finally allowed to rejoin society, she must undergo some ceremony intended to return her (and sometimes also the hut and her possessions) to a state of ritual cleanliness. Xhosa, Mfengu and Mpondo women prepare a special brew of beer. The Mpondo and Zulu woman must springclean the hut and, in the case of the Zulu, she is then sprinkled with purifying *intelezi* medicine. The Venda mother is formally visited in the hut by her husband and must present him with a bracelet before he can accept food or sit down. If this is not done he will develop a fatal shivering disease.

The attitude to the birth of twins differs between the groups. Generally they are considered unnatural or in a potentially dangerous state. Among the Xhosa and Bomvana young euphorbia trees are planted next to the hut and watered with the twins' bathwater. A mystical association is believed to exist between a twin and a tree so that if one fails to flourish, so will the other (Cook 1927: 97; Soga 1932: 292–5). To the Sotho and Venda, twins are dangerous to the community, causing the country to become 'hot'. They were formerly killed (Mönnig 1967: 101 (Pedi); Stayt 1931a: 91 (Venda); Krige and Krige, 1943: 218 (Lobedu); Schapera 1927 (General)).

The mother's reincorporation into her group is usually marked by a feast. This feast may be to thank the midwives (beer among the Zulu or a sheep among the South Sotho), or it may be part of a ritual dedicated to the ancestors in gratitude, especially if it is a first child or first son. A common custom among the Cape Nguni, Tsonga and Pedi is the killing of a goat, known among the Cape Nguni as the *imbeleko* goat (from the term *ukubeleka*, to carry a child on the back). Among the Cape Nguni this goat is usually provided by the child's father; among the Pedi and Tsonga the mother's brother must provide it. The goat is skinned, and the hide used as a carrying blanket or mat for the infant. Nowadays the child may be provided instead with a blanket bought, among the Xhosa and Mfengu, from the proceeds of the sale of the goat's skin. Portions of the slaughtered animal may also be mixed with medicines or made into amulets and given to the child to strengthen and protect him.

Apart from the general treatment of the child with medicines and protective amulets, special rites are sometimes performed at this stage. The Bhaca, and some Xesibe and Mfengu groups, incise the child's face (*chaza*) for protection and because the ancestors wish it, while the South Sotho and Pedi shave the child's head. Among the Pedi this rite is performed by a doctor, the child's head being washed with water and medicine and then shaved, preparatory to forming the traditional hairstyle. Xhosa and Thembu children have the top joint of the little finger of the left hand amputated to ensure health, a custom apparently borrowed from the San (Bushmen). Other rites performed in this period of early infancy include, among the Tsonga, Venda, South Sotho, Pedi and Swazi, a ceremony, sometimes repeated monthly, in which the baby is shown to the moon. The explanation for this is not certain, but Kuper suggests that it symbolically introduces the child to the world of nature (Kuper 1963: 50). Junod explains it as a rite of passage which the Tsonga regard as necessary to the child's mental growth. 'When a child is not intelligent, it is usual to say to him: You have not been shown your moon!' (Junod 1927 I: 53).

The rites marking the end of the seclusion of the mother also mark the 'social birth' of the child—his recognition as a new member of the community, often symbolized by naming him at this stage. Mönnig describes the ritual of incorporation among the Pedi as follows:

> On the afternoon of the day in which the seclusion of the mother and child is ended, a special feast called *ngwana o tšwa ntlong*—the child appears at the home—is usually held. This is a feast in which only the parents and the paternal relatives take part, and is the final initiation of the child into its father's group. It is a very joyous feast for which much meat and beer is prepared. The child is introduced to the group by its name. Towards the end of the feasting a special dance will be held in honour of the child, and also to set an example for its future conduct [the traditional men's dance being led by a man noted for his

bravery and industry in the case of a son, the dance of women being led by a woman with a hoe, noted as a worker, in the case of a daughter.] These dances are not peculiar to the ceremony, but are the characteristic fashion of male and female dancing seen at all ordinary feasts and are, therefore, an introduction of the child into the normal family life. This ceremony concludes the initiation of the child into the family, and thereby, in the case of a first child, also of the mother into her new status (Mönnig 1967: 104).

Naming practices vary considerably from group to group. The baby may be named at the end of this seclusion period amidst quite elaborate ceremony (Venda) or the name may simply be made public before a small group of people when the child is a few weeks old (Zulu). The name given in infancy is often changed when the child goes through initiation at puberty, or if the child fails to make progress, and incorrect naming is diagnosed to be the cause of these misfortunes. Often, in Christian families, the child is given a 'school' name at baptism, and even pagan families may give the child a European name in addition to a tribal one, either as an infant, or when he goes to school, to avoid difficulties with vernacular names. Ashton mentions that the South Sotho commonly take European names when seeking employment 'to avoid the derogatory modes of address so often used by Europeans, such as "Sixpence" or "Jim"' (Ashton 1952: 32).

The basis for choosing a name also varies from group to group. Peoples such as the South Sotho and Zulu commonly name children after grandfathers or important lineage members. The 'school' Mpondo also follow the custom of naming after grandparents, but the pagan Mpondo do not. The Venda believe the baby is a reincarnation of a dead relative and it is particularly important to choose the right name, lest by calling the child by the wrong one the wrath of the offended ancestor be incurred and illness brought to the child. Often the child is called after some important event which occurred around the time of the birth or after some personal characteristic.

Names are often not flattering. The Bhaca, for instance, favour derogatory names: 'Children who are given good names do not live' (Hammond-Tooke 1962: 76). Both the Venda and the South Sotho prefer derogatory or unflattering names. Among the latter group this is especially so where the death of previous children is believed to be due to sorcery. The child is given a name such as 'dog' or 'human excrement' and deliberately left looking neglected in order not to arouse the sorcerer's interest. Where a boy is born after a long succession of girls, and especially where other male children have died young, the boy is often dressed as a girl, given an 'unpleasant' name and sent away to his maternal grandparents for safety.

Should it die before passing through the rite of passage acknowledging its 'social birth', the child in some tribes may be ignored as never having been born. Among the Swazi, for instance, no public mourning is allowed and the

Venda will bury the body in a cool place in the same way as children killed at birth because they were not fully human, i.e. twins or deformed infants.

Infancy

From the time when the child is introduced into the community until he is weaned (usually between one and three years of age) he leads a warm, secure, pampered existence. Attention to his needs and well-being are more important than any rigid attempts to train or discipline him. Most peoples still see the infant as weak and in need of special treatment and protection, in the form of medicines and amulets against specific childhood dangers. The Tsonga, for instance, believe that milk alone is not sufficient to make a child grow and Junod quotes the Tsonga adage: 'The child grows by medicine' (Junod 1927 I: 48). For this reason the Tsonga mother always carries with her a reed containing the black powder which protects the infant on her back against the dangers of the bush, and a little calabash filled with medicated water which guards the child against the two most prevalent and feared childhood ills, convulsions and infantile diarrhoea. Both these illnesses are believed to be caused by an internal snake or worm (*nyoka*) and, unless checked by the routine use of medicine, will cause the child's death.

For the first few months, and sometimes longer, the infant is almost constantly with the mother. Carried on her back in a skin or blanket, it goes wherever she goes. Blacking writes:

> During the first year of his life, a Venda spends much of his time on his mother's back, and shares many of her experiences: he is shaken violently as she dances to the rhythms of a beer-song, pressed against her in a crowd at the installation of a headman, or squeezed during the finale of a *domba* initiation, when she and other married women join the 'chain' dance of the initiates; he is almost deafened by the sound of drums and reed-pipes playing the Venda national dance, *tshikona*, jogged regularly to the rhythm of his mother's work, as she pounds maize, hoes a field, or plays a drum, and lulled to sleep by the sound of someone telling a folk tale on a winter's night, when there is no work to be done on the following day and people can get up late (Blacking 1964: 25).

The baby in our society is, for the most part, cut off from contact with anyone but his immediate family. The African baby, by contrast, is from an early age drawn into the life of the community. At first this means going about with his mother, but very soon he will be given, at least partly, into the care of a child-nurse, typically an older sister, cousin or girl of the household. These young nurses, usually five to ten years old, often congregate in or near the village with their young charges, and the baby is thus introduced into a play-group of contemporaries. Sometimes, as among the Lobedu, the baby may also be left in the care of its grandmother, while the mother stamps or hoes. The women in the extended homestead all take an interest in the child and, after the first few months, the father too will usually play with the child, carrying him and singing to him when he needs consoling.

Babies, except in exceptional circumstances, are all breast-fed. Watery porridge is customarily fed as a supplement to breast-feeding and the baby is gradually introduced to other foods so that, by the time he is weaned, he is accustomed to an adult diet and the change is more psychological than dietary in impact.

Toilet training, for the few tribes where reference is made to it, seems on the whole rather less of a problem than in our society, largely because the mother does not expect the child to have control of his functions until he is two or three years old, and occasional lapses are treated with tolerance.

The whole technique of infant rearing seems to follow this rather lenient pattern—to the point where Hammond-Tooke, commenting on Bhaca babies, writes: 'They are hopelessly spoilt, their every whim being attended to, and at the slightest whimper they are given the breast.' Junod, too, says of the Tsonga that 'they would deem it cruelty to refuse the breast to a crying child' and the Lobedu child is also indulged for, as the Lobedu say: 'Care for it, for tomorrow it will care for you' (Hammond-Tooke 1962: 76–7; Junod 1927 I: 47; Krige and Krige 1943: 102). If the mother should be over-strict or careless in her handling of the child, the older women and, among the Venda, even strangers, will often admonish her. Blacking explains this for the Venda by saying 'a baby is not the property of an individual but of the group' (Blacking 1964: 21). Schapera mentions that this was traditionally also true for the Tswana but that the attitude is changing.

> The right to punish children formerly extended also to the community in general. Any man or woman insulted or otherwise injured by a child was entitled to thrash it on the spot. Nowadays, parents are growing apt to resent this, and it is more usual for the offended adult to complain to them, so that they may themselves punish the child (Schapera 1938a: 181).

The indulgence shown the young child is probably partly due to the environment in which he grows up. Unconfined by the limitations and hazards of life in town, with the whole homestead, plus his own nurse, to keep him out of danger, the restrictions which circumscribe the Western child need not be applied to him. 'There is little equipment in a traditional Venda home to make either parents or children anxious; and only three rules are strictly enforced: children must not play with knives or fire, and they must always show respect to others, especially their seniors' (Blacking 1964:29).

This last rule—showing respect to others—underlies much of the training. It is essential to the functioning of the entire social system (see chapter 11—morality). Political, religious, kinship and social relations are all organized around the principles of seniority and male dominance, demanding that each individual know his position in the hierarchy, and the appropriate respect relations to every other member of the group. The Bantu believe that certain basic rules of respect and politeness can be learned even before a child is weaned. We are told of the Swazi that people deliberately try to teach the young child basic kinship terms and correct behaviour. 'Obedience and politeness are inculcated from the beginning of awareness. Little achievements meet with warm encouragement and such stereotyped praise as "Chief", or "Now you are really a man"—or "a woman"' (H. Kuper 1963: 50).

Weaning and Early Childhood

The age of weaning varies a good deal from group to group[1] and has probably changed considerably over recent years.[2] Usually, a mother decides to wean a child either because she considers him old enough (the Tsonga believe, for instance, that when a child can be sent to a neighbouring hut to borrow snuff he is sufficiently mature) or because custom pronounces that he is old enough and the mother should leave off suckling him and have another child. Sometimes, despite the taboo on full intercourse during lactation, the woman falls pregnant and weaning must be hurried. A common method of weaning is to smear the nipples with some unpleasant-tasting substance such as bitter aloe, pipe oil, Jamaica pepper or chili. Sometimes herbs are mixed with the child's food or tied around his neck to wean him away from the breast, or the mother may simply wrap a blanket around her breasts and refuse to allow him to suckle. Among the Lobedu, Venda and South Sotho the child's companions may mock him for continuing to drink from his mother like a baby. Some groups, e.g. the Zulu, Mpondo, Tsonga and South Sotho, combine weaning with sending the child away from home to live with his maternal or paternal grandparents.[3]

On the whole, weaning as a stage of the life cycle is not attended by much ritual. The Mpondo may slaughter a goat or beer is made 'but this is not a ritual killing, the omission of which might make the child sick, but only meat or drink for rejoicing' (Hunter 1936: 158). The Zulu slaughter a goat 'for the purification of the mother and child, whereupon sexual intercourse may again take place' (Krige 1936a: 73). Probably the most elaborate ritualization occurs among the Tsonga, where a doctor is called in and the child treated with special medicines in an involved ritual (Junod 1927 I: 58–9). The rite is similar to that performed for purposes of purification at the conclusion of treatment for a serious illness. That it should follow weaning gives some insight into the Tsonga conception of infancy, for it suggests that they regard these first three years as a period in which the child's life is constantly in danger. 'He is during the whole time under the supervision of the physician, who takes leave of the little patient on the day of weaning' (Junod 1927 I: 59).

Weaning brings the period of infantile dependency to an end, and the child joins a group of toddlers of about his own age. For the next two to four years he lives a relatively carefree, irresponsible life, with small jobs like chasing chickens and running errands being the only demands made on him. It is, however, a valuable period from the point of view of the child's socialization.

His circle of acquaintances increases and he ventures further afield in the exploration of his environment. Unlike Western children, he is seldom lonely or lacking companions; the typical homestead has a number of women of similar age to his mother, who will themselves have children of about his age. This stage is important in that it lays the foundations for much of his future adult behaviour, which will require his co-operation within a group of contemporaries. His peer group, watched over by those just a little older, lay down rules for acceptable conduct and are in a strong position to see that they are obeyed. Sanctions such as mockery and ostracism enable them to deal effectively with displays of bad temper, selfishness and poor sportsmanship.

Up to the age of six there is little difference between the day-to-day lives of boys and girls; play-groups include children of both sexes and they share the same games and pastimes.

From Six Years Old to Puberty

From about five or six years old the lives of boys and girls diverge. Boys more and more go off with other boys of about their own age to herd livestock, while girls remain in or near the homestead, occupied with 'women's work'. Sometimes, when the boys come in from the veld in the evenings, they may play together but a boy who spends too much time with the girls is usually ridiculed by his friends.[4]

The young boys gain their first experience of herding with the less valuable stock. They may stay around the village tending calves (Pedi), but more commonly they go out, in the company of older boys, with the sheep, goats, donkeys and calves. Herding cattle is usually left to boys of ten or older. At first, the young boy may be loath to leave behind the easy, irresponsible existence of early childhood for the responsibilities and rough life of a herdboy. However, ridicule from other boys, and beating, or threats of beatings, from his father, older brother or one of the older herdboys normally brings him into line. Herding is an essential experience for a boy (besides its obvious economic necessity) as it weans him psychologically from his life in the women's world. The Swazi express this by saying that boys 'must not grow up under the skin skirts of their mothers' (H. Kuper 1963: 51).

The herdboy certainly faces a tougher time among the other boys than he experienced in the village or homestead. He is thrown together, not only with his contemporaries but also with the older herdboys, often youths of seventeen or eighteen years. Rather like 'new boys' in a Western boarding school, the young herdboy may be bullied and teased by the older ones. A system of 'fagging' is fairly common and unpleasant jobs are usually delegated to the children. Among the Venda:

> Little boys . . . of four or five go out herding, and become involved in a separate micro-society which operates within the larger framework of Venda society. The senior boys organize the herding as they choose,

which often means that they sit under a tree playing competitive games such as cattle-raiding (*mufuvha*), while the juniors look after the animals. Adults never interfere with this system unless animals damage crops or property: then the senior boy is punished, and he in turn will take it out of the juniors to whom he delegated the work, unless they have already run away! (Blacking 1964: 32).

This term 'micro-society' can be usefully employed among peoples other than the Venda. The herdboys form a definite group, with a sub-culture of their own. Like the adolescent sub-culture in our own society, they have their own norms, often in conflict with those of their elders. Among the South Sotho: 'The boys' group is free and easy and is not bound by the conventions and standards of their elders' (Ashton 1952: 37). One standard of behaviour, enforced among adults but broken regularly by herd-boys, is respect for the property of others. Pilfering as a major pastime among the herdboys, sometimes on the orders of the gang leader, is mentioned for Lobedu, Pedi, South Sotho and Tsonga. If the culprits are caught redhanded punishment may follow, but on the whole adults tend to shrug off this petty theft as boyish mischievousness. Usually only food is stolen, though the gang leader may also demand tobacco.

While this type of boys' sub-culture flourishes in most of the tribes, it appears to be particularly strong among the Pedi and Xhosa.[5] Among the Pedi, gang leadership is formalized by a contest usually taking the form of fighting with switches made from slender, tapering roots of the *moretlwa* tree (*Grewia flava*). At first the boys of one *kgôrô*[6] will fight each other; they will then begin to challenge those of other *kgôrôs*, the older boys encouraging even the smaller ones to join in. Finally three groups emerge—'a group of smaller boys who cannot compete for the ultimate leadership, a group of larger boys who do not feel themselves able to contend for the leadership, and the final group of big boys who are striving for the general leadership' (Mönnig 1967: 108).

When the groups reach this stage the boys make a formal application to the chief for permission to complete the fight for leadership of the age group. An extended contest, in which switch fights determine the leader for each group, is held.[7] The winner of the final fight among the bigger boys will become the general leader, with the two other winners as go-betweens between him and the other groups. Mönnig writes: 'The uninitiated boys and girls[8] form a transitional group. They are not yet members of the tribe, but they have to a large extent outgrown parental control. They form a society of their own, which is not fully integrated with the tribal society.' Although they are outside the control of the tribal courts at this stage, and insubordination and stealing are encouraged, they are strictly, often harshly, controlled by their own leaders. 'The leader of the boys forms a "court" with councillors of his own. These are usually the boys who came second and third in the fighting, who are deputy leaders. The youths, both boys and girls, are brought before his "court" and punished for their misdeeds. As they own no property, punishment is either corporal or through the ridicule of other youths' (Mönnig 1967: 108–9).

Despite the fact that this period is marked by delinquent behaviour, which the adults find offensive, it is nevertheless a period in which valuable lessons for the future are learned. The boys develop an intimate and accurate knowledge of the veld and its wild-life. The Kriges, writing of the Lobedu, comment: 'A herdboy walking along with you will give you the name and uses of almost every tree or shrub you pass in that rich bushveld environment, and once a boy of fifteen astonished us by being able to name over 200 specimens of plants from that area' (Krige and Krige 1943: 108). Hunting birds and small animals, and making use of the wild fruits of the veld, boys become very self-sufficient. Co-operation with peers and obedience to the authority of those only slightly older than oneself are instilled during this period, but, with the exception of the Venda *thondo*,[9] this is not a period where formal institutionalized instruction is given.

The life of the girls does not change radically in the years between weaning and puberty. Unlike the boys, a girl remains for the most part tied to the household in the role of assistant housewife. In the early years her main occupation is usually that of nursemaid, but gradually she learns all the other skills she will need to run her own home. At first, her contributions are small; being physically not strong enough to carry an adult load of water or firewood, she may bring only a miniature calabash or bundles of kindling. She is taught those techniques which match her strength. Grinding corn or maize, smearing walls and floors, hoeing, cooking, making fires, winnowing, collecting relishes and stamping are all skills acquired gradually over this period. Usually long before puberty, the girl is fully able to run a household.

Although today many of the youths and some girls leave home soon after puberty to work in the cities at jobs for which they have had little or no preparation, traditional society saw the child in these pre-adolescent years almost fully trained for his future economic role. Rather than consciously passing on knowledge in an artificial situation, traditional education was by imitation. The Kriges' statement on the Lobedu may well sum up the situation in Bantu societies generally:[10]

> Children learn the tasks required of adults simply by doing them. They are anxious to imitate their elders, and there is never any compulsory element in the teaching of these skills. Moreover, in their education they have this advantage, that it is not carried on in an institution divorced from everyday adult activities. The child feels that he is an essential part of the society; all he does is a direct contribution to the domestic economy (Krige and Krige 1943: 105).

Imitating adult life carries through into children's games as well. Little girls with real babies to mind will still make themselves dolls out of mealie cobs or plant stems and rags; little boys will make clay models of oxen and homesteads and imitate ceremonies witnessed in the village. Singing, dancing, drumming and playing musical instruments are favourite pastimes, and many games involve songs or rhythmic movements. Often activities which are looked on merely as games by the children are in fact valuable aids in developing skills. Imitating adult behaviour obviously falls into this category but so, too, does a game such as that played by Zulu, Lobedu, Venda and Tsonga boys in which a tuber, or, in the Tsonga case, a grass disc, is rolled downhill and the boys attempt to spear it, developing in the process excellent hand-eye co-ordination and exactness of aim (Raum 1953: 105). Making their own toys—bows and arrows, 'hockey' sticks, musical instruments, spinning tops, sleds, hats and models of everything from oxen, wagons and lorries to imitations of the visiting anthropologist's possessions (the Kriges mention spectacles and watches as being the fashion for a while during their stay among the Lobedu)—develops the children's knowledge of the raw materials available to them and the manual skills they will need for later adult tasks. Another common pastime with herdboys is riding oxen (Berglund 1968; Wilson and Thompson 1969: 108, 143). Usually one or two in the herd are specially trained for this purpose.

Many games found among Bantu children are very similar to those played by Western children. This similarity occasionally may be due to contact with missions and schools, but many of these games are found throughout the world. Among the Bantu hopscotch, hockey, hide-and-seek, cat-and-mouse, tag, leap-frog, clap-hands, Ring o' Roses, cat's cradle (a string game), tops and jacks all exist in modified forms.

Playing 'house', a favourite Western game, is a very common pastime among Bantu children. Among the Lobedu, Venda and Pedi, it has developed into a highly formalized imitation of a real marriage, of some duration, with the construction of miniature villages and 'husbands' and 'wives' fulfilling the obligations to spouse and kin which would be expected in the real thing.[11]

An important feature of the herdboys' lives, especially among the Cape Nguni, is stickfighting. Hunter, describing the practice among the Mpondo, writes:[12]

> Fighting with sticks is as constant an occupation of the Mpondo as is playing with a ball of the English. I have seen a mother playing with her son of 2 or 3, pretending to hit him so that he put up one arm for defence and tried to hit back; boys of 4 and 5 have their knobkerries, and begin to scrap. When out herding the elder boys arrange contests, pairing off couples and forcing them to fight; the combats between individuals are constant; the boys of one *umzi* [homestead] fight those of another, the herds of one set of *imizi*, the herds of another, one district another. Often two neighbouring districts are in such a state of war, that if a boy from one enters the other he is immediately attacked (Hunter 1936: 160).

Games like these involving not only imitation of adult economic roles but adherence to accepted norms and to the rituals of social relations, are valuable training for the young. As with economic behaviour, social values, attitudes and behaviour are not taught in any formal sense at this stage. Rather the child picks them up in his daily social intercourse. Listening to folk-tales which point a moral or hearing proverbs designed as correctives to misbehaviour—'lies do not make one wealthy', 'the cow is helped which helps itself' (Ashton 1952: 44)—the child picks up values unconsciously.

Certain values are commonly stressed throughout Bantu society. Respect for elders, obedience to those in authority, generosity, responsibility, willingness to share (particularly food), and the ability to live in peace with others, because they are basic to adult relationships, are heavily emphasized in childhood. Girls tend to conform to these norms earlier and more easily than boys, who temporarily suspend obedience to some degree during the lawless, insubordinate herdboy stage.

Sanctions against those who do not conform are applied from two directions: by the peer group and by adults, with the father being the main authority and disciplinarian in the family. Adults, peers or older children may all threaten a child with a beating in cases of disobedience, but these threats are generally not carried out. The Mpondo, for instance, though they constantly threaten, very seldom administer a hiding. 'Children are precious and to beat a child is to "spoil" it' (Hunter 1936: 164). Naturally some parents will be more likely to favour corporal punishment than others; the child's discipline is a function of his parents' personality. Among the Tswana, in former times, a particularly potent parental sanction was the belief in the power of the curse. Schapera writes: 'If a child shamefully and persistently neglected his father, or indeed any senior relative, the latter would deliberately invoke some evil upon him, and it was firmly believed that the curse would take effect' (Schapera 1940a: 254). A commonly used sanction, particularly in the hands of the peer group, is mockery or ridicule, often in the form of chants or songs. The threat of ostracism is also a powerful force for conformity. As in our society, bogeys or threats of supernatural punishments are often resorted to in an attempt to frighten a child into obedience. The South Sotho child is told he will turn into a monkey if he does not stop crying or sits with his back to the fire, or that wandering off or making a nuisance of himself will bring the wolves,[13] *thokolosi* or the police after him. Crying or disobedient Mpondo children are told, '*Thikoloshe* will get you', 'a murderer will come and cut your heads off', or (during Monica Hunter's fieldwork), 'Here's the white woman: she will bite you.'

Generally, the strictest discipline during these years is at the hands of other children. The Kriges remark this among the Lobedu, and add: 'Children learn more easily and more willingly from other children than from adults, and every boy knows that soon he too will enjoy the privilege of authority over those younger than he is' (Krige and Krige 1943: 107).

The pre-puberty years, then, are years in which the child learns his future economic role and much of the social behaviour that will be expected of him as an adult. They are years of development, little marked by any ritualization of status changes, though a few rites do occur. For instance, among the Swazi at about the age of six and the Zulu 'before reaching puberty', a ceremony is held at which the child's earlobes are pierced.[14] In both tribes, it is believed that after this ceremony, the child should be more mature, more responsible for his or her actions. The Zulu child is finally incorporated as a full member of his family by going through this ritual (Krige 1936a: 81–2).[15]

Among the Pedi, a communal name-giving rite (*rela maina*) is reported. Mönnig writes:

> It is generally said that children should be named (i.e. given new names) soon after they are weaned, but in practice such ceremonies are usually held when the time for tribal initiation draws near, and there are un-named children eligible for that initiation. Usually when *rela maina* ceremonies are held quite a number of children are named, their ages ranging from about three years upwards to about sixteen (1967: 105–6).

The ceremony publicly initiates them into membership of the corporate lineage group, symbolically reinforced by the fact that the rite takes place at the spot where the ancestors are buried; also, by naming each participant in order of rank, first boys then girls, their exact status relative to one another, is underlined.[16]

Although rites centred specifically on the child are infrequent, pre-pubertal children are often essential to communal rituals (see chapter 11). Many rites require participants who have not been contaminated by sexual intercourse or menstruation. For instance, among Venda, Kgatla and Lobedu, immature girls and boys must sprinkle the country with medicines to bring the rains; the Venda baby must be brought out of the birth hut and presented to his relatives by a little girl who 'has not yet menstruated and is therefore ritually cold, and safe' (Blacking 1964: 18). This participation in ceremonies, whether it be as key actor or merely as an observer, systematically introduces the growing child to the ritual of social relations and draws him into the social world of the adults.

By the time he reaches adolescence the Bantu child is thus economically and socially fairly well equipped for his future adult life. All that remains is for the change to adulthood to be effected. The onset of puberty, in most Bantu societies, is marked by a period of intensive ritualization aimed at integrating the child formally into the adult world.

Puberty

Many Bantu peoples have rites marking the first physical signs of puberty, particularly in the case of girls. Among Venda, Tsonga, Zulu and, formerly, the Lobedu, the boy's first nocturnal emission signals physical maturity. Among Lobedu and Tsonga (Mpfumo clan) the occasion is marked simply by treating him with medicine to strengthen and protect him. The Zulu surround the event with an extensive ritual, the *thomba*, in which the boy, having been treated with strengthening medicine, is secluded in a hut with companions who have already gone through the ceremony. He must observe food taboos and avoid contact with women. A certain amount of instruction concerning sexual behaviour is given, but in general the isolation period is uneventful. Seclusion is usually terminated the day after a ritual sacrifice of a beast or goat has been made to the ancestors, with the rest of the community joining in feasting, singing and dancing, when the boy is taken down to the river by his comrades to wash and is given a new name by which he will be known for the rest of his life by people of his own age or younger. (Older people will still call him by his boyhood name, but it would be abusive for the younger ones not to recognize his new status by using his new name.) The seclusion hut is freshly smeared, the boy is given new clothes and, amidst much singing, dancing and beer drinking, he is reincorporated into the society as a mature man and may start courting girls.[17]

The Venda boys' puberty ceremony, *vhutamba vhutuka*, differs from the others in that a boy who experiences his first emission must wait until a number of boys have reached the same stage before the rite takes place. They are then put through six days of physical hardening by the initiates of the previous ceremony—the main ordeal being a daily three- to four-hour immersion in icy river water—and given sexual instruction and taught tribal etiquette and customs. This is regarded as the first stage on their 'journey towards manhood' and they are now encouraged to indulge in 'playful familiarities' with girls—a practice hitherto strictly forbidden (Stayt 1931a: 106).

Puberty ceremonies for girls usually occur at the time of first menstruation, although this is not invariably so. For instance, the Mpondo ceremony, *ukuthombisa*, must be held sometime between a girl's first menstruation and marriage. Not to perform the ceremony might incur the wrath of the ancestors, so that where a married woman who has not been through the ceremony falls ill, the rite is sometimes carried out after marriage to appease the spirits.[18] The Venda rite, *vhusha*, may be postponed until two or three girls have begun to menstruate, and they then go through the ceremony together (see Plate 9a) (Stayt 1931a: 106–10).

Most common in the case of the girls is an initiation rite which includes seclusion for the duration of the first menstrual period. Ceremonies of this type occur, for instance, among Pedi, Lobedu, the northern Tsonga clans,[19] Zulu and Cape Nguni. The rites all follow a basically similar pattern, though the Pedi nowadays practise a very much simplified form with minimal community involvement (Mönnig 1967: 124–5).

Among the other tribes the first menstruation is usually not reported directly to the mother, but through an intermediary, or, indirectly, by the girl crying or running away and hiding. When the fact becomes known, the girl is secluded in a hut, often attended by a friend or a number of other girls. The Lobedu girl must not only be secluded for her own first menstruation, but she is made to go through the entire ceremony with four to six subsequent initiates before her change of status is recognized (Krige and Krige 1943: 111). During this period—anything from three or four days (Pedi) to a month (Tsonga)—she must not be seen by the community, especially not by men. Often she is covered by a blanket and when she goes outside to relieve herself she must remain covered and unidentifiable. Although she may be cut off from normal social intercourse, the girls who are with her spend the evenings singing, dancing and feasting. During seclusion, the girl may be subjected to certain hardships. Among the Tsonga and Lobedu she is forced to sit in icy river water for long periods, and she may be beaten or forced to eat porridge without relishes (Lobedu) or scratched, pinched and teased (Tsonga). Zulu and Bhaca girls are more leniently treated, but must observe a taboo on sour milk which is lifted at the end of the seclusion period by the killing of a goat. Pedi, Lobedu and Tsonga give a certain amount of sex instruction during the seclusion period, including warnings on how to behave during menstruation, but there is no mention of instruction given among the Cape Nguni or Zulu. At the end of the seclusion period the girl is reincorporated into the community by means of a feast and a beer drink. Her emergence from childhood is recognized by some symbolic act, for instance the wearing of new clothes (Pedi) or of clothes normally reserved for married women (Zulu and formerly Bhaca), by having her head shaved (Lobedu and Zulu) or by the destruction of something associated with the seclusion period—e.g. the grass of the seclusion hut floor is burned (Bhaca) or the veil worn during seclusion is removed (Tsonga).

Among the Zulu, the *udwa* ceremony associated with first menstruation is followed, often years later when the girl is already engaged and ready for marriage, by the *omula* or coming-of-age rites. The ceremony is associated with marriage and is held only in the case of a virgin. Although the ritual does not follow the usual pattern of rites of passage—separation, marginal transition phase and reincorporation—it nevertheless marks the transition of the girl to a fully marriageable state. The most important aspect of the *omula* is the singing of special songs often seemingly very vulgar and obscene. Krige writes: 'In general, the songs may be said to make clear the meaning and purpose of menstruation; they depict the sex act and its relation to procreation, extol the penis and warn against full intercourse before marriage.' These songs also play a very important part in many Zulu fertility rites (Krige 1968: 176-7).

Initiation Schools

The most dramatic examples of puberty rites occur in the initiation schools where there is a *collective* status change, surrounded by elaborate ceremonial. These schools are, however, not always associated with physical maturity. In some male schools very young boys or mature men may go through them together with boys who have just reached puberty. This type of age distribution occurs, for instance, in societies where adolescent boys are likely to be away at school or working when the ideal time for initiation approaches or in societies where initiations are held very irregularly e.g. the Lobedu, where tribal ceremonies are only held every twelve to fifteen years (Krige and Krige 1943: 114).[20]

The popularity and importance of initiation schools has gone through periods of decline and resurgence in many Bantu societies. A tendency noted by a number of writers is for circumcision schools to be abandoned in times of war and social upheaval, either because the lodges interfere with the mobilization of men or it is feared that the initiates would be unable to escape in the event of an attack.[21]

Apart from pressure being applied from outside for schools to be discontinued e.g. by missionary or government action, they may lose their importance spontaneously or through the introduction of some functional substitute. The Mpondo, for instance, say that one reason for the disappearance of initiation schools in their society was the deleterious effect on health— 'circumcision wears out people'—although the immediate cause was a fiat by a chief (Hunter 1936: 165). Schapera writes that a Tswana boy no longer has to go through even the very modified initiation to be accepted into an age-regiment. 'Schoolboys are exempted, and those away working consider themselves as a matter of course members of the same regiment as their age-mates' (Schapera 1940: 259). Going to work in town has become a way of proving one's manhood in many tribes, even where initiation ceremonies exist, but where they do not a period in town may by itself entitle the boy to claim adult status, e.g. the Bhaca (Hammond-Tooke 1962: 79).

In some areas, there appears to be a resurgence of interest in initiation schools. Hammond-Tooke remarks that Hlubi circumcision schools are drawing more Bhaca every year, especially in areas close to Hlubi locations, and that Mpondo often have the circumcision performed at a mission hospital. Mpondo students at Fort Hare and Lovedale frequently return home circumcised, probably because they have been in contact with Xhosa and Thembu girls who refuse to have anything to do with uncircumcised men (Hammond-Tooke 1962: 81–2). The South Sotho also appear to be reviving the custom. Chadwick (1958: 9) and John Perry[22] have mentioned this trend. Perry ascribes it to the growth of Sotho nationalism and a new enthusiasm for old customs. In many tribes the schools are encouraged by chiefs who stand to benefit financially from the dues paid to them.

Circumcision

A custom commonly associated with male initiation ceremonies in South Africa is circumcision. Krige gives the following note on the distribution of the custom.

> The present distribution of circumcision cannot be fully plotted out, owing to complete lack of information on many tribes. We do, however,

know from published sources that it is practised by Xhosa, Thembu, Fingo and Bomvana; some of the Tswana tribes; the Southern Sotho; the Pedi, Masemola, Lemba, Ndebele, Matlala of North-West Transvaal, Mmamabola of Woodbush, Transvaal Shangana-Tonga, Venda and Lobedu, Xananwa, Letswalo and Khaha. In Portuguese East Africa it is practised by Chopi and some Shangana-Tonga (Krige 1937b: 100).

All Cape Nguni circumcise except the Bhaca, Mpondo, Xesibe and Ntlangwini. The Mpondo used to have initiation schools with circumcision rites (Hunter 1936: 165) and Hammond-Tooke mentions that there is evidence to suggest that the Bhaca formerly practised the custom (Hammond-Tooke 1962: 81). Natal Bhaca 'still slit the frenulum or cut it off with a horse-hair as a hygienic measure' (Kohler 1933: 10).[23] Similarly the Zulu cut the string under the foreskin at about nine years of age, but this is not a ritual occasion.

Boys' Initiation Schools

In broad outline, boys' initiation schools follow a similar pattern in all tribes. Prior to the opening of the schools, the boys often spend time together. Among the Lobedu they spend a fortnight out in the veld learning songs in preparation for the opening of the school; among the South Sotho they meet daily going out with the cattle and returning at night, collecting firewood and making ropes for the lodge, and learning a number of secret songs. Pedi initiates must spend this preparatory period working for the chief. The schools are under the control of an appointed 'father' (usually a man of high rank), a guardian or guardians (often the boys who were themselves initiated at the previous session) and a doctor or skilled 'surgeon' who will perform the actual circumcision. Among the Cape Nguni the ceremony is a much more local affair than among the other groups. Boys of a local area are circumcised together and their schools are usually smaller, the 'father' of the school being the father of one of the initiates. Although the chief will be informed of the intention to hold an initiation, there is no organization at a chiefdom or national level as one finds among the Sotho groups. In preparation for the school the fathers of the Cape Nguni initiates will kill a goat; among the Xhosa and Mfengu the boy will be given meat from the right foreleg, a practice said to prevent the boy going mad or dying during the initiation.

An essential feature of the initiation schools is that the boys should be physically separated from the rest of the community for at least some part of the duration of the school. Accordingly, a lodge is built in a secluded place some distance from the village.[24] The separation period itself is sometimes preceded by a symbolic act signifying the separation of the initiate from his former state.[25] The Pedi, Tlokwa, Venda, Tsonga and Bomvana, for instance, shave the boys' heads; the South Sotho and Bomvana hold a ritual killing and a feast.

Where circumcision is practised, it is this operation which finally separates the boy from his childhood. There is often specific reference to this change by the boy or the onlookers at the moment the operation is completed. For instance, among the Xhosa and Mfengu, after he is cut the boy is told to say 'I am a man' and the surgeon answers 'You are a man' (Wilson *et al.* 1952: 208).

Among the Cape Nguni, the initiate must demonstrate his new manliness by not flinching or crying out at the operation. South Sotho and Venda boys are not expected to give such a stoic performance, and cries are drowned by the loud singing of the onlookers.

After circumcision, the wound is usually treated, the medicine applied varying from healing leaves to antibiotic creams, brandy and paraffin in recent years. The initiates are then taken to the seclusion lodge where they spend between two and three months cut off from normal community life. The degree of isolation varies, but is far less strict among the Cape Nguni than for the northern Bantu tribes. The Nguni initiates, for instance, may work in the fields, and costumed dancing in neighbouring villages is central to the ceremonies among Bomvana and Xhosa. Besides this physical separation from the past and the everyday, their special state is further underlined by numerous taboos and observances. In many tribes the initiates' bodies are painted with white clay (e.g. Pedi, Tswana, Venda, Tsonga and Cape Nguni); often a special language or special words for common objects and actions are used (e.g. South Sotho, Pedi, Tswana, Venda, Tsonga and Bomvana); contact with women is almost always forbidden or severely curtailed, although Cape Nguni initiates are not deprived of the company of their girlfriends.

A feature of all the initiation schools is the subjection of the initiates to various hardships and ordeals. Beatings—either routine or for some real contravention of the laws of the lodge—unsavoury food, a prohibition on the drinking of water, uncomfortable sleeping conditions (the schools are traditionally held in winter), and long, cold sessions bathing in the icy rivers are the ordeals most commonly encountered. They are intended to discipline the boys and prepare them for the hardships of manhood (see Plate 9b). Occasionally this severe treatment leads to the death of an initiate; usually when this happens the body is buried secretly and the parents only informed at the end of the school. Like a baby which had died before naming, the dead initiate may often not be publicly mourned, suggesting that the boy they had known was 'dead' anyway and the 'man' had not yet been born.[26]

An important feature of many of the initiation schools is the formal teaching which is given during the period of seclusion by the men of the tribe. The stress on teaching varies. Among the Cape Nguni, instruction is minimal. The Xhosa and Mfengu receive some sex instruction, but among the Bomvana, Cook writes, 'there is no curriculum of learning' (Cook 1931: 58). In the other tribes, the boys are often made to learn secret formulae and songs, the esoteric nature of many of these making them useful passwords in establishing one's identity as an initiated tribesman when travelling among strangers. Among the Sotho groups, teaching has a strong nationalistic flavour; tribal loyalty and values and the rights and obligations of citizenship are emphasized. An important occupation in all the male initiation schools is hunting; however, this is not usually a 'new' skill learned in the school, since the initiates are likely to have mastered the art during the days spent in the veld as herdboys. Dancing is often a feature of the separation period, particularly spectacular and important in the reed-costumed *abakhwetha* dances of the Cape Nguni (see Plate 10).[27]

The end of the seclusion period is marked by rites releasing the boy from the marginal status of the previous months. The white clay is washed away in the river and, in all groups except the Lobedu, the boy is smeared with red ochre. Often their heads are again shaved (South Sotho, Lobedu, Venda, Tsonga and Pedi) and they are given new clothes (Pedi, Tswana, Tsonga, Bomvana, Thembu, Mpondomise, Mfengu, Xhosa). One rite common to all the schools is the ritual burning of the seclusion lodge and all the contents including the clothes and utensils used by the boys during their stay; the retreating boys are forbidden to look back as their past is burnt behind them.

The boys now return to the community and are received with feasting and celebration, often accompanied by exhortations delivered by the older men. In many cases the boys do not return to their own homesteads immediately. Among the Bomvana, for instance, they spend three or four days in the kraal of the 'father' of the school. The Pedi youth spends ten days in the royal kraal during which time he is reminded of his new duties and responsibilities; the Venda boy must spend six days working for the chief before he is allowed to go home.

Although the boy is now re-incorporated in the community and his changed status is recognized, he is not necessarily regarded as being completely adult in all spheres of community life. Initiation may prepare him for one or many of his adult roles: for example, military, political, religious, legal, marital or sexual—the emphasis varies from society to society. However, where initiation schools are held, they are an essential stage through which the boy must pass before he can attain higher status.

'Supplementary' Schools

A number of the North Sotho (e.g. Pedi, Lobedu, Mmamabolo of Woodbush, Letswala and Matlala) and Tswana groups hold supplementary schools some time after the initial circumcision.[28]

Schapera describes the Tswana 'black' *bogwêra* which takes place a year or so after the 'white' *bogwêra*[29] as follows:

> It was held in the great cattle-kraal adjoining the Chief's council place. The boys remained here for a few days only, during which they were made to go over the laws they had previously been taught, and received some additional instruction, accompanied as usual by many painful forms of discipline. After this they were given their first task to perform as a regiment: they might be sent on a cattle raid or to kill a lion, or to

hunt for the Chief. They were then regarded as men and were free to marry, after their leader had done so (Schapera 1940a: 257-8).

The Pedi *bogwera* usually takes place one to two years after the *bodika* or circumcision school. Although the *bodika* initiates the boy into tribal status with limited political rights, it is only once he has been through the *bogwera* that he attains full politico-jural status.[30] Mönnig writes of the school: 'The word *bogwera* means friendship and, apart from its politico-jural function . . . its purpose is to cement the lasting bond between the members of the regiment which was created during the previous session . . . a strong bond of solidarity and mutual cooperation is created during the latter session, a bond which lasts throughout the life of its members' (Mönnig 1967: 122).

The routine of the *bogwera* is largely a repetition of that of the *bodika* but is not as formal or harsh as the circumcision school. A small lodge is built for the boys, close to the village, where they receive instruction during the day; at night they sleep in the chief's gathering place. The school is terminated after a month by a ceremony in which a pole, topped by a woven grass bird, and representing the regiment, is planted by the boys near the tribal fire in the chief's gathering place. Mönnig writes: 'This is the formal incorporation of the members of the regiment, as a unit, into the society of men' (Mönnig 1967: 124). The boys remain a further ten days at the chief's place spending most of their time in his service. Near the end of this period a senior councillor will address them, and with the words 'On this day you are men' officially recognize their new status.

The Lobedu *buhwera* school, unlike the Pedi and Tswana schools described above, centres not on the consolidation of a regiment and tribal status, but rather on introducing the boys to the mysteries of the Bird, the ruling spirit of the *byali* or girls' initiation (see below p. 233). The boys spend their time in an enclosure built next to that which houses the Bird.[31] The Kriges write of the *buhwera* school:

> They are taught a few 'laws' or formulae associated with the *vuhwera*, but their main activities are learning to make the elaborately woven costumes[32] and later to dance in the *vyali* courtyard. Towards the end of the initiation they spend most of their time going about to dance,[33] accepting invitations from other district heads and paying their respects at the royal village . . . The *vuhwera* is a kind of finishing school, an initiation into the secret of what the Bird is and how the costumes are made. It is almost as though this is an esoteric art, the preservation of which has become the main function of the *vuhwera* (Krige and Krige 1943: 135).[34]

Girls' Initiation Schools

Schools for girls of the scope and size associated with the boys' circumcision lodges are found among the Lobedu, Venda, Pedi, South Sotho and Tswana.[35]

The Tswana, Lobedu, Pedi and Venda schools are closely linked with the schools held for boys of the same age. Thus the Tswana girls' school initiates a new girls' regiment shortly after the boys' regiment is formed, the two regiments sharing the same name. The Lobedu *byali* or girls' initiation takes place at the same time and in conjunction with the boys' *buhwera*; the Pedi *byale* starts at the close of the boys' *bogwera*, and also brings a new women's regiment into being; the Venda *domba*[36] is in fact a combined school for boys and girls, though more emphasis is placed on the compulsory attendance of girls than of boys.

The schools vary in their duration. Traditional Tswana and Pedi schools lasted only one month; the Lobedu school lasts a year, taking in a full agricultural cycle; the Venda *domba* lasts anything from three months to two years. Although special areas are set aside for the initiates and a lodge may be built, the element of complete isolation at a distance from the village is missing. While the girls' initiation is usually the concern of the women of the community, the Lobedu *byali* and the Venda *domba* are both organized by both men and women.

Analogous to circumcision in the boys' schools, the girls' schools usually also have some suggestion of a genital operation included in the rites. Ashton writes of the South Sotho: 'They may . . . undergo some physical operation, the hymen perhaps being broken either by the insertion of a horn or of a woman's finger' (Ashton 1952: 57). The Lobedu girl is given a tiny cut above the clitoris (Krige and Krige 1943: 138). The Tswana and Pedi, while not actually performing a genital operation, do have rites imitating such an operation. In former times the Tswana girl was cut on the inside of the thigh and a burning stick applied to the wound (Schapera 1940a: 259). The Pedi have an elaborate ceremony in which girls go through a rite imitating circumcision. A knife is pressed between the girl's legs while she lies under a blanket; although she is not actually injured, the girl cries in fright, and the other initiates, seeing the women who perform the operation with their hands covered in plant juices to simulate blood, are probably as impressed by the ordeal as the boys who undergo an actual operation (Mönnig 1967: 126).

Like the boys, girl initiates must observe certain taboos and are subjected to hardships and ordeals, but on the whole they are less harshly treated than male initiates. Singing and dancing are very important in girls' initiation schools, the 'python' dance of the Venda girls being a particularly noteworthy example (see Plates 12a and 12b). As in boys' initiation schools, the initiation period is also a time for formal education into tribal laws and values, although the Kriges point out that this is not a very important part of Lobedu girls' initiation. In general, the teaching focuses on the woman's roles and duties—domestic, agricultural and marital—and sex education is emphasized.

The Lobedu and South Sotho lodges are associated with specific animals.[38] Among the Lobedu, the Bird is the ruling spirit of the *buhwera-byali* ceremonies, and his wishes and commands dominate the whole course of the *byali* school. The girls must feed, dance and sing for him and may desist only with his permission. The supernatural aspect of the initiation carries over into the important rites of showing the initiates the sacred objects or 'mysteries' of the tribe. Among the Tswana and South Sotho there is little information concerning this, though Schapera does remark on 'semi-public masquerades in honour of various "deities" forming a conspicuous part of their routine' (Schapera 1940a: 259).

Among the Pedi, and more particularly the Venda and Lobedu, this revelation of the sacred is central to the whole school. The mysteries may take a number of forms—masked figures, mummeries, clay, wooden or other models of animals and people or simply interesting and elaborately decorated objects (Lobedu, *digoma*; Pedi, *dikgomana*; Venda, *dzingoma*). Among the Lobedu, the greatest *goma* of all is the Bird who rules the *byali*. The Venda *dzingoma* are associated with teaching regarding tribal norms and values (Stayt 1931a: 116–22; Blacking 1969: pt. 3).

The girls' schools are often considered to be a necessary preliminary to marriage. For the South Sotho and Lobedu they have overtones of a fertility rite. For this reason, though the South Sotho do not usually enforce attendance at an initiation school, a man who marries and discovers that his wife has not been initiated, might send her to the next *bale* held in the district.

The Function of Initiation Schools and Rituals

Although in most Bantu societies where initiation schools or rituals are held they are considered to be of central importance in the life cycle of the individual, the specific significance of the institution in any particular group is often difficult to determine. Many ethnographers carry interpretation only so far as to say that initiation confers adulthood or manhood on the initiate, without defining whether this means sexual, jural, social, religious, political or economic adulthood, or a combination of these statuses.[39] Detailed analysis of particular rites, songs or formulae within each school or ceremony is rare.

Attempting to explain initiation rites in terms of theories believed to have universal application[40] is a difficult and often unsatisfactory procedure. It is difficult in that material on many aspects of socialization is lacking in the standard monographs, e.g. details of the mother-son sleeping arrangements necessary to Whiting and associates' hypothesis (Whiting *et al.* 1958: 19), and unsatisfactory in that, though they may partially explain the significance of initiation, much of what makes a ceremony important in a particular tribe is culture-specific, e.g. the creation of regiments among the Pedi and Tswana or the importance of the Bird in the Lobedu *buhwera-byali* complex. In the discussion of the significance of initiation schools which follows, these cautionary remarks must be borne in mind.

The extent to which initiation schools can be regarded as institutions for formal education varies. However, even where teaching plays an important part, the schools do not offer training for economic roles. Blacking's comment on the Venda could equally well be applied to Bantu peoples as a whole. He

PLATE II
Zulu wedding dance

PLATE 12
Initiation

a and b Scenes from the Venda *domba* (initiation) dance

writes: 'Formal public education in traditional Venda society was never intended to give people technological training for earning a living: domestic crafts were learnt in families, and other techniques were acquired by serving apprenticeships privately to specialists (who often happened to be close kinsmen)' (Blacking 1969: (pt. 2) 71). Deliberate teaching of tribal norms and values occurs in most of the societies, but appears to be less developed among the Cape Nguni and Lobedu, and is more emphasized and straightforward in girls' schools, where it usually focuses on the woman's rights, obligations and etiquette in marriage. Even where an attempt to convey formal instruction is obviously being made, there is no guarantee that the initiate benefits from the teaching. Much of the information is given in obscure and esoteric formulae and rituals, and the initiate, confronted with them for the first time, fails to comprehend their meaning. His, or her, participation in later ceremonies, often as an assistant or teacher, may help the individual to begin to understand the meaning of the lessons.

The behaviour and values which the schools do try to inculcate will depend on the place of the school within the total social structure. Among the South Sotho, Tswana and Pedi, for instance, the schools focus on the establishment of a new age regiment, formerly with military functions; teaching stresses loyalty to the chief and the tribe rather than one's kin or local group. Among the South Sotho the ochre used to smear the boys is mixed with certain of the chief's medicines 'to secure the loyalty of the boys, strengthen their allegiance to the tribe and chief and (in the old days) unite them to their fellow-warriors' (Ashton 1952: 53). Schapera writes of the formation of Tswana age regiments: 'Through them a child was removed from the sole control of his parents, and made to assume responsibilities towards the Chief and the tribe that previously did not apply to him' (Schapera 1940a: 255). The Cape Nguni initiate, by contrast, receives only very general instruction regarding the behaviour proper to a man. Speeches made at the Mfengu and Xhosa re-incorporation ceremonies, for instance, 'mentioned the new status attained by the initiates and the behaviour expected of them as men, but by far the greater eloquence of the speakers went into telling them in what concrete manner they must build their homes—by buying cattle' (Wilson et al. 1952: 216–17).

Among the 'Red' Xhosa, initiation is intended to make a boy more mature in his handling of social relationships especially those involving conflicts of interest. 'When Red Xhosa talk about education or maturing there is no theme they harp upon more constantly than that "boys settle things by the stick"[41] but "men should settle things by the law" (or "by words" implying judicial or quasi-judicial disputing). This is supposed to be a prime lesson of initiation' (Mayer and Mayer 1970: 173).

Whatever the nature of the formal education which these schools attempt to give, they all share one common element—the teaching is administered under unusual and dramatic circumstances. The degree of drama varies from the relatively unspectacular act of secluding girls in the village for a month, to the elaborate public masked dancing of the Cape Nguni and Lobedu boys, involving the whole community, and, among the Lobedu, absorbing their attention for an entire year.

Young sees initiation rites as a dramatic production aimed at helping the community accept the boy's new status. 'If the audience can be led to imagine the new situation with the help of a little staging, it will find it easier to continue doing so and will then finally be so taken in by the whole thing that it comes to accept the change as permanent, real and legitimate' (Young 1965: 74). The drama of the initiation situation must also affect the way in which the initiate perceives the importance of the instructions and revelations of the school. Sargant has gone so far as to compare initiation with the modern techniques of 'brainwashing' in which isolation and hardships disorientate the subject, destroy or weaken his old personality and make him amenable to the learning of new beliefs and behaviour patterns; the technique would be particularly effective during puberty, when the individual is already experiencing a certain degree of physical and, possibly, emotional upheaval (Sargant 1959: 97–9). Young sees the boy's experience in less traumatic terms; he writes:

> In the crowded and emotionally charged situation that usually develops in initiations, the boy's thoughts are caught up. Even if he is not personally impressed, he still contributes to the performance by submitting to the ritual. But he cannot fail to realize one significant fact: For the first time in his life he is 'backstage' looking at the women and the uninitiated from the standpoint of the men (Young 1965: 26).

An aspect of Bantu initiation ceremonies which has been over-emphasized by those who would like the schools banned—missionaries, teachers and government officials—is the association of the schools with sex instruction and the frequent, often 'obscene', allusions to sexual functions. Nudity, or near-nudity, on the part of the initiates in many groups has brought similar condemnation. Blacking quotes an early comment on the Venda: 'The effect of *domba* is to teach the young folk the complete Venda vocabulary of foul language and to acquaint them with all the aspects of sexual life, and that from a very sordid point of view' (Blacking 1969: (pt. 3) 151). While sex instruction is often an important aspect of the teaching of the schools, particularly those for girls, they never promote or condone sexual licence. Although the traditional attitude to sex is devoid of the concept of sin associated with it in Western society, and relations between the sexes are seen as natural and good, sexual relations are regulated within a strict social framework and the rules are usually clearly enunciated during the initiation schools. Pregnancy prior to marriage is contrary to the norms of traditional society, and often the obscene songs sung at initiation are intended to be used later to ridicule any girl who finds herself in this predicament. In many groups, full sexual intercourse prior to marriage is avoided by the practice of intra-crural intercourse; often the girls are regularly examined by their mothers or the older women to ensure that they have not been deflowered. Defloration would bring shame not only on the girl but, as among the Zulu and Mpondo, on her whole age-group, who would punish her for her fall from grace. The Venda initiate is examined at the end of the *domba* by the old women and, if she proves to be *virgo intacta*, is carried home in triumph on the back of her mother or one of the older women. Her return is greeted with trilling and rejoicing, while the girl who has been deflowered is deprived of the traditional adornments of the newly-initiated, and spat on and derided by the other girls and the community at large (Stayt 1931a: 123).

The question of sanctions against premarital pregnancy among the Red Xhosa is examined by the Mayers, who point out that the liaisons among *abafana*, who have been through initiation and now belong to the *intlombe* youth organization, and girls of a similar age, while encouraged as normal and desirable by the peer-group, are nevertheless strictly controlled by the group itself.

> Throughout the youth organization 'private love' (a stock phrase) is vigorously discouraged. There are various ways of ensuring publicity . . . one of the young people's stated objections to 'private' love is that a girl might have more than one lover at a time. This would be a bad training for marriage (in which the woman must confine herself to one sexual partner though the man need not). The other objection is that the couple might be tempted to full intercourse instead of *metsha* [intra-crural intercourse], with danger of pregnancy ensuing (Mayer and Mayer 1970: 176).

The adult world will penalize the girl who becomes pregnant by ruling that she may not marry, but must become an *inkazana*—a woman available for love affairs, usually with married men. The peer group will add their own sanctions to this ruling. The girl will be seen as 'adult' from the moment she is pregnant and the young must then *hlonipha* (respect) her; the nature of this *hlonipha* relationship makes it impossible for her to join in the normal activities of an *intlombe* group and, as the Mayers point out, 'the girl who becomes pregnant must expect a dull, lonely life' (Mayer and Mayer 1970: 177). Thus, despite the encouragement to sexual liaisons which the *intlombe* gives, its power to control its members results in fewer premarital pregnancies among the Red girls than among either School (Christianized) or urban Xhosa girls (Mayer and Mayer 1970: 163).

The emphasis on sex in many initiation schools, then, rather than encouraging immorality, is in fact a method of teaching the future behaviour required by the mores of the society concerned. The threat of sanctions such as ridicule, isolation or fines for those who do not observe the rules in the period following initiation, or later in married life, is usually made clear during the schools.

Apart from sex behaviour, initiation normally demands that the behaviour of the newly initiated be generally more mature and responsible. Bearing in mind the anti-social behaviour common among herd-boys, initiation could be seen as a mechanism for nipping delinquency in the bud.[42] The period just before initiation, among for instance the Pedi, Mpondomise and Xhosa, is marked by a rapid deterioration of behaviour on the part of the initiates-to-be. Mönnig writes of the Pedi boys:

> The behaviour of the boys becomes increasingly worse. They steal openly and will take, with force, any melons or sugarcane from a woman returning from the lands. They make lewd suggestions to women, and are slovenly and uncouth in their dress. In this manner the boys create a situation where the initiation has to start to rid the community of their objectionable behaviour (Mönnig 1967: 111–12).

The pre-initiation period in Bantu society is marked by intensive peer-group interaction, especially among boys. Gottlieb, Reeves and Ten Houten have remarked the same tendency in Western societies. 'The adolescent becomes oriented to his peers, and seeks goals within his peer sub-culture even at the risk of social rejection from adult referents' (Gottlieb, Reeves, and Ten Houten 1966: 27). In Bantu society, initiation helps to prevent prolonged alienation by suddenly and dramatically cutting the youth off from this transition period and aligning him solidly with the adult world. The initiation schools, with adult norms and adult teachers as referents, sever his connections with the non-initiated, and provide a mechanism by which the adolescent can identify with his new adult role. The Mayers suggest that the sharp break between the Red Xhosa pre-initiation *mtshotsho* youth organization and the post-initiation *intlombe* youth organization, which begin to participate fully in the adult world, is a valuable force for preventing disruptive 'ganging up' by the youth; 'it may be said to score a point for the gerontocracy on the principle of divide and rule (Mayer and Mayer 1970: 185–6).[43] The Mayers contrast the Xhosa situation with that in Mpondo society in which the boys do not go through an initiation school.

> Besides the traditional-style Red youth groups (*igubura*), which somewhat resemble the *intlombe*, there are in Pondoland the so-called 'rascal' youth groups, *indlavini*, which are truly sectarian and much more dangerous. *Indlavini* are organized in all-male gangs, which meet secretly in lonely places. They defy adult standards of dress and manners, and they not only clash with rival gangs but sometimes terrorize home people, elders and girls, as well. An interpretation suggested here is that Xhosa initiation offers youth a flattering reception by adult society at just the age (eighteen on) when *indlavini* are pitting their wits against it (Mayer and Mayer 1970: 186).[44]

Initiation schools are bound up with the widening social horizons of the adolescent group. The schools themselves often serve to bring together boys and girls who had previously not known one another; 'graduation' from these schools normally entitles the initiate to participate in the adult world to a far greater extent than he did previously.

Cohen has pointed out that, in societies where organization is based on a kinship group wider than the nuclear family, some mechanism must be found for breaking the strong nuclear family bond and attaching the child to the wider group (Cohen 1964: 51). Initiation ceremonies provide one such mechanism. The initiate is removed from the protection and authority of the nuclear family and subjected to the control of a relatively unfamiliar group. This 'estrangement' is less marked among the Nguni groups because of the smaller, more local, nature of their schools and the less 'nationalistic' flavour of the initiation as a whole.

In the school, the initiate forms new associations which will cross-cut not only nuclear family ties but also lineage and rank ties; in some areas these ties will even extend across ethnic boundaries e.g. Mfengu and Xhosa, Bhaca and Hlubi, and, in the north, Pedi, Tsonga, South Sotho, Venda and Lemba, may attend the same school, forming bonds of interest and friendship. The wide area from which a new age-regiment is recruited among the Sotho and Tswana groups extends the boy's effective range of social relations far more than the more local Nguni schools; however, the Mayers have pointed out that among the Xhosa, once the boys are initiated and form *intlombe* groups, they have a wide visiting circuit where they can expect hospitality, not only as a group but individually. 'It is a fundamental rule that a young man "can dance at any *intlombe*" regardless of whether he or his group has had any relations there before. In principle, "an *umfana* can ask for *intlombe* anywhere from right across the Bashee to right across the Great Fish River"' (Mayer and Mayer 1970: 179).

Participation in the initiation schools not only brings the initiate into contact with a wide range of contemporaries but also, in the Sotho and Tswana groups especially, forges those who go through initiation together into a group, who will henceforth have certain rights and obligations to one another. The formation of age-sets is less marked among the Cape Nguni; though the Red Xhosa *intlombe* group is an 'age-grade' comprised of initiated men, they were not all initiated together, and the group loses members at the top as men marry off and give up *intlombe* activities, taking in new members from the ranks of the recently initiated. Wilson *et al.*, writing of this aspect of initiation among the Xhosa and Mfengu, comment that the boys initiated together 'do not form a group with a distinctive name, among whom specific obligations of mutual help obtain. They perform no communal tasks, nor are there any social occasions when they are entitled to special treatment as a group' (Wilson *et al.* 1952: 115).

Young maintains that affiliations formed in initiation schools extend beyond those initiated together. The schools tend to create a general feeling of solidarity between all males or all females who pass through them (Young 1965: 26–7). Bantu initiation schools all have elements which suggest that they are aimed at drawing the boy into the society of men in contrast with that of women and the uninitiated; letting the boy in on the secrets of school and of events which he had witnessed but not previously understood may well serve to create a bond between the men of the group. The exclusion of women and the uninitiated emphasizes his acceptance into the world of men and the new loyalties he must develop. Blacking remarks on the same function in relation to girls passing through *domba*: '*Domba* opens the door to full participation in the society of women by incorporating girls in informal age-sets. Seniority of age is an important principle of Venda social organization and as women grow older they become more powerful and respected and play a leading role in ritual and ceremonial' (Blacking 1969: (pt. 3) 151). The grouping of girls into a formal unit with continuity of co-operation and obligation, however, is limited in Bantu societies where the girls are scattered by virilocal marriage.

Initiation, then, can be seen as a valuable mechanism for adjusting social relations and defining roles and statuses. Despite these important functions, initiation in itself need not, as mentioned above, confer instant adulthood in all social roles. Rather, it may be seen as an essential preliminary qualification, a *sine qua non* of later acceptance into complete adult status. The boy who refused to go through initiation, for instance, would be barred from many political and jural activities and be unlikely to find a bride in his community. Where initiation entitles the initiate to marry, marriage and parenthood may confer the privileges of full adult status; in many tribes, full political, jural and religious status are often only attained after middle-age. The Kriges, in describing the attainment of status among the Lobedu, make this clear.

> The rites of the *vudiga* and *khɔba* do not . . . change boys and girls from youth to full-fledged manhood (or womanhood). The transition is gradual. The *khɔba* becomes a bride; the bride after the birth of her first child is a *mudwana*; and she in turn, when her children marry is a venerable old woman (*mukhegulu*). The bride is of small consequence even in her own home; for long she serves an apprenticeship under the control of her mother-in-law, who also takes her child out of her hands, baths it and feeds it. Only as an old woman does she reach the peak of her life. With a man the position is no different. After the *vudiga* he has a kind of legal status. After marriage he advances a further stage, but in his marital relations and as a father he is a child dependent upon advice from his elders. In public activities, such as in the courts, he still sits and listens, but the old men may entrust a case to him and his age-mates to teach them a sense of responsibility (Krige and Krige 1943: 123).[45]

Advancing age brings increased power and authority to men and women. The gloomy spectre of old age which haunts our society is kept at bay among the Bantu by the prospect of new roles to suit the aging individual's capacities and aptitudes. For the man, his age will call for respect, and the young will accept the judgments of his experience and his religious authority. For the woman middle-age and the menopause mark a period of increased influence not only in domestic but often also in community affairs.

The initiation schools, then, do not mark the final stage of the development of the individual; they do, however, equip and entitle him to accept the roles which maturity will bring.

Notes

1 Weaning may occur at any time from one to five years of age. The Venda for instance wean at three or four years, the Bhaca between eighteen months and two years, the Zulu and Bomvana between two and three, the Tsonga after '3 hoeing seasons', the South Sotho between one and three, the Pedi in the child's third or fourth year. The Lobedu child normally leaves off suckling without any positive steps to wean him; he may suckle for four or five years if there are no younger siblings.

2 Stayt, for instance, mentions weaning at three or four years old, though even boys already out herding sometimes suckled when they came home in the evening (Stayt 1931a: 94). Blacking's study, thirty-three years later, showed that weaning now occurs at about a year. Mpondo weaning, formerly 'after three hoeing seasons', now occurs at eighteen months to two years. This might possibly be due to a decrease in polygamy, and consequently more difficulties involved for the parents in observing the taboo on full intercourse, which accompanies lactation in most tribes.

3 Hunter writes of this custom among the Mpondo: 'Where the father is an eldest son, with his own *umzi* [homestead], the eldest child is sent after weaning to the paternal grandparents, but this is not solely to facilitate weaning, but because it is customary for the eldest grandson to live with his paternal grandparents and inherit his grandfather's property. Occasionally a child is sent to the maternal grandmother for a few weeks after weaning' (Hunter 1936: 158). Also see Junod (1927 I: 61, 171) for details of this custom among the Tsonga.

4 This pattern is to some extent modified by the increasing tendency for children to attend Western-type schools, which are almost invariably co-educational.

5 It is possible that the phenomenon exists equally strongly among other tribes, but ethnographers have not given it much attention. For descriptions of youth organizations among the Xhosa see Wilson *et al.* 1952: 158–65, and Mayer and Mayer 1970: 159–89.

6 'The *kgoro* is tentatively described as a lineage group although . . . it is not necessarily a lineage. But it does always originate, and usually remains largely as a group of patrilineal relatives' (Mönnig 1967: 104 footnote).

7 It is imperative that all boys proposing to go through the next initiation school should attend, since the general leader who emerges at this contest will have specific functions during initiation (Mönnig 1967: 108).

8 'A leader among the girls . . . is also chosen. She is chosen for her ability to sing and dance, and leads the girls in the feasts at which the girls entertain guests with singing and dancing' (Mönnig 1967: 109).

9 A school essentially military in character now fast disappearing or extinct in much of

Vendaland, this institution was perhaps the closest thing to a Western-type school in Bantu society. It was a permanent educational institution with boys of 7 or 8 coming in and leaving at puberty (Stayt 1931a: 101–5). It is being rapidly replaced by the non-indigenous *murundu* or circumcision school. Venda chiefs encourage participation in the *murundu*, since the chiefs may not be circumcised and this sets them apart from commoners who have been through the school (Blacking 1964: 32).

10 Margaret Mead comments on this fundamental difference between primitive and Western education. She writes: 'Perhaps the most important [difference] is the shift from the need for an individual to learn something which everyone agrees he would wish to know, to the will of some individual to teach something which it is not agreed that anyone has any desire to know' (Mead 1943: 311).

11 Sexual intercourse is rigidly forbidden in the Pedi 'village' but the Kriges talk of 'play intercourse' among the Lobedu. Stayt does not discuss this aspect for the Venda. For descriptions of these villages see: (Lobedu) Krige and Krige 1943: 109; (Pedi) Mönnig 1967: 110–11; (Venda) Stayt 1931a: 99–100.

12 For a detailed analysis of the importance of stickfighting in the functioning of Red Xhosa youth organizations, see Mayer and Mayer 1970.

13 A reference to the costumed 'wolves' of the initiation schools.

14 Ear piercing is also carried out on nubile girls and on boys in the year preceding initiation among the Tlokoa group of the South Sotho (Ashton 1952: 47).

15 For a detailed description of the ceremony among the Zulu see Krige 1936a: 81–7.

16 For a description of the ceremony, see Mönnig 1967: 104–7.

17 In the old days, he was still not allowed to marry until two further rites—incorporation into a regiment and the sewing on of the headring—had been performed. For a full description of the *thomba* and its modifications in the urban setting see Krige 1936a: 87–100.

18 For a detailed description of the seclusion, sacrifices and rituals of the *ukuthombisa* see Hunter 1936: 165–74.

19 Although a girl's first menstruation is the cause for a *khomba* or puberty ceremony, Junod writes: 'Three or four girls receive the initiation together' (1927 I: 177). It is not clear from this whether the ceremony thus resembles the Venda *vhusha* (above) or the Lobedu rite described below in the recruitment of initiates.

20 Female initiation schools usually recruit only physically mature girls. Among the Pedi and Venda they are only attended after the girl has gone through her own puberty ceremony. The South Sotho girls must be between 15 and 20 years old, i.e. in all probability also physically mature. There is no clear indication of age in the Tswana material but since ceremonies were held at irregular intervals it is probable that the age range was quite wide.

21 See Junod 1927 I: 72 on Zulu and Tsonga; Hunter 1936: 165 on Mpondo; Krige 1936a: 116–17 on the Zulu; Hammond-Tooke 1962: 80–1 on the Bhaca.

22 Personal communication.

23 Other references to circumcision for reasons of hygiene appear in S. M. Guma's article on the South Sotho, who believe that the practice prevented the man from passing on infections to a woman during intercourse—'an uncircumcized boy smells' (1965: 241), and in Pitje's paper on the Pedi (1950: 118).

24 The Bomvana lodge is exceptional in this respect as it is often built only a hundred yards from the kraal of the 'father' of the school. The period of seclusion is also atypical. Whereas seclusion in most schools lasts 2–3 months the Bomvana seclusion, though not as strict as for other groups, lasts for approximately eight months (Cook 1931: 52).

25 See A. van Gennep *Rites of Passage* (1909) for an analysis of the rituals surrounding the life cycle and their division into three stages—rites of separation, transition and reincorporation. Also Gluckman's criticism and further analysis of the significance of these rites (1962).

26 See van Gennep (1909) on the concept of death and re-birth applied to rites of passage.

27 See Cook's description (1931) for the Bomvana. Wilson *et al.*, in their study of male initiation among the Xhosa and Mfengu, comment, however: 'The dancing which formed such an important part of the traditional ceremonies has disappeared in the Keiskammahoek District' (Wilson *et al.* 1952: 203).

28 The Venda boy may take part in the *domba* after going through the *murundu*. *Domba* is atypical of Bantu initiation schools in that boys and girls attend together, though it is today essentially a girls' school.

29 The terms 'white' and 'black' refer to the white lime with which the initiate is smeared during the circumcision school and the black charcoal and fat with which he is smeared at the subsequent school.

30 Mönnig points out that Pedi girls have only one initiation school, comparable to the first of the boys, which entitles them to tribal membership. He comments: 'They are never initiated further and are thus barred from participation in politico-jural activities' (Mönnig 1967: 140).

31 The Bird's costume 'consists of a light, semi-circular framework about 4 ft. high, over which are put strings of the *muga* thorntree . . . which have been placed in water to become black. Surmounting it all is a small head crowned with an ostrich or other feather. It is seen only occasionally, when it comes dancing into the *byali* courtyard at night, and, in spite of bright moonlight, its black colour makes it difficult to discern clearly. It speaks and sings by whistling through an instrument . . . made of the leg-bone of cattle' (Krige and Krige 1943: 135).

32 'These are of two types: a light one, said to be for hunting, and a heavy one. Both costumes have skirts of loose-hanging grass, flung out in a circle by the gyrations of the dancer, as well as comely waist, arm, and leg bands and underskirts of woven grass. The light costume has in addition broad shoulder bands crossing over chest and back and a mask resting upon the shoulders, veiling the face and open at the top. The heavy costume is far more imposing. Besides a woven waistcoat, there is an immense covering for head and shoulders, rising to a crested summit, flanked by what gives the impression of scales arranged in rows or projecting wings, and fronted by a snout like that of a crocodile. The dance reminds one now of the prancings of a male bird courting

its mate, now of a lizard convulsively shaking its whole body as it rests upon a rock' (Krige and Krige 1943: 138).

33 Compare this with *abakhwetha* dances among the Cape Nguni, e.g. Cook's description of the Bomvana (Cook 1931: 58ff.).

34 The Lobedu also hold a further school, the *gomana*, which like the *buhwera* is concerned with the introduction of the boys into the deepest secrets of the tribe. It is held twice a year and lasts only a few weeks; during the school the boys receive four semi-circular cuts from mouth to cheekbone, after which they are shown the sacred drums and learn that the supposed ancestor spirits who 'return' to the earth and communicate with men in the whistling language are in fact old men in disguise (Krige and Krige 1943: 126–30).

35 Tswana girls' initiation schools still existed at the time of Schapera's research, but in very attenuated form (Schapera 1940a: 259–60).

36 Attendance at the *domba* is ideally preceded by a month spent at *tshikanda*, a girls' initiation school. Blacking comments that the songs, dances and 'laws' learned at *tshikanda* are essentially the same as those of the *vhusha* or puberty ceremony. He believes that this 'ensures that every noble woman knows all about the commoners' schools . . . as well as about her own school, which a commoner may not attend, 'and which differ markedly from the commoners' *vhusha* (Blacking 1969: 24).

37 Although the Venda *domba* does not involve an operation, the girls' *musevetho* or *sungwi* ceremony, believed to have been introduced from the South Sotho, incorporates a rite in which the initiate is cut on the clitoris and branded on the thigh (Stayt 1931a: 138–41). Venda boys are also circumcised at a non-indigenous school, the *murundu*, probably Lemba in origin (Stayt 1931a: 125–38).

38 As the South Sotho boys' initiation is associated with the 'wolves' (Ashton 1952: 51) and the Lobedu *buhwera* with the Bird (see above).

39 A paragraph from Mayer's introduction to the ASA monograph on socialization illustrates this difficulty. He writes: '[Audrey Richards] remarks *inter alia* that initiation rituals have too often been assumed to have normative functions when the assumption has not been tested empirically in the field. . . . She applies her stricture even to her own work, recalling that she failed to speak to the two Bemba girls whom she watched being initiated in a three-week-long ceremony, "yet I blithely declared that the rites were used to inculcate the values of marriage and parenthood"' (Mayer 1970: xv).

40 For example, Whiting, Kluckhohn and Anthony's psychogenic theory which postulates that a close mother-son sleeping arrangement leads a boy to identify with both male and female roles, and consequently the society must provide some means for resolving the role conflict—namely, initiation schools in which the boy is removed from the women's world and identified with that of the men (Whiting, Kluckhohn and Anthony 1958: 359–70); or Young's theory that initiation dramatizes sex role and creates solidarity among the initiates (Young 1962: 379–96 and Young 1965); or Cohen's theory that initiation schools aim at severing the links between a child and his nuclear family in order to anchor him a wider kin network (Cohen 1964: 11–155).

41 This refers to the stickfighting of the *mtshotsho* youth groups.

42 Youth organizations, even prior to initiation, may serve a similar controlling function

in preventing delinquency. See Mayer and Mayer 1970: 187; Wilson *et al.* 1952: 158–65; Mönnig 1967: 108–11.

43 Though initiation may assist the integration of the boy into the adult world it is not the only mechanism which closes the 'generation gap' and controls delinquent tendencies. The conservatism and economic organization of traditional Bantu society forced the boy to comply with adult requirements in order to acquire a wife and, more particularly, land, which is controlled by the older men.

44 Hammond-Tooke mentions the formation of *iindlavini* gangs among the Bhaca—also a society without initiation schools—mainly composed of youths who have done a stint on the mines and, on coming back, assume the status of *umfana* (young man). The gangs, also anti-social in much of their behaviour, seem to place more emphasis on dances and amours than the Mpondo and are typically 'school' rather than 'Red'. Hammond-Tooke points out that 'the institution of *iindlavini* appears to be analogous to the Xhosa and Mfengu "Parliament" (but not the *iBavu* or Boys' Association) described for the Keiskammahoek district.' Among the Bhaca there is a separate organization of traditionalist youth (*iintsizwe*) which appears to be closer to the Xhosa model described by the Mayers in that they are less 'anti-social' (Hammond-Tooke 1962: 79–80). (The nature of the Xhosa 'Parliament' youth organization is discussed in Wilson *et al.* 1952: 158–65).

Although initiation might well serve the function of curbing delinquency in most of the Bantu societies the Kriges write of the Lobedu initiation: 'From the almost outlaw play-gang, he [the initiate] must be conducted to the fringes of responsible society or be placed in a position from which he can gradually make his way into society. It would be an exaggeration to say that the *vudiga* is designed to cope with the turbulence of youth; for even the circumcized are still wild' (Krige and Krige 1943: 115).

45 The Mayers make a similar point regarding the participation of the initiated *abafana* in the politico-jural world of the Red Xhosa (Mayer and Mayer 1970: 185).

Chapter 8

Traditional Rulers and their Realms
Basil Sansom

This chapter is about traditional rulers, their realms and their regimes of government. It is designed to show how Southern Bantu rulers established and maintained authority over subject tribesmen. Their task—in Weber's terms—was to achieve co-ordination in a structure of imperative, and therefore legitimate, command.

Southern Africa was a region in which Bantu peoples set up an astonishing variety of primitive states. At one extreme there were the pocket chiefdoms that harboured tribelets, say, Makapan's people in the Transvaal or the Bhaca in Southern Nguni lands. At the other, there were great kingdoms, Shaka's Zululand being the prime example. In European terms, the scale of this contrast is that between the Duchy of Luxemburg and the French Republic.

Further, these contrasts of polity unfolded in time. The precursors of kingdoms were lesser chiefdoms that were expanded by conquest or through the peaceful assimilation of refugees. Once established, kingdoms were subject to depletions. They lost splinter groups whose members moved off to establish new and usually minor polities. Indeed, a series of acts of enlargement by incorporation, and diminution by secession and migration, spread the Bantu peoples over the face of the sub-continent and produced the political variety that we must comprehend in this discussion. We are faced with a congested history of political development and a range in types of polity. In time, this discussion will be limited to the traditional states of the last century. Within this provenance, the states are made subject to a six-fold typology. I show the means used by rulers to co-ordinate authority in the six kinds of state that were characteristic of Southern Africa in the nineteenth century. The traditional era ends as the Bantu polity is effectively incorporated into the domain of white overrule (see chapter 12).

This chapter is divided into three sections. In the first, the general scheme for classifying the Bantu states is outlined. The second section deals with a set of political processes and problems that were common to Bantu polities. In this section the implications of the scheme for classification are worked out. Finally, a number of case studies are presented. The third task is to show how general ideas about Bantu polities are worked out in specific instances.

I The Types of Bantu State

Dimensions of command

This scheme for typing Bantu states is necessary to comprehend the political variety of the Southern African scene. The organizing idea which it serves is this: there are three dimensions to a ruler's command and these can vary independently. His powers have a measurable span, they have scope and, third, they are found located in particular institutions and sets of relationships. By their interplay, span, scope and location of powers created the species of the Southern Bantu state. Kingdoms are not the same merely because they are kingdoms. Nor is the difference between pocket chiefdom and kingly state a contrast of size alone. Instead, there are realms of similarity and difference that the three notions of span, scope and location can express.

Span of command is a notion allied to size. It refers to the extent of a ruler's command measured by the population that is, for defined purposes, subject to his central jurisdiction. In Southern Africa, variations in the span of command have already been mentioned and are easy to illustrate. Independent but petty chiefs to the north and west of what is now the Transvaal ruled but a few thousand people (Massie 1905). In 1870, the Zulu king Mpande held sway over a nation estimated to number some 210,000 souls (Gluckman, cited by Stevenson 1968: 40). Size of the subject population differed greatly from state to state.

Irrespective of the span of their command, the Bantu rulers differed in their ability to intervene in the affairs of their subjects. Scope of command enables one to describe this range in variation. The scope of a ruler's command is the degree to which his authority extends to influence the actions of his subjects in their various fields of endeavour. Absolute authority represents the upper limit when the ruler is all-powerful and the scope of his command is exhaustive. It was achieved in Southern Africa during Shaka's tyranny over the Zulu kingdom. Then, there was no field of activity into which the ruler could not extend his controlling hand. In contrast, Casalis could write of the 'haughty vassals' of South Sotho kings. These vassals 'safeguarded their immunities', enlarging their own powers at the expense of those of the monarch (Casalis 1861: 214). Again, when Schapera (1938a: 84) describes how a modern Tswana chief can be fined in his own court for exceeding his powers, we are made witness to an exercise in which the scope of a ruler's command is defined against the immunities of subjects. Thus, the more immunities that subjects enjoy, the more the scope of the ruler's authority declines. In Southern Africa, the scope of command enjoyed by traditional rulers ranged from Shaka's embracing tyranny to the comfortable and uncomprehensive rule of the Lobedu rain queen.

Location of command specifies the base of a ruler's authority and fixes it in specific departments of tribal life—tribal cults, the regiments, councils, administration of lands, etc. By identifying loci of command, one is able to compare the means towards imperative co-ordination that various rulers employ. To exemplify: the Zulu and the Lobedu realms provide a contrast between a regnant general and a priestess-queen. Army and cult were, respectively, these monarchs' prime loci of command. Further, this distinction is one of emphasis. Just as Lobedu tribesmen could gird themselves as warriors to serve their queen, the Zulu king could put on the ornaments and clothing of the occult or ritual practitioner to work magical or priestly acts. The distinction is in the relative weighting of tribal institutions, some of which may be elaborated at the expense of others to provide the avenues of command. The sanctity of the Lobedu queen had primacy. Because of it she could legitimize her secular commands. The Zulu king was first a general but he could be strengthened by ritual performance. For this monarch, the spiritual basis of power was secondary, used to buttress the edifice of military might.

Because the Zulu tyranny provides an example of absolute rule in Southern Africa, it is convenient to comment on the relationship between scope and location of powers in terms of it. When scope of command is expanded towards absolutism, the ruler monopolizes control of the totality of the state. The absolute ruler's power is made pervasive by extending its scope to the point where it is universally and exhaustively located. He can modify action in each and every department of life; for his people there are no immunities. But, when dealing with absolute power, the idea of location is still important. When comptroller of all, a ruler can promote or demote institutions by laying emphasis on particular avenues of command. For Zulu kings, the military continued as the first source of power, their primary locus of absolute command.

The ideas of span and scope provide yardsticks for comparative treatment of Bantu states. Using them, the powers of the ruler to influence a given set of people to act in a specific set of ways, may be expressed. Location of command comprehends the particular institutional developments in various states. It enables discrimination of the means that rulers employ towards the imperative co-ordination of their subjects' activities.

Three grades of polity

Historical developments in Southern Africa allow definition of three grades of polity. In ascending order, these were: independent chiefdoms, federations of chiefdoms and, finally, kingdoms in which erstwhile chiefdoms became districts. The independent chiefdom is the prototype for Southern Bantu political development. To the best of our knowledge, it is the political form which the Bantu brought with them to Southern Africa in the course of their southward migrations. Federations and kingdoms grew out of independent chiefdoms and used the chiefdom as a constituent part of the enlarged polity. Finally, the independent chiefdom was also a reversionary type. When the larger polities fragmented or lost members through secession, the independent chiefdom was normally the type of polity in which defectors or survivors re-arranged their political affairs.

Independent chiefdoms were able to expand by the assimilation of relatively small groups of people normally seen as 'refugees' from other tribes. But political expansion on the larger scale always involved a wider integration of established units—the jointure of chiefdoms to form larger political units, federations or kingdoms. Thus in Southern Africa, significant increases in the span of a ruler's command normally entailed the conquest or assimilation of constituent chiefdoms. The distinction between tribal federations and kingdoms depends on an assessment of the extent to which central control was established in a composite dominion.

In the nineteenth century, Southern Africa saw the expansion of key Bantu states. The expansionist states started as independent chiefdoms whose rulers came to dominate other chiefdoms that they assimilated to their rule. In the literature, Southern Bantu super-states are called nations and writers dignify their rulers with the title of 'king' (Schapera 1956; Kuper 1947a; Gluckman 1940). The Zulu under Shaka, the South Sotho under Moshesh and the Swazi, governed by scions of Mswati, all qualify as African nations that were governed by kings.

Chiefs such as Kgama of the Ngwato and Sekwati of the Pedi also extended their powers to exercise a measure of control over previously independent peoples. Ngwato and Pedi polities were probably moving towards nationhood when autochthonous political development was checked and their history became bound up with the progress of white expansion in Southern Africa. Kgama and Sekwati were paramount chiefs who set themselves over lesser chiefs in polities best described as federations. The Southern Bantu federations were congeries of chiefdoms in which one chiefdom was unquestionably dominant. There was a centre of dominance but control was unevenly exercised from this centre. The central ruler's powers declined towards the periphery of his realm and his control of the peoples of the periphery was sporadic rather than regular.

While significant increases in span are thus associated with accretion of chiefdoms, the distinction between federation and kingdom is based on a consideration of the scope of the central ruler's powers in a composite and enlarged domain. The ruler's power was always immediate and at its most comprehensive in his home district. But, in federations, the opposition between centre and periphery, original grouping and accretions, was the central structural feature. In kingdoms, this was subordinated to the wider unity of the nation. Subordinate chiefs were vassals and, through them, the ruler reached into the district chiefdoms of the nation. In kingdoms, tribesmen enjoyed a common status as subjects who could be commanded by their king. This is a comment on the scope of a king's command: all men were equally subject to him as nationals of the state.

Independent chiefdom, federation and nation are the first components of the scheme for classifying Southern Bantu states.

Ecology and the state

Bantu states in Southern Africa were established on terrain that may be divided into two vast ecological zones. These zones have already been discussed in chapter 5. Conveniently described as the Bantu East and West, these zones exercised an influence on the character of rule and the potential for politics in the states set up within them. It is no accident that conciliar government and a penchant for arbitration characterize Sotho who are peoples of the West. Eastern peoples are more ready to take to arms, more violent in their political oppositions, and their rulers more evidently the commanders of their subjects. This is both a cultural and a regional difference. I am going to argue that ecology affected the location of a ruler's powers. In the West, the ruler was a chief of bounds and grants. He derived power from the centralization of his administration of lands and through control of the seasonal cycle of work. In the East, economic decentralization was the norm. The ruler had, therefore, to counter decentralizing trends in the economy in order to maintain his central control.

Presiding over their tribal economies, rulers in East and West faced different problems and solved them in characteristically Eastern and Western modes. Contrasting ecologies led to contrasting emphases in administration. The economy of the East made cattle highly relevant as a form of political capital. In the West, the grain economy was more important. This corresponds with an East versus West opposition between the value of cattle as capital and of people as labour. These baldly stated differences were the basis for differential location of political power. In sum, the contrast may be stated in this way: Western rulers located command in systems designed to distribute the means of production, while Eastern rulers sited power in systems for redistributing the products of labour and investment. Thus, it is fruitless, in

TABLE 8.1 *A classification of Southern Bantu polities*

Ecological zone	Grade of polity		
	Independent chiefdoms	Federations	Kingdoms
A. 'Eastern' ecology: scattered settlements	Small Nguni tribes Phalaborwa	Venda Mpondo	Swazi Zulu Lobedu
B. 'Western' ecology: compact settlements	Small Tswana and North Sotho tribes	Pedi Ngwato Tawana	South Sotho

Southern Africa, to deal with 'the economic powers of the chief' without discriminating between widely differing types of tribal economy.

Political expansion occurred in both the Eastern and Western divisions of Bantu South Africa. Thus in the classification of states proffered in Table 8.1, distinctions on the grounds of historical development and of ecology are combined. It segregates the independent chiefdoms, the federations and the nations of the East from those of the West. The ecological adaptations referred to were more accurately defined in chapter 5 as adaptations of Type A (Eastern) and Type B (Western). What remains is to show the relevance of this scheme, in combination with the notions of span, scope and location of command, to an understanding of Southern Bantu statecraft and statehood.

II Political Themes and Processes

Ecology and government

The economy is worked into the exercise of central authority in so far as the ruler enjoys the capacity to discriminate between subjects by re-allocating desired commodities among them. In Southern Africa there were two patterns for authoritative intervention in economic affairs. Sotho rulers followed one course while the Nguni, Venda and Lobedu authorities pursued another. These patterns can be conceptualized by regarding the re-allocation of economic resources as the common goal of potentates who play the game of politics on two types of gaming board. The map of Mochudi and its environs (Map 5.2, reproduced on page 143) stands for one kind of board. It depicts a Tribal Estate managed from a central town in which tribespeople are concentrated, an arrangement germane to the organization of Sotho peoples. In contrast, other Southern Bantu rulers governed Chequerboard Realms in which people were distributed over blocks of territory. This disposition is illustrated in Maps 5.1 (page 142) and 8.1 (page 277), the first depicting a Bhaca settlement and the other showing Lobedu country. We can now consider the consequences of 'plays' made according to two sets of rules that govern political gamesmanship in the separate contexts of Tribal Estate and Chequerboard Realm.

My analysis is guided by a thesis about the location of authority. Rulers of Tribal Estates were manipulators of bounds and grants. The bias in their power was towards governance exercised over access to territory and over seasonal regulation of work. Authorities in Chequerboard Realms were less able to adjust bounds and grants. They located their powers in their ability to mulct the subject population. Chiefs of the Chequerboard re-allocated products rather than the means of production acting, by turn, as exactors and providers.

On the 'board' that is the Tribal Estate, the ruler's manoeuvres depend on the segregation of three types of territory. A residential area is set apart from the fields which, in turn, are separated from areas exploited from hunting and grazing posts. The ruler is at pains to oversee and confirm all allocations of rights to all classes of land. As the three classes of land are separate, rights in each are allocated separately to individuals. Several pastures, or plural grants in blocks of arable, can be given to any subordinate official. These are the ground-rules for a ruler's ability to discriminate among his subordinates.

The Sotho players of second rank are headmen who control residential wards within the town. Each headman desires control of good arable and good pasturage that, furthermore, is distributed in lots over the tribal territory. Distribution enables the headman's followers, first, to spread risk as they exploit scattered holdings and, second, to take advantage of the local variety in soil types and the seasonal grass cover in different zones. Inevitably, headmen compete with one another in efforts to gain, not simply the 'best' resources, but a satisfactory mix of resources. For a headman in one Tribal Estate this may mean (1) having a Southern pasture, (2) a Northern pasture, (3) fields near the river and (4) arable land at the foot of a scarp. This combination is designed to secure an optimum share of local assets. At a particular moment, our headman may feel content, apart from a shortage of Southern grazing. He must then work to extend his holdings in Southern pasture. Thus the requirements of headmen are particular and their particularity varies over time. There are good reasons for variation. Arable lands can be worked out, herds fluctuate in size, demand for land will increase or decrease among a headman's followers as their numbers dwindle or swell. These are the grounds underlying the competitive demands for re-apportionment that are made by headmen who supplicate for resources in competition with one another. A headman who wins chiefly favour wins at the expense of his rivals and one man's loss is always another's gain.

Southwold (1969), invoking the modern theory of games which provides mathematical formulations for the analysis of competitive human action, argues that tribal politics is, in general, susceptible to analysis as a 'zero-sum game'. The prime condition of zero-sum games is that the losses of those beaten in a competitive struggle equal the sum of all winners' gains. One man's success is thus always contingent on another's failure. After any number of plays in a game, the sum of losers' minus scores, added to the positive scores of winners, yields the uncompromising zero that is the characteristic of the zero-sum game. Southwold's general argument fits the conditions sketched above, in which headmen compete for a finite set of scarce resources. For a less abstract justification of this contention one can turn to the writings of the redoubtable missionary-explorer, Andrew Mackenzie.

In his account of ten years spent north of the Orange River, Mackenzie reports on his visit paid to the Ndebele. His account is particularly valuable for he witnessed a peculiar situation in which the warriors of a delinquent Zulu regiment were recreating community life by establishing a tribal polity. The regiment had fled from the wrath of the Zulu king, penetrating the country north of the Vaal, despoiling tribal settlements, forcefully recruiting youngsters and, more significantly, the women who were to supply an Ndebele stock. Undoubtedly the inherent consequences of favouritism and competition were heightened by the peculiarities of the Ndebele situation in which a society of men, women and children had to be built about a regiment of men. Always perspicacious, Mackenzie observed that:

> the private soldier has little in possession or enjoyment but he has also little care. The officer, on the other hand, knows that jealous eyes are upon him. His equals in rank and status covet his possessions, and regard the favours which he receives as so much personal loss to themselves (Mackenzie 1871: 325).

Particularly noteworthy is the way in which Mackenzie is in no doubt about the warriors' own view of things. The Zulu deserters' appreciation of their situation is precisely that which can be expressed as 'zero-sum'.

What I have noted is the ruler's incipient power to make a headman's holdings more or less attractive to potential followers and, in consequence, to influence the headman's ability to draw people to him. The ruler alters the face of the tribal territory by supervising its division into land of various classes which is allocated to competing officers. He also has the power to take resources 'out of competition'. Thus the right to hunt wild animals and gather wild products throughout the Tribal Estate was always guaranteed to all subjects. Where these products are concerned, the ruler surrendered the power to make discriminating allocations. In addition, he could declare particular pastures open to tribal use. Schapera observed that, in the modern Ngwaketse Reserve, 'a few districts are used as common grazing ground, where anybody is free to bring his cattle without permission' (Schapera 1943c: 234). Schapera also provides a clue to an explanation of why rulers should surrender certain assets to general exploitation. 'Such an "open" district usually contains the only good surface waters for many miles around, and presumably it has been felt undesirable to limit their use to certain people' (Schapera 1943c: 225). The political effects of control over a grazing district thus situated would be profound. The ruler cannot afford to favour any one official to the extent of allowing him to monopolize its use. By adjusting seasonal bounds and limiting the amount of time that could be spent in cultivation, the ruler also limits competition for agricultural labour, evening out the production of grain. This point was fully developed in chapter 5. The ruler thus has devices by which he can remove certain assets (pastures and labour) from the competitive arena by throwing them open to universal use. He thus exercises a control on the amount and nature of the stakes for which headmen may legitimately compete. The overall effect is to prevent untoward aggrandizement of the office of headman. As a category, headmen are kept in their place.

Next, I note an important limitation on the ruler's ability to re-allocate resources. There are few known instances of Sotho-Tswana rulers dispossessing headmen (or even subjects) of their holdings in land, whether arable or pasture. Rulers discriminated positively by making grants to one subject as against all others. They seldom deprived by taking away grants that had already been made (see Schapera 1943c: 192). When they did, it was the result of particularly bitter political strife, an ultimate measure. Yet this does not destroy the argument about authoritative discrimination. The work of high office concerned the regular rearrangement of rights in resources. In this process, marginal adjustments were regularly made. For instance, when a headman applied for a new pasture, he would propose a location for it. Inevitably, the proposed pasture was sited in relation to the established pastures of others. It had thus to be inserted among them. Pastures were areas in a radius about a cattle post with a water supply. The central post was the established holding, rather than any precise tract of land about it. Insertion of a new cattle post modified the boundaries of existing pastures: more cattle, or cattle of different ownership, would now graze in a general locale. While rulers, therefore, generally made marginal adjustments, it is marginal adjustments that are normally at issue in political life. Unless whole systems of allocation are overturned, the usual business of government is with the marginal losses or increments of power experienced by persons who occupy relatively stable positions.

The 'gaming board' of the Tribal Estate has been set up and the rules of the game set out. We may now examine the political consequences of locating a ruler's power in his ability to make adjustments in the distribution of a set of boundaries in terms of which he relates people to resources.

The first consequence is that the Sotho ruler must, at all costs, preserve the integrity of the pattern of settlement. If tribespeople desert the Sotho towns, authority must fail. This consequence was first noted by Mackenzie, who reported a conversation with a Tswana chief. The chief expressed wonderment at the powers of her Britannic Majesty, Queen Victoria. The Queen, he saw, continued to command her subjects though they had left the homeland and come to South Africa. In his own territory, the chief was plagued by the wanderlust of his people. Tribal wars had been stifled by European presence and, under new conditions of peace, tribesmen were tempted to desert their central town. The chief had constantly to recall 'Bantu Nimrods' from hunting posts and insist that they return to civic duties in the town. He said that he could not rule if such absences went unchecked. Since Mackenzie's day, successive observers have noted the correspondence between dispersal of Sotho populations and the slackening of the ruler's authority (Mackenzie on Thlaping (1887); Sillery on Ngwato (1952); Ashton on Tawana (1937); Breutz on Vryburg and Mafeking tribes (1955 and 1959)). The evidence collected in a variety of polities is overwhelming: towns are integral to the maintenance of authority in the Sotho-Tswana system of administration.

A second consequence of the Sotho dispensation is a conflict of interests between headman and subjects. In their exploitation of resources, it benefited tribesmen to pursue a ranging, open strategy (see chapter 5). This could lead a follower of one headman to seek access to resources that were under the control of another. This is why the headman's best policy was to aim at variety (the optimum mix) in his own combination of grants. To the extent that his followers exploited areas outside a headman's control, they were less dependent upon him and his power over them was weakened. Dispersal of this kind strengthened the ruler *vis-à-vis* headmen. The more officials a tribesman could play off against each other, the greater the likelihood of an appeal to the ruler to intervene in any disputes. Again, to the extent that ward members did not exploit only those resources allocated to their own ward headmen, the ward was less a consolidated group with discrete interests. The overall effect, I suggest, would be to promote sentiments of a tribal rather than a sectional identity (cf. Gluckman 1965: 140).

Third, it must be recognized that Sotho peoples bought peace at a price. Working rural resources from a town is not the most efficient way of exploiting them. This is evidenced by the actions of people who are tempted to stay away from town in order to spend time at cattle posts or fields. The people need, at once, to exploit a ranging strategy and to deal with the problem of keeping the peace in a territory over which a tribal population moves and whose members, in moving, have to negotiate around islands of ownership. The cost of living in towns was part of the price of peace. In principle, all disputes were settled in civilized fashion in the courts of the town.[1]

The fourth consequence is that centralization inheres in the system for allocation of natural resources. A Tribal Estate is a unit of exploitation and management on which the ruler is continually involved in the business of relating his people to the area they use.

Fifth, the possibilities for mobility of personnel between local political groupings is enhanced. Precisely because boundaries are flexible and people live in towns, change of adherence to a headman and his ward was not hindered by ineluctable problems about contiguity of dwellings and agricultural land.

Sixth, I note that Sotho defensive arrangements in time of war were based on the towns. Towns were often built in the shadow of hills or mountains, and ramparts were maintained on the high ground above the town. Town settlement had the advantage of providing tribesmen with a base where they could leave family members when they went out hunting or to cattle posts. The mode of warfare was assimilated to living in towns but should not, as some suggest, be considered their *raison d'être*. A weakness of the system was that while it protected people in residence, cattle were not put out of the reach of raiders.

Finally, a conciliar system of government prevailed in Sotho towns. Schapera (1956: 44) suggests that the frequency with which councils met may have had something to do with the concentration and availability of tribesmen. However, the links in this causal chain are more deliberately forged. Sotho lived in towns in order to conciliate, and this because conciliation was a necessary part of their day-to-day lives. Given the presence of people on a specific territory plus their desire to range over and exploit its varied amenities, then an intermingling of people in their economic pursuits must result. There is interspersal of holdings, a complication of borders and the necessity for arbitration when these are disputed. Nor are interests segmented into blocks that correspond with self-contained territories. In a sense, everyone is interested in every allocation because interests are generally dispersed. Take away conciliar government and you would have to take away the dispersal of interests and commingling of persons that is part of a total system in which the ruler is a guardian of a mode of adaptation to the ranching country of the South African hinterland.

A neglected aspect of politics in Western lands is that there was a specialization of offices to effect the administration of local resources. The specialization occurred where one would expect it—in the department of tribal life which was the ruler's prime locus of command. The creation of the office of *modisa*, or comptroller of pastures, is a signal example (Schapera 1943c: 224ff.). As more specialized offices are established, the ruler's powers of discrimination and intervention increase, especially when offices and titles are of different types and are independent of one another.

Among Kwena and Ngwato, the office of *modisa* was a grant in itself and was not contingent on the holding of other grants or titles. In particular, headmanship did not necessarily entail title to special pastures (*naga*). Detailed information on this score is limited to the modern period. After fieldwork in the Ngwaketse Reserve during the 1930s, Schapera (1943c: 225) reported that: 'There are altogether 127 overseers, of whom only 59 (including the chief) are headmen of wards. The overseers represent all the main elements of the population, and are not drawn exclusively or even mainly from any particular section.' Indeed, 'some wards contain more than one overseer, and others none at all' (Schapera 1943c: 225). This introduces possibilities for the combination and clustering of offices and grants. Tables 8.2 and 8.3 indicate how these were realized in modern times. Note that eighty-four ward heads do not hold offices as *modisa*. Also, thirty-five men held plural grants in pastures. These are the statistics of both special favour and discrimination.

Schapera detailed lists of allocation of grants to individuals. A man called Balone Serurubele is named as the comptroller of four pastures. Balone Serurubele was not the headman of a ward. How then does Balone's political position compare with that of any of the eight-four pastureless wardheads? While these headmen are accredited with followers, Balone enjoys grants in pasturage. Men like Balone must become the focus of dealings in which followers of pastureless headmen appeal for the right to graze cattle on the lands under their control. Incumbency of any one office was thus modified by grants of other types. The most powerful men held a cluster of grants and offices. Consequently, one headman cannot be equated with another. Headmanship is a matter involving size of following, grants in arable, grants in pasture and other economic relationships between the incumbent and his ruler (see Schapera 1943c: 225ff.).

TABLE 8.2 *Number of pasture comptrollers per ward*

No. of comptrollers per ward	0	1	2	3	4	5	6	7	8
No. of wards	84	53	17	7	0	1	1	0	1

TABLE 8.3 *Number of pastures per comptroller*

No. of pastures per comptroller	1	2	3	4	5	6	7
No. of comptrollers	92	21	5	4	3	1	1

Schapera described a recent state of affairs. None the less, his data illustrate a principle. In their allocation of grants of various types, the Western rulers had the power to discriminate among their subjects in a variety of ways. Men could be favoured on one count and deprived on another. A man's status was not contingent on the holding of one particular office. One would always have to ask what cluster of rights and grants were his to administer. Competition over a plurality of grants was the essence of Sotho politics.

Some writers fail to realize the salience of ecological management for political control. Writing about Tswana politics, Stevenson has remained purblind to the location of a Tswana ruler's powers. Indeed, he wonders whether Tswana polities should be called states at all. But then, Stevenson believes that 'Specialized political status among the Ngwato and other Tswana was limited to the office of chief and headman, which were both ascribed by primogeniture in the agnatic line' (Stevenson 1968: 83). The point is that, among Tswana, there is not merely headmanship, but headmanship with pastures and headmanship without them. There is headmanship with one pasture and headmanship with several. The value of office is further modified by yet other grants, this time in arable. Finally, in some Tswana chiefdoms, there was further differentiation that will be discussed later. To the untutored, power by virtue of management of bounds and grants can be invisible. One the lands of the Tribal Estate, the manipulation of bounds and grants in relation to people was the basis of political life.

On the lands of Chequerboard Realms, boundaries confine men to areas in which they concentrate their social and political investments. The administration of access to land is decentralized and there is an inflexibility of boundaries. Because different classes of land are bundled together—a man's home, fields and pastures are in close proximity—the ruler abdicates the ability to supervene in a continuous round of re-allocation of bounds. The first political consequence is that the potential to centralize authority through re-allocation of natural resources is taken out of the system. The ruler must use other devices to achieve discrimination among his subjects.

Rulers of the Chequerboard are deprived of a locus of authority, but that is not all. The properties of the Chequerboard itself create further problems for anyone who seeks to establish central authority. On it, territorial oppositions are clear and more fiercely expressed. The contiguity of squares on the board creates problems when there is pressure on resources. The incorporation of groupings contained within bounded districts makes their mutual opposition more absolute. The disposition of persons over a chequerboard territory fosters a tendency towards predation.[2]

On the Chequerboard, political association was expressed territorially in a direct and unambiguous way. The people of a headman were the people of his district. If tribesmen removed from the district, they moved from one ambit of control into that of another headman. The extent of a headman's district was directly related to the number of followers he could hold. Followers had to satisfy their need for resources within district bounds.

The tendency towards predation is a result of the linkage between territorial occupation and political control. When a tribal territory is an expression of segments of authority, difficulties arise once districts of the tribal domain become contained, surrounded by bounds that separate one headman's ambit from that of another. A contained district can expand over territory only at the expense of its neighbours. Alternatively, the population of an entire district can be resited on land at the edge of the tribal territory. Resiting has a cost: the district's population must be willing to rebuild homes, clear new fields, and move from known to unknown pastures.

Chequerboard rights are exclusive rights. What the borders of a district enclose, the people of that district hold. Competition for land rights is competition for a more total exclusion of others from localities than in the Tribal Estate. Zulu say that, like vultures, they pick out the eyes of the land. They seek out the choice parts and use them up. An eye of land is land that will yield everything that people pursuing a mixed economy can want. In eyes, variety of natural resources was contained in small compass. Unlike the Sotho-Tswana, the chequerboard peoples could not easily supplement inadequate holdings in one place by using holdings situated elsewhere. Although there was probably no absolute shortage of land before the white man came, dearth of lands was experienced in localities because shortage is always reckoned in relative terms. People are not satisfied with mere land, all would like eyes, and given eyes, would like to choose the best.

Thus competition for land was the territorial expression of competition for control of people who had to be held in contiguity by an official who otherwise lost them to another's overrule. As the ruler's domain was a chequerboard of districts, so larger areas were chequerboards of chiefdoms. The same tendency towards predation prevailed once chiefdoms became embattled within boundaries.

Territorial corporateness was also an expression of a group's wealth. The significant role of cattle in Nguni diet has been remarked (chapter 5). They supply the staple of milk and sporadic feasts of meat. There is temptation in cattle, and this temptation was enhanced by the great worth of cattle in the East where they are more thoroughly and completely integrated into economic life. The opposition of territorial blocks was an opposition of holdings in cattle, each group protecting its own.

Contrasting Tribal Estate and Chequerboard Realm, we may note that boundaries resolve a ruler's problems in the former while they seem to create and exacerbate difficulties in establishing central command within Chequerboard Realms. The ruler of the Tribal Estate uses bounds as a means towards central control and the creation of sentiments of tribal identity. In adjusting bounds, he discriminates among and controls his headmen. The Chequerboard ruler surrenders boundaries as a means to these ends. Instead, they become lines for the consolidation of sectional interests. Reader (1966: 286) has described how, in modern times, Makhanya regiments mobilized and faced each other across the boundary dividing one section of the tribe from another. This is the style of thinking when people are distributed on the chequerboard pattern where boundaries are used by small groupings against outsiders. In either case, boundaries are essential but one kind of ruler finds in them a source and location of power. The other locates this strength elsewhere in order to overcome the sectional strength which boundaries enclose.

Chequerboard chiefs were forced to elaborate the means towards direct control over material goods and the status of persons. This can be appreciated when descriptions of the Nguni cattle economy are considered. Nguni rulers made progresses through the land and they expected to be welcomed with feasting and gifts. Their visits demanded a subject's expenditure of both cattle and grain. Nguni subjects were wont to send cattle to the ruler's capital, appreciations or unsolicited expressions of their fealty. Among Nguni, cattle patronage was common. Furthermore, the dispossession of the wealthy is reported, usually on the grounds that they are guilty of witchcraft. Shaka punished disloyalty (which he judged on his own terms) by killing a man and all his kraal and taking their property into the royal exchequer. Finally, the courts provided a source of income in livestock—just as they did in the West. However, where I have been able to make comparisons, the Nguni scale of fining seems higher than that imposed elsewhere. Nguni rulers all worked a spoils system, discriminating among subjects by acts of gift and deprivation. What ensured its operation was the ruler's control of the means to violence. Through the spoils system and by special decrees and adjustments, they also intervened in an economy of status—an area of behaviour that will concern us later.

In conclusion, the contrast between East and West is a contrast in political style that is the result of differential location of power. Exercise of power by a Chequerboard ruler is more visible and obvious and, consequently, seems more arbitrary, direct and cruel. Benefit to the ruler is patent because it involves handling material goods or visibly disposing the trappings of status. The people are ruled and can see how they are ruled. On the pattern of the Tribal Estate, benefits derived by the ruler are less obvious. He is 'paid' at a standard rate of tribute in produce and labour: his income from the people is made up of fees and legal dues. He is not often seen to be making exactions. When he adjusts bounds and defines lands there is no obvious material advantage to him: the ruler is not seen to be on the make. Nevertheless, these adjustments are crucial to the management of political relations. It is easier for the ruler to appear as a third party mediating the conflicting claims of subjects. Chequerboard Realm and Tribal Estate thus produce contrary trends in government. The two patterns of territory lead to different emphases in the location of political control.

Ecology and the great ceremonies

Fortes and Evans-Pritchard (1940: 6–22) have provided the classic description of the political significance of the ritual that surrounds high office in African states. South of the Sahara, kingship, chiefship and subordinate office was normally cloaked with mystical legitimation. Among Southern Bantu, the head of state represented his clan and his people to the ghosts of departed chiefs or kings. His association with the land was both religious and secular. He was involved in rain-making and the magical doctoring of fields. He was also custodian of the strongest magic in the polity. Above all, the head of state participated in the great ceremonies. The great ceremonies had political import that is conveniently discussed at this point. I hold that the style of their celebration can be related to patterns of settlement, to the contrasting arrangements in Chequerboard Realm and Tribal Estate.

The great ceremonies are those that either involve all members of the polity as participants or are celebrated by an officiant who represents the the common weal. Great ceremonies are enacted for the good of the state. In Chequerboard Realms, the great ceremonies were used to emphasize the unity of a people around their ruler. In polities of the Tribal Estate, the great ceremonies expressed the sectional diversity that was contained within the overall unity of the tribe.

Chequerboard Realm and Tribal Estate are two vast and contrasting images of society. The Chequerboard is a pattern of divisions. The central town of the Tribal Estate is a statement of collective identity: the town is a people. Chequerboard and Tribal Estate beget in men's minds their respective and distinct conceptions of identity. In Western lands, one can stand on a knoll and view a prospect that is, at once, town and polity. The tribe is caught up in residence about one. Society is comprehended, real and virtual to the eye. In Chequerboard Realms, the prospect is always a division. To make up the tribe or nation, the pieces must be put together, a synthetic exercise. Town life contains a people and includes a perception of collective identity. The people of districts have a primary identity that is sectional. These two separate realities are constantly before the eyes of those who experience them; their perception is a continuing renewal. The contrast can be put this way: townsmen see a whole which must be broken into its parts, district dwellers must always constitute the tribe or nation out of the divisions with which they are familiar.

In ritual, potentates of the chequerboard are a human synthesis of the realm. The great ceremonies are structured around chiefship or kingship, and ritual emphasis is placed on the ruler's uniqueness. Medicines are used to strengthen the ruler and the polity is strengthened by his ministration. The ruler's health is part of political destiny; when he is sick, the land becomes 'hot' in sympathy and everyone is endangered. In this vein, the Lobedu queens had—like priests of Israel—to be without physical blemish. Perfection of body perfected their political action (Krige 1938: 271). Descriptions of great ceremonies in the kingdoms of the Zulu (Gluckman 1954), Swazi (Kuper 1947), and the Lobedu (Krige 1931) show how the ruler is put at the centre. Representatives of the people address the ruler in a national dialogue about high office. In small Chequerboard chiefdoms, though a smaller political community must be drawn together, the accent is similar. For the Bhaca, the first fruits ceremony is a scaled-down version of the Zulu *incwala* (Hammond-Tooke 1962). And, through an event of their history, the Bhaca illustrate the threat and danger imminent in large gatherings of people who normally live scattered abroad, separated by the bounds of their districts. During the ceremony, a Bhaca chief was stabbed above the eye by a candidate for office. In their ceremonies, Chequerboard people celebrate a mystical union that is the state, a union that is maintained despite the inherent divisiveness of their dispersed settlement on tribal lands.

In contrast, the people of Tribal Estates are at pains to express diversity by identifying the segments out of which the polity is constituted. Pedi initiation ceremonies provide an example. The youths of the tribe are taken together to a secret place where, after being circumcised, they live in seclusion. But they are circumcised in order of rank and are allocated places within the lodge on the basis of rank. The emphasis is on the uniqueness of individuals within the tribal group. Segmentation of groups of initiates is expressed by the way in which they are fed. Platters of food are sent to the mountain lodge from the village settlement below. The initiates divide into commensual groups and those who eat together come from political divisions within the tribe. Celebration of the first fruits has a similar segmental structure. In all this, the ruler takes precedence and acts as sponsor of ceremonies. But the ceremonies are not primarily about the ruler's office. The stress is analytic, the tribe in the unity of ceremony is anatomized.

I cannot, in short compass, present a detailed case to substantiate this general thesis finally, although the evidence is abundant. The political consequence for contrasting types of realm is this: one should look for spectacular elaboration of rituals of high office in Chequerboard Realms where great ceremonies provide the legitimation for overrule. On the Tribal Estate, there is an organic unity: the ruler's control is immanent in the system for allocating resources which is centred on him.

The prototype of polity

For Southern Bantu, the independent chiefdom was the prototype of polity. It enshrines a basic set of constitutional arrangements that were adapted to the ecological exigencies of particular zones, that presented a rationale for political association and defined a framework for administration. The independent chiefdom was also the matrix out of which more complicated states were born. Though the traditional era has passed, ideas of polity live on among Southern Bantu with whom they may be discussed today. When dealing with the Bantu concept of polity, I write in the present tense.

Inhabitants of an independent chiefdom make up a tribe. And 'tribe' is a Southern Bantu concept of a people properly joined in common political association. A tribe is also an ethnic idea, its members sharing in a language and a culture. Ethnic identity is always coupled with ideas about a people's common origin and their collective ethnic history. In this, Southern Bantu conceptions become complicated. The point is this: tribes are associations of political convenience. They are founded by historical figures, they come into being at known moments in time and in places that are remembered. Tribes rise and fall, they can fragment and re-form, swell or shrink in size. Tribes are not eternal, and collective memories reach way back, past the founding of a particular chiefdom, to a time when a person's ancestors lived in other polities. In Southern Africa, ethnic origin transcends tribe. The original groupings of Southern Bantu are groups of common stock and any tribe is a collection of stock-groups. First and foremost, ideas of political association among Southern Bantu relate tribe to stock-group.

Southern Bantu see the genesis of political association in groups of common stock. For them, these are the prime and 'natural' political groupings. Among the Nguni, the significant stock-group is the clan whose members share a common name (*isibongo*). Clan names pass from father to child like surnames in Europe. These names are highly significant because there is a ban on marriage between persons of the same clan name. The Nguni clans are thus exogamous and membership is determined by birth into patrilineal descent groups. Although most fellow-clansmen cannot say exactly how they are related, the possession of a common name is accepted as an earnest of common stock. Within clans, there are descent groups made up of people who can trace relationship with one another. Within descent groups, descent lines are recognized and ranked on patrilineal principles. The first-born son of a man's senior wife outranks all brothers and half-brothers. The brothers, in turn, are ranked by order of birth and the relative rank of half-brothers is determined by the seniority of their mothers in a polygynous household. A senior brother's son outranks the son of any junior brother. By extension of these principles, all men of a descent group are given relative rank. Ideally, seniors should command juniors. Kinship principles thus provide the paradigm for authority. Fathers command sons and fathers are succeeded by the first-born of their great houses which are the homes of senior wives. High office should vest in senior lines.

Within clans, there is a continual process of division of descent groups, new and distinct groupings hiving off from established groups. Descent groups have leaders—ideally the most senior kinsman by agnatic reckoning. Proliferation of descent groups is thus also a proliferation of leaders. The leader of a new group, again ideally, is the senior kinsman. Offshoots from established groupings are, inevitably, junior to their stem group. Within clans, therefore, the descent groups can be given appropriate rank and one group will have pre-eminence because its seniors represent direct lines of original founding ancestors. At a higher level, clans can also divide. As with descent groups, original founder clans outrank those that stem from them. When Nguni clans split, marriages can take place across the new clan divide.

Stock-groups among the Sotho were distinguished as groupings of people who sang and danced to (*gobina*) a particular animal. The Kwena celebrated the crocodile, the Pedi the porcupine etc. In one respect, Sotho stock-groups differ radically from those of Nguni peoples—they are not exogamous groupings. Indeed Sotho custom enjoins the marriage of near kin.

The Southern Bantu tribe can now be described as a collection of stock-groups. In each chiefdom, one stock-group is politically dominant. This dominant group supplies the noble line of chiefs. Often, the dominant group supplies the tribal name. When describing their tribal allegiance, all tribesmen take the name of the dominant stock-group. Kgatla, Kwena, Kone are—at once—the names of tribes and the clan-names of chiefs. For tribal purposes, diverse clans are gathered together and their identity is subsumed in the name of the noble clan. But for internal use, in arranging marriages, in founding settlements, the diverse clan identities are asserted again.

In the history of the Bantu of the south, migration interrupts periods of settled existence. A tribe is attached to a locale. It exists while its people are together. Migration often meant a breaking of association when a tribal fragment would follow a new route to a new settlement. Groupings from one tribe could join the settlement of another or secessionists could establish themselves as a new tribe in a new place. A complexity of such movements in time meant that the people of a single tribe never shared a single origin. The history of Bantu origins is a history of stock-groups. And the embracing history of political association that joins the tribal membership is always outlived by the exclusive stock histories that divide them.

When political association between fellow-clanspeople ends, common origins are not forgotten. Founder clans are recognized, though their representatives may live far away. Thus among the Tswana, the Huruthse are honoured as originals, the most senior of Tswana groupings (Schapera 1952: 8). In Zululand, the Qwabe take pride of place (Gluckman 1940: 36). And pride is the lot of these senior groups. Their honour gives them an eminence because they are scions of founding ancestors: they are first in ritual rank but there is no correlate of authority or power.

Within polities, ethnicity, or origin by stock-group, is significant as it provides grounds for political discrimination. Everywhere, the dominant stock-group of chiefs and their noble kinsmen is set apart. Then, other stock-groups are ranged about it, the way this is done differing from polity to polity. The Tswana and North Sotho peoples relate dominant to subordinate stocks in the following manner. They recognize three broad classes of tribesmen. There are nobles (*dikgoshana*), their vassals (*batlhanka/bashimane*), and people called 'refugees' (*bafaladi*). Vassals are tried and trusted servants of the chief. Their stock-groups have been incorporated into the tribe some generations back. The vassals are tribesmen by assimilation whose linkage with the noble house has become part of a tribal destiny. Refugees are more recent arrivals. They must serve their time hoping in the end, by proof of constant allegiance, to join the ranks of vassals. Between chief and refugee there is a residue of reserve that will only drain away with time. Tswana and North Sotho rank all men within the tribe. Nobles are ranked by the seniority of kinship. Within stock-groups, kinship ranking again applies. Between stock-groups that are not linked by kinship in the male line, rank is still established. In this case, rank is determined by the order in which groups were incorporated into the tribe. Like Elizabethan Englishmen, Sotho conceived of polities where 'men, by degree, stand in authentic place' (*Troilus and Cressida* I: 3). Macgregor noted that 'genealogical precedence has been reduced to such a science with these people that it is hardly too much to say that if two Basuto were taken haphazard out of the street in Johannesburg or any large town, in a very few minutes they would have decided without cavil or dispute which of them was the senior' (in Ellenberger and Macgregor 1912: 281).

To illustrate the political significance of clans among a Nguni people, I step out of context for a moment and cite a description of clans in the developed Swazi kingdom, rather than in a rudimentary polity. Kuper writes that:

> The centralized monarchy is built on a network of ties between the royal Nkosi Dlamini and commoners. The clans, over seventy in number, fall roughly into four major grades. At the apex is the Nkosi Dlamini in which the lineage of the king known as the *Malangeni* ('Children of the Sun') is pre-eminent; then there come clans known as 'Bearers of the Kings', which overlap with other clans that predominate in certain local centres and retain minor roles of chieftainship. Third come clans whose members hold hereditary official positions . . . and, finally, clans between whose members there is a minimum of social interaction [because they live apart] (Kuper 1965: 497).

In all the Southern Bantu polities, stock-groups were of political moment. For the tribesman, ascribed ethnic identity could spell political advantage or disability.

The rationale of political association demands ideas about legitimate authority as well as conceptions of proper groupings. We have seen that birth and origin provide a basis for the formation of groupings. The authorities set over them owed their position, in part, to the same hereditary and kinship principles that were the foundation of group membership. This poses a problem. How does a ruler exact obedience from subordinates who are bound in loyalty to their kinsmen at the core of each following?

Colson has compared the positions that tribal officials occupy with an ideal of bureaucratic office. She notes that, in South African kingdoms, the ruler did not command a national cadre of appointive officials who could be put into office, dismissed or promoted at will. 'If the king alienated a lord, he alienated his following as well, and a lord could not lightly be set aside to be replaced by another man' (Colson 1958: 43). The kingdoms did not show 'any strong tendency towards bureaucratic organization. The hereditary right to office was too entrenched for this' (Colson 1958: 43). Southern Bantu rulers could not easily control men by giving office, withholding office and taking office away. The bureaucratic picture is one in which men are sanctioned or rewarded by being moved in and out of office. But in this, note that the office remains intact. Men, as incumbents, come and go.

Southern Bantu officials were amenable to the ruler not as bureaucrats, but as leaders of followings (see Schapera 1956: 220). Barth (1969: 28) has remarked that 'in a bureaucratic office the incumbent is provided with those assets that are required for the performance of his role'. Assets are attached to office and the integrity of this attachment is maintained. To sanction the incumbent of bureaucratic office, the rule is 'move the man'. To sanction the behaviour of leaders of followings, the rule is 'modify their access to those assets necessary for the performance of their role'. Southern Bantu rulers attacked men or favoured them with assets. The extent of the ruler's power over subordinates is then measured by the extent to which he can deprive them or add to their store. And assets include the gamut of things material and things human as well as intangibles—values such as honour and reputation. The kings and chiefs with whom we are concerned proceeded by reducing or enlarging the positions held by subordinates. Headmanship, for instance, could be aggrandized or diminished. The man remained, his powers waxed or waned.

Leaders of followings are both supported and threatened from below. The direct threat to their position is a loss of followers. From ruler down to lowly headman, every official is subject to possible desertions of his people. Within the polity, the ruler's acts of discrimination can make one leader more attractive than another. The ruler's power lies in his ability to cause a headman to gain or lose followers. While descent was a prime principle of association in local groups, kinship loyalties do not override all considerations of interest and advantage. If pressed, men move to join other groupings. Schapera's *Ethnic Composition of Tswana Tribes* (1952) shows the extent to which different stock-groups are mixed within local units.

Having defined a major source of the ruler's power, I can also indicate how power was enlarged and extended in developed polities. To gain greater control, the ruler brought a greater variety of assets under his command. This involves the differentiation of classes of rights. Land is not merely land, it is land of defined types. Women to be given in marriage are distinguished from one another so that one type of marriage has different consequences from another. New systems for conferring honours are devised. The greater the variety of assets at a ruler's command, the more subtle his grants and deprivations become.[3]

Indeed, this is how the location of powers can be conceived. Power is located in the control of a specified class of assets, its provision and distribution. When a ruler assimilates a new class of assets to his command, he has found a new location for power. That location is the system for provision and distribution of the commodity in question.

Rulers of independent chiefdoms presided over segmented realms. In structure and organization, the divisions of the chiefdom were a small-scale version of the polity itself. Thus, as Ashton (1952: 209) remarks of the South Sotho, 'the duties of the various authorities are essentially the same in all the different grades, the senior ones merely having wider jurisdiction and greater responsibility than their juniors'.

The chief was religious head of the tribe, the first judicial officer, the president of the tribal councils, prime administrator of lands, leader of the army. Correspondingly, a subordinate official had judicial powers, led his councillors in debate, administered an estate in land, and commanded a section within each regiment. The segmented realm is a decentralized polity because the ruler must make a simultaneous concession of clustered powers to his subordinates. He reserves few unique powers entirely to himself. Constant secessions of groupings and the regular division of tribes is a result. The history of Southern Bantu political development is a progress towards centralization. This involved the aggrandizement of rulers who added to their powers by reducing the immunities of their subjects and modifying the office of subordinates to make them dependent on the central power. The last section of this chapter is a study of cases of political development. In it, I try to indicate the means by which rulers brought about the enlargement of realms, increasing their span of command by extending the scope of their powers. To achieve this end, they modify tribal institutions to make them preponderant loci of central control. The effect was, in each case, to transform the polity.

E. J. Krige notes that 'The great power of the chief in the three most important tribes of the Lowveld lies in rain-making' (1938: 271). Then, she comments on the consequences of this specific location of power: 'Here we find as in so many other aspects of their culture an intensification of a feature present in modified form in many other tribes, *leading to a difference as great or greater than the complete absence of the trait*' (1938: 271; my italics). Other Bantu chiefs make rain, but the Lobedu chiefs make rain-making the star in the constellation of their powers. This makes their polity unique. And in this way, each developed polity was a unique constellation of powers. Political development was particular because rulers in different places made much of dissimilar means towards central control. Hence the expansion of polity can only be understood by considering cases.

III Case-studies in the Expansion of Polity

The traditional ruler faced his people or their representatives in the councils of the tribe or nation. His closest advisers were privy to him, and their meetings with the ruler were held in secret. Subordinate officials, local headmen or the chiefs in a kingdom, could be called to advise or consult with the ruler. Finally, the entire population of tribesmen could be brought together to witness deliberations of great moment. A ruler was, therefore, answerable to his people. He had always to contend with two possible threats to his status and position. Rebellious subjects could try to oust him and place a rival claimant (normally a man of noble stock and a close kinsman) in office. Secessionists could desert the ruler, moving away, often under the lead of a disaffected kinsman of the ruler.

Unpopularity is a consequence of the discriminations of authority (Gluckman 1955b). To some extent, the ruler was insulated and protected from the onus of responsibility. Important decisions, when made in the council, were given the appearance of unanimous acceptance. Matters were talked out until voices of disagreement were stilled. Delegation of administrative tasks exposed the ruler's minions rather than the ruler to popular wrath. When functionaries satisfied the people, the ruler took the credit; when their actions led to dissension, the functionary took the blame. A fascinating example is the management of rain-making by Lobedu queens. The queens, one would suppose, were highly vulnerable—if the rains did not come, they had failed. But the stigma of failure belonged to a court official. The queen delegated the rain-making function to a chief who continued in office until drought proved his incompetence. Incompetence led to dismissal and replacement. Nor could rulers be directly approached by subjects, an intermediary always stood between supplicant or complainant and the head of state. The etiquette of a ruler's court, designed to protect and nurture his authoritative standing, is a study in itself. The point is this: rulers were vulnerable and their statecraft entailed keeping a balance between competing sections within the polity. The more assets they could distribute, and the more varied the assets at their command, the greater the ruler's potential for holding both his office and his people. He had to maintain a state in which it was evident that subjects would lose more than they could gain by promoting acts of usurpation or schism. The focus in this chapter has been the ruler's power to intervene and the means that rulers used in intervention. The final point in the general argument about power is this: the ruler intervened to create and promote satisfaction and stability in his realm, and this was an exercise in self-preservation. When men came to council, they were differentiated in terms of their command over people and assets. They were measured by the strength of their followings and the wealth that they and their supporters could dispose. To a degree, the ruler could make men and unmake them, adding to or subtracting from their political stature. In acts of aggrandizement or diminution of stature, the ruler worked in a field of relationships—he modified and adjusted a distribution of power among men of the polity. In presenting these case-studies in political expansion, my business is with development of the means to hold subjects in an expanding dominion by the elaboration of the institutions for a ruler's authoritative intervention. Mackenzie caught the mood of political competition in this description of the excitement of Ngwato on their way to confront their ruler:

> In assembling at one of these public gatherings, the men march under their headmen; and in cases of dispute the headmen range themselves under the chiefs they prefer, and thus march to the council. The relative strength of their parties is thus discovered and such things as *coups d'état* are not unknown in the history of the Bamangwato (Mackenzie 1871: 373).

Of the cases that follow, two concern developments in polities of the Tribal Estate; the remaining two are instances of the expansion of Chequerboard Realms.

(1) *The Pedi federation* (c. *1824–79*)

The Pedi polity was a federation of Tribal Estates located in the central Transvaal in an area bounded by the Olifants (*Lepelle*) River and the range of the Lulu mountains. In the federation, each Tribal Estate was geographically distinct and separate and governed by a chief. These chiefs had once been independent but were brought into subjection by the Pedi tribe under Sekwati, who became paramount in the region. The Pedi domain is now known as Sekhukhuneland after Sekwati's successor. As is usual in these cases, the events surrounding the emergence of the dominant group, that would explain why they became conquerors, are obscure. We can, however, examine the means that Pedi rulers developed in order to hold their dominion.

The first point is to note that Pedi expansion did not involve the widening of polity to embrace the entire federation within a single Tribal Estate. Local conditions worked against such development. To explain this, we turn to the idea of a tribal *unit of exploitation* which was explained in chapter 5. The limits of a unit of exploitation are established as the largest area over which members of a given population would wish to range in furthering their productive activities. In Sekhukhuneland, the conditions of the West apply but the convenient unit of exploitation is not as large as it needs to be further westward in Tswana lands. The ideal Pedi Tribal Estate is exemplified by the Valley of Tjati where Sekhukhune I lived until his defeat by Sir Garnet Wolseley in 1879 (Hunt 1931). Tjati contains a variety of soil types on the valley floor, and the surrounding highlands provide seasonal mountain pasture. There are good water sources. For Pedi, the best Tribal Estate is located where a judicious combination of highland, lowland and water is available. Juxtaposition of mountain and lowland provides an ideal catchment area for rain which waters land for the production of crops. In their exploitation of the region, people need to range and have access to distributed natural resources. But their ranges are neatly pocketed, more contained than the ranges of the Tswana in the West. The political consequences of this configuration were that Pedi paramounts had to join Tribal Estates: they could not manage the whole locale of their domain as a single estate. Subjects would find little economic advantage in such an arrangement. Hence, while the paramount and his subordinate chiefs could play politics and make the discriminations of the Estate gaming board within their chiefdoms, relationships between chiefdoms had to be set on a new and different footing.

To federate the separate chiefdoms of the region, the Pedi paramounts ran a system that depended on the interplay of ritual legitimation of their rule and the exercise of military might.

The Pedi announced that they were the ritual superiors of all the chiefs of the federation. Every ritual performance that involved chieftainship was done only with the consent, knowledge and patronage of the paramount. Every year, the subordinate chiefs supplicated that they might eat the first fruits in their chiefdoms. At intervals of four to six years they sought permission to 'castrate their bulls', a euphemism for the circumcision of tribal youths in the great ceremony of initiation. Such supplications were accompanied by gifts sent from subordinate chief to the paramount. The paramount exacted certain token offerings from regions especially endowed—clay from Tsopaneng, thatching grass from the south, buck from the flat lands, and so on. In the ritual legitimation of office, all chiefs were made dependent. Ritual acts, too, were underlined as the idiom in which inter-chiefdom relationships were expressed. 'Castrating bulls', eating first fruits, tilling the first sod of the year, if done without permission, are the tokens of denial of federal authority. The paramount could withhold permission and, hence, endanger the wellbeing of a chief's people. He could show disfavour by forcing a chief to postpone those rituals—such as initiation—that were not tied to the agricultural round.

Most significant of all, the Pedi established themselves as wife-givers to all subordinate chiefs. When a chief succeeded to office, he had to marry the wife who would bear the heir to chieftainship. She was always a Pedi of the paramount's house (Hunt 1931: 282). Without such a wife, a chief was not confirmed in office. Thus the paramount had a hand in the matter of local succession: the new chief was the man to whom the paramount allocated a bride. The advent of the bride was the occasion for a great ceremony in the chiefdom. The fire in every hearth was put out and then rekindled by hearth-owners in order of rank. They used fire that was carried by runners from the paramount's hearth. Brides given by the paramount had two titles: *Setimo Mello*, the Snuffer of Fires, and *Lebone*, the Light (Harries 1929: 34). Such women put out the powers of one reign and brought in the flame of its successor. By supplying brides, the paramount gave recognition to the successors of chiefs and he could create new chiefs, incorporating new groups into the federation or recognizing the division of one chiefdom into several new political groupings.

This political use of women was also a feature within chiefdoms where a headman could be elevated by marriage with a woman of the chief's house. Bothma (1962: 67) has shown the local logic of this arrangement. When a man marries a woman who both outranks him and is given to him by a superior authority, he receives a devolution of powers with his wife. He now 'has a princess to feed' and can collect tribute from his following that, otherwise, would have gone directly to the chief. The headman with a noble wife makes a single prestation to the chief on behalf of his following. This only results when men *receive brides from superiors*. If subordinates give brides to their superiors, who thus become affines, the relationship is of a different order. Affines are of two kinds: bride-givers and bride-receivers. For political purposes, passage of brides from a junior to a senior does not alter the prerogatives of their respective offices in a hierarchy. Passing wives downward is another matter. This is a concession of authority.

The concession is bought at a price. The bridewealth paid for noble wives is great: they are a capital investment and the marriage yields interest for as long as both parties live. The Pedi paramount had, in his sisters and lineage sisters, a source of economic and political capital. When they were given to subordinate chiefs, the subordinate's people all contributed to the herd that enabled their ruler to marry. In this economy of women and cattle, the ruler could not be prodigal. He gained cattle at the expense of concessions of authority and had to strike a balance in his dealings. Because the political economy was truck in women, rank and status, the paramount had to watch his qualifications. The local rationale demanded that he must be the dispenser of rank. Hence his bride, and consequently his heirs, should rank highest in all the land. When the paramount Sekhukhune sought the highest-ranking woman in the land, he found her already a wife and mother in the house of a lesser chief. He voided her marriage and claimed this Pedi *non-pareil* for his own (Harries 1929).

The structures of ritual legitimacy and of delegations by marriage-alliance, are one aspect of the Pedi paramount's power. The second was in military might. Faced with a recalcitrant chief, the paramount could try to subdue him by force. But this was not easily achieved for the Pedi paramount did not have a large fighting-force at his disposal. He could command the regiments of his home chiefdom. For certain victory, he had to mobilize other chiefs against the offender, for other chiefs might even join the offender and overturn the federal association itself. The paramount's manner of internal control by arms was in the organization of 'punishment commandos' (Wangemann 1957: 98). These were made up of the regiments of an alliance of chiefdoms and the composite army descended on the chiefdom of a lonely victim to despoil it. An account of one raid by a 'punishment commando' has been supplied by the missionaries who witnessed its prosecution in 1862 (Wangemann 1957: 97ff.).

Thus the Pedi federation was a loosely bound collectivity of chiefdoms whose paramount enjoyed limited federal powers. His federal discriminations were expressed in the idiom of rank and ritual and could only be backed by force if he could sponsor an alliance of chiefs against a victim chiefdom. There are limits to internal predations of this type, for everyone is a potential victim if the raids occur too frequently.

Within the chiefdoms of the federation, powers were located in the manner of powers in a Tribal Estate. But between chiefdoms a second system was established. In the Pedi case, I note a commentary on one of my general themes: while separate chiefdoms were Tribal Estates, the federation was a chequerboard of chiefdoms. Federal land was not managed as a great economic venture. In joining the federation of Tribal Estates, the emphasis on ritual legitimation of office and the mystical union of polity is emphasized. In effective discrimination and intervention among chiefs, the ruler must, in the end, resort to despoliation, arms and the threat of war. At the level of federal organization, Pedi behaved like rulers of Chequerboard Realms.

(2) *The Ngwato federation* (c. *1850–85*)

The federation of the Ngwato stands for the ultimate expansion of the Tribal Estate in Southern Africa. In this federation, the paramount continued to treat his domain as a single, vast unit of exploitation. The development of the Ngwato state is a story of the diversification of powers by the creation of new commodities or strictly defined sets of assets that the ruler could command. At the same time as the ruler managed new commodities, he concentrated control over their administration in the hands of the group of nobles —the true Ngwato who, today, make up about a fifth of the population in Ngwato territory (Schapera 1940b: 57).

Ngwato lands are now defined as the Ngwato Reserve in the north-east part of Botswana. As the traditional Ngwato state expanded in the last century, its rulers benefited from political disturbances in the rest of Southern Africa. Depredations of Ndebele, Boers, Britons and others, put pressure on tribal peoples. To the north, many fled to Ngwato territory where they were received as refugees. For the latter part of their history, the Ngwato people did not need to expand by conquest. As it came to include more people, the territory of the state was enlarged and came to include a diversity of ecological zones. In this situation where peace reigned over a large western area, its Tswana inhabitants ranged further and wider to promote economic and political advantage. They were presented with the opportunity for pursuing a traditional strategy on an unprecedented scale. The characteristics of the Tribal Estate were writ large and exaggerated.

In an article on 'Land and Chiefship in the Tati Concession', Werbner provides the telling and definitive analysis of the requirements of paramount chieftainship in the pattern of what I call the Tribal Estate:

> A tribal ruler had a relative span of authority in north-eastern Botswana. It was greater the more he was able to provide and allocate the resources which his people needed to meet extreme hazards in production, in the raising of their crops and in the herding of their livestock. To rank above chieftains of petty territories, a paramount ruler or chief had to play a qualitatively distinct part in the management of the economy. He had to co-ordinate a significantly greater and more enduring diversity of productive resources than the others. His village had to be able to provide against a run of bad years, or a severe drought, such as scorched the way for the retreat of a paramount chief, the Khurutse Rauwe, from the high veld. A paramount chief had to control such productive resources as would allow him a greater concentration of subjects and make him secure against their scattering. He could not be continually in danger of being reduced to the condition of the lesser chieftains, liable like them to fluctuations in the numbers of his subjects due to temporary variation in economic production and in the serviceability of resources. There was a systematic relation between paramount rank, settlement in a concentrated or nucleated village, and a distinct mode of production in separate zones of pasture and cultivation. For a paramount chief it was a case of all or nothing (Werbner 1970: 6).

How then, did the Ngwato chief gain embracing control of all? First, he had greater variety of ecological opportunity to offer. He could give more because his domain was great and contained more. The pattern of organization of the Tribal Estate allowed for the necessary definition and allocation of scattered resources among a population. Operating on an enlarged scale, the Tribal Estate became richer in possibilities.

Differentiation was not only a matter of putting boundaries around zones distinguished by specific natural resources. The Ngwato built the herding arrangements for their cattle into chiefly dispensations in a formal and legalistic manner. The status of *batlhanka* was established: 'These men . . . were placed as common headmen in charge of the chief's cattle-posts. The cattle entrusted to them were the hereditary property of the chieftainship, so that the *batlhanka* were always attached to the ruling chief himself' (Schapera 1940b: 77). This amounted to a fief based on cattle for: 'The entire property of a *motlhanka* was regarded as *kgamêlô* ["milk pail" cattle provided by the chief]; and since the chief could withdraw his *kgamêlô* whenever he wished, he could at any time ruin the holder' (Schapera 1940b: 78).

To the three classes of nobles, vassals and refugees found in Tswana communities, the Ngwato added a fourth, the hereditary serfs who were 'attached to prominent men' (Schapera 1952: v). There is evidence that these serfs could be transferred from one holder to another (Lloyd n.d.). Serfs, like grants in pasture, could be used to aggrandize the holdings of a subordinate.

While managing a large Tribal Estate with a diversity of assets at his command, the Ngwato paramount elevated the members of the ruling group by making them the agents of centralization. Ngwato were appointed to high office and held a disproportionate number of posts in the administration. In other Tswana tribes, the ruler tended to form alliances with vassals (*batlhanka*), often to consolidate his position against rival factions within the noble group. Numerous marriages between nobles and vassals attest to the political relevance of vassal-noble alliances (Schapera 1957). In contrast, there was a marked tendency towards endogamy within the noble group among the Ngwato. As so many headmen and minor chiefs were, in any case, Ngwato, marriage between Ngwato and Ngwato in official positions spelt alliance between political sections within the realm (see Schapera 1957). Thus, after Kgama became a Christian and abandoned polygyny, he was

> still able to consolidate his hold over the tribe by marrying off his sisters and daughters to headmen with large followings. Kgama carried this policy into effect by marrying three of his daughters to the local chieftains of the Khurutse, Kaa and Talaote respectively, and three others to prominent royal headmen, two of whom were important enough to be appointed district governors (Schapera 1940b: 76).

The picture of the Ngwato federation is thus one of chiefly powers located in the ability to administer a highly diversified economy. Political status and position can be measured as a holding of assets. In addition, chiefly favour could be extended in other ways—by marriage, gift of servants etc.

(3) *The Lobedu kingdom (1800–94)*

The Lobedu state is set apart in Southern Africa by the combination of two features: sacred kingship and the non-corporate nature of Lobedu local groups. Nguni and Sotho-Tswana local groups cluster about holdings in property, and members are recruited on the basis of patrilineal descent. Lobedu stress affinity rather than descent, and have a rule of cross-cousin marriage that perpetuates alliances through generations. The society is integrated by chains of exchange in which brides are passed against cattle. The Lobedu local group is a group of workers rather than a group of people who hold exclusive rights in durable property. For my purposes, the Lobedu queen is the ruler of a Chequerboard Realm in which economic security is gained by establishing networks of exchange relationships. Political power accrues to individuals at the centre of ramifying networks of exchange relationships. The powerful can call in and supply more items for exchange than can persons of lesser standing. Command is located in systems of prestation and counter-prestation. The ruler is unique because she has control of unique resources with which to establish links between herself and her subjects.

Leach (1951) has provided what is, to my mind, a convincing interpretation of aspects of exchange and politics among Lobedu. Yet, as Southall has noted (1965: 114), Leach's elegant model remains a model as all the information necessary to test it is not available. Despite gaps in information and Krige's scepticism (1964: 164), Leach's interpretation cannot be ignored. What I have done is to use those propositions and deductions that, on the basis of available evidence, seem to be incontestable. In addition, I have put the political consequences of exchange in a broader context of a regional ecology and of Lobedu economic life.

Two emphases in Lobedu culture can be related and explained with reference to the agricultural bias of the Lobedu economy. The first emphasis is on the queen's ability to make rain, the second is the stress on reciprocity and exchange in social relationships. The queen's ritual activities provide security through traffic with the occult. As the Kriges state: 'The queen is thus the foundation stone of the security of the cultural structure. Her rain-making powers safeguard not only agriculture from the caprices of nature, but the whole country from the attacks of its enemies' (1943: 283). Chains of exchange relationships provide security by redistributing consumption goods between producers whose success varies from year to year with the vagaries of rainfall, management of production, and the changing social composition of labour force and unit of consumption.

The drive to maintain security must be related to the commodities that Lobedu produce and consume. First, milk and beef are not significant in diet (E. J. Krige 1938: 269). Meat is supplied by slaughter of small stock. Grain, garden produce and wild products are the major sources of food. Though the Kriges studied the Lobedu after the rinderpest epidemic of 1895 and after the epidemic of Texas fever in 1910 had decimated Transvaal herds, these events do not account for the small size of herds in Lobedu country. The Lobedu occupy an ecological niche, a retreat in the mountains better suited to agriculture than to cattle-raising. Their apparent immunity to the raids of bands that disturbed other Transvaal groups has been attributed to the awe which the sacred queen inspired in would-be attackers (Krige and Krige 1943: 1–5). But Lobedu country is, in itself, only attractive as a prospect for occupation to those who would be willing to farm without herding significant numbers of cattle. As a prospect for raiding, the relative dearth of cattle in Lobedu country makes it unattractive. Occupancy of an ecological niche as well as the queen's sacredness won Lobedu an immunity from outside interference. At the same time, the political security of the kingdom had a cost. A grain-reliant economy was established with no significant internal provision of cattle-surety against times of poor harvest and drought. Further, Lobedu systems of storage were inadequate and their granaries were prey to depredation of termites and weevils in the humid atmosphere of the mountains. The year was the significant unit for economic activity, and there was no emphasis on stores that would tide people over a bad year of drought. Lobedu were not only grain-reliant, but also reliant on each year's harvest. In this context, the rain-cult makes sense. So does emphasis on the exchange of produce.

Each Lobedu production-unit was linked to others by the marriages of its members. Marriages were established by exchanging women against cattle and this primary exchange was the paradigm for further exchanges that continued and flourished between in-laws over the years. The formal expression of this (documented in modern times) was that bride-givers honoured their sons-in-law with beer in great quantities at least once a year. On receipt of beer, the son-in-law responded with a gift of small stock. In the formal gift-giving, the value of the beer exceeded the value of the small stock (Krige and Krige 1943: 63). In the formal exchange, the son-in-law seems to get more than he gives. At this point, Leach introduces his proposition that bride-receivers outrank bride-givers: sons-in-law appear to get wives and yearly tribute as well. An inequality between givers and receivers of brides is, in Leach's view, assimilated to politics. Men of authority stand in a bride-receiving relationship with subordinates. It is this element in Leach's model that Krige has contested.

The relative ranking of affines apart, it is clear from all accounts that affinal links gave people of one consumption unit access to the produce of another. The emphasis in exchange is on 'small-change', perishable commodities such as grain and beer, and small stock destined for slaughter. These exchanges were made 'within the year' and a redistribution of presently available consumption goods was effected. Mutual access of affines to one another gives people an idiom of kinship for making demands (*hu lova*) on their affines. And the demands they make represent their present needs. The shortages in each production-unit can thus be compensated. Reciprocity is a surety against uneven production of commodities.

Cattle, the 'big notes' of Lobedu exchange, are almost wholly reserved for bridewealth transactions (Krige and Krige 1943: 66). In a key sentence—quoted by Leach—the Kriges epitomize the Lobedu allocation of value between cattle and beer: 'ownership of cattle is not the chief or even a very important method of reckoning status. A man will complain, not because he has no cattle, but because he cannot brew beer to maintain his prestige' (Krige and Krige 1943: 42). Beer demands that labour be expended for production of grain and for brewing: it can also be acquired from a man's bride-giving group. Cattle and women are invested in social relationships: they create links of affinity. This investment yields interest in goods for consumption purposes. Further, there was a form of 'fighting with property'. Men with pretensions to status can be forced to feast groups of visitors who come to honour them by dancing at their homesteads. These dancing groups are sponsored by leaders: they come from a locality in the name of a prominent kinsman or neighbour. Sending a group invites a retaliatory visit. However, this consequence can be commuted. The dancing group demands expenditure of meat from its hosts. If the group's sponsor sends beer after the visit of his dancers, he forestalls retaliation. The obligation to reciprocate is commuted and it is cheaper to send beer than to give a feast (Krige and Krige 1943: 83). Why then should the receipt of beer be accepted as recompense for expenditure of meat?

This is another shred of evidence that adds plausibility to Leach's case. If the gift of beer was a token of subordination as well as an exchange commodity, the original sponsor is seen to buy meat for his people at the price of subordination to a superior. It should be noted that the commodities exchanged reflect the idiom of affinal relationships: sons-in-law give meat or small stock, the bride's group, beer. In Leach's thesis, bride-givers rank below bride-receivers.

The Lobedu queen thus reigned over an agricultural people who had devices for evening out differential accumulation of surpluses from year to year between local groups within the population. In the balance-sheet of transactions, the Kriges insist that an equality in exchanges of products was achieved, at least in the long term. Leach, contrariwise, argues that, on logical grounds, the balance was achieved by adding the intangibles of prestige and political power to the equation.

Indisputably, the queen commanded an intangible—her control of the elements. And headmen came, one by one, to beg her for rain, paying tribute for her service. This rain-tribute was a source of wealth that supplemented the agricultural income of the people of the capital. As a great magical practitioner, the queen was set apart from ordinary people, first by her sex—a woman instead of a man in an authoritative position. She was incestuously conceived and did not die, but committed ritual suicide after the fourth initiation school of her reign. She controlled awful magic in which skin and body-dirt of departed rulers were ingredients. She had access to rain-making ancestors and the sacred groves in which they were buried. In her relationship with the occult, the queen legitimated her position and could exchange ministration for goods.

At a more practical level, the queen was connected through marriage to all the important political officers in the tribe. As 'cattle beget children', woman-to-woman marriage is possible in Africa. 'Every Lobedu induna [headman] sends a daughter to be a *mothanoni* [wife] of the queen as do any of the nobility who wish to be on a good footing with her' (E. J. Krige 1938: 272). The queen only keeps a proportion of the many wives she receives: others are given by her to important subjects. She stands in wife-giving and wife-receiving relationships with the important people of the land. The women she gives confer status and can elevate ordinary men (Mönnig 1963b: 60). It will be remembered that Pedi chiefs took brides from subjects as a matter of course. However, they gave brides to transform the political status of recipients who had 'to feed a princess' and, to feed her, took tribute from followers. A Pedi chief gives more than a bride: he gives away the authority to command a section of his people. The Pedi practice accords with Leach's ideas about distinguishing status by the direction of transfer of women. In the South African context, it enhances Leach's case with reference to the Lobedu. If the major thesis is accepted, the queen is seen to accept wives from all headmen, but to distinguish and raise some headmen by giving them women.

Lobedu headmen controlled small districts. On Map 8.1 these are seen to

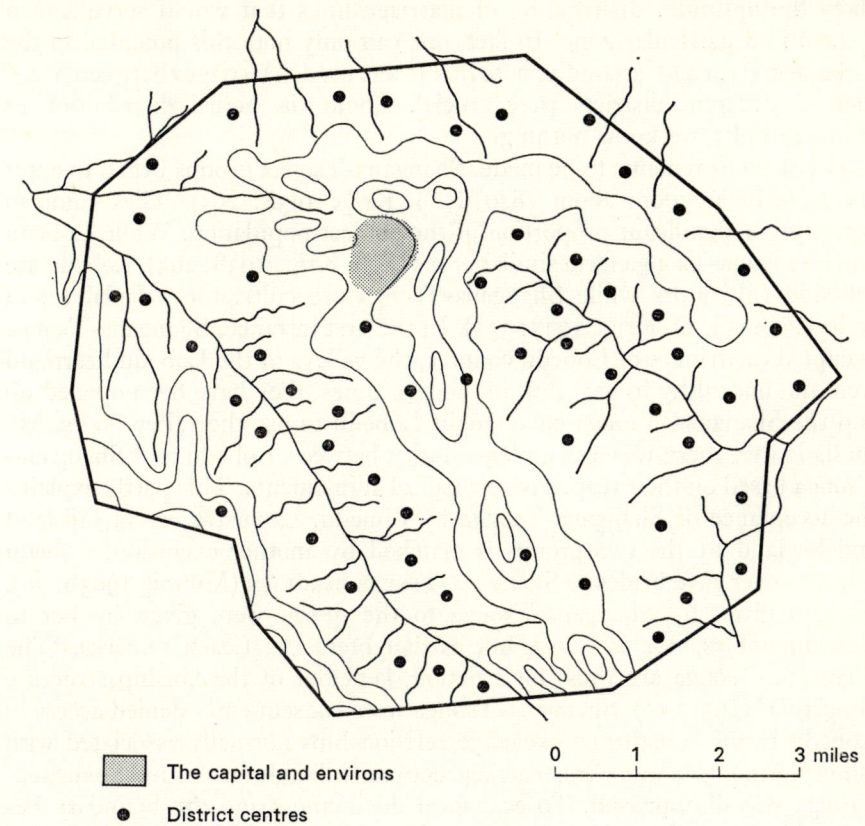

MAP 8.1 *Lobedu country and settlement pattern (after J. D. and E. J. Krige 1943)*

be divided by topographical features, especially the tributary streams of the Lobedu rivers. The districts correspond with a small unit of exploitation. Without many cattle, Lobedu did not need to range in search of pasture. As good cultivators, they did distribute their fields which, today, can be as much as ten miles apart (E. J. Krige 1938: 269). A multitude of tiny districts thus focus on the capital and the queen. She presides, I argue, over a country where the queen's rain and the queen's peace provide a context in which people can gain access to different areas by striking relationships with their inhabitants. On the Tribal Estate, a man distributed his investments by gaining access to different locations for pasturage and fields as well as by establishing relationships with other herders, farmers, etc. In Lobedu country, access to zones is through the people who work them, and is access to produce, the result of labour. Affinal links that span districts, carry produce of one district into another. At a theoretical level, one could draw up a 'marriage strategy' to show the optimum distribution of marriage links that would serve a man located in a particular zone. In fact, one can only note this potential in the Lobedu system and, secondly, note that it was used. Marriages between headmen of different districts were crucial. About the actual distribution of marriage links, we know nothing.

A last point remains to be made. Shangana-Tsonga groups began to enter the Lobedu kingdom about 1840 (E. J. Krige 1938: 265). They came to constitute a significant proportion of the subject population. While Lobedu and Shangana-Tsonga farm similar crops (E. J. Krige 1938: 265), Lobedu are hill-side cultivators while Shangana-Tsonga are cultivators of plains and valley-floors (J. D. Krige 1937: 355). In the first instance, Shangana-Tsonga occupied the fringes of Lobedu country, the valleys of the Lobedu heartland were too unhealthy to use. But, in modern times, they have been opened up and the Shangana-Tsonga have taught Lobedu to use the valley floors. My thesis is that there was a complementarity between Lobedu and Shangana-Tsonga based on their respective ecological adjustments. This partly explains the acceptance of Shangana-Tsonga by Lobedu. Exclusive use of hill-land and lowland by the two groups is matched by another exclusion. Lobedu queens never gave brides to Shangana-Tsonga headmen (Mönnig 1963b: 56). Women given by Shangana-Tsonga to the queen were given by her to Lobedu nobles, not as wives, but as daughters. As Leach remarks, 'The Shangana-Tsonga are thus, by a fiction, kept out of the kinship structure altogether' (1951: 50). Shangana-Tsonga were consequently denied access to Lobedu in the constituted exchange relationships normally associated with affinity. Among commoners, marriage between hill-side farmer and Shangana-Tsonga was disapproved. To ecological distinctness and the boundary between kinship and outsider, one may add a third point. Lobedu believe that Shangana-Tsonga manage transactions on extrinsic rather than intrinsic grounds, that they exchange commodities for gain rather than making regular transactions within culturally defined relationships with rules of reciprocity (Krige and Krige 1943: 68.) I suggest that this adds up to a situation favouring limited trade transactions between two separate peoples occupying their distinct ecological niches in the Transvaal. There are obvious mutual advantages to the contact of peoples who exploit the environment along different lines—their surpluses and shortfalls can be complementary.

To conclude, the span of a Lobedu queen's command was partly limited by given ecological circumstances. In the first instance, she ruled a nation of hill-side farmers and the possible area for their occupancy was determinate. Working from the mountains, the queen also entered into political relationships with alien groups whose members followed a pattern of exploitation that was distinct from, and to some extent, a complement to Lobedu agriculture. The location of the queen's command was in her power to make rain and in her control of the exchange of women as wives. The queen had 'the power to withhold rain from the undeserving or to drop it gently upon the deserving with mathematical precision' (Krige and Krige 1943: 2). This is a power to discriminate. It gives the queen the ability to sanction the 'undeserving' and is the basis for demands for tribute from each district. Second, the queen was the centre of a network of affinal ties. She only had access to all the districts of the kingdom because she alone had affinal relationships with all headmen. Her power to arrange marriages extended to the ability to create ties between district headmen. When the queen gave a bride received as tribute from one headman to another headman, the queen created a tie of affinity between two districts: the headmen concerned became affines. By arranging marriages, the queen intervened significantly, structuring interdistrict relationships: 'in general, the father's relatives live largely in the same district, the mother's or the wife's in some other area and visits and gifts of beer serve as an introduction to the districts in which they live' (Krige and Krige 1943: 83). The scope of the queen's power was limited to managing the effects and consequences of rain-making and alliance. It is important to note that the capital did not become a great redistribution centre for produce and grain, there was no management of a national surplus in produce. Surplus and shortfall were experienced by small units and adjustments were made between them. Centralization of exchange could not have occurred unless holdings in land were allocated on a feudal basis, or unless political authorities could gain access to the labour of the subjects, or unless the ruler extended her powers to tax subjects. Any of these developments would require the use of force to sustain them. The Lobedu kingdom was a polity in which the ruler expanded the scope of her powers to the maximum degree commensurate with a rejection of recourse to force in the normal business of government.

(4) *The Shakan tyranny (1821–8)*

Shaka's Zululand was a state in which the ruler extended the span of his command beyond any prior conceptions of Southern Bantu expansion. The Zulu nation was contained within a *cordon sanitaire*, a great expanse of waste land that separated the Zulu peoples from other, lesser, tribal polities. The *cordon* was managed like a tribal iron curtain. It prevented defections and gave the ruler utter control over relationships between his realm and the world outside. Secession, and hence the threat of depletion of the span of command, was virtually impossible. Shaka extended the scope of his command. Referring to him and his successors, Gluckman (1940: 46) writes that 'During the time of the kings, the State bulked large in the people's lives.' Walter (1969: 218) remarks that 'there was no private sphere'. The power of the monarch was universally located, its scope was absolute. To achieve universal location of power, the Zulu kings modified tribal institutions. Their reforms followed the logic of the separation and centralization of powers. First, they clearly separated departments of social life and, within those departments, created distinctions of rank and status. Second, they centred each department on the monarchy. The distribution of honour and of resources in each department was in the ruler's gift. Finally, Shaka, the arch-tyrant among Zulu kings, countered all tendencies to reduce the span and scope of his command, cancelled any trend towards locating immunities from his thrall, by maintenance of terror.

There were white witnesses to Zulu tyranny. Men such as Fynn and Isaacs left vivid accounts of the ruler's behaviour and of the military machine in which the ruler's power was located. Their accounts and the work of later scholars has led to an appreciation of the 'constitutional' and administrative reforms that enabled successive rulers to govern South Africa's largest kingdom. There is a standard picture of the kingdom: at the centre is the capital surrounded by barracks in which a standing army was maintained. The royal district was both the place of the army and a place of cattle, for large herds attached to regiments were kept there, making the capital the centre of wealth and might. The king controlled the maturation of men who were only allowed to marry when released from military service. Male initiation, once a local affair on the traditional Nguni pattern, was abolished and the king gave each tribesman his majority. The great ceremonies were militarized and men attended them in regimental formation: 'The ceremonies were chiefly designed to strengthen the Zulu at the expense of other people' (Gluckman 1940: 31). The king controlled a monopoly in national magic, thus 'Shaka expelled all rainmakers from his kingdom, saying only he could control the heavens' (Gluckman 1940: 31). Gluckman (1955b) has emphasized administrative reforms that gave subjects a plurality of allegiances. In military organization, each man belonged to a 'head', a unit for recruitment in which membership was fixed and hereditary. The heads, drawn from the districts of the nation, were represented in each regiment. Thus a man owed loyalty to his 'head', to the regimental commander, and to the chief of his district. Plural allegiance led to 'cross-cutting ties' of loyalty that gave cohesion to the nation and countered traditional segmentation of authority where officials commanded homologous units. Inevitably, only the king could mobilize regiments and give them orders. By introducing a variety of offices, the king separated powers and allowed separate powers to converge only in the kingship. For the elaboration of the complexities of the standard picture of administration, standard works may be consulted (Gluckman 1940; E. J. Krige 1936a; Omer-Cooper 1966). I am concerned with the advertisement of a work of another order. In his *Terror and Resistance*, Walter (1969) has provided a compelling analysis of political process in the Zulu state, using the Zulu case to support general propositions about terror in political organization.

The Zulu terror was directed outwards as predation on other peoples. Directed inwards, terror subserved a régime of despoliation and redistribution of spoils among subjects. Walter argues that 'the impression left by violence was the linchpin in Shaka's system of power. Terroristic despotism depends on the impact that violence makes on the consciousness of witnesses and on the communication of this fear to others more remote' (Walter 1969: 132).

In directing terror outwards, Shaka 'discarded the limited warfare of Dingiswayo's era for the *impi ebomvu*—literally 'red impi'—a war of extermination' (Walter 1969: 137). He took what he wanted from victim tribes, be it recruits to his regiments, women, or cattle. What he did not want, Shaka destroyed. Within the realm, people were put to death at the tyrant's command. The property of victims was forfeit to the king who generally gave it away, often to those who had served as executioners. Nor were victims slaughtered singly. When the ruler saw danger in the following of a subject he exterminated the leader and all his people. Apart from these obviously political executions, the terror was maintained by apparently whimsical selection of subjects to be put to death. In this connection, it is significant that the king became the smeller-out of witches and evildoers in the tribe. He often killed to eliminate mystically defined 'enemies within'—persons who endangered the nation by breaking taboos and harbouring evil, mystically conceived as a contagion. There is no news in the butchery instigated by Zulu kings. But Walter has demonstrated that even Alice-in-Wonderland whimsicality in selection of victims was a craft of state. The régime was integrated *by* the ruler's arbitrary behaviour.

It is impossible to recount Walter's argument in full, but we can note some of its elements. First, the terror was exercised within and from a state contained within secure bounds. Second, the conception of the ruler was that of a great despoiler-provider. Third, administrative reforms prevented consolidated opposition. 'In the Zulu system, persons, relations, and events with a potential for limitation impinged on the despot from time to time, but their effect was isolated, scattered and systematically deprived of the conditions necessary to organize them as institutional restraints' (Walter 1969: 249). Finally, terroristic despotism was structured around the tension between a fiction and the reality which could reveal the fiction to be a lie. The fiction was a vision of the ruler as omnipotent, infinite in power, with uncountable wealth in cattle, and the commander of a military nation whose members could not be numbered. The lie was given by any act of popular disapproval, by any uncomfortable fact that denied the primary image. In fact, the ruler's powers declined towards the periphery of his realm. In fact, his cattle could be counted and men did not have as many cattle at their disposal as they could wish. The nation was not one people but a new creation of disparate elements, and there was incipient threat of fragmentation. But, Walter argues, 'continual violence and the enchantment of the grand performance drew attention away from the discrepancies between fiction and reality' (Walter 1969: 258). The drama of kingship, as well as its terror, was used to imprint the fiction and obscure the reality. This is not an abstract conception: drama and terror were events to be witnessed. Terrific acts overshadowed other possibilities, an image of the enormity of kingship was maintained. The terror served to overcome the successive crises of integration inherent in the new composite nation.

The Chequerboard Realms of the Zulu and Lobedu hold their fascination for contrary reasons. The sources of the Lobedu ruler's powers and the relative immunity of Lobedu in their mountain retreat seem, at first, to defy explanation. The sources of the might of Zulu kings is evident: the problem here is to define its limits rather than its extent. Events among both the Lobedu and the Zulu have attracted scholars less interested in South Africa as a region, than in the relevance of South African polities for political and anthropological theory. Lobedu and Zulu, in the intricacy of contrasting institutions, represent the range of political expression in Southern Africa.

Conclusion

This chapter is structured around the proposition that a ruler's command can be defined as his ability to intervene in political process in order to discriminate among his subjects by making invidious allocations of value amongst them. Given this, the next task was to locate the ruler's powers for discrimination and to define their scope. The powers are located in institutional forms that differ in the emphasis placed upon them and in their articulation, from polity to polity. This approach leads one to point up the variety inherent in systems of control within the polities of Southern Africa. In this chapter, that variety has been illustrated, it could not be exhaustively comprehended. However the propositions put forward here have implications for the understanding of political process in all the polities of Southern Africa. I have drawn attention to the territorial and spatial expression of political relationships, and I insist that territorial arrangements relate to local ecological conditions, whether or not there is an absolute shortage of land. The models of the Tribal Estate and the Chequerboard Realm have a general significance. The interplay of span, scope and location of command in each polity is the key to the understanding of political process.

There is an important general thesis contained in this chapter. It relates commodities and their definition to styles of government and links the substance of the chapter on Economic Life with the present argument. Direct access to transferable capital goods is a precondition for discrimination among subjects by distribution of spoils. The Nguni polities were spoliation states, not merely in relations between polities, but in the internal relationships between leaders and their followers. Force and violence are part of this package. The Lobedu, though constituting a Chequerboard polity, did not provide the ruler with opportunity for spoliation—the necessary commodities were not available. When, on the Tribal Estate, the ruler had access to value mainly by allocating the means of production through manipulation of bounds, this prime locus of authority determined the nature of his government. The ruler of the Tribal Estate did not generally effect immediate allocations and transfers of actual wealth: he modified the potential for the creation of wealth. The effects of his actions were in the long-term, they were seen in the building up of herds and at harvest-time. One can say that the ruler of the Tribal Estate assumed peaceful economic exploitation to realize the results of his work.

The despoiler-rulers constantly entertained the possibility of violence, internecine or otherwise. Addressing Shepstone, the Zulu king Cetywayo said: 'My people will not listen unless they are killed' (cited by Walter 1969: 231).

Notes

1 I owe this point to a discussion with Dr R. P. Werbner. I had thought only in terms of benefits rather than the costs of Tswana settlement patterns.

2 Sahlins (1961) has written a suggestive essay on the relationship between territory and predation among peoples without rulers. My formulation benefited from his analysis.

3 In arriving at this conceptualization of power, I have benefited greatly from discussions with Professor E. L. Peters.

Chapter 9*
Law and Justice
A. C. Myburgh

Introduction

Law and culture

Law is that aspect of culture of which the function is the maintenance of order; its connection with the other aspects will become clear in the course of our discussion. The traditional legal systems of the South African Bantu peoples may be described as non-specialized since they are typical of small-scale societies having non-specialized cultures (Myburgh 1965: 7).

Like all culture, law is subject to constant change; among the South African Bantu the modifications have been largely due more to contact with the West than to factors arising among the peoples themselves.

This contact has resulted in the simultaneous operation of Bantu legal systems and a Western system with which they are sometimes incompatible. This phenomenon, to which we shall draw attention where necessary, is often referred to as the conflict of laws, but somewhat unfortunately so, since the same expression is often used for private international law.

Sources of law

Sources may refer to origins or to stores of information, and may be termed sources of origin and sources of reference respectively.

The sources of origin are custom and legislation. Among the South African Bantu, legislation occurred but exceptionally (Warner 1858: 62; Kropf 1889: 168; Schapera 1937b: 178, 179; Schapera 1938a: 41; Breutz 1941: 83), leaving a preponderance of customary law (Schapera 1937c: 197). Legislative enactments were the decrees of rulers acting in consultation with their counsellors or in terms of a mandate from a general assembly of their followers (page 291 below). Examples are Kgama's abolition of the marriage payment known as *bogadi* for the Ngwato (Schapera 1938a: 145, 146) and various measures among the Cape Nguni such as Gaika's (or rather Ngqika's) laws against slaying an adulterer caught in the act (Brownlee 1858: 113) and removing virgins to the capital for sensual purposes (Brownlee 1858: 129), Sandile's abrogation of the requirement that a man cover his head when approaching the capital (Brownlee 1858: 128), and abolition of circumcision by Faku and other Mpondo chiefs (Hunter 1936: 165, 396).[1]

The only sources of reference yielding data on the customary law and legislation of the South African Bantu, and on the interpretations of these given by their courts, are the peoples themselves and such records as have been compiled after recourse to them. It is hardly necessary to remind the reader that the legal systems in question are essentially unwritten (Schapera 1937c: 197) and that the available records, vernacular and other, are the result of initiative originally taken by persons of Western origin.

Law and justice

Among the peoples under discussion, as elsewhere, law is not synonymous with justice, although the latter is always the ultimate objective of a legal system, as is exemplified by the data on the Pedi (Mönnig 1967: 300). So, for instance, Kgama's prohibition of *bogadi* among the Ngwato (page 284 above) and the restriction of marriage to members of authorized regiments among the Zulu (Krige 1936a: 38, 119, 252; Myburgh 1944: 32, 33, 48, 267, 270, 272) must have conflicted with the people's sense of justice; nevertheless, both were recognized as valid law. Kgama's measure has remained in force, being acquiesced in by the Ngwato, although the occasional deviations (Schapera 1938a: 146) show a continued sense of injustice; when the death penalty could no longer be imposed for violation of the Zulu rule, the latter was abrogated because the people's sense of justice prevailed over their legal convictions (Myburgh 1944: 33).

Law and observance

We see, then, that legal conviction is distinct from the sense of justice; and it is to the former that observance of law is to be attributed. Violation of the law is the exception everywhere, as is litigation; among the South African Bantu it is often most difficult to find judicial authority for a legal precept or jural principle. The reason is that people are law-abiding because their legal convictions are formed and reinforced by factors derived from various cultural aspects.

The Bantu are taught the requirements of the law at home and in the formal schools (see chapter 7). They also learn these in association with their coevals as they pass through the different age-grades. Their knowledge is constantly replenished and supplemented by observation and by participation in sacrifices to expiate wrongs and in the many ceremonies connected with matters such as marriage, death and succession, and the ruler's control over the crops. Assemblies at the capital remind them of the system underlying order and good government. Topics involving the law are frequently discussed; and the leaders, such as the head of the household or the ward, never cease to enjoin compliance with the law in direct terms or indirectly by giving advice. The individual comes to realize that falling foul of the law is met with the disapproval of the living, and to believe that the ancestral spirits uphold the law and will punish unlawful conduct. Finally, he becomes acquainted with the functions of the courts and the means by which their orders are enforced (Schapera 1938a: 36, 37).

Observance of law is therefore not only due to the provision of measures peculiar to the legal system, but largely to the influence of education, social organization, political organization, economy, religion, and language.

Obviously, too, the law may be inferred from what people comply with because they defer to the ancestors, public opinion, the leaders, or the courts.

Law and the courts

It should now be clear that a legal system comprises what is accepted by the people concerned for the maintenance of order. To ascertain this is the function of the courts. When matters are brought before them they must find, state, interpret, and make orders in terms of, the law as established by the people. Law does not, therefore, owe its validity to judicial recognition.

Nor are a court's pronouncements necessarily correct statements of the law; indeed, courts everywhere have often departed from one another's decisions. Moreover, the courts are unable to remedy deficiencies in situations for which the law contains no provision. Much has been said about 'judge-made law'; the fact remains, however, that the judgments of the courts are no more than what they consider to be the law already in operation.

The authority of court decisions varies; among the South African Bantu no court is compelled to take cognizance of or abide by its own decisions or the decisions of any other court (Schapera 1938a: 40), although considerable weight is attached to such decisions.

Law and sanctions

The various coercive factors we have mentioned as contributing to the observance of law may be termed sanctions. Nevertheless, legal sanctions must be distinguished; it is these that we shall now discuss.

Sanctions of the law may be divided into two classes: approbatory and disapprobatory. The former has the effect of confirming or upholding an act such as the nomination of one's successor to the position at the head of a household.[2] The latter may occur as a refusal to recognize an act as valid (such as the converse of the example given above), as punishment, or as an order for restitution in favour of another or others.

Legal sanctions may normally be enforced only by the executive organs acting on the orders of a competent court. Among some South African Bantu, however, certain extra-judicial sanctions are, or at least were, lawful. Sorcerers, traitors, murderers, and persons committing incest or bestiality used to be killed without being brought before a court (Krige 1936a: 223, 224; Schapera 1937c: 211, 212; page 295 below); for personal injury self-help was often resorted to without interference, property being seized and the adversary or his group being attacked and even killed by members of the injured person's group (Myburgh 1969: 148, 149).

Law, rights, and duties

An important legal concept is that of rights. A right is distinct from a competency, which is derived from the law, and a power, which may be derived from the law or from a right (Myburgh 1969: 145).

Among the South African Bantu rights are vested in agnatic groups (Myburgh 1969: 146). A right produces a legal relationship between those in whom it vests and all others, since the latter are in duty bound to respect it.

Four categories of rights are observable in South African Bantu legal systems: real rights (over things), rights of guardianship or authority (over persons), obligatory rights (to performance), and rights of personality (protecting human integrity). An obligatory right is the concomitant of an obligation, to wit, the relationship between creditors and debtors (Myburgh 1969: 145).

Rights of the first-named three classes are collectively known as patrimonial rights because they are constituents of the aggregates of rights and duties known as estates; and since the South African Bantu share their duties as well as their rights within agnatic groups, the only estates known to their legal systems are those of such groups.

From the above it follows that any patrimonial liability incurred for an unlawful act, whether criminal or delictual, is shared by all the members of the guilty person's group (Myburgh 1969: 146).

Public and private law

There are distinct analogies between public and private law among the South African Bantu (Marwick 1940: 259, 268; Myburgh 1959: 41, 42); this clearly emerges from their figurative speech (Schapera 1937b: 178), such as calling a chief the father of his people or the owner of their territory.

Nevertheless, a ruler is not the father of his people since he is usually not even related to most of them, and their territory is not subject to ownership since no civil action can be brought in connection with it. Nor can one describe paternal authority as legislative or judicial or executive.

It is clear, therefore, that one must distinguish between public and private law, however difficult it may on occasion be to recognize the phenomena belonging to, and find their proper place in, each of the two divisions.

Public Law

Public law is closely connected with political organization although it includes more than what is usually meant by the latter term.

Constitutional law

Constitutional law is concerned with the structure of government. It defines the homeland, the composition and powers of the organs performing legislative, executive, and judicial functions, and the position of those governed. Among the South African Bantu the functions of rule are not performed by different organs (Dugmore 1858: 34; Post 1887 I: 215) and the judicature is not separated from the executive, even at the highest levels (Language 1943a: 124; Myburgh 1965: 9). The territorial borders are defined by natural features such as rivers and eminences (Schapera 1937b: 191) and power over public land is derived from the constitution, not from ownership (cf. Kerr 1953: 16–20; Hammond-Tooke 1962: 145, 146).

The nucleus of the typical South African Bantu constitution is the ruling family (Schapera 1937b: 173), whose influence is entrenched by rules ensuring authority for its members. Its representative, usually a chief or king, but among the Lobedu regularly and among other Sotho occasionally a chieftainess (Post 1887 I: 133; Schapera 1937b: 175), is the legislative, executive, and judicial head; in a word, the constitutional head and ruler (Schapera 1937b: 176; Schapera 1938a: 62). He (we shall use masculine forms only) can demand respect, must be obeyed in the exercise of his functions, can conscript regiments for public labour, has sole power to order national ceremonies, lead the army in combat, and can alone banish, impose the death penalty, and convene national assemblies (Schapera 1937b: 176, 177; Schapera 1938a: 62, 63). His position is hereditary in accordance with well-established rules (Post 1887 I: 142, 143; Schapera 1937b: 174; Schapera 1938a: 53–6), is often coupled with a distinctive name or special forms of address (Post 1887 I: 170; Krige 1936a: 233; Schapera 1937b: 176, 177; Schapera 1938a: 62, 63), is marked by insignia (Post 1887 I: 128; Krige 1936a: 243; Schapera 1937b: 177; Schapera 1938a: 60), and may be coupled with an exclusive salute (Schapera 1937b: 177). It is doubtful whether he could be deposed (Post 1887 I: 5, 6, 250, 251; Schapera 1938a: 85; Marwick 1940: 259); as a rule no judicial proceedings can be instituted against him (Post 1887 II: 83; cf. Bantu Administration Act, 1927, sect. 4; Schapera 1937b: 184; Kerr 1953: 12); among the Swazi and certain Tswana, for whom prosecution of the ruler is reported, members of the ruling family will be among those to whom he is mainly answerable (Schapera 1937b: 184; Schapera 1938a: 84; Marwick 1940: 260, 263, 264–6). In the final analysis, however, the effectiveness of the constitution depends on the people's loyalty to the dynasty, for their lack of faith in a regime may, when constitutional means fail, result in large-scale defection or civil war or assassination (Post 1887 I: 153; Schapera 1937b: 184; Schapera 1938a: 85; Marwick 1940: 259). Provision has accordingly been made for safeguards against incompetence, aloofness, and despotism.

The ruler must be old enough and adequately trained. This is often ensured, at least partly, by the requirement that the successor apparent pass through the initiation school before assuming office (Schapera 1937b: 176; Schapera 1938a: 61). Should he not yet be ready to succeed when his predecessor's rule ends, a member of the ruling family must act as regent and head of such family (Post 1887 I: 146, 147; Schapera 1937b: 175, 176;

Schapera 1938a: 61, 62). If the successor qualifies before the ruler's position becomes vacant he may be required to perform regular public tasks and to act when the incumbent is unable to discharge his duties. For misconduct, especially attempts to hasten his succession, he may be disinherited with the concurrence of the tribe (Schapera 1938a: 57, 58); and an unsatisfactory regent may be replaced (Schapera 1937b: 176; Schapera 1938a: 61). A new ruler, whether permanent or acting, must be presented to the people and admonished in their presence (Schapera 1938a: 60, 61) at a formal installation. A ruler in office may on certain occasions be publicly criticized with impunity (Post 1887 I: 116; Krige 1936a: 260; Schapera 1937b: 183; Hammond-Tooke 1962: 204). He is regularly assisted and advised by a council on which different sections of the people are represented by their leaders (Post 1887 I: 196, 228; Schapera 1937b: 182), while among the Sotho serious situations, such as discord within the ruling family or among the people, are dealt with by an assembly of all the available men, who are commanded by the chief to attend and are usually armed to forestall disorder (Post 1887 I: 79–81; Schapera 1937b: 183; Schapera 1938a: 82).

Within the realm all persons are subject to and protected by the constituted authorities, but they are not equally affected. Strangers need not render tribute but are precluded from settling without the ruler's or his representative's permission and from acquiring land. They may avail themselves of the law, but if they infringe it they are treated with less clemency than the people of the homeland (Schapera 1937b: 192; Schapera 1938a: 52, 118). Belonging to the latter implies allegiance to the ruler and fitness to be accommodated with residential, agricultural, and pastoral land as well as relief in emergency. It is brought about by birth, conquest, or voluntary submission, and entails payment of levies (Schapera 1937b: 187; Schapera 1938a: 118–21, 123) in service and in goods or value (Schapera 1938a: 63, 64). Conquered and immigrant groups might for generations suffer disabilities such as servility and ineligibility for high office (Post 1887 I: 106; Schapera 1937b: 188; Schapera 1938a: 31, 32, 119–21). Subjects must live in the division to which they belong and obtain the ruler's permission to go abroad; the ruler could restrict their movement or banish them and have their property confiscated or distributed among their kin. Permission to emigrate might be conditional on payment of debts, and authorized return after banishment or flight need not be followed by restoration of property confiscated or distributed (Schapera 1938a: 121–4).

Military service was compulsory for every subject (Post 1887 I: 279; Schapera 1937b: 187). The regiments were territorially organized among the Mpondo (Hunter 1936: 400), based on clan membership among other Cape Nguni and on age elsewhere (Schapera 1937b: 194). These were used for combat, for the tasks performed by the police in modern states, and for public works (Bryant 1929: 78; Schapera 1937a: 195; Schapera 1938a: 286). The surviving regimental systems have, of course, lost their martial functions. Where the regiments are age-groups and circumcision is practised, recruitment coincides with the periodic initiation schools. Among the Sotho and Ndebele the leader of each group of initiates and of the corresponding regiment is a member of the ruling family (Post 1887 I: 165, 290; Fourie 1921: 126, 136; Schapera 1937b: 195).

Levies are of various kinds, the sources from which revenue is derived still largely belonging to the traditional order, although confiscated property and spoils of war were last added to treasuries in pre-European times. Unclaimed stray cattle, heirless property, administrative dues (such as death dues and dues from immigrants and initiates), and whatever is furnished in terms of a court order (except so much as accrues to a litigant in a civil suit) become part of the public resources. Tribute is the main source of public revenue and must be rendered to the ruler or to the heads of the respective jural communities, who may be allowed to keep part of what they receive to defray local expenditure. It includes parts from the carcases of game such as choice cuts, tusks, skins, and feathers, as well as agricultural produce, livestock, meat from slaughtered domestic animals, labour for public works and, nowadays, cash from subjects working abroad (Post 1887 I: 118, 264, 265, 266, 275; Post 1887 II: 33; Hunter 1936: 385; Schapera 1937b: 177; Schapera 1938a: 63–6, 118–19, 221–3). Like public land, these resources are not controlled by virtue of ownership but of the constitution. Similarly, arrangements (such as those pertaining to the *kgamelo* cattle of the Tswana) by which tribesmen's property is merged with public resources (Schapera 1938a: 67, 248–50) are not contractual but constitutional, and control of the whole is not private but official.

The people may live in more or less small homesteads or, among the Sotho, in what may be called villages and towns. The realm is subdivided into a hierarchy of smaller jural communities, each usually headed by a person immediately answerable to the head of the smallest community of which it forms part and governed in council like the realm (Maclean 1858b: 145, 146; Schapera 1937b: 174; Schapera 1938a: 53; cf. Mönnig 1967: 280–3, 310–12). The position of a head is normally hereditary and he is often a member of the ruling family (Schapera 1937b: 185).

The realm may include a number of chiefdoms (Post 1887 I: 208; Hunter 1936: 378; Krige 1936a: 218; Schapera 1937b: 192–4; Marwick 1940: 267; Myburgh 1944: 157; Ashton 1952: 186) termed, in Zulu, *izifunda* (singular: *isifunda*), but in the Tswana and Cape Nguni systems the chiefdoms subject to the senior ruling family are so only in ritual matters such as the feast of the first fruits, by which economic activity is controlled, and (among Tswana) initiation, which is bound up with the formation of regiments (Schapera 1937b: 192; Schapera 1938a: 4; Hammond-Tooke 1965a: 156).

A chiefdom may be divided into districts (Maclean 1858b: 146; Krige 1936a: 218; Language 1943a: 25) termed, in Zulu, *izigodi* (singular: *isigodi*) and, where there are towns or villages, into wards or wards and sections (Post 1887 I: 195, 196: Schapera 1938a: 19–28) or other units of common membership (Post 1887 I: 196; Mönnig 1967: 224, 245). Among most Nguni the headman in charge of a district is immediately subordinate to the chief (Post 1887 I: 196, 197; Marx 1903: 355; Hunter 1936: 378; Krige 1936a: 218; Hammond-Tooke 1962: 209); among the Tswana a headman of a ward in the capital may be subject to a senior headman of another ward, who is usually the head of a section and directly responsible to the chief's establishment. In a village a junior headman falls under the village headman. The latter may be responsible to the chief directly or intermediately through the head of a district, who is often the traditional head of an immigrant or subjugated group to whom the district has been allotted for occupation. The district head's immediate superior is either the chief's resident representative in the district or his accredited representative at the capital (Schapera 1938a: 94–103, 119, 120). The Pedi system operates through intermediaries between the heads of the constituent jural communities and the chief (Post 1887 I: 123; Mönnig 1967: 282, 283).

The head of a jural community and his counsellors are not only an administrative body but also a court of law, and the hierarchical scheme outlined applies whenever matters are referred upwards on the initiative of the head or on appeal emanating from those dissatisfied with a judicial verdict (Fourie 1921: 153; Schapera 1937b: 213, 214; Schapera 1938a: 290–2). The criminal jurisdiction of the lower courts never included matters involving obedience to the ruler or the death penalty, banishment, or confiscation (Schapera 1937b: 176, 177; Schapera 1938a: 63, 181; Van Niekerk 1966: 38); while administrative matters such as immigration, emigration (Schapera 1937b: 192; Schapera 1938a: 118–23), national ceremonies, the formation of regiments (Schapera 1937b: 177; Schapera 1938a: 63, 69, 106–8), and fresh appointments to positions tending to become hereditary (for example, those of the heads of jural communities), as well as the suspension or removal of men holding such positions, were reserved for the ruler-in-council (Schapera 1938a: 97), who must also be informed of deaths (Brownlee 1858: 128; Breutz 1941: 82) and visits from abroad (Schapera 1937b: 178; Schapera 1938a: 69).

The legislature was headed by the ruler and comprised either the people's assembly, as was the case among the Tswana (Schapera 1938a: 41, 70; Language 1943a: 64), or the general council, which consisted of the ruler's private advisers, certain of his less immediate kin, heads of jural communities, and influential commoners of ability (Dugmore 1858: 34; Kropf 1889: 168; Fourie 1921: 147–8; Schapera 1937b: 183, 184, 198; Hammond-Tooke 1969b: 248ff). No proposed measure could become law unless it was adopted by the recognized body as a whole. Promulgation of laws not passed at a general assembly was effected in different ways. Among the Swazi local chiefs were required to inform their followers (Marwick 1940: 280), while laws for the Zulu empire were proclaimed at an army parade during the ceremony of the first fruits (Krige 1936a: 259).

Contact with the West has brought considerable constitutional modification. The chiefs have acquired greater security, but they have lost their legislative and military power as well as much of their judicial authority

(Schapera 1938a: 41, 42, 49, 71, 72, 86–8), especially in criminal matters.

In the Republic of South Africa they cannot order banishment,[3] the death penalty, severe corporal punishment, or even (unless they hold sway in the districts of the northern Cape Province, known as British Bechuanaland) heavy patrimonial sacrifice.[4] As far as offences known to Bantu legal systems (page 295 below) are concerned, their power to punish is limited to violation of allegiance, disobedience to orders, breach of official discipline, contempt of court, breach of taboo, common assault, abuse of seniors, and neglect of the sick.[5] But their immunity from litigation has been largely preserved[6] and they can now be represented in urban areas beyond their territories.[7] The original system of rule-in-council has been given statutory recognition in a modified form, whilst provision has been made for participation of the rulers and their councils in government on a larger scale[8] and self-government has already been granted the peoples of the Transkei. The old order figures prominently in the constitution of this area. Transkeian chiefs constitute a parliamentary majority, their original functions amongst their people remain intact until altered by or on the recommendation of the Transkeian legislature or executive, and there is provision for the establishment of a High Court which will replace the superior courts of South Africa and be required to apply recognized Bantu law in civil suits concerned with it.[9]

The former High Commission territories have been granted constitutions comparable to those of modern states but retaining features of the indigenous systems. Lesotho and Swaziland are independent monarchies. The constitutions have retained the traditional kings as heads of state, regency being determined by procedures compatible with the old order.[10] Two-thirds of the Lesotho senate are chiefs, the remaining third being the king's nominees,[11] while in Swaziland a quarter of the assembly (if the membership of the attorney-general is not taken into account) and half of the senate are members appointed by the king.[12] The superior courts of Lesotho have jurisdiction under any law and therefore also under Sotho law;[13] powers over land must be exercised in accordance with Bantu law in both Lesotho and Swaziland;[14] and Swazi law is to remain operative in regard to the appointment, suspension, and dismissal of chiefs and to the Swazi National Council, the royal ceremony of the first fruits, and the regimental system.[15] Botswana is a republic. The House of Chiefs takes the place of a senate.[16]

Administrative law

Administrative law governs the exercise of executive powers, the connected responsibility and procedures, and the relations between the functionaries and the people.

As chief executive the ruler is ultimately concerned with all administrative matters. These include immigration and emigration, allocation of land, death notices, revenue, petititions, welfare services such as ceremonies and poor relief, mediation, initiation schools, the army, public works, and staffing

(Schapera 1937b: 177–9; Schapera 1938a: 68–71; Breutz 1941: 82). Among the Nguni he could apparently take action in former times against persons whom he and his council had administratively found to be public enemies involved in violation of allegiance, sorcery, or incest and other sexual offences (Krige 1936a: 224; Schapera 1937c: 211, 212).

The head of each constituent jural community must function as the ruler's representative among the people of his area and as their representative at the capital, watching over the interests of both the government and the governed and refraining from action prejudicial to either (Schapera 1937b: 185; Schapera 1938a: 91, 92; Language 1943a: 21).

The exercise of administrative functions must accord with correct procedure, which is closely bound up with the relative powers of the different functionaries. The ruler must be approached through the administrative chancellor (Post 1887 I: 123; Marx 1903: 355; Schapera 1937b: 182) at the capital by heads of jural communities, and should go through the proper channels when issuing instructions. For example, he could communicate directly with the headman of a ward in the capital, passing by the headman of the section within which the ward fell, but would have to instruct a junior headman in an outlying village through the village headman (Schapera 1938a: 102), the reason being, of course, that the permissibility of short cuts depends on whether all concerned live within easy reach of one another. Subordinate heads should refer matters upwards through their immediate superiors since the latter are responsible for all the affairs within the subdivisions constituting their areas (Schapera 1938a: 89). Seniors must in turn observe the correct procedure towards their subordinates unless circumstances analogous to those sketched above warrant simpler methods.

Executive functions involve the exercise of discretion, which means consideration of all the circumstances. This may be illustrated by reference to emigration and immigration among the Tswana. Permission to leave for good could be granted or refused by the ruler-in-council on considerations such as payment of debts, removal of valuables, and defection on a large scale or support of a hostile people (Schapera 1938a: 121, 122). Permission to settle should depend on whether there is room and applicants are acceptable, and the head of the jural community to which those admitted are referred and his counsellors must, in allocating residential and agricultural land to the newcomers, have regard to their and other people's present and probable future needs, the nature of the terrain (rocky, wooded, steep, eroded, etc.), and the availability of water, timber, clay, and pasture in areas not yet occupied (Schapera 1938a: 118, 119). The allocation may be brought before the chief-in-council by way of petition at any of the regular sessions (Schapera 1938a: 68, 93). The result will largely turn on the question whether the subordinate authority has acted with proper discretion—that is, reasonably in the circumstances.

Mediation is an important administrative function. In the event of differences between a chief and his tribe the chief of a neighbouring tribe may be invited to the capital by either side for conciliatory action, which means that he becomes an official mediator (Schapera 1937b: 192; Schapera 1938a: 85). In a sub-district a headman who has administrative but no judicial powers is helped by his elders to settle disputes; if the disputants belong to different sub-districts the two headmen try to reconcile them at the headman's in the sub-district of those against whom the allegations are made (Language 1943a: 9, 13, 14). A member of a ward court may be entrusted with the duty of introducing civil matters to the court; his opinion often has the effect of a settlement without trial (Van Niekerk 1966: 39). It has even been reported that courts themselves attempt to bring about settlement rather than subject parties to trial (Breutz 1941: 50).

Discipline is enforced in various ways. A counsellor to a divisional head absenting himself from duty or otherwise disobeying the head's orders may be prosecuted (Schapera 1937c: 211; Schapera 1938a: 273); if the head is himself unsatisfactory, his council may reprimand him or report him to the ruler, who may have him prosecuted or suspend or even dismiss him (Schapera 1937b: 186; Schapera 1938a: 93, 94, 98; Language 1943a: 18). A subordinate who by-passed his senior could obviously be made to face similar action at the instance of the former or of the ruler himself. The decisions of subordinate authorities are presumably subject to review. The ruler may dispense with the services of his administrative chancellor or any member of his private council for disloyalty, neglect of duty, or criminal conduct by ceasing to consult him, and dismiss a member of the general council for repeated absence from meetings or other neglect of duty (Language 1943a: 39, 51–3). If the ruler acted despotically or arbitrarily he could be called to account by his council; if he persisted, he would risk defection or assassination; if he and his council became corrupt, the people would be left to their own resources and the peace would be gravely threatened (page 288 above). Dismissal and suspension are usually followed by the appointment of the person next in order of succession (Schapera 1938a: 94, 97); suspension among the Tswana usually takes the form of orders from the ruler to move to a stated place in the capital (Schapera 1938a: 95).

What are often termed military courts or courts martial were not courts in the true sense but bodies empowered to take disciplinary action (Fourie 1921: 152) against the members of men's and women's regiments, including punishment by thrashing or fining (Schapera 1937c: 213; Schapera 1938a: 114, 115, 117, 258). The initiation schools are of the same order; the hardships inflicted on the intiates by the supervisors (Post 1887 I: 291; Schapera 1938a: 106, 116) were part of the lawful administrative measures associated with their training. Among the Zulu forcible disciplinary action could be taken by the age-group of a seduced girl, who was scolded, derided, and beaten. The girls could thrash the seducer; at his kraal they could demand or seize an animal for ritual slaughter (Krige 1936a: 157, 158). His conduct was seen as encroachment on the affairs of the group for which they could take summary action.

We shall not enter into detail about the collection, custody, and control of the revenue. Suffice it to mention that much of this was left to the authorities in charge of the various jural communities and that unauthorized acts on their part could lead to the disciplinary action already discussed (Schapera 1937b: 185; Schapera 1938a: 63, 91, 95, 96). Attention should, however, be directed to those whose property was merged with public resources (Schapera 1938a: 67, 248–50): they all became officials under their headman, and all the property with which each was entrusted could be withdrawn by the ruler for dereliction of duty, to the utter ruin of the unfortunate one and his family.

The state of affairs described above has undergone various changes. In the Republic of South Africa the allocation of land is now largely governed by proclamation,[17] as are courts in which prosecutions may be brought;[18] recognized officials can no longer be dismissed by traditional authorities;[19] some of the measures that could formerly be lawfully adopted for the purposes of regimental and similar groups would today be illicit. In Botswana merging of tribesmen's property with public resources was abolished by Kgama for the Ngwato and modified for the Tawana by the Administration (Schapera 1938a: 249, 250); most of the control under which traditional authorities' powers were brought from time to time (page 291 above) has remained under the new Republic.[20] Lesotho and Swaziland have retained some original features. The constitution of Lesotho not only preserves the power of the king and the chiefs to allocate land but makes provision on traditional lines for appeals against decisions on land allocation.[21] In Swaziland the appointment, dismissal, and suspension of chiefs is still governed by Swazi law.[22]

Criminal law

A crime or offence is an infringement of a precept or prohibition, intentional or negligent, for which the law provides a penalty. It is therefore an unlawful act or omission to which the law attaches a disapprobatory sanction in the form of punishment. Since crime conflicts with the interests of the public it falls within the realm of public law and action is taken against it at the public instance.

Public and private interests could, of course, be violated simultaneously. Among the South African Bantu the latter cannot be separately served by settlement, such action being construed against the wronged party as criminal participation (Myburgh 1944: 270); the infringement must be adjudicated in accordance with private as well as public law in a single set of proceedings (Schapera 1937c: 199; Van Niekerk 1966: 38).

The South African Bantu recognize a variety of crimes.[28] They may be classified as those branding the perpetrators as public enemies and depriving them of the protection of the law (treasonable violation of allegiance, incest, bestiality, murder, sorcery) and the rest; alternatively, as those against authority (violation of allegiance, flouting of authority, contravention of decrees, non-observance of customary duties such as rendering tribute and reporting deaths, disobedience to orders, breach of official discipline, contempt of court), those against persons (murder, culpable homicide, assault, rape, abortion, verbal abuse of seniors, neglect of the sick by failing to call a doctor to a patient who has died), that against property (theft), those against public decency (incest, sodomy, bestiality, self-exposure and the like), and those against public beliefs (sorcery, breach of taboo). The list does not, however, apply as a whole to all groups. Theft is not a crime among the Cape Nguni but a wrong of private law (Brownlee 1858: 115, 116). The same applies to assault among the North Sotho and South Sotho (Schapera 1937c: 210). Failing to report deaths, failing to call a doctor, self-exposure, and offences similar to the last-mentioned are reported for certain Cape Nguni only (Post 1887 II: 97; Brownlee 1858: 128, 129). As we have seen, participation in crime is punishable; but nowhere has evidence been found of criminal consequences attaching to attempt.

It seems, on the whole, that accidental violation is excused and that intent is viewed more seriously than negligence (Krige 1936a: 228; Schapera 1937c: 209, 210; Schapera 1938a: 261; Ashton 1952: 255; cf. Post 1887 II: 55, 56). Intent is, of course, essential to treason, contempt of court, murder, assault, rape, abortion, verbal abuse of seniors, incest, sodomy, bestiality, self-exposure, and sorcery. There are indications that infancy and lunacy exclude responsibility (Myburgh 1944: 15; Ashton 1952: 244); and normally criminal conduct could be justified on grounds of severe provocation, self-defence or the defence of others (Schapera 1938a: 261) or their property or the property of one's own group, obstruction in the performance of a public duty, or protection of the public safety. A man would therefore not be guilty of murder or culpable homicide if he killed another who resisted him while helping to carry out an order for confiscation (Warner 1858: 76) or whom he could consider a public enemy, such as one doing a person to death in his presence or engaged in acts recognized as sorcery, especially if such acts were committed in his home at night and could therefore be seen as a threat to his family and their belongings. The same would apply if he acted to prevent theft of other people's cattle or of the family herd, or under the severe provocation of catching the deceased in adultery with his wife (Schapera 1937c: 210; Schapera 1938a: 261); and persons believed to be monsters, such as an infant born deformed (Post 1887 I: 285; Schapera 1937c: 210) or feet first, or cutting the upper teeth first (Post 1887 I: 287; Schapera 1937c: 210; Schapera 1938a: 261), and either or both of twins (Post 1887 I: 282, 283; Schapera 1937c: 210; Schapera 1938a: 261) were considered dangerous and could be put to death with impunity. Nor would a man be guilty of assault if he attacked another committing rape or theft or mortally insulting him (Myburgh 1969: 155) or someone approaching a grave he was ordered to keep free from intruders (Brownlee 1858: 125).

Punishment took the form of death, banishment, confiscation of some or all of the guilty person's family property, bodily correction, or a fine in livestock. Corporal punishment is commonest among the Sotho (Schapera 1937c: 200), but is also reported for the Cape Nguni (Post 1887 II: 85). Imprisonment was unknown (Post 1887 II: 51; Soga 1932: 44). The order for punishment rested with the discretion of the court, but the death penalty, banishment, and confiscation were usually confined to treason, murder, sorcery, and incest.[24]

A guilty person's group share his patrimonial liability on grounds already mentioned (page 287 above; Post 1887 I: 46; Post 1887 II: 35; Marx 1903: 348), but obviously they cannot share corporal punishment with him (Schapera 1938a: 50). The fact that in former times the family of a person condemned for sorcery or violation of allegiance were massacred (Dugmore 1858: 22; Post 1887 I: 48; Krige 1936b: 224, 227) must be attributed to outlawry, the whole group being deemed participants and therefore public enemies.

Sorcery and the beliefs associated with it have lost recognition everywhere, as has justification on grounds other than those accepted in Western systems.

The law of procedure

The procedure followed in the traditional courts of the South African Bantu is simple and free from technicality. We are not aware of a single verdict arrived at by an indigenous court on procedural grounds, the main function of the judiciary being to decide all matters on the merits.

Each court comprises the head of the jural community over which it has jurisdiction and his counsellors, the former usually acting as president unless he is involved (pages 288, 294 above) or cannot be present, in which case his place is taken by a senior counsellor (see Plates 13a and 13b); (Schapera 1938a: 281). Among the Tswana and Pedi no verdict of the ruler's court is final without his concurrence, although his deputy may preside (Schapera 1938a: 282, 283; Harries 1929: 99; Van Niekerk 1966: 39). The Zulu king never presided and was only required to assent when important persons were involved (Krige 1936a: 232).

All proceedings are conducted orally and in public (Post 1887 I: 259), usually out of doors (Schapera 1938a: 292), and are open to the participation of all men (Krige 1936a: 229) by way of questioning and comment, females being excluded (Schapera 1937c: 215; Schapera 1938a: 287, 288) except as complainants, witnesses (Hunter 1936: 415), and, of course, accused. Those primarily involved in a trial are accompanied by their supporters (Post 1887 I: 256; Schapera 1937c: 214); these invariably include their kin (Harries 1929: 100; Van Niekerk 1966: 39) since the latter will share any liability resulting from the outcome, but there is no professional representation.[25] Witnesses (Post 1887 II: 133) are not sworn (Fourie 1921: 154; Harries 1929: 100; Krige 1936a: 231; Schapera 1937c: 216; Schapera 1938a: 289; Marwick 1940: 286), and there is no closing of a case other than termination of the hearing by the president of the court when he considers the evidence and comments disposed of (Krige 1936a: 231). There are various officers of the court. One of these is often an experienced man who regularly arranges for trials and introduces each matter in turn (Harries 1929: 98; Schapera 1937c: 212; Schapera 1938a: 283; Language 1943a: 125; Van Niekerk 1966: 39). Messengers (Harries 1929: 100; Language 1943a: 125) are usually selected from men attending the sessions (Schapera 1937c: 213; Schapera 1938a: 286).

In civil matters litigants are agnatic groups led by their respective heads or by substitutes for these. There may be only one litigant group; this is the case in a declaratory action (pages 301, 305 below). Usually, however, there are two. Where the parties belong to different constituent jural communities the court of first instance is that of the defendants' constituent jural community (Schapera 1937c: 214; Schapera 1938a: 284, 285; Van Niekerk 1966: 38) and the plaintiffs must give notice at this court, where they are told the day of trial and warned to be present with their witnesses. The messengers then inform and warn the defendants in similar terms (Marx 1903: 357; Schapera 1938a: 284). Both parties must be present; there is no provision for judgment by default. Should either party or any material witness fail to appear on the appointed day, the case is postponed and the messengers warn the defaulter or defaulters to appear on the new date. Absence then entails the risk of prosecution for contempt of court (Harries 1929: 99; Schapera 1937c: 215; Schapera 1938a: 288; Language 1943a: 135; van Niekerk 1966: 39). The court may dispose of the civil matter or refer it to a higher court; and either side may appeal (Post 1887 II: 134; Schapera 1937c: 213–16; Schapera 1938a: 298). The decision is pronounced by the president and should represent the preponderance of the members' findings, but there is no count and therefore no division (Harries 1929: 99, 100; Krige 1936a: 229–31; Schapera 1937c: 215).

Criminal proceedings are instituted by the officer who introduces matters for trial (Schapera 1938a: 286; Language 1943a: 141); his functions are sometimes performed by the presiding officer himself (Dugmore 1858: 39; Language 1943a: 141). The court of first instance is, it seems, that of the accused's constituent jural community if the matter lies within its jurisdiction. The messengers or the officer referred to above must warn the accused, the complainant, if any, and the witnesses, to appear (Schapera 1937c: 213; Schapera 1938a: 286, 288). If the complainant belongs to a constituent jural community other than that of the accused, he or she should be accompanied by the head of his or her constituent jural community or his representative (cf. Schapera 1938a: 285, 286; Marwick 1940: 286). The accused must be present, and may be required to plead (Harries 1929: 91; *contra* Mönnig 1967: 318). If he or she cannot be found, a military detachment may be ordered to carry out a search (Schapera 1938a: 286). Should the matter lie beyond the jurisdiction of the court of the accused's constituent jural community, it must be referred to the higher court having jurisdiction after an enquiry conducted by the first-named court or, if there is a complainant, by the court of his or her constituent jural community. A lower court may refer a criminal matter to a higher court, and an accused may appeal against his or her conviction in a lower court (Schapera 1937c: 213; Schapera 1938a: 281, 282, 285).

Civil and criminal appeals and referred matters must be placed before the court of immediately higher jurisdiction in accordance with the hierarchy outlined above (Schapera 1937c: 213; Language 1943a: 126). This must be done by the president of the lower court or his representative, who must be present at the hearing to render an account of the earlier proceedings (Schapera 1937c: 216; Schapera 1938a: 292; Language 1943a: 141; Mönnig 1967: 318). Lower courts of unequal jurisdiction may simplify the appeal procedure by sitting together (Schapera 1938a: 101; Van Niekerk 1966: 40).

The order of court will, in matters that are both criminal and civil, clearly distinguish or indicate the connection between the punishment and the award. It will, for instance, specify which of the livestock to be delivered will be the fine (Ashton 1952: 273), or allow the victim of an assault to inflict on his assailant an injury similar to the one he has suffered (Schapera 1937c: 200, 210); in the old days it would often order a murderer to be put to death in the same manner as the deceased (Fourie 1921: 155; Schapera 1938a: 261). In each of the two cases last mentioned the order comprises punishment as well as an award of satisfaction to the complainants.

Costs must be paid by successful litigants among some Cape Nguni (Brownlee 1858: 127), but are usually met from fines and from awards against unsuccessful litigants, part of which is used to pay messengers (Post 1887 II: 33–5; Schapera 1937c: 217) and feed members of the court, at least some of the animals ordered to be delivered being slaughtered for meat, while their skins may be used to obtain beer (Harries 1929: 100; Schapera 1938a: 281, 294; Marwick 1940: 285).

Execution is stayed where notice of appeal has been given; final orders are enforced in different ways. Compliance with an order for delivery of livestock must follow with the least possible delay. The animals must be left with the head of the judgment debtors' constituent jural community, who must send for any party to whom an award may have been made to take delivery. If the order was made by a higher court, the head takes them to the seat of that court for similar disposal (Schapera 1938a: 294). In the event of undue delay in delivering stock after a final order, messengers of the court may be instructed to attach the number of animals specified, the defaulter being liable to prosecution for contempt of court (Schapera 1937c: 217; Schapera 1938a: 294), while the messengers must be remunerated by either the debtors (Myburgh 1944: 236) or the creditors (Marwick 1940: 287). Orders for confiscation were executed at once, as was the death sentence and still is a final order for corporal punishment (Post 1887 I: 257; Post 1887 II: 138; Schapera 1937c: 217; Schapera 1938a: 49; Language 1943a: 145), and in public. Death was brought about by stabbing, clubbing, impalement, decapitation, hanging, strangulation, stoning, burning, or exposure to ants or hot stones

(Post 1887 II: 40, 42–5, 66–8; Krige 1936a: 226, 227); confiscation was usually entrusted to a regimental detachment (Warner 1858: 76). Corporal punishment may take the form of talion, as we have seen (page 299 above), or of a thrashing (Schapera 1937c: 217; Schapera 1938a: 49), or, where the offence is abortion or infanticide, of a covering of highly irritant substances (Schapera 1938a: 261–3); and formerly a thief's hands were cut off or burnt away (Schapera 1937c: 207; Schapera 1938a: 271).

Both intercession and asylum are known to the South African Bantu. Among the Tswana lashing must be stopped if an onlooker intercedes for the sufferer, and a person under sentence for any crime except homicide finds asylum and escapes punishment if he manages to flee to the ruler's mother or, if the sentence is whipping, to her or to the ruler's wife (Schapera 1938a: 294, 295), while the Nguni variously recognize the ruler's or his mother's quarters (Hunter 1936: 419; Marwick 1940: 247), a ruler's grave (Post 1887 II: 38; Krige 1936a: 227), or the person or home of the chief counsellor (Kropf 1889: 173) as havens of safety from punishment.

Considerable change has been brought about in procedural matters, which are now largely governed by legislation.[26] In the Republic of South Africa the original position has, however, been left more or less undisturbed for chiefs' and headmen's criminal courts,[27] and although it is preserved for their civil courts, there is provision for written records and judgment by default beyond the borders of the former British Bechuanaland.[28]

The law of evidence

Most South African Bantu have no rules relating to the burden or the quantum of proof in either civil or criminal cases, although the Cape Nguni (Dugmore 1858: 39; Warner 1858: 60; Post 1887 II: 135) and the Pedi (Harries 1929: 101) seem to place on an accused person the burden of proving his innocence. There is no theory of relevance and admissibility; hearsay (Harries 1929: 101; Krige 1936a: 231; Marwick 1940: 286), confessions under torture (Warner 1858: 93; Brownlee 1858: 126; Post 1887 II: 66, 107), the results of divination and ordeals (Post 1887 II: 146, 159; Krige 1936a: 225–7; Schapera 1937c: 216), evidence of character (Schapera 1937c: 216), the appearance of a child in questions of paternity (Schapera 1938a: 265; Seymour 1970: 332), and unsworn statements (Harries 1929: 100; Krige 1936a: 231; Schapera 1937c: 216; Schapera 1938a: 289) were all admitted, although the weight attached to any particular detail depended on its context and the aggregate was measured by the impression it left after thorough testing by various methods such as the examination of witnesses.

Strong credence is often given to circumstantial evidence. A garment or other article produced by plaintiffs, particularly where redress is sought for seduction or adultery (Schapera 1937c: 215, 216; Schapera 1938a: 288; Seymour 1970: 321, 346), often proves decisive, while the effect of the 'spoor law' is to render the inmates of a kraal or village to which the tracks of stolen cattle are traced liable for restitution unless they can show that they have followed these past their home (Brownlee 1858: 122; Post 1887 I: 77; Krige 1936a: 229); and unreasonable delay in taking action against an adversary is seen as an indication that his claim was not sound when it is alleged to have arisen (Seymour 1970: 61–4, 332, 333).

We shall not dwell upon the subject but merely point out that torture, divination, and ordeals are illegal, that all evidence tendered in criminal courts having jurisdiction higher than that of chiefs' and headmen's courts must conform to the requirements of typically Western systems (page 300 above), and that in civil courts having such jurisdiction the proceedings may 'not be opposed to the principles of public policy or natural justice'.[29]

Private Law

Private law has much in common with social organization. Its scope is, however, somewhat wider and overlaps economic organization as well.

An important feature of private law is its involvement with rights, which, like duties, are shared by agnatic groups, as we have seen (page 287 above). An agnatic group must be understood to include non-agnates under the authority of such a group.

It is essential to distinguish the relationships between groups from those between members of a group. The former are attributable to the rights and duties of groups; the latter, to the respective shares of members in the rights and duties of their group.

Litigation occurs between groups alone, it being understood that certain constituent groups, such as a deceased head's houses (wives with their families) are seen as separate groups (Schapera 1937b: 188). Conflicts between members of the same group are diposed of within that group (page 305 below) or by the head of a jural community acting administratively according to custom (Seymour 1970: 283) or judicially (van Warmelo 1949: 735; cf. Seymour 1970: 284) in what seems to be a declaratory action (page 298 above) brought on behalf of the group.

Western influence is evident from the increasing tendency in legislation to take cognizance of the individual rather than the group. This will become clear in the course of our discussions.

The law of persons

The law of persons defines persons and governs their status. A person is a being having rights and duties, and a person's status is his position in respect of rights, competencies, and duties as a member of a class.

We have already introduced the reader to rights and duties. Competencies are of two orders: first, competency to act, which means the capacity to conclude juristic acts (that is, acts to which the law gives effect, such as entering into a contract, marrying, adopting a child, or assuming a hereditary position); and second, competency to litigate (that is, to sue or be sued as a party in a civil suit).

In modern legal systems two broad classes of persons having dissimilar status may be distinguished, to wit, natural and fictitious (or juristic) persons. The former are human beings; the latter, aggregates of property, known as foundations, or groups of persons such as the state, universities, and public companies. Juristic persons lack human attributes and the rights, competencies, incompetencies, and duties associated with these, such as a right of personality for protection of the body, the duty to obey parents or guardians, the competency to marry, and the incompetencies of youth. A juristic person is, or has, an estate quite distinct from the estates of its managers or members, and these do not share its liability. The matter need not detain us further, since the concept of a juristic person is foreign to the South African Bantu (Myburgh 1965: 10). An agnatic group is not a juristic person because the estate of the group is that of its members and its liability is shared by them; nor is a kingdom or chiefdom or any other jural community, because it does not figure in private law: for instance, it is never involved in civil litigation;[30] and nothing can be found in the legal systems of the South African Bantu that could be mistaken for a foundation.

The South African Bantu, then, know only natural persons. All natural persons have rights of personality, to wit, rights protecting the body, the dignity, and the reputation, as well as the duty to obey those in lawful authority over them while they are young; most have other rights and duties as well. But the South African Bantu share their rights and the duties associated with these, as is apparent, for example, from the consultations preceding the slaughter of an animal (Hunter 1936: 31, 32) and from the division of its meat (Hunter 1936: 364; Krige 1936a: 56, 57; Myburgh 1944: 9), all demonstrating participation in ownership, and from the fact that during negotiations, disputes, and litigation all the available group members lend their support as listeners, witnesses, questioners, or contributors to the proceedings (page 297 above), which demonstrates participation in obligatory rights and the duties corresponding to such rights.

Legislation has affected this by providing for individual ownership, in Natal, of property acquired by an emancipated woman,[31] of a kraal,[32] of kraal property,[33] and of the mother's beast,[34] and for competency, in the case of an emancipated woman, to contract and to sue and be sued alone.[35] The effect of legislative provisions fixing the age of majority at 21 years (page 303 below) has also been to stress the individual as against the group.

A group member's share in the rights of the group (that is, in the powers derived from these) corresponds, as do such member's duties, to his or her competencies, and the last-mentioned depend on the factors by which persons are placed in different status classes, viz mental and physical maturity, sex, marriage, and rank.

An infant cannot participate in the representation of its group for purposes of juristic acts or litigation, but it shares the group's ownership by deriving its maintenance from their movable and immovable property, and its share in their obligatory rights and rights of authority and personality are exercised on its behalf by the members in charge of it. The measure in which it must itself discharge duties increases with its discernment (Myburgh 1944: 14, 15). A youngster may, for example, be allowed to testify (Myburgh 1944: 280); a girl must help her mother with household tasks, while a boy must tend the domestic animals (Schapera and Goodwin 1937: 149, 150). After puberty both sexes can marry and participate in the choice of a bride or bridegroom (Post 1887 I: 290, 384; Marx 1903: 354; Schapera 1937c: 202). Mentally incapacitated persons are in the position of infants (Myburgh 1944: 15; Seymour 1970: 283).

A change has been effected by legislation. In the Transkei a male or female[36] and in Natal a male [37] is a major from the age of 21; in Natal, however, the man remains subject to the kraal head in kraal matters.[38] The effect is liberation from the group unless, in Natal, the man chooses to remain with it. By marrying, however, a female joins her husband's group (Seymour 1970: 220).

A female cannot become the head of an agnatic group (Seymour 1970: xix) and so can never represent such group in court or in the conclusion of juristic acts or be charged with the duties connected with such representation. But a girl can exercise her share of the group's right of authority over her by offering herself in marriage to a group of her choice subject to confirmation by the head of her group (Krige 1936a: 123, 125; Krige 1937b: 112; Myburgh 1944: 22, 48). Among the Zulu she demonstrates her share in the power to transfer the right of authority over her, as well as her continuing share in the ownership of property belonging to her mother's house, by tapping each of the cattle delivered for her by her suitor's group (Krige 1936a: 130; Myburgh 1944: 53). Her share in her group's rights of personality and obligatory rights is apparent from her power to take an active part in steps to obtain redress when she or a woman of her group is the victim of a delict such as seduction or an accusation of misconduct with the father-in-law (Krige 1936a: 31; Schapera 1938a: 265; Seymour 1970: 330-2, 335-8). At the same time she has duties: she must grind, sweep, plaster, cook, and till the soil (Schapera and Goodwin 1937: 149, 150).

In terms of legislation for Natal a spinster, widow, or divorced woman may under certain circumstances be vested with the powers of a kraal head.[39]

A male can become the head of an agnatic group or of several such groups (Post 1887 I: 56; Seymour 1970: xix, 67); if he is not the head of his group, he exercises his share in their right of authority by playing a leading part in the transfer of the marital right over female members (Myburgh 1944: 64, 68, 72, 73, 89; page 306 below). He shares ownership of the family cattle, some of which he can require to be placed at his disposal for the acquisition of a wife (Krige 1937b: 114; Seymour 1970: 71, 153); he participates in the group's rights of personality, taking an active part in the seizure of animals for slaughter when such rights are violated (Myburgh 1969: 148); and when steps are taken for the enforcement of the group's obligatory rights his participation is evident from the support he lends the head (page 297 above). His duties towards the group include building, clearing new soil, herding, milking, and assisting the head when the group is faced with a claim (Schapera and Goodwin 1937: 149, 150; page 297 above).

Marriage confers a special status on both sexes. A married woman can exercise her major share in the right of authority over her children by punishing them (Schapera 1937b: 189; Schapera 1938a: 128, 175) and her minor share in the right of authority over other members of her marital group by demanding that they protect and provide for her and her children (Post 1887 I: 52, 53; Schapera 1938a: 151; Seymour 1970: 72); this she does through the head's wife or mother, who must then take up the matter with her husband or son (Myburgh 1944: 285, 286). She has an important share in the ownership of property belonging to her house and must be consulted by the head before he deals with any of it (Seymour 1970: 66, 71). She has sole control of the daily rations for her family and bears full responsibility for their adequacy and for the safekeeping of her stores (Krige 1936a: 47, 177; Schapera and Goodwin 1937: 159). Her share in the ownership of the fields allocated to her house empowers her to take summary action against depredators (Myburgh 1969: 149). She also shares in the ownership of livestock belonging to her house and can require the senior participants to prevent her husband or, if he is not the head of the group, even such head, from exceeding his share by such conduct as killing or other squandering or by farming out to the detriment of her family (Seymour 1970: 72, 136, 206). Should her husband die, her share in the ownership of the homestead and agricultural land entitles her to remain in her quarters and cultivate her fields (Krige 1937b: 117; Kerr 1953: 63). She shares in the group's rights of personality and takes an active part in obtaining satisfaction when a girl is seduced (Whitfield 1948: 116, 148; Hammond-Tooke 1962: 96, 101). But the other members of the group can demand, in terms of their share in the right of authority over her, that she make her reproductive capacity and her services available. She must have children if she can (Krige 1937b: 116; Schapera 1938a: 151; Seymour 1970: 134), rear the children in her charge, cook, maintain her quarters, and till the soil (Hoernlé 1937a: 77; Schapera and Goodwin 1937: 149, 150; Schapera 1938a: 151; Seymour 1970: 134).

The status of a male is enhanced by marriage in that he becomes the group's principal representative in the domestic affairs of his family. He is especially empowered to exercise their right of authority over his wife and children, if necessary by moderate castigation (Post 1887 I: 52, 53; Schapera 1938a: 151, 175; Seymour 1970: 134, 230); and it is his duty to clear new soil for their needs and help with their building operations (see above). An unmarried male cannot, as a rule, become the head of an agnatic group (Seymour 1970: xix) and cannot therefore qualify for the major share in the group's rights or represent the group in litigation or the conclusion of juristic acts. A senior member usually acts on behalf of a successor designate until the latter marries (Schapera 1937b: 189; van Warmelo 1949: 943, 971, 972).

In Natal the effect of marriage is, in terms of legislation, that the husband becomes a major but remains subordinate to his kraal head in kraal matters.[40] This means that he can free himself from the group by simply leaving them.

Rank affects status. A man's share in the group's right of authority empowers him to give orders to his younger brothers (Junod 1927 I: 229); the position among sisters is similar (Hunter 1936: 34). The share of an eldest son in the rights of his constituent group is demonstrated by the fact that as successor apparent to the head's position in such a group he is consulted by the head in matters involving such rights (Hunter 1936: 31; Seymour 1970: 66); and the fact that he (van Warmelo 1949: 901) and the general successor apparent and the latter's mother as the great wife (Seymour 1970: 66) are similarly consulted in matters concerning the whole group shows that they participate in the rights of that group. Adopted children, children of auxiliary wives, leviratic and other vicarious children, children of unmarried females, adulterine children, incestuous children (Whitfield 1948: 51, 52; Stafford and Franklin 1950: 69, 70; Seymour 1970: 260–5, 270, 274, 275), and persons attached to a group as dependants (Post 1887 I: 42; Schapera 1937b: 191) are of inferior rank; if there are other members, these will have a greater share in the rights of the group.

The status of the head of an agnatic group is that of maximum competency. As a mentally sound married male and the person ranking highest in the group he is fit to serve and control members of all classes, to have the largest share of the powers derived from their rights, and to represent them in litigation and the conclusion of juristic acts. He decides on the site for the home of each house (family) and allots land for cultivation and livestock to each (Schapera and Goodwin 1937: 157; Seymour 1970: 128); he can, if he is a Zulu, determine the rank of all or some of his houses (Myburgh 1944: 299–301; Seymour 1970: 122, 123); he can disinherit a successor apparent to his position as head of the group as a whole or as head of a constituent group (Schapera and Goodwin 1937: 162; Seymour 1970: 282, 283), whether it be a house or a section (a house with its junior houses), adopt a child (Schapera 1937b: 189; Seymour 1970: 226), give a daughter in marriage (Seymour 1970: 101, 102), and enter into contracts for farming out livestock (Schapera 1937c: 201). But as we have shown, he must consult the senior members of the group (above and page 304) and is answerable to them if he does not or if he acts unreasonably, partially, or inhumanely. Persistence could lead to dangerous friction within the group, especially if he entered into contracts with other groups (Seymour 1970: 71, 72), and even to administrative or judicial involvement with the authorities (page 301 above) or to dissolution of marriage (Schapera 1937b: 190; Schapera 1938a: 151; Seymour 1970: 134, 181, 182) and, where there has been cruelty, to prosecution (Schapera 1938a: 151) for assault.

Family law

The term 'family law' is self-explanatory in that it denotes that division of law pertaining to the family; that is, to spouses, parents and children, guardians and wards.

We have already spoken of guardianship or authority as a shared right, of agnatic groups in which polygyny is prominent, and of puberty as a prerequisite for marriage (pages 301, 303 above). We may add that persons within the prohibited degrees of relationship cannot marry; broadly speaking, consanguineous unions are forbidden among the Nguni and Tsonga, but among the Sotho cousins may marry and among the Venda a woman's son may marry her brother's daughter, affinity being nowhere a bar to marriage except between actual or classificatory parents- and children-in-law (Hoernlé 1937a: 77, 87; Schapera 1937c: 202; Myburgh 1944: 219–24; Seymour 1970: 117–19; Olivier 1969: 2–8).

An agreement assuming great importance when implemented is that entered into between the group of a bride-to-be and her suitor's group, providing for transfer of authority over her for the purpose of establishing and maintaining a family against transfer of goods or value (known by the Zulu word *ukulobola*, the goods or value being termed *ilobolo*) and, among some peoples, rendering of service (Krige 1937b: 115). Performance or partial performance (Post 1887 I: 346, 374; Kropf 1915: 303, s.v. *isi-Nyaniso*; Soga 1932: 228, 229; Krige 1936a: 130; Seymour 1970: 93, 94, 96, 99) on the part of the man's group brings about betrothal; performance on the part of the woman's group, marriage, the act of transferring authority (Post 1887 I: 387) ending with, and culminating in, the beginning of cohabitation, which need not involve sexual relations (Post 1887 I: 396; Olivier 1969: 52).

Betrothal renders the woman's group liable; blameworthy non-performance on their part or misconduct on her part leading to justified repudiation entails the return of what has been received, together with any increase and the equivalent of unreported (or even all) losses (Soga 1932: 229; Schapera 1938a: 133, 134; Seymour 1970: 97). The man's group is not liable, but as a rule blameworthy rejection of the bride entails forfeiture of what has been transferred to the value of an earnest (Seymour 1970: 97–100). The death of either prospective spouse terminates betrothal and the bride's group are normally liable for restoration (Seymour 1970: 96) unless it has been agreed, or custom decrees, that a substitute be found for the deceased if possible (Myburgh 1944: 255; Schapera 1938a: 134). When betrothal is terminated by consent between the groups and there is no agreement as to the consequences, the suitor's group, being freed from their duties, can demand the return of what they have transferred with increase and less unavoidable losses (Seymour 1970: 96).

Marriage renders the husband's group liable for unpaid *lobolo*, the question of which constantly arises where perpetual piecemeal delivery is an institution, as among some Nguni (Myburgh 1944: 227–9; Seymour 1970: 155,

158). We have said that marriage is brought about by transfer of authority over the bride. This involves giving her person into the custody of her suitor's group and agrees with the recognized way of transferring membership from one group to another: the right of guardianship or authority is transferred together with custody of the person concerned. But in the case of the bride the purpose of the transfer, and therefore of the right, is limited to the establishment and maintenance of a family (Myburgh 1965: 11): the man's group will not, for example, derive from it the power to give her in adoption (Whitfield 1948: 68) or in marriage (Myburgh 1944: 236; *Mtiyane v. Mate*, 1957 N.A.C. 49, N.E.) as do her group from their plenary right of guardianship or authority. We shall call this limited right the marital right of guardianship or authority.

The effect of the transfer is not to terminate the bride's membership of her group of origin but to confer membership of a second group on her (Myburgh 1965: 11). She now shares all her rights, including the right of authority over her own person, with each group in a measure commensurate with her position in such group (pages 303–5 above). This is clear in the transfer of gifts from her old group to the new in proportion to the amount of *lobolo* (Post 1887 I: 354; Marx 1903: 351; Hunter 1936: 199; Myburgh 1944: 111; Hammond-Tooke 1962: 121), showing their intention to emphasize that they have not lost her and cannot therefore accept the equivalent of a plenary right over her person; the old group's continued exercise of authority over her by taking disciplinary measures against her for misbehaving towards her new group (Marx 1903: 351–3; Schapera 1938a: 158; Myburgh 1944: 289; Ashton 1952: 86; Seymour 1970: 175); her continued share in the resources of the old group when she is with them (Myburgh 1944: 110) and in their rights of personality when she joins in taking revenge on a person who has impeached the honour of one of their female members (Krige 1936a: 31).

It has often been alleged that formerly neither the bride's nor the bridegroom's consent to their marriage was required, and it is true that their share in their group's rights, including the right of authority, is limited. We have shown, however, that it is not lacking (page 303 above); and acquiescence, even under duress (Schapera 1938a: 128; Myburgh 1944: 49, 242, 247, 250), is consent, though not voluntary. That freedom is not essential to validity in the legal systems under discussion is clear from what we have observed in the law of evidence (page 300 above). In a word, as the most important members of their respective groups in the matter of their marriage they are bound to co-operate (Marx 1903: 349; Schapera 1938a: 129). This they cannot do unless they acquiesce; but acquiescence is sufficient consent.

Wedding ceremonies are not essential, but they serve as notice to the public and facilitate proof of marriage should this later be required (Seymour 1970: 111). They depict the nature of the juristic act and are therefore most instructive. The constant show of reluctance and antagonism on the part of the bride and her group (Post 1887 I: 327, 328; Krige 1937b: 116; Hoernlé

1925) demonstrates their continued solidarity and their obligatory right as against the bridegroom's group; the gifts (Krige 1937b: 116) show the duty to preserve harmony and goodwill; various actions (such as showing objects connected with household duties and chastisement) symbolize the group's authority over wives (Myburgh 1944: 77-9); rites are performed to confirm acceptance of the bride, secure her permanently for the receiving group, and help her to have a child without delay (Myburgh 1944: 82, 83, 87, 95, 96, 99, 100-4, 106).

The spouses must, of course, accord each other marital privileges at all reasonable times and perform their household duties (Seymour 1970: 134). Fertility is not essential to the validity of marriage; a female known to be barren or malformed may be taken and given as a wife (Myburgh 1944: 140, 245, 246, 259, 284). A family is therefore sufficiently established by the union of husband and wife and the services (Seymour 1970: 189) accruing to the husband's group in terms of their obligatory right need not include the production of issue. But although progeniture is not the decisive purpose of marriage its importance is so great that unless the husband's group have waived it they can demand its accomplishment among many peoples, if necessary by substitution in the form of a measure such as the sororate or levirate, otherwise the marriage can be dissolved.

Dissolution of marriage is brought about by termination of the woman's membership of her new group. This may be due to her death (subject to the sororate, etc.) or to abandonment or forfeiture of such group's marital right of authority over her or by its retrocession with the consent of both groups (Seymour 1970: 194). Either group may repudiate the marriage on good grounds such as the serious misconduct, impotence, or sterility of a spouse (Schapera 1937c: 204; Seymour 1970: 169ff.), unless, in the case of a barren wife, the defect has been remedied by the sororate or similar means (Krige 1937b: 116, 117) or condoned. Whether delivery or restoration of any *lobolo* can be claimed will depend on the extent to which the wife and her group have discharged their duties (Schapera 1937c: 204). Generally speaking, marriage is not dissolved by the husband's death, for the widow is required to comply with the levirate. Certain Cape tribes, Xhosa, for example, disallow cohabitation with the deceased's brother but expect the widow to have children fathered by unrelated men (Krige 1937b: 117).

A child is a member of the agnatic group into which it is born or to which it is transferred. A child born to an unmarried female is a member of her father's group by virtue of their plenary right over her; one born to a wife, a member of her husband's group by virtue of their marital right over her (Schapera 1937b: 189). A child may be adopted or, in the Cape Province, transferred to its natural father's group on payment for the delict by which it was conceived and reimbursement of its mother's group for its maintenance (Schapera 1937b: 189; Bryant 1949: 233; Seymour 1970: 226, 234, 235); among the Venda a child of an unmarried mother follows her into her husband's group when she marries (van Warmelo 1949: 803-7); among the Pedi a girl's child is transferred to the group of the man marrying her for valuable consideration (Harries 1929: 29); in terms of the *go ralala* and *go gorosa* of the Tswana and the *go lata* and *go beka* of the Pedi a girl regularly has children by cohabiting with her betrothed at her home and these become members of their mother's husband's group when she marries, for they are transferred with her (Post 1887 I: 374; Harries 1929: 9; Schapera 1938a: 135). The right of guardianship or authority over a child is always plenary and vests in the group having plenary or marital authority over its mother, unless it is transferred.

Amongst the peoples who do not allow marriage between cousins, for example, Nguni and Tsonga, a child born to a husband and wife never belongs to its mother's group and the well-known freedom and cordiality towards the maternal uncle (Hoernlé 1937a: 72, 88) must be seen in the light of the fact that he has no share in the plenary right over his sister's children.

Although a wife's group never have rights of authority over her children amongst the Nguni, some of the Cape tribes recognize what is generally known as *ukutheleka*. In terms of this a group to whom *lobolo* is owing may, if the woman concerned or any of her children should come into their custody (for example, by visiting them), retain such custody until reasonable payment is made. They may even, it seems, sue for custody, give a girl in marriage, and receive her *lobolo*, provided that they transfer to her father's group any balance left after discharge of the debt.[41]

We have already referred to the position of children in the group and the relationship between them, their parents, and other members (page 302 above). It is only necessary to add that all their earnings accrue to their group by virtue of the latter's plenary right over them, just as do their mother's earnings by virtue of the marital right over her (Myburgh 1965: 11).

Membership of the agnatic group is terminated by expulsion (Post 1887 I: 53; Post 1887 II: 25; Marx 1903: 349; Myburgh 1944: 285, 287; Seymour 1970: 285), of which disherison is a form (Schapera 1938a: 129; Seymour 1970: 285), by death (see, too, pages 286, 295 above), or, as has been shown, by transfer.

Much of the foregoing has been affected by legislation. The term marriage is reserved for the monogamous union known as Christian or civil marriage, the institution described above being termed the customary union.[42] In Natal a customary union is void unless the bride publicly declares that she freely consents to and wishes it;[43] death of the husband terminates the union,[44] which can otherwise only be dissolved by a Bantu Affairs Commissioner's court on fixed grounds, which do not include sterility;[45] and the union can be declared void by such court on certain grounds, including impotence.[46]

Certain legislation is the result of problems connected with the differences between the two types of union; for example, that safeguarding a family or families established by customary union should the man enter into a monogamous union,[47] and that providing the widow of a customary union with an action against a person causing the death of her partner.[48]

The law of things

The law of things is that division of law in which things are defined and the rules and principles governing the rights in things (that is, real rights) are enunciated. The things concerned are material things, and may fall, as may real rights, into a number of recognized categories.

For the South African Bantu we may distinguish between movable and immovable things. The latter term denotes areas of land and things attached to these such as plants or structures; the former, things that are neither land nor so attached. Ownership is known among these peoples and vests in agnatic groups, as explained; whether other real rights are distinguishable needs brief discussion.

Ownership may be acquired by original means[49] such as appropriation of ownerless things (wild fruit, game, clay, timber, etc.), manufacture (pottery, working in wood, etc.), cultivation, and administrative action (allocation of residential and arable land, reward from public resources) or by derivative means, to wit, by transfer such as is required for *ukulobola*, exchange of movables or fields, payment for delict, etc. (pages 311, 312 below). It is lost by alienation, abandonment, surrender to the authorities, confiscation, or destruction. Ownership of land vests in an agnatic group when an area is allocated by the ruler or on his behalf; allotment to the constituent groups (houses) is made by the head in consultation with the family council. Such land cannot be given away to foreigners or sold, but otherwise it remains the property of the group unless abandoned or surrendered to or requisitioned or confiscated by the authorities (Schapera and Goodwin 1937: 157; Schapera 1938a: 197ff.; Ashton 1952: 149; Mönnig 1967: 340, 341; van Warmelo 1967: 1085).

Whether real rights other than ownership were known is doubtful (Soga 1932: 384). That a widow may continue to use and occupy residential and agricultural land available to her before her husband's death has been ascribed to a personal servitude in her favour (Kerr 1953: 62ff.). We believe, however, that it is part of the powers constituting her share in the patrimonial rights of her late husband's group, and particularly in their ownership, since her membership of such group continues (page 304 above). The custom that owners of adjoining fields may alone cut grass on the strips in between and that these may not be cultivated (Kerr 1953: 62) presents difficulty. The owners' powers are probably derived from ownership (see Kerr), the owners of each field being co-owners of the dividing strip; perhaps the prohibition is a penal one designed to ensure clear demarcation and forestall disputes over boundaries. There is at least one problem involving movables. It seems that in the Transkei a movable thing may be delivered to creditors by their debtors, who cannot claim return before settlement in full but can sue for the thing or for damages if it has been wrongfully alienated or lost; and that on default the thing is forfeited to the creditors (Whitfield 1948: 489, 490; Seymour 1970: 309, 310). We do not, however, know whether the debtors remain the owners in the meanwhile or, if they do, whether the creditors have a real right in the thing operative against other creditors. The juristic act is known as pledge, but may well be a fiduciary transfer of ownership. The same uncertainty prevails where a thing is merely pointed out as a guarantee (Seymour 1970: 309, 310).

Land tenure has been profoundly affected by legislation, the effect being mainly to control allocation and recognize individual ownership (page 295 above; Kerr 1953: 34ff.; Hammond-Tooke 1962: 147).

The law of obligations: contract

A contract is an agreement entailing liability; among the South African Bantu such agreements always occur between groups. Modern systems recognize consensual contracts requiring no more than mutual understanding between the parties; among the South African Bantu, however, liability is not, as a rule, incurred until performance or part-performance is made. In other words, the contract typical for these peoples is the real contract.

This is illustrated by *ukulobola*, which we have already discussed (page 306ff. above): delivery of *lobolo* entails liability for transfer of the bride or return of the goods; transfer of the bride, liability for delivery of any *lobolo* owing. The same principles apply to the well-known South African Bantu contracts of exchange[50] and loan[51] of movables (such as cattle for *ukulobola*, the loan being termed *ukwenzelela*), or immovables (for example, a field for cultivation), farming out[52] of livestock (*ukusisa, ukunqoma, go fiša*, etc.). In cases of agency (Seymour 1970: 313, 314) and other service contracts (Marx 1903: 359; Schapera 1937c: 201; Schapera 1938a: 253) liability is brought about by performance of the service on the part of the servants.

Where a contract is entered into for securing payment, the effect of performance on the part of the debtors is to render the creditors liable, if payment is made as agreed, in the case of bodily delivery (Seymour 1970: 309; page 310 above) of a thing, for return or indemnification; in the case of verbal delivery (Seymour 1970: 309), for making good loss resulting from wrongful alienation.

The custom known as *ukufakwa* seems to be a mode of performance peculiar to a loan for a girl's needs. By indicating (Seymour 1970: 103, 152, 157, 308) the expected *lobolo* (Seymour 1970: 310, 313) and 'putting the creditors into' it, the debtors confer co-ownership on the former with immediate effect if and when delivery takes place. Performance may also consist in the transfer of plenary authority over a girl to the creditor group (Seymour 1970: 310), the latter then being entitled to her *lobolo*.

Contracts of suretyship have been mentioned (Whitfield 1948: 489), but in the absence of data we cannot discover their nature.

There is reason to believe that service in the ruling establishment (Schapera 1938b: 66) is not contractual but a matter of public law.

The law of obligations: quasi-contract

In quasi-contract liability is unconnected with agreement and arises from performance alone. This happens in cases of necessary service (the *negotiorum gestio* of Western systems) and unjust enrichment. Examples for the South African Bantu are maintenance (Seymour 1970: 232ff.) or *isondlo* (basis: necessary service) and 'tributariness' or *ukwethula* of a group towards another (Seymour 1970: 310, 311) because property belonging to the latter has been used for the former's benefit (basis: enrichment); it being understood that liability would be contractual (Schapera 1937c: 201) where *isondlo* or *ukwethula* had been agreed upon.

The law of obligations: delict

A delict is the unjustified violation of a right, intentional or negligent, entailing liability (Myburgh 1969: 146, 147). Among the South African Bantu, as elsewhere, infants and lunatics are incapable of intent or negligence and therefore of delict (Myburgh 1969: 147). The creditors are the injured group; the debtors, the group of the culprit (Myburgh 1969: 146). A group is delictually liable when any of its members intentionally or negligently violates a right by his own activity or through the activities of others or of animals (Myburgh 1969: 147; Seymour 1970: 323). The remedy to be achieved by performance is satisfaction (amends) for personal injury or damages for patrimonial loss. Personal injury results from violation of rights of personality but may result from violation of patrimonial rights; patrimonial loss results from violation of patrimonial rights but may result from violation of rights of personality (Myburgh 1969: 146) and includes increase of duties involving an estate (Myburgh 1969: 152).

Rights of personality are violated by assault, negligent injury of the body, threats involving imprecation (such as 'Go, and your belly will swell!'), insult, and defamation; rights of personality and of authority by homicide, rape, seduction, adultery, courting a married woman, abducting a wife, and kidnapping a girl; ownership by theft, damaging property, and encroachment on fields by cultivating these. Each of the delicts last mentioned may entail satisfaction of the creditors for shock or trouble (that is, for personal injury caused by the violation of a patrimonial right) besides mulcting of the debtors in damages, while assault or negligent injury of the body may entail payment of medical expenses (that is, of damages for patrimonial loss caused by the violation of a right of personality) and of an amount to make amends for the suffering (Myburgh 1969: 148-53).

What is compensation and what satisfaction is deducible from various circumstances? In the old days satisfaction was often obtained by self-help: an unprovoked insult could be met with violence; a thief or adulterer could be thrashed or killed; for allowing cattle to damage crops herdboys could be thrashed and the animals driven into their owners' fields; an animal or animals could be seized for ritual slaughter from the group of a homicide or a person discrediting or otherwise violating a female's decency, the purpose being not patrimonial restitution but healing of the injury by lustration (Myburgh 1969: 148, 149). Where a court awarded many times the value of a stolen thing, the actual value would be compensation and the rest amends, while mutilation of the thief's hands might be ordered to satisfy the injured; for abduction of a wife seizure of an unlimited number of cattle might be authorized to cover both damages and satisfaction; an apology might be adjudged sufficient amends for an assault or a verbal insult (Myburgh 1969: 149-53).

The amount of relief may be fixed by custom. If it is not, the court must exercise its discretion. In doing so it considers (Myburgh 1969: 154) the social standing of the parties, the culprit's general character, the means he used for committing the delict, his condition at the time of commission (for example, drunken), his subsequent conduct (for example, hostile or conciliatory), the circumstances under which the delict was committed (for example, in the presence of persons who did not connect defamatory words with the plaintiffs), and the plaintiffs' conduct (for example, suggestive of abuse in view of repeated claims for seduction or adultery in respect of the same woman).

An act may be justified and therefore free from delictual unlawfulness. The truth of a statement makes it non-defamatory; injuries inflicted in the course of recognized activities such as ceremonies and games are lawful, as are all acts falling within the class of summary remedies; and all the factors excluding criminality (page 296 above) also exclude delictual liability (Myburgh 1969: 154, 155).

Self-help and mutilation would not be recognized today; otherwise the position has remained comparatively undisturbed (Seymour 1970: 318ff.).

The law of succession

The law of succession comprises such provisions of a legal system as are concerned with deceased estates. For the South African Bantu this has limited meaning. Their estates vest in agnatic groups who are not, in principle, subject to decease and therefore exclude the notion of inheritance except in the sense that members' shares in the patrimonial rights of their group increase when their number decreases through death. Succession merely means succession to the position of the deceased head of an agnatic group in accordance with well-established rules.

An estate may comprise the patrimonial rights and duties shared by an agnatic group known as a 'house' (page 301 above): that is, a wife, her children, and members by adoption or by transfer from another house, the head being the husband or his male successor, ideally the spouses' eldest son. Such an estate is termed house property. It includes ownership in movables, fields, and residential quarters, and may be increased by the earnings of, and *lobolo* for, members of the house (Seymour 1970: 69).

A house may be a constituent of a comprehensive agnatic group, usually referred to as a kraal, of which the head is often, but need not be, the husband of all the wives: some of these could, for example, be married to other members such as his brothers or sons or to unrelated adherents (Hoernlé 1937a: 69, 75). The estate shared by such a group is termed kraal property. It often consists of contributions from the estate of the head's mother's house and that of his father's kraal. The cattle brought by the mother when she married and the mother's beast for each married sister are, for example, often reserved for the youngest son's establishment and may be supplemented with kraal cattle (Marwick 1940: 179; Myburgh 1944: 302, 303; cf. Schapera and Goodwin 1937: 163).

Rights of personality, which are excluded from any estate (page 287 above), are apparently shared within the comprehensive group (pages 203, 204, 307 above).

A comprehensive group may consist of sections in order of rank for succession to the head's position, each comprising a single house or several houses in order of rank for succession to the position of its head and to that of head of the whole group (Schapera 1937c: 203, 204; Seymour 1970: 254ff.); an individual house may have a house attached to it for purposes of succession to the position of head of the combined houses (Seymour 1970: 258ff.). Succession to the position of head of a house or a section or the kraal or more than one of these is confined to males and governed, between members of a house, by primogeniture. Descendants are preferred to ascendants; relatives of the direct line are preferred to collaterals; collaterals of the full blood are preferred to those of the half blood; the latter succeed in order of house rank (Schapera and Goodwin 1937: 162, 163; Schapera 1938a: 54; Bryant 1949: 438; Seymour 1970: 253; cf. Natal Code, sect. 110).

A son of an attached house is preceded by a son of the parent house (Seymour 1970: 258–62); a leviratic son is excluded only by a son of his mother and the deceased (Seymour 1970: 270); a man's natural son transferred to his group and an adopted son are excluded by a son of a marriage (Seymour 1970: 263, 264); among certain Cape Nguni a wife's adulterine son seems by custom to rank as a son she has borne her husband (Seymour 1970: 274), but the Zulu seem to exclude him altogether (Myburgh 1944: 274, 275); a son of an unmarried female either succeeds in her father's group only when males of other ranks are wanting (Hunter 1936: 208; Seymour 1970: 275) or, apparently among the Zulu, does not qualify at all (Myburgh 1944: 274, 275).

It seems that unrelated adherents can never succeed within the group of their hosts, but that their head can be succeeded by the head of such group if he dies without male relatives (Myburgh 1944: 305). Reports also mention that a group lacking male issue may fall to the ruler with their estate (Post 1887 I: 425; Post 1887 II: 7; Bryant 1949: 439; Seymour 1970: 254); the patrimonial rights, including guardianship or authority, then presumably cease to be rights and become part of the public resources, but in the absence of data we cannot be certain. Adoption (Seymour 1970: 265) and disherison

(Seymour 1970: 265, 283) are juristic acts for which formalities have to be observed.

Legislation now provides for testamentary disposition in respect of all but individually held quitrent land and property accruing to the testator's wives' houses.[53] Quitrent land devolves in accordance with prescribed rules[54] as does devisable property in respect of which there is no will;[55] and disherison in respect of quitrent land is governed by regulation.[56]

Notes

* This chapter was completed in April 1970. It does not take into account legislative changes occurring after that date.

1 See, too, Kerr 1953: 11.

2 *Masela Mpolo v. Cawe Nozihamba*, 1964 B.A.C. 75, S.

3 Bantu Administration Act, 1927, sect. 5.

4 *Ibid.*, sects 20, 21.

5 *Ibid.*, sect. 21 & Third Schedule.

6 *Ibid.*, sect. 4.

7 Urban Bantu Councils Act, 1961, sect. 5.

8 Bantu Authorities Act, 1951; Promotion of Bantu Self-Government Act, 1959.

9 Transkei Constitution Act, 1963, sects 23, 43–6, 50.

10 Lesotho Independence Order 1966, sects 32–4; Swaziland Independence Order 1968, Schedule, sects 1, 28–30.

11 Lesotho Independence Order 1966, Schedule, sect. 41.

12 Swaziland Independence Order 1968, Schedule, sects 38, 40, 42.

13 Lesotho Independence Order 1966, Schedule, sect. 110.

14 Lesotho Independence Order 1966, Schedule, sects 93, 95; Swaziland Independence Order 1968, Schedule, sects 35, 94.

15 Swaziland Independence Order 1968, Schedule 3 ff.

16 Botswana Independence Order 1966, Schedule, sect. 86.

17 Bantu Administration Act, 1927, sect. 25.

18 *Ibid.*, sect. 20.

19 *Ibid.*, sect. 2.

20 Botswana Independence Act 1966, sect. 2.

21 Lesotho Independence Order 1966, sects 92, 93, 95-9.

22 Swaziland Indepencence Order 1968, Schedule 3 ff.

23 Warner 1858: 64; Brownlee 1858: 113-15, 124, 125, 128, 129; Post 1887 II: 33, 34, 54, 55, 70, 97; Fourie 1921: 155-6; Harries 1929: 109-10; Schapera 1937c: 207-9, 211, 212, 216; Schapera and Goodwin 1937: 166; Schapera 1938a: 39, 63, 146, 273, 278, 312; Myburgh 1944: 271; Ashton 1952: 266-81; pages 288, 294 above.

24 Warner 1858: 94; Brownlee 1858: 126; Post 1887 II: 25, 32, 54, 56, 57, 65, 66, 91, 96, 149; Marx 1903: 357; Fourie 1921: 156; Harries 1929: 101; Krige 1936a: 224; Schapera 1937c: 209, 211; Schapera 1938a: 219; Myburgh 1944: 257; Mönnig 1967: 327.

25 Brookes 1924: 176; Marwick 1940: 286; Govt Notice R. 2082 of 29/12/1967, Schedule, rule 5.

26 Schapera 1938c: 279; Bantu Administration Act, 1927, sects 9, 11, 12, 13, 20, 21; Govt Notices R. 20833 & 2084 of 29/12/1967.

27 Govt Notice 45 of 13/1/1961.

28 Govt Notice R. 2082 of 29/12/1967.

29 Bantu Administration Act, 1927, sect. 11.

30 Cf. Bantu Administration Act, 1927, sect. 4.

31 Natal Code, sects 28, 42.

32 *Ibid.*, sect. 33.

33 *Ibid.*, sect. 36.

34 *Ibid.*, sect. 96.

35 *Ibid.*, sects 28, 42.

36 Proc. 112 of 1879, regn 39; proc. 140 of 1885, regn 38.

37 Natal Code, sect. 27.

38 *Ibid.*, sect. 38.

39 *Ibid.*, sects 28, 42.

40 *Ibid.*, sects 27, 38.

41 Warner 1858: 71, Soga 1932: 268, 284; Hunter 1936: 191; Krige 1937b: 114; Whitfield 1948: 138, 148; Hammond-Tooke 1962: 133, 135; Seymour 1970: 155-8.

42 Bantu Administration Act, 1927, sect. 35.

43 Natal Code, sect. 59.

44 *Ibid.*, sect. 57.

45 *Ibid.*, sects 76, 78.

46 *Ibid.*, sect. 77.

47 Bantu Administration Act, 1927, sect. 22.

48 Bantu Laws Amendment Act, 1963, sect. 31.

49 Post 1887 II: 162, 163, 169; Marx 1903: 358; Schapera and Goodwin 1937: 131ff., 141, 142, 144ff., 157; Schapera 1938a: 66, 216, 217; Hammond-Tooke 1962: 145ff.

50 Marx 1903: 359; Schapera and Goodwin 1937: 153ff.; Ashton 1952: 149.

51 Schapera and Goodwin 1937: 157; Schapera 1938a: 205; Ashton 1952: 149; Mönnig 1967: 340; Seymour 1970: 312; cf. Marwick 1940: 162.

52 Marx 1903: 358; Krige 1936a: 186, 187; Schapera 1937c: 201; Schapera 1938a: 246–8; Mönnig 1967: 165; Seymour 1970: 314–17.

53 Bantu Administration Act, 1927, sect. 23.

54 Proc. R. 188 of 11/7/1969, sects 35–40 and annexure 24.

55 Govt Notice R. 34 of 7/1/1966, regn 2.

56 Proc. R. 188 of 11/7/1969, sect. 40.

Chapter 10
World-view I:
A System of Beliefs
W. D. Hammond-Tooke

Like people everywhere the Southern Bantu are not only concerned with the prosaic business of wresting a living from the soil, tending their herds, giving and receiving in marriage or settling disputes. They, too, ask the 'big questions': how and by whom was the world created, what is man's place in the universe, what happens after death and, perhaps most important of all, what are the causes of evil and misfortune and how to cope with the exigencies of life? The answers they give to these questions are fundamental to an understanding of tribal life and thought. Confused and unsystematic as they sometimes are, they express the deepest longings and most basic values of the society. We are concerned in the following two chapters with the traditional world-view, the answers given to the 'big questions', the sphere of what is usually termed 'religion'.

Religion has many functions. It provides emotional support in times of distress, it contributes to the coherence of social groups, it sanctions and supports moral codes, and it provides an authoritative explanatory theory for the ultimate questions that man asks himself. Its contributions are thus both social and personal. South African traditional religions do all these things and provide a more or less coherent system which enables the tribesman to cope with the uncertainties and apprehensions which are the price man pays for the self-awareness of his humanity. But the traditional systems differ markedly from the so-called 'World Religions'. They are all firmly rooted in the social structure, and membership of cult groups is determined by birth (they are thus, by their very nature, non-proselytizing), the objects of worship are structurally determined, and they are quite unashamedly this-worldly in orientation. Unlike Christianity, for example, which accepts suffering as inevitable and indeed necessary, merely promising grace to face it, all Bantu religions are concerned with attaining the good life here on earth, and their rituals tend to be essentially pragmatic. A dualism is recognized, as in Christianity, between good and evil, but the war waged between them, with its resulting rewards and penalties, is essentially here and now, and not in an apocalyptic future existence. The witch and sorcerer, the very embodiment of evil, is a constant threat to the well-being of man and beast, and the whole complex of witch beliefs, with its related institution of divination, must thus be seen as an integral part of the religious system.

These two chapters must be read, then, as a whole. The first is concerned with the Bantu world-view as a system of beliefs, of concepts about the nature of the supernatural, the life after death, the causes of misfortune and the efficacy of magic; the second deals with the working out of this system in everyday life, as a system of action. The concern here is with the symbolic expression of these beliefs in ritual (both 'religious' and 'magical'), the emergence of 'religious' roles, with the interpretation of misfortune by divination and other means and with the relationship of these beliefs to social life, especially to the coherence of kinship groups. The complex relationship between religion and the moral code will also be discussed.

Creation, Impersonal Nature and High-Gods

One of the most striking features of traditional belief systems is the almost complete absence of what might be called a 'theology'. There is little speculation as to the nature of the spirit world or of the life after death and, unlike some other peoples, a rather poorly developed corpus of myths. But all groups have some form of creation myth, however exiguous, and, with it, some conception of a Creator who brought the universe into being. He is always named, and the act of creation is described, but there the matter ends. He is *deus otiosus* and no longer takes much interest in the affairs of his creation. There are no rituals directed to his worship, he is seldom if ever invoked by his creatures and he does not constitute an important factor in the religious system. The Kriges' description of the Lobedu Supreme Being is typical.

> The Lovedu are not given to speculation about first beginnings and final causes. . . . A vague, hardly ever evoked myth attributes the creation of the world and man to *Khuzwane*. . . . But the act of creation, like *Khuzwane* himself, is too remote, too unrelated to present realities, to be of any concern to men; and they find no place in, nor do they in any way influence, the Lovedu philosophy of the cosmos or of society. The Lovedu apparently feel the need to posit a first or final cause but such a cause has not continued to operate as a force (Krige and Krige 1954: 59).

The same can be said for the Xhosa *Dali* or *Qamatha*, the Zulu *Nkulunkulu*, the Venda *Raluvhimba* and the Sotho *Modimo*. There also seems to be little or no connection between the creator god and the ancestral spirits, although there is evidence that the Sotho believe that *Modimo* can be approached through the medium of the ancestors (Mönnig 1967: 57; Willoughby 1923: 79) and one of the names of the Zulu *Nkulunkulu* is *Mvelangqangi* ('The First to Emerge'). For some he is the first ancestor (Callaway 1868–70: 47 and *passim*.) The creation myths themselves are of engaging simplicity. The Zulu maintain that Nkulunkulu 'broke off the nations' from a bed of reeds (*ohlangeni*) (Callaway 1868–70: 2), and a similar myth is recorded for the Swazi (Kuper 1947: 191), Mpondomise (Brownlee 1923: 116) and Tsonga (Junod 1927 II: 348), The South Sotho, perhaps influenced by Nguni beliefs, 'claim that all true Basuto originate from the same place, namely, a reed bed at Ntsuanatsatsi, where the first man emerged' (Ashton 1952: 10). Callaway explains the symbolism, for the Zulu at least, by the analogy drawn between the giving off of reed shoots and the segmentation of the family, with its resultant proliferation of descent groups and tribes. The Mpondo do not appear to have any origin myths and all Alberti, the first systematic observer of the Xhosa, could ascertain from them was a legend that all people, stock and all forms of animal life, came out of a cavern 'in the land in which the sun rises' (Alberti 1810: 13). Casalis reports a similar myth from the South Sotho (Casalis 1861: 240). The Tswana speak of a hole or holes in a rock at Lowe, near Mochudi, from which the tribal ancestors are said to have emerged and point to footprints in the rock as proof. The Lobedu also believe that *Khuzwane* left his footprints on certain rocks when they were yet soft, and this association of the name *Khuzwane* with footprints is also found as a subsidiary belief among the Venda. Stayt refers to the Venda *Khuzwane* as 'another deity', in addition to the main god, *Raluvhimba*, 'also vaguely connected with the creation' (Stayt 1931a: 236). The Tsonga also speak of early human footprints (Junod 1927 II: 349). Although no specific creation myths have been recorded for the Pedi, there is an alternative name for *Modimo*, *Mmopabatho*, which derives from the verb *bopa*, 'the moulding a pot out of clay' (Mönnig 1967: 46). The Pedi are unusual in that they believe that *Modimo* (also called *Kgobe*) had a son, *Kgobeane*, who created man after *Kgobe* created the world. It would appear, then, that, although among all the groups the Supreme Being is connected with creation in a general way, only the Zulu and Swazi (and perhaps the Pedi) explicitly describe the method of creation.

Another myth, significant for its wide distribution among the tribes, is the explanation of death by the well-known story of the chameleon and the lizard. In the beginning the Creator sent the chameleon to tell mankind that it would live forever. Subsequently he changed his mind and dispatched the lizard with a message of mortality. The chameleon dawdled on the way and it was the lizard's message that became effective. The myth has been specifically recorded from among the Zulu, Pedi, Tsonga, and South Sotho, among whom the principals are referred to as a chief's son, Leoba, and his servant Khatoane (Ashton 1952: 100–6; Casalis 1861: 242). It is significant, though, that *khatoane* also means 'lizard', and *lenoaba* 'chameleon', and it would appear that this is a modification of the original zoomorphic myth.

All the South African Bantu, then, conceptualize creation in terms of a personified first cause. But the explanatory functions of the Supreme Being may go further than this. In particular he is thought by some tribes to be responsible for the working of nature, especially in its more majestic and dangerous aspects of storm, drought and flood. These phenomena do not involve interpersonal relations between tribesmen, but are impersonal, capricious and vital to man's well-being. Thus among the South Sotho *Modimo* 'was sometimes seen to manifest Himself as lightning or as a thunderbolt'

(Ashton 1952: 116), and, among the Pedi, '*Modimo* is very closely associated with the elements of nature, wind, rain, hail and lightning. In fact there is more than an association. To a large extent these elements are personified by *Modimo*', for the same root *-dimo* is found in the word for 'sky' and *ledimo* means a whirlwind, a hurricane or storm (Mönnig 1967: 46–7). Here again the function of the beliefs is explanatory, rather than instrumental. Submission, in most cases, is fatalistic, and few rituals have been developed to influence this manifestation of the god. The Venda deity *Raluvhimba* is also believed to be 'connected with all astronomical and physical phenomena' (Stayt 1931a: 230) and is identified with *Mwari* the widely-revered Shona oracle and rain-maker. In this case, however, there is evidence that during the time of Chief Muthivhi he was actually worshipped in caves.

Sometimes the two aspects, First Cause and Sky God, are split between two or more deities. Thus the Tsonga, who attribute the creation of the world to 'Nature' (*Ntumbuluko*), speak of an impersonal power, *Tilo*, apparently a personification of the sky, who controls life and death, sends storms and rain, afflicts children with convulsions, and is propitiated in times of drought by watering the graves of twins. The Zulu also seem to have a personified Sky God, other than *Nkulunkulu*, called the 'Chief of the Sky', who brings storms and kills by lightning those who offend him, but the evidence for this is confused. It appears that this complex of beliefs is related to two separate concepts, viz. creation, and nature in its impersonal, cosmic and more dangerous aspects. Neither, however, involves interaction between tribesmen on the personal level. To meet this need there is another complex of beliefs, that of the ancestral shades and witchcraft and sorcery.

Local and Nature Spirits

Apart from the Supreme Being and the ancestral shades (see below), most South African Bantu peoples believe in spirits or spirit-like manifestations which are 'free' in that they do not fit into the structurally-determined system of ancestors proper, linked, as they are, with descent and kinship groups. Some tribes do not have such beliefs ('Nature spirits and hero-gods have no place in the Lovedu scheme of things' (Krige and Krige 1943: 231), but they seem to be in the minority.

Whereas it is possible to generalize, to some extent, about the Supreme Being and the ancestor cult, this is not so for the 'free' spirits. They appear to be *ad hoc* beliefs that, as far as can be ascertained, are unique to different tribes and are presumably the result of local speculation on the awesome or uncanny impression given by such things as caves, mountains and groves, or are attempts to explain natural phenomena such as the seasons.

The Venda appear to have developed the belief in local spirits to a greater extent than other South African peoples. Apart from the groves inhabited by the spirits of dead chiefs (see below), Stayt writes of spirits who live in rivers and lakes (especially Lake Fundudzi, associated with the ancestral spirits of the guardian of the lake). There is also a large pool below the Phiphidi Falls, inhabited by the spirits of the Ngona autochthones, who can be heard dancing under the water. Offerings of hair and ornaments are made to these spirits by people crossing above the falls. Apart from this

> A great many rivers and mountains are supposed to be inhabited by spirits not directly connected with any particular lineage. . . . There are mountain spirits, *zwidhadyani* [properly *zwiḍahadzhane* cf. Lobedu *zwiḍajani*, 'ancestral spirits come to join in the joy and revelry of the living'], who are mostly of foreign origin, often BaSutho. . . . These creatures, though credited with human reasoning, do not appear in complete human form; one spirit is a leg, another an arm, another a body without a head. . . .[1] These dismembered monstrosities are all so dangerous to the traveller that if he only catches a glimpse of one of them he is bound to die. In addition to *zwidhadyani*, there are spirits living in streams and pools, a small and war-like people with human form; they are always armed with bows and arrows and . . . bring death to anyone who has the misfortune to encounter them (Stayt 1931a: 238–9).

The Venda also believe that individuals, particularly chiefs, return to earth in the form of animals.

The Nguni generally do not have this proliferation of nature spirits. But certain Cape Nguni, especially the Xhosa, speak of 'people of the river' (*abantu bomlambo*), who 'are believed to live in deep pools and to work harm on victims, particularly at night; even when they remain invisible to their victims, they cause illness, blindness, or mental derangement' (Wilson *et al.* 1952: 191). In Pondoland the 'people of the river' (*abantu base mlanjeni*) are clan ancestors but this does not seem to be true of the Xhosa, although there is evidence that certain of their clans, especially the Ngqosini, are somehow connected with them (De Jager and Gitywa 1963: 110). Sacrifices of maize, sorghum and tobacco are made at intervals at the deep pools associated with the *abantu bomlambo*. Diviners are frequently believed to be initiated by the 'people of the river', being called into the river for several days and emerging as fully-fledged specialists. The Ciskeian Xhosa believe that crocodiles (long extinct in the area) are the messengers of the *abantu bomlambo* and lure people into the pools (Hunter 1936: 488). It is difficult to place this complex of ideas. It appears to operate separately from the ancestor cult and, even in Pondoland, there is evidence that the cult of *ukunikelo emlanjeni*, in which sacrifices are made to propitiate the river, is giving way to magical treatment to 'push away' the people of the river, who are often conceptualized as snakes. Hunter states that the river people are seldom if ever referred to as *amathongo* (ancestral shades) but as *amatshologu*, which she defines as 'an evil manifestation of the ancestral spirits' and that 'the thing to which the offering is made in the river is predominantly harmful' (Hunter 1936: 263).

The Zulu are unique in possessing a nature goddess, *Nomkhubulwana*, the Princess of Heaven, who was honoured by the women and girls of local districts of Zululand and Natal when the crops began to shoot.[2] Samuelson, a missionary, describes the Princess as being

> robed with light as a garment and having come down from heaven to teach people to make beer, to plant, to harvest, and all the useful arts. . . . She is a maiden and she makes her visit to the earth in the Spring of the year. She is also described as presenting the appearance of a beautiful landscape with verdant forests on some parts of her body, grass-covered slopes on others, and cultivated slopes on others. She is said to be the maker of rain (Samuelson 1929: 303).

If no rites were performed for her she was offended and blighted the grain: she is thus a goddess of the same kind as the corn gods and goddesses of the ancient world, although obviously no direct connection can be postulated. The main rites in propitiation of *Nomkhubulwana* involved transvestisism and a role reversal in which girls put on male attire and herded and milked the normally tabooed cattle, while their mothers planted a garden out in the veld and poured a libation of beer over it. Thereafter this garden was neglected. 'At various stages of the ceremonies women and girls went naked, and sang lewd songs. Men and boys hid and might not go near' (Gluckman 1954: 5).[3] *Nomkhubulwana* is unique among South African deities in that she is female and is obviously a personification of the spring. Privileged access to cattle and ritual obscenities are found among Tsonga, Thembu and Bhaca, but the Thembu instances are associated with a girl's first menstruation (Maclean 1858a: 102), and the others mentioned in the literature are connected with the driving away of an insect pest.

The Sotho tribes appear not to have developed the concept of nature spirits to the same degree as the Zulu and Venda, although the Pedi speak of a cave in the mountains called *Mašankotane* inhabited by certain *badimo* [spirits] to whom people of the nearby village regularly sacrifice, and certain valleys and woods are described as dwelling places of the *badimo* (Mönnig 1967: 62). The Tswana also refer to *Lôwê, Tintibane, Matsieng* and *Thobêga*, 'demi-gods associated with caves and archaic footprints' who appear to be deified chiefs of peoples occupying the country long before the present inhabitants arrived. 'Offerings are occasionally made to them of meat, corn and beer, accompanied by prayers for rain, fertility of crops, and success in war' (Willoughby 1932: 36–40; Brown 1926: 101ff.). The treeless mountains of Lesotho do not seem to have stimulated the creation of nature spirits.

The function of these nature and local spirits would appear to be to provide explanations for aspects of the environment which, for various reasons, instil an emotion of awe and sense of the uncanny. Caves, woods, silent reaches of water and secluded pools, fossilized footprints, all impress with fear or intellectual interest and demand explanation, and this is made in terms of spirit beings. The exception is *Nomkhubulwana* who is quite clearly, as we have seen, the personification of the spring. It is strange that no other Bantu tribe has felt the need to make this apotheosis.

Among Swazi (Kuper 1947: 193-6), Tsonga (Junod 1927 II: 376), Venda (Stayt 1931a: 236), and some Mpondo groups, certain woods are considered sacred as they are the burial places of chiefs. Kuper's description of the Swazi sacred groves is particularly graphic:

> Kings are buried in caves far from their villages. Round the caves are dense forests with impenetrable undergrowth broken by narrow footpaths. The air is full of noises. . . . Huge snakes glide through the trees and are praised as kings. The groves can only be entered in safety with the assistance of the keepers, trusted men appointed as chiefs over the surrounding locality. . . . Woe betide the man who stumbles unaware into the grove, for he will not be able to get out unless the keeper hears his call and releases him with the sacrifice of a beast to the powerful captors (Kuper 1947: 194).

Among the imiZizi of Pondoland the custom of burying chiefs in woods is said to have been borrowed from the Zulu (each chief is buried in a different wood and no one may approach or gather wood there), but the Mpondo proper bury a chief at the gate of his cattle byre—and this also appears to have been Zulu custom (Krige 1936a: 172). Among the Pedi 'certain valleys or woods [are] described as dwelling places of the *badimo*', apparently conceptualized as ancestral spirits; these places are avoided, except when sacrifices are made.

The Ancestral Spirits

The spiritual beings discussed above are in reality peripheral to South African tribal religions. Their function is to provide intellectually and emotionally satisfying explanations for certain important aspects of impersonal nature and awe-inspiring phenomena. But most of man's personal problems flow, not from the natural environment, however hostile, but from his relationships with his fellow men. The mere fact of living together in society divides man from man in families, lineages and territorial units, each with its own sense of solidarity, bought at the price of hostility to other, like, groups. In addition, there is always differential access to desired goods and competition for scarce resources, whether they be land, cattle or women. Men are always in competition with one another and the great human problem is that of good interpersonal relations. Religious and moral systems everywhere have something to say about this; everywhere they lay down norms of behaviour and provide occasions for the symbolic expression of these norms—and sanctions to prevent their breach. There are, of course, other social mechanisms for coping with conflict situations. All South African tribes have hierarchies of courts for dispute settlement, and joking relations, in some tribes, provide an outlet for possible frustrations and psychological tensions arising from 'difficult' relationships, as between in-laws and between patrilineal and matrilineal kin. Social pressures such as ridicule, ostracism and the like work towards conformity. But these mechanisms are imperfect: the fundamental norms and values must be restated with a greater than human authority—and everywhere this authority is conceptualized as residing in supernatural or super-empirical beings. Among the Bantu these beings are the ancestors (Zulu: *amadlozi* or *amathongo*; Cape Nguni: *amathongo* or *izi(imi)nyanya*; Tsonga: *shikwembu*; Lobedu: *vadimo* or *zwiḑajani*; Tswana: *medimo* or *badimo*; Venda: *midzimu*; Pedi and South Sotho: *badimo*).

The ancestors are the spirits of the dead members of the lineage or clan. The nature of these unilineal descent groups has been discussed in chapter 6: suffice it to say here that in all tribes the clan is widely dispersed and does not have any corporate functions, its main role being to define exogamic rules (among the Nguni) and provide scattered kin from whom hospitality can be expected when on a journey. Lineages are *demonstrated* descent groups in which actual relationships to an apical ancestor can be traced. They differ in generation depth and geographical dispersion. Among the strongly patrilineal Nguni the Mpondomise lineages are from five to six generations (Hammond-Tooke 1968a: 30), the Ndlambe from three to five generations (Bigalke 1969: 48), the Mfengu three to four generations (Wilson *et al.* 1952: 56). They probably, therefore, average four to six generations in depth, although royal lineages tend, of course, to be deeper. Lineages were almost certainly deeper in the past. It appears that the lineage depth of other South African tribes tends to be much the same. Although we have no actual figures for lineage depth among the Pedi, examples given refer to lineages (or lineage remnants) of three or four generations (Mönnig 1967: 231), and Ashton speaks of lineages with 'the common ancestor no more than three or four or five generations removed' among the South Sotho (1952: 16). It is explicitly stated that, among the Pedi, 'An ordinary family will not worship its ancestors for more than two or three generations back, while lineage heads may be recalled for as many as five generations. The ancestors of the chiefs are naturally remembered the longest' (Mönnig 1967: 57). Among the Lobedu, Tsonga and Venda the patrilineal emphasis is not as unequivocal as among Nguni and Sotho. Among the Lobedu 'the lineages pale into insignificance beside the marriage or the bilateral kin groups' (Krige and Krige 1943: 86) and, according to Stayt, among the Venda, although descent, succession and inheritance are reckoned through the father, 'every individual is also a member of a parallel lineage on the mother's side, very important in social and religious life'. Whereas the lineage ancestors in the male line are the effective shades among the Nguni and Sotho, among the Lobedu, Venda and Tsonga both paternal and maternal ancestors are remembered and have influence over their descendants (see below). Among the Lobedu the bilateral recognition of ancestors involves a much more limited section of the lineage, the cult being extended instead to all four lines of grandparents; in fact

> The spirits that cause most trouble are one's grandparents, and in religious practices these tend to be the most important. Both sides of the family,

that of one's father and that of one's mother, are equally important. . . . Even when a spirit in the line of the father's father is being placated, the line of the father's mother may also be mentioned (Krige and Krige 1943: 239).

Among the Venda only paternal ancestors are normally addressed, but female ancestors of the patrilineage, standing in the relationship of *makhadzi* (father's sister) are sometimes included in invocations (van Warmelo 1932: 186, 174, 160; Stayt 1931a: 242).

This raises the question as to who become ancestors. Although among the Pedi 'There is no question of the spirit of any person being barred from the world of the ancestral spirits (*badimong*)' (Mönnig 1967: 55), this generalization does not hold for all groups and, certainly, not all dead kinsmen are invoked at rituals. To answer this question something must be said of traditional beliefs in the afterlife.

All groups believe in a life after death. A dualism is recognized between the body and what may perhaps be called the 'soul', although this, of course, is imposing Western categories on a traditional concept which need not necessarily have the same semantic range. Among the South Sotho 'Man (*motho*) is believed to be composed of two elements: the corporeal body ('*mele*) or flesh (*nama*), and the incorporeal spirit (*moea*, which also means the wind) or shadow (*seriti*)' (Ashton 1952: 112). The Venda also 'think the soul is a combination of the breath and the shadow' and Stayt comments: 'It is curious how fixed the idea is among them that a corpse throws no shadow' (1931a: 241). Mönnig's exegesis of Pedi beliefs defines a tripartite conception —that of body (*mmele*), *moya* (soul) and spirit (*sereti*), in which the breath and the shadow are clearly distinguished. *Moya* (lit. 'breath', 'wind'), the life principle, is suffused throughout the whole body and the body cannot live without it, while the shadow can leave the body temporarily. He equates the *sereti* concept with, among other things, the personality (Mönnig 1967: 48–50). The Zulu call the 'soul' *idlozi* or *ithongo*, but here again there is a strong association with a 'hazily defined something called *isiThunzi* (shadow or personality)' which is intimately connected with the spirit 'for they say that the shadow is that which will ultimately become the *ithongo* or spirit when the body dies' (Krige 1936a: 284). Among the Cape Nguni concepts are vaguer. Among the Mpondo there 'is no orthodox theory as to what becomes the *ithongo*', although some associate it with the breath (*umphefumlo*) (Hunter 1936: 232), as do the Bhaca and Xhosa, who also use the word *umoya* (wind) for this posthumous manifestation of the breath (Hammond-Tooke 1962: 227; Bigalke 1969: 75). Among the Cape Nguni generally the shadow does not appear to be so clearly linked with the spirit as in most of the other tribes. The term *isithunzi* is used among them to describe the slightly sinister and malevolent aura that inheres in the personality of powerful men, especially chiefs. Among the Tsonga a 'third name for the soul' is *ntjhuti*, or *shitjhuti*, which means 'shadow' (Junod 1927 II: 362).

There is often lack of clarity as to whether all deceased persons in fact achieve immortality. Among the Mpondo

> All 'old people' (*abantu abadala*) who die become *amathongo* (ancestral spirits), and can influence the lives of their descendants. What happens to children and young persons after death is not clear. Most think that they also become *amathongo*, but add, 'We do not know what happens to them. We only hear about old people asking for meat'. . . . The dividing line is not between those who have had children and those who have had none, but between those who had weight and influence before their death and those who died while still children, or young men and women (Hunter 1936: 231).

The Bhaca are similarly vague, but some maintain that only married people become ancestors, and Ashton implies the same for the South Sotho (Ashton 1952: 114 fnt. 2). The Tsonga believe that every human being becomes an ancestor (*shikwembu*), but the fate of children dying in infancy 'is one of the points about which there is no very clear explanation' (Junod 1927 II: 373-4). The information on the Pedi is more explicit. The 'spirits of young people, and particularly of children, go to their forefathers, but do not become *badimo*'. All, however, live in the world of the dead, the only exception being those buried without the necessary rites being performed. 'Such spirits become ghosts (*setšhoša*). . . . They haunt their graves in the form of a bright light, and also haunt the homes of their descendants, making life unpleasant for them' (Mönnig 1967: 55).

The body itself is disposed of by burial—except among the Xhosa among whom, Alberti relates, corpses of commoners were exposed in the veld to be devoured by hyenas, although chiefs were buried in the cattle byre (Alberti 1810: 93–5). In most groups family heads and important people are buried in the cattle kraal or close to its fence, less important men, women and children in the hut or, more commonly, in some convenient place nearby. Variations occur in the positioning of the body but a recess is commonly dug in the side of the grave and the corpse is placed in a sitting position, often accompanied by its more intimate personal belongings and other objects. Thus, among the South Sotho, kaffir-corn, gourds and pumpkin seeds (said to be the original food of the Sotho) are placed on or near the body, with wisps of *mohloa*, a grass symbolizing family and community life because it grows near settlements, and *molile* grass, both plaited into miniature platters. A man's snuffbox, milking pail and thong, and a woman's porridge stick, are also buried with the corpse (Ashton 1952: 106). Both the Zulu and Sotho chiefs were buried on occasion with some of their councillors and body servants to accompany them and, according to Samuelson (1929: 291), some of the wives of a Zulu king might be buried with him. Among the Mpondomise a number of chiefs were buried in rivers to prevent molestation by witches.

But the mere fact of death and interment does not necessarily make an ancestral spirit. Although among the Mpondo 'Since the living person is a potential *ithongo* there is no hiatus between death and the possibility of the deceased influencing his descendants' (Hunter 1936: 232), in some other tribes a special ritual is needed to effect the change of status. Perhaps that with the most explicit symbolism is the *ukubuyisa idlozi* ritual of the Zulu, 'the bringing home of the spirit of the deceased', which takes place a year or two after his death. The ritual is only performed for men, especially the kraal head, and its neglect can bring about misfortune. An ox is sacrificed and choice portions are placed on the *umsamo*, the sacred place at the back of the hut especially associated with the ancestors. At the ritual the name of the deceased is included in the praises of the ancestors for the first time after his death and he is specifically requested to return to his home and care for his descendants. 'Often, as a further measure to ensure his return, the officiator, his eldest son, takes the branch of a tree and drags it from the grave into the house, by this process bringing him home' (Krige 1936a: 169–70). A similar ritual occurs among the Xhosa among whom the burial is followed by the ritual killing of an ox to *khapha* (accompany) the deceased to the land of the spirits and, a year or so later, the *ukuguqula* or *ukubuyisa* ritual ('to cause to turn back', 'to cause to return') which re-integrates him into the corporation of the lineage (Bigalke 1969: 80). This formal re-incorporation of the spirit appears to be typically Nguni, although the Kriges quote 'an interesting though unusual killing among the Lobedu called the "bringing home" of a spirit', in this case a young man stabbed to death in a Johannesburg compound, who was 'complaining' and bringing illness to his brother's children. It is not associated with mortuary rituals, however (Krige and Krige 1943: 238).

Ideas about the abode of the dead are vague, but the most generally accepted view is that it is underground (Pedi, Venda, South Sotho, Tswana, Tsonga, Mpondo, Bhaca, Zulu). However, there are alternative theories, often held by individuals. Among the Pedi 'Some say it is underground, others say it is in the skies above, others again that it lies where the sun sets, in the west. The latter seems to be the largest consensus of opinion' (Mönnig 1967: 53–4). Ashton states that present-day Sotho deny that the future life is lived underground, but both he and Casalis stress that this was the original Sotho belief (Ashton 1952: 113; Casalis, 1861: 247). Tsonga ideas are confused and contradictory. 'Some say that the departed go to a great village *under the earth*, where they live in abundance and have many cattle, but there is also the idea that the spirit remains in the grave' (Junod 1927 II: 375–6). A similar belief is found among the Venda (Stayt 1931a: 241). Among the Cape Nguni there is the idea that the spirits brood over the homestead (Bigalke 1969: 76). Life in the spirit world is much like that on earth but is idealized as a land of plenty: for the Pedi it is also a shadow world, 'where the shadows are longest' (Mönnig 1967: 54).

The ancestral spirits, then, are the collective lineage dead. This aspect of collectivity is important and is expressed in the fact that the vernacular term for them is almost never used in the singular form. This has been specifically noted for the South Sotho (Ashton 1952: 114 footnote), Tswana (Brown

1926: 109), Pedi, (Mönnig 1967: 54), Mpondomise (Hammond-Tooke 1968a: 41) and Xhosa (Bigalke 1969: 76), and is implicit for all tribes. Within this undifferentiated group of ancestral spirits it would seem analytically useful to distinguish between the 'shades', or ancestors as a whole, and 'communicating ancestors', those specifically invoked in rituals.[4] The ancestor cult operates, then, against a general background of lineage dead who are often thought to be present at rituals, even although a particular ritual is not being performed for them.

The communicating ancestors are more specifically determined by the social structure. Among the Nguni generally they tend to be those who occupy nodal positions in the articulation of lineage segments. It seems that whether or not a person becomes a communicating ancestor depends on his position in the lineage structure, particularly on whether he forms a point of segmentation between segments in the lineage genealogies. Among the Mpondo

> The officiant begins with the name of his nearest direct ascendant who is dead (his father or grandfather) and continues with what names in the family tree he remembers, working back to the founder of the clan, or further. Personal names, not *izibongo* (praise names), are used. A general invitation to all the *amathongo* is given, although one may have been particularly diagnosed as sending sickness (Hunter 1936: 248).

Among the Zulu

> the *amaThongo* are called upon in order of age, beginning with the first known ancestor and going down the line on the *indlunkulu* [great house] side. Then all those on the *iKhohlwa* side that are known to the officiator are mentioned, and finally at the end, the priest may say to the ancestors, 'Call all of our sib, do not leave anyone out, but call those that I have not mentioned, and those that I do not know' (E. J. Krige 1936a: 292–3).

The Mpondomise, however, never pray to or call on any specific lineage shade, but always to the lineage dead as a whole. Ritual killings are made on a large number of occasions, but it is only at specific killings to propitiate a spirit who has been divined as causing sickness (called by the genetic term *iidini*) that the calling of the names of ancestors (*nqula*) is done. In no case is the name of any of the dead lineage members, represented on the family tree, even mentioned, but always the names of four or five *clan* ancestors, with their praises. Often a discussion is held before the ritual to make sure of the names to be called, or a member versed in these matters is told off to do the actual calling. This ignoring of individual lineage dead is explicitly confirmed by informants. 'When a person makes a sacrifice he prays to no particular shade but does it for all the dead people of his home. We never speak of *isinyanya* [singular]—it is always in the plural.' 'You do not call all the names because by calling the older names you include them all. Even if you recognize an ancestor in a dream, and you know that he is asking for meat, you will not specially call his name. He is included in the invocation of the clan ancestors' (Hammond-Tooke 1968a: 40–1).

Now this raises several important issues. It means that, ideally, among the Mpondomise the lineage is conceptualized as a unitary group, under one ritual leader and that the constituent segments have no ritual status of their own. Second, the lineage is an undifferentiated unit in respect of its object of worship. One does not find, as among the Mpondo, members of each segment worshipping their own particular 'set' of segment shades, e.g. father, grandfather, and great-grandfather, until the names unite with the lineage genealogy at the point of bifurcation. The integrity of the lineage as a whole is thus at all times symbolically insisted upon (Hammond-Tooke 1968a). Among the Cape Nguni generally a woman, if she marries, is influenced by two sets of shades—those of her own lineage and those of her husband's. 'If my mother is sick the sickness might be sent from two places: either from her own *umti* [homestead] or from her husband's place' (Hammond-Tooke 1962: 234).

Among other tribes the emphasis is more on *particular* ancestors, probably reflecting the lesser importance of the lineage among them. Among the Pedi, 'The immortality of the ancestral spirits is of practical and religious importance for a few generations only. Beyond that they are hardly remembered. An ordinary family will not worship its ancestors for more than two or three generations back, while lineage heads may be recalled for as many as five generations' (Mönnig 1967: 57). The position for the Lobedu is strikingly similar: 'The immortality of Lovedu spirits is of practical importance in their working religion only for two or three generations back; beyond this they are hardly remembered' (Krige and Krige 1943: 239), and, as we have seen, in this tribe both sides of the family are important. Among the Pedi, Lobedu and Tswana, we are told that the spirits of the more recent deceased are the most important: among the South Sotho, on the other hand, 'It was believed that the earlier gods were more powerful than the more recent ancestors so that many prayers began . . . "New gods pray to us to the gods of old"' (Ashton 1952: 115).

There does seem to be an important difference here between the Nguni and all other South African Bantu peoples. On the one hand we have a fairly undifferentiated group of ancestors, all of whom are called to sacrifices, and which reflects the importance of lineage and clan solidarity in Nguni social structure. On the other hand, among the other groups the patrilineage is not as important (among the Sotho, including the Lobedu, it is not exogamous) and religious emphasis is on particular, specified ancestors, usually a father or grandfather, and, among Venda and Lobedu, also on maternal ancestors (see below). It would appear that the Nguni fit more clearly than the others into Fortes's explanation of the impersonality of the ancestor cult (and the relative lack of interest in the after life) as being due to the fact that what is being worshipped is not the total personality of the deceased, but a jural principle that underlies the society, viz. the importance of paternal authority and filial piety (Fortes 1965).

The importance of the ancestors is that they continue to take close interest

WORLD-VIEW I: A SYSTEM OF BELIEFS

in the affairs of their descendants. But their attitude and actions tend to be unpredictable, and this is reflected in a marked ambiguity towards them on the part of their worshippers. Generally speaking they are benevolent and cast in the role of mentors and protectors. Among the Lobedu, 'They are one's protectors and no harm can befall one unless they . . . are neglectful. Witches, powerful as they are, can neither enter the village nor cause sickness without their connivance. . . . Disease cannot enter nor epidemic break out if only the ancestors are watchful enough and well disposed.' They are responsible for the fertility of crops (Krige and Krige 1943: 231–2). Ashton comments for the South Sotho that

> In spite of the apprehension with which they are regarded individually, the spirits of the dead are not regarded as necessarily malevolent. On the contrary, the *balimo* are expected to take an interest in their survivors' material well-being. They have some influence over the crops and can improve the harvest if they want to. . . . Their help is both sought and acknowledged at the end of each season by . . . gifts (Ashton 1952: 114).

The picture is similar for the Mpondo. 'On the whole the *amathongo* are propitious to their descendants. They see and hear everything that is done. They have the power to send health to man and beast, to increase property, to ensure good crops. Men returning from a fight praised (*ukubonga*) their ancestors for having saved them. . . . If they were to desert a man, misfortune would befall him at once', and 'Although the *amathongo* cannot secure a man against sorcery or witchcraft, and are never appealed to through a ritual killing when the sickness is diagnosed as due to either, they are some defence against it' (Hunter 1936: 234).

But if the ancestors were merely benevolent they would not play such a vital part in Bantu religion. The fact of the matter is that the ancestors are capricious, jealous and easily offended, and their wrath is an important explanation for misfortune. The South Sotho ancestors appear to be particularly troublesome, for Ashton states that formerly *all* illness was attributed to them 'in the belief that they continually tried to compass the death of the living in order to secure their companionship' but that only a few maladies, such as hysteria, insomnia and epilepsy, are ascribed to them today (Ashton 1952: 115). This seems to be an extreme case. More usually, they complain of neglect, especially neglect of custom. Among the Nguni they also complain of being hungry, but this is not common among other tribes. Lobedu ancestors, for instance, never complain of being hungry but desire rather to be remembered; 'they want their beads worn, their name revived, a beast or goat dedicated or named after them' (Krige and Krige 1943: 233).

The general attitude of the living to the dead reflects a certain irritation with the idiosyncracies of the gods—in fact Pedi rituals are explicitly stated as being aimed at preventing them from interfering in the lives of their descendants, 'to keep them away or to get rid of them' (Mönnig 1967: 60). The general attitude between worshipped and worshipper lacks the aura of reverence and adoration associated with, for instance, Christianity. The Lobedu are typical of the Bantu generally. 'We must not expect a behaviour pattern of humble worshipper to omnipotent good. . . . People pray to ancestors as man to man, scolding them or reminding them of their duties to their children. . . . As the gods have human attributes, "worship" is not characterized by humility or formality. . . . Religion is cheerful' (Krige and Krige 1943: 239–40), and Junod says of the Tsonga: 'The attitude of the worshippers . . . the freedom they show in insulting their gods, indicates that they consider them as exactly on the same level as themselves' (1927 II: 425). What we know of the Venda would seem to indicate, however, a greater reverence towards the spirits of the deceased.

Ancestors make their wishes known in two main ways—either through dreams or by illness that is subsequently divined as being 'sent' by them. Dreams are reported for all the tribes, although the Kriges comment that this is far less true for the Lobedu than for Nguni (Krige and Krige 1943: 232). Among the South Sotho: 'If the dead are only just glimpsed in a dream, it may not mean much more than that they are still interested in and fond of one; but if they appear looking cross or loving, it is serious and means either that they are angry with one or longing for one to join them' (Ashton 1952: 114). Wrath caused by neglect of ritual and custom will be discussed more fully in the following chapter.

A further peculiarity in some tribes is a belief that ancestors sometimes appear in the form of animals. This is true especially for the Venda, Zulu and some Cape Nguni. Among the Venda it is typically a chiefly ancestor that returns after death in the form of an animal, usually a lion, but two headmen had leopards 'connected with their ancestors' and one lineage believes that its ancestors turn into snakes (Stayt 1931a: 239–40). The Zulu associate snakes with a visiting spirit (Krige 1936a):

> A chief or village head turns into a black or green *mamba*. . . . When such a snake visits a kraal, the daughters-in-law of the deceased put on their veils and *hlonipha*, and a beast is usually slaughtered for it. . . . A young *mamba* is, however, the spirit of a male child and the Zulus believe this to be distinct species, calling it *umHlwazi*. Chieftainesses turn into an *umSenene*, a large, brown, non-poisonous snake, and common people may become . . . another light brown, non-poisonous and rather sluggish snake, or . . . a small harmless brown snake, very fond of sleeping in huts. . . . The spirit-snake is usually known by the resemblance it bears to the man whom it represents: a lame man is known by the lameness of the snake: anyone with only one eye will turn into a snake with only one eye: while most snakes are recognized by the marks of injuries which they bear, injuries that they received when alive on earth.

Another characteristic of the spirit-snake is that 'when looking at a man it does not look like an animal that fears to be killed, it looks without alarm. . . . It moves about the whole house and fears nothing' (Krige 1936a: 285–6).

WORLD-VIEW I: A SYSTEM OF BELIEFS

Among the Mpondo the ancestral spirit responsible for the 'calling' of a diviner may take the shape of an *ityala*, i.e. a wild animal such as a lion, leopard or elephant, but this manifestation is confined to this context. The diviner and her relatives show respect towards her *ityala* by not killing it, eating its flesh or mentioning its name (Hunter 1936: 321–2).

Although no buildings as such are dedicated to the ancestors, all tribes have certain places associated specially with them. Among the Nguni these are the cattle byre itself, in which all killings are made, and the raised niche found at the back of the great hut, above which the entrails of the sacrifice are hung (see e.g. Hammond-Tooke 1962: 240). Dieterlen mentions that 'as part of their domestic cult, some Basuto have a little niche at the back of their hut, where they store the gall bladders of sacrificial animals and keep overnight beer used on semi-religious occasions' (Dieterlen 1930: 141), but the nearest approach to this that Ashton could discover in the 1940s was 'the practice of pouring some of the bile of sacrificial or ceremonial animals (such as the sheep killed to celebrate a birth) on the floor at the back of the hut' (Ashton 1952: 116). Among the Pedi 'There are no shrines erected to the ancestors' (Mönnig 1967: 62).

The Lobedu make shrines 'which are to be found generally on the left-hand side of the entrance to the sleeping hut of the chief wife'. They vary greatly in form and may consist of a small mound of earth, containing the bones of a sacrificial goat, a sacred plant or tree, a black river stone or a piece of ant heap (Krige and Krige 1943: 234).

The Venda have a number of ritual objects associated with the cult. Many important lineages have a black bull, 'regarded as the embodiment of all the ancestral spirits' (see Plates 15a and 15b), and those of lesser importance have large, cylindrical river stones to represent the actual animal. Both bull and stone are addressed as *makhulu* (grandfather). Maternal ancestors are represented by a black female goat, and there are other sacred objects, called collectively *zwitungulo*, such as axes, hoes, *masila* cloth, old horns, copper ingots, beads, etc. which formerly belonged to the ancestors, which are guarded jealously and regarded with awe. They are often used in ritual 'and are addressed in a personal manner as though they were actually the homes of the person whom they represent' (Stayt 1931a: 242–9). The Lobedu have similar objects called *thugula* (Krige and Krige 1943: 233) and the Tsonga 'altar' (*gandjelo*) is a small pot placed at the right side of the entrance to the village (Junod 1927 I: 320; II: 388).

Extra-Descent Group Ancestors

Although all South African societies are patrilineal and worship primarily the ancestors in the male line, there remain the ancestors of the mother's lineage called, by McKnight, 'extra-descent group ancestors' (McKnight 1967: 1). Among some tribes, for example the Venda, Lobedu and Tsonga, ancestors on both sides appear to enjoy equal standing. Stayt records that

'The ancestral spirits which can affect the lives of individuals are divided into two groups, those of the father's lineage and those of the mother's group', and specifies particularly the mother's brother, mother's mother, mother's mother's brother and mother's mother's sister. 'The spirits of the mothers play a separate and peculiar role in the ancestor cult of the BaVenda.' They are represented by a black female goat, in contrast to the sacred cattle or stones of the paternal spirits and, in fact, 'The ancestral spirits of the mothers' group have the most powerful influence on their descendants.' The reason for this is to be found in Venda conceptions of the composition of the body, specifically that the body of the child is built up from menstrual blood, so that all illnesses connected with blood, with a few rare exceptions, come from the mother's side of the family. In this case sacrifice is made by the mother's brother (Stayt 1931a: 240–1, 259–61, 251). 'We have then two effective groups of spirits, one confined to the father and his ancestors in the male line and the other to the mother and her ancestors in the female line, forming a dual organization whose spirits inhabit respectively the sacred bull and the sacred goat' (Stayt 1931a: 260).

The Tsonga also stress the importance of the maternal ancestors and both father's and mother's ancestors are of 'equal dignity', but here the attitude of maternal ancestors to their descendants is ostensibly the reverse of that reported for the Venda. Junod comments: 'It would seem, however, as if the gods of the mother's side were more tender-hearted and popular than those of the father's' (Junod 1927 II: 374). Yet he gives a detailed description of a sacrifice for a sister's son by a mother's brother because the disease was being caused by the maternal ancestors (1927 II: 396) and, in discussing misfortunes sent by the ancestors in general, quotes, 'perhaps the gods of your mother have done this, because you had not given your paternal uncle the tjumba part of the lobolo, which he has a right to claim' (1912 ed. I: 360–1). Although the Tsonga extra-descent group ancestors are not, as among the Venda, 'more important' (in the sense of being a major cause of trouble), it is clear that they, too, can directly affect the life of their daughter's children.

For the Lobedu, as we have seen, the picture is similar. 'Both sides of the family, that of one's father and that of one's mother are equally important; both cause trouble and both must be placated; and this is an accurate reflection of the social structure, of relationships reckoned bilaterally, and of the cattle links' (Krige and Krige 1943: 239).

Among the Pedi, Tswana and Sotho generally, there does not appear to be this bilateral emphasis, although, among the South Sotho, 'A few special cases, notably ulcers called *setsoa*, are curable only by the maternal ancestors who have to be approached through the patient's maternal uncle or his representative' (Ashton 1952: 115).

The position among the Nguni is similar to the Sotho. Hunter writes that 'An old diviner commented on the fact that a mother's *amathongo* are not thought to influence her child', in the sense of healing it, but it seems that the mother's spirits can send sickness.

WORLD-VIEW I: A SYSTEM OF BELIEFS

A child is never sacrificed for to its mother's *amathongo* even though it is sometimes obvious that the child has inherited the disease from its mother, (that is, that its mother's *amathongo* are troubling it). In such a case a ritual killing is made at the father's *umzi* to the *amathongo* of the child's father. If the child does not recover people say, 'That proves it, the *amathongo* of the mother are responsible,' yet no ritual killing is made for them (Hunter 1936: 233).

The Bhaca also do not sacrifice to the maternal ancestors although, here too, they may cause sickness and even death to a wife's children (Hammond-Tooke 1962: 119–20). Where maternal ancestors *are* important among the Nguni is in connection with divination which, among them, is closely connected with the ancestor cult and involves possession by an ancestral spirit (see chapter 11). Here it is almost invariably the maternal ancestors who 'call' the novice to her profession. McKnight has suggested that the power attributed to the extra-descent group ancestors is a means of enforcing rights over members of an affinally-related descent group, particularly as the sister's son is in an ambiguous position between two descent-groups.

> It is therefore not surprising that the sister's son may be used as a vehicle of revenge by the bridewealth-receiving group to enforce their rights. . . . To settle quarrels and disputes with affines solely by means of physical force would mean the destruction of the affinal ties. This is resolved to some degree by the use of mystical sanctions, by the actions of the extra-descent group ancestors (1967: 16).

Witchcraft, Sorcery and the Problem of Evil

Both religious and magico-witchcraft belief systems provide alternative theories as to the causes of evil, illness and misfortune—and whether one or other is employed raises important questions of values and structural relations. It is as if both religion and the witch myth recognize a duality in the universe, that between a state of affairs that is right, moral, normal, good, healthy and safe, and one which is wrong, immoral, bad, unhealthy, abnormal and dangerous—and provide explanations for them and techniques for converting one to the other. A state of negative imbalance between natural and social forces must be returned to an equilibrium in which good relationship to the gods, to the forces of nature and to one's fellowman, must be re-achieved. The signs of this imbalance are essentially, among the South African Bantu, immediate, obvious and physical. Sickness, misfortune, drought, are all signs that the balance has been upset, and one of the main objects of religious ritual and the resort to divination and protective magic is to restore it. Both religious and witchcraft beliefs are utilized to explain and control misfortune but, as we have seen, it is the witch beliefs which more specifically handle the problem of evil in the universe.

There is thus a strong similarity in aim between indigenous religion and witchcraft. They are merely two different theoretical explanations of the phenomena, with different techniques for coping with it. Both reject the Western idea of chance. The concept of chance is an important (and necessary) one in our scientific Western world-view. We have been taught to explain events by means of a complicated chain of cause and effect sequences which explain *how* things happen. But we cannot explain by this means *why* something happens. We know that a man contracts malaria through being infected by a micro-organism, and that this organism was introduced through the bite of an insect vector, but we do not know why this particular man and not another (subjected to the same environmental and nutritional risks) escaped infection. We say it was by chance. But that this is an emotionally unsatisfactory explanation, especially for the sufferer, is shown by the reluctance to let the explanation rest there. Perhaps most people, struck down by illness, ask themselves further questions—what have *they* done to deserve this affliction or (if they are religious) in what way have they sinned?

None of the South African Bantu have the concept of chance in their world-view. Apart from death from extreme age and minor illnesses such as chills and stomach upsets, all deaths and occasions of misfortune are believed to be caused ('sent') by some external agent. This agent may be a supernatural being in its own right, or a human being using supernatural means. In the first case it is the ancestors who are sending the misfortune, in punishment for some breach of custom: in the latter the agent is human, a witch or sorcerer.

There is an important difference between these two sources of misfortune. Ancestrally sent misfortune is an explicit punishment for breach of religious or kinship duty which a man brings upon himself by his own actions. The diagnosis of an ancestral origin of misfortune, therefore, points squarely to the blameworthiness of the victim or his guardian and (presumably) gives rise to guilt feelings. If, however, the misfortune is diagnosed as due to the operation of witchcraft or sorcery, no fault attaches to the victim. He is a target of malevolence from outside himself. This could be explained as a projection of hate and envy existing in the victim's own mind, in which there might well be repressed feelings of guilt. Often a man believes another is antagonistic to him because he himself has negative feelings towards the other.

The other difference is that whereas ancestrally sent illness is bad, it is not evil. Illness caused naturally or by the ancestors is generally curable: it is only witchcraft and sorcery that really kill. Ancestral wrath is more in the nature of paternal admonition of a neglectful and recalcitrant son. It is in the nature of fathers to become impatient and chastise their offspring for neglected duty. Witchcraft or sorcery, on the other hand, is entirely evil. It represents the dark, malevolent urgings that lie at the heart of man—the product of hate, envy, revenge and malice. It threatens the very basis of social life and must be detected and combated with every means at one's disposal. It represents the African version of medieval demonology with which it has, of course, close parallels.

Witch Beliefs

The witch and the sorcerer are individuals who use their powers and the forces of nature to harm other people. Anthropologists usually reserve the term 'witch' for someone who harms others by means of a psychic force or manifestation. Apparently this may be unconscious, as among the Tsonga and Venda, or quite explicitly conscious as among the Lobedu, Nguni and Sotho. In both cases, however, witchcraft proclivities are believed to be inherited and, interestingly, the witch is usually believed to be a woman. The Venda and Tsonga believe that the witch (*muloi*) is quite unaware of her powers and is perfectly normal during the day, but at night her spirit leaves her sleeping body and goes out naked to wreak harm on her victim. Witches know each other and meet in the bush to eat human flesh and discuss their deeds. 'The more powerful may compel the less powerful to bring them human flesh and the witch must often kill her own loved ones': it is this idea of treason against the kin group itself, an attack on the very basis of the social structure, which makes witch-activity such a heinous offence. It is the quintessence of immorality.

Among other groups the conscious factor of malevolence and bad faith is crucial: an explicit use of these dark powers to harm an enemy. Anthropologists distinguish between this use of a psychic, personalized power, either used by the witch herself or through the vehicle of familiars (*witchcraft*) from *sorcery*, the use of magical substances, e.g. medicines, charms, etc., often used with excrement, nail parings, hair clippings and other bodily parts of the victim. Sorcerers are not born to their role, as are witches: they are ordinary tribesmen who obtain 'strong medicines' from a herbalist or diviner and use them in an *ad hoc* fashion to harm an enemy. This important analytical distinction is not always expressed terminologically by the Bantu. Both witches and sorcerers tend to be classified together under one term: *abathakathi* (Zulu and Xhosa); *baloi* (Sotho and Lobedu). Among some tribes the distinction can, if necessary, be specifically made by qualifying the general term. Thus the Lobedu and Pedi distinguish between 'night witches' and 'day witches' (sorcerers) and the Mpondo and Bhaca sometimes discriminate between *ukuthakatha ngesilwana* ('to bewitch with animals') and *ukuthakatha ngobuthi* ('to bewitch with evil drugs') (Krige and Krige 1943: 250; Mönnig 1967: 75–6; Hunter 1936: 275; Hammond-Tooke 1962: 278).

Sorcery is a fairly straightforward attempt to influence the course of nature by magical means—the manipulation of spells, medicine and other objects. It forms part of the more general use of magical techniques, but is distinguished analytically from the magic of protection and cure by its antisocial character. Although in the nature of the case it can have no pragmatic effectiveness, the use of poisons, which is sometimes, and increasingly, being resorted to, obviously has.

Witch beliefs are broadly similar in all South African Bantu societies. In all one finds the notion of the magical leaving of the body, the association of witches in covens (associations to further their operations) and the themes of nakedness, cannibalism, invisibility and the use of familiars as agents of harm. These latter are usually animals among the Sotho and Venda, especially the hyena, snake, owl, crow and polecat (*muishond*) and the baboon and wildcat among the Zulu and Xhosa. In addition, the Nguni have an elaborate bestiary of mythical beings such as the *thikoloshe, ichanti, impundulu* or 'lightning bird' and *mamlambo*, some of which, especially the *thikoloshe*, have been borrowed by the South Sotho (Hunter 1936: 275-90; Hammond-Tooke 1962: 278-89). Perhaps the most dreaded familiar in all groups is the zombi, the living dead (Xhosa: *isithunzela*; Pedi: *setseetse*; Zulu: *umkhovu*; Lobedu: *khiduduwane*), dug up by witches after interment and sent to do their bidding. Xhosa-speakers believe that the tongue is cut out, and a wooden peg driven through the brain, and that the huge black *isithunzela* has an hypnotic effect on its victim. The Kriges report that 'The most fearful of all familiars is . . . the *khidudwane*, a human being who has been killed by a witch to be its slave' (Krige and Krige 1943: 251-2). Of recent importation is the European idea of a ghost (Xhosa: *isiporo*; Lobedu: *khipogo*), from the Afrikaans 'spook'.

Among the Mpondo, and the Nguni generally, there appears to be a strong sexual element in witchcraft beliefs. *Thikoloshe*, in particular, with his enormous penis, is believed to have sex relations with his owner and Ashton reports for the South Sotho that he is blamed for women's sexual troubles. Thus frigidity is attributed to his destroying a woman's natural desires by giving her secret sexual gratification, and Wilson has correlated this erotic element in Mpondo witch beliefs with the institution of clan exogamy which effectively excludes a large number of locally situated persons from possible sexual access (Wilson 1951). It is possible, perhaps, to explain this conceptualization of the witch as a woman, and her familiars as beings with abnormal sexual endowments, as a projection of male fantasies and guilt feelings in a strongly patrilineal society, where women are accorded a subordinate role and where they do not have the sexual freedom enjoyed by men. Looked at from this point of view, witch beliefs among the Nguni are a projection of the men's guilty recognition of the relative deprivation of women in the field of sex and the symbolization of the resentments and aggressions that they know that *they* would feel if subjected to the same conditions. This psychoanalytic hypothesis is, of course, difficult to test.[5] Among the Lobedu

> Night-witches employ familiars (*dithomya*) such as the hyena, the snake, the *muishond* (*Poecilogale albinucha*), and, to a lesser extent, owls and the striped *muishond*. . . . How the witch tames these animals is not known, but . . . they come at night to ask for food and call the witch their 'mother', but there is no sexual relationship between witch and familiar as is reported for the Pondo (Krige and Krige 1943: 251).

Throughout the tribes witches are almost invariably believed to be women while sorcerers are men. Sorcery is not normally inherited (although there is a vague Pedi belief that it is passed from father to son) and anyone can become a sorcerer if he possesses the right medicines. This emphasis on medicines (Sotho: *dihlare*; Xhosa: *amayeza*; Mpondo, Bhaca and Zulu: *imithi*) is crucial. Unlike some other peoples, e.g. the Polynesians, where the faultless pronouncement of a spell is the most important aspect of magical procedures, among the Bantu having the right medicine is all-important, and the spell is merely an exhortation to it to do its work well. Most medicines are derived from plants (the Nguni term, *imithi*, and the Sotho, *dihlare*, are derived from the word for 'tree') and, among the Lobedu, 'Fully 80 per cent of medicines are of vegetable origin' (Krige and Krige 1943: 215). Magical techniques can, of course, be used in a socially approved way to assist man (see below). The sorcerer, however, uses medicines to harm and perhaps kill a victim. The Cape Nguni distinguish between these two uses of medicines. *Umthi* refers to all medicines, however used, but '*ubuthi* (the prefix is that of the class of abstract nouns) means the material of magic used for illegal ends only' (Hunter 1936: 290).

There are a number of methods of harming people by sorcery. Perhaps the commonest is to obtain some essence of the person to be harmed, their excrement, nail parings or hair clippings, which is then mixed with the medicines—although this is not always essential.

'The Pedi are unanimous in saying that they fear day-witchcraft [sorcery] far more than they do night-witchcraft' (Mönnig 1967: 75-6), and this appears general among the Sotho-speakers. It is reversed among the Nguni, among whom the witch is greatly dreaded, and Hunter states that accusations of sorcery are fewer than accusations of witchcraft among the Mpondo (1936: 310).

The incidence of witchcraft and sorcery accusations and the public reaction to a witch will be discussed in the following chapter when this belief system is seen as a system of action.

Magic of Protection and Cure: The Herbalist

The belief system described above is essentially explanatory and provides more or less satisfying reasons for the ills and misfortunes that befall one. But explanation is not enough. Something must be done to alleviate or ward off the harm, whether caused by ancestors, witches or sorcerers. Methods differ with the cause. In cases diagnosed by the diviner as being caused by the ancestors, the appropriate action is to perform a sacrificial killing or other ritual: where caused by witch or sorcerer, magical techniques are resorted to, both as a cure and as a prophylactic. Magical techniques are also used to protect against the vagaries of impersonal nature—blight, drought, hail, lightning—and all South African tribes have a vast range of protective charms and medicines to cover every contingency. As we have seen, all emphasize the importance of medicine, rather than the spell, which is mainly, although not exclusively, derived from vegetable products. The Kriges comment that among the Lobedu 'There is hardly a plant in that rich lowveld vegetation which is not used in the pharmacopoeia of some herbalist or doctor.'

Before discussing in more detail the nature of the magical belief system, something must be said of the logic behind it. First of all it must be stressed that there is a substantial knowledge of nature and its workings that is essentially non-magical and empirical. The tribesman plants his crops in bushy country or along river banks where the luxuriance of the vegetation is proof of fertile soil, he observes the seasons and gears his agricultural cycle to them, he has an exact and extensive knowledge of the nutritional and practical uses of plants and wild fruits and he is a skilful animal husbandman. If he did not have this expertise he would be unable to survive. It would be incorrect to describe this knowledge as 'scientific', if by this we mean that he explains these properties in terms of explicit theories which postulate logical connections between the phenomena. But this knowledge is empirical in the sense that it is the product of trial-and-error experimentation achieved over centuries and handed down in the technological tradition. This is also true for the treatment of minor ailments, which are frequently dealt with in much the same way as among whites. Among the Lobedu 'sniffing up water is used for colds, the milk of a certain euphorbia is supplied [applied?] to draw out deep-lying thorns; splints of strips of wood are used for broken limbs or sprains' and teeth are levered out with a poker-like instrument. Enemas and emetics are commonly used among the Nguni, but not typically among the other tribes.

But these pragmatic techniques form an insignificant proportion of the total. There soon comes a stage where the tribesman's knowledge ends and the vagaries of weather, pestilence, sickness and death become unpredictable. In the absence of scientific knowledge and controls magic takes over. It is obvious that some medicines do, in fact, have therapeutic properties, but the Bantu do not distinguish between the purely medicinal and the magical. All one can say is that measures taken for protection are obviously purely magical, in our sense, while treatments for sickness may be partly therapeutic.[6]

As Frazer pointed out long ago the logic behind magical beliefs is based on the association of ideas, particularly the concepts that like produces like and that things that have once been in contact can continue to affect one another. Thus, among the Zulu,

> For spasms and the twitching of flesh, twitching animals are used. . . .
> If blood comes out of the body through the nose or mouth, it is necessary to take the bark of trees which have juice like blood. . . .
> To cure fear and nervousness, the heart, eyes, fat and flesh of the lion, elephant, and other powerful animals are mixed with the bark of many trees (Krige 1936a: 334).

Among the Mpondo a key is tied round the neck of an ailing child to 'lock up the cough', while patients with mumps address the *msenge* tree which has knobbly lumps on its trunk (Hunter 1936: 304). Like, then, can also combat like, as well as producing it. The importance of contagious magic is seen especially in the use of bodily exuviae in sorcery (see page 337). The symbolism of other magical procedures is not always so obvious, but there is practically no plant whose bark, twigs, roots, bulbs or leaves are not at one time or another pressed into service as an ingredient in some magical concoction. And not only plants are used. Among many in the materia medica that have been recorded in the literature are lion and elephant dung, powdered shark's fin, seawater, various animal fats (among the Bhaca pig's fat is a particularly potent protective medicine as pigs are impervious to snake bite), *thikoloshe* fat, snake venom, 'powdered belly of the crocodile' and so on, to name only a few. These may be drunk in infusions, inhaled, rubbed into cuts on the body, smeared on pegs and buried, washed with or used as enemas.

Medicine for socially approved purposes falls roughly into three categories, viz. that used to promote the solidarity and well-being of the tribe; for the protection of huts, stock, crops and other personal property; and in interpersonal relations. Among the Bhaca, for example, the chief, assisted by the *inyanga yempi* (tribal herbalist), ensured the fertility of the crops by the great ceremony before planting,

> the tribal territory was protected against lightning and hail, the lifegiving rain was wooed by the chief in the former rain-making ceremonies, and the knees of the warriors are still strengthened and the tribe bastioned against the attacks of hostile tribes at the spectacular *ingcubhe* festival [first fruits—see chapter 11]. Sometimes semi-religious in character, these ceremonies rest on a solid foundation of magic (Hammond-Tooke 1962: 267).

On the more local level *isiphephetho* medicines are burned in the fields to protect the crops against birds, and mixed with the seed to prevent it from rotting. A widespread method of stimulating healthy plant growth is to take a piece of whale bone, *isiphephetho*, elephant dung, ostrich bone and a type of succulent plant called *umavumbuka*, grind them, mix with water and sprinkle on the seed. The horn of a dark-coloured sheep is dug into the corners of gardens to promote fertility and the bones of the sand shark are used to protect stock against the *thikoloshe*. The Bhaca also use medicines to protect gardens from human thieves. One type, called *intivelo* (trap), is buried among the growing crops so that when a thief tries to uproot a plant he will be transfixed to the ground and be unable to move until the owner comes. The Bhaca, like all Cape Nguni, have a vast range of love potions, philtres and charms to obtain and retain affection, including *ibhekamnandedwa* ('look-at-me-alone'), a root bitten and rubbed on face and hands to attract girls, and hippopotamus fat, which is rubbed on the fingers so that, when a girl is caught round the waist, she will desire the man and come to him at night 'even if at first she did not want him' (Hammond-Tooke 1962: 267–77;

Hunter 1936: 295–306). Defendants use medicines in court to soften the hearts of judges. Bhaca medicines fall into distinct categories according to their properties. *Isihlambeto* (from *ukuhlamba*, to wash) is used by children and pregnant women to purify and protect, while *intseleti* ('slippery medicines') are used against familiars and by the chief in the first fruit rituals. *Umsizi* are 'black medicines' used as a protection against the *impundulu* or lightning bird, while *ubulawu* 'brings good luck' and is used particularly by diviners. Further details of this rich and varied pharmacopoeia (which differs widely from tribe to tribe in idiosyncratic detail, e.g. the Lobedu have a poorly-developed corpus of love magic (Krige and Krige 1943: 258)) will be found in the monographs quoted.

Although some families have their own medicines, handed down for generations from father to son, most tribesmen obtain theirs from specialist herbalists (Zulu and Bhaca: *inyanga*; Xhosa: *ixhwele*; Tsonga: *nyanga*; Sotho: *ngaka*; Lobedu: *ŋaga*; Venda: *ŋanga*). The profession of herbalist must not be confused with that of diviner, to be discussed in the following chapter. Herbalists are ordinary people who have acquired an extensive knowledge of magical technique and who do not, typically, possess occult powers. Frequently they inherit their knowledge, but it can also be obtained through apprenticeship or purchase. Herbalists differ greatly in their knowledge and in public esteem. Some specialize in one or two medicines while others are renowned for their vast knowledge. Some herbalists specialize as lightning doctors, cleansing a homestead and its inhabitants after it has been struck, burying a man or beast who has been killed by lightning and providing protective medicines; others can make rain (see Plate 14b), or are renowned as healers. Although not as closely associated with the ancestors as is the diviner, reputable herbalists appear to be aware of the importance of ancestral favour. Once a Swazi herbalist qualifies, 'he calls on his own and his master's spirits for success and, periodically renews the power of his "bags of medicine" in an elaborate ritual reaffirming his dependence on the dead' (Kuper 1947: 162). Although distinct from one another, the two professions of herbalist and diviner are mutually dependent 'and the practitioners cooperate in much the same way as the general practitioner and the specialist in Western society' (Kuper 1947: 162).

Notes

1 Van Warmelo (personal communication) informs me that this description is incorrect. The *zwidahadzhane* are beings with one eye, arm and leg apiece.

2 The evidence as to whether or not the Swazi had *Nomkhubulwana* is conflicting (see Gluckman 1954: footnote 15).

3 See also E. J. Krige (1968) for discussion of the role of women in these ceremonies.

4 These terms are used by Bigalke (1969). They are not ideal but we have been unable to suggest more suitable ones.

5 For a theoretical reformulation of this argument see W. D. Hammond-Tooke, 'The Cape Nguni witch familiar as a mediatory construct', *Man* N.S., 9, 1974.

6 An analysis of the active principle of the plants shows that they contain acids, alkaloids, oils, gums, resins, etc., but only about 5 per cent of the ingredients have a pharmacologically specific reaction (Watt and Breyer-Brandwijk, 1932).

Chapter 11
World-view II:
A System of Action
W. D. Hammond-Tooke

The previous chapter surveyed the world-views of the Southern Bantu peoples, looking at them as systems of beliefs in the supernatural (or, rather, the super-empirical) and as explanatory theories which seek to answer certain fundamental questions about man and the world he lives in. But beliefs must find expression in action. The African tribesman does not contemplate the supernatural world passively. He interacts with it. The ancestors must be honoured, or propitiated and 'kept away' if they are troublesome; the witch and sorcerer must be detected and dealt with; impersonal nature must be manipulated by magico-religious means and the society strengthened and protected against harm. We here enter the realm of ritual, both religious and magical, the techniques man has devised to manage satisfactorily his relations with gods, nature and other men. Ritual forms the articulation point between the belief system and the network of day-to-day interactions between men which is society. It is here that the social and ideational interpenetrate. In this chapter, then, we shall be concerned with ritual actions *per se*, on the one hand; on the other with the effect of the belief system on social relations. For the belief system gives rise to specialized social roles, e.g. the office of 'priest', or officiator at rituals, and that of diviner, the interpreter of misfortune—and these, in their turn, interact with their 'publics'—the priest with his 'congregation' and the diviner with his clientele. Then, too, the kind of person accused of being a witch or sorcerer tells us much about the society, particularly its built-in stresses and strains.

What is ritual? There have been many attempts at a satisfactory definition, but for our purposes it can be defined as a stereotyped behaviour pattern, usually expressing its aim symbolically, that is believed to maintain or to effect a significant change in man's relationship with the supernatural. Professor Wilson (1954a: 240) has suggested a useful distinction between the, often identified, concepts of *ritual* and *ceremonial*. Ritual is always believed to affect the relationship between man and the supernatural: ceremonial is merely a conventional form of action which is considered an appropriate clothing for the ritual proper. Thus, in the Christian Eucharist, the ritual is the unvarying liturgical form which *must* be performed for the action to be successful; ceremonial concerns the musical setting, incense, processionals, genuflexions, and so on, that mark special occasions of particular import and dignity. It is essentially the greater elaboration of ceremonial that distinguishes 'high' mass from 'low' mass. Like ritual, ceremonial, too, makes extensive use of symbolism. As we shall see, the comparative poverty of 'theological' speculation among the Bantu is amply made up for by the importance of ritual.

World-view and Social Roles

The 'congregation'

'Congregation' is used here in the Durkheimian sense of the group of worshippers who have a common god or gods as the object of their worship. As we saw in the previous chapter, the Supreme Being is not usually the object of any cult activity and the effective gods are the ancestors, deceased members of lineage or bilateral kin group. It follows from this that, strictly speaking, the tribe as a whole does not form a congregation. Each lineage among the Nguni and Sotho, and each cognatic group among the bilaterally-organized Venda, Lobedu and Tsonga, forms a separate and discrete cult group worshipping its own particular set of ancestors who only have influence over their own descendants. Membership of the cult group is thus strictly determined by the social structure. It is ascribed by birth in the first instance and can only be achieved (in some tribes)[1] by marriage or adoption. Thus among the Mpondo and Bhaca, and probably all the Cape Nguni, a married woman comes under the influence of her husband's ancestors and is thus influenced by two sets of shades, those of her own lineage and those of her husband's (Hunter 1936: 233; Hammond-Tooke 1962: 234). On the other hand, 'Amongst Thongas the wife does not adopt the gods of her husband's family' (Junod 1927 II: 412). The nearest approach to a *tribal* religion is the invocation, by the chief, on the tribe's behalf, of the august spirits of dead chiefs at times of national danger and at the *communal rituals*, to be discussed below. But, strictly speaking, the worshippers here are the members of the royal lineage: commoners do not pray to or invoke the names of the royal dead—although, of course, they benefit from the results of this invocation.

The picture emerges, for all the tribes, of a large number of discrete cult groups, each worshipping its own set of shades. Religion on this level, then, is not a strong force for tribal integration, except in the rather simplistic sense that a common belief in ancestors can have a general unifying effect. Rather would it seem to be divisive. The ancestor cult's main effect, then, is on the coherence of unilineal descent groups (especially among Nguni and Sotho) or families, for at the rituals all members are expected to attend, under the leadership of the family, or lineage, head. In addition there is evidence that rituals can be effective only when peace and harmony prevail between kinsmen. Brown records for the Tswana that

> the sacrifice itself is not considered sufficient. It must be accompanied by confession, and the confession usually, if not always, precedes the

sacrifice. . . . In the case of a child on whose behalf the doctor has been called in, confession of possible strife between the parents, or their failure in any respect towards the recognized customs of their tribe, is required (Brown 1926: 151)

and Schapera states that 'a special ceremony of reconciliation' was necessary if a member had quarrelled with a family head, before he would approach the ancestors on their behalf (Schapera 1940: 306). The Tsonga also have a ceremony of reconciliation, called *ku hahlela madjieta* (Junod 1927 II: 398–400), as do the Zulu (Krige 1936a: 59).

It is interesting, in the light of comparative material from other parts of Africa,[2] that this reconciliation is sometimes accompanied by spitting. Brown records for the Tswana that

Spittle plays an important part in some of the sacrifices of the Bechuana, especially in those in which sickness is said to be caused . . . by ill-feeling on the part of the relatives of the sick person, or a feeling of injury in their hearts. When the sacrifice is slain the contents of the stomach will be taken and into them each relative called by the medicine man will expectorate, and the idea is that with the expectorated spittle whatever feelings of hurt or evil that may be in the heart will be expelled (Brown 1926: 158).

The Tsonga reconciliation rite also includes spitting (Junod 1927 II: 399), as does the Lobedu and Venda ritual of *hu phasa*. The Kriges quote an instance of this ritual being performed by a mother who took water and squirted it on the ground with the words 'You people of ours, I myself, mother of the girl, *phasa* lest they say I remained with a dissatisfied heart'. They comment: 'By intimating that she had no grievance, she tried to safeguard herself from being, at some future date, found in the dice as the cause of her daughter's barrenness' (Krige and Krige 1943: 240).

The 'priest'

Strictly speaking the term 'priest' for the leader of the cult group is a misnomer if by it is meant a specially consecrated individual, set aside by training and by special vocation to serve the god. The priest, or officiator at a ritual, is typically a senior kinsman who plays this role among a number of others. But always there is the sacrificial and mediatory aspect, whether there be a blood sacrifice, as among the Nguni and Sotho, or a libation of beer or consecrated gruel, which makes the term more or less appropriate.

Among the Nguni the priest is the lineage head, the genealogically senior male member of the descent group. Ideally only he can invoke the ancestral spirits. Among the Mpondomise

His main functions are those of ritual leader and 'chairman' of the lineage court. . . . His homestead is not a special meeting place (he may, and often does, discharge his office at the home of a member who is sick or who is giving trouble) and he must, on occasion, travel long distances. Dates of all ritual killings must be arranged with him, he must see to it that all members are notified so that they can attend and he must be present in person (Hammond-Tooke 1968: 38).

Occasionally, if the *inkulu* (lineage head) is unable to be present, his younger brother, or even the head of the family immediately concerned in the rite, may officiate. Among the Mpondo, informants state that an elderly female agnate of the homestead head, past the age of childbearing and therefore not subject to women's taboos, may officiate (Hunter 1936: 247).

Among the South Sotho, Pedi and Tswana there is also this emphasis on the male line. 'The head of the family, as senior living representative of the ancestors, conducted the rites. . . . His role of family priest gave him considerable authority over his dependants' (Schapera 1940a: 306).

Among the other tribes this strong agnatic and male emphasis is not so marked. Among the Tsonga where, as we have seen, the mother's family are of equal importance, the mother's brother plays an extremely important role in the religious life of his sister's son with whom there exists a joking relationship which includes the 'snatching' of the meat of the beast sacrificed on his behalf by the mother's brother (Junod 1927 I: 269; Radcliffe-Brown 1924; Goody 1959). Junod comments that 'Maternal relatives have a special religious duty towards their nephews. They act as their priests, offerings being frequently made to the gods of the mother's family through the agency of the maternal uncle' (Junod 1927 II: 410 fnt.). But of course the family is also under the patrilineal priestship of the senior male through whom all offerings must be made (Junod 1927 II: 411).

Among the Venda

> The sister of the head of the lineage . . . plays an equally important part in its religious affairs. She is the priestess of her lineage, and except on rare occasions paternal ancestor spirits may only be approached through her. Any person requiring her ministrations, in order to commune with an ancestor, must inform the head of the lineage, who summons his sister. If it is quite impossible for her to appear, her brother, the *ndumi*, may act in her place; failing him, the headman . . . but in either of these two contingencies the substitute must use the name of his sister, the true priestess. On the death of the priestess her daughter or son may act in her place, but always using the 'mouth' of their mother (Stayt 1931a: 249-50).

This strong emphasis on the father's sister (*makhadzi*) in Venda society is partly explained by Stayt (and the Venda themselves) by the fact that she is the primary factor in bringing cattle into the family, by means of which her brother was able to obtain a wife, and she is therefore responsible for the establishment and, therefore, the good health, of her brother's family (Stayt 1931a: 174).

Among the Lobedu, where the role of the father's sister is similar to that of the Venda, she also has an important position in ritual. 'The influence of a sister is reinforced by her religious position. At the annual harvest offering to the gods, it is always the eldest sister in the family who has to officiate. She is the one best able to intercede with the spirits' and any grievance on her part against her brother may cause the spirits to be 'stirred up' and bring illness to his children. But, although every sister is potentially a priestess, different sisters may be called upon to officiate in different rituals. If the ritual affects the family as a whole, the eldest daughter of the chief wife must officiate, but in cases of illness this would be done more appropriately by a man's uterine sister. 'It is a man's uterine sister that plays the biggest part in his life, for in this, as in everything, the individual family is always asserting itself as against the larger, polygynous family group' (Krige and Krige 1943: 76). At the *hu phasa* ritual (see below), however, 'the officiator may be male or female, whomsoever the [divining] dice have indicated' (Krige and Krige 1943: 235).

It is clear that the role of priest is closely related to the social structure. Among the strongly patrilineal Nguni and Sotho it is always the genealogical senior male; among the Tsonga there is the special relationship of the maternal kin, reflected in the important position of the mother's brother; and among the Venda and Lobedu, who stress cattle-linking and affinal ties, the father's sister predominates in this role. It is perhaps significant that both Venda and Lobedu had early contacts with the Rhodesian Karanga, Lozwi and Nyai (Krige and Krige 1943: 305).

The diviner

But perhaps the most important religious functionary is the diviner (Zulu: *isangoma, isanusi*; Bhaca: *isangoma*; Mpondo, Xhosa: *igqira*; South Sotho: *selaoli, senohe*; Pedi: *ngaka*; Venda, Tsonga: *mungome*; Lobedu: *mugome*) (see frontispiece). His importance derives from the fact that it is he who has the power to interpret the causes of misfortune, to establish whether it has been caused by ancestral wrath or by the machinations of witch or sorcerer. The divination situation and the methods used will be discussed more fully below: here we are concerned with recruitment to the profession.

Among all the Nguni peoples the status of diviner is closely associated with the ancestral spirits. Not only does the vocation stem from a special 'calling' by the ancestors, but the divination itself consists of direct communion with the shades who are believed to speak through the diviner, who is thus, in effect, a medium. The call comes in the form of a specific sickness (*ukuthwasa*), divined as being sent by the ancestors. It is characterized by *iinkathazo* ('troubles'), pains in the body, uncontrollable nervous twitchings and sporadic periods of dissociation. As one Zulu informant memorably expressed it: 'He [the diviner] becomes a house of dreams' (Callaway 1868: 260). The novice thereupon apprentices herself (by far the great majority of Nguni diviners are women) to a diviner and undergoes an extended period of training, involving the use of certain medicines and, especially, the performance of certain dances (*ukuxhentsa*) designed to induce trance. Anyone may fall ill of *ukuthwasa*, although there is a strong tendency for the profession to run in families. During her novitiate the novice is in danger of ritual pollution and observes numerous food and other taboos, avoiding contact with the community as much as possible. At the completion of the initiation period, which may last one or two years, the novice undergoes an elaborate initiation and emerges as a fully-fledged diviner. The association with the ancestors is strong. Among the Mpondo the *inkathazo*

> may be caused in a man not only by the *amathongo* of his father, but also by the *amathongo* of his mother or father's mother, and in a woman not only by the *amathongo* of her father and husband, but also the *amathongo* of her mother. The *amathongo* of a man's father or a woman's father or husband, however, are always mainly responsible.

Among the Zulu the *isanuse* is a specialist in finding lost property and Krige records a number of different types of diviner, e.g. the *izinyanga zesithupha*, the *amabukulazinti*, or stick diviners, the *amathambo*, or bone diviners, and the *abalozi* who are ventriloquists. Soga records a similar variety for the Xhosa (Hunter 1936: 320–35; Hammond-Tooke 1955; 1962: 244–56; Krige 1936a: 299–310; Kuper 1947: 161–6; Soga 1932: 160–9).

This 'Nguni' pattern is found among the Tsonga and also, today, as an intrusive element, among the South Sotho and Pedi. These diviners, among the South Sotho called *lethuela*, *leqetha* or *mokoma*, 'are similar to the Pondo *amagqira* and represent a foreign culture trait introduced by Thembus and others, who have come in from the Cape Colony. They are mainly to be found in the southern and eastern parts of Basutoland' (Ashton 1952: 283). The traditional South Sotho diviner is called *selaoli* and uses bones in his diagnosis and treatment. The skill is acquired from another *selaoli* who is paid for his instruction. There is also the 'seer' or *senohe* who finds lost or hidden objects, diagnoses illness and foretells the future. His power of second sight cannot be acquired: 'It is a gift from God or the ancestors and is exercised intuitively' (Ashton 1952: 283). The *mapala* diviners of the Pedi, who dress in ankle-rattles and feathered headdresses and who 'divine through direct spiritual contact with the ancestors', are also of foreign (Nguni?) provenance. They, too, are mainly women, dancing plays an important part in their training and 'the cure from affliction by such a spirit also forms the initiation into the cult' (Mönnig 1967: 87). Generally speaking, the Sotho as a group do not seem to distinguish as clearly as the Nguni between diviner and herbalist ('The Pedi *ngaka* . . . may be described as diviner, witch-doctor, priest, medicine man and magician'), and divination by bone-throwing is the most common technique of Sotho doctors, who are usually men. But in all groups there seems to have been a general tendency to adopt, in addition, Nguni-type mediumistic divination by female diviners, who directly interpret ancestral and spirit demands. This is also true of the Lobedu, who formerly resorted to the ordeal (*mureu*), especially the drinking of poison, to implicate those accused of witchcraft. The Lobedu no longer rely on *mureu* because it involves too great publicity and danger of white intervention, and, since the beginning of the century, they have tended to consult the 'smelling-out diviner' (*mugome*), an institution borrowed from the Tsonga (Krige and Krige 1943: 204).

The Venda have a number of types of diviner. Although the *ŋanga*, the most numerous, possess the divining dice, they apparently do not have occult powers. The 'true' diviners are the *mingome*, 'especially skilled in the use of the magic dice and the magic bowl. Among them are the *vhabvumbi*, the smellers-out, who specialize in discovering articles which have been stolen. There are also fortune-tellers; but by far the greater number of *mingome* are *maine vha lufhali*, the diviners who discover the identity of the *vhaloi* [witches].' *Mingome* can be of either sex and their apprenticeship must be acceptable to the ancestors, as shown in the fall of the dice. A man may be both an *ŋanga* and a *mungome* (Stayt 1931a: 264).

The importance of the dance, with its accompanying drumming, is reflected in the names for mediumistic diviners which all have the root *-goma* (Zulu: *isangoma*; Sotho: *mokome*; Tsonga and Venda: *mungome*; Lobedu: *mugome*) meaning basically, 'a drum', and the tendency for this institution to diffuse to other groups is striking.

The mystical powers of the chief

Although the South African Bantu chief is primarily a political officer, he also stands at the apex of the religious system. This is often expressed in the literature in the phrase 'the chief is chief priest of the tribe'. His relationship with the supernatural derives from two sources, viz. his structural position as the genealogical senior representative of the ruling lineage and the fact that high political office everywhere tends to accrete to itself certain mystical attributes.[3]

We have already touched on the chief's role in the ancestor cult. Only he can perform the propitiatory sacrifices to the shades of the dead chiefs in time of national emergency, and it is in this sense that he can be described as a 'tribal' priest. Among the Venda, for example, he offers thanks to the ancestral spirits collectively at the festival of the first fruits, and his ancestors 'although actually propitiated by the chief's lineage alone, are felt to be associated with all the people' (Stayt 1931a: 241). Among the South Sotho, 'In the old days, each family was considered to be under the direct influence and protection of its ancestors and the tribe as a whole under those of the ancestors of its chief' (Ashton 1952: 114–15). Mönnig states that the Pedi go further and believe that the chief forms a bridge between his people and the Supreme Being, *Modimo* (1967: 252).

But, in addition, the role of supreme ruler itself is a consecrated, set apart, one. The extent to which the role is sacralized differs between the groups and is less developed among the Nguni, Sotho and Tsonga, although the Pedi refer to their chief as '*Modimo wa lefase*' ('God of the Earth'). The furthest development towards a sacred kingship is found among the Lobedu and Venda. The Lobedu queen is a rain-maker who was expected to commit ritual suicide at the end of the fourth initiation school of her reign. The Kriges stress, however, that, unlike the kings of Sofala described by Don Santos in 1607, who formerly had to take poison when disaster or ill-health overtook them, physical defects in Mujaji are not believed to affect the country (Krige and Krige 1943: 165–7). But the queen's death causes the country to 'heat' and dry up, bringing drought and famine. Perhaps the closest approach to a divine kingship is the chiefship of the Venda.

> His very person is sacred: he must be approached on hands and knees.
> . . . The chief's person is so sacred that it is no rare thing to see people rub on their own bodies, by way of a strengthening drug, sweat and mucus of which the chief has got rid. . . . But not only is the chief thus regarded as semi-divine during the greater part of his life: towards the end of it, or sometimes long before, he actually confers godhead upon himself, when after abjuring all contact with women, and putting away his wives, he performs a solemn solitary dance (*u pembela*) which makes him in very truth a god (*Mudzimu*) [lit. ancestral spirit] (Lestrade 1932: v).

In contrast to their purely religious role Southern Bantu chiefs were seldom, if ever, herbalists or diviners in their own right. The Pedi chief possesses an inherited divination set, but he is not able to interpret it, and generally speaking, in the communal rituals to be described below, the services of special herbalists are engaged to prepare the strong medicines necessary. An exception was the Xhosa chief, Gcaleka, who was a renowned diviner (Soga 1930: 142–5; Hammond-Tooke 1957: 34).

The magico-religious role of the chief will be discussed more fully below, when the cyclical communal rituals are described.

The Occasions for Ritual Action

As we have seen, traditional religion is expressed basically in ritual rather than in complicated metaphysical speculation: there is practically no aspect of life which is not ritualized at one time or another. Professor Monica Wilson has suggested a classification of rituals as *rituals of kinship* and *communal rituals* which reflects important categories and will be used here (Wilson 1957; 1959a). Purely magical ritual has been touched on in the previous chapter.

Rituals of kinship

These are the rituals associated *par excellence* with the ancestral cult and are confined to the family- and lineage-centred congregations already described. They can be divided into (a) *life-cycle rituals*, the sacralization of important stages in the life of the individual, and (b) *piacular* or *contingent rituals*, those performed in response to specific stimuli, in particular to illness divined as sent by the ancestors for some neglect of custom.

Among all the groups the various changes of status—birth, initiation, marriage and death—are accompanied by symbolic actions, of greater or lesser complexity, that serve to express publicly the transformation and invoke the blessing of the dead. They are discussed in some detail in the chapter on Individual Development and in chapter 10, to which reference is made. These are the rituals, usually involving the sacrifice of an animal or the making of a libation and accompanied by some invocation of the spirits, which stress amity between kinsmen, and the neglect of which is a potent source of ancestral wrath. Often the diviner's explanation of ancestrally sent illness or misfortune specifies the ritual which has been omitted, perhaps most commonly the non-observance of the re-integration ritual for the spirit (Xhosa: *guqula*; Zulu: *ukubuyisa*).

It is in the piacular rituals that the interaction between living and dead is at its most intense. Here the individual and his group have been assailed and there is the urgent desire to seek the cause. Resort is made to divination (see below) and, if diagnosis indicates ancestral wrath, a sacrifice is made to propitiate the spirits.

Among the Nguni, Tsonga and Sotho (except the Lobedu and Pedi) ritual essentially involves a blood sacrifice. Cattle are the preferred sacrificial animals but goats are frequently substituted or, among the poorer Tsonga, fowls. Sheep are seldom if ever slaughtered by the Nguni or Tswana (except among the Zulu, where they are used in sacrifices for protection against lightning) as they do not cry out or bellow when killed, thus calling the ancestors, but they are preferred to goats among the South Sotho and Pedi and, among the Tsonga, may only be sacrificed by chiefs. In all these groups beer offerings are also made, indeed, among the Pedi 'Beer is nearly always the medium of sacrifice, and may be accompanied by goats, sheep or cattle, and occasionally by game and even vegetable matter. Usually, however, beer is considered sufficient by itself. When other things are sacrificed they are nearly always accompanied by beer' (Mönnig 1967: 61).

Libations of water and sprouted grain are the main elements in Venda and Lobedu ritual (see Plates 15a and 15b). Called *u phasa* among the Lobedu (Vendu: *hu phasa*), the rite consists of a prayer and the pouring on to the earth or *thugula* of a mixture of ground, sprouted grain and water, sometimes accompanied by spitting. If the *u phasa* ritual is not effective the Venda sacrifice a black goat. For the Lobedu the Kriges state:

> Ritual killings of all kinds are insignificant by contrast with the beer offering. There are, first, killings especially for the ancestors, but they are so rare that many people have never seen them. Secondly, there are

occasions when the killings, clearly ritual, are not thought of as an offering or sacrifice [?]. . . . And, thirdly, there are killings, not associated with the ancestors or religion, in which small pieces of meat may nevertheless be set aside to 'tell' (*hu suma*) the gods of some event or to propitiate them (Krige and Krige 1943: 237).

Differences between tribes appear to be broadly correlated with the differential importance of cattle-keeping as opposed to hoe-culture.

For the details of rituals the reader is referred to the relevant monographs. Space only permits one or two examples.

Among the Zulu the officiator first praises the ancestors loudly in the cattle byre, then reports (*bika*) to them in a normal voice what beast he is going to give them. The beast is then thrown and stabbed with the sacrificial spear and as it bellows the officiator says, 'Cry, ox of the *amadlozi*!' and again mentions the shades by name. The victim is then skinned, great care being taken to avoid spilling the blood and chyme on the ground. Before anyone partakes, the spirits must be first given their share. This consists of two main parts, viz. (a) that which is burned, with the flower of the yellow everlasting as incense, usually including part of the fourth stomach (*inanzi* or *injeke*), and (b) that set aside for the ancestors to 'lick' and placed for this purpose on the *umsamo* niche at the back of the great hut. The rest of the meat is distributed among those present and must be eaten on the same day: all that remains of the victim, the skin and bones, is burned. In piacular rites the gall is smeared on the sick person so that the shades will lick him and make him well (Krige 1936a: 292–6). Gall is also prominent in Cape Nguni and Tswana ritual and among the former the *intsonyama* (Bhaca: *imbethfu*), a muscle attached to the right foreleg, is of special significance and is ritually tasted by the patient. One of the effects of ritual killings is to ensure a steady consumption of meat by the community as, in most cases, all are welcome to join the feast. Bigalke recorded fifty-eight ritual killings in one Ndlambe headman's area during a period of two years, representing only a portion of those which actually took place. He comments: 'Few weekends pass without some ceremonial being held in each village' (Bigalke 1969: 104–5).

In all sacrifices it is commensalism which is being expressed, a communion meal which symbolically unites the living and the dead. As Hunter says: 'To kill a beast or a goat, or brew beer, is the Pondo way of honouring a guest. . . . The dead, like the living, are honoured by a feast. It is said that "the *amathongo* are hungry. They wish to eat". . . . Every Pondo questioned emphatically denied any idea of replacement. "An *ithongo* does not want a person, he wants a beast"' (Hunter 1936: 245). This is supported by Willoughby. 'The Bantu,' he writes, 'appear to have no idea of the transferring of the sin of the worshipper to the victim, or of substituting the death of the victim for the merited death of the sinner. Their idea of sacrifice is rather that of communion with the spirit' (Willoughby 1928: 74–5). The only evidence for a possible substitutionary element, as is found, for example, among the Nuer of the Sudan (Evans-Pritchard 1956: 260–2), is the recorded invocation at a Bhaca sacrifice ('Leave this person; take this beast'—Hammond-Tooke 1962: 239), but this may not in fact involve the identification of the sick person with the sacrifice.

Apart from these propitiatory sacrifices, killings are also made to thank the ancestors, particularly after the completion of a journey or a spell at the labour centres.

Communal rituals

The rituals of kinship all express symbolically the unity of family and descent group and handle the problems of individuals in the specific domestic sphere, both in terms of life-cycle and health. But the chiefdom itself is not merely the sum of its descent groups: it is an important social entity in its own right and its members, although of heterogeneous provenance, are welded together by their allegiance to the chief, possession of a common culture and tradition and the occupation of a particular territory. Loyalty to the tribe is second only to loyalty to the kin group and these values, too, must be restated in religious terms. Thus all tribes in the past sought to secure and maintain tribal well-being by the performance of (usually) annual rituals in which all members participated, however vicariously. Some of these communal rituals were essentially religious in that they quite explicitly invoked the shades of deceased chiefs: in others the magical element was more pronounced—and frequently there was a blend of both. The main communal rituals were rain-making, the securing of fertility of land and crops, the protection of the country against lightning and hail, the celebration of the harvest and the strengthening of the chief and army.

In Southern Africa, where rainfall is uncertain over large areas and the fear of drought ever present, rain-making rites are found in all groups. The ultimate responsibility lies squarely with the chief, although he is usually assisted by special rain-doctors. The exception appears to be the Zulu for whom Krige states: 'The Zulu kings did not encourage rain-doctors in their kingdom because they said that they themselves controlled the heavens' (Krige 1936a: 320). The rites seem to be generally directed to the tribal ancestors, but among the Venda and Pedi it is believed that the Supreme Being ultimately controls the rain (Stayt 1931a: 232; Mönnig 1967: 157). In the latter case rain is begged from Kgobeane, the son of God, through his wife, but in times of severe drought here, too, sacrifices are made to the chiefs' shades. Among both Tsonga and Mpondo the chief's ancestors are upbraided at their graves for withholding rain and the Tsonga beat the royal graves in the sacred groves with sticks (Junod 1927 II: 316; Thelejane 1963).

Among Tsonga, Venda, Pedi, Mpondo, Bhaca, Zulu, Bomvana, Lobedu (and, indeed, probably in all other tribes) the rain rite involves the immolation of a black-coloured animal, an obvious example of sympathetic magic. Among the Pedi the rain medicines are kept in large pots (*mphoko*) behind the hut of the chief's principal wife and at the annual rain ceremony (*mothokgo*) young girls from all over the country proceed to the capital carrying small pots of water drawn from their local areas. This water is poured into large pots, rain medicine is added and the small pots refilled with the medicated water. The girls then return home and sprinkle the earth with this concoction (Mönnig 1967: 155-8). This rite bears a strong resemblance to the Bhaca ritual of blessing the seed (Hammond-Tooke 1962: 176-7). Mpondomise chiefs relied for rain-making on certain San (Bushman) families who lived in the Tsolo area until 1910, and who subsisted on tribal charity in recognition of their services.

But the famed rain-maker, to whom supplicants for rain came from far and wide, was the Lobedu Mujaji.

> During life, she is not merely the Transformer of the Clouds, but she is regarded as the changer of the seasons and guarantor of their cyclic regularity. . . . Her very emotions affect the rain. . . . Her rain-making is not confined to dramatic ceremonies in time of severe drought; it is conceived of as continuous care throughout the summer . . . the Lobedu do not attribute every fall of rain to some special activity or volition on the part of their queen, but rather believe that the queen exercises some general control or care which ensures a good season (Krige and Krige 1943: 271).

As among the Pedi, the rain medicines are kept in rain-pots, and include as a chief ingredient the skin of the deceased chief and of important councillors. But the power of the queen is not absolute and she can only control rain 'in agreement with her ancestors'. She also does not work alone and, like other chiefs, always collaborates with a rain-doctor, who takes the blame if the rain is bad, i.e. is insufficient or accompanied by too many thunderstorms.

Space does not permit detailed discussion of the rituals designed to protect the country from lightning and hail. Among the Bhaca, for example, the country was doctored against hail and lightning by a herbalist, using pegs smeared with the chief's medicines. After all the approaches to the country had been protected in this way, he came down from the mountains and, clad only in a prepuce covering, ran through the fields waving two sticks smeared with *umnyenya* medicine (Hammond-Tooke 1962: 177-8; cf. Jackson 1969: 239 for comparative data on the Langa Ndebele). Among the Mpondo, Thembu, Bhaca and Zulu the crops were protected from maize blight by a ceremony in which young girls ran through the fields clad in bead aprons (Gluckman 1935; Hunter 1936: 78; Hammond-Tooke 1962: 178).

But perhaps the most important communal ritual is the annual festival of the first fruits. It is found as an explicit harvest festival among all the tribes and, among the Tsonga, Mpondo, Bomvana, Zulu, Swazi and Bhaca it combines, in addition, a specific strengthening of the chief and army at the capital. Common to all is the basic ritual action of 'biting' (Nguni: *luma*; Sotho; *loma*) the first fruits, accompanied by spitting (*shwama*), before the new crops can be freely eaten by tribesmen. It is also universally a symbolic expression of genealogical seniority and political authority, for the sequence of rites must be initiated by the chief (within individual tribes) and by the paramount (in a chiefdom cluster). It thus has a very direct function in symbolizing dramatically the hierarchical authority structure of Bantu chiefdoms and relative rank. No one can partake of the new crops until this first has been done by his political senior. Among the Nguni and Sotho the first fruits are typically pumpkins, gourds and sweetreed, but also kaffir corn and maize; the Ronga *luma* kaffir corn and the greatest Tsonga ritual involves the fruit of the marula (*Sclerocarya caffra* (Sond)) (Junod 1927 I: 397).

Among the Tsonga, Zulu, Mpondo, Bomvana, Swazi and Bhaca (in fact probably all the Nguni) the rite was integrated with an elaborate strengthening of the chief and doctoring of the army with strong medicines in a magnificent series of rites that involved *inter alia* the killing of a bull by unarmed warriors and, among the Zulu, Swazi and Bhaca at least, the institutionalized criticism of the chief which has caused these rites to be called by Gluckman 'Rituals of Rebellion'.[4]

Divination and the Interpretation of Misfortune

In the previous chapter the nature of causal explanation of misfortune in terms of ancestral wrath and witch-sorcery beliefs was discussed. These concepts become crucial in human relations when misfortune or sickness overtakes a man and the highly-charged emotions crystallize around the divination situation. It is here that the latent tensions within the social structure are brought into focus and, more or less adequately, dealt with.

Techniques of divination

A great variety of divinatory techniques is used by the South African Bantu peoples. Generally speaking all Nguni and some Tsonga divine by the mediumistic involvement of the diviner with tutelary ancestral shades, while the Sotho, Tsonga and Venda favour the divining dice. The Venda are unique in the possession of the divining bowl and the Lobedu (formerly) and the Tsonga and Zulu also relied on the ordeal. As we have seen, there has been a certain amount of borrowing of Nguni methods.

In addition to the séance, the Nguni also practise the *ukuvumisa* method of divination. Hunter has described it for the Mpondo as follows:

> The inquirers sit down in a hut or in the *inkundla*, the *igqira* squatting directly opposite them. . . . The *igqira* first has to find out the inquirers' reason for coming—who is ill, and what the symptoms are. Then he tells who has caused the trouble, and how. The *igqira*'s method is to make statements; after each statement the inquirers clap and shout, '*Siyavuma!*' (We agree!). The *igqira* judges from the heartiness of the assent whether or not he is on the right track. If he

has established a point satisfactorily, the inquirers say: '*Phosa ngemva*' (Put it behind you). If he is wrong they say '*Asiva*' (We do not hear). An *igqira* is not discredited if he makes some wrong statements, but if he is slow the inquirers take up their money and go off to try elsewhere (Hunter 1936: 336).

Sotho and Venda divination depends on the fall of four specially carved dice which form the basis of the system but are usually also used with knuckle bones and other objects (see Plate 14a). Among the Venda the four main dice are used alone for tribal matters. The dice must be carved by a specialist to the accompaniment of a definite ritual. In the simplest system, in which four dice only are used, there are sixteen possible combinations in which the dice can fall: each combination has its own praise name. Sotho divining sets tend to be more complex in that other forms of dice are added, such as knuckle bones, roots etc. The Venda divining bowl is carved of wood, with a wide, flat rim on which are cut, in relief, figures representing the various totem groups found among them, as well as figures representing persons and objects in tribal life. In the centre of the bowl a cowrie shell covers a cavity in which magical substances have been secreted. The bowl is filled with water and fruit kernels or seeds are floated: the position where they come to rest against the side allows the diviner to interpret.[5]

Whatever the method of divination, the reaction to a discovered witch was violent, especially among the Nguni, Tsonga and Sotho. Death was the penalty, sometimes preceded by torture. Among the Zulu, Tsonga and Mpondomise, witches were impaled on a stake or, among the Zulu, tied in a skin and thrown to the crocodiles or garrotted with a thong (E. J. Krige 1936a: 227). A Mpondomise and Xhosa refinement was to peg the victim down, smear him with water or honey and break a nest of vicious black tree-ants over him (Hammond-Tooke, 1969b: 255; Soga 1932: 180). Among all the Nguni a witch's homestead was razed by fire. Tsonga witches were either impaled or drowned, although a flogging or banishment was resorted to 'when the crime [was] not so heinous' (Junod 1927 II: 534). Zulu and Bomvana witches were clubbed and thrown over a precipice (Krige 1936a; Cook 1931: 153). Casalis recounts the brutal torture and execution of an accused sorcerer by the South Sotho (Casalis 1861: 351).

The reaction of the Venda and Lobedu was not so physically violent. The Venda use counter-magic to encompass the death of a *muloi* or (formerly) challenged the accused to take the poison ordeal: if found guilty he was belaboured with sticks until he fled (Stayt 1931a: 282–3). Among the Lobedu the victim, or his consulting diviner, resorted to an indefinite warning to publicly 'shame' the witch, and a suspected witch could be taken to court (Krige and Krige 1943: 259–60).

The sociology of witch beliefs

But the theoretical importance of witch accusations is the insights they give into stresses and strains in the social structure. When misfortune falls, and is believed to be caused by a fellow tribesman, the kind of person who is selected as a target for accusations is presumably one occupying a social position that brings him into conflict with the accuser, or whose behaviour is unacceptable.

Unfortunately not much work on this aspect has been done in South Africa and the only quantitative material we have is for the Lobedu, Mfengu, Dushane and Ndlambe. We learn from the literature that, among the Swazi, witchcraft emanates typically from a jealous co-wife or unscrupulous half-brother, ambitious for inheritance, from commoners jealous of a more successful fellow man and from princes ranged against each other and against chiefs or the King (Kuper 1947: 175), and that, among the Mpondo, the vast number of accusations are against women. 'A study of the accusations shows that they are almost invariably against some woman of the *umzi* [homestead] who is a wife, not a daughter, of that *umzi*, or against a former lover or a rival in love, or a neighbour' (Hunter 1936: 307).

More specifically the Kriges found that 70 per cent of cases of witch and sorcery accusations recorded by them among the Lobedu involved close relatives and that, contrary to the position among the Nguni, both men and women are equally liable to harm one. The most prolific single source of witchcraft is the conflict of co-wives (24 per cent of all cases), reflecting tensions in the polygynous household. Spouses also bewitch one another, but wives kill and injure husbands more frequently than do husbands their wives. There are also unexpected aspects of their findings. Despite the potential conflict between in-laws, only 20 per cent of cases involved wives or their relatives bewitching a husband or his relatives, and only 16 per cent of a husband or his relatives bewitching wives or their relatives. Nor do 'easily aggrieved relatives' who are 'very sensitive' (e.g. cattle-linked brothers and sisters, father's sisters, fathers, father's brothers and grandparents) readily bewitch:

> they are believed to have repressed complaints, but they cannot project as witchcraft the displeasures or misfortunes or failures upon those who must, but do not, respect and humour them. They can and do cause illness, but it is not by way of witchcraft, and the resolution of the conflict is by pardon and *hu phasa*, through the gods, not through *vuloi*.

Only 30 per cent of cases were against strangers (Krige and Krige 1943: 263–4).

Professor Wilson and her associates found in Keiskammahoek that those accused of witchcraft or sorcery were related to their victims either by blood or marriage in 82 per cent of cases recorded and that the person most often accused was a wife and, second to her, a mother-in-law. Cases of conflict between in-laws constituted 52 per cent of the total and by far the greater number of accused in this category were women. Percentages of cases involving a wife's bewitching of her husband's people, and *vice versa*, are almost identical among Lobedu and Mfengu, but the proportion of non-kin accused among the Lobedu is almost double that of the Keiskammahoek Mfengu. Recent work among the Dushane and Ndlambe of the Xhosa tribal cluster shows a higher incidence of non-kin accusation (about 40 per cent) and a concentration of accusations against wives of lineage members. Among the Dushane, 38 per cent of accusations against kin occurred between a woman and her husband's brother's son, three cases against the husband's brother himself and two with the husband's brother's son's son. The reason for the prevalence of the father's brother's wife as a target for witch-accusations is probably due to the fact that she is the nearest lineage affine (and therefore stranger) not the actual wife or mother of the victim (Wilson *et al.* 1952: 170–86; Hammond-Tooke 1970a; Bigalke 1969: 136–46).

World-view and Morality

The relationship between the magico-religious system and morality is a complex and difficult one. Religious behaviour may be defined as that involving right relations between man and the supernatural; moral behaviour right behaviour between man and his fellow man. Conceptually they are distinct: in practice religion supports and gives authoritative backing to the moral code. Moral norms must be universifiable, they have a 'given' quality (so that they do not essentially need sanctioning) and they are founded on a people's conception of the nature of things, of the world and of reality. We should expect, therefore, that moral codes reflect the social structure and idea systems of traditional societies, and refer to absolutely basic values, the very essence of social life, without which the society would cease to be what it is. Not all norms are moral. The breach of rules of etiquette, for example, does not normally carry with it moral reprobation. Moral behaviour is concerned with the 'good' life, and Bantu morality, like Christian morality, is closely intertwined with Bantu religion. Both 'religion' and 'morality' are firmly rooted in the world-view.

How do the Southern Bantu conceive the 'good' man?

Basic to traditional cosmological ideas is the great value placed on health and the well-being of man, beast and crops: one complex of values involves, then, health and fertility. Another involves harmonious social life, the elimination of discord, and the ensurance of co-operation and mutual goodwill between man and man. These two idea complexes are interrelated. We saw how illness and misfortune are almost inevitably interpreted in human terms. A failure in health or fortune is typically caused by some failure in social relations, either with the ancestors or with one's kin or neighbours. The worlds of nature and society are not distinct. Rather do they form one moral universe in which action and attitude in one sector affect the other. A premium is thus placed on good social behaviour, for failure here might have drastic consequences for the whole of life. For the Bantu, the comment that 'the wicked flourish like the green bay tree' is patently untrue.

This emphasis on man-to-man relationships as a basis of moral behaviour is, of course, the foundation of all ethical systems. But the nature of these traditional societies, with their small-scale relationships, means that even stronger pressures operate to eliminate conflict that might disrupt the group than is the case in modern industrialized society. As we have seen, illness and misfortune are conceived in moral terms, and the same is true for gift-exchange, economic relations, family relations, and so on.

It was said that the moral code is rooted in the basic values of the society. What are these?

All Southern African tribes are patrilineal, with strong emphasis on male authority. They are all highly stratified into both kinship and political hierarchies. This gives rise to two basic principles in social life—patrilineal descent and rank. Coupled with this is the (universal) generation gap with its strong dominance pattern. These basic ideas—agnation, ranking and generation—are fundamental, and we should expect to find them reflected in the moral code.

This is indeed so. Perhaps the most fundamental moral prescription is the need to show respect (Xhosa: *intlonipho*) to lineage seniors and, indeed, to all members of the senior generation. This respect is inculcated from the earliest years. Children are taught absolute obedience to parents, they must always use formal modes of address to them, they may not interrupt while grown-ups are talking, nor shout at them nor call across to them. Among the Xhosa, parents whose children fail to behave well are said to feel *intloni* (shame).

Initiation brings a change in moral responsibility. Before this important ritual children are alleged 'to have no sense', to be morally irresponsible: afterwards they are adults and fully responsible for their actions. Frequently, when a boy becomes difficult to handle, the older men will say that he needs to be initiated and the ritual usually does, in fact, effect a personality change. The unbridled sexuality of youth must give way to the gentleness, responsibility and *gravitas* that is expected from the mature man in Bantu society. Respect towards seniors is now no longer subject to parental sanctions. The sanctions are now supernatural and, Xhosa say, misfortune will befall him who 'plays the fool with the old people' (*edlala ngabantu abadala nje*). Younger brothers must respect elder brothers and lineage members their head. The outward sign of this respect is partly verbal, but is also shown in the many 'customs' of the homestead, notably the killings at the various life-cycle rituals. This emphasis on respect runs through all the kinship and descent groups, from family to clan, and associated with it is the prescription of kinship loyalty and mutual assistance. The importance of safe-guarding kin group interests is greater than the value of truth-telling as an absolute—and this has led to the widespread charge of Bantu mendacity. Respectful behaviour to seniors is a moral good in itself but, as we have seen, it is also given expression on the religious plane. Every time a killing is made for the ancestors the officiant is stating in symbolic action this basic principle of filial piety and respect for seniors. The moral rule is restated at the religious level and backed by religious sanctions.

But respect is expected towards all seniors, whether related or not. At beer drinks or meat feasts there is no intermingling of individuals who belong to different age groups. Each group sits by itself and, in particular, young men do not eat from the same dish as older men. The way of sitting reinforces this. A junior may not sit on something while a senior sits on the ground. And, always, women respect men. It is 'wrong' for a woman to join a man's group unless specifically invited to do so, for this would give rise to the suspicion of loose behaviour. Young brides, in particular, should not attend beer drinks without their husbands, and their relationship with in-laws is hedged about by *hlonipha* taboos.

Sexual morality again reflects basic values, in this instance the importance of fertility. It is the procreational aspect of sex which is sacred and must be handled with respect and circumspection. Mere love-making is morally neutral, and indeed good, and a young person who has no lover is ridiculed. African sex morality can only be understood in terms of marriage. Marriage is essentially a 'diplomatic' alliance between families in which rights in the woman and in her children are vested in the husband and his group respectively. From this rises the institution of the levirate. Pre-marital sex does not itself involve the basic value of fertility (as long as it conforms to strict customary controls) and thus has no moral connotations. Seduction, on the other hand, is 'wrong' and punishable in the courts and by the ridicule of age mates. Adultery is wrong for women and here, as in seduction, there is a double standard, reflecting male dominance.

The importance of lineage solidarity is reflected in the husband-wife relationship. It is somehow thought wrong for a man to be too closely involved with his wife, as this may conflict with his loyalty to his kinsmen. Husband and wife do not spend their leisure time together (men and women are segregated at beer drinks and other functions) and a man who walks beside his spouse or shows too much affection for her in public is suspected of being bewitched. This cluster of moral prescriptions, then, is based on the values of kin solidarity and fertility.

But the 'good' man is not only he who respects seniors and is loyal to his kin group: he is also a good neighbour. How is this expressed in the moral code?

Here the great rule is harmonious living together and co-operation. Particularly today, with the heterogeneous nature of local groupings, this means co-operation with non-related neighbours. Indeed, the Mpondomise say that it is from neighbours, rather than kinsmen, that one can really expect assistance in time of trouble. Neighbours assist one another in working their fields, in bringing home the harvest, and in times of sickness. The good man is he who is generous—with his time, his concern and his worldly goods. Generosity is the virtue of chiefs *par excellence*, and every man strives to act like a chief. Here again there are sanctions. People assist one another, not only because it is the morally right thing to do, or because of the glow of self-satisfaction that comes from knowing that one has behaved correctly. They do so because, if they do not, they themselves may be refused assistance later. This reciprocity is inculcated from childhood and constantly practised. The fact of living together and being intimately involved in the same small piece of country, gives rise to loyalties almost as strong as those of kinship. But living together in close proximity also raises problems. There is always the possibility of jealousies arising from differential success in agriculture, and in life in general. This is the area of witchcraft accusations, reflecting these tensions, but the extreme condemnation of the witch points up the high moral value of neighbourly co-operation. A good man is one who is a good neighbour, untainted by the least suspicion of witchcraft.

The importance of moral behaviour between neighbours is given expression in the work of the courts. As the Kriges say for the Lobedu court: 'All the procedures aim, not at settling legal issues, but at effecting compromises and reconciliations. The *khoro* . . . relies, not on force, but on friendly adjustments' (Krige and Krige 1943: 186). Important here is the Lobedu custom of *hu khumelwa* ('to beg pardon of one another'), by which reconciliation is reached by an emissary who intervenes between the two parties, usually accompanied by the slaughtering of a goat (cf. Nguni *hlamba* ritual). This granting of pardon stops court procedure and the Kriges estimate that about 80 per cent of disputes are solved in this way without ever coming to court. Gluckman has shown for the Barotse of Zambia the importance of moral behaviour, and, although detailed material is not available for the Southern African tribes, there are strong indications that a similar system operates. Gluckman states that in Barotse courts the judges test the behaviour of the litigants against the concept of the 'reasonable' man in determining whether their actions are legally right or not. But mere legality is not enough. The judges expect actions also to be *morally* right—and Gluckman defines morality as right and generous behaviour towards one's fellow man. It is that extra which comes, not merely from obeying the letter of the law, but from going the second mile: that extra 'goodness' that is not due to fear of sanctions (Gluckman 1955: 229).

The widest territorial area in which morality operates is the chiefdom, and here loyalty to the chief and his political officers is a supreme good. The good man is he who is prepared to die for his chief—and van Warmelo has recorded the epical saga of the Ngwane which poignantly illustrates this (van Warmelo 1938). Connected with this is the prohibition against manslaughter within the chiefdom, for this involves killing the chief's man.

The virtues of a good man are, then, respect for seniors, loyalty to kinsmen, assistance to neighbours, freedom from the suspicion of witchcraft, generosity, meticulous observance of custom, loyalty to chief and political officers, kindness and forbearance. Perhaps it can all be summed up as good neighbourliness. Most writers on the Bantu maintain that morality among them is confined to within kin groups. We have seen that it is wider than this and that it includes all those who are thought of as members of the community, whether it be household, neighbourhood (village), district or tribe. Formerly

PLATE 19
Municipal housing in Soweto, Johannesburg, 1972

PLATE 20
Urban life

a Single men's hostels, Soweto, Johannesburg, 1972
b A wealthy man's home in Soweto

it does seem that there was a tendency for the moral community to end with the chiefdom and that loyalty, truth-telling and so on were only enjoined within it, but against this there is the hospitality universally enjoined towards strangers, expressed in the Xhosa proverb *Unyawo alunompumlo* ('the foot has no nose'). Strangers, being defenceless, are particularly under the protection of the chief or headman and are accorded special privileges. Bantu maintain that today moral behaviour, such as hospitality, respect and truthfulness, is expected among all Bantu, of whatever tribe. It is only the white man who is outside the moral community.

Notes

1 This is certainly true of the Nguni and Junod notes that the Rev. P. Ramseyer assured him 'on very good evidence' that in Basutoland 'a wife takes the family name (*seboko*) of her husband and abandons her *midimo*' (Junod 1927 II: 412 fnt.).

2 See M. Wilson (1959).

3 See M. Fortes and E. Evans-Pritchard, *African Political Systems* (1940), Introduction, for a discussion of this phenomenon.

4 See Gluckman (1954) for the original formulation. The theory is based on Kuper's magnificent description of the still existent Swazi ritual (*incwala*) (Kuper 1947: 197–225) and on Bryant (1949: 622 ff) and Marwick (1940). The Bhaca ritual (*ingcubhe*) was still being performed in the 1940s (Hammond-Tooke 1962: 179–97). See also Hunter (1936: 404–6) for the Mpondo and Cook (1931: 141–5) for the Bomvana. Gluckman's original interpretation has come in for some re-evaluation, notably by Turner 1955; Wilson 1959; Reay 1959; Worsley 1961; Norbeck 1963; Beidelman 1966; E. J. Krige 1968.

5 For further details see Giesekke 1930–1: 299ff; Stayt 1931a: 279ff; Junod 1927 II: 536ff; Mönnig 1967: 78–88.

III
Incorporation in the Wider Society

Chapter 12
The Process of Political Incorporation
J. A. Benyon

I The Southern Nguni and the Moving Frontier: First Stage

From the first contact between black and white in the early eighteenth century, some two hundred years of fluctuating and often turbulent relations have made the process of political incorporation of the Southern Bantu a major theme of South African history. It was a process with a set general pattern, but infinite variety of detail. At first, competition for land between pastoral peoples and the disruptive influence of white traders, missionaries, and government agencies upon traditional society generated friction which quasi-diplomatic methods failed to neutralize. The subordination of black by the superior military skills and technology of white ensued; and Western structures of political and judicial authority appeared in the conquered zones (though suitably modified, white-controlled indigenous institutions might be retained). Frequently, the advent of white government provoked formidable 'primary resistance movements' which anchored themselves to surviving features of the old Bantu polity, such as the ancient ruling lineages or tribal religion. The elaboration of white administrative institutions usually followed the quelling of such resistance. Finally, belated attempts were made to provide increasingly detribalized blacks with some form of 'representation' to compensate them for a loss of control over the shaping agencies of their everyday life.

The first reaction of the Dutch Company officials of the eighteenth century to the presence of dense Southern Bantu settlement in the south-east of Africa was exclusionist: the problem was to be shut out by the proclamation of a government line which would divide Boer pastoralist society from the Southern Bantu chiefdoms to the east. After several early changes this boundary came to be fixed along the Great Fish River in 1780, with all forms of trade or contact across the frontier strictly prohibited (Jeffreys 1928: 93–4: C. of P. resolution; Naudé 1949 III: 76–8, 90, 186–9; Cape Colony 1827).

It is one thing to proclaim a line; another, to keep it inviolate. The Fish river is easily fordable at most times; and only its lower reaches, in their deep, arid trench, could serve as any kind of demographic barrier. Upstream, the river flows for many miles from west to east (parallel to the dynamics of both white and Southern Bantu migration), and the insubstantial obstacle of its northern reaches was early ignored by white farmers covetous of rich pasture land around the Winterberg. Besides, it would be wrong to suppose that the Fish marked the westernmost extremity of Southern Bantu settlement. Even when the first hostile contact between white and black took place in 1702,[1] elements of the Xhosa tribal cluster of the Southern Nguni had probed far into the present-day eastern Cape. In the southern (Zuurveld) zone these minor chiefdoms, notably the Gqunukhwebe, were well established at the time of the Fish river's proclamation as boundary (Wilson and Thompson 1969 I: 103, 236–7). Nor was the resultant frontier situation solely one of interspersed white and black, for many Khoikhoi (Hottentots) had become sandwiched between the converging axes of white and black migration. They had long interacted with the Bantu—with consequent limited assimilation—and were to act as the main intermediaries in this south-eastern contact-zone (*ibid.*, 68–9, 93, 234, 246–9; Harinck 1969: 145–69).

Between 1779 and 1802 the border was chronically disturbed. Raid and counter-raid, sometimes escalating into minor 'kaffir wars', were part of the daily round. Tenuous Dutch East India Company authority was expressed in boundary proclamations, the appointment of a Boer commandant to direct the farmers' military operations, and the creation of a *landdrostdy* at Graaff-Reinet in 1786. Yet little order resulted: Boer pastoralism under the *leeningplaats*[2] system required broad acres; and the tendency towards fission in Southern Nguni political units encouraged a high rate of population growth and land occupation (Hammond-Tooke 1965a: 143–66 *passim*). Frontier turbulence was the inevitable consequence. Shortage of land determined the problem; cattle-lifting was merely a symptom—but an acute one. When Britain occupied the Cape temporarily in 1795 and permanently in 1806, these sharp antagonisms were to be an inescapable part of her frontier inheritance.

The Cape was not earmarked by Britain for either settlement or commercial development: its imperial purpose was strategic. Owning the southern tip of Africa would render the sea-route to British oriental possessions invulnerable. Yet, willy-nilly, turbulence on the Cape frontier acted as a spur to expansion in the African interior (Galbraith 1959: 167–8). The first major British response to this stimulus followed the recommendations of a certain Colonel Collins and involved the expulsion of Xhosa in the Bushmans-Sundays river area across the Fish by Colonel Graham in 1811. But the measure only perpetuated the exclusionist approach of the Dutch. In 1812 Grahamstown was founded; and the consolidation of the frontier by an efficient white military power began. Where, previously, only a thin screen of Boers had contained the Xhosa, now appeared permanent cantonments for the redcoats, small signalling stations on the heights and larger forts at the Fish drifts, to be followed, in time, by the military highways which the ageing Duke of Wellington recommended.[3]

In the coastal areas vacated by retreating Xhosa the British settlers of 1820 were placed with the purpose of further consolidation. Though many of these settlers soon left their locations and flowed into the neighbouring villages, the overall consequence was a vastly increased white population on the frontier. In spite of government decrees there had been trade by barter between black and white for decades. Now these commercial tendencies were greatly stimulated, and increasing numbers of missionaries, some of them 1820 settlers like W. Shaw and J. Ayliff, also moved into Xhosa territory. Far from being an effective barrier, the Fish river was in fact a line of interaction where friction was often, but not always, in evidence (Wilson and Thompson 1969 I: Ch. IV-1, 233–46).

Nevertheless, friction and turbulence were inherent in the situation—the frequency of open hostilities is easily explicable in such general terms. On the other hand, some assessment of the degree of unity and consistency in Xhosa resistance must be made, and this, in turn, implies a detailed investigation of at least some of the causes and consequences of the successive frontier wars. One fundamental fact is immediately clear: interaction across the Fish made it impossible for the British colonial government to abstain from trans-frontier contacts. Perhaps inevitably, these tentative contacts soon developed into close involvement—first in the domestic wrangle over the Rarabe-Xhosa succession between the chief Ngqika (Gaika) and his uncle, Ndlambe. Espousing the cause of the former, whom it chose to regard as the general representative of the frontier Xhosa, the colony helped harry the latter. The Ndlambes and associated chiefdoms had long experienced the growing pressure on land and the psychological tensions rising from contact with the advance-agencies of European civilization. It needed little to fuse them together for at least one supreme act of aggression against the white threat. A prophet and war doctor named Makanda (Nxele) acted as this catalyst, but his massed attack on Grahamstown in 1819 failed; no help came from the sky as he had prophesied.

Governor Somerset exploited this defeat by obtaining the cession of a belt of territory beyond the Fish boundary. This was henceforth supposed to remain empty and neutral.[4] Yet Britain's ally in the recent war, Ngqika, who verbally arranged with Somerset for the western boundary of Xhosa occupation to be fixed along the Keiskamma-Tyhume line—by implication ceding the tribal land beyond, as far as the colonial boundary of the Fish—was not really entitled by Southern Bantu custom to give such a commitment. Admittedly, Ngqika ranked as the paramount chief of the western (Rarabe) Xhosa, but at the level of his own chiefdom he was obliged to act as the trustee and allocator, rather than disposer, of tribal land. At the level of the loosely knit Xhosa cluster—and much of the Ceded Territory had been held by chiefdoms other than Ngqika's—it has been shown that the senior chiefdoms did *not* exercise *political* control over those more junior (Hammond-Tooke 1965a: 149–52, 155–7; MacMillan 1963: 98). Outright cession by Ngqika was therefore invalid according to the Xhosa interpretation, though it seems probable he intended nothing so definite. Following normal custom, he could have seen the transaction as a loan, or grant of usufruct, of a portion of his chiefdom's land to the colony. But he had no right—nor apparently did he claim any—to do this on behalf of the other Xhosa chiefdoms.

No sooner was it established, than this Ceded—or 'Neutral'—Territory was violated: first, by the establishment of Fredericksburg (Cory 1913 II: 108–12); second, by the institution of trade-fairs at Fort Willshire in 1824 (Cape Colony 1827: 23 July 1924); third, by the extension of magisterial district boundaries across the Fish (*ibid.*, 13 October 1820 and Advertisement 11 March 1825); and, last, by the encroachments of whites, Xhosa, and Khoikhoi in the northern section watered by the Kat and Koonap rivers. In 1829 it was, for instance, found necessary to expel Maqoma and, later, Tyali, Ngqika's powerful half-brothers, from the Kat and Mancazana valleys; but in their place was established the Kat River Settlement of Cape Coloureds (Marais 1939: 216–45). Contrary to information conveyed in several well-known general histories, the colonial boundary does not appear, in fact, to have been formally extended in the same year to the Keiskamma-Tyhume line. However, the Ceded—or 'Neutral'—Territory was henceforth *treated* as part of the colony.[5] Nor did the system of reprisal raids under a modified spoor law cease.

The ultimate consequence of all these anomalies and uncertainties was the British imperial government's decision to seek formal written agreements with a *number* of Xhosa chiefs. Ngqika's death in 1828 had ended colonial insistence that there could be only one representative figure among the frontier Xhosa. Indeed this pretence had actually undermined the general respect, if not authority, which might have been Ngqika's as paramount. Tribal resistance had, therefore, never focused upon him. It was now logical for the colony to look to the chiefs separately. Ngqika's heir, Sandile, was young, and his fiery uncle, Maqoma, had yet to show his hand as the new champion of the Xhosa traditional order. Developing out of recommendations by Governor Lowry Cole for written agreements (Hunt 1970: 196), strongly supported by Cape humanitarians, notably Dr Philip (MacMillan 1963: 105–10), and apparently cross-fertilized by the principles of the British Indian subsidiary treaty system (Walker 1957: 183), London's carefully conceived project for diplomatic agreements had really become unavoidable with the demand, from 1830 on, by the Whig party at Westminster for stricter economy in the handling of colonial affairs (Muller 1948: 27–8).

The whole scheme was almost jeopardized by the course of the frontier war of 1834–5. Instead of treaties, British authority proper was extended by the disobedient governor, D'Urban, on his personal initiative, to the lands of conquered Xhosa between the Keiskamma and Kei rivers in May 1835 (Galbraith 1963: 113–14). By September D'Urban had dropped his ill-conceived plans for expelling the still hostile Xhosa chiefdoms from this new 'Province of Queen Adelaide' and had taken steps, through Colonel Harry Smith, for the *direct* rule of the tribesmen between the rivers (Bell and Morrell 1928: 459–63).

Though it proved ephemeral, the Queen Adelaide venture has a momentous historical significance. It marked the first attempt at incorporation of Southern Bantu chiefdoms within the colonial sphere by political and administrative action—as distinct from extrusion beyond the frontier by crude military means. Consequently, it elicited from British officials the first serious thought on the practical implications of actually *ruling* an African people whose socio-political system was so vastly different from their own. Additionally significant is the fact that the dominant theme of future Cape 'native policy'—the subversion of the traditional structure of chiefly authority—emerged as early as this 'Queen Adelaide' interlude. While Smith might have moved carefully at first, he was in no doubt about his long term objective:

> To attach the people to the new order of things was of vast importance; to lessen the power of the chiefs equally so; but this had to be gradual, for, if I removed the hereditary restraint of the chiefs, I should open the gates to an anarchy which I might not be able to quell (Moore-Smith (ed) 1902: 435).

As the best means of averting the feared anarchy, Smith saw that the main elements of tribal law, modified to meet 'civilized usages', would have to apply for a long time ahead (*Br. Parl. Papers* 1837, XLIII (503) 251: Smith's notes). Another dominant theme of Cape 'native policy', the utilization of modified customary law—later embodied in special codes—therefore traces its source to 1836. But Smith did not have time to devise such a code because, for various reasons, the 'Queen Adelaide' scheme foundered in 1837. British authorities then reverted to the original idea of formal treaties with *independent* chiefdoms in the Keiskamma-Kei area (Galbraith 1963: Ch. 8, 123–50 *passim*).

This so-called 'Stockenström Treaty System' was not a return to the old exclusionist policies. Under it Andries Stockenström became Lieutenant-Governor of the Eastern Districts, with special responsibility for the frontier. His position carried with it a diplomatic status *vis-à-vis* the Xhosa, which was reinforced by the establishment of resident agents with the chiefdoms. Men like Charles Stretch, agent on the Tyhume, appear to have carried out their work of liaison with conscience and tact. Allegations of cattle-theft—claim and counter-claim—were, for instance, carefully investigated (see Crankshaw 1960: *passim*). Thus the abuses inherent in the old 'spoor law', under which stolen cattle were often incorrectly traced and innocent kraals raided by irate white farmers, were largely eradicated. Nevertheless, these treaty relations were breaking down by 1846. Perhaps it was being too optimistic to expect that two such disparate entities as a European colony and an African chiefdom could subsist side-by-side on a basis of diplomatic equality. In the context of persistent drought and perennial competition for land, the innately hostile forces of frontiersmen and Xhosa were hardly to be so easily reconciled. Besides, Stockenström's dismissal (Galbraith 1963: 149–50), the subsequent modification of the treaties (Crankshaw 1960: 54–8), and Maqoma's mounting irritation at the threat of white settlement in his near-neighbourhood had made the Xhosa increasingly distrustful of white *bona fides*.

The expensive 'War of the Axe' of 1846–7 finally convinced the Imperial

Government that the Bantu-inhabited frontier zone had to be incorporated and internally administered. The Permanent Under-Secretary for Colonies, Sir James Stephen, guided London thinking:

> The Chiefs and their tribes should acknowledge the Queen as the Protector of their nation and should receive a British military officer as Commander-in-Chief. . . . [This officer] should, in effect, exercise the supreme authority in their state with such concessions as might be calculated to secure their willing obedience.

Last, Stephen did not contemplate 'the introduction . . . of English Law, of English institutions or of European settlers'.[6]

Consequently, a new frontier dependency, British Kaffraria, was established between the Keiskamma and Kei in 1847. Its essentials of rule were very largely those which Stephen had spelled out: first, imperial control, but the deliberate omission of those institutions which were characteristic of British colonies proper; and second, as the logical corollary, a relatively uncomplicated system of government which would at least be intelligible to the Xhosa. Certain elements of the existing tribal system, such as African customary law, were found to be particularly useful foundations to build upon. In their initial experiments with this indigenous law Cape administrators could, moreover, exploit the anomalous constitutional position of British Kaffraria—neither full colony, nor protectorate. Special codes of modified tribal law became thus a feature of the 'native policy' followed in the black territories which came successively under Cape colonial sway.

Two further important developments lie in this period. In 1846 the Governor of the Cape became 'High Commissioner' expressly entrusted with the solution of frontier questions (*Br. Parl. Papers* 1847–8, XLIII (912) 5), and, second, this new post went to Harry Smith. In British Kaffraria he was to use it as his main instrument for implementing the same plans for magisterial control which he had earlier been obliged to shelve in 'Queen Adelaide'.

As a suitable model for the establishment of the magisterial system Smith looked to the functioning of his 'superintendents' in the Mfengu locations of the 'Victoria District' (annexed to the Cape proper in 1847 and therefore lying west of the Keiskamma-Tyhume frontier line). These Mfengu were the best allies the Cape had found among the Nguni. As tribal remnants from the Shakan wars, or *Mfecane*, they had fled south from Natal and entered into various client relationships with the Xhosa. After the 1834–5 war D'Urban had settled 17,000 Mfengu in the old Ceded Territory, near Fort Peddie. They now changed their clientship to the Cape government and developed into useful allies in the wars against the Xhosa, who deeply resented the Mfengu occupying their old lands. Understandably, their precarious position made the Mfengu amenable to white control; so their magistrate, Calderwood, could soon begin experiments to convert them into peasant, as distinct from tribal, cultivators holding land on individual tenure (*Br. Parl. Papers* 1850,

XXXVIII (1288) 1–4, 12–13: Despatches 15 March and 24 May 1849, and enclosures).

Xhosa resistance and his own impatience defeated Smith. The deposition of Ngqika's son, Sandile, and his replacement by a white official reveal how little the High Commissioner understood the tribal society he sought to control. His military villages in the Tyhume valley were considered a standing threat by the Xhosa, hard-pressed now by the steady consolidation of alien white forces opposite them and, indeed, in their own midst. Again there arose a prophet, Mlanjeni, to fan up the war spirit for what proved to be the most debilitating of all eastern frontier struggles. Lasting from 1850 to 1853, it even caused Smith's own recall in 1852. The tenacity which the Xhosa displayed in bush-fighting and the degree of unity and co-ordination achieved by the chiefdoms and a number of Cape Coloured allies will need much closer investigation by historians before a satisfactory picture of this sustained conflict can emerge. A good place to begin may be the fevered vision behind Mlanjeni's prediction that British guns would fire only hot water!

As part of Sir George Cathcart's military solution after the war, Sandile and his Ngqikas were expelled from the Amatole mountains, and the frontier road-and-garrison system was then elaborated (Du Toit 1954 I: 66–85 *passim*; Cathcart 1857: 381–4). This greatly facilitated the task of Sir George Grey, who became High Commissioner in 1854.

Grey was a civilian whose mind recoiled instinctively from rigid military solutions to frontier problems. But his experience in New Zealand had attached him to the school which thought the 'advance of civilization' among primitive societies could only be secured by close contact with whites. Loose or indirect methods of control were to be eschewed. European education, medicine, religion, culture, and, ultimately, law were to diffuse among the Xhosa, who were to be so placed as to observe closely what the whites derived from these benefits (Rutherford 1961: 304, 312–39). In fine, Grey's approach was 'assimilationist', rather than rigidly segregationist, with this rider that the acculturation of the Xhosa to the habits and behavioural pattern of the European was primarily intended as the final way around the problem of Cape frontier insecurity (Rutherford 1961: 325–6).

Through Maclean, Chief Commissioner for British Kaffraria, Grey began to implement his plans. First, the chiefs were to be lured into retirement by the promise of stipends (Du Toit 1954: 94–6). Their judicial functions would be gradually usurped by white 'special magistrates', who would initially act as mere assessors with the chiefs (*Br. Parl. Papers* 1856, XLII (C 2096) 16–17: Despatches and enclosures). The magistrates were to be guided by tribal custom, which was digested into a small handbook known as *Maclean's Compendium* (for extracts see: G4 of '83, Appendix B 1). To forward the grand design the High Commissioner meanwhile secured an imperial grant-in-aid of £40,000 per annum (P.R.O., C.O. 48/365: Draft Despatch, 19 May 1855).

The profoundly disruptive effect of the 'Cattle-killing' of 1857 upon Xhosa society greatly assisted Grey's scheme. Twice before—in the wars of Makanda and Mlanjeni—the Xhosa had invoked the supernatural to help halt the advance of European civilization. Now, encouraged by the visions of a teenage prophetess, Nongqawuse, and her uncle, Mhlakaza, the Xhosa committed themselves to the destruction of their cattle and crops under the delusion that their ancestors would rise up and support their resistance to white penetration. There is no ground for believing that either Grey or Sarili (Kreli), the Gcaleka-Xhosa paramount, encouraged the work of destruction for Machiavellian purposes. Rather, Xhosa resistance had at last 'turned awry' under the repetitive blows of defeat to 'lose the name of action' in a maze of primitive millenarianism (see Moorcroft 1967: *passim*; Wilson and Thompson 1969 I: 256–60).

The 'Cattle-killing' caused widespread starvation, with many Xhosa crossing into the Cape to take service. In the disaster Maclean saw the opportunity of finally breaking the power of the chiefs. Some were duly banished for their part in the 'national suicide' of their people (Du Toit 1954: 103–4). Grey could then begin inserting wedges of white settlement into the vacant parts (*ibid.* 109; Rutherford 1961: 380–1). Together with provision for African education—as witnessed by government encouragement and subsidy of missionary institutions like Lovedale—this white colonization had, indeed, always been Grey's final answer to the problem of 'civilizing' the frontier chiefdoms (see Shepherd 1940: 131–5; P.R.O., C.O. 48/365: Despatch No. 17 March 1855, encl. Speech). After the 'Cattle-killing' the success of these plans seemed certain. When Grey left the Cape in 1861, the focus of attention had already shifted forward from a quiescent British Kaffraria to the land beyond the Kei. Here Grey wished to extend the same methods that had given such rapid results in British Kaffraria (Rutherford 1961: 430–3). But the loss of the imperial grant-in-aid, the mounting frontier difficulties of the new High Commissioner, Wodehouse, and the hesitations of the Secretary of State, Cardwell, combined to halt the process of *formal* political incorporation on the Kei river for more than a decade in the 1860s and early 1870s (Du Toit 1954: Ch. 13, 179–95 *passim*).

In British Kaffraria the Cape had achieved its first substantial success upon the frontier. The colony could now lay claim to a 'native policy' in many respects superior to that developed either in Natal or the Boer republics. Admittedly, the Xhosa chiefs' powers waned fast. The agreement of October 1855 for judicial sessions of chief and magistrate sitting jointly soon gave way to the magistrate acting alone. From their initial position as assessors, the magistrates graduated after 1857 to the free exercise of the chiefs' 'forfeited' jurisdiction. Fines henceforth went to the Crown; and not only the chiefs, but also the headmen were incorporated in the government's stipendiary system. Moreover, the government took the initiative in allocating districts within the chiefdom's lands to these headmen. They were to be the responsible parties in the districts—but this responsibility was no longer to the chief. In addition, the government's concentration of the population in villages from 1856 also brought the Xhosa under the close surveillance of the growing mounted police force (Du Toit 1954: 86–110 *passim*).

At least this Cape policy did involve providing some alternative to the traditional structure which it set out to undermine. For instance, once British Kaffraria was officially annexed to the Cape Colony in 1865, both the privileges under the law which had been secured to persons of colour by the legislation of 1828–34 and the 'colour-blind' franchise of the Cape constitution of 1853 were extended to the incorporated African (MacMillan 1963: 18; Marais 1937: 337). After a long period of tentative experiments and partial solutions, Cape policy under Grey had taken a positive direction. The weakness of his policy was that his white settlers still threatened the tribesman's land (Rutherford 1961: 425–9). But, at least, education and possibilities of employment in the colony were now available as an alternative to inevitable defeat in war or delusions of despair which led only to self-destruction. Xhosa losses might have been grievous between 1778 and 1865, but they were not entirely unrelieved.

II Natal and Zululand

In studies of native administration the 'Natal' and 'Cape' systems are generally differentiated. However, it would be wrong to suppose that these differences had their origin in some fundamental divergence in theory between the officials of the two British colonies. Rather, the direction which political incorporation took in Natal was mainly determined by local circumstances.

Among the most powerful of the factors which governed historical trends in Natal was the formidable Zulu monarchy which Shaka had built up in the early nineteenth century. His ferocious campaigns to reduce all in his vicinity to subjection and the consequent internecine wars—the *Mfecane* of the 1820s (see Omer-Cooper 1966: *passim*)—either led to the incorporation of the Nguni chiefdoms of Natal in the Zulu system or broke them into detribalized remnants which fled their exposed positions near Shaka southward, to the present Transkei, or north-west, toward and over the Drakensberg escarpment. When the exploratory *Kommissie Trek* of the Voortrekkers appeared in the early 1830s, Natal therefore wore the smiling face of open, underpopulated land to the prospective Boer migrant (Walker 1948: 96, 139, 142–3, 148–9). But, to the north, the Zulu proved themselves an insupportable menace to the Voortrekkers. Consequently, Boer commandoes together with dissident Zulu allies overthrew Shaka's successor, Dingane, in 1838–40, though the potential threat of the *impis* across the Buffalo and Tukela rivers was no more than neutralized for a time. The white frontiersmen then settled down to establish their 'Republic of Natalia' in the relatively open country, and to break up its coveted land into farms.

This loose-knit republic was, however, short-lived. Concerned about her South African paramountcy, Britain hastened to stake out her imperial claim to the area. In 1845 she established at Pietermaritzburg an embryo colonial administration, which was initially to depend on the parent colony of the Cape (see Bird (ed.) 1888 I: 380: Despatch, 25 May 1844). Disheartened at this turn of events and at the disorganization of 1843–8, most of the republican-minded Boers trekked back to the Highveld, leaving much of the land again open and inviting to the thousands of original Nguni inhabitants who had been steadily seeping back from their refuges of the *Mfecane*. In these years some 80,000 re-appeared.

Much of the process of incorporation of Natal Africans turns on the personality of Theophilus Shepstone. With a missionary and 1820 settler background and some experience of Cape native administration, he arrived in Natal to take up the post of Diplomatic Agent to the tribes in 1846 (for detail see Gordon 1968: 86–115). His assumptions about the African might have been paternalistic, but he was also a calm, able, and remarkably self-sufficient man.

Shepstone's variant of an old Voortrekker scheme—involving the shifting of 'surplus' Natal Nguni into the Griqualand East region and ruling them himself as 'Great Chief'—soon proved impracticable. Therefore he embraced the alternative of reserve African settlements inside Natal. In their initial stages, these were supposed to follow the lines of the Ayliff-Calderwood Mfengu settlements of the Cape frontier. But Shepstone and his fellows on the Natal Native Affairs Commission of 1846–7 lacked the necessary funds for this policy of betterment—though he did have singular success in leading 80,000 of the returning Nguni into the areas which were to serve as 'locations'.[7] By 1849 there were seven of these reserves, all of which took some time to be surveyed. At the end of the Shepstone era altogether some 2,000,000 acres of this 'Location land' had been set aside in Natal—to which must be added 146,571 acres of mission reserves (Brookes and Hurwitz 1957: 6). This was, however, only about a sixth of the total acreage of Natal, much of the better land having been already pre-empted by white farmers. In the early years the reserves might have just supported their populations; later, overcrowding and the attendant ills of overstocking and erosion were to present themselves as serious problems. Yet, ironically, the reserve policy was unpopular among white Natal colonists at first—because it seemed to set aside too much land, thereby potentially restricting both the farmers' labour supply and acreage available for land speculation (Brookes 1924: 53–6).

So far as it had gone by 1851, the location system was no more than a pragmatic reaction to the problem of returning refugees. The chief point to notice is Shepstone's success in launching the scheme administratively. And, once afloat, it had to be kept buoyant by a series of shifts and expedients which came to be dignified as 'Shepstonian Native Policy'. One contrivance was Shepstone's semi-artificial tribal system, which pyramided up from 'headmen' and 'chiefs', via himself as Diplomatic Agent and, later, Native Secretary, to the Lieutenant-Governor of Natal at the apex as Supreme Chief. With the finance for magisterial supervision lacking, this was an intelligent solution to the problem of government in the locations. But, having thus established a pre-Lugardian form of 'indirect rule', Shepstone faced the closely related problem of law-enforcement. Perhaps his recollection of the Queen Adelaide venture suggested to him the possibilities of indigenous Natal Nguni custom, shorn of certain unacceptable tribalisms. In spite of strong initial opposition by Natal's Recorder (Judge), Henry Cloete, suitably modified 'Native Law' was accordingly recognized in the Ordinance of 23 June 1849. But Shepstone decided to keep a close control over its application (Gordon 1968: 145-9).

This, substantially, was the Shepstone 'policy' of legal differentiation and territorial segregation. Only three further important facts need to be added. First, the legal title to reserve land was vested in the hands of a Natal Native Trust in 1864—which was only the Executive Council of Natal acting in another capacity (Brookes and Hurwitz 1957: 9). Second, a Native High Court of dubious merits (mainly because it depersonalized the legal side of Shepstone's system) came into existence in 1875, and the codifying of native law was initiated. Two codes, those of 1878 and 1891, were to appear, though Shepstone was known to disapprove of this step—preferring the flexibility of informal arrangements. Finally, provision was made in 1865 for the exemption of detribalized Africans from native law and, under certain further conditions, for a grant of the franchise to them (Brookes 1924: 58-60). Only a handful of Africans ever cast their votes in Natal elections; so it is fair to conclude that the Shepstonian policy of racial differentiation had fortified itself against major changes in fundamentals by the time Shepstone himself passed from the Natal political scene in 1875.

During the years from 1875 to 1903 the apparent efficacy—or, rather, 'reputation'—of Shepstonianism inhibited adjustment and improvement. In his own day, Shepstone had often been criticized. On his departure, his latter, more conservative, ideas on administration entrenched themselves so deeply that they reacted unfavourably upon any proposed improvement of the kind which he and the 1846-7 Native Commission had originally considered essential in location policy. The pace of life in the locations simply did not match the acceleration outside; and the Natal Native Secretaryship—which continued in the Shepstone family—lost that close contact with tribal life which had given some warmth and humanity to Shepstone's tenure of it.

The most dramatic event of the post-Shepstone era was the demolition of the Zulu military system and hereditary monarchy in the Zulu War of 1879. The stabilization of south-east Africa as the groundwork of a subcontinental confederation was the British war aim. However, the conflict began inauspiciously for the redcoats and Natal auxiliaries, who experienced a devastating setback at Isandhlwana. Militarily, the defeat was soon retrieved, but, politically, it broke the British government's commitment to confederation—from which a consistent 'native policy' might have emerged. Zululand was left to drift, rudderless, in a narrowing strait. Britain's mistake in refusing to annex and replace the shattered authority of Cetshwayo, the last Zulu king, was further compounded by Wolseley's postwar settlement. The latter's 'kinglets', the creation of a Zulu 'Reserve', and the half-hearted restoration of

Cetshwayo in 1883 were all futile expedients. Even the establishment of the Boer 'New Republic' on Zulu soil and some tentative German probing failed to distract the British government from its perennial Irish problem. Only in 1887 did Britain finally annex Zululand; but this was followed by incorporation in colonial Natal in 1897. By that time the old Zulu 'kingdom' had virtually lost its identity (see Webb 1969: 302-23; Brookes and Webb 1965: 146-55, 185-8).

It would perhaps have been too much to expect that Natal—having achieved 'Responsible Government' (i.e. a colonial executive) in 1893—would follow a more imaginative policy in Zululand than she was pursuing in her own reserves. The rinderpest epidemic of 1897-8 and the apparent fragmentation of Zulu society into its numerous pre-Shakan units made resistance to white penetration seem unlikely. Predictably, Zululand was partitioned into white farmland, Crown land, and African reserves by the Zululand Delimitation Commission of 1902-4. While the Zulu retained a more generous proportion of land than that assigned to the neighbouring Nguni of Natal, many of the typical features of latter-day Shepstonianism made their appearance north of the Tukela. By the early 1900s this policy was generating severe tensions, not least in the locations of Natal proper, where its shortcomings were being sharply highlighted against a backdrop of overcrowding and a changing economic pattern. As in Xhosa resistance, so in Zulu: from a ferment of primitive millenarianism there at last emerged the messiah—in this case Dinuzulu, last scion of the Shakan house. Whatever his precise role in the so-called Bambatha rebellion of 1906-7 (this still remains doubtful), he was the only available focus of a rising which, at bottom, expressed pent-up 'pan-Zulu' frustrations at the protracted and painful nature of incorporation and at the steady ossification of Natal 'native policy' (see Marks 1970: *passim*; Brookes and Webb 1965: 221).

The system which circumstances forced on Shepstone has had a sustained influence on the subsequent 'native policies' of Southern Africa (Welsh 1971). Certainly, it cannot be neglected in any study of the origins of the policy of *Apartheid*. But in its early stages it was merely a series of rather obvious formulae devised by one of the few white men who had a working knowledge of Southern Bantu society. Had Shepstone ever set his mind more vigorously to the business of educating and bettering the African, he might today be a less controversial historical figure. But it is well to remember there was always a land shortage (admittedly artificially induced) in 'colonial' Natal, and Shepstone always had white critics who resented the way he walled off his administrative activity from petty local politics and jealousies. And, to achieve this coveted extra-political position, Shepstone's system involuntarily came to rest upon a cheap, semi-traditional, and—*ipso facto*—conservative base.

III The Genesis of the High Commission Territories

To the two forms of African government so far discussed, a third must be added—the High Commission Territory. In a sense, the administration evolved for the three High Commission Territories, Basutoland, Bechuanaland, and Swaziland, was a blend of elements from the Cape and Natal systems, together with the further ingredient of protection and supervision by the British imperial government. Political independence has since entrenched the individuality of the successor-states to the High Commission Territories; yet the early historical development of these territories—and particularly that of Basutoland, which was the first—has had an abiding influence upon their subsequent progress in both the domestic and external fields.

Basutoland was essentially a product of the *Mfecane* (or *Difaqane* as this great upheaval is known in Sotho dialects). West of the Drakensberg the distribution and organization of the Sotho peoples, who, together with the Nguni, form the bulk of the Southern Bantu, were as vitally affected as the coastal chiefdoms adjacent to the Zulu (Lye 1967: 107–31; Lye 1969: 191–206). To escape the marauders who scoured the Highveld during the 'Troubles', groups of South Sotho—and other refugees—congregated along the Maloti spur of the Drakensberg, where they were drawn together into a species of federation by Moshweshwe, who had come to dominate his father's minor Mokotedi chiefdom (Ellenberger and MacGregor 1912: 128–236 *passim*). With singular skill Moshweshwe consolidated his power. Cattle lifted in several profitable raids were distributed on loan to an ever-widening circle of clients under the *mafisa* system. To Moshweshwe's fame as a warrior was thus added an abiding reputation for generosity. He then set about 'placing' his sons in strategic spots in the emergent *Lesotho*, contracting judicious marriages, occupying the hill-fortress of Thaba Bosiu as the impregnable base for Sotho expansion, neutralizing the Tlokwa threat of Sekonyela, and 'importing' Paris Evangelical missionaries to instruct his people and act as advisers in his relations with the Boer trekkers and British government (Sanders 1969: 439–55). From 1836 these relations were to be his chief preoccupation.

The Great Trek created a new frontier between black and white beyond the Orange. At first, the imperial government moved hesitatingly in its search for stability in the area. Moshweshwe and the Griqua, Adam Kok, were drawn into alliances with the British by Governor Napier in 1843 (P.R.O., C.O. 48/243: Despatch No. 69, 22 July 1844, encl. Treaties), but these treaties had to be elaborated at Touwfontein in 1846. A British Resident—entrusted with considerable diplomatic and mediatory duties—was established in the vicinity of the Griqua and Sotho, at Bloemfontein (Eybers, G. W. (ed.) 1918: 262ff.). Finally, the process was taken to its logical conclusion in 1848 with the proclamation of British sovereignty between the Orange and Vaal rivers by the impulsive and expansionistic Sir Harry Smith (*ibid.*, 270–3). Moshweshwe and the lands of his tribal federation in the Caledon river area were thereby half-incorporated, though the Sotho were not supposed to lose any powers of internal self-government. Only their external relations were henceforth to be carefully regulated.

Moshweshwe's first close contacts with British over-rule were disillusioning. Major Warden, the British Resident in the Orange River Sovereignty, proved unnecessarily high-handed in his dealings. Fighting between Sotho and imperial troops followed in 1852; and two years later the expense of its South African responsibilities caused an exasperated British government to shake off the Sovereignty (*ibid.*, 281–5). The Boer-inhabited area became the Orange Free State and was left to sort out its relationship with the sulky Sotho as best it could. Turbulence on the Sotho frontier became endemic. As one war between Free State and Sotho in 1858 gave way to another in 1864, Moshweshwe came therefore to appreciate that the British government, with its strategic interest in subcontinental stability, was his best potential ally against the land-hungry Boers.

In the 1860s this British interest was represented by three semi-distinct authorities—the Cape and Natal colonial governments and the imperial High Commissioner, Sir Philip Wodehouse. Moshweshwe's appeals for succour were initially directed to the latter, but he soon called also on Shepstone in Natal to protect and annex him (Axelson 1934: 46–7). To Wodehouse, a supporter of the Cape system of magisterial supervision in tribal areas, Natal's 'native policy' was anathema.[8] Worried that Sotho turbulence might communicate itself to the Cape's eastern frontier, fearing also that the Free Staters might secure a route to the sea after their conquest of Moshweshwe, and apprehensive that Shepstonianism might gain acceptance as the general formula for rule in incorporated territories, Wodehouse exceeded his instructions from London by bringing Basutoland under the authority of his High Commission in March 1868 (Theal (ed.) 1883 III: 894).

The imposition of British over-rule saved the South Sotho from despoliation by the Free State. In addition, the segmentation of the tribal federation along typical Southern Bantu lines, which might have followed disputes over the succession to Moshweshwe, was inhibited by the establishment of permanent boundaries and by this over-rule. Conflicts between the leading chiefs of the paramount's first house became 'internalized', helping the federation to survive (Atmore 1969: 300–1).

In Downing Street Wodehouse's action was eventually accepted as a *fait accompli*, though there was a general feeling that, with Cape Responsible Government in the offing, the colony should shoulder the burden of Basutoland, as well as of British Kaffraria. Accordingly, Basutoland was annexed to the Cape in 1871 (Eybers 1819: 61–2). But the interim period 1868–71, when boundaries were under negotiation and the situation inside Basutoland was fluid, had witnessed the appearance of only a skeletal magisterial establishment under the High Commissioner's Agent. Consequently, the chiefs of Moshweshwe's first house (the old paramount died in 1870) had enjoyed a considerable latitude. When the magistrates of the Cape period, after 1871, began to erode their authority, these chiefs therefore looked nostalgically back to the 'High Commission' period of 1868–71 (see G6 of '83, 35: Report, 18 October 1882). Their resentment was probably not strong enough in itself to have generated a full-scale rising against white over-rule. However, when the dual threat of 1878-9—that the Sotho would be disarmed of rifles acquired at the Diamond Fields and that white settlers might appear in the south—was added to it, rebellion became inevitable (Tylden 1950: 128-44).

The so-called 'Gun War' of 1880-1 was the greatest and most successful 'primary resistance movement' mounted in Southern Africa. Historically, it can be interpreted as Lesotho's War of Independence. When the widely dispersed and inadequate Cape colonial forces eventually acknowledged that they could make little headway in hostile country, a truce was arranged on the High Commissioner's initiative (P.R.O., C.O. 48/500: Despatch No. 178, 19 April 1881, encl. Tel. 18 April; *Br. Parl. Papers* 1881, LXVII (C 2964) 25-6). In these circumstances it was impossible for the Cape colony's magisterial system to re-establish itself (Benyon 1968: 485-586). On the other hand, the Sotho feared that complete independence would recreate the Free State-Sotho border situation of 1854-68. They therefore requested the Queen to resume their external protection and to supply a scratch 'High Commission' establishment like that of 1868-71. Prompted by the strategic consideration of the British paramountcy and by the philanthropists, the imperial government reluctantly agreed.

The first High Commission Territory came gradually into its own from 1884 onwards. Its administration was based upon a compromise between white magisterial and 'indirect' tribal forms of authority, and functioned largely through the exercise of 'moral suasion' by successive, enlightened Resident Commissioners, like Marshall Clarke and Godfrey Lagden (Benyon 1968: 587-631 and Appendix C). Under imperial protection Basutoland was to remain a tribal preserve at the geographical centre of Southern Africa—surrounded by white colonies, Boer republics, and increasingly incorporated black trans-Keian territories.

The precedent established in the case of Basutoland exercised a strong fascination upon the men who were responsible for the establishment of the Bechuanaland Protectorate shortly afterwards. The idea that there was an alternative formula to white colonial incorporation or the elaborate legal apparatus of Crown Colony Government for ruling strategically placed black territories took root in British administrative circles, especially as humanitarian imperialists, like the Rev. John Mackenzie of the L.M.S., were skilful in propagandizing their plan for such imperial protectorates or 'territories'. These would depend directly on the British High Commissioner, to the exclusion of colonial governments (see Mackenzie 1887 I: 119-23, 131-78 *passim*).

In the case of Bechuanaland many of the elements of the Basutoland situation were duplicated. The Tswana chiefdoms straddled the strategic route into the interior. At the edges of this territory, 'filibusters' and Boer settlers soon began to nibble. Characteristically, they contracted 'alliances' with dissident chiefs and pretenders who had their private axes to grind against the main chiefdoms of the 'Keate Award' area. Lying north of Griqualand West and west of the Transvaal, both of which had been earmarked for incorporation in Britain's proposed confederation, this zone had not escaped some informal British control between 1878 and 1881. But the retrocession of the Transvaal to the Boers and the collapse of confederation left a vacuum which resurrected the old problem of encroachment in aggravated form. Inside the line of the Pretoria Convention of 1881 certain Tswana and Griqua groups were automatically incorporated under Transvaal rule, while two petty Boer republics, Stellaland and Goshen, were quickly constituted outside the line, on lands claimed by the Thlaping under Mankurwane and the Tshidi-Rolong of Montshiwa (Sillery 1952: 47-8). With this deteriorating situation as background, Mackenzie's publicist campaign in England in 1882 swung a substantial body of philanthropical opinion behind the cry for protection of the Tswana. While Boer delegates achieved some extension of the 1881 line in the London Convention of 1884, an awakened public opinion and the recommendations of Sir H. Robinson, the High Commissioner, deprived the Transvaal of the 'Road to the North' (see Schreuder 1969: 388-427 *passim*).

The loose protectorate envisaged in the London Convention did not entirely eliminate the threat of Boer expansion. Among the leading figures of Gladstone's second ministry, Joseph Chamberlain was soon doubly concerned at the potential threat posed, from the other side, by the new German protectorate in South West Africa. If German and Boer joined hands, the 'Road to the North' might yet be blocked. In October 1884 Chamberlain succeeded in drawing the British Cabinet round to an acceptance of greater responsibility (Garvin 1935 I: 492; Benyon 1968: 632, esp. footnote 3). Sir Charles Warren was deputed to take a substantial military force into Bechuanaland in 1885 to impress upon the Boers that Britain meant business (Agar-Hamilton 1937: 359-62, 386-423). The main incidental result of this complex manoeuvring by the white powers was the political incorporation of the Tswana (see Wilson and Thompson 1971 II: 271-2).

To begin with, only the area south of the Molopo river came effectively under British protection. In 1885 it became the Crown Colony of British Bechuanaland and was incorporated in the Cape Colony in 1895. North of the Molopo, in Bechuanaland 'proper', the Protectorate was established in 1885, and then in very tenuous form and extending north only to 22°S latitude (Sillery 1965: 40, 43). Mackenzie and the High Commissioner had clashed the previous year over the future of the protectorate south of the Molopo, and subsequent intrigue cost the former the Deputy Commissionership to which he had been appointed. Sidney Shippard became the first Deputy Commissioner of the Northern Protectorate, and in 1887 John S. Moffat appeared as Assistant Commissioner north of the Molopo (*ibid.*, 99).

By this time Cecil Rhodes was taking the initial steps which were to lead to the formation of the British South Africa Charter Company. Indeed, from 1889, the issue in Bechuanaland was whether Rhodes's commercial interests would convert the Protectorate into a launching pad for his schemes in the interior, or whether Mackenzie's ideal of direct imperial rule and entrenched protection for the Africans would prevail. The foremost protagonist of the latter system was Sir Henry Loch, High Commissioner from 1889. In 1890 he had persuaded the Colonial Office in London to introduce an Order in Council enabling him to legislate in the Protectorate and extending the scope of protection to the Caprivi strip and the Zambezi. To this was added a further and more explicit Order in Council in May 1891. In terms of proclamations by Loch, which exploited these Orders to their fullest extent, an administrative cadre was then established for the Protectorate (*ibid.*, 145-6, 148-58). Inclined largely through missionary activity to consider the 'Imperial Factor' as their ally in the struggle to save their land and at least a respectable number of their old prerogatives from Boer or Charter Company encroachment, the chiefs of the Ngwato, Ngwaketse and Kwena duly accepted Loch's dispensation.

After 1891 Rhodes's Charter Company nevertheless had reason to anticipate that the Protectorate administration would shortly be entrusted to it. But Rhodes was checkmated by the visit of the chiefs Kgama, Sebele and Bathoen to England in late 1895. Impressed by the chiefs' fear of being incorporated by the Company, Chamberlain, as Secretary of State for the Colonies, ruled that the protection through imperial officials, which they asked of the Queen, would be maintained (*ibid.*, 217-34). The hopes of absorption still entertained by the Company were than dissipated, shortly afterwards, by Jameson's disastrous 'Raid', in which Rhodes was so deeply implicated. By 1896 Bechuanaland had achieved much the shape of modern Botswana and was reasonably established as one of the new-type, internally-governed imperial protectorates in which the legal status of citizens, the simpler administrative forms, and the survival of considerable chiefly prerogatives were the only noteworthy differences from Crown Colony rule (for legal status see Polack 1963: 138-55). Recognition of African rights in land and law was thus secured.

Beyond Bechuanaland lay Lobengula's Ndebele 'kingdom'. Its experience of incorporation was to be much more traumatic than that of the Protectorate chiefdoms. After their flight from Zululand in 1823, and in the course of a sanguinary Odyssey across Southern Africa under Mzilikazi's guidance, the Ndebele had assimilated numerous Sotho tribal remnants, yet retained the essence of a centralized military monarchy on Zulu lines (Lye 1969: 87-104; Bekker 1962: *passim*). With the rise of Kruger's Boer republic and the opening of the Bechuanaland route to Rhodes's aggressive brand of Cape-De Beers imperialism, the final Ndebele settlement round Bulawayo then became strategically important to white powers.

Owing to profound apprehensions among the Ndebele, white penetration of Lobengula's 'kingdom' had been insignificant by the mid-eighties. But the swiftly accelerating pace of the African scramble obliged Lobengula to open the door—albeit grudgingly. While his initial treaty with J. S. Moffat merely brought the Ndebele within the British sphere of influence, the Rudd Concession of 1888 was to be the Trojan horse which let in the Charter Company and compassed the military downfall of the Ndebele within five years (Brown in Stokes and Brown (eds) 1966: 63–93; Glass 1968: *passim*). However, the Ndebele war of 1893 was merely the initial phase of the incorporative process. It was followed by the suppression—through negotiation and force—of the rebellions of 1896–7 in Matabeleland and Mashonaland. The co-ordination of this widespread resistance to white pioneer settlement and alien rule was the remarkable work of the Mwari-Mlimo religious cults and Shona spirit mediums—whose roots went far back to the Rozwi and Mwene Mutapa 'empires' (Ranger 1967: *passim*). Nevertheless, the end of the rebellions opened even Shona society to Christian conversion and left the Charter Company free to continue, though more cautiously, its policies of land partition and reservation. As the Company and its pioneers had shouldered the burden of conquest and incorporation, the High Commissioner proved unable, and the Crown unwilling, to intervene effectively. Rhodesia was therefore to develop on widely divergent lines from those of the High Commission Territories.

Swaziland in the late nineteenth century differed markedly from the cases of Basutoland and Bechuanaland. The hegemony of the Dhlamini chieftainship had been steadily undermined by an extremely wide-ranging series of concessions and monopoly grants to enterprising whites who had penetrated the Swazi country, mainly from the Transvaal, since the 1860s (Hailey 1953 V: 360–4). The territory did not, therefore, remain a relatively consolidated block of tribal land. Because a possible route of republican egress to the sea lay through Swaziland to Kosi Bay, strategic factors were also soon involved (Garson 1957 II: *passim*). In the Anglo-Transvaal conventions of 1881 and 1884 some attempt had been made to secure the independence of the country. When these provisions proved insufficient, a system of joint Anglo-Transvaal control over external Swazi affairs was inaugurated in 1890, only to give way in 1894 to a convention which conceded the Transvaal sole rights of protection and jurisdiction (Hailey 1953 V: 365–8). But Britain quickly closed the potential exit to the sea by proclaiming a protectorate over coastal Tongaland in 1895. Simultaneously, the Transvaal appointed a Resident Commissioner in Swaziland, who remained till the outbreak of the Anglo-Boer War in 1899. During that war the Swazi Queen Regent again asked for British protection. Incorporation in the Transvaal *Colony* might have lost Swaziland its semi-independent status; so its administration was based, instead, upon an Order in Council of June 1903 in terms of the Foreign Jurisdiction Acts (*ibid.*, 370). Thereby it became the third High Commission Territory and Britain's second 'imperial' protectorate in South Africa. As in the other two cases, a governmental system of white commissioners was established to work in harness with indigenous 'traditional' authorities. But so much land had been alienated to whites that Swaziland never became an African preserve in the Basutoland sense (Wilson and Thompson 1971 II: 278). Until the moves for their independence were well under way in the 1960s, all three territories remained under the imperial High Commissioner's authority.

IV The Boer Republics

The Transvaal—or 'South African Republic'—and the Orange Free State were products of the Great Trek. One of the political motives behind this great exodus of 1835–7 was the desire of the Boers to preserve the peculiar ethos of the frontier from the threatening corrosion of British philanthropical thought and metropolitan legislative interference (Muller 1948: 35–50, 66–80). The stated desire to maintain the 'proper relations between master and servant' (Retief's Manifesto, *Grahamstown Journal*, 2 February 1837) was therefore a strong influence in determining the character of Trekker 'native policy'. In an age when the colour-line was also a rough civilization test the constitution of the South African Republic even found it necessary to provide that there should be no equality between white and black in the state (Eybers 1918: 364).

As far as the Orange Free State was concerned, the British–Sotho solutions of 1868–70 and 1884 largely solved the 'native problem'. Much of the land into which the Trekkers had moved had been open or sparsely populated owing to the depredations of 'Mantatee'[9] hordes in the *Mfecane* (See Lye 1969: 191–206). After the Sotho territory passed under the Crown's protection, there remained only one or two minor tribal reserves, such as those at Thaba N'chu and Witzie's Hoek, and the broken-up African 'squatter' population on white farms. For these it was not felt necessary to evolve any special 'native policy'.

In the Transvaal the Trekkers based their claim to land either upon their conquest of the Ndebele in the Marico area in 1837 or upon the treaties of 'cession' from local chiefs which have characterized South Africa's moving frontier lines throughout their history. Farm boundaries were then unilaterally arranged, and the land and any Bantu population it carried submerged under the encroaching white ownership. In this situation the African generally entered into the Boer's service as a labourer, or as a tenant-at-will, or under some other form of client relationship. But there were pockets of indigenous tribal land which escaped absorption. These were to be found far from the main areas of Boer settlement. For instance, the strength of the Pedi 'super-chiefdom', both in numbers (it had absorbed numerous Sotho refugees) and in the defensive advantages of its 'perimeter' in the broken country on the Steelpoort river, enabled its paramount, Sekhukhune, to retain a temporary independence. The same went for the Venda chiefdoms of the Zoutpansberg. Central republican authority was generally weak; indeed, there was no formal political unity before 1860. By the time Shepstone annexed the Transvaal no consistent 'native policy' had therefore emerged. A certain amount of labour was expected from the client African, and, if this was not forthcoming, the Boer sometimes resorted to a much-suspect system of 'apprenticing' young tribal orphans, thereby securing the necessary number of hands on his farm (Agar-Hamilton 1928: 169–95; cf. Kistner 1952: 226–43).

After 1877 Shepstone took the first steps in introducing some organization into Transvaal 'native policy'. His son, Henrique, became Secretary for Native Affairs and the elements of Natal Reserve policy were introduced (Brookes 1924: 123–7). Two years later Wolseley, with Swazi help, finally crushed Sekhukhune in a bloody encounter (Smith 1969: 237–54). By 1898 the Venda resistance had also been brought to an end by Boer commandoes under Piet Joubert (Wilson and Thompson 1971 II: 283). After the retrocession of 1881 Shepstone's own work lived on in the Republic's Law 4 of 1885. The chiefs in the surviving tribal areas retained limited jurisdiction, and their reserves were gradually—and not very carefully—beaconed off. They lay mainly along an east-west axis north of Pretoria and along a north-south axis down the eastern side of the Transvaal. Like the trans-Keian territories, they became 'Union Native Reserves' after 1910.

V The Southern Nguni and the Moving Frontier: Second Stage

The 1860s were a period of indecision in the area between the Cape and Natal borders. British authorities were agreed on only one point—the miscellaneous territories of the region were ultimately to come within the Empire. But there the consensus ended: the imperial government disliked the plans of Grey for extending the British Kaffrarian system so rapidly to the trans-Kei; without Responsible Government the Cape Colonists were at first hesitant about taking a strong line themselves; and Natal's ambitions in Griqualand East threw that colony foul of the austere Philip Wodehouse, High Commissioner 1862–70.

Between the Kei and the Mbashe (Bashee) a vacuum had been created by the expulsion of the Gcaleka paramount, Sarili (Kreli), in 1858. Eventually he was allowed back, but only to the coastal strip. In the midland area, round Idutywa, was located a mixed population, many of whom were colonial Mfengu with 'British citizenship'. The emigrant Thembu from the Cape settled the northern semi-mountainous area, east of the Indwe river, while Tembuland proper extended from the headwaters of the Mbashe east to the Mthatha (Umtata) and south to Bomvanaland on the coast. There remained only two other territorial units south of Natal—Pondoland, neatly divided by the St John's estuary and Mzimvubu river, and the mountainous 'Nomansland', later Griqualand East, sprawling across the headwaters of all the many tributaries which feed the Mzimvubu. The trans-Keian territories therefore formed a heterogeneous patchwork of unbroken Southern Nguni tribal clusters, such as the Mpondo and Mpondomise, of great cluster-segments, like the Gcaleka, and of scattered, semi-detribalized peoples in Fingoland, the Idutywa reserve, and 'Nomansland', after the Griqua had made their hazardous trek there in 1862.[10]

In the 1860s Wodehouse relied upon a system of resident agents and typical mid-Victorian 'influence' to secure reasonable stability in the area (Campbell 1959 I: 59–61). 'British subjects', like the Mfengu and Griqua, were a useful prop to British prestige, and the old treaty of 1844 between the Cape Governor and Faku of the Mpondo continued in force (Brownlee (ed.) 1923: 92–5). But circumstances such as Faku's age, the character of his main heir, Mqikela, the unfortunate segmentation into a western and an eastern Mpondo after 1868, the death of the principal missionary adviser, Jenkins, and Governor Frere's expansionist policies combined later to rob the agreement of much of its effectiveness (Cragg 1959: 286–452 *passim*).

Such a loose-knit diplomatic system clearly had grave defects from the British point of view; and circumstances were conspiring by the late sixties and early seventies to encourage change (Campbell 1959: ch. 9, 77–99). Increasingly, Cape and Natal politicians were showing themselves prepared— for commercial and other reasons—to incorporate tribal land (the Cape took over British Kaffraria in 1865 and Natal absorbed the County of Alfred the following year). Moreover, Fingoland had more or less constituted an informal colonial administration for itself and, urged on by the formidable Captain Blyth, Mfengu magistrate 1870–6,[11] had begun schemes aimed at social and economic advance. Griqualand East, too, felt the tightening grip of the Cape government when, in 1875, Adam Kok agreed to share his authority with a British commissioner (Campbell 1959: 134). But no legal act of full annexation and incorporation had been effected beyond the Kei by the outbreak of the Cape-Xhosa war of 1877–8. British authority still rested on varying diplomatic and indirect controls.

In the war of 1877–8 the Gcaleka-Xhosa made another, and final, effort to stem the tide of white incorporation. Though it proved vain, this war fitted logically into the larger, sub-continental pattern of military resistance and rebellion of the next few years—Moorosi's Phuti revolt in southern Basutoland in 1879, the Sotho 'Gun War' of 1880–1, the Zulu War of 1879, the Transvaal's (and Britain's) Pedi war of 1876–9, and the Mpondomise-Thembu rebellion of 1880. Yet, significantly, this patterned sequence seems to have been caused more by the reinforced political thrust of whites in the late seventies than by any commonly-experienced adverse economic conditions among the surviving tribal units, or by secret liaison for concerted action among blacks (Saunders n.d.).

After the war of 1877–8 the High Commissioner, Sir Bartle Frere, concluded that the British policy of confederation, which he had been sent to South Africa to implement, could only succeed if the fighting potential of the trans-Keian territories was permanently neutralized by formal annexation and incorporation. For this purpose he proposed extending the Cape magisterial system as it functioned in Basutoland alongside tribal representative forms, such as the national *Pitso*, to the entire block of still semi-independent territories (*Br. Parl. Papers* 1878, LVI (C 2144) 154ff.). An African-staffed civil service and provision for special parliamentary representation was also envisaged (*ibid.*, 220ff.; Despatch 1 June 1878, 233, rules). But the bold conception was partly destroyed by the delay of the imperial government in considering the scheme and by the collapse of confederation after the Zulu war. Frere himself lost authority and was obliged to accept the alternative plans of his Cape ministry for the steady, systematic absorption of the territories into the colony (Benyon 1968: 356, quoting Frere to Hicks-Beach, 1 April 1880). Already, in 1877, certain local acts for the colonial incorporation of Fingoland and Griqualand East had been passed. These were, accordingly, put into effect by proclamation in 1879 (Campbell 1959: 135, 143).

Nevertheless, Frere's grand conception for a system of carefully integrated 'extraordinary' rule for the trans-Keian territories was never entirely lost sight of. In 1880 the British government's complacence was shaken by the Mpondomise-Thembu rebellion against encroaching white control. It coincided with, and was partly inspired by, the neighbouring Sotho revolt (the 'Gun War'). Gladstone's second Liberal ministry had already concluded that the Cape was mismanaging its 'native policy' in the affair of Sotho disarmament. It appeared essential to 'take security'[12] that similar mistakes would not follow in the disturbed trans-Kei. The imperial government therefore laid down that a satisfactory code of indigenous law should in future be linked legislatively to any colonial Acts of incorporation which might be forwarded to London for approval (*Br. Parl. Papers* 1882, XLVII (C 3112) 26: Letters Patent).

Simultaneously a Cape parliamentary faction was pressing for greater care in handling the 'native question'. John X. Merriman had crystallized the feelings of his fellow colonial M.P.s by moving in 1880 for a commission to examine the laws and customs of the Cape Nguni (*Cape Argus*, reporting Cape Assembly, 17 and 23 July 1880). From this initiative there later stemmed the great *Report on Native Laws and Customs*—or Barry Report—of 1883 (G4 of '83). It was a masterpiece of careful enquiry and sound academic reasoning which smoothed the way for taking over the remaining trans-Keian territories and helped rationalize the forms of rule introduced into them. This process of absorption had been halted half-way in the case of the 'St John's Territory', Gcalekaland, the two Tembulands, and Bomvanaland by the understandable delay involved in the production of the report and by a growing hesitation in Scanlen's colonial ministry over accepting these districts after the Cape's failure in Basutoland. But in 1884–5 they were all annexed to the Cape by the more confident ministry of Upington (Campbell 1959: 143, 146).

Pondoland, the last remaining territory, came reluctantly under Cape rule. To stall the inevitable, Mqikela's chief adviser, Mhlangaso, tried to play off the Cape against Natal. However, the protectorate which Britain declared along the Pondoland coast in 1885 was the portent of things to come. Mhlangaso and Sigcawu, the new East Mpondo paramount, then fell out; and their squabbling emphasized to the Rhodes Cape ministry how anachronistic an independent tribal Pondoland was in the *milieu* of the 1890s. In 1894 Major Elliot and W. Stanford persuaded Sigcawu to submit to Cape rule without actually having to deploy *force majeure*. That force was in reserve all parties were aware, though it is myth that Rhodes had a mealie field shot down by a Maxim to intimidate Sigcawu (Saunders n.d., ch. 6 *passim*, esp. footnote on 'mealieland incident'). The annexation of Pondoland completed the process of incorporation in the trans-Kei. Limited white immigration and land-acquisition followed in the sparsely settled mountainous areas of the territories, but they remained predominantly a black, semi-tribal preserve.

The trans-Kei was ultimately divided into twenty-seven magisterial districts, which were, in turn, formed into three Chief Magistracies—Transkei proper, Tembuland, and East Griqualand (with Pondoland) (Hammond-Tooke 1968c: 457). In 1903 a Chief Magistrate at Umtata, responsible to Cape Town, came to preside over the 'United Transkeian Territories'. The magisterial elements of the system were clearly derived from the old experimental policies of British Kaffraria. Chiefs received stipends and their powers were curtailed, particularly in criminal matters, where the work of the Barry Commission issued in the Native Territories Penal Code (Act 24 of 1886).

The old idea of a distinct and special government for the Transkei, which could claim a distinguished line of proponents in Blyth, Frere, and even General 'Chinese' Gordon (see G5 of '83: Gordon to Col. Sec. 27 June 1882 and Memo), was not adequately reflected in the magisterial system described above. As the emphasis fell mainly on executive authority, the means of securing a modicum of 'consent' from the governed African was essentially lacking. In time, a growing affluence might have brought many tribesmen within the pale of the Cape constitution—where they could, to some extent, have controlled their destiny by exercising their votes. However, it was precisely this 'blanket' vote which worried the politicians of the Cape parliament. Not surprisingly, they reverted to the idea of giving a special, or 'extraordinary', status to the Transkei. But one hand gave, and the other took away: while two parliamentary seats were created for Tembuland and Griqualand East, another bill excluded communal tenure from the electoral occupational qualifications (which had themselves been recently raised) both in the Cape and the Transkei (Hammond-Tooke 1968c: 459).

The next step in the process was Rhodes's Glen Grey Act of 1894. Aimed partly at curing socio-economic problems, this legislation provided for allotments under individual tenure. While the allotments would not be considered a franchisal qualification (being still defined as 'communal land'), a District Council with a small electoral element and supervised by the magistrate was simultaneously created (*ibid.*, 460–1). In time and in modified form the district conciliar system was extended to the entire Transkei (*ibid.*, 461–4, 466). By the 1930s the United Transkeian Territories General Council (or *Bunga*) had developed above these District Councils. Indeed, the Barry Report had envisaged such an organization, though not as large as the *Bunga* (G4 of '83, 45–6). The latter body finally consisted of the Chief Magistrate, twenty-six other magistrates, three *ex officio* paramount chiefs, and three tribal representatives appointed by each District Council. The white-black ratio was 27:81; the elected-official 78:30. Revenue came mainly from hut tax and was received by the District Councils on a *pro rata* basis. With executive approval they could use these funds for local improvement, leaving the larger questions of conservation, communications, and health to the *Bunga* (Hammond-Tooke 1968c: 462–5).

As in the more positive aspects of Cape BaSotho policy 1871–83, so too in the Transkei—some attempt had been made to gain the consent of the governed. But it was policy to keep *Bunga* discussion away from controversial political issues. While the *Bunga's* role was thus limited, this cautious experiment and the magisterial executive to which it was harnessed helped give the Transkei—one of the largest relatively consolidated blocks of surviving black territory in Southern Africa—a status which was *sui generis*. The fair success of this experiment in 'local government' encouraged its extension in modified form to the Ciskeian and Transvaal reserves and other African territories. When the project for establishing Bantu 'Homelands'—admittedly on differing governmental principles—was inaugurated, it is therefore not surprising to find that the area which featured first and most prominently in the planning and early developmental stages was the Transkei.

The outbreak of the Anglo-Boer War in 1899 followed hard upon the last major incorporations of Southern Bantu tribal territory. The protracted process of extending white over-rule had thrown up collaborators and resisters, conquistadores and statesmen, martyrs and philanthropists, winners and losers, heroes and villains. But it had also created a new society with new values, a new economy, and a new technology. That the explosive force of white expansion should have prevailed over the individual Southern Bantu chiefdoms, clusters, and even 'kingdoms' was, probably, inevitable. But the *way* in which the whites had prevailed—and then *organized* the incorporated black peoples—have their abiding historical importance in the twentieth century.

VI Union and After: 'Homelands' and Heartland

When delegates to the National Convention on Union gathered in 1908, the process of political incorporation was over. True, further developments were to stem from a changing political and demographic situation, but the Southern Bantu, throughout the sub-continent, had already come under some form of direct or indirect white control. What follows is, therefore, in the nature of a postscript.

The Union of 1910 brought the separate and divergent native policies of the Cape, Natal, and ex-Boer republics under a single Native Affairs Department. While the policies which each had developed toward the incorporated African continued in their general pre-Union directions, the possibility henceforth existed that they would be amalgamated into a uniform and inclusive policy. With this contingency in view, it became a question whether the Cape policy of the colour-blind franchise—already limited by the legislation of the

1880s and 1890s—would prevail against the differential or segregationist policies of the Transvaal, Free State, and—to a lesser extent—of Natal. Ultimately it was the Cape which lost.

The first attempt to deal with the native problem on a South African scale pre-dated the Union. The Lagden Inter-Colonial Commission on Native Affairs of 1903-5 worked against the background of Milnerian reconstruction after the Anglo-Boer War. Many recommendations were therefore directed toward encouraging black labour to nodal points of industrial growth (see *Br. Parl. Papers* LV (Cd. 2399)). While the Glen Grey system of individual tenure was to be encouraged, native purchase right or lease should, the commission majority felt, be limited to certain areas. In fine, the document took a decidedly conservative line, though it was not acted upon during the meetings of the National Convention.

In the negotiations for Union it was understood that the controversial 'native question' should be shelved as far as possible. Apart from agreeing that the High Commission Territories might later—with British permission—be incorporated in the Union and that qualifying Africans should remain upon the common voters' roll in the Cape (subsequently entrenched in the draft Union Act), the Convention was loath to interfere with the *status quo* (Eybers 1918: 528, 554; S.A. Act, Cls 35, 151).

Amongst early significant legislation of the Union Parliament was Sauer's Native Land Act of 1913 (Act 27 of 1913). It was aimed both at reducing the squatter problem and at preventing whites from acquiring land in African 'areas' and *vice versa*—though this principle did not initially apply to the Cape where the right to acquire land was reckoned to go with the franchise (App. Div. 1917: Thompson and Stilwell *v* Kama). As the ownership of land now rested overwhelmingly in white hands, some redistribution was, however, called for. The Beaumont Commission was appointed to investigate this question. In 1916 its report proposed that 22,000,000 acres should be added to the 17,660,000 of the existing reserves (Vol. I, U.G. 19, 1916; Vol. II, U.G. 22, 1916). But the commission encountered many objections from land owners and found other difficulties in the way of effecting this transfer. Subsequently, provincial commissions investigated the same question, but legislation on the land problem was shelved in 1917. In the meanwhile, on the industrial front, the colour-bar was established on a Union-wide basis by the Mines and Works Act of 1911 (Act 12 of 1911) and by subsequent amending legislation passed in response to the continuing expansion of the African urban and industrial population. The implications of the emergent pattern were therefore unmistakable: within the Union the incorporated Bantu were likely to be subject to a system of thoroughgoing territorial and economic segregation.

The coalition of Hertzog's Nationalists and Labour, which gained power as the 'Pact' ministry of 1924, was based on the protection of 'civilized labour'. But Hertzog had to find some alternative outlet for the African, and he therefore bethought himself of the 'additional areas' of the Beaumont Report. He conceived measures in this and other fields of native affairs in 1926, though the only significant legislation passed—in the following year—was a Native Administration Act which, echoing Shepstonianism, gave the Supreme Chief (i.e. the Minister of Native Affairs) greatly extended administrative powers in all provinces except the Cape.

The legislation of the 1930s opened with the Natives' Urban Areas Amendment Act which further restricted movement of Africans into towns. It was followed by the 'Fusion' ministry's legislation of 1936, which Hertzog had waited a decade to pass. The Native Trust and Land Act (Act 18 of 1936) established a machinery whereby the problematical additional land in the 'released areas' outside the reserves, with which the Lagden and Beaumont Commissions had both dealt, could be transferred. But the proportion of Bantu reserve land in the Union even at the hypothetical end of the process would clearly still be seriously out of relation to the proportion of Union Bantu inhabitants. The Representation of Natives Act (Act 12 of 1936), while it left the Cape Africans their individual vote, put them on a separate roll for the election of three white MPs. It further created four semi-provincial constituencies for the election of four white senators to represent native interests in the Union Parliament, as well as of twelve Africans to sit on a Native Representative Council. This council was to be strengthened by various appointees, the five native commissioners, and the Secretary for Native Affairs. Finally, an indirect electoral machinery through 'colleges' was to fill up the remaining seats on the Council, which was to have only advisory functions. The vital change to note is the qualified African's removal from his 'entrenched' position on the common roll—which, by implication, removed his right to acquire land where he wished in the Cape. In 1937 a third measure, the Native Laws Amendment Act (Act 36 of 1937), gave the government, through its magistrates and native commissioners, even greater powers over movements from the reserves to the towns and *vice versa*.

There can be little doubt the black African was more comprehensively 'incorporated' by the outbreak of the Second World War than in 1910. But the process, particularly in the thirties, had worked against him. Well before the Union the Cape policy was being modified; after 1910 it had proved unable to resist the pressure of the northern provinces. In its limited sphere the *Bunga* might have progressed, but that was not enough.

The years after the Second World War have been dominated by the evolution of the policy of *Apartheid* or separate development. In terms of this policy Bantu are to be encouraged to live in their own areas and to develop as far as possible along 'their own lines'. Even when consolidated, these areas of development will, however, comprise only 13·7 per cent—admittedly fairly good land—of the total area, much of it drier, of the country. In view of this fact and the large African population which has settled on white farms or around white urban areas, the policy faces the most formidable pitfalls and obstacles, not least the opposition it has engendered in Africa and the world in the context of a general imperial retraction by European powers.

THE PROCESS OF POLITICAL INCORPORATION

The *apartheid* policy actually rests very largely on the rough pattern of segregation established by the process of political and economic incorporation of former years. But there has been a much more thoroughgoing emphasis on this pattern of segregation. The Tomlinson Commission which reported in October 1954 sketched out the main guidelines for the socio-economic development of the reserves or, as they have been renamed, 'Bantu Homelands' (U.G. 61/1955). However, socio-economic development has also been closely linked to political change. Starting with the Bantu Authorities Act of 1951 (Act 68 of 1951), a new structure of local authority based—Shepstone-like—on the old tribal and ethnic divisions has been erected in the Homelands to dovetail with the existing magisterial system. At the base of the pyramid is the tribal authority, above it the district or regional authority, and, finally, the territorial authority. In 1959 this process reached an important turning-point with the Promotion of Bantu Self-Government Act which enabled the central government, through its Department of Bantu Administration and Development and appointed Commissioners-General, to broaden the scope of the earlier Act to include the establishment and recognition of Bantu 'national' units—North Sotho (Lebowa), South Sotho (Basotho-Qwaqwa), Tswana (Bophuthatswana), Zulu (Kwazulu), Cape Nguni (Trans-Kei, Ciskei), Tsonga (Gazankulu) and Venda (Act 46 of 1959).

Having contributed its part to the political development and unification of the Transkei, the *Bunga* accepted the new dispensation of Bantu Authorities in 1955. This made the Transkei the most obvious field in which to test the policy. In 1963 the Transkeian Constitution Act (Act 48 of 1963) was passed to establish a government for the territory and a legislative assembly with strong traditional and limited elective elements. As a preliminary to this development the election of whites to the central parliament by Africans on a separate roll ceased in 1959. The hypothetical terminal point of this process of creating territorial parliaments is supposed to be the voluntary participation of homelands enjoying political autonomy, together with the ex-High Commission territories, in a kind of Southern African Common Market with the axial 'white' area.

The grants of independence by Britain, which converted Basutoland into Lesotho, Bechuanaland into Botswana in 1966, and Swaziland into an independent African monarchy in 1968, have also significantly altered the sub-continental situation. Instead of politically incorporating these countries—as was expected in the years after Union—Republican South Africa has had to adjust to the presence of independent territorial entities half-embedded within her body-politic. Though she can exert great political leverage upon them, the reverse is also true. The ex-High Commission territories may now sensibly affect the developing situation in their powerful neighbour-state.

This chapter is not concerned with prognostication. Clearly the development of the Homelands, as sketched out above, the independence of the ex-High Commission territories and the growing weight of the black population in white areas pose questions which the architects of Republican governmental policy will find increasingly taxing and problematical. However, it is obvious that 'political incorporation', based on a pattern of segregation, is still a central fact of the present situation in South Africa proper. Nor is it likely that the Republic of South Africa will easily bring itself to the point of surrendering full external sovereignty to the Homelands—which may be the inescapable consequence of the present policy of granting internal autonomy. And, finally, the Africans resident in the white areas continue to be incorporated under rigid and uncompromisingly segregationist terms. Apart from Botswana, Lesotho, and Swaziland, the process of politically incorporating the Southern Bantu under white authority—inaugurated more than 150 years ago—is only in the initial stage of reversal (1971).

Notes

1 First contact between *individuals* took place early in the eighteenth century—a trading expedition from the Cape Colony clashed with the Xhosa in 1702—but the confrontation of the main migratory movements came only in the latter half of that century.

2 The *leeningplaats*, or 'loan place', was a quitrent farm of some 6,000 acres (generally its size was determined by riding out from a central point for a half-hour in all directions). Theoretically, these farms reverted to the government on non-payment of the quitrent; further, they could not be sub-divided—factors which combined with the size of Boer families and the needs of the pastoral farmer for winter and summer grazing to bring about an extremely rapid occupation of available land.

3 See Public Record Office, London, C.O. 48/326: Confidential Memorandum for the Cabinet by Wellington, n.d., *circa* June 1852, following Cathcart to Earl Grey, No. 41, 20 April 1852.

4 The treaty was informal; it was not committed to paper in precise terms and, consequently, left the way open to all manner of interpretation by administrators and authors. See, for information: *Treaties with Native Chiefs 1803–54*, presented to Parliament 1857, 9–12: Cape Gazette report of Somerset's treaty; Hutton (1887), *The Autobiography of Sir Andries Stockenström, Bart*, I: 126-7, 336-7.

5 The belief that the colonial frontier was formally extended to the heights west of the Tyhume in 1829 seems to have originated with E. A. Walker. In his chapter in Holland Rose et al. (1936), *The Cambridge History of the British Empire* VIII: 304, he cites his *Historical Atlas* (1922) as his source for his statement on the 1829 Frontier extension. In his *Atlas*, in turn, he cites on p. 15 a reference to a proclamation dealing with the question ('No 617 C. Archives, *Apr. 17*, 1829'). Miss Joan Davies, chief of the Cape Archives depot, kindly checked this reference for me (apparently it is now referenced under 'C.O. 367'). Both items (nos 13 and 14 in this category) are dated 17 April 1829, but are merely documents received from the Commissioner-General of the East frontier. Neither is in any sense a formal government proclamation. Document 14, a memo by Stockenström, contains certain 'Hints' for the government, and in it the author mentions that the Ceded Territory 'is now . . . looked upon as part of the Colony'. The whole tenor of Stockenström's remarks leads the reader to infer that

PLATE 21
Urban life

a Sunday afternoon in a Soweto side-street, 1970
b Selling grilled maize cobs, Soweto

PLATE 22
Urban life

a Municipal beer hall in Soweto, with municipal police
b A 'Red' migrant in town. Transvaal Ndebele woman selling groundnuts near Orlando station Soweto

THE PROCESS OF POLITICAL INCORPORATION

this situation had come about quite informally as a development of the arrangement of 1819. Apart from Miss Davies, I am grateful to Dr A. M. Lewin Robinson, Director of the S.A. Library, for the information that the Cape Govt. *Gazette* contains no proclamation on or round 17 April 1829 extending the frontier. In default of any further citation, Walker's assertion regarding a formal frontier extension in 1829 has therefore to be respectfully contradicted.

6 Even though this quotation is from a cancelled portion of the Governor's instructions, it most clearly illustrates the direction of Stephen's thought at the time. See British Public Record Office, C.O. 48/264: Draft instructions to Pottinger, n.d., prepared by Stephen.

7 In Natal the word 'location' denotes a rural reserve, but in the remainder of South Africa today is generally taken to denote an urban Bantu township.

8 This information is from an unpublished source. Br. Col. Office Library, 13015 Wodehouse Papers: Wodehouse to Newcastle, No. 9, 20 August 1862, Private.

9 The word 'Mantatee' is derived from MaNthatisi, mother and—for a period—guardian of the Tlokwa chief Sekonyela. The ravaging hordes of the *Mfecane* have indiscriminately been labelled 'Mantatee', though it has lately become clear that Sekonyela's Tlokwa were responsible for very little of the disruption originally attributed to them and their formidable chieftainess.

10 The failure in the Bloemfontein Convention to link Britain's abandonment of the Orange River Sovereignty with any provision for Griqua land rights and the continuation of the process of alienation to white farmers had reduced the Eastern Griqua at Philippolis to a parlous condition by 1860. It was at Sir George Grey's instigation that A. Kok III and his clan trekked from Philippolis over the Drakensberg to the 'Nomansland' area in 1862. Thereby the High Commissioner secured an ally in independent Kaffraria and the Griqua had a better chance of retaining sufficient land for their support.

11 Captain Matthew Blyth was actually elected by the Mfengu to rule them. He governed with a strong hand through a native police force. Later, in 1874, he persuaded the Mfengu to pay a 10s. Hut Tax, like that of Basutoland, to support his establishment (Campbell 1959: 122).

12 The quotation is a personal observation by Kimberley, Secretary of State for the Colonies, Br. Public Record Office. C.O. 48/494: Frere to Kimberley, Confidential, 14 June 1880, Minute by Kimberley, 11 July 1880.

Suggestions for further reading

BROOKES, E. H. (1924) *The History of Native Policy in South Africa*.
DU TOIT, A. E. (1954) *The Cape Frontier, 1847–1866*.
HAILEY, BARON (1953) *Native Administration in the British African Territories*, Part V.
HAMMOND-TOOKE, W. D. (1968) 'The Transkeian Council System, 1895-1955: An Appraisal', *J. Afr. History*, IX, 3.
MACMILLAN, W. M. (1963) *Bantu, Boer and Briton*.
OMER-COOPER, J. D. (1966) *The Zulu Aftermath*.

J. A. BENYON

RUTHERFORD, J. (1961) *Sir George Grey*.
SILLERY, A. (1965) *Founding a Protectorate*.
THOMPSON, L. M. (ed.) (1969) *African Societies in Southern Africa*.
WALKER, E. A. (1957) *History of Southern Africa*.
WELSH, D. (1971) *The Roots of Segregation: Native Policy in Colonial Natal, 1845–1910*.
WILSON, M. and THOMPSON, L. M. (1969 and 1971) *The Oxford History of South Africa*, Vols. I and II.

Chapter 13
The Process of Economic Incorporation
D. Hobart Houghton

The title of this chapter covers two distinct but interrelated processes of economic incorporation. One of these is the process by which members of the Bantu-speaking peoples of Southern Africa were gradually drawn into the economy which the white colonists built up in the southern tip of the continent. The other is the process by which this initially agricultural and pastoral economy, directed mainly towards the self-subsistence of the local population of all races, was drawn into the international exchange economy and transformed from one of extensive agriculture to a highly developed industrial economy based on mining and manufacture. This change greatly increased the demand for labour, and the employment opportunities offered by the gold-mining complex of the Witwatersrand attracted African workers from all the Bantu-speaking tribes of Southern Africa, drawing some from territories far outside the area of what is now the Republic of South Africa. This process, which is still continuing, accelerated the economic incorporation of Bantu-speaking peoples in the modern exchange economy which was created and is still dominated by the descendants of the original white colonists, and it offered Africans who were successful in making the transition a standard of living much greater than the majority could have obtained in their traditional economies.

The account of these two processes can conveniently be divided into three phases. In the first, the economy of the white settlers was almost wholly based upon farming, which in the vicinity of the ports was moderately intensive, but in the interior it was extensive cattle and sheep ranching, which had much in common with the traditional Bantu economies described in chapter 5. This phase lasted from the foundation of the white settlement in 1652 to the 1860s.

The second phase was when large-scale mining activities were added to farming and became a major industry. Mining in no way replaced farming; indeed it had the effect of stimulating it and transforming agriculture to make it more market-orientated because the large populations of the mining areas had to be fed. Both diamond-mining and gold-mining were highly labour-intensive and within a few years of the mineral discoveries Kimberley and the Witwatersrand had attracted the largest concentrations of people yet known in Southern Africa. Skilled labour was largely provided by immigrants from Europe and America, and the Bantu-speaking African people provided the unskilled labour. From the 1860s to the First World War, farming and mining were the main generators of income and employers of labour.

In the 1920s manufacturing industry began to expand and to take its place beside the other two as the third basic sector of the economy. In this third phase, which lasted from the twenties to the present time, manufacturing grew in absolute and relative importance and now occupies first place as a generator of income and in providing opportunity of wage-employment for people of all races.

Mention has been made only of farming, mining and manufacturing, but in all three phases, trade, commerce, and service activities played their role. Commercial activities were centred on the sea ports, and the white settlers from the Netherlands and Britain (which were then the most advanced trading nations of the world) brought with them the concept of a developed exchange economy which was a major innovation in Southern Africa The physical geography of the country, however, made transport and communications difficult, and this placed severe restraints upon trade in the interior where family units had perforce to rely largely upon their own efforts for the provision of the necessities of life. As transport facilities developed with railway and road construction, and more recently with the coming of air services, the isolating factors have been reduced and the industrial centres have been able to find wider markets. In spite of customary and legal restraints, more and more Africans have been drawn into the secondary and tertiary sectors of the economy, and their standard of living has risen as a result of the general growth of the economy despite a relatively high rate of natural increase and the influx of large numbers from adjacent less-developed territories, because the growth-rate has been sufficient to expand employment opportunities. The process of economic incorporation during each of these three phases of development will now be considered in greater detail.

Two Centuries of Farming

Up to the middle of the nineteenth century few Bantu-speaking Africans had been drawn into the economy of the white settlers at the Cape. The population of the Colony was racially mixed, consisting, as it did, of descendants of the white settlers from northern Europe, indigenous yellow-skinned Khoikhoi (Hottentots), slaves imported from Batavia and Madagascar, and people of mixed blood; but the Bantu-speaking people had not penetrated to the western Cape at the time of the white settlement there, and significant contact between white and Bantu did not occur until the latter part of the eighteenth century. From 1778 onwards the Fish river was both a territorial and a racial frontier between the Colony and the Bantu-speaking tribes who inhabited the land to the east of this river. Although successive governments at the Cape attempted to prevent the expansion of the Colony and reduce contact between white and black to a minimum, the frontier was far from being inviolate, as the repeated *placaats* prohibiting intercourse indicate, and even the chain of forts built by the British along the Fish river failed to keep the races apart. Hunters, missionaries and traders crossed the frontier, and cattle-stealing forays and sporadic warfare indicate that contacts of one sort or another were being established between the two groups. The basic conflict, as H. M. Robertson has pointed out, was the struggle between white and black pastoralists for more grazing-land to support their growing herds of cattle (Robertson 1934: 404). There is evidence that some Bantu-speaking individuals had come into the Colony to work on white farms (*ibid.*, 408, 409), but prior to the Cattle Killing of 1857 their numbers were small.

The annexation after the War of 1845 of the territory between the Fish and the Kei rivers and the establishment of British Kaffraria as a military bulwark to the Colony, brought, for the first time, significant numbers of Bantu-speaking people under British rule. 'So ended the long sustained attempt to maintain territorial segregation along the line of a river and so began the attempt to rule black and white as inhabitants of one country' (Walker 1928: 238). Here in British Kaffraria, Sir George Grey initiated a policy of settlement of white farmers and of Mfengu among the Xhosa to exert a civilizing influence upon the latter, and he encouraged missionary effort and the building of schools and hospitals and other public works. Meanwhile the Mfengu, who had allied themselves with the white settlers against the Xhosa, had begun to work on white farms in the eastern districts of the Colony. In 1855, Mr Calderwood, Commissioner to the Mfengu, reported that 'the crops of Lower Albany . . . must have, to a considerable extent, perished without the labour of the Fingoes' (Robertson 1934: 419).

It was the disaster of the Cattle Killing in 1857[1] which first impelled the Xhosa people to seek employment in the Colony in significant numbers, and Margaret Roberts, when conducting a survey of farm labour in the Albany and Bathurst districts in 1957, found that many of the African families resident on the farms stated that their forebears had come at the time of the Cattle Killing (Roberts 1959). H. M. Robertson states that the population of British Kaffraria was reduced from 105,000 to 37,000 between January and July 1857 and that 'in the first seven months of 1857, upwards of 19,000 Kaffirs are supposed to have taken refuge in British territory, and by the end of the year an immigration of 33,000 was noted' (Robertson 1934: 421–2).

The economy of the Cape Colony at this time offered only limited employment opportunities. Crop cultivation, which is relatively labour-intensive, was limited to the growing of food for the local population, but the innovation which was transforming South African farming and establishing an export market for its product was the introduction of the Merino sheep. Wool exports rose from £178,000 in 1846 to £2,082,000 in 1866 (Schumann 1938: 47), but the labour demands of sheep-farming were limited to a relatively small number of shepherds. The very limited entry of Bantu-speaking people into the economy of the Cape Colony even as late as 1865 is clearly seen from the census returns of that year. Their penetration into the Western Districts of the Colony was negligible, and only in the Eastern Districts and in Kaffraria were they present in significant numbers.[2]

TABLE 13.1 *Census of Cape Colony, 1865*

	European	*Hottentots*	*Kafir*	*Other*	*Total*
Western Districts	105,348	52,637	9,176	69,139	236,300
Eastern Districts	76,244	28,961	91,360	63,516	260,081
Total for Cape Colony	181,592	81,598	100,536	132,655	496,381

The designations of the various groups are as given in Table 13.1. 'Kafir' probably included all Bantu-speaking inhabitants, and 'Other' embraces the descendants of the slaves and people of mixed blood. It will be noted that, in the Western Districts, the Bantu people numbered only 9,000 out of a total population of 236,000 (3·8 per cent), whereas in the Eastern Districts they numbered 91,000 out of a total of 260,000 (35 per cent).

In British Kaffraria, where an enumeration was conducted in 1858, the position was shown as in Table 13.2.

TABLE 13.2 *Inhabitants of British Kaffraria, 1858 (excluding British soldiers in the forces)*

Total native population	*German military settlers*	*Other Europeans*	*Total inhabitants*
38,559	1,154	2,994	42,707

The 'Total native population' may have included a few Hottentots, but was comprised almost wholly of Bantu-speaking people. These account for 38,000 out of a total population of 43,000 (90 per cent).

The exodus in the thirties of Dutch-speaking farmers from the Cape to the north extended greatly the area of contact between white and black in the Orange Free State, the Transvaal and Natal, but it led to little change in the economic condition of the Bantu-speaking people with whom they came into contact because the economic life of the Voortrekkers was even less market-oriented than that of the farmers in the interior of the Cape. H. M. Robertson comments on this point:

> Yet it cannot be said that any marked changes in the *economic* life of the Native occurred as a result of Boer expansion. The very extent of the territorial claims of the Transvaal remained indeterminate before the first British occupation, and, even up to the present day, tribal life has

continued on Crown lands in the Northern Transvaal. Elsewhere in the Transvaal, it is true, and in most of the Orange Free State, tribal occupation did not survive the division of the land into large European-owned farms. But Natives continued to occupy land as 'squatters' of one sort or another, with little change in their agriculture (Robertson 1935: 5).

Many Africans worked for the farmers, but there was little wage-paid labour, and share-cropping and payments in kind appear to have been the normal custom.

In Natal, however, after the British annexation, the settlers experimented with a variety of cash crops and, when sugar-cane was proved to be a success, the demand for labour could not be met from the indigenous African population. The Zulu wars had decimated the African people, and the large reserves created by Shepstone gave the remnants adequate land so that they had no need to seek work on the white farms. Thus the advent of this important cash crop did not draw the indigenous people into the growing market economy, and the labour needs for cane production were met by the introduction of agricultural workers from India.

The general conclusion must therefore be that during the purely agricultural period of white settlement in South Africa, between 1652 and the 1860s, relatively few of the Bantu-speaking people of the continent were drawn into the new type of economy which was developing. Economic and cultural contact was taking place through the activities of traders and missionaries, Bantu languages were being given a written form, the Bible and other works were being translated and printed, and the people were introduced to wider horizons both in the matter of consumption commodities and in techniques of production. Firearms for the hunters, wagons drawn by oxen for the pastoralists, and ploughs for the cultivators of the soil,[3] were transforming the traditional African economy, but it was not until the discovery of mineral wealth that the Bantu-speaking peoples were incorporated into the modern economy on a large scale.

The Mining Revolution

Although the quest for mineral wealth had been undertaken ever since the first white settlement, and mining on a small scale had been carried out by Africans centuries before the advent of white settlers,[4] it was not until 1867 that a spectacular find occurred. In that year diamonds were discovered near where the town of Kimberley now stands, and the consequences provided ample justification of the remark of the Colonial Secretary when he placed one of the earliest diamonds upon the table of the House of Assembly in Cape Town: 'Gentlemen, this is the rock on which the future success of South Africa will be built.'[5]

When it was discovered that diamonds were to be found not only in the alluvial sands of the Orange River but also in some of the volcanic pipes of

Kimberlite, the industry was given a secure and permanent foundation, and large numbers of workers of all races flocked to the area where a population of 40,000 soon came into being.

Within two decades the diamond discoveries were overshadowed by the discovery of gold on the Witwatersrand and the greatest gold-mining area the world has known commenced production. Within ten years the number of Africans employed on the Witwatersrand had risen from 15,000 in 1889 to 97,000 in 1899 (Robertson 1935: 15) and numbers have increased as the mining industry expanded until by 1969 mining and quarrying gave employment to over 500,000 African men, whose earnings exceeded R100,000,000 per annum.[6]

For almost a century hundreds of thousands of Africans have been employed annually in the mining industry.

> They come on foot, on horseback, on bicycles, by dug-out canoe, by lake and river steamers, in lorries, by train, and some even by air. They came from as far afield as 2,000 miles. They came from all points of the compass —from the peaceful hills of the Transkei, from the lion country of the Bechuanaland bush, down the broad reaches of the Zambesi, from the tropical shores of Lake Nyasa and the mountain fastnesses of Basutoland. They come, too, in their thousands from the hills and valleys of Portuguese East Africa, from the rocky uplands of Sekukuniland, the tangled swamp country of the Okavango delta and the green hills of Swaziland. From these far corners of southern Africa men from more than 100 tribes are attracted every year to the Witwatersrand by the magnet of the mining industry.[7]

Most of the African workers in mining are temporary migrants who leave their tribal homelands for a stint of nine to eighteen months on the mines and then return home until poverty or boredom sends them off to the industrial centres once again. The greater part of their working lives is spent in the industrial areas, but their families and their permanent domicile are in the tribal areas. Thus the 557,000 Africans employed in mining in June 1969[8] constituted a permanent labour force whose members are temporary and transient workers. Therefore in the course of a few years, the number of Africans who have been to Egoli[9] is many times greater than the number employed at a given moment of time so that, today, there is hardly an able-bodied African man in South Africa who has not at some time in his life worked in modern industry.

Employment in the mines has probably exerted a greater influence upon the Bantu-speaking peoples of Southern Africa than anything else, not excluding the dedicated efforts of thousands of teachers and missionaries of all denominations. For the tribesman it provided an introduction to urban life and an environment wholly different from anything he had previously encountered; there he worked under the discipline imposed by the use of power-driven precision machinery and the dictates of the clock; there he learned the elements of modern hygiene and first aid; at work he rubbed shoulders with thousands of fellow Africans from many different tribes, speaking many languages, and a patois, *fanakalo*, was evolved to aid communication.

In the early days of the mining camps at Kimberley and the Witwatersrand there was an unruly element, and law and order was not always effectively maintained.[10] African migrant workers, who came to earn money to buy cattle and firearms, were ill-housed and often ill-fed, but some of them did well for themselves on the diamond fields.[11] Restrictions to prevent the theft of diamonds were imposed at an early date, and the housing of African workers in compounds was instituted and various other restrictions imposed (Doxey 1961: 32ff.). This compound system was also adopted on the gold fields, and initially conditions left much to be desired. A great improvement has taken place in recent years, and on the modern mines the living, eating and recreational facilities are of a high standard.

Initially tribesmen came to work on the mines on their own initiative, many having to walk hundreds of miles through hostile peoples. On their return journey they were often set upon and robbed of their hard-won earnings. Various individuals began recruiting labour and offering chiefs gifts to enlist their support for these efforts, and some of these recruiting agents were unscrupulous. The mining companies then took a hand, and the Rand Labour Association was formed in 1897. It was re-formed as the Witwatersrand Native Labour Association in 1901 with the sole recruiting agency in Mozambique (Robertson 1935: 16). Later the Native Recruiting Corporation was established by the Chamber of Mines to recruit labour in the Union and the High Commission Territories. Undoubtedly these monopoly recruiting organizations have done much good by facilitating the transport of workers from their homes to the mines and back again; and the system of deferred pay, by which a portion of a man's pay was withheld and paid on his return home or remitted to his family, reduced the danger of robbery. But the system has been criticized on the ground that it is a monopoly which has tended to inhibit the rise in African wages and to prevent them from being forced up as a result of competitition between the various mines. African mine wages have risen during the last half-century by much less than wages in other categories of employment.[12]

The Chamber of Mines has often maintained that if African miners' wages were to be raised this would decrease the supply of African workers offering their services, because the migrant mine-worker is a target worker. He desires to earn a certain sum to augment his traditional economy and, if wages are higher, he can remain at home longer before the need arises for him to go out to work again. This phenomenon, described by economists as a backward-sloping supply curve for labour, may have held in the early days of the mining industry, but it is doubtful whether it still prevails today (Berg 1961). The role of Africans in the gold-mining industry is well presented in F. Wilson's doctorate thesis.[13]

The Growth of Manufacturing Industry

The nineteen twenties was a difficult period in South Africa as it was in many other countries. There was the aftermath of the First World War to contend with, and South Africa's two major industries, farming and gold-mining, were particularly hard hit. The instability of agricultural prices and technical changes in the methods of farming were driving many white people from the land. This drift to the towns of large numbers of men and women without skills suitable to an urban environment, together with the lack of employment opportunities, gave rise to what was referred to as 'the poor white problem'. It was on such a large scale as to dominate both the economic and the political fields at that time. Various legislative measures were enacted with the overt or covert intent of preserving skilled employment in manufacturing industry for white persons.[14] Because of the world depression little growth occurred in manufacturing in the 1920s, but in the 1930s it began to expand rapidly, and during and since the Second World War its growth has been phenomenal.

Although the original intention was to provide employment for whites, manufacturing has advanced so rapidly that it has far outstripped the capacity of the whites to man the factories and machines, and the non-white peoples of South Africa have increasingly been drawn into this sector of the economy. Many have moved into semi-skilled and skilled occupations in spite of the legislative and customary impediments to their doing skilled work. The transformation of the situation is clearly revealed in Table 13.3.

TABLE 13.3 *Employment in manufacturing and construction industries*[15]

Years	Whites	Coloured	Asians	Africans	All races
1924–5	43,000	23,000	9,000	56,000	131,000
1929–30	58,000	25,000	9,000	70,000	162,000
1934–5	83,000	25,000	10,000	90,000	208,000
1944–5	119,000	55,000	17,000	208,000	399,000
1954–5	210,000	103,000	27,000	433,000	773,000
1964	231,700	144,000	44,800	534,300	954,800
1969 (June)	325,000	222,000	72,000	796,000	1,414,000

From Table 13.3 it is seen that the total labour force in manufacturing and construction increased between 1925 and 1969 a little over ten-fold (from 131,000 to 1,414,000), and the number of Africans employed rose from 56,000 to 796,000—an increase of more than fourteen-fold. In this latter year Africans employed in manfuacturing and construction greatly exceeded Africans employed in mining (796,000 compared with 557,000). This represents a major change from the situation in the nineteen twenties when mining was the main avenue of employment other than agriculture for Africans.

The movement of Africans into secondary industry has had deep social implications because manufacturing makes more diversified demands upon its labour force than mining and, for the rank and file worker, requires a higher standard of general education, greater technical training and a greater commitment on the worker's part to the industrial system. Most of the labour employed in mining was migrant labour working only intermittently on the mines, where the system appears to have had only minor adverse consequences on productivity and some positive advantage from the health point of view, for the periodic return to the rural areas reduced the danger of contracting silicosis. In manufacturing the adverse effects of intermittent work and a high labour turnover are more pronounced, and a stable, highly committed labour force is essential if a high level of labour productivity is to be achieved.

On looking at the changing role of the African in the modern industrial economy of South Africa two things strike one with great force. The first is the enormous extent of the African's penetration into all sectors of the modern economy. Compared with most other countries in Africa this is truly remarkable. The second is that, in spite of the fact that, according to the 1960 census figures, three-and-a-half million Africans are employed in the modern market-oriented sectors of the national economy, where they constitute 65 per cent of the economically employed population, their economic integration in the industrial process is far from complete and many glaring imperfections in the labour market are apparent. Three examples illustrate this point. The first is the continued persistence on a large scale of the migratory labour system. The second is the existence of numerous customary and legal barriers to the vertical mobility of the African worker, and the third is the marked disparity between the earnings of Africans compared with members of other racial groups, particularly the whites. These matters are briefly considered in the following sections.

The Migratory Labour System

The migratory labour system had its origin at the very inception of the mining era. It must be remembered that at that time few would have been so bold as to suggest that the mines at Kimberley and the Witwatersrand were likely to remain in production for almost a century. Previous experience in other countries had shown many mining booms to have been of short duration, and a policy designed to bring the families of tens of thousands of African workers to the mines would have certainly been regarded as most ill considered. It is not the rise of the migratory system that requires explanation, but its persistence for almost a century. As the Fagan Commission remarked, the migratory system has been described as a useful bridge between the traditional and the modern economy, but 'a bridge is intended to be crossed, not to serve as a permanent abode'.[16] One would have expected a permanent movement of population out of the low-productivity traditional agriculture to the industrial centres where greater employment opportunities and higher remuneration were offered. In this way the marked disparity between the progressive industrial sectors and the static traditional sector would have been reduced and a more balanced economy would have replaced the marked dualism at present existing. That this has not occurred to a greater degree than has been the case may be attributed to two sets of forces. On the one hand, there is the strong cohesive force of the traditional society which in a variety of ways maintains its hold on the man who goes to town and tends to draw him back after his work stint is over;[17] and on the other hand, various legal restraints have been imposed on permanent migration of families to towns under the Urban Areas and Group Areas legislation, which was motivated in part at least by the notion that the industrial areas were brought into being by the initiative of the whites and that Africans should not become dominant there.

The migratory labour system still prevails on a large scale. Writing on this matter, D. K. Chisiza (1962: 35, 37) has this comment to make:

> An African, who has been brought up in an extended family system under which family ties are very strong, cannot bear to be away from his family and relations for long. Those who are brought up in horizontal family systems may not fully appreciate its intensity. But it is there—real, intense, merciless. . . . Encouraging workers to bring their families with them to town would be an effective solution were it that the African family consisted of husband, wife and children. Unfortunately, it includes parents, uncles, aunts, brothers, sisters, nephews and cousins. . . .
>
> Any solution of this problem must take into account the reasons advanced above, namely, that (a) the rural African feels lonely in urban areas, (b) he suffers from a sense of insecurity, (c) he has obligations to his rural relatives which can be fulfilled only in person, (d) he finds it trying to adjust himself to urban life, (e) he feels he cannot bring up his children in towns, and (f) his economic goals are quickly realized.

In spite of the strong cultural forces drawing them back to their rural homes, including the desire to own cattle the keeping of which is not possible in the cities, many African families have taken up their abode in the urban areas and have become more fully a part of modern urban industrial society. Many more would undoubtedly have done so were it not for the formidable array of restrictive measures, both legislative and administrative (Doxey 1961: 168–71), the results of which have been to retard the process of full urbanization. In the words of H. R. Burrows,[18]

> Though the traditional structure of African family and tribal life is disintegrating because of its inadequacy when brought into close contact with the developing exchange economy with the implicit wage system, its breakdown is being protracted by the system of segregation and migrant labour. The social disadvantages of sudden disruption have

been avoided at the cost of delaying specialization. As a result, there is today no self-supporting peasant economy, no permanent agricultural labour force, and no stable urban population.

The magnitude of the migration of workers is difficult to express as a specific number because they represent a flow through a period of time, but the Tomlinson Commission gave figures from which it is evident that at any moment of time some 900,000 temporary migrant workers are probably employed in the modern sectors of the South African economy—400,000 in mining, 210,000 extra-Republican workers in agriculture, and a large, but undefined number in industry, commerce and transport. The Commission commented upon the loss of manpower involved in the system: 'that on the average 600,000 man-years of labour available were not economically applied'.[19] In these 'wasted' man-years are included the time spent in travel and the period at home which many regard as a period of rest before returning to their next urban job. On the other hand many returned migrants are actually engaged in peasant farming operations, especially if their time at home coincides with the planting season.

The total number of migrant workers must be of the order of one-and-a-half to two million, and they spend their working lives circulating between industrial and commercial occupations in the cities and peasant agriculture. They have been described as 'Men of Two Worlds' (Houghton 1967: Chapter 4) and the employment histories of individuals which result from this system show a fantastic variety of occupations. Apart from the waste of manpower, the economic disadvantages of the system are that it leads to high labour turnover and the resulting instability prevents the acquisition of industrial skills and the formation of a skilled and committed labour force of Africans. The social evils are the break-up of family life and the undesirable consequences of the very high masculinity rates in the cities, such as prostitution and drink. In short the system inhibits the growth of a stable settled urban population of industrial workers in the towns, while in the rural areas the absence of so many able-bodied men militates against efforts to improve farming and raise the productivity of agriculture, and this led the Tomlinson Commission to recommend that the migrant (partly farmer and partly industrial worker) be encouraged to specialize. 'The first essential is the development of a true Bantu farming class, settled on farm units which will ensure the full means of existence to each family, and in the second place it is necessary to develop a true urban population.'[20]

But the migratory system is so deep-rooted that it will not be easy to dissolve it. Many of the Bantu areas depend upon the earnings of migrant workers to supplement their income from farming to the extent of about half their cash income. From the gold mines alone support for these areas was estimated in 1965 (Houghton 1967: 105) to have been as shown in Table 13.4.

In order to prevent the very large influx of Bantu-speaking peoples to the existing industrial centres which the movement of their families to town would

TABLE 13.4 *Migrant workers' earnings (in rands)*

		R
South Africa	Transkei	4,153,000
	Ciskei	852,000
	Natal	414,000
	Other	985,000
Foreign Countries	Lesotho	2,571,000
	Botswana	1,693,000
	Swaziland	550,000
	Mozambique	4,717,000
	Zambia	630,000
	Malawi	3,781,000
	Total	20,346,000

necessitate, and yet to provide industrial employment for those who can no longer be accommodated in peasant agriculture, the government, since 1960, has embarked upon a vast programme of establishing factories in or near the 'homelands'. New industrial complexes are arising in areas bordering upon the Bantu areas, and in some cases within the areas themselves, and industrialists are being offered considerable incentives to locate their factories there. The policy is to bring industry to the people rather than require the people to move to the existing industrial centres. Even if the policy meets with success it is, however, doubtful that the migratory labour system will be eliminated. Mining must always be carried on where the mineral deposits occur, and many other industries are bound by great locational advantage to a particular area. Nevertheless, the movement of industry nearer to where the people live will save time spent in travel and may to some extent reduce the disruption of family life.

Vertical Labour Mobility of Africans

In mining and manufacturing the skilled work is still largely done by white workers and semi-skilled and unskilled jobs are filled by people of other races —Coloureds, Indians and Africans. This is partly a matter of history because in the early mining days no skilled workers were available in South Africa, and skilled men were recruited from Europe, America and Australia. It was thus customary for skilled workers to be white, but there was no legal restriction on anyone acquiring skilled status. In order to get the Transvaal mines into full production again after the Anglo-Boer War, the British administration sanctioned the introduction of Chinese workers;[21] and, by 1906, the labour force on the mines was 18,000 whites, 94,000 Africans and 51,000 Chinese. Because of the wide educational and cultural gulf, the white skilled miners had not regarded the African as a potential threat to their position, but the Chinese were a different matter. To allay the fears of the white miners, the first industrial colour bar legislation was introduced by the British administration of the Transvaal in 1904 in an Ordinance restricting the employment of non-European immigrants to unskilled labour.[22] The colour bar in mining was further entrenched in 1911 when, allegedly in the interests of safety, blasting certificates were by law withheld from non-white miners.[23]

After the First World War the proposal that Britain should return to the gold standard at the pre-war parity raised serious difficulties for the gold-mining companies whose costs had risen considerably. A government commission[24] had recommended that greater use should be made of African labour to reduce costs but, when the mining companies attempted to put this into effect, they were met with strong opposition from the white miners. Civil war broke out along the Witwatersrand, and the military had to be called in to put down the rebellion.[25]

As a result of the widespread poverty in the country at that time, and fanned by the events of the Rand rebellion, popular feeling turned against the government of General Smuts, and a coalition of the National Party and the Labour Party won the election of 1924. They took office pledged to safeguard the interests of white skilled workers and to take action to relieve what was then referred to as 'the poor white problem'. Various laws were passed[26] many of which had excellent features, but which collectively tended to restrict the rise of non-white workers to the skilled ranks. Administrative action was taken under what was called 'the civilized labour policy' and the powers to restrict the entry of Africans into urban areas under the Natives (Urban Areas) Act were more strictly applied. On the more positive side action was taken to expand manufacturing industries with a view to providing employment for the poor whites. This aspect was crowned with such outstanding success in the nineteen thirties that the white population soon proved too small to meet the growing demand for white industrial workers, and non-whites were increasingly called upon to augment the industrial labour force. During the Second World War many non-white workers moved into semi-skilled and skilled occupations because of the growing demand and the absence on active service of many skilled men. Moreover technical progress and more advanced industrial machinery brought about a major change in the structure of the labour force. In place of the old categories of skilled craftsman, semi-skilled and unskilled, the labour force came, in all industrialized countries, to consist of a relatively small number of highly qualified men and a large number of machine operators. With proper training the African has proved to be a very satisfactory worker of this class and his place as a machine-minder has been firmly established.

Controversy has now moved to the advance of non-white workers into the skilled ranks. The skilled white workers are highly sensitive to anything which seems to them like the 'dilution' of the skilled ranks; and any government dependent upon the votes of an all-white electorate must be highly sensitive to the views of the white trade unions, bearing in mind the insurrection of 1922. Skilled workers naturally wish to protect their position, and the trade union movement is divided into two main camps—those who seek to protect the skilled man by insistence upon 'the rate for the job' irrespective of race, and those who want a reinforcement of the colour bar.

The latter policy received support in the Industrial Conciliation Act of 1956 with its controversial 'job reservation clause', which empowers the Minister of Labour to reserve certain occupations for members of a particular race. This might have been expected to limit severely the vertical mobility of the African worker, but in fact this has not been the case. The national economy has been expanding so rapidly since 1945 that an acute shortage of skilled workers has arisen. The restrictions of the job reservation clause have in practice been largely circumvented by the granting of exemptions and the reclassification of jobs so that those formerly performed by whites are now open to people of other races. Indeed the existence of the job reservation clause has in some cases given the white workers a sense of security as a result of which they have been less firmly opposed to non-white advancement.

A legalistic review of colour bar legislation in South Africa would certainly give the impression that the structure of the labour market was extremely rigid and that vertical mobility for Africans was impossible. This is not the case and, although many difficulties and frustrations occur, so long as the national economy continues to expand at a rapid rate, the operation of the laws of supply and demand will provide opportunities for the advance of the competent African worker.

Earnings and Standard of Living

As a result of the rapid growth in the national economy, average real income per capita has risen during the last half century by over 2 per cent per annum, and all sections of the population have benefited from this advance, although not to the same degree. Distribution of income between the different racial groups is unequal. The whites are the wealthiest group, and the 'poor white problem' of the nineteen twenties is a thing of the past. In general the white incomes are four to six times those of the other groups, and their average standard of living ranks with that of the wealthy countries of the world. Next to the whites in order of wealth come the Asians and Coloureds, followed by the urban African workers, and at the bottom of the scale are the African peasants still engaged in traditional agriculture. Their cash income is distressingly low, although in good seasons they harvest crops and they have other non-monetary satisfactions from their way of life. In most cases, however, they are subsidized by remittances from members of their families at work in the industrial areas, as was indicated in the section above on migrant labour.

In Table 13.5 aggregate employment and earnings for the main racial groups are given for the month of June 1969 and the approximate annual rate is calculated in the last column. The figure in this column for African mine workers is, however, misleading as it does not include the free board and lodging which they receive.

TABLE 13.5 *Employment and earnings*[27]

	No. employed June 1969 (000)	Earnings in June 1969 (R000)	Earnings per worker June 1969	Approx. annual earnings per worker 1969
Manufacturing				
Whites	270	74,138	R274·6	R3,295
Coloured	180	11,665	R 64·8	R 778
Asian	68	4,654	R 68·4	R 821
African	581	27,704	R 47·7	R 572
All workers	1,099	118,162	R107·5	R1,290
Construction				
Whites	55	15,359	R279·3	R3,354
Coloured	42	4,090	R 97·4	R1,174
Asian	4	513	R128·3	R1,540
African	215	10,024	R 46·6	R 559
All workers	315	29,986	R 95·2	R1,142
Mining				
White	62	20,469	R330·1	R3,961
Coloured	6	377	R 62·8	R 754
Asian	1	51	R 51·0	R 612
African	557	9,408	R 17·0	R 204
All workers	626	30,305	R 48·4	R 581

Earnings in Table 13.5 include overtime pay, etc. but exclude payments in kind, which is highly significant in the case of African mine workers who receive free board and lodging in the mine compounds. From the table it is clear that the earnings of African workers in manufacturing and construction are on the average about one-sixth of the earnings of white workers. The reason for this is that the majority of Africans are in unskilled or semi-skilled jobs while the majority of white workers are skilled. The wide disparity between skilled and unskilled rates of pay has been adversely commented upon by many government commissions. It is in large measure the result of the considerable pressure in lower ranks of industry caused by the movement of Africans out of subsistence farming and, particularly in the case of mining, the influx of Africans from adjacent territories.

African family incomes are considerably larger than the earnings per worker would indicate, because in most families there is more than one breadwinner. Considerable research has recently been done on this matter but it is not possible to review it here.[28]

Population Growth and Economic Development

In the Republic of South Africa population has been increasing fairly rapidly. The total population increased from six million in 1911 to seventeen million in 1960, but the rate of growth differed for the different racial groups. Whites increased at an average rate of 1·82 per cent, African 2·07 per cent, Coloureds, 2·16 per cent and Asians 2·35 per cent.[29] In 1968 the population was increasing by about 430,000 persons per annum of whom 83,000 were white, 297,000 African and 50,000 Coloured and Asian. The government, aware of this fact and of the social evils and political dangers inherent in poverty and mass unemployment, has sought to maintain a high growth rate in the national economy. It has been estimated that an average real growth rate of 5·5 per cent is within the bounds of possibility without generating inflationary pressure, and an even higher rate has successfully been achieved in recent years. If population growth remains below 2·5 per cent per annum this provides for a significant rise in average real income, which can be expected to double every thirty-three years.

Such a rate of growth will make increasing demands upon skilled manpower, so that if effective growth is to be maintained and the increasing population of all races is to be absorbed and given remunerative employment, there will have to be a considerable upward movement of non-white workers into more responsible and higher paid jobs.[30]

Notes

1 A heart-rending contemporary account of this event is to be found in J. A. Chalmers, *Tiyo Soga*, chapter 9, and a more scholarly historical appraisal of these events in A. E. du Toit, 'The Cape Frontier—a study of native policy with special reference to the years 1847–1866', *Archives Yearbook for South African History*, 1954, vol. 1.

2 *Census of Cape Colony, 1865. Population Return, Etc. of British Kaffraria, 1858.*

3 William Shaw in *The Story of My Mission in Southern Africa*, 1860, 419, writes of the introduction of a plough which he was demonstrating to the people. 'A neighbouring chief . . . seemed very much interested: he said nothing, however, for a while, but watched the plough in silence: at length, he could no longer avoid expressing his satisfaction, but, clapping his hands, and shouting to a man who was standing at some distance on the hill side, he said, "This thing that the white people have brought into the country is as good as ten wives". Of course he meant that it would do as much work in the same time as ten women could do.'

4 See Brian Fagan 'The later Iron Age in South Africa' in *African Societies in Southern Africa*, ed. L. M. Thompson, 50–70; and R. R. Inskeep in *Oxford History of South Africa* ed. Monica Wilson and Leonard Thompson, vol. I, 31ff.

5 S. H. Frankel, *Capital Investment in Africa*, 52.

6 R9,538,000 in the month of May 1969. *Statistical News Release*, Department of Statistics, 11 December 1969.

7 *Mining Survey*, Transvaal Chamber of Mines, June 1951.

8 *Statistical News Release*, Department of Statistics, Pretoria, 11 December 1969.

9 Egoli is the African name for the Witwatersrand.

10 A lively account of conditions on the diamond fields in the early days is to be found in *Incwadi Yami or Twenty Years Personal Experience in South Africa*, by J. W. Matthews, New York, 1887, chapters 12–16.

11 *Ibid.*, 192. Matthews records how in order to combat theft of diamonds 'It has become a very general practice even among respectable diggers and companies to give a percentage to native servants on the value of any diamond which they may bring. One company at Du Toit's Pan in particular by this means increased their returns to such an extent that they found it paid them to promise each "Happy Child of Ham" twenty-five per cent commission on whatever gem he might unearth.'

12 See Sheila van der Horst, 'The Economic Implications of Political Democracy', *Optima*, June 1960, D. Hobart Houghton, *The South African Economy*, 139, 157–63; W. F. J. Steenkamp 'Bantu Wages in South Africa', *South African Journal of Economics*, 30,2, 1962.

13 F. Wilson, *The Economics of Labour in the South African Gold Mines 1930–1965*.

14 For details see Sheila van der Horst, *Native Labour in South Africa*; G. V. Doxey, *The Industrial Colour Bar*; D. Hobart Houghton, *The South African Economy*, 138–65.

15 Source up to 1954–5, *Union Statistics for Fifty Years*, Bureau of Census and Statistics, 1960, G6, G7; for 1964, *Statistical Year Book 1965*, H24, H30; and for 1969 *Statistical News Release*, 11 December 1969, Department of Statistics. Except for 1964, all figures are taken to the nearest 1,000. This accounts for discrepancies between 'All races' and the total of individual race figures for 1934–5 and 1969.

16 *Native Laws Commission Report*, U.G. 28/1948, 43.

17 For an account of various ways in which contact is maintained between those in town and their traditional society see Monica Wilson and Archie Mafeje, *Langa*; I. Schapera, *Migrant Labour and Tribal Life*; Philip Mayer, *Townsmen and Tribesmen*.

18 In *Native Laws Commission Report*, U.G. 28/1948, 23.

19 *Socio-economic Development of the Bantu Areas within the Union of South Africa*, U.G. 61/1955, Summary Report, 96.

20 *Socio-economic Development of the Bantu Areas within the Union of South Africa*, U.G. 61/1955, Summary Report, 208.

21 The gold mines in 1899 had employed 12,000 whites and 107,000 Africans. In 1902

all that could be mustered were 10,000 whites and 45,000 Africans. Source: *Transvaal Labour Commission*, ed. 1896, 1904, para. 101.

22 Transvaal Ordinance Number 17 of 1904.

23 Mines and Works Act, No. 12, 1911.

24 *The Low Grade Mines Commission*, U.G. 34, 1920.

25 For a somewhat partisan account of these events see *2,000 Casualties* by I. L. Walker and B. Weinbren.

26 Industrial Conciliation Act, No. 11, 1924; The Wage Act, No. 27, 1925; Mines and Works Amendment Act, 1926. For the inhibiting effect of these on African advance see Sheila van der Horst, *Native Labour in South Africa*, chapter 13.

27 Source: *Statistical News Release* Department of Census, 11 December 1969. Slight discrepancies between totals ('All workers') and sums of items are due to rounding off to the nearest 1,000.

28 See the publications of the Bureau of Market Research, University of South Africa, Pretoria.

29 *Statistical Year Book*, 1966, A–10.

30 Since this chapter was written data from the 1970 Census has become available. It gives the total population of the Republic of South Africa as 2½ million and reveals an intercensal increase in the African population of 3·81 per cent as contrasted with the figure of 2·07 per cent quoted above. This lends further weight to what has been said about the need to maintain a higher growth rate in the pastoral economy and expand employment opportunities for the whole population, particularly the Africans.

Chapter 14
The Influence of Christianity
B. A. Pauw

This chapter primarily concerns Christianity in the reserves and other rural areas set aside for exclusive occupation by Bantu-speaking peoples, where they often live under chiefs or headmen, and are involved in forms of local or regional government reflecting some continuity with tradition. Generally speaking these are the areas in which the Bantu-speakers lived in numerous independent chiefdoms and a few larger political units, sometimes referred to as kingdoms, when they were encountered by the first missionaries. In these 'tribal' areas churches were founded and began developing before large numbers of Bantu-speakers started migrating to towns, and many features of urban church life still have to be seen against the background of Christianity in the tribal areas. This is probably true of Christianity among those settled on white farms as well (cf. Hunter 1936: 536-43), but information on the religious life of this sector of the population is still very meagre.

Christianity among South African Bantu peoples presents a complex picture that cannot be understood without reference to the historical development of Christian missions and churches, which again must be studied against the background of the earlier chapter on the classification of cultural groups and the map on page xx. With awareness of church history in the context of cultural grouping we proceed to a consideration of different patterns of acceptance and growth of Christianity in different situations. A discussion of the mission station and of the church congregation as a distinct group in tribal society leads to a more general consideration of the position of Christians in the social structure, and of belief and ritual among Bantu Christians, with reference to the two types of cultural tradition, Bantu and Western Christian, with which they now have ties. In this connection it should be noted that 'tradition' and 'traditional' will usually refer to Bantu tradition, with due regard to the fact, however, that Christianity also has its traditions, and that much that is traditional to Christianity or certain branches of it is today shared by large numbers of Bantu. Christianity among urban Bantu will be briefly discussed in a final section.

I Historical Outline of Missions and Churches

At the present time (1970) Christianity has a history of just about a century and a half among the Bantu-speaking peoples of South Africa (Du Plessis 1911: *passim*; Gerdener 1958: *passim*), the Xhosa and the Tswana being the first groups among whom missionaries settled. Among the latter, sustained missionary activity dates from Robert Moffat's settling at Kuruman to found a mission of the London Missionary Society in 1821, after several intermittent attempts by other missionaries. Methodists (Wesleyans) and missionaries of the L.M.S. and the Glasgow Missionary Society (Presbyterian) started work among the Xhosa at about the same time. By the end of the decade Moravians and the Berlin Missionary Society (Lutheran) had also founded stations among the Xhosa and other Cape Nguni peoples in what is now the Ciskei. The Methodists extended their work rapidly among the Nguni of the Ciskei and Transkei, while the L.M.S. churches, bearing a Congregationalist character, have remained predominant among the Tswana of the northern Cape Province and Botswana. During the fourth decade of the nineteenth century churches were established among the South Sotho and Natal Nguni: the Paris Evangelical Missionary Society (Reformed) founded a mission in Lesotho (1833), and in 1835 the American Board of Commissioners for Foreign Missions (Congregationalist) started working with Port Natal as base.

By 1850 the Methodists had extended their work to the Rolong (Tswana) at Thaba 'Nchu in the Orange Free State and to Natal, and the Norwegian Missionary Society (Lutheran) had started work in Natal, north of the American Board missions. The peoples of the Transvaal and Swaziland as yet had no settled mission stations. Zululand proper was still relatively untouched, but the Norwegian Missionary Society was seeking entry and was able to found a number of stations in subsequent years.

The Berlin Mission commenced work among the Pedi of the Transvaal in 1860, gradually extending its work to other North Sotho groups, and in 1872 founded a mission among the Venda. Meanwhile the Hermannsburg Mission (Lutheran) was forging a chain of stations among the Tswana of the western Transvaal who were outside the L.M.S. sphere of influence. A Swiss mission began working among the Tsonga in 1875, founding churches of the Reformed type. Later in the century Methodist missionaries settled among the Swazi.

Although Anglicans were relative late-comers among the Bantu, the Anglican Church developed in many places during this half-century and, like the Methodist Church (which continued its expansion), is today well represented in nearly every tribal area. The Dutch Reformed Church had a few mission stations in the Transvaal by 1900 but has greatly expanded its work in diverse regions since 1950. The Roman Catholic Church started work among the Bantu even later than the Anglican Church, and in respect of tribal areas has its largest following in Natal and Lesotho. The Lutheran element, introduced among the Natal Nguni by the Norwegians, was strengthened by the arrival of the Berlin Mission, the Hermannsburg Mission and the Church of Sweden Mission.

The first phase of missionary work among the Bantu coincided with a period of widespread violence and unsettled conditions in South Africa. There were successive clashes on the frontier between the white farmers and the Xhosa and other Cape Nguni, and Shaka's Zulu warriors wrought havoc in Natal and farther afield, giving rise to large population movements like that of the Natal remnants who moved south-westward to become absorbed by the Cape Nguni, who called them *amaMfengu* (destitute wanderers). Mzilikazi, one of Shaka's lieutenants who fled his domain, dispersed the population in large parts of the northern territories, and warriors of the greatly feared Mantatisi attacked as far west as Kuruman. Meanwhile the white Voortrekkers migrated from the Cape Colony to settle in the Orange Free State, Natal and the Transvaal. These conditions, making for insecurity, fear and suspicion among chiefs and their followers, were not favourable to the work of the missionaries who often had to flee for their lives and sacrifice homes and other property.

During this early phase a number of prophets, more or less influenced by Christian ideas, played a significant role among the Xhosa (Raum 1965a: 51–60). Ntsikana is said to have witnessed the visits of Van der Kemp (1799–1800) and other missionaries to chief Ngqika. He is popularly represented among the Xhosa, however, as a purely indigenous forerunner of Christianity, who received his insights independently. His prophetic utterances are interpreted as having advised, amongst other things, monogamy and acceptance of the Bible, and he is held in honour by Xhosa Christians of independent as well as other churches.

Other prophets, however, represent a reaction against whites and Western influences, including Christianity, and their activities reached a tragic climax in the Cattle-killing of 1857, resulting from the prophecies of Mhlakaza and his brother's daughter, Nongqawuse. The ancestors were supposed to have sent messages promising salvation from the supremacy of the whites. They would return to life, while the whites would be driven into the sea and the people would become rich in cattle, corn, and all the good things of the whites if they stopped practising witchcraft and sorcery, killed all their cattle, destroyed all their grain, and ceased cultivating their lands. A large proportion of the Xhosa believed these prophecies and complied with the conditions, and thousands perished in the ensuing famine.

It was only after these events, which broke the power and opposition of a number of hostile chiefs and resulted in many people's seeking assistance from the missionaries, that the missions made a definite break-through among the Xhosa. In other cases the collapse of opposition was the result of military defeat. Among the Pedi the Berlin Mission met with fierce opposition from chief Sekhukhune, and within his domain could make headway only after his people had suffered a severe defeat at the hands of white and Swazi forces in 1878.

By 1880, although Christians still formed a distinct minority of the population, the Church was well established in most tribal areas, counting many literate Bantu, including teachers, evangelists, and a number of ordained ministers among its members. Migration to towns had begun, and urban communities were developing. Some missions attempted to extend their work to the towns to care for their expatriate members, but they usually remained predominantly rural-oriented.

At this stage of development the missions were faced with a new form of unrest, this time within the ranks of the Church itself. A separatist movement, seeking independence from whites in church matters, developed among Bantu church members (Sundkler 1961a: 38ff.). The churches that arose from the movement are usually designated either 'independent' or 'separatist', but the terms in fact indicate two distinct features. The urge for independence from white control was initially manifested in a secessionist trend. Some of the seceding groups, however, eventually developed a degree of stability and, later, also readiness to co-operate with other churches, which render the qualification 'separatist' inappropriate in their case. On the other hand many further schisms took place, often involving separation from groups already independent of white churches, to such an extent that the number of known independent groups in the Republic of South Africa has grown to over 2,000. The separatist trend therefore continues in many independent churches.

The independence movement is characterized by three successive but continuing waves, each associated with a distinct type of church. The first independent churches were the result of secessions from the orthodox type of Western church, represented by the pioneer missions, and sought to adhere closely to the orthodox forms of worship and church government introduced by the missionaries, but emphasizing freedom from any form of control by white Christians.

The first to be recorded was a minor secession from the Paris Mission in Lesotho in 1872. In 1882 a Methodist minister, the Rev. Nehemiah Tile, founded the Thembu Church which was to be a national church of the Thembu people (Cape Nguni) with their own king (*uKumkani*) as head. In 1885 church members in the Maidi chiefdom of the Tlhaping of Taung seceded from the L.M.S., which had its headquarters in the neighbouring chiefdom, to form the Native Independent Congregational Church for the Maidi (Pauw 1960a: 52–3). The Lutheran Bapedi Church, founded in 1889, was a secession from the Berlin Mission, initially under the leadership of a young white missionary.

In Pretoria an Ethiopian Church was founded in 1892 under the leadership of another Methodist, the Rev. Mangena M. Mokone. Both the place of origin—in town and not in a tribal area—and the name, were significant. The reference to Ethiopia in Ps. 68:31 (A.V.) was taken to foreshadow an independent African church. The reference was obviously wider than any particular 'tribe' or people. From now on 'Ethiopian' or 'African' often appeared in the names of new groups, and those independent churches which retain the character of orthodox Western churches are now commonly referred to as an *Ethiopian type* of church (Hayward (ed.) 1963: 71). Important subsequent developments were the incorporation in 1896 of most of the members of the Ethiopian Church into the (American Negro) African Methodist Episcopal Church, and the acceptance in 1900 of many A.M.E.C.

members, mostly in the Ciskei, into the Church of the Province of South Africa (Anglican) with retention of a semi-independent identity as the 'Order of Ethiopia'. In Natal the Zulu Congregational Church sprang from a secession from the American Board in 1896, and in the Ciskei the Rev. P. J. Mzimba and some followers left the Free Church of Scotland Mission in 1898 to form the Presbyterian Church of Africa. Despite the fact that some of the important Ethiopian developments took place in towns or educational centres, their influence extended to the tribal areas as well. Although another type of independent church now made its appearance, this did not spell the end of secessions of the Ethiopian type. However, opposition to the dominance of whites in South African society gradually found expression in organizations with primarily political aims rather than in the Ethiopian churches.

The development of Christianity among the Bantu during the first part of the twentieth century was characterized by a multiplication of the agencies involved. Many of these were new missions, some South African in origin but most of them European or American, and included Baptists, Sabbatarians, and Pentacostalists. By far the greater number of new bodies, however, resulted from a continuing schismatic tendency.

The second wave in the independence movement gave rise to a *Sabbatarian-Baptist type* of independent church, stimulated by American Negro missionary influence (Pauw, forthcoming). Albert Christian, one of the early Negro Baptist missionaries to South Africa, when back in the USA, was converted to a Negro group, the Church of God and Saints of Christ, calling themselves 'Israelites'. Christian returned to South Africa in 1903 as an Israelite Bishop to propagate the Sabbatarian and Baptist doctrines of his newly-adopted church, introducing its Old Testament practices and terminology associated with the belief that the Negroes were descended from the ten lost tribes of Israel. Enoch Mgijima and some followers later separated from this group and eventually clashed with the police at Bulhoek near Queenstown in 1921 on account of their refusal to move from illegally occupied land. Defying police fire in the belief that the bullets would turn to water, 163 Israelites were killed (Schlosser 1958: 131–49). Further secessions took place, and there are now a number of independent groups using the same name as the original group. In 1906 W. W. Oliphant, also under American influence, founded an independent Sabbatarian-Baptist group called the Church of Christ. There were a number of secessions from this group or its offshoots, of which the Bantu Church of Christ, with headquarters in Port Elizabeth, gained prominence under Bishop James Limba, who died in 1963.

These Sabbatarian-Baptist independent churches do not have a large following outside the Cape Province. They tend to use the Bible in a literal and fragmentary manner, and to place legalistic emphasis on observing Saturday as sabbath and on adult baptism by immersion, the Israelite groups having a particularly strong Old Testament bias. The hymns in a number of these churches consist of Scripture portions sung to original tunes.

In the third phase of the independence movement a host of small, and a few larger, groups developed, which are now commonly collectively called Zionists. This phase was stimulated by mission work of the Christian Catholic Apostolic Church in Zion from the USA, and the Apostolic Faith Mission. The emphasis on divine healing, adult baptism by immersion, Christ's second coming, and baptism in the Holy Spirit was taken up and elaborated by leaders of these movements, who from 1914 onward started forming independent groups of the *Zionist type*, characterized by a syncretistic combination of Pentecostalist elements with Bantu tradition (Sundkler 1961a: 47–50, 55). Initially Zionism made its strongest impact in the northern areas but in later years movements of this type also spread to the Transkei and Ciskei. In the extraordinary variety of names of groups of this type references to Zion, Jerusalem, the Apostles, and Pentecost often reappear. It should be noted that not all independent offshoots from the Pentecostalist movement are of the syncretistic Zionist type. A group of some size like the African Pentecostal Church, for example, in its teaching, worship and ritual, has remained close to Pentecostalism among the white population.

II Patterns of Acceptance and Growth of Christianity[1]

Statistics of religious affiliation of the population of tribal areas alone are not available, but the figures in Table 14.1 show the position for all rural Bantu-speakers in the Republic of South Africa in 1960 (South Africa 1963: 31).

TABLE 14.1 *Religious affiliation of rural Bantu-speakers (1960)*

	Number	%
Methodist	828,217	11·1
Roman Catholic	422,568	5·7
Anglican	419,531	5·6
Dutch Reformed	363,669	4·9
Lutheran	352,417	4·7
Apostolic	218,993	2·9
Presbyterian	123,415	1·6
Congregational	95,761	1·3
'Bantu churches'	1,325,942	17·8
Other Christian	307,347	4·1
Other and unspecified	3,005,979	40·3
Total	7,463,839	100·0

Excepting the Roman Catholic Church, these names do not represent single organizations, but the great majority of Methodists, Anglicans and Dutch Reformed adherents belong to the Methodist Church of South Africa, the Church of the Province of South Africa, and the 'Nederduitse Gereformeerde

Kerk in Afrika' respectively. The category 'Bantu churches' approximately coincides with independent or separatist churches, while it can safely be accepted that the 'other and unspecified' persons nearly all adhere primarily to traditional belief and ritual.

The figures for the rural population of those economic regions in which the major reserves are situated, suggest that the proportion of Christians in the Bantu population varies roughly between 40 per cent and 60 per cent in the territories of Cape and Natal Nguni peoples. Within a specific territory there may be considerable variation, however. In the Transkei, for example, there are districts where the proportion of Christians is considerably larger than 60 per cent, and others where it is much smaller than 40 per cent. The figure for the northern and eastern Transvaal, where Venda and Tsonga are found, but North Sotho predominate, is well below 40 per cent, whereas the Tswana areas of the western Transvaal and northern Cape Province have a much higher proportion of Christians than the territories of any other group. Detailed studies of two major North Sotho groups also refer to exceptionally low proportions of Christians in certain important chiefdoms (Krige and Krige 1943: 314; Mönnig 1967: viii). The proportion of Christians in Swaziland approximates to the South African African average, but Zionist churches have an unusually large following (Hughes 1964: 161). More than 70 per cent of the Bantu population of Lesotho were enumerated as Christians in 1956, independent churches having a much smaller following than in the Republic of South Africa (Basutoland 1963: 23). Botswana has a relatively low proportion of Christians, but in some chiefdoms the position is comparable to that in the Tswana areas in the Republic of South Africa (Schapera 1958: 2, 4). It is worth noting that the South Sotho and the Tswana (West Sotho) represent the most christianized peoples, whereas the culturally closely related North Sotho, are among the least christianized.

The Methodists have a significant following in most tribal areas, but owe their overall numerical lead to their very marked predominance among the Cape Nguni. Anglicans are fairly evenly distributed. Roman Catholics are concentrated in central and southern Natal, the north-eastern Transkei, and Lesotho, and have a numerical lead in some of these parts. In Lesotho the great majority of Christians belong to one of only three major churches: in 1956 33.8 per cent of the Bantu population were enumerated as Roman Catholics, 21.9 per cent as 'French Protestant' (Paris Mission, now *Kereke ea Lesotho*), and 9.4 per cent as Anglicans, while other Christians accounted for only 5.8 per cent (Basutoland 1963: 23). Other churches particularly associated with groups or areas in which they predominate are the Berlin Lutherans among the North Sotho and Venda, the Reformed church of the Swiss Mission among the Tsonga, the Hermannsburg Lutherans among the Tswana of the western Transvaal, and the Congregationalist churches associated with the L.M.S. among other Tswana. Diverse Lutheran groups of German and Scandinavian origin, which are becoming increasingly integrated, predominate in Zululand and adjacent areas of Natal.

Some of the large independent churches are also concentrated among certain peoples, for example the Shembes' Church of the Nazarites among Natal Nguni (Schlosser 1958: 252), Limba's Church of Christ (though predominantly urban) among Cape Nguni, and Edward Lekganyane's Zion Christian Church among North Sotho (Schlosser 1958: 197). The latter possibly has even more North Sotho followers than the Berlin Lutherans.

In spite of such association of certain missions or churches with particular peoples and regions, a wide diversity of groups is usually represented in even a single district or chiefdom. Moreover, most of the churches mentioned as being associated with particular peoples have followers among others as well.

The contrast between the nominal christianization of whole chiefdoms that occurred among the Tswana, and the pattern found among other groups, where a distinct cleavage developed between Christians, often forming a minority, and the rest who definitely resisted christianization, is discussed in a later section.

Differing fortunes in earlier periods of upheaval have also affected the reaction to missions. Although conflict and unrest initially hindered mission work, the eventual outcome was often that groups dislocated or disintegrated through conflicts with other Bantu peoples eventually readily accepted Christianity. This clearly happened in the case of the Mfengu. Not only did they have to flee from the Zulu under Shaka, but for a time held a less privileged position among the Xhosa and other Cape Nguni. Peoples like the Bhaca and Hlubi of East Griqualand also went through periods of dislocation and disintegration. The proportion of Christians among these groups is distinctly higher than among other Cape Nguni. Among the Xhosa, who bore the brunt of the series of military clashes with the white colonists, a substantial core have resisted christianization, although the overthrow of the chiefs' power did lead to a limited break-through for the missions.

Differences in social status have also produced different attitudes to formal acceptance of Christianity among people of the same chiefdom. In a study of churches in a Tswana chiefdom where women formed 72 per cent of the total membership of the churches, attention has been drawn to the marked preponderance of women in church membership in diverse Bantu tribal areas (Pauw 1960a: 86). In the earlier stages of mission work traditional ideals of manliness associated with war and fighting, the herding activities of boys (preventing them from attending Christian schools), and the strictures against polygyny, which in some cases prevented husbands, but not their wives, from becoming church members, were obstacles to men joining the churches. Although these factors have lost much of their direct effect, they fostered the persisting attitude among men that the church is the concern of women. Traditional ritual and ceremonial, in which women are less directly and inevitably involved than men, form another impediment. On the other hand the churches offered women greater opportunities for leadership and self-expression than traditional Bantu society did. Migrancy further interferes with men's church activities and exposes them more to secularizing influences than women.

Among different peoples royalty and others associated with traditional political leadership have not joined the churches as readily as the rest of their people (Blacking 1964: 43; Kuper 1946: 178–80, 183; Pauw 1960a: 93–4, 115). Traditional obligations in connection with customs forbidden to church members, such as initiation or puberty ceremonies, rain rituals and agricultural ceremonial, are a more serious impediment to them than to commoners, since many of their subjects expect them to perform these duties. Polygynous marriages of chiefs often have a political function, making it more essential for them than for their subjects to have more than one wife (cf. Blacking 1964: 44–6). On the other hand identification with the church may offer to commoners a means of avoiding irksome obligations to chiefs and headmen. Some chiefs have nevertheless openly become Christians, thereby fostering the acceptance of Christianity among their people (Schapera 1958: 9; Vilakazi 1962: 13).

A less elaborate and virile ancestor cult among the Tswana and South Sotho peoples (cf. Sheddick 1953: 66) could be a factor responsible for the typically larger proportion of Christians among them than among Nguni peoples.

Among the Tswana and Cape Nguni higher proportions of non-Christians are found in less accessible areas. Since topographical features often determine accessibility, these must also be held responsible for differences in the degree of christianization (Pauw 1965: 245–7, 252).

The methods, attitudes, and 'secular' activities of missionaries have no doubt also affected the process. In earlier stages missionaries and their activities were welcomed for the sake of the political and economic advantages their presence entailed, although the people concerned often remained reluctant to profess Christianity openly. At later stages educational and medical work have helped to bring people into the churches. The ability of missionaries or clergy of one denomination to spend more time, energy and funds, and consequently to offer more impressive services and amenities, than others working beside them, also fostered growth in numbers. This is particularly evident in the case of the Roman Catholic Church (Ashton 1952: 8; Kuper 1946: 181–2; Pauw 1960a: 56; Vilakazi 1962: 12–13).

III The Local Church Group

In discussing the nature of the church group and its organization it is necessary to distinguish between mission station and church group. The mission station originated as a physical entity external to the life of the local population, although often within their territory. The nature and layout of its buildings, the missionaries who settled there, and their manners, ideas and technical equipment came from outside Bantu society. Foreign religious, educational, industrial, agricultural and other economic activities were performed at the station. Early converts were generally collected to live on or around the station, where they followed Western customs, forming a closed community with the white missionaries. The leading missionary exercised authority within the group and organized religious and educational as well as economic activities. Such early mission village communities, which largely coincided with local church groups, although including persons drawn from the surrounding population, were external or marginal to tribal society.

In the course of time increasing numbers of converts remained living with their families and kin, many of them becoming members of local church groups organized at out-stations of the mission, so that today the life of the majority of church members in tribal areas is more or less integrated with that of people not belonging to the Church. The mission station itself, now often without any white missionary, has also become more integrated, but less so than the local church at the out-station. In spite of its initial external nature, the mission has had a profound influence in changing the life of Christians as well as non-Christians through the wide range of activities carried on in churches, schools, dwellings, clinics, workshops, and bookshops, and through agricultural activities, trading and building.

Mission stations have of course not all passed through the same cycle of development. Those of later origin did not develop into the closed communities of the early stations. Older stations that have become centres for advanced education, with large boarding institutions drawing their students from an extensive area, have remained more external to the life of their local communities. Among the Tswana, who live concentrated in large compact settlements, the segregated mission village of Christians was unusual, and the mission buildings could form an integral part of the main settlement in a chiefdom. Altogether the mission station, among them, tended to be less external from the beginning.

Most stations today fall between the extreme external type of early mission village and the integrated out-station, each retaining a central position in the life of the churches of its area as the seat of the ordained minister and the place where the churches of the neighbourhood gather on special occasions. The school, although no longer controlled by the mission or church, usually remains closely associated with it.

The independent churches and some smaller missions of recent origin have dispensed with mission stations, often even doing without special church buildings. Many such churches have been introduced into a chiefdom or smaller community by a local resident who joined the church while abroad, and in whose homestead services are conducted. Although such groups do not have the same external character of the early mission communities, their appearance sometimes involves conflict with established church groups, some of whose members may defect to the new group whose teachings often deviate from that of earlier established groups.

Many of the administrative and supervisory church duties that used to be performed by the white missionary are now usually the responsibility of a

Bantu minister who may have to serve ten or more local churches, visiting them in turn to administer the sacraments and co-ordinate activities. He also is therefore relatively marginal to the life of the local church group, and the regular continuation of church activities depends largely on local lay preachers, elders or catechists.

Church government usually conforms to the system of some Western church, or a combination of such systems. It is largely through missions and churches that the Bantu have learned Western patterns of organizing groups based on association. There is a tendency in independent churches to simplify organization and to establish hierarchies or emphasize existing ones. Some Zionist groups have an extensive range of hierarchical offices. Discipline is exercised by a church council or by a whole local group acting as a court and tending to follow traditional patterns of judicial procedure.

Missionaries have generally required that converts abstain from certain customs like polygynous marriage, inheritance of wives, traditionally recognized forms of extra-marital sexual intercourse, dancing, sacrificial rituals and recourse to diviners and other traditional practitioners. Some also opposed marriage payments, initiation and beer drinking (cf. Ashton 1952: 119; Blacking 1964: 42–8; Krige and Krige 1943: 316; Vilakazi 1962: 101–3, 125). A legalistic system of controlled contributions in the form of regular fixed amounts is a tradition of long standing in many churches. Pre-marital sex relations, often dealt with only when pregnancy results, are the most common transgression for which the sacraments are withheld from the erring member, who in addition may have to attend a special class and take a back seat in the church. A girl may be denied wearing a veil and white dress for her wedding and may have to be married in the vestry or minister's study instead of in church (cf. Vilakazi 1962: 57; Hammond-Tooke 1962: 97).

Independent churches occasionally openly recognize a custom like polygyny or initiation, opposed by other churches. On the whole, though, they avoid open recognition, which might lend substance to accusations of a return to paganism, but also desist from explicit opposition. Zionists, who are definitely syncretistic and have their own methods of countering witchcraft and sorcery and other dangers, are emphatically opposed to recourse to diviners and other medicine-men.

Local church groups are small in size, often counting less than a hundred registered adults. In groups of long-established churches members baptized in infancy and brought up as Christians in home and school, some of them third-generation Christians, now usually predominate. Associations (*imimanyano, mekgatlo*) for different age and sex categories of church members are common, and the Manyanos of mature married women, which in each church have their distinctive uniform, often form the core of local churches. Differential status is reflected in the pattern of seating in church, adult males, females, and children occupying separate parts of the building, and Manyano women and male office bearers often being distinguishable from the rest.

For many active church members the local church group offers the most important field of joint activity outside the home. Services and association meetings, preceded and followed by informal social contacts, figure prominently in their weekly routine, and concerts and other fund-raising activities provide entertainment. Major religious festivals have strong social overtones and are usually occasions for communal meals. The small size of the group and the informal character of services make for intimate relations, the more so when services take place in a homestead. When members in addition receive encouragement and assistance from the close-knit church group or one of its associations in time of illness, bereavement and other troubles, it fulfills many of the functions of kinship groups in traditional Bantu society. This is particularly evident where kinship has lost much of its traditional significance, as among some Tswana, or where Christians, by their separation from the pagan part of their society, have been separated from a large part of their kinsmen (Vilakazi 1962: 27–9, 94, 102).

Where much of the traditional ceremonial and other excitement have disappeared, or where Christians are prohibited from participating in these, church activities now help to break the monotony of routine activities. The large number of church offices in relation to the small size of church groups, and the many opportunities for any member to preach, pray or deliver testimonies, particularly in Zionist and Pentecostalist churches, offer ample scope for self-expression and for exercising public leadership, even to persons who on account of sex or genealogical status have little opportunity for this in that part of public life governed by Bantu tradition.

The local church group has regular contacts with other local churches in the same area, the church at the original mission station often symbolizing the unity of a group of local churches. Contacts with larger regional and national divisions of the church are few, but in well-established churches members are well aware of these. Direct contact with non-Bantu Christians is very limited, but members of churches of missionary origin are in varying degrees aware of such contacts, as well as of international contacts at one or more levels of church organization beyond the local area. When missionaries played a more prominent role in church life there was often more real contact with, and dependence on, an overseas body than with white Christians in South Africa. Moves toward greater autonomy and responsibility for the 'mission' churches sometimes met with the complaint that they were being deserted by the 'fathers'. In small independent churches the links with the rest of the church are often very tenuous.

Organized ecumenical activity is remote to the life of the local church, but Bantu Christians are not keenly aware of doctrinal differences between their churches. There is occasional spontaneous contact between the local groups of different denominations in the same neighbourhood, and office bearers and members of different churches often co-operate on occasions like night watches, funerals, prayers for rain and fund-raising activities.

IV Christians in Tribal Society

The impact of Christianity on tribal social structure involves much more than the emergence of groups with a purpose, structure, beliefs and activities foreign to Bantu tradition. Among different peoples it has produced a pervasive division within chiefdoms and communities. Although most Christians nowadays do not live in communities segregated from non-Christians, a distinct division of Christians from pagans is often unmistakable. This cleavage has been well documented for the Cape and Natal Nguni (e.g. Dubb 1966: *passim*; Hammond-Tooke 1962: 63-5 *et passim*; Hunter 1936: 6, 351, 377 *et passim*; Mayer 1961: 20-41 *et passim*; Reader 1966: 338-42; Vilakazi 1962: *passim*), and for the Lobedu (Krige and Krige 1943: 314-22), and there is evidence of it among the Pedi (Mönnig 1967: viii) and the Venda (Blacking 1964: 33-4, 43, 47-9).

This division of society may be contrasted with the position in a number of Tswana chiefdoms in which chief and people have formally associated themselves with Christianity or the great majority of the people are nominal Christians. In reserves of the northern Cape Province a large proportion of the people are registered members or catechumens of a church, many others are distinguished as *barati*, people who are sympathetically disposed to (lit. like or love) the Church, while only a small minority are not associated with the Church. The distinction between these categories is very vague in comparison with that found among the other peoples mentioned.

The differing patterns among Tswana and Nguni peoples has been related to differences in social structure. The Tswana live in large, relatively compact settlements, not in scattered homesteads like the Nguni, and it is not unusual for a Tswana chief to have the majority of his people living in the capital with him. This fosters strong central authority, and solidarity among the chief's followers, and is unfavourable to the entry of multiple religious agencies (Pauw 1965: 245). In a number of chiefdoms the conversion of the chief further fostered nominal christianization of a whole chiefdom (Schapera 1958: 9).

The remarkably contrasting position among the North Sotho, who are culturally closely related to the Tswana, still requires investigation but might be partly related to the mission policy of isolating Christians in separate settlements and to such a radical rejection of the indigenous culture by the Berlin mission that opposition from the political leaders was inevitable (cf. Krige and Krige 1943: 314-18; Mönnig 1967: viii). The Lobedu, in fact, do not conform to the residential pattern of the Tswana and some North Sotho, but live in scattered villages (Krige and Krige 1943: 17). Among the Pedi segregation of converts might have been difficult to avoid after the eruption of chief Sekhukhune's violent opposition in 1864, at whose hands Pedi Christians actually suffered persecution. Moreover Sekhukhune was later involved in serious conflicts with Boer and British forces, that ended in his imprisonment and the crushing of his empire (Mönnig 1967: 27-31). These conditions would obviously have militated against a policy of integration adapted to the centralized social structure of the Pedi. Even the founding of the Pedi Lutheran Church by a former member of the Berlin Mission, who sought greater participation for Pedi Christians in the control of church affairs and adopted 'the Pedi way of life' (Mönnig 1967: 31-2), did not lead to extensive 'tribal' christianization.

The people of Lesotho seem to be far advanced towards a universal nominal acceptance of Christianity (cf. Sheddick 1953: 65 n.1) but the Tlokoa are characterized by their conservative adherence to tradition, and as late as 1930 were still unanimous in their resistance to christianization (Ashton 1952: 117 *et passim*). In Swaziland putting on Western dress used to be a sign of conversion, and Christians tended to assume an attitude of superiority towards pagans, but the cleavage is less definite than among other Nguni peoples. Kuper ascribes this to 'the strength of the national organization' and to the fact that there has not been such a close correlation between Christianity and school education, so that there are many non-Christians who have been to school and many uneducated converts among the Swazi (Kuper 1946: 184-5).

The Cape Nguni commonly distinguish between School people or *amagqoboka* (people who have been pierced through; a designation for Christians) and Red people or *amaqaba* (the ones who smear). The latter are the pagan traditionalists who wear red blankets and dress, and smear or paint their bodies with a mixture of fat and red ochre. The basic contrast is between the acceptance of Christianity and seeking school education on the one hand, and choosing to remain illiterate pagans on the other. Other overt signs are Western-style as opposed to traditional-style dress, especially in the case of women, rectangular houses instead of round huts, and different forms of entertainment and of etiquette. Vilakazi describes similar distinctions among Natal Nguni.

The contrast is one of polarity rather than dichotomy, involving intermediate types. Among Xhosa-speaking people, for example, the name *inxiba* (dressed person) signifies a person who in dress and otherwise deviates from ideal Red patterns but does not identify himself with the Church. Hammond-Tooke refers to a neo-pagan type (Hammond-Tooke 1962: 64) similar to the *igxagxa* defined by Vilakazi as 'a person who is culturally neither a Christian nor a traditionalist' (Vilakazi 1962: 76). Some of the distinctions marking the cleavage are also becoming less clear-cut than they used to be. Most people, however, identify themselves with either the Christian or the pagan sector, the Christian or School sector being more inclusive than the organized church group.

Despite this cleavage Christians and pagans usually participate in the same political institutions, excepting Christians living on land belonging to missions or a type of mission reserve where they do not come under the jurisdiction of traditional chiefs (Krige and Krige 1943: 314, 317; Vilakazi 1962: 97). Some of the Natal reserves have developed into separate Christian chiefdoms with their own chiefs. A more exceptional kind of chiefdom developed among the Pedi during the previous century, when a Christian half-brother of chief Sekhukhune became disillusioned with life in the mission community, settled on his own and collected Christians from different chiefdoms under his rule (Mönnig 1967: 28).

Christians and pagans mostly pursue the same basic agricultural and pastoral activities, which they supplement by wages, usually earned in migrant labour. Christians, however, having developed a much more extensive need for Western goods, are more dependent on income in cash. Further, missionary emphasis on the dignity of labour and efforts to foster economic diversification and enterprise have had effect. In contrasting Christians and pagans in a Natal reserve, Vilakazi writes that Christians work more readily for wages and that the enterprising people are all Christians. By fencing their fields, charging a fee for grazing on their reaped fields and selling milk and manure —all of which run counter to Zulu tradition—Christians incur the disapproval of pagans who regard these individualist trends as mean and selfish (Vilakazi 1962: 120–1; cf. Reader 1966: 71). Similar contrasts have been observed among the Lobedu (Krige and Krige 1943: 319–20).

Christianity has affected social structure and organization in many other ways. Missionary opposition to traditional rites of passage have for some Christians led to the disappearance of such rites and the consequent fading of the distinctions between the successive statuses an individual occupies as the life cycle proceeds, but substitutes have also developed. Everywhere Christian marriage and funeral ritual have been introduced, but not without adaptations to Bantu tradition, as in the washing of hands after a funeral, services of condolence and commemoration at later stages, and competitive Western-type dancing in the place of traditional competitive dancing at weddings (cf. Vilakazi 1962: 75). Initiation ceremonies have been officially prohibited by some Tswana chiefs (Schapera 1958: 3). In chiefdoms where this has not happened, some Christians comply with the church rules prohibiting participation. Modified ceremonial culminating in a church festival for boys developed among the Kgatla (Schapera 1934e: 48–9). In Lesotho Moshoeshoe promised the missionaries not to let his children and grandchildren be initiated. Some of them later became important chiefs who could not hold their own initiation ceremonies or attend those held by other chiefs, and either neglected or opposed the institution (Ashton 1952: 55–6). Among the Xhosa and other Cape Nguni, whose initiation ceremonies are less secret than those of the Sotho peoples, initiation is attended by many boys from Christian homes. Features of girls' initiation, to which there was more objection, are often incorporated in a Christian bride's preparation for marriage.

Some Christians have replaced traditional ceremonies to recognize an infant as a social person by a service to take the child out of the house, or a baptismal dinner in connection with which an animal may be slaughtered in deference to the ancestors.

In extreme instances the church has taken the place of the wider kinship group for Christians (Vilakazi 1962: 97, 102). Conversion to Christianity involved at least an additional allegiance, the church competing with kinsmen and other traditional groups for the Christian's loyalty. Prohibition of participation in traditional kinship rituals involving sacrifices to the ancestors undermined the solidarity of lineages. Nevertheless, many traditional kinship duties are still observed by Christians, and most of them are involved in a kinship network that is more extensive and close-knit than that of Western peoples. Even where the Christian-pagan cleavage is evident, whole lineages of Christians living in the same neighbourhood, acting together in ritual, ceremonial, economic and judicial activities are not unusual (cf. Reader 1966: 61), but there are signs of a greater concern with the interests of the nuclear family at the expense of the lineage (cf. Vilakazi 1962: 30–1).

In a detailed study of a Zulu reserve, Vilakazi has contrasted trends among Christians in respect of marriage and the family with the patterns still observed by pagan traditionalists (Vilakazi 1962: *passim*). Whereas traditionalists publicly recognize and control pre-marital relationships, taking a lover is an individual affair that is kept a secret from parents and church officials among Christians.

In Christian marriage negotiations there is less reticence between prospective in-laws than among traditionalists, and parents more commonly participate directly instead of using go-betweens. The tensions and emotional flare-ups that characterize traditional Zulu ceremonial are less in evidence among Christians, who conduct negotiations with cold politeness. Christians require more to be given as marriage goods (*lobolo*) but use the proceeds to meet the costs of trousseau, furniture, household equipment and food for the wedding feast, which are regarded as social necessities. Marriage has become more personal and individual, although parents and other kinsmen are still involved in negotiations.

For the Christian wife monogamy eliminates the rivalries experienced by co-wives in traditionalist polygynous families. Christian wives can also usually expect more respect and less superiority from their husbands and share more activities with them than the wives of traditionalists.

Unlike their pagan counterparts, daughters in a Christian family can become economically independent, and are able to contribute to the care of their parents. Thus they obtain a greater say in the economic affairs of the home and may become eligible for inheritance.

Much of the reticence between in-laws prescribed by Zulu tradition is disregarded by Christians, to the extent that a man will not refrain from eating with his mother-in-law. Christian married women do not have to observe the numerous traditional avoidances in language, dress, and movement around the husband's home.

V Belief and Ritual: Christianity and Bantu Tradition

We finally consider the more specifically religious content of contemporary

Christianity in tribal society. In approaching the subject from the angle of continuity with the two traditions involved, we do not propose a mechanical sorting out of elements belonging to either of the two traditions. The dynamic nature of the process of change and the need to study the present manifestations of social structure and culture in their own right, as they are now found to be functioning, is fully recognized. Nevertheless, continuity with either of the two traditions is often immediately apparent, particularly in the field of belief and ritual. To a certain extent Christianity has replaced Bantu religious tradition among Christians, but the latter tradition has by no means been eliminated. We shall try to indicate to what extent the two traditions have remained constant or have changed, and to what extent they have remained separate or have been synthesized or adapted to each other, and how these trends are functionally related to the social structure.

Contemporary religion among the South African Bantu, even of any particular cultural group, is characterized by a considerable degree of diversity. First there is the distinction between those that profess Christianity, and those that do not. It is of course among the latter that traditional religious ideas and practices are adhered to most 'purely' and extensively, but even their religion has been influenced by Christianity. The God of whom Christians speak is, for example, identified with the single supreme being Bantu peoples vaguely acknowledged before the missionaries came, and many non-Christians no longer think of him as distant and unapproachable (cf. Ashton 1952: 116–17; Sheddick 1953: 67). Even pagan traditionalists occasionally pray to him directly. This kind of influence of Christianity among non-Christians still awaits detailed investigation. Further there is among Christians the diversity resulting from differences in the national and denominational background of the missionaries who introduced Christianity, increased by separatist tendencies. In addition traditional religion has not lost its effect among Christians.

Certain broad distinctions can, however, be drawn. There are the Christians of the churches in which the respective types of Christianity introduced from Europe or America have continued without spectacular adaptation or syncretization. These are primarily the established orthodox churches, Protestant as well as Roman Catholic, but also including Baptist, Pentecostalist and Sabbatarian groups. Many members of these churches, however, combine their attachment to these Western forms of Christianity with adherence to elements of traditional Bantu religion, keeping the two traditions relatively separate. With this broad category, which includes the independent churches maintaining a considerable degree of continuity with Western forms of Christianity, we contrast churches of the Zionist type, in which Baptist and Pentecostalist beliefs and practices have been definitely syncretized with Bantu tradition.

In orthodox churches Christian services were occasionally introduced to provide a substitute for traditional ritual. Special prayers for rain were conducted to discourage traditional rain ritual. The official role played by some chiefs in such services parallels their traditional responsibility for rain ritual (cf. Ashton 1952: 117). For many people Roman Catholic rites of blessing and sprinkling have taken the place of indigenous rituals to safeguard homes, stock pens, fields, and food at feasts against witchcraft and sorcery, or to terminate conditions of impurity. Blessed medallions could easily be substituted for Bantu amulets (cf. Ashton 1952: 296, 316; Kuper 1946: 182, 187). This kind of adaptation has, however, been superficial and, except in the case of the Roman Catholic Church, uncommon. The use of traditional patterns in church music, architecture, and decoration has been exceptional. In the field of ideas and beliefs, however, it is possible to indicate particular emphases or themes that characterize Bantu Christians' interpretation of the Christian tradition.

Interpretation of Christian tradition

To many Bantu Christians awareness of the nearness of God and his concern with the personal circumstances of believers is an essential feature of their faith. God's care as the loving Father of his children who may approach him directly and personally in prayer, is enthusiastically accepted as a new insight contrasting with traditional belief in a distant and unconcerned supreme being. Regard for his transcendence as almighty Creator and Father is, however, not absent. The efficacy of prayer against troubles and difficulties is particularly emphasized in the women's Manyanos of the orthodox churches, by Zionists and other Pentecostalists, and by charismatic leaders around whom prayer-movements develop without becoming separate churches. Among Zionists and some others, however, prayer becomes a magical technique of tapping extraordinary power.

Ideas about God centre on God the Father, with less emphasis on Christ as the Son of God. Jesus is recognized as mediator who suffered and died for man's salvation and set an example of humility, endurance, love and compassion, but He is seen more as the Son of man than the Son of God, at the level of the ancestors, as the great ancestor of the Church, rather than at the level of God the Father (cf. Reader 1966: 284). In orthodox churches even less attention is paid to the Holy Spirit as third person in the Trinity. In Pentecostalist and Zionist churches, however, there is special concern with the Spirit. Possession of the Spirit as source of knowledge and power is eagerly sought, and speaking with tongues and the use of violent gestures is interpreted as evidence of the working of the Spirit from whom knowledge hidden to others is received through prophecy, visions and dreams. The Spirit is also the source of power by which Zionists overcome the forces inimical to life, and by which vitality is enhanced. Knowledge and power are, however, increasingly possessed and controlled by the Zionist prophet in a magical way.

A moralistic or legalistic trend, placing greater emphasis on adhering to laws and doing good works than on grace, is also evident. This might well be related to traditional beliefs that the assistance and goodwill of the ancestors depend on correct behaviour of the living. It has, however, no doubt been fostered by the prohibitions and other rules laid down by missionaries as conditions for admission into a Christian congregation, and by the legalistic system of contributions. Apart from these rules morality is not clearly defined, but restraint, love and peace are emphasized in a general way. At the level of the local church in tribal society there is not much expression of concern with larger social and political issues, which is often a feature of deliberations at national and regional levels.

A secretive attitude has developed in connection with some prohibitions, to the extent that many church members are satisfied that no wrong is done by the relevant acts as such, as long as these do not become public knowledge (cf. Ashton 1952: 305–6, 313; Krige and Krige 1943: 316; Sheddick 1953: 66; Vilakazi 1962: 101, 103, 125). This kind of formalism emerges also in a tendency to disguise traditional sacrifices with Western forms of behaviour and new names, as in the case of sacrificial meals that are shorn of certain traditional details, served in Western fashion and called dinners instead of *amadini* (sacrifices) by Xhosa-speaking Christians.

Some writers have associated the legalistic emphasis with a preference for the Old Testament. In my own experience this preference is difficult to prove, except in the case of some Sabbatarian groups, especially those of the 'Israelite' type, which played a particularly prominent role in the history of church separatism in South Africa, but have today lost much of their significance. A literal and fragmentary use and interpretation of the Bible with reference to particular doctrines and practices is common to Zionists and other Pentecostalist and Sabbatarian groups, who particularly emphasize their Biblical foundation.

There is further a trend toward sensuous experience in connection with religion, in the form of emotionalism or the elaboration of ritual. The emotionalism of early Methodism is perpetuated in rural Methodist churches, and has found its way into other churches that lack this tradition of emotionalism. The lively, rhythmic singing to the accompaniment of the clapping of hands, stamping of feet, speaking with tongues, shouting, and other ecstatic behaviour typical of many Pentecostalist and Apostolic groups have spread from these to others, and have moreover been elaborated in Zionist practices. In a different way Anglican and Roman Catholic ritual have a special emotional appeal (cf. Kuper 1946: 182).

Christian teaching attaching direct efficacy to the sacraments and other liturgical activities, which easily lends itself to a magical interpretation of ritual, has also found ready acceptance. This has probably contributed to the spread of Roman Catholicism, Pentecostalism and Baptist teaching and practices. The magical nature of Zionist belief and ritual is self-evident.

Orthodox Christians have tended to interpret Christianity as primarily concerned with other-worldly salvation. The trust in prayer and in God's care in everyday life serves more to alleviate hardships than to remove them completely. Other types of churches tend to react by offering salvation here and now. A few outstanding charismatic leaders have become messianic figures for their followers, being regarded as the indispensable channels through whom this salvation is attained (Sundkler 1961a: 323ff.). In Zionist churches it is primarily a salvation in terms of health and vitality. In Bishop Limba's church again there is greater concern with economic advancement in the Western context. A leader like Bishop Edward Lekganyane represented both kinds of blessing (Schlosser 1958: 200).

The preceding paragraphs and the rest of this chapter are not intended to convey the impression that Christianity among the Bantu is altogether deviant. Different points of view will, of course, lead to different evaluations, but in my own view there is among Bantu Christians a core of genuine faith in the grace of God manifest in Jesus Christ.

Zionist syncretism

In his study of Zulu independent churches Sundkler emphasized the syncretistic tendencies of Zulu Zionist groups, indicating a whole range of parallels between the activities and ideas of Zionists and Zulu diviners (Sundkler 1961a: *passim*). Just as a special form of illness ascribed to possession by an ancestor spirit leads to initiation as a diviner, so an illness is usually the starting-point for joining a Zionist group, and a Zionist's development implies possession by the Holy Spirit. In both instances food and other taboos play an important role. During initiation the diviner regularly undergoes purification by vomiting by the riverside, and he has to enter the river to find a mystical snake under which he searches for white clay with which to anoint himself. For baptism and regular purifications Zionists visit pools full of dangerous creatures from which the 'Lord of the Waters' protects them (see Plates 17a and 17b). Prophet and diviner both promote health and vitality, recognizing witchcraft and sorcery as an important source of illness. In prophesying Zionists follow the same procedure of asking leading questions as does the most typical kind of Zulu diviner. They also recognize the ability of the ancestor spirits to cause ill-health and barrenness, and the need to satisfy or propitiate them with sacrifices.

The Zionists' prayer with laying on of hands often becomes a violent and emotional activity carried on in an atmosphere of suspense to drive out evil spirits, witchcraft familiars or the powers of sorcery. They shun traditional techniques of healing as well as Western medicine. Water over which prayers have been said, ashes, consecrated sticks, staffs, flags, anklets and wristlets believed to have been prescribed by the Spirit are often used to sustain or restore health. Many Zionists wear special dresses or cassocks, girdles, cloaks and headdresses adorned with crosses, crescents, circles, stars, and angels, as the Spirit prescribes. There is some variation in colour and form, but a sufficient uniformity to distinguish an overall type (see Plates 16, 18a and 18b).

The largest and best-known Zulu syncretistic group, the Nazareth Baptist

Church founded by Isaiah Shembe, who was succeeded by his son, J. G. Shembe, has an identity distinct from the smaller Zulu Zionist groups. In this group special revelation, taboos and healing through the leader's touch or contact with a ritual object such as the founder's veil, are also particularly significant. The leader combines the functions of the traditional Zulu doctor-diviner with those of a chief, and the founder has become a black messiah for his people. The living leader is approached by his followers with attitudes of extreme submission, mostly through intermediaries, like a chief, and is greeted with royal praises. Group dancing to the accompaniment of drum and song at the church headquarters, where the leader's home is, is highly organized on an age-group basis. Dance groups have special uniforms, in some of which extensive use is made of traditional skin clothing, shields and bead ornaments. All this is suggestive of traditional dancing at the chief's kraal. There is also a parallel to the traditional Zulu festival of the first-fruits in which chief or king had to take the initiative. Church members may not partake of the new crop before Shembe has blessed the first fruits (Oosthuizen 1967: *passim*; Schlosser 1958: 221 ff.; Sundkler 1961a: *passim*).

The ritual and belief of Zulu Zionism have spread not only to other Nguni peoples, whose traditions have the same parallels as the Zulu with the Zionist practices and ideas mentioned, but also to Sotho peoples whose traditions differ in significant respects. Zionists with the same forms of divining, healing, and purification are found among the Tswana, for example, whereas the typical Tswana technique of divining by throwing bones, and their purification rites consisting of sprinkling, do not form such neat parallels to the Zionist practices described. However, some of the Zionist groups that predominate among the Sotho peoples (which include the Tswana) deviate from Zulu Zionist patterns in notable respects. The St Paul Apostolic Faith Morning Star group and the Zion Apostolic Church have different forms of dress, and perform rituals of sprinkling that conform closer to Sotho tradition, while their divination is less developed and not clearly patterned on the Zulu practice of asking leading questions (Pauw 1960a: *passim*).

The largest and best-known Sotho Zionist church, the Zion Christian Church, that came to prominence under Bishop Edward Lekganyane, also has typical forms of ritual that distinguish it from Zulu Zionism. Church apparel is a more definite uniform—khaki for men—and fanning with small bits of paper is their typical method of purification and healing (Schlosser 1958: 193 ff.).

Although Zionism among Sotho peoples cannot be correlated with Sotho tradition as clearly as Nguni Zionism with Nguni tradition, such parallels are not altogether lacking. Moreover the magical nature of rituals and beliefs is unmistakable, and in this there is affinity with Sotho as well as other Bantu traditions. The characterization of Zionism as a syncretization of Pentecostalism and Bantu tradition is not invalidated by the variations found among Sotho peoples.

In spite of the close affinity with Bantu tradition, Zionists strongly emphasize the Biblical foundation of their beliefs and practices. Their singing, clapping, dancing, shouting, prophesying, laying on of hands and possession by the Spirit are all 'in the Bible'.

Orthodox Christians and Bantu tradition

Although Bantu tradition has not been allowed much opportunity for expression in the corporate life of non-Zionist churches, there is evidence from diverse cultural groups that Bantu religious tradition asserts itself in the private and family life of many Christians (e.g. Ashton 1952: 305–6, 313, 316; Pauw 1960a: 39; Sheddick 1953: 66; Vilakazi 1962: 32, 103, 125). For a more detailed assessment of the significance of Bantu religious tradition for Christians we refer to a recent study among Xhosa-speaking Christians in a Transkeian district (Pauw, forthcoming). The position among non-Zionist Pentecostalists and Sabbatarian-Baptists varies; here we concentrate on Christians associated with orthodox churches.

The study indicated that a substantial majority believed that their ancestors would send misfortune if they neglected certain important traditional duties or customs. A majority also interpreted dreams or other experiences from their own life as visitations from their ancestors, or regarded certain fortunate events as blessings from the ancestors. Some had taken an active part in the performance of ancestor rituals.

Christians' deference to Xhosa customs relating to death and the dead emerges in the home and family activities. Often church office bearers and a substantial part of the local church members participate, but interest is centred on the family concerned. Many Christians slaughter a beast 'to accompany' the dead, using the meat to feed the guests attending the funeral. To some people the washing of hands performed after almost every funeral signifies purification from the contamination of death. Rural Christians, especially women after the death of their husbands, strictly follow mourning observances like wearing black, acting with restraint, and keeping to the home. An initial lifting of some of these is occasioned by a service conducted by church office bearers, associated with a traditional ceremony of bringing the wives back to the homestead from the veld or forest where they had to remain after their husband's death. Neglect of the ritual to accompany the dead, and of certain mourning customs, is commonly regarded as a potential reason for the ancestors to send misfortune.

What is ostensibly a Christian ritual may be performed with an unpublicized motive implying Xhosa religious beliefs. The erection of a tombstone, unveiled at a service conducted by a minister, attended by a large number of kinsmen and church members, and followed by a dinner in Western style, for which a beast has been slaughtered, sometimes has the purpose of pacifying or pleasing the dead. It is commonly regarded as a substitute for a traditional sacrifice 'to bring back' the dead.

The form of the ritual behaviour by which Christians recognize their ancestors varies considerably. Some perform rituals that are not much different from those of pagans, but usually some of the traditional details are eliminated, often in a conscious attempt to disguise the traditional significance. Certain details of Xhosa tradition may be observed on the day an animal is slaughtered in the relative privacy of the circle of close kin, to be followed on the next day by activities of a Christian or Western nature.

Belief in sorcery and witchcraft is also common among Christians. Many ascribe certain events in their own life to such causes. Although Western medical treatment is readily sought in other cases, it is generally regarded as ineffective against witchcraft and sorcery, except in cases ascribed to *idliso*, a form of sorcery effected by surreptitious administration of harmful medicine in food or drink, which is commonly equated with poisoning. Medical treatment is also sought for relief of immediately dangerous or painful symptoms or injuries ascribed to a witch or sorcerer. Otherwise Christians rather seek assistance from diviners and medicine-men when witchcraft or sorcery is suspected, but some have accepted prayer as an alternative way of countering such misfortune.

Most orthodox Christians are not particularly concerned with the relation between the teaching of the Church and the traditional Xhosa religious beliefs they still hold. Superficial synthesis of the two traditions is not lacking. It is often said that God and the ancestors work together, with the recognition that the ancestors are on a different plane from that of God. Ancestor belief and ritual are also justified with reference to the commandment to honour one's parents or to Christian ideas of life after death. In a general way traditional belief and ritual are justified by the argument that Jesus said he did not come to destroy people's customs—obviously a reference to Matt. 5:17. Witchcraft familiars are commonly identified with the demons and evil spirits Jesus drove out. Diviners and medicine-men are considered as supplementing God's aid to man, so that neglecting their assistance would be a way of tempting God by taking unnecessary risks. Further, Xhosa techniques of healing are considered to be essentially of the same nature as Western medicine, so that it is equally justified for a Christian to avail himself of the services of traditional specialists and of medical doctors. On the whole, however, there are no very distinct attempts at reconciling the two traditions, but neither is there a strong awareness of conflict.

That many Christians adhere to traditions that to an outsider investigating their beliefs appear to conflict with the Bible, need not imply insincerity on their part. Concern with intellectual consistency within an inclusive unitary system of knowledge is a value of large-scale Western society foreign to the magical explanations of small-scale societies. Even the kind of society in which Bantu Christians are involved has large-scale as well as small-scale features. Admittedly the Western education in which most Christians have shared could be expected to cause uneasiness about logical inconsistency, but the education most of them have had is still relatively limited. What awareness there is of the significance of overall consistency is either satisfied by a superficial synthesis or formalistic adaptation of the two religious traditions, or is not acute enough to disturb people's minds.

The absence of a sense of conflict is further explained by the complementary social functions of Christianity and Bantu tradition. It is significant that the ancestor rituals of Christians emerge in the homestead, in the context of family and kin, and not in the corporate life of the church group. Bantu tradition functions in the context of small-scale, face-to-face relationships: the ancestor cult is relevant to family and kinship ties, and witchcraft beliefs explain misfortune with reference to strained relations with persons with whom one is in close contact. These particularistic beliefs of Bantu tradition therefore function mainly in relation to the small-scale features of society. The Church, on the other hand, although it has attained some significance for the small-scale features, and has even taken over some of the functions of kinship groups, in the orthodox forms established by missionaries, primarily represents wide-ranging relationships typical of the large-scale society into which the Bantu peoples have been drawn. Admittedly there is not much explicit expression of concern with national and international problems and organized ecumenical activity, but there is keen awareness of participation in a universalistic faith in one God concerned with all peoples, and one Saviour and one book in which the way of salvation is revealed. Moreover, this faith has not yet penetrated the small-scale forms of social life to such an extent that it has replaced Bantu tradition. The two traditions therefore function in predominantly different contexts or situations. Further, Bantu tradition's orientation to salvation from ill-health and other forms of immediate misfortune related to the personal relationships of every-day life, supplements the other-wordly orientation of the orthodox churches.

Zionists, however, find their own this-worldly salvation in a more definite syncretism. It is suggested that this syncretism is also functionally related to a social structure that is partly small-scale and partly large-scale. In close-knit, face-to-face groups they practise a predominantly magical religion closely akin to the particularistic Bantu tradition associated with small-scale forms of society. Their inevitable involvement in large-scale society outside the church group finds expression in an interpretation of their beliefs and practices in terms of the more universalistic tradition of the Bible.

VI Christianity among Urban Bantu

In 1960 18·7 per cent of urban Bantu in the Republic of South Africa were not enumerated as Christians (South Africa 1963: 31). For census purposes the category of urban Bantu includes the permanent as well as the temporary population of large and small towns. Of the settled urban Bantu population even a smaller minority do not at least nominally associate themselves with a church. This is borne out by the fact that there is a distinctly higher than average proportion of non-Christians in urban areas carrying a large mine compound population, consisting largely of migrants. For the urban Bantu of the West Rand economic region, for example, the figure is 38·8 per cent, and for those of the region which includes the Free State gold fields 39·5 per cent (South Africa 1963: 36, 37).

The same different types of churches discussed earlier are found in the urban areas. The pioneer missions usually followed their members who migrated to the towns, but some of the churches that began working among Bantu later, started their work in towns and subsequently moved into rural areas.

In the larger towns the pioneer orthodox churches have large local groups running into several hundreds of members, and frequent mass gatherings of single churches or of an inter-denominational nature, running into thousands, are a feature distinguishing urban church life from that of rural Christians. In addition urban Christians are involved in a larger variety of extra-domestic group activities besides those of their church. The intimate and close-knit relations typical of rural churches, are therefore generally lacking in large urban church groups, but are characteristic of the women's Manyanos (Brandel-Syrier 1962: 231 *et passim*), even within the larger churches, and of Zionist and other small groups.

A few movements that have not made a spectacular impact in rural areas, have gathered large congregations in urban areas, comparable to, and sometimes even exceeding, those of the orthodox pioneer churches in numbers. This is the case, for example, with the Rev. N. B. H. Bhengu's Assembly of God in East London (cf. Dubb 1961: *passim*; Mayer 1963: *passim*; Schlosser 1958: 36 ff.), Bishop Limba's Church of Christ in Port Elizabeth (cf. Mqotsi and Mkele 1946: *passim*) and the Old Apostolic Church in a number of urban centres. In spite of their mass character the groups mentioned are characterized by strong social control and solidarity of the local church group. Much of the members' activities takes place within the context of the church group, which is of a closed nature, and within which there is a close-knit network of relationships. These groups are not strongly syncretistic in their forms of ritual, but are characterized by selective emphasis on Pentecostalist, Baptist, or Sabbatarian teaching.

The small minority of highly educated professional people mostly belong to the orthodox churches that have made the greatest contribution to the school education of the Bantu. Some of them also belong to independent orthodox churches, but hardly any belong to Zionist churches.

The orthodox churches in town have until recently been strongly rural-oriented, with older rural-minded members often calling the tune, but some of the emphases indicated in respect of rural churches in tribal areas are not as explicit among urban Christians. This is the case particularly with the other-worldy emphasis and the lack of concern with race relations and national politics.

Although adherence to traditional Bantu belief and ritual is somewhat less among urban Christians than those in tribal areas, it is by no means lacking. Performance of ancestor rituals is not uncommon and beliefs about the ancestors have been adapted to the urban situation in remarkable ways. If the ancestors turn their backs on one, one is unable to save money or remain in employment, or one may be overtaken by accidents or arrested. Good fortune in gambling and betting at the races may be ascribed to the favour of the ancestors. Urban Christians also still ascribe some misfortunes to the action of witches and sorcerers, and have recourse to diviners and traditional Bantu medical techniques. The overall impression is that Bantu Christianity has somewhat more large-scale features in the towns than in tribal areas, but in social structure and culture urban Bantu Christians are essentially also intermediate between small-scale tribal society and the type of thoroughly large-scale society associated with Western urban élites.

Note

1 Much of the rest of this chapter is based on my own research among Tswana and Cape Nguni peoples (cf. Pauw 1960a; 1963b; 1965; forthcoming) in which I could proceed from the valuable work of predecessors among these peoples (cf. e.g. Hammond-Tooke 1962; Hunter 1936; Schapera 1953, 1958; Wilson *et al.* 1952). References to other sources of supplementary and comparative data are given in the text.

Chapter 15

The Impact of the City
Allie A. Dubb

Introduction

The present chapter deals with what may be regarded as one of the most dramatic aspects of change in Africa: the large-scale migration of tribesmen to white towns and the establishment of large permanent urban African populations. This movement has resulted in the development of new institutions, neither traditional nor wholly Western, and has necessitated rapid and often considerable changes in the individual migrant's outlook, social relations and way of life.

In this chapter, an overview of urban African life in the Republic of South Africa will be presented. It will be primarily descriptive, insofar as the reader will be made acquainted with the substantive findings of the most important available researches. At the same time, and in order to render these data more meaningful, there will also be some discussion of basic concepts. In this presentation, detail is, of necessity, frequently sacrificed in the interests of greater coverage, and the reader is referred to the bibliography for fuller discussions of both particular topics and particular towns.[1]

African Settlement in Town

Official censuses show that in 1911 there were 677,000 whites in the urban areas as against 524,000 Africans. By 1960, however, these numbers had increased to 2·6 million whites and 3·5 million Africans. Thus, while, as Table 15.1 shows, two-thirds of Africans still lived in rural areas in 1960 as compared with only 16 per cent of whites, there were, in actual numbers, 1·3 Africans in town to every white. Projecting these trends into the future, the Tomlinson Commission (1955: 34) estimated that the population of the four major urban industrial areas in the year 2000 would be 4·2 million whites and 13·2 million Africans. Table 15.2 shows the populations of selected urban areas.

One of the problems consequent upon this large and constantly increasing influx of Africans into the towns is that of accommodation. Attempts to solve it must be seen in terms of two factors: official policy and economics. Official policy has been and is, in the first place, that Africans in towns are migrants and not immigrants—i.e. they are temporary sojourners rather than permanent residents. In the second place, it is a fundamental principle that Africans should reside in segregated townships,[2] away from the white parts of town.

TABLE 15.1 *Population of urban areas in South Africa 1911–60: Whites and Africans—in thousands**

	1911	1921	1936	1946	1960
Whites	677	908	1,367	1,793	2,582
% of total S.A. White population	53·0	59·7	68·2	75·6	83·6
Africans	524	658	1,252	1,902	3,471
% of total S.A. African population	13·0	14·0	19·0	24·3	31·8

* From *Statistical Year Book 1964*, Bureau of Statistics, Pretoria, Tables A–12 (i) and A–14 (ii).

Note: Although the official census of the white population is probably accurate, this cannot be said for the enumeration of Africans. Many, particularly in town, extend their fear of official enquiries to census-taking, so that the information obtained is probably an underestimate (see Reader 1961a: 41–3; Sadie 1970).

TABLE 15.2 *Population of principal urban areas 1951 and 1960: Whites and Africans—in thousands**

| | 1951 | | | 1960 | | |
Town	Whites	Africans	All races	Whites	Africans	All races
Johannesburg	366	492	919	413	651	1,153
Cape Town (a)	267	60	632	305	75	807
Durban	153	162	498	196	222	681
Pretoria	151	122	285	207	200	423
Port Elizabeth	79	70	199	95	123	291
Bloemfontein	49	57	109	63	76	145
East London	44	40(b)	91	49	57	116

* From *Statistical Year Book 1964*, Bureau of Statistics, Pretoria, Table A–15.

Note: (a) The Coloureds are the largest population group in Cape Town with 417,881 in 1960 and 297,018 in 1951.
(b) Reader (1961a: 42) on the basis of a 1 in 10 survey estimated the total African population of East London at 78,000. See also Table 15.1, Note.

The second factor, the economic, is a consequence of the extremely low wages earned by Africans, particularly up to the end of the 1950s. This meant that either white employers or local authorities had to provide housing, or that the people themselves would have to erect whatever dwellings they could. These principles of policy, as well as the economic reality, were embodied in the Natives' (Urban Areas) Act of 1923, and subsequent amendments, which empowered local authorities to set aside land and to build houses for Africans. In fact very little was done to provide these people with adequate accommodation until after World War II. Thus at the end of 1951, the Tomlinson Commission (1955: 28) reported that there were approximately 314,000 families permanently settled in town—and a shortage of some 167,000 family dwellings, the cost of building which would be approximately R70 million. For more than half a century, then, Africans in town were variously accommodated in compounds provided by large employers such as the mining companies, municipalities, railways and others; in 'single' men's hostels—many of whose inmates were, in fact, married with wives and families in the country; in large scale housing schemes erected by local or central authorities; and, for the most part, in slums comprising crowded and ramshackle shanties put up by the people themselves. The appalling story of the authorities' attitude of *laissez-faire* in one city, East London, and of its consequences, is described by Reader (1961a: chapter 2). This is echoed in studies of other cities such as Cape Town (Wilson and Mafeje 1963: chapter 1 *passim*), and Johannesburg (Hellmann 1948).

Since the end of World War II, however, there has been considerable progress. While there is still a backlog, there are centres like Port Elizabeth and Johannesburg, for example, in which the shanty towns have all but ceased to exist and where the African population is housed in relatively decent brick or concrete houses. Nevertheless, while conditions are undoubtedly far better than they were, they still leave much to be desired: apart from the drabness and monotony of large economic and sub-economic housing schemes, few Africans enjoy the luxury of indoor water-taps and sanitation or of electricity; streets are, for the most part, unpaved, and become muddy and hazardous during the rainy season; street-lighting is frequently inadequate; sanitary facilities, where provided on a block basis, are usually overstrained and in filthy condition; and, because of the continued housing backlog, dwellings are still overcrowded—though by no means to the same extent as previously (see Plates 19, 20a and 20b). From another point of view, what is perhaps as serious as the harshness of the physical environment, is the fact that township dwellers have no choice of area or neighbours. If they want a decent roof over their heads, they are obliged to accept whatever is offered them from what becomes available. This makes it difficult for respectable 'middle-class' families to bring up their children in a decent atmosphere.[3]

Perhaps the most serious disability faced by Africans in town is the consequence of a progressive hardening of official policy regarding permanent residence. While, as has already been indicated, the Tomlinson Commission conceded that over one million Africans were permanently settled in urban areas by the end of 1951 (1955: 34), the National Party Government has made it clear through successive legislation that, *de jure*, no African has the right to remain in white towns. Whereas it was once possible for an African to own both land and a house in town, today he may, in some townships, build his own home—but on ground that will always belong to the municipality (see Plate 20b). The expropriation of African freeholdings in towns was, in fact, *one* of the motives behind the slum-clearance schemes. But not only is an African debarred from owning land, he is also subject to deportation[4] for any of a number of reasons, by order of a municipal or government official, with little or no right of appeal. Thus, while on the one hand there is a large and increasing *de facto* permanent African population in the towns, there is, on the other hand, a very real sense of insecurity constantly hanging over the location-dwellers. It is not surprising that, in this atmosphere of poverty, insecurity and impotence, crime should flourish and the safety of human life and property is precarious. In particular, the *tsotsi*, with his especially vicious brand of youthful delinquency, is a product of this environment.

Most local authorities, however, acknowledge the reality of their large African populations and have increasingly recognized the needs of these populations beyond the provision of housing. Most of the major cities, therefore, have provided a range of amenities, more or less adequate, such as playgrounds, clinics, sports fields, social centres, swimming pools, health and welfare services, libraries, and so on. In addition, plots are allocated to various religious denominations for the erection of churches and, in some cases, congregational centres, while central government provides facilities for primary and secondary schooling.[5]

Why Africans come to Town

Why, despite the unpleasant realities of town life, do Africans continue to flood into the urban areas? Throughout Africa the answer is the same: to earn money. Traditionally, African economies were subsistence economies— i.e. people produced as much as they needed to live on and little more. There was no occupational specialization apart from herbalists, diviners and, in some cases, iron-smiths, so that everyone was engaged in agriculture and/or animal husbandry. These traditional African economies depended to a large extent on the ability to move on as old pastures become exhausted and agricultural land worked out.

With the arrival of the whites, and the setting up of boundaries, territorial freedom was limited although production methods remained the same. Tribal lands thus became more and more impoverished, and it became progressively more difficult for people to subsist in the old way. Furthermore, the attitude among many African peoples that every man had a right to some land led to the fragmentation of plots to the extent that individual holdings often became too small to support a family. In South Africa, where land was generally held communally, and allocated by the headman to each married man, the availability of plots simply could not meet the demand, and there gradually emerged a category of temporarily or permanently landless men. Thus, writing of the Keiskammahoek region of the Eastern Cape Province, Houghton and Walton (1952: 176-7) state that 19 per cent (i.e. 5,000 out of 26,500) of people originating in the area had to leave home permanently, while 20 per cent of the remainder were migrant labourers. A very good harvest, they found, provided about half the nutritional requirements of the population, while in time of drought this was reduced to about one-twentieth. There is no question that this represents the general situation in the Republic of South Africa. It is therefore clear that whatever other reasons there may be for Africans going to town, the primary motivation is to supplement a failing subsistence economy in the rural areas.

Pressure on land was not, however, the only important consequence of white colonization. In the first place, administrations imposed taxes on the indigenous population partly because the revenue would enable them to meet the costs of administration and to carry out certain public works, and partly to compel Africans—who were, on the whole, hard-put to meet their tax obligations from sales of cattle or produce—to offer themselves for paid employment. In the second place, through the agency of missionaries, traders, administrators and settlers, familiarity with and a demand for European artefacts and foodstuffs emerged and grew. Rural Africans desired, and frequently, in a very real sense, needed such things as manufactured textiles, sewing machines, salt, bicycles, sugar, various articles of clothing, iron pots and knives, tobacco, milled cereals, soap, sweets, paraffin cookers, and so on. Taxation and newly-developed needs, then, are further incentives for going to town and earning money.

Personal motives, not necessarily directly economic, must also be mentioned. Among the Xhosa, for example, a period spent on the mines or working in town after initiation is known as 'changing of clothes' and is regarded as an essential part of the transition from boyhood to manhood. There are also those who go to town out of curiosity, a sense of adventure, or a desire to experience the excitement of city life. And, finally, there are those for whom town provides an escape from unwanted obligations or lowered status: a son who finds the authority of his father irksome; an unmarried mother, divorcee or widow whose dependent status is often resented by kinsmen and is unpleasant for herself; a younger son with no prospect of inheriting land; a man who has fallen foul of his chief or headman; or one who has been accused of witchcraft or sorcery.[6]

To sum up, Africans in the Republic migrate to the towns for one or several of the following reasons:

(i) Intermittent shortage of food in the tribal economy occasioned by drought or other adverse factors (the principal reason).
(ii) To purchase cattle for *lobola* (bride price) or other reason.
(iii) To earn money to pay tax.
(iv) Curiosity.
(v) To buy tools and implements of agriculture.
(vi) Over-population in the Native Reserves.
(vii) To attain social prestige (ILI 1957: 42).

The Urban Milieu

For approximately a century, then, Africans have been moving in increasing numbers from rural to urban areas. While much of this movement has been purely migratory, many Africans have settled permanently in town, set up families and produced an ever-increasing town-born population. During the course of this long period of settlement and in response to the specific occupational, economic, social, residential and other environmental characteristics of urban, as distinct from rural life, new urban institutions have come into being. These are not simply extensions or modifications of traditional tribal institutions: they are, as Mitchell says (1966: 47-8), new institutions, developed by urban dwellers to meet their needs in town and which, 'because of their different contexts differ from rural institutions meeting the same need in the tribal social system. An urban social institution is not a changed rural institution; it is a separate social phenomenon existing as part of a separate social system.' The behaviour of the migrant in town, therefore, differs from his behaviour in his rural home because of the different situation in which he finds himself. Thus while tribal customs and norms continue to survive in town, it is essential to view the urban milieu as a system in its own right.

What, then, in broad outline, are the major characteristics of urban life as compared with the rural tribal setting?

In the first place, the economic system of the town contrasts sharply with that of the rural areas. In town the African worker becomes involved in a system which demands regular, prolonged and consistent participation during the major part of his waking hours. Most frequently the nature of his work is such that its immediate and even long-term results may have little meaning or importance to him and he is motivated largely, if not solely, by the wages he will receive. In this situation, furthermore, he is frequently compelled to work and co-operate with people who, in terms of traditional criteria of association such as kinship, neighbourhood, tribe or political allegiance, could never have been part of his social universe. Also, in terms of the urban economic system, economic relations are largely impersonal and are based on monetary exchange —in contrast to the greater emphasis on reciprocity between neighbours and kinsmen in terms of tribal norms.

Residential arrangements in town may be determined by a variety of factors: one may live with kinsmen or people from the same rural area; one may be accommodated in a 'single men's hostel' (see Plate 20a) or mining compound where one's room-mates may even be of a different tribe, speaking a different language, and being more or less traditionalist than oneself; one may become a tenant of anyone who may have an available room; one may set up an independent home with one's family; one may live in a tribally homogeneous area or a multitribal one; in short, one may choose (or be forced to choose) from a wide range of possibilities.

The most important area of free choice in town, and perhaps one of the most significant differences from the relatively closed rural situation, is the field of formal and informal associations. In town, a man may choose his friends from kinsmen or *amakhaya* (Xhosa, people from the same rural area), from fellow employees, from neighbours or, in fact, from the whole range of people with whom, one way or another, he may come into contact. More formally, he may choose to spend his leisure time with his *iseti* (Xhosa, men of more or less the same age from the same rural area who habitually drink together); in church activities, both nuclear and peripheral; in participating in sports or social activities and clubs; and perhaps even in civic associations. He may also belong to a variety of burial societies, credit rings, and mutual aid, savings or benevolent associations. At one time, but no longer, he may even have belonged to some kind of trade union or political party.

To summarize, we may say that traditional tribal institutions were developed in a rural setting in which there was a simple technology and a simple division of labour. Relatively small closed groups co-operated on the bases of kinship and/or neighbourhood, while authority was based on age, seniority and political position. In town, however, migrants come as individuals and, in general, have to fend for themselves as individuals (see Plate 22b). Kinship, neighbourhood and, frequently, even common tribal affiliations have receded in importance as new systems of norms for defining and regulating relations have developed to meet the needs of urban life.

Urbanization: Some Important Concepts

What happens to Africans in town, or how town-based and town-born Africans differ from 'tribal' Africans, has been discussed at great length in the literature. An early conceptualization was that Africans became 'detribalized' in town: that is, they became less tribal as they became more urban or western. Even where the terms 'tribal', 'urban' and 'western' have been fairly clearly defined, however, it is abundantly clear that no such process as detribalization can be empirically demonstrated. Thus in 1948 Hellmann wrote as follows about the population of one Johannesburg township:

> That the process of detribalization and assimilation to western civilization are not one and the same is shown by a more careful analysis of a sample urban population such as the Natives of Rooiyard.
>
> The average European would unhesitatingly classify these Natives as detribalized. And in doing so he would advance as proof the various manifestations of the adoption of European material culture which he would perceive in Rooiyard. But what is detribalization? I have taken as my standard the following three criteria: permanent residence in an area other than that of the chief to whom a man would normally pay allegiance; complete severance of the relationship to the chief; and independence of rural relatives both for support during periods of unemployment and poor health or for the performance of ceremonies connected with the major crises of life. It seems to me that complete detribalization is never attained (if these criteria are not met) (1948: 110).

Hellmann further suggests (1948: 115-17) that, with reference to the replacement of 'Native' material and non-material culture, 'the rapidity and completeness of the process of detribalization has been exaggerated.' Nevertheless, one of the conclusions to which she comes, is: 'finally, I am compelled to seek refuge in a platitude and to sum up in saying that the longer the period of urban residence and the fewer the visits to the country, the more rapid and complete the process of detribalization' (1948: 112-13).

There is little doubt that during the thirty-five years since Hellmann's pioneering study,[7] it has become increasingly obvious that the concept of detribalization was founded on false assumptions, imprecise definitions and did not help in explaining the facts. In the first place—and this is implicit in the quotation from Hellmann—a distinction must be made on the one hand between social, political and economic bonds with the tribe, and, on the other hand, the preservation of tribal customs, language and other cultural characteristics in town. Second, there is abundant evidence (some of which we shall examine presently) that length of residence in town does not necessarily result in diminution of tribal identity or of adherence to at least some tribal customs. And, finally, it is possible for a highly Westernized person, for example a doctor or teacher, to work in a rural tribal area and, therefore, not to be urbanized. It is clear, then, that we would do well to discard the term 'detribalization', in favour of simpler and more precise concepts.

As a first step we shall examine two basic terms: stabilization and urbanization. The first of these, stabilization, is essentially demographic and, as Mitchell (1956a: 697) defines it, refers to the extent to which individuals cease to return to the point of origin of their migration; it is a statement of the change-over from the circulation of people between town and country to their permanent settlement in town. It is possible to express the degree of an individual's stabilization quantitatively as a ratio of the years spent in town to his total age.[8] What is important, however, is that stabilization makes no assumptions about any changes which the individual may undergo during the course of his living in town.

Urbanization, however, is a sociological concept and refers to changes in behaviour consequent upon coming to town. Just what these changes are, how and when they occur, and whether or not they are permanent has led to the development of a number of different approaches. Thus Gluckman's assertion (1960: 57) that 'an African miner is a miner' stems from the view that in town the African is involved in a social system independent of the rural tribal system, and that his behaviour is determined primarily by the roles he plays there. When he returns to his rural home, his behaviour is once more determined by the roles he plays within the tribal social system. As Mayer (1962: 579) puts it: 'Gluckman thus postulates . . . a switching back and forth between two distinct social fields or systems.'

Another type of alternation, termed by Gluckman 'situational selection', recognizes more explicitly the continued influence of the tribal culture and social system in town, and postulates involvement in different sets of relations which in themselves call forth different patterns of behaviour. The model brings out that a man even while actually in town can still . . . switch back and forth between urban and tribal behaviour according to the immediate situation (Mayer 1962: 579).

Thus Epstein (1958: chapter 4, 229-40), for example, shows how Africans on the Zambian Copperbelt rejected a tribal system of representation for dealing with white management on the mines in favour of a trade union, while, on the other hand, the struggle for power *within* the trade union was cast in tribal terms. Another example of situational selection is Mitchell's (1960: 15) description of William, a relatively educated and sophisticated African, and also a practising *ng'anga* ('witchdoctor'), who had lived outside his tribal area for twenty-five years. William conceded 'that in some circumstances the White man's medicine is definitely best', as for instance, when his wife was confined. Yet on the other hand, he argued, there were situations in which *his* medicine was superior. Thus the trader who wished to attract customers, the scholar who desired an easy examination paper, the ambitious clerk, the flirt—all would come to William for some charm to ensure their success. Both Epstein and Mitchell, then, show how Africans in town select those modes of behaviour which seem most advantageous or fitting in terms of a particular situation and relationship.

Mayer (1962: 580) chooses to define urbanization strictly in terms of relationships: a person is fully urbanized when his extra-town ties—i.e. with people in the rural tribal areas—are of minimal importance or have completely disappeared, in comparison with his social relationships in the town itself. Put in another way, the migrant becomes a townsman when he is no longer subject to the pull of the country home but is fully committed to the town and its people. But while Mayer is primarily concerned with the structural aspect of urbanization—i.e. patterns of social relations—he does not ignore the cultural dimension. This is, to some extent, dictated by the nature of his material since the Red Xhosa[9] themselves distinguish between the structural and cultural aspects of urbanization. They speak of two types of response to the city: *ukutshipa* (to abscond) and *ukurumsha* (to adopt town ways). The *itshipa* is a person who severs his ties with the people at home as well as with his *amakhaya* (people of the same rural area) in town. The *irumsha* is one who adopts town ways at the expense of Red traditions though he may not, at once, sever his home ties. Both manifestations are abhorred—in particular the *itshipa*—and although they are seen as separate and logically independent, it is generally believed that one state will lead to the other. Mayer therefore concludes that in practice it was necessary to examine both aspects of urbanization and extends his definition accordingly. It is possible, he writes (1961: 6)

> to assess a person's urbanization in terms of his 'way of life' his institutionalized activities, and especially his values and attitudes. The truly urbanized person, in this [cultural] definition, would be one who is fully

confirmed in 'urban' modes of behaviour—private life included—and (above all) in valuing these positively.

We have now selected and discussed several concepts which are useful in understanding the African in town, and which will provide a framework for the ensuing discussion.

Urbanization: the structural aspect

To repeat Mayer's (1962: 580) definition of urbanization: a person is fully urbanized as his extra-town ties disappear and his within-town ties become paramount. From another point of view, the individual has become, or is, urban-centred rather than rural-centred. It is this which differentiates the migrant from the townsman. The balance between within-town ties and extra-town ties, as well as their quality, can be measured by means of the network concept developed by Barnes (1954) and Bott (1957).[10] Both Mayer (1961) and Pauw (1963a) employed this concept in their analyses of migrants and townsmen in East London. Epstein, applying it in his study of the Zambian Copperbelt, defines the concept most clearly (1961: 31, 56):

> each individual African is involved in a network of social ties which ramify throughout the urban community and extend to other towns and to the tribal areas. . . . A network, in this sense, is always egocentric: it exists only and is defined with reference to a particular individual. As Barnes remarks, each person sees himself as the centre of a collection of friends. It follows therefore that the network is always 'personal', for the set of links that make it up are unique for each individual. . . . Since it is essentially 'personal' the network allows of many different configurations. . . . A close-knit network is defined as one in which there are many relationships between its component units: in a family which has a close-knit network many of its friends, neighbours and kinsfolk will know one another. . . . By contrast, a loose-knit network exists where friends, neighbours and kin are not known to each other and the degree of connectedness is therefore slight.

In any given network not every link is characterized by the same degree of intensity so that some parts of it will be more close-knit than others. Epstein distinguishes between the *effective* network which 'consists of clusters of persons fairly closely knitted together' and the *extended* network which is less connected and within which relationships are less intense.

Using this concept Mayer (1961: *passim*) distinguishes between the close-knittedness of rural networks as compared with urban ones. Furthermore, he suggests that rural networks also tend to be closed—that is, recruitment is limited to a small number of criteria such as kinship and neighbourhood—whereas in town a large number of criteria such as employment and occupation, church-membership, common sports and other interests come into play. The migrant, according to Mayer, retains his rural network in town, 'stretching' it to include town-based kinsmen and other *amakhaya*, but maintaining its closed character in relation to other categories of people. To the extent that this pattern is maintained the migrant remains country-rooted and, in terms of Mayer's criteria, non-urbanized. To the extent, however, that outsiders are recruited into the network, while rural relationships gradually assume less and less importance, to that extent the migrant is becoming a townsman. The born townsman, as Pauw (1963a: 187ff.) shows, exhibits a characteristically open network which includes almost entirely other town-born, or at least, town-centered people. The following cases will illustrate various types of networks among Africans in town.[11]

Kleinbooi M. is a Pedi from the Northern Transvaal. He has been in Johannesburg for twenty years and works as a gardener and odd-jobber in three European homes. He lives in a room in an outbuilding of one of these. His wife and children live in his home area and have visited him twice in the past four years. Neither he nor his wife are Christians, while the latter speaks neither English nor Afrikaans, and wears traditional dress even when visiting her husband in town. For his part, Kleinbooi goes home at least once a year for several weeks, usually around ploughing time, or on other occasions as well if there is any urgent matter to attend to such as a death or rebuilding a hut.

Kleinbooi rises daily at about 5.30 a.m. and generally begins work about an hour later. During most of the day he has, in some of the homes, the African maid for company though whilst working outdoors he carries on a shouted conversation with the gardener next door. Friends and acquaintances also drop by to chat to him over the fence—unless the mistress of the house happens to be close at hand. He stops work at five in the afternoon and, when he has money, usually goes to a bottle-store for Bantu beer.[12] From there he either returns to his room or goes to visit his brothers—both of whom work and live at a nearby European primary school. They prepare the evening meal together over a paraffin cooker, drink beer and talk. Some evenings Kleinbooi, with or without his brothers, goes to visit home-boys working in the same area. He also visits, from time to time an accommodating house-maid—not a Pedi, but also Sotho-speaking—living in the yard of one of the houses at which he works. He is usually home and in bed by 9 p.m. or, at times, by 10 p.m. He seldom has occasion to visit the townships as he has neither close friends nor relatives there, and most of his leisure time is spent in the back-yards of white residences.

Thomas N. was born in Langa location Cape Town. His parents and older siblings had come to Cape Town some thirty years ago, when his father decided to leave the employ of a white farmer in the Ciskei and to make his home in town. Although Thomas's parents were pagans and uneducated they realized that it was essential for their children to receive some education and they were sent to a mission school which operated in the location. Thomas completed standard V there, but at the age of fourteen left school, albeit much against his parents' wishes. He also attended church services and instruction classes, since this was a requirement of the mission, although he has never become a full communicant.

As a child Thomas's friends were, for the most part, town-born youngsters or, at least, youngsters who had come to town at an early age. Like most of his friends, Thomas was left to his own devices after school as both parents worked in town in order to support the family. He and his friends amused themselves playing ball and other games in the street, or simply hanging around the township smoking cigarette ends, stealing trifles or begging from passers-by.

After leaving school Thomas worked on and off as a newspaper boy, but was unable to find steady employment as he was not willing to do manual work. Finally, at the age of twenty, he got a job as a delivery boy in a store in Cape Town. At twenty-six Thomas has changed jobs three times, the last of which he took up only eight months ago. All have been of the same type.

In his leisure time Thomas goes about with other town-boys several of whom are old school-friends. All these boys have girl-friends, also town-born. Thomas's girl-friend has already had one child by him and it is likely that they will marry when Thomas can afford to pay *lobolo* (bride-wealth). The boys and their girl-friends frequently participate in such activities as dances and jazz sessions and are avid cinema-goers. On the weekends Thomas and his friends watch soccer in the township, although, if there is a big game in town, they may go there. Thomas regards himself as a Capetonian and has no desire to even visit the Ciskei whence his parents came and where he still has some relatives. Since childhood he has had no direct connection with these people and has, in any case, always regarded people from the country as gauche and backward.

Joseph X. is a thirty-five-year-old Xhosa-speaking teacher in a secondary school in Port Elizabeth. His parents were Anglicans and he attended a mission school in the Transkei. He later attended the University of Fort Hare gaining a B.A. and teaching diploma. His present post, which was also his first, he has now held for ten years. He lives in a self-built house and his wife is a nurse at the Livingstone Hospital. Their two children attend a local primary school.

Joseph spends most of his working day at school, and his most frequent contacts are with his fellow-teachers. His closest friend is John I., a Sotho journalist with whom he studied at Fort Hare, and whom he sees several times a week. Among other things, the two share an interest in rugby and are committee members of the same club. Joseph spends a good deal of his leisure time in this and other organizational activities. He attends church regularly and is on the church roster for visiting sick members. He is also an office-bearer in the local branch of the African teachers' association. Joseph is regarded as one of the important men in the location and he is frequently consulted by members of the Urban Bantu Council and by others. He is invited to all the important functions in the township: the opening of a new school, a reception in honour of a visiting dignitary, a church convention and, of course, the smart social events and dances.

Joseph's professional and other interests, then, mean that his most frequent social relations are with those who may be regarded as the African élite of Port Elizabeth—other professionals and educated business men. From time to time, however, Joseph also visits relatives and old friends from his home area. He enjoys these occasions, talking about home affairs, crops and cattle, sitting on the floor, propped up against the wall drinking beer with these less educated kinsmen and home boys. They, too, are perfectly at ease with Joseph although they regard his visits as a singular honour. About once every two years, Joseph spends a week or two with his parents in the country, and although he is much involved with the affairs of the township, he often speaks about returning to the Transkei when he reaches retirement age.

These three accounts illustrate some different kinds of network which occur among town Africans. In the case of Kleinbooi, it was found that in town he interacted mainly with his closest kinsfolk and with other people from the same rural area. Kleinbooi, we might say, has not *extended* his network but has simply *stretched* an existing rural network into the town. Kleinbooi then remains essentially bound to his rural home and works in town as a necessary expedient. He is, in terms of Mayer's definition, certainly no townsman, and, to use Mayer's terminology once again, is incapsulated within a circle of rurally-oriented *amakhaya* (home people) (1961: chapter 5). By contrast, Thomas is a townsman: he was born and bred in town and regards the town alone as his home. His friends are likewise townsmen and regard country people, with some amusement, as bumpkins. The most interesting of the three cases, however, is that of Joseph. Joseph is a highly educated and sophisticated man and yet retains some links with the country which he still visits and to which he says he will retire. Furthermore, Joseph maintains contact with less educated kinsmen and home-boys in town. Joseph, then, resembles Kleinbooi in some respects and Thomas in others. His case has been quoted in order to illustrate the fact that, in terms of Mayer's criteria, being a townsman does not necessarily imply being highly-educated, sophisticated or 'Westernized'. Thomas is more fully urbanized than Joseph, but Joseph is unquestionably more Westernized. Thus ranking the three men on a continuum of urbanization we would place Kleinbooi at the one extreme, Thomas at the other and Joseph somewhere in between.

Urbanization: the cultural dimension

Changing now from a structural to a cultural frame of reference, it has already been suggested in the previous discussions that urbanization is not synonymous with Westernization. One who is born in town or who has made the town his home is, presumably, urbanized inasmuch as his behaviour patterns have been moulded in an urban milieu. But we cannot assume that these patterns are necessarily 'Western'! The concept of situational selection might help to clarify this point. In the pursuit of health, which is always an important concern, there are various alternative courses of action to deal with illness. These include: consultation with a diviner to establish whether the misfortune is due to the ancestors, evil spirits, witchcraft or sorcery; consultation with a herbalist from whom appropriate magico-medical remedies may be obtained; visiting a doctor, clinic or hospital; consulting a pharmacist; or having a special prayer said at church. All these alternatives, or combinations thereof, are available in a case of ill-health—but it is not always possible to predict which will be selected. A teacher in a rural area might go directly to the local white doctor without visiting either a diviner or a herbalist. Yet, on the other hand, a town-born man such as Thomas, may go to a white chemist for some medication and at the same time consult a diviner about the possible supernatural causes of his illness. Even education does not necessarily enable us to predict what choice will be made as there is a good deal of evidence that diviners' clienteles comprise not only traditionalists, but also middle-class Africans, professionals and, even, Whites. Nor does it seem possible to postulate that the longer a person has been in town the more likely he will be to choose the 'Western' alternative.[13] We cannot say that if a man would have consulted *only* a diviner when he first came to town, he might consult *both* a diviner *and* a white doctor after having been in town for some years, and that perhaps after many many years in town would *only* consult a white doctor. Generalizing beyond our example, then, the alternatives from which an individual may select in any given situation, will be determined by his education, experience and beliefs. What he actually does select will, presumably, reflect his assessment of the situation and of the best possible way to cope with it. The alternatives, however, need not necessarily be seen in terms of the categories traditional and Western but may also be distinguished in terms of rural and urban. Thus a rural alternative may be Western while an urban one may be a modification of a traditional form. We cannot say, therefore, that a person is more urbanized because he selects Western modes of behaviour more frequently than traditional ones.

What we have said underlines the fact that it is impossible to speak of *an* urban African culture even where as in East London and Durban, for example, there is a high degree of tribal homogeneity. As Pauw (1963a: 28) says:

> hardly any clear patterns seem to have crystallized yet, and the variations in patterns of behaviour, values and beliefs, and the different combinations of these in different regions of the culture, seem to defy systematization. At this stage it is impossible to give a complete picture of the culture of the urban Bantu.

THE IMPACT OF THE CITY

The following case-histories from Johannesburg illustrate some of the variations in dress, style of life, adherence to tribal custom, interests and values.

Mr. N. is a Tsonga from Sibasa. He has worked in Johannesburg since 1946. He met us at the door of his typical 4-roomed Council house in Chiawelo.[14] At the time of calling, 5.30 p.m., he was dressed in trousers and shirt sleeves, the picture of any Western husband at the end of a hard day's work. However, on entering the house, we were transported to the interior of a hut in a rural area. The smoke-filled living room revealed 2 rough wooden benches and one or two grass mats. Mrs. N. emerged from the kitchen where she had been cooking the evening meal over an open brazier, barefooted and wearing her tribal dress. During the interview that followed Mr. N. sat on one of the benches and Mrs. N. squatted on the floor. Our discussion revealed that Mr. N. is a confirmed practising traditionalist and after 20 years of town life, has made only the most superficial concessions and whenever possible these do not extend to his home life. Thus his 'domestic relations are governed by tribal norms, though industrial relations are not'.[15] He is still a pagan and is polygamously married by *lobolo* only. He maintains the strongest ties with the rural area where wife No. 2, who is the sister of wife No. 1, lives. His leisure time is spent discussing tribal affairs with fellow tribesmen.

Mr. N. sees no necessity to adapt his traditional social and cultural patterns to that of White society and, therefore, the urban environment. Correct observance of tribal customs makes life easier even in the townships—'it is the right thing to do to live the right way'. Any change is, therefore, only skin deep. He regards his 20 years in Johannesburg as a sojourn. When he can no longer work, he will return 'home'—his enforced exile will be at an end.

Mrs. P. is the complete antithesis of Mr. N., the traditionalist. She asserts that she and her family do not practise any tribal customs and that in fact 'tribal customs are of no purpose or value in the urban area . . . the whole procedure of tribal custom is always complicated and there is no place for their observance in the urban area'.

Entering the house of Mrs. P. in Tladi, the visitor sees an amply furnished home no different from that of the average lower class European. The living room was filled with a lounge and a dining room suite; the kitchen boasted a coal stove, a dresser and a table. Mrs. P. is Tswana speaking, and was born in Johannesburg 28 years ago. She has a standard VI education and together with her family is an active member of the Roman Catholic Church. She belongs to a ballroom dancing club and her husband is a member of a judo, weight-lifting and physical training club. She is opposed to children of urban parents living in a rural area because they would make 'no progress in education. What educational benefit do you get from herding cattle and hoeing lands?'. In short Mrs. P. feels that the observance of tribal customs is 'a waste of good precious time'.

Mrs. M. of Dube combines both traditional Bantu customs and Western customs in her way of life. She is, however, not simply gradually exchanging her traditional institutions for Western ways and customs. She regards both the old customs and the new as being of equal importance, and neither conflicts in any way with the other. She takes an equally active part, for example, in both her church activities and Ancestor Worship. She has, however, adapted traditional customs, firstly by selecting certain of them and secondly by modifying these to suit the urban situation.

Mrs. M. is Zulu speaking and was born in the Bergville area of Natal where she was educated up to standard VI level. She has lived in Johannesburg since 1949 and is now 36 years of age. She is married by *lobolo*, civil and Christian rites. She and all her family attend the Methodist church and are active members. Her husband is a member of a football club and one of her sons is a boy scout. When we visited Mrs. M.'s house she was busy sewing by machine in her kitchen, which, like the living room, was furnished in contemporary style. Over a cup of tea Mrs. M. talked freely and showed herself to be most progressive in outlook. Her very definite views on the importance of maintaining certain tribal customs—'it is a very good thing'—struck us most forcibly, since at the same time Mrs. M. revealed herself as being completely urban-centred. In her own words 'I would like to live in Dube when I'm old—I prefer living in the urban area because I like urban life—rural life is opposed to my way of life' (NEAD 1965: 1–3).

Aspects of Town Life

In the remainder of this chapter we shall examine some institutions and groups characterizing urban African life in South Africa (see Plates 21a, 21b, 22a and 22b). These include marriage and the family, kinship, social stratification and voluntary associations.

Marriage and the family in town

Among all the south-eastern Bantu-speaking people, the domestic unit was, traditionally, the patrilineally extended family rather than the nuclear family.[16] Ideally, this unit comprised a man, his wife or wives,[17] his unmarried children, his married sons and their families, and various other dependent relatives. But while this arrangement still exists, it is no longer universal even in the rural areas. In the first place, Christian missionaries tended to emphasize the nuclear family unit, while the very act of conversion led to a degree of withdrawal from the extended families to which converts belonged. In the second place, the migration of male work-seekers to European farms and towns led either to temporarily husbandless and fatherless homes in the reserves, or to the removal of wives and children to the migrants' places of employment. In the towns the traditional type of extended family is virtually non-existent.

First, it is either an individual or a couple—with or without children—who migrate to town, rather than a complete extended family. In the second place, urban housing conditions would, in any case, make it extremely difficult for such a large group to establish common residence.

Pauw (1963a: chapter 8) in his study of East London distinguished four types of household.[18] The first, and most common, comprises the nuclear family plus, possibly, one or two other relatives or dependants. The second type is the multi-generational male-headed household in which the nuclear family is augmented by the children of an unmarried daughter or daughters. Third, the mother-child household comprises an unattached woman (widowed, divorced, separated or an unmarried mother), and her unmarried children. In course of time, this may develop into the fourth type, the multi-generational female-headed household, in which the mother-child unit is extended to include the offspring of unmarried daughters and even granddaughters. This type of family—which is made up of a chain of mothers and daughters without any permanently attached male, and which is becoming increasingly widespread—is especially interesting since, contrary to the traditional principle of patrilineality, the links between members of this group are entirely through females. Similarly, it is the materfamilias rather than a male, who wields authority in the household.[19]

While many female-headed households have a succession of male consorts, a relationship which is frequently encountered is known as *ukushweshwa* (Xhosa, concubinage).[20] A man who has, or expects to have, a wife and children in the country will, if he is able, often also set up a fairly permanent relationship with a woman in town. They establish a common home to which the man contributes financially, and often they have children together. This is not, however, marriage, and neither has any legal rights in the other. As might be expected, some women will try to wean their lovers away from their legal wives, while on the other hand the *shweshwe* might resist the man's desire to marry her, preferring to retain her independence. Under such an arrangement, the man may form a strong attachment to the *shweshwe*'s children and will assist in their support, but he has no jural rights in them nor they in him. His primary obligations are to his own heirs and successors, the children of his legal wife in the country. The *shweshwe*'s children, as any children of an unmarried woman, will be members of their maternal grandfather's lineage though, for practical purposes, this is often of little importance.

Another important aspect of the family relates to economics. In tribal society the family was the unit of production and consumption and was essentially self-sufficient. Today, probably, the larger proportion of households in rural areas rely on remittances by migrant labourers. Nevertheless even though they are no longer self-supporting, they must still produce a good deal of their own food as well as satisfy other needs by their own efforts. As the unit of production, the rural family is knit together by the mutual interdependence of its members, amongst whom those economic activities necessary for survival are divided. Most of the major roles—various types of work in the fields, house-building, tending the stock, milking, domestic chores—are age- and sex-specific. In town the family, or more precisely the domestic group, is still an important unit of consumption, but no longer of production. Here members of the household are involved in the economic life of the city as a whole, and their contribution to the household is in the form of cash rather than services. While the wife, mother or oldest daughter may, if she herself is not forced to take a job, devote her full time to servicing the other members, any individual who earns money can perform most of these services himself and purchase others. The relative unimportance of a formal division of labour within the urban family makes its members less dependent on one another than in the rural setting.

This change in the economic role of the family and in economic relations between its members—together with such factors as the loosening of kinship ties and the decline of the patrilineally extended household—has had important consequences for husband-wife and parent-child relationships. Thus Hellmann (1967a: 6ff.) writes that in the towns

> the family is on its own, no longer embedded in the web of kinship which was the basis of the traditional system. . . . Parents are called on to accept responsibilities and functions—educational, economic and emotional—that were formerly carried out by a group of kin. In a number of families, new patterns of behaviour between husband and wife and between parents and children have developed which meet the demands of these new conditions. In such households, there is close co-operation between husband and wife, consultation about money matters, the children's education and other concerns. . . . It seems to me that this pattern is regarded as the ideal to be aimed at by professional and middle class women, although by no means all men of the same status share this aspiration and its attainment is very infrequent. . . . It is far more common to find families under strain because of the unresolved conflict between the husband's patriarchal conduct and the wife's new role as wage-earner, manager of the household budget and educator of the children. Men, including educated men, seem to resist the emancipation of women which modern conditions promote.[21]

In similar vein, a journalist, Jenny Ndale, writes in the African paper *Post* of 2 May 1965:

> Men are still bogged down in the tribal notion that taking little Enoch out for a walk is none of their business. . . . The idea of sharing everything that marriage and children mean . . . our African husbands just don't [accept]. . . . Maybe if our husbands would move up a notch into this modern age and could be persuaded to take more interest in their children, less of these would leave home for delinquency. Maybe if they paid their wives a little more attention, there'd be fewer lovers let in through the back door when they're away.

THE IMPACT OF THE CITY

Another respect in which the urban family differs from the rural one also arises out of economic factors. Whereas in the rural areas economic activity is centred around the home and family fields, in town it takes place entirely outside of the household. In the country, then, there is always some responsible adult at hand to watch over the children whereas in the town, with its smaller nuclear family and one or both parents working, there is often no one to supervise them. With insufficient creche and nursery school facilities, as well as a critical shortage of space in primary and secondary schools, township children roam the streets and get into all kinds of mischief. As Hellmann (1967a: 11–12) points out, many children 'fail to find in their homes the emotional security they need or in their parents the models with whom they will want to identify themselves. . . . Parental control has weakened and youthful indiscipline has grown.' The *tsotsis*—town youths characterized by their total disrespect for authority and cynical disregard for the lives and property of others—are the bitter fruit of family breakdown in an unfavourable physical, social, economic and political environment.[22]

A final topic related to marriage and the family which we shall discuss is sexual gratification and love. Africans, generally, take a pragmatic view of sex: it is a natural urge which everyone is entitled to satisfy within socially defined limits. The limit placed on pre-marital sex by the south-eastern Bantu is, simply, that an unmarried girl should not fall pregnant. Thus among the Zulu and Xhosa, for example, an unmarried girl may indulge in sex play leading to external intercourse (*ukumetsha* in Xhosa, and *ukusoma* in Zulu), but must not permit actual penetration. To ensure observance of this rule, older women, usually grandmothers or aunts though never her mother, subject her to periodic inspection of her virginity. Although it is doubtful whether this examination has any objective validity, it appears to have the desired psychological effect.[23]

In the towns, girls who are not prepared to allow full intercourse are ridiculed, while parents do not, and did not traditionally, directly concern themselves with their children's sex instruction and supervision. Thus a girl, a mother at the age of fifteen, told Pauw (1963a: 112): 'My mother used to tell me that babies are bought in the market when you are grown-up. But what puzzled me is that I never saw babies on beds in the market.' Pauw points out that sexual activity in town begins around the age of eleven or twelve and that by the time a girl reaches fifteen it is almost certain that she has had intercourse. In his sample of seventy-four unmarried town-born women aged fifteen years and over, six out of ten were mothers, while of those between twenty to thirty-five years old, three-quarters had had children (Pauw 1963a: 118). Attitudes to pre-marital pregnancy are ambivalent: while Pauw records that some girls have even contemplated suicide (1963a: 119), Wilson and Mafeje (1963: 43) quote the resignation of a father in Langa:

> Look at M., my own child. This is the second child she is expecting. What shall I do with her? Shall I kill her or drive her out of the house? Of what

use would that be? The best thing is to let my daughter enjoy life so long as she cares for her children properly. When God wills these bad conditions in society will all be over.

But there is another aspect of pre-marital pregnancy. A young man asked by Pauw (1963a: 118) whether he was going to marry his girl-friend replied that he would like to but that he suspected she was barren. They had been sweethearts for some years and had been having sexual relations all that time but 'without any results'. While the custom of paying *lobolo* (bride-wealth) is still widespread, even among urbanized and Westernized people, it no longer safeguards the husband's rights to a fertile wife. In the first place, since *lobolo* is paid in money rather than cattle, it is virtually irrecoverable. Second, if the couple are married by Christian or civil rights, barrenness does not constitute a ground for divorce, while plural marriage is out of the question. A young man will, therefore, often wait until the girl has had a child before marrying her and handing over the marriage payment.

One final comment should be made: traditionally, marriage was arranged between the two sets of parents. While a young person was generally not forced to marry someone whom he or she did not like, the most important criteria of suitability were family status, wealth, probable fertility and the woman's robustness and ability to work, rather than romantic love. In the towns, however—although this was already the practice among rural Christians—choice of spouses has become a personal matter for the two young people involved, and notions of romantic love are already very common. Nevertheless, as we have seen, prospective bridegrooms are still concerned with such practicalities as child-bearing capacity, faithfulness and family background.

Kinship

Anthropologists have shown that, traditionally, kinship played a key role in organizing relationships—social, economic, political and jural—among the south-eastern Bantu-speaking peoples. Inheritance and succession, residence, marriage rules, mutual aid and hospitality, ancestor cult ritual and even proper conduct were, to a great extent, defined in terms of kinship. For most purposes it was the patrilineage—a group of kinsmen, related in the male line, who could trace descent from a common ancestor—which was of prime importance, although a person had rights and obligations within the wider group of cognates and affines as well.

Today, among conservative traditionalists, the *ideology* of kinship solidarity and amity remains although, in the day-to-day business of living, other categories may assume greater importance. Thus in the Transkei, for example, a man has no right to land in any particular area simply because his father or other agnatic (patrilineal) kinsfolk live there, nor is his only claim based on inheritance. It is as the subject of a particular headman—and whether or not they are kin is irrelevant—that he will apply for an allotment when he marries. Furthermore, since lineages are usually widely dispersed and local settlements include families belonging to several lineages and clans, non-agnates and unrelated neighbours assist each other more frequently and intensely than faraway kinsmen.[24] The corporateness of the patrilineage and, to a lesser degree, the clan is manifested on ritual occasions; in the expectation that members of the lineage will be informed of and invited to participate in each others' births, marriages, funerals and similar important events; and in defining preferred and prohibited marriages.

When the migrant comes to town he will, not unnaturally, seek out kinsmen or people from the same rural area both for companionship and because he can expect help from them in securing accommodation and employment.[25] As we have already pointed out, the Red (or traditionalist) migrant tends to confine his social relationships to these *amakhaya* (home-boys) and kinsmen unless he decides deliberately to sever his rural ties and/or adopt town ways. Within the *amakhaya* group, where conversation centres on the country, its people and their affairs, traditional values are retained and reinforced. At the same time the migrant maintains direct links with the rural home through his rurally-based wife, children and other relatives, to whom he remits part of his earnings, and through his participation in ancestor cult rituals. Thus for the Red migrant, kinship plays much the same role in town as it does in the country.

The country-rooted Christian (or School) migrant also maintains strong bonds with kinsmen and *amakhaya* as well as with his rural home. However, his network is, *ab initio*, potentially wider than that of the pagan since it also includes fellow-Christians who may be neither kinsmen nor neighbours. It is clear, then, that kinship and neighbourhood may diminish in importance if Christianity becomes the primary criterion of network recruitment.

Turning now from the migrant to the townsman proper, Hellmann (1948), Pauw (1963a: chapter 9) and Wilson and Mafeje (1963: chapter 4) are agreed that kinship continues to play an important role. However, as Wilson and Mafeje point out: 'kinsmen are bound by personal ties, but they do not now form defined corporate groups other than the elementary family' (1963: 75). Pauw (1963a: chapter 9) found that, in East London, most townsmen had locally-based kin, many being close neighbours. Kinsmen towards whom obligations were recognized and from whom help and support could be expected, were, however, selected much more on the basis of personal preference than of agnation (patrilineality) or genealogical closeness. Furthermore —as a consequence of the widespread development of the matrifocal household—maternal kin had assumed far greater importance than in the traditional system. These kin included the mother's patrilineage, other cognates related mainly through women and even the wife's parents and family. Finally, both Pauw and Wilson and Mafeje found that while clan exogamy was generally observed in town, its validity was being questioned by some. All these changes in kinship patterns were reflected in corresponding changes in terminology in which traditionally-recognized categories were now being ignored while new ones had been created (Wilson and Mafeje 1963: 86ff).

Despite these changes it is clear that townsmen include a number of kin in their social networks. In fact as they become settled and marry in town, they become involved in a gradually widening web of kinship. Given that their kinship group is not necessarily corporate or patrilineal, townsmen have, therefore, more immediate access to kinsmen than do the rurally-centered migrants (Pauw 1963a: chapter 9). Kinship, then, is an important basis of social relationships for both pagan and Christian, migrant and townsman. For the townsman, however, kinship is not a *primary* basis of association as it tends to be for the migrant.

Stratification in town[26]

The pagan-Christian cleavage—or what the Xhosa refer to as Red-School—represents one of the earliest effects of European influence on African life in the Republic. Developing in the rural areas with the establishment of missions and schools, it involves every aspect of culture: values and attitudes, observance of custom, religion, Western education and way of life, dress, sex and marriage, interests and activities, etiquette and manners. Structurally, despite cross-cutting ties of kinship, the two categories generally live in separate neighbourhoods, keep their children apart, and spend most of their working and leisure hours with people of their own kind. That this cleavage continues to exist in town is evident from the data on Cape Town and East London and may be confirmed by casual observation in other townships. Certainly in East London, Durban and Johannesburg, traditionalists in tribal dress are not an uncommon sight.

The division which is most basic in town, however, is that between migrants and townsmen. As we have seen, it cuts across the pagan-Christian cleavage, and in Cape Town, according to Wilson and Mafeje (1963: 18), to a large extent overrides it. Neither of these cleavages is static: there is, all the time, movement from pagan to Christian and from country-rootedness to town-rootedness. This means that in town there is always an intermediate group of would-be townsmen and these are, frequently though not invariably, either Christians or becoming Christians.[27] Wilson and Mafeje (1963: 15ff) describe the various categories of town-dwellers in Cape Town in terms of the migrant-townsman dimension.

In the first place, the migrant is

> readily identified by his dress, his gait and manners, and his speech. Typically, he wears shabby trousers and a dilapidated hat, carries a billy-can, and smokes a long pipe filled with *twak*—a rank tobacco popular in the country. He walks with the grace and dignity of those who have spent their childhood on the veld, barefoot, but stares around him in town and is nervous crossing a street. He speaks the traditional Xhosa with relatively

little modification, and in addressing people there is a certain formality and courtesy in his speech and manner. As for food, the migrants live mainly on mealies and bread, with beans or curdled milk, and small quantities of meat, tea, and sugar when they can afford it (1963: 16-17).

The semi-urbanized people, the *iibari* (probably from the English 'barbarians'), seek absorption into the town. Many of them have little education although some are more educated than a good proportion of townsmen. There are two types of semi-urbanized people: the stereotypical *iibari*, who imitate the slick and flashy *ooMac* (see below), and those (often School people) who wish to be regarded as respectable people. Finally there are the townsmen proper—the 'townees' and the 'decent people'.

> The *townees* or *tsotsis* are also called '*location boys*', or *ooclever, bright boys*, and *spoilers*. . . . This type of urbanized young man is distinguished by his dress: wide-bottomed trousers without any turn-up, called *ivups* [from the sound they make], which might be translated 'flappers'; 'skipper' shirts, sports coat, no collar or tie, and pointed shoes. He uses a mixture of Afrikaans and Xhosa slang—indeed the language of the *tsotsis* in Johannesburg, *mensetaal*, is said to be identical with that of white 'ducktails'. . . . The age-set from 15 to about 25 of the *tsotsi* type are called *ikhaba*, from *ikhaba* a half grown mealie stalk (1963: 22-3).

The *tsotsis* are violent and boisterous, smoke dagga, fight with knives and are anathema to the decent people. They look for jobs which are neither too dirty nor involve too much hard work but which provide opportunities for pilfering. As they get older, from about 25 to 35, the *ikhaba* are called *ooMac* and are expected to be more reasonable and responsible than when they were boys, while their wives must behave as befits married women.

> The second section of townsmen are the respectable people—the 'decent people' as they are called—who are very critical of the behaviour of *tsotsi* boys and girls. Many of them are educated and essentially middle class, and some, indeed, suggest that all the 'decent people' are educated, but this is not strictly true. The educated people are referred to by others, somewhat derogatorily as *ooscuse-me*, and accused of being aloof and conceited. They pride themselves on being respectably dressed, and gentle and polite in their manner (1963: 26).

With regard to relative status, there is no unanimously agreed system of ranking. Thus in East London, Mayer (1961: 76ff.) points out that School people and townsmen have a system of ranking which includes all Africans in the township and which is based primarily on education and adaptation to the town. Reds, who are on the lowest rung of this hierarchy, accept its validity in relation to School people but deny that it applies to themselves whom they see 'as standing outside this essentially non-Red system.' (1961: 77). In Cape Town, Wilson and Mafeje found similar discrepancies between systems of ranking:

Townsmen look down on the migrants and partly assimilated: 'They are ignorant pagans (*amaqaba*)', 'barbarians', 'country bumpkins', (*oonolali*), and so on. The migrants for their part, despise the townsmen in general for their wickedness and lack of discipline, but if one probes a bit further it emerges that it is really the *tsotsi* section which is despised. The attitude of those who remain incapsulated in groups of home-boys is 'thank God we are not as those townees are', and the migrants would never admit themselves to be lower in status than the *tsotsis*, though they show a reluctant respect for their 'cleverness' in making money and in evading the police. The *tsotsis* regard the migrants as lower, and the fact that many migrants seek to be absorbed into the ranks of townsmen, but no townsman ever wishes to become a migrant, suggests that there are, at least, the beginnings of a class distinction in the urban environment. Gay young men from the country aspire to be accepted as 'bright boys' by the *ooMac*, and many more countrymen gradually merge with the 'decent people' of the town. They show respect for 'those who have been here a long time', and seek to copy their behaviour. . . . Status in town and in the country are by no means identical, but there is some correspondence between them. Wealth and professional qualifications carry prestige everywhere, and membership of a middle-class family; but the status of hereditary chiefs is ambiguous (1963: 138–41).

In the emerging class structure of the towns, it is the wealthy self-employed businessmen, professionals and higher-paid white-collar workers who constitute the élite (by African township standards) or middle-class (by white standards) (Brandel-Syrier 1971: xxvi). In both Reeftown and Grahamstown, Brandel-Syrier (*ibid.*, xxx, 301) and Nyquist (n.d.: 827–8) found, respectively, that those belonging to this stratum could be more or less readily identified by other residents, and that they 'serve as an important reference group for other urban Africans' (Nyquist n.d.: 832). Nyquist describes the élite as a 'multi-bonded group' (*ibid.*, chapter 19, *passim*) sharing common conceptions of home and family life; similar achievements and interests in education, occupation, religious affiliation, leisure-time activities, and membership of voluntary associations; common attitudes which are characteristically success-oriented in terms of European-type goals; and, above all, being bound together as a 'distinct and closely interacting group' (*ibid.*, 831). Brandel-Syrier's findings for Reeftown are similar, but Nyquist goes on to point out that the élite are particularly disadvantaged by the discriminatory laws of the land.

As a success-oriented stratum strongly aspiring to a Europeanized mode of life, the *abaphakamileyo* (élite) are in a special position of marginality, trapped between European-imposed barriers to upward mobility and continued pressure from lower-ranking Africans seeking higher status. . . . As a result of their special marginal situation, the upper stratum experiences stronger feelings than other Africans of suffering and unhappiness, of ambivalence and antagonism toward Europeans, of hostility toward European-imposed laws and the European court system, of job dissatisfaction, and of inferiority (*ibid.*: 836, 838).

Tribal affiliation, a significant criterion of stratification in Central and West Africa,[28] has hardly been investigated in the Republic of South Africa. This is, to some extent, a reflection of its limited relevance in the two most thoroughly researched cities, East London and Cape Town which are tribally homogeneous, and its probable irrelevance in most other major urban centres.[29] It is Johannesburg, which has the largest and most heterogeneous African population, in which the significance of tribal affiliation must be examined.

Regrettably, as should be clear from the preceding discussions, relatively little research has been undertaken in Johannesburg and none at all on the specific problem of 'tribalism' (in the sense of self-identification and categorization of others). The data presented, therefore, are gleaned from scattered sources and their synthesis must be regarded with some reservation.[30]

In a sample of 175 residents of Soweto (the huge complex of African townships in Johannesburg), it was found that people preferred fellow-tribesmen as neighbours,[31] while Walther (1968: 43ff.) suggests that there is a tendency among domestic servants for particular tribes to predominate in particular areas. Verster, in a personal communication, comments that the various types of mutual-aid societies among women (see below) tend to be tribally homogeneous as they are generally limited in size and recruited within a neighbourhood. Other indications of the relevance of tribal affiliation are large- and small-scale intertribal disputes and fighting;[32] the tendency for many independent African church congregations to be drawn from a particular tribal group (Verster: personal communication; Dubb 1962); the existence of tribal sterotypes (Longmore 1959: 27ff.); the preference for tribal endogamy (Longmore 1959: 27ff.) and its actual predominance (NEAD 1965: 30). In a more general sense, a greater feeling of 'belonging' in relation to one's own tribal group as compared with others emerges from a study by Dubb, Melamed and Majodina (1973).[33]

But while 'tribalism' does appear to affect relationships at the most intimate levels of association and in certain situations, it is not all-pervasive. Thus intermarriages *do* occur (NEAD 1965: 30—about one-third of cases; Hellmann 1948: 12–13—over half the cases); enforced residential separation of tribes (officially styled: 'ethnic grouping') is disapproved of (NEAD 1965: 74–6); mission and other major church congregations are multi-tribal; election of members of the Urban Bantu Council does not appear to be affected by 'tribalism' (Verster: personal communication); sports and social clubs are heterogeneous (Verster: personal communication). It appears, then, that in large formal associations, tribal affiliation is of little importance, while despite the fact that people seem to 'feel more at home' with fellow-tribesmen and, therefore, prefer them, they are opposed to any formal, compulsory separation. It is also probable—though there is no documentary evidence—that 'tribalism' decreases with education and urbanization and that it is greatest where communication with others is easy only in one's own language and cultural idiom.

There are, then, several categories of town-dwellers, defined in terms of such criteria as country- or town-rootedness, religion, tribe, education, wealth, respectability, traditionalism, and so on. These categories may be viewed either horizontally or vertically—though from the latter point of view there is no unanimity. The cleavage between the categories is manifested generally in style of life and social relationships but in particular it may be observed in leisure-time activities and in membership of clubs and other voluntary associations. Thus pagans and migrants tend to spend their leisure with home-boys rather than in formally organized clubs; sports clubs are frequently made up exclusively of home-boys; the choirs of respectable and conservative School people will specialize in church and traditional music rather than in the more modern secular and 'catchy' numbers of townsmen's choirs; and the *iibari* and *ooMac* will patronize clubs which allow drinking and play jive music, whereas the *ooscuse-me* prefer more conservative and disciplined activities. It is where people may select with whom they wish to associate, that class distinctions are most vividly apparent.

Voluntary associations

Leisure-time activity depends on free choice and is therefore an important index of people's interests and of the ways in which they interrelate. It reveals those categories of people who choose to associate with one another—whether in organized groups or informally—as well as the criteria of their association. In addition, in the present context, it reflects changes in African life resulting from contact with Whites and from coming to town.[34]

In this section, we shall discuss the more structured aspect of leisure-time activity, the voluntary association. Such associations are brought about by people wishing to foster a common purpose or interest. Structurally, they may range from a loosely-organized drinking set to a regional rugby board with a constitution, officials and considerable funds, while the purposes they pursue may be social (clubs, dancing groups, choirs, picnics), sport, economic (welfare organizations, thrift clubs, burial societies, mutual-aid societies), political, or civic (ratepayers' associations, vigilantes).

The role of the voluntary association in South African towns has been summarized by Dubb (1961: xii):

> Broadly speaking, urban populations may express their common material, social and cultural needs in three ways: through establishment of and participation in a system of local government, the formation of sub-urban communities, and through membership of voluntary associations. In the East Bank location [East London], as in many other African townships in

South Africa and elsewhere, Africans have little or no say in local government while neighbourhood groups are rare. [Furthermore, Africans are not permitted to organize either trade unions or political parties.] The only real expression of common interests and needs, therefore, is within the voluntary associations.

Two additional factors which contribute to the importance of voluntary associations are employment conditions and poverty. With regard to the first, there is only a very small percentage of Africans employed in jobs otherwise than as labourers,[35] so that relatively few find meaning or satisfaction either in their work as such or in their job situations[36] and, therefore, often look for these in voluntary associations. The second factor, poverty,[37] has given rise to a variety of savings and other financial-aid clubs which will be discussed below.

Probably the largest group of associations—and that which is readily available to migrant and townsman alike—is the churches. In East London, Reader (1961b) found that about two-thirds of the adult African population (24,660 out of 33,030) claimed allegiance to Christianity, and of these Dubb (1961: 38) estimated that from one-fifteenth to one-fifth (between 1,500 and 5,000) actually participated in church activities. These activities extend beyond the purely religious and cover a variety of interests and needs: the churches provide a meeting place for adherents and, as such, the opportunity for making friends; through their various offices, church societies and undertakings they provide an outlet for leadership and other abilities;[38] and in some churches an attempt is made to provide a sufficient variety of activities to occupy most of their members' leisure time.[39]

Perhaps one of the most interesting facets of African urban church life—since it characterizes associational life generally—is the tendency towards fission. Since the end of the nineteenth century, sects have split from parent mission churches and from each other so that today there are many thousands of these independent churches[40]—and the process still continues. The reasons given for these secessions include race discrimination, disagreement over use of funds, theological differences, and disputes over leadership. On analysis, however, it appears that instigators of a seccession are generally men who are desirous of taking over leadership but are unsuccessful. It is probable that the paucity of positions of leadership and responsibility in employment, trade unions, politics and civic affairs makes such positions in the churches so highly prized. In fact, of course, it becomes a matter of diminishing returns for many, since secession may promise leadership but not followers.

The same pattern is to be found in other voluntary associations and, in particular, the sports clubs. There is constant conflict between sports administrators at every level, and splitting is therefore extremely common. Mayer (1961: 220ff.) and Wilson and Mafeje (1963: 114ff.) describe this process in East London and Cape Town respectively.

Next to the churches, sport is the most popular leisure-time activity.[41]

Many thousands of people participate in or are spectators at weekend sports events. There are scores of clubs—the most popular by far being those for rugby, soccer and cricket. In Cape Town most of the clubs are recruited on a home-boy basis, and this is reflected in their names. On the other hand, tennis and golf clubs attract the middle-class people irrespective of place of origin. Mayer (1961: 221) and Verster (personal communication), however, attach less significance to tribe and region in East London and Johannesburg respectively.

Mutual aid, funeral, credit and similar associations with an economic function are widespread. A common arrangement is for a group of men working in the same firm to contribute a portion of their weekly wages into a pool which is taken by each member in turn. Thus at regular intervals members receive a relatively large lump-sum of money. The burial societies generally operate on a subscription basis although additional fund-raising activities may be organized. Another means of raising money, either for the benefit of an individual or an association, is the concert. Not only do people pay for admission and refreshments, but they may also 'purchase' particular turns— or pay for an item *not* to be performed.[42]

Townsmen also have their dancing and social clubs. As Wilson and Mafeje (1963: 126ff.) show, membership tends to follow class lines. Bands also claim membership from a particular class, though a good musician would be in general demand. Pauw (1963a: *passim*) makes similar observations about these activities in East London.

It is clear that a wide variety of voluntary associations exists in town and that either they are based on white counterparts or else they represent responses to specifically African urban needs.

Conclusion

An overview such as this calls for no conclusions: it presents neither new material nor new hypotheses. In the same way, a summary would be superfluous since this chapter is in itself a summary. The purpose of this concluding section, therefore, is simply to draw the reader's attention to lacunae in the data and in this overview.

There is no doubt that since Ellen Hellmann wrote her chapter 'The Native in the Towns' in the original 1937 edition of *The Bantu-Speaking Tribes of South Africa*, urban studies have come a long way. The work of Mitchell, Epstein and others on the Zambian Copperbelt, Mayer in East London, and other anthropologists in East and West Africa, have contributed many new and useful concepts to the study of migrancy, urbanization and related problems. The data for these studies, however, have been collected largely in countries north of the Limpopo. In the Republic of South Africa, Mayer (1961), Reader (1961a), Pauw (1963a) and Wilson and Mafeje (1963) have provided the most substantial general studies available, and they deal *only* with East London and Cape Town. No comparable studies of any other major

THE IMPACT OF THE CITY

South African city exist, so that the scholar must content himself with what he can glean from more specialized studies such as those of Longmore (1959) and Brandel-Syrier (1962 and 1971); scattered articles, papers, mimeographed lectures and personal communications; and postgraduate theses. Analysis, comparison and synthesis of these scattered data is not only difficult but, often, of dubious validity. This is because the quality of both data collection and subsequent analysis and interpretation varies considerably: sample selection and size, time and place within the same general area, theoretical sophistication, research techniques, the changing climate of the research situation[43] —all may differ from study to study. There are, therefore, serious gaps in the data on Africans in town, in the Republic, while even what is available must often be regarded with circumspection.

Despite the paucity of material, it has by no means been exhausted in the present chapter. A considerable body of social-psychological data on Africans as workers, for example, has been published by the National Institute for Personnel Research.[44] Because this was beyond the scope of the chapter no reference has been made to these publications—though there is much of interest relating to attitudes, urbanization, and so on. In a limited review, such omissions are, in a sense, necessary, but they have nevertheless been included in the Bibliography for the sake of completeness.[45]

Notes

1 It should also be noted that sources will not be specifically acknowledged each time material from them is used. It should always be clear from previous references, however, what the source of any information is.

2 African townships are also commonly referred to as 'locations'.

3 Writing of a township on the Witwatersrand which she identifies as 'Reeftown', Brandel-Syrier (1971: 20-5) points out that residential differentiation along 'class' lines was encouraged by the authorities since the establishment of the township some years after World War II. After some initial resistance, mainly for economic reasons, professionals and businessmen are increasingly moving into the more fashionable areas.

4 An African may, on various grounds, be expelled from the town and sent back to the rural area from which he originated. 'Deportation', in this context, does not therefore imply the expulsion of foreigners from the Republic. A more common term is 'to be endorsed out' which refers to an endorsement made in the identity book carried by every African, to the effect that he is prohibited from remaining in town. It should be noted that even town-born people, as well as those who have totally severed their rural connections, may be 'endorsed out' to a tribal 'homeland'.

5 The administration of African affairs throughout the country is being taken over by the government Bantu Administration Department. The relevant Act—Act 45 of 1971 —provides for the division of the country into areas under Bantu Affairs Administration Boards, whose responsibilities will include the running of existing townships, presently largely under the jurisdiction of the municipalities of the White towns to which they are attached. One much-publicized advantage of the take-over, will be that Africans will be permitted to sell their labour in a wider area than at present.

Whereas they are now confined to a particular municipal area, a number of such areas will in future be combined into a single area under its own Board, and Africans within it will be able to circulate more freely. Apart from this, however, the consequences of the take-over cannot be predicted.

6 For discussions of causes of migration in South Africa see Schapera 1947: chapter 3; Reader 1961a: 71ff. For a review of the question for Africa as a whole, see ILI 1957.

7 Although published in 1948, *Rooiyard* was presented as an M.A. thesis in 1935.

8 Alverson (1967) discusses various indices of stabilization.

9 The Xhosa-speaking peoples have for long distinguished between *abantu ababomvu* (Red people) and *abantu basesikolweni* (School people). The former are traditionalists, vigorously committed to the preservation and continuation of Xhosa customs and the traditional way of life. School people, on the other hand, through the Church and Western education, have come to value European culture. The division between the two groups is both rural and urban. A full discussion of this topic is to be found in Mayer (1961: chapter 2). Dubb (1966) should also be consulted.

10 Network has since been used increasingly in the analysis of urban situations. The reader is referred to Mitchell (1969) for a discussion of the development and uses of the concept as well as for specific network analyses.

11 Kleinbooi, Thomas and Joseph are fictitious characters, but their networks are none the less real. See also Houghton 1960a.

12 Traditional beer, made from maize or sorghum, now brewed and sold commercially in pint-size cartons.

13 See Wilson and Mafeje (1963: 110–12); Pauw (1963a: 56–7, 87); Longmore (1959: chapter 8).

14 The predominantly Venda section of Soweto, the vast complex of townships southwest of Johannesburg.

15 Pauw 1963a (cited, without page reference).

16 The nuclear (or elementary) family is a group consisting of a man and a woman—whose union is recognized in terms of the rules of the society—and their legitimate children, own or adopted.

17 Polygyny was highly valued although, in practice, only the wealthier men were able to marry more than one wife. Among pagans polygyny still occurs, but is declining. See, for example, Hunter 1936: *passim*; and Hammond-Tooke 1962: *passim*.

18 It should be noted that although we refer to Pauw's findings, these domestic arrangements are common to all South African townships. For information on Johannesburg, see Longmore 1959: *passim*. Verster (1965: 158) gives a breakdown of types of marriage in a sample of 2,416 mothers in Soweto. She found that 2·11 per cent were living together, 9·61 per cent had been married by civil or Christian rites, 43·32 per cent by civil or Christian as well as customary rites, 28·78 per cent by customary rites, and 16·18 per cent had never been married. Some discussion of the family in Cape Town may be found in Wilson and Mafeje 1963: 76–82.

19 There is a fairly widespread belief that there is an extremely high masculinity rate among urban Africans and that this accounts for the large number of unmarried mothers. It might therefore be noted that in Johannesburg the masculinity rate was 94·1 (Verster 1965: 166), in East London 108 (Reader 1961a: 150) and in Cape Town (Langa 86·6. (Wilson and Mafeje 1963: 4). However, masculinity is only one demographic factor which *may* contribute to the conditions described.

20 See Mayer 1961: 256–265; Longmore 1959: 68–75.

21 Brandel-Syrier (1971:83) points out that the wives of the Reeftown élite were important 'status symbols' as well as co-earners, and that it 'was generally agreed in Reeftown that "a wife can pull her husband up"' (*ibid*., 84). At the same time she records a high degree of marital strife and instability (83) as well as noting that 'A great number, probably the majority, were known by their wives to be "unfaithful", at more or less regular intervals in extra-marital relationships' (91).

22 See Pauw 1963a: *passim*; Mayer 1961: *passim*; Wilson and Mafeje 1963: *passim*; Longmore 1959: *passim*.

23 The practice still prevails among pagans in the rural areas but not among Christians, since the missionaries regarded it as a disgusting and evil custom. One of the consequences has been that, among the Xhosa at any rate, it is generally acknowledged that Christian girls have more pre-marital pregnancies than do pagan girls.

24 See Hammond-Tooke 1968a and b.

25 See Reader 1961a: 73f. and chapter 8.

26 The term 'stratification' is used here in its broader sense to include both vertical and horizontal 'strata'. Thus both the pagan—Christian cleavage, and the emergence of socio-economic classes, are discussed.

27 Mayer 1961: 180ff., chapters 12 and 13; Dubb 1966.

28 See Mitchell 1966, for bibliographical references.

29 East London, Port Elizabeth and Cape Town are largely Xhosa; Durban—Zulu; Bloemfontein—Sotho.

30 Sources include a personal communication from Miss Joan Verster, formerly of the Non-European Affairs Department, Johannesburg Municipality.

31 Unpublished material in connection with NEAD 1965, and communicated to the author by Verster.

32 During the 1940s there was fighting almost every weekend between the Zulus and 'the Russians' (Sotho men). Hellmann (1948: 92) mentions tribal alignments in personal disputes.

33 One hundred Africans—one-third each Zulu, Xhosa and Sotho—were asked to rate 'myself', each of the three tribes, whites, urban Africans and rural Africans on a Semantic Differential Scale. The semantic distance between 'myself' and own tribe was consistently and significantly less than between 'myself' and other categories. It may be mentioned too, though not relevant here, that the distance between 'myself'

and 'rural person' was very much less than between 'myself' and 'urban person' suggesting some kind of ideal typology with 'rural' representing an optimum type and 'urban' the very much less desirable contrasting type.

34 It may be mentioned that Mayer's 1961 study of East London was based entirely on leisure-time activities and patterns of association.

35 According to Bureau of Statistics (1964: H5) about 2·5 per cent of all Bantu (as against over 50 per cent whites, 8 per cent Coloureds and 35 per cent Asiatics) were white-collar workers. See also Reader 1961a: 63–5.

36 See Reader 1961a: Chapter 5, and SAIRR 1962 onwards: *A Survey of Race Relations in South Africa*.

37 See Reader 1961a: 65–9 and SAIRR 1962 onwards.

38 Most churches have an *umanyano* (Women's Guild or Mother's Union) and organize bazaars and concerts. See Dubb 1961: Part I and Part II, chapters 5–7; Brandel-Syrier 1962.

39 This is especially true of some of the smaller sects but applies also to a few larger churches such as the Assemblies of God ('Bhengu's Church'). In such cases, the church often becomes a community rather than simply a limited-purpose association. See Dubb 1961: Part I, chapter 4 and Part II.

40 Sundkler (1961a: 354ff.) lists the names of 1,156 independent churches and mentions a further 123.

41 Mayer 1961: 220f.; Pauw 1963a: 44f.; Wilson and Mafeje 1963: 113.

42 See Kuper and Kaplan 1944 for descriptions of two common types of association. See also Ardner 1964.

43 This refers to the possibility of participant observation when the white anthropologist's right of access to African townships is limited both by the authorities and by considerations of personal safety. It also refers to the climate of attitudes towards whites in general and research in particular.

44 A particularly interesting study is Grant 1969 in which an attempt is made to construct an urbanization scale.

45 See, in particular, the first section of Bibliographical references.

Bibliographical Index

Bibliographical

The bibliography lists all references appearing in the text and includes a number of more important sources, not so appearing. Figures in square brackets refer to page numbers in the present book. For further bibliographical information the reader is referred to the following works:

ASCHENBORN, H. J. (1961) 'Anthropological and Archaeological Journals in South African Libraries' (mimeograph), Pretoria: State Library

BACK, J. (1958) 'South African Native Life and Problems: Modern Status and Conditions 1950–1958; A Select Bibliography' (mimeograph), Cape Town: University School of Librarianship

COMHAIRE, J. (1952) *Urban Conditions in Africa: A Select Reading List on Urban Problems in Africa*

DE JAGER, E. J. (1966) 'A Select Bibliography of the Anthropology of the Cape Nguni Tribes' (mimeograph), Johannesburg: Africana Museum

GIFFEN, R. (1958) 'A Select Bibliography of South African Life and Problems: Modern Status and Conditions 1950–1958' (mimeograph), Cape Town: University School of Librarianship

HAMMOND-TOOKE, W. D. (1969) 'The present state of Cape Nguni ethnographic studies' in *Ethnological and Linguistic Studies in Honour of N. J. van Warmelo*, Pretoria: Government Printer, pp. 81–97

HOLDEN, M. A. (1949) 'A Select Bibliography of South African Native Life and Problems: Modern Status and Conditions, 1939–1949' (mimeograph), Cape Town: School of Librarianship

JACOBY, A. (1950) 'Select Bibliography of South African Native Life and Problems: Modern Status and Conditions' (mimeograph), Cape Town: University School of Librarianship

KUPER, B. M. (1962) 'A Bibliography of Native Law in South Africa 1941–1961' (mimeograph), Johannesburg: University of the Witwatersrand

LURIE, A. S. (1969) 'Urban Africans in the Republic of South Africa; 1950–1966' (mimeograph), Johannesburg: University of the Witwatersrand, Department of Bibliography, Librarianship and Typography

NIPR (National Institute for Personnel Research) (1970) *NIPR List of Publications 1946–1968* (and supplements for 1969 and 1970), Johannesburg: NIPR/Council for Scientific and Industrial Research [469]

SCHAPERA I. (1934) 'The present state and future development of ethnographical research in South Africa', *Bantu Studies* 8, 219–342

—— (1941) *Select Bibliography of South African Native Life and Problems*, London: Oxford University Press

SOLOMON, C. (1964) 'A Select Bibliography of South African Native Life and Problems: Modern Status and Conditions, 1958–1963', (mimeograph), Cape Town: University School of Librarianship (a supplement to I. Schapera (1941))

WILLETS, R. J. (1952) 'The Urbanization of the Native in South Africa, 1910–1952: A Bibliography' (mimeograph), Cape Town: School of Librarianship

Official Documents

Bantu Administration Act (1940) [288, 301, 315-17 *passim*]
Bantu Affairs Administration Act 45 (1971) [469]
Bantu Authorities Act (1951) [315, 393]
Botswana Independence Order (1966) [315, 316]
Cape Colony Archives C.O. 367 [394]
Cape Colony Census (1865) [412]
—— (1946) [59]
—— (1960) [59]
Government Notice R 2082 (1967) [316 *bis*]
—— R 2084 [316]
—— R 34 (1966) [317]
—— R 2257 (1928) [317 *bis*]
—— R 20833 (1967) [316 *bis*]
Industrial Conciliation Act, No. 11 (1924) [414]
Industrial Conciliation Act (1956) [410]
Lesotho Independence Order (1966) [315-16 *passim*]
Low Grade Mines Commission, U.G. 34 (1920) [409, 414]
Mines and Works Act, No. 12 (1911) [391, 409, 414]
Mines and Works Amendment Act (1926) [414]
Mining Survey (Transvaal Chamber of Mines) [413]
Natal Code (1942) [314, 316-17 *passim*]
Native Land Act (1913) [391]
Native Laws Amendment Act (1937) [392]
Native Laws and Customs (Barry Report) (1883) [388]
Native Territories Penal Code (1886) [389]
Native Trust and Land Act (1936) [392]
Natives' (Urban Areas) Act (1923) [409, 443]
Preliminary Survey of Bantu Tribes of South Africa, A (1935) [57-8]
Population Return of British Kaffraria (1858) [412]
Promotion of Bantu Self Government Act (1959) [315]
Representation of Natives Act (1936) [392]
Swaziland Independence Order (1968) [315-16 *passim*]
Transkeian Constitution Act (1963) [393]
Transvaal Labour Commission (1898) [413]
—— (1904) [413]
Transvaal Ordinance, No. 17 (1904) [409, 414]
Urban Bantu Councils Act (1961) [315]
Wage Act, No. 27 (1925) [414]
(*See also under* South Africa)

British Parliamentary Papers

1837, XLIII (503) [371]
1847-8, XLIII (912) [372]
1850, XXXVIII (1288) [372-3]
1856, XLII (C 2096) [373]
1878, LVI (C 2144) [387 *bis*]
1881, LXVII (C 2964) [381]
1882, XLVII (C 3112) [388]
1905, LV (Cd 2399) [391]

British Public Records Office

C.O. 48/243 (1844) [379]
C.O. 48/264 [395]
C.O. 48/326 (1852) [394]
C.O. 48/365 (1855) [373–4]
C.O. 48/500 (1881) [381]

Books and Journal Articles

ABELSON, P. H. (1969) 'Malnutrition, learning and behaviour', *Science*, 164, 17 [30]
ACOCKS, J. P. H. (1953) 'Veld types of South Africa', *Mem. Bot. Surv. S. Afr.*, 28 [50, 54, 149]
AGAR-HAMILTON, J. A. I. (1928) *The Native Policy of the Voortrekkers*, Cape Town: Maskew Miller
—— (1937) *The Road to the North*, London: Longmans [382, 385]
ALBERTI, L. (1810) *De Kaffers aan de Zuidkust van Afrika, Natuur-en Geschiedkundig beschreven*, Amsterdam: Maaskamp (trans. from original German MS of 1807 by W. Fehr as *Ludwig Alberti's Account of the Tribal Life and Customs of the Xhosa in 1807*, Cape Town: Balkema, 1968) [128, 129–30 *passim*, 320, 327]
ALBERTO, M. S. and A. D. BARRETO (1952) 'Occurrence of the congenital blue or mongolic spot in the new-born Negroes of Mozambique' (MS. only), presented to the Annual Congress S. Afr. Assoc. Adv. Sci., Lourenço Marques, 1952, 1–6 [20 *bis*]
ALLBROOK, D. B. (1956) 'Size of adrenal cortex in East African males', *Lancet*, 2 606–7 [44]
—— (1958) 'Addendum on the measurements of specimens of the female bony pelvis', *J. Obst. and Gynae. of the British Empire*, 65,4, 600–5
—— (1962) 'Some problems associated with pelvic form and size in the Ganda of East Africa', *J. Roy. Anthrop. Inst.*, 92, 1, 102–14 [16]
ALLISON, A. C. (1954) 'The distribution of the sickle-cell trait in East Africa and elsewhere, and its apparent relationship to the incidence of subtertian malaria', *Trans. Roy. Soc. Trop. Med. Hyg.*, 48, 312–18 [27]
ALVERSON, H. S. (1967) 'Time series analysis of migratory stabilization', *African Studies*, 26, 3, 139–44 [470]
ANGAS, G. F. (1849) *The Kaffirs Illustrated*, London: Hogarth [129, 130]
ANKERMANN, B. (1915) 'Verbreitung und Formen des Totemismus in Afrika', *Z. f. Ethnol.*, 47, 114–80
—— (1918) 'Totenkult und Seelenglaube bei afrikanischen Völkern', *Z. f. Ethnol.*, 50, 89–153
ARDNER, S. (1964) 'Comparative study of rotating credit associations', *J. Roy. Anthrop. Inst.*, 94, 2, 201–27 [472]
ARGYLE, W. J. (1969) 'European nationalism and African tribalism' in P. H. Gulliver (ed.) (1969a), pp. 41–57 [xix]
ARKIN, M. (1960) 'Strikes, boycotts—and the history of their impact on South Africa', *S. Afr. J. Econ.*, 28, 4, 303–18
ASHTON, E. H. (1937) 'Notes on the political and judicial organization of the Tawana', *Bantu Studies*, 11, 67–83 [254]
—— (1938) 'Political organization of the Southern Sotho', *Bantu Studies*, 12, 287–320
—— (1939) 'A sociological sketch of Sotho diet', *Trans. Roy. Soc. S. Afr.*, 27, 2, 147–214 [45]
—— (1943) *Medicine, Magic and Sorcery among the Southern Sotho* (Communications from the School of African Studies, University of Cape Town, New Series, No. 10), Cape Town

BIBLIOGRAPHICAL INDEX

—— (1946) *The Social Structure of the Southern Sotho Ward* (Communications from the School of African Studies, U.C.T. No. 15), Cape Town [128]

—— (1952) *The Basuto: A study of traditional and modern Lesotho*, London: Oxford University Press (2nd ed. 1967) [128, 129–30 *passim*, 193, 195, 205, 216, 221, 224–5 *passim*, 233, 235, 242, 244, 266, 290, 296 *bis*, 299, 307, 310, 316, 317 *bis*, 320–1 *passim*, 325–6 *passim*, 330–4 *passim*, 349, 350, 423, 425, 428, 429, 431–3 *passim*, 436]

ATMORE, A. (1969) 'The passing of Sotho independence 1865–70' in L. M. Thompson (ed.) (1969), pp. 282–301 [380]

AXELSON, E. (1934) 'Natal and the Annexation of Basutoland 1865–70', unpublished M.A. thesis, University of Natal [380]

AYLWARD, A. (1878) *The Transvaal of Today*, Edinburgh: Blackwood [171]

BAANDERS-VAN HALEWIJN, E. A. and F. DE WAARD (1968) 'Menstrual cycles shortly after menarche in European and Bantu girls', *Human Biol.*, 40, 3, 314–30

BACKER, W. (ed.) (1970) *The Economic Development of the Transkei*, Alice, Cape Province: Fort Hare

BAIN, A. G. (1829) *Journal of Andrew Geddes Bain* (ed. M. H. Lister), Cape Town: Van Riebeeck Society Publ. No. 30 (1949)

BARAITSER, M. and D. E. EVANS (1969) 'The effect of undernutrition on brain-rythm development', *S. Afr. Med. J.*, 43, 56–8 [45]

BARNES, J. A. (1954) 'Class and committees in a Norwegian island parish', *Human Relations*, 7, 1, 39–58 [450]

BARNICOT, N. A. (1958) 'Reflectometry of the skin in southern Nigerians and in some Mulattoes', *Human Biol.*, 30, 150–60 [18 *bis*]

BARETTO, A. D. (1955) 'Contribution to the study of the pelvis of native females of Mozambique', *S. Afr. J. Sci.*, 52, 21–2 [15]

BARTH, F. (1960) 'Nomadism in the mountain and plateau areas of South West Asia' in *The Problems of the Arid Zone*, UNESCO [176]

—— (1969) 'Introduction' in F. Barth (ed.), *Ethnic Groups and Boundaries*, London: Allen & Unwin [265]

BASUTOLAND (1963) *Basutoland: Report for the Year 1961*, London: HMSO

BAUMANN, M. (1919) 'Ancient tin mines of the Transvaal', *J. Chem. Metall. and Min. Soc. S. Afr.*, 19, 120–32; 20, 32–4 [130]

BECKER, P. (1962) *Path of Blood*, London: Longmans

BEEMER, H. (1939) 'Notes on the diet of the Swazi in the Protectorate', *Bantu Studies*, 13, 199–236 [45, 151, 153, 156]

BEET, E. A. (1946) 'Sickle-cell disease in the Balovale District of Northern Rhodesia', *East Afr. Med. J.*, 23, 75–86

—— (1947) 'Sickle-cell disease in Northern Rhodesia', *East Afr. Med. J.*, 24, 212–22

BEIDELMAN, T. O. (1966) 'Swazi royal ritual', *Africa*, 36, 4, 373–405 [363]

BELL, K. N. and W. P. MORRELL (1928) *Select Documents on British Colonial Policy, 1830–1860*, Oxford: Clarendon Press [370]

BENNIE, W. G. (1939) 'The Ciskeian and Southern Transkei Tribes' in A. M. Duggan-Cronin, *The Bantu Tribes of South Africa*, III, Sect. 1, London: Cambridge University Press

BENYON, J. A. (1968) 'Basutoland and the High Commission, 1868–1884', unpublished D.Phil. thesis, University of Oxford [381 *bis*, 382, 388]

BERG, E. (1961) 'Backward-sloping labour supply functions in dual economies—the Africa case', *Quart. J. Econ.*, August [403]

BERGLUND, A.-I. (1968) 'Pack oxen and cattle-riding amongst the Zulus', *African Studies*, 27, 1, 29–30 [129, 223]

BEUKES, W. T. H. (1931) 'Der Häuptling in der Gesellschaft der Süd, Öst und Zentral Bantuvölker', dissertation, Hamburg

BIGALKE, E. H. (1966) 'Notes on the place of domestic and indigenous animals in Cape Nguni life', *Ann. Cape Prov. Mus.*, 6, 1, 1–16

—— (1969) 'The Religious System of the Ndlambe of East London', unpublished M.A. thesis, Rhodes University, Grahamstown [325–6, 328–9 passim, 342, 353, 359]
BIRD, J. (1888) Annals of Natal, 1495–1845, Cape Town [376]
BIRDSELL, J. B. (1963) 'The origin of human races', Quart. Rev. Biol., 38, 2, 178–85
BLACKING, J. (1961) 'The social value of Venda riddles', African Studies, 20, 1, 1–33
—— (1964) Black Background, New York: Abelard-Schuman [217–19 passim, 221, 225, 234, 240, 241, 242, 423 bis, 425, 427]
—— (1967) Venda Children's Songs, Johannesburg: Witwatersrand University Press
—— (1969) 'Songs, dances, mimes and symbolism of Venda girls' initiation schools. 1. Vhusha, 2. Milayo, 3. Domba, 4. The great Domba song', African Studies, 28 [235–6, 244]
BLOHM, H. (1933a) 'Das Opfer und dessen Sinn bei den Xosa in Südafrika', Archiv. Anthrop., N.F. 23, 150–3
—— (1933b) 'Die Christliche Familien-Gesellschaft im Xosa-Volkstum', Africa, 6, 431–55
—— (1935) 'The African explains witchcraft: Pt VI Xhosa', Africa, 8, 522–5
BODENSTEIN, W. and O. F. RAUM (1960) 'A present day Zulu philosopher', Africa, 30, 2, 166–81
BONATZ, A. (1834) 'Description of the mission settlement of Shiloh', Periodical Accounts ... of the ... United Brethren 13, 302–8, 347–52, London [129]
BOSHIER, A. K. (1969) 'Mining genesis', Mining Survey, 64, 21–8 [83]
BOTHMA, C. V. (1962) Ntshabeleng Social Structure, Pretoria: Government Printer [197 bis, 270]
—— (1969) 'Pedi origins' in Ethnological and Linguistic Studies, Pretoria: Government Printer [84]
BOTT, E. (1957) Family and Social Network, London: Tavistock [450]
BOURQUIN, W. (1951) 'Click-words which Xhosa, Zulu and Sotho have in common', African Studies, 10, 2, 59–81 [84]
BOYD, W. C. (1964) 'Modern ideas on race, in the light of our knowledge of blood groups and other characters with known mode of inheritance' in C. A. Leone (ed.), Taxonomic Biochemistry and Serology, New York: Ronald Press, pp. 119–69 [45]
BRAATVEDT, H. P. (1927) 'Zulu marriage customs and ceremonies', S. Afr. J. Sci., 24, 553–65
BRAIN, P. (1953) 'The sickle-cell trait: a possible mode of introduction into Africa', Man, contr. No. 233 [28]
BRANDEL, M. (1958) 'Urban lobolo attitudes: a preliminary report', African Studies, 17, 1, 34–51
BRANDEL-SYRIER, M. (1962) Black Woman In Search of God, London: Lutterworth [425, 439, 469]
—— (1971) Reeftown Elite, London: Routledge & Kegan Paul [464–5 passim, 469 bis, 471, 472]
BREUTZ, P.-L. (1941) Die politischen und gesellschaftlichen Verhältnisse der Sotho-Tswana in Transvaal und Betschuanaland, Hamburg [284, 291, 293–4]
—— (1953a) The Tribes of Marico District, Pretoria: Government Printer
—— (1953b) The Tribes of Rustenburg and Pilansburg Districts, Pretoria: Government Printer
—— (1955) The Tribes of Mafeking District, Pretoria: Government Printer [254]
—— (1956) 'Stone kraal settlements in South Africa', African Studies, 15, 4, 157–76 [83]
—— (1959) The Tribes of Vryburg District, Pretoria: Government Printer [254]
—— (1963) The Tribes of Kuruman and Postmasburg Districts, Pretoria: Government Printer
—— (1969) 'Sotho-Tswana celestial concepts' in Ethnological and Linguistic Studies, Pretoria: Government Printer

BREWER, G. J. (1967) 'Genetic and population studies of quantitative levels of adinosine triphosphate in human erythrocytes' *Biochem. Genet.*, 1, 25–34
BROCK, J. F. (1961) *Recent Advances in Human Nutrition*, London: Churchill [45]
BROOKES, E. H. (1924) *The History of Native Policy in South Africa*, Cape Town (2nd ed 1927, Pretoria: Van Schaik) [316, 376–7, 386, 395]
BROOKES, E. H. and N. HURWITZ (1957) *The Native Reserves of Natal*, Vol. 7, Natal Regional Survey, Cape Town: Oxford University Press [376–7]
BROOKES, E. H. and C. de B. WEBB (1965) *A History of Natal*, Pietermaritzburg: University of Natal [378 *bis*]
BROWN, J. T. (1921) 'Circumcision rites of the Becwana tribes', *J. Roy. Anthrop. Inst.* 51, 419–27
—— (1926) *Among the Bantu Nomads. A Record of Forty Years Spent among the Bechuana*, London: Seeley, Service [323, 328–9, 345, 346 *bis*]
BROWN, R. E. (1966) 'Organ weight in malnutrition with special reference to brain weight', *Develop. Med. Child. Neurol.*, 8, 512–22 [45]
BROWNLEE, C. (1858) 'Notes' in J. Maclean (ed.) (1858a) [284 *bis*, 291, 296, 299–301 *passim*, 316 *bis*]
—— (1896) *Reminiscences of Kaffir Life and History*, Lovedale: Mission Press
—— (1955) 'A fragment of Xhosa religious beliefs', *African Studies*, 14, 1, 37–41
BROWNLEE, F. (ed) (1923) *The Transkeian Native Territories: Historical Records*, Cape Town: Maskew Miller [319, 387]
—— (1940) 'Some experiences of Native superstition and witchcraft', *J. African Society*, 39, 54–60
—— (1944) 'Burial places of chiefs', *J. African Society*, 43, 23–4
BROWNLEE, J. (1827) 'Account of the Amakosae, or Southern Caffres' in G. Thompson (1827)
BRUWER, J. P. (1957) *Die Bantoe in Suid Afrika*, Johannesburg: Afrikaanse Pers
BRYANT, A. T. (1909) 'Zulu medicines and medicine men', *Annals Natal Museum*, 2, 1–103
—— (1917) 'The Zulu cult of the dead', *Man*, 17, 140–5
—— (1919–20) 'The religion of the Zulus', *Native Teachers' J.*, 1, 44–50
—— (1923) 'The Zulu state and family organization', *Bantu Studies*, 2, 47–51
—— (1929) *Olden Times in Zululand and Natal*, London: Longmans [61, 64, 289]
—— (1939) *Description of Native Foodstuffs and their Preparation*, Pretoria: Government Printer
—— (1949) *The Zulu People as they were before the White Man Came*, Pietermaritzburg: Shooter & Shuter [128, 308, 314 *bis*, 363]
BUDTZ-OLSEN, M. D. and A. C. J. BURGERS (1955) 'The sickle-cell trait in the South African Bantu', *S. Afr. Med. J.*, 29, 109–10 [35, 45]
BUITENDAG, F. W. C. (1951) 'The emergence of the urban African', *Race Rel. J.*, 18, 3, 205–11
BURCHELL, W. J. (1822–24) *Travels in the Interior of South Africa*, 2 vols, London: Longmans [129 *bis*]
BUREAU OF STATISTICS (1964) *Statistical Year Book*, Pretoria: Government Printer [472]
CALLAWAY, H. (1866–8) *Nursery Tales, Traditions and Histories of the Zulus*, Springvale, Natal: Blair [319, 320]
—— (1868–70) *The Religious System of the Amazulu*, Springvale, Natal: Blair [348]
—— (1871–2) 'Divination and analogous phenomena among the Natives of Natal', *J. Roy. Anthrop. Inst.*, 1, 163–85
CAMPBELL, A. C. (1965) '*Ubukhwetha* among the amaXhosa', *Nada*, 9, 2, 52–8
CAMPBELL, J. (1815) *Travels in South Africa*, London: Black, Parry [129 *bis*, 130]
CAMPBELL, W. B. (1959) 'The South African Frontier, 1865–85', *Archives Yearbook for South African History*, 1, Pretoria: Government Printer [386–8 *passim*, 395]

BIBLIOGRAPHICAL INDEX

CAPE COLONY (1827) *Proclamations 1806–1825* [367, 370 bis]
—— (1873) *Report and Evidence of Commission on Native Laws and Customs of the Basutos*, Cape Town: Saul Solomon
—— (1883) *Annexures to Votes and Proceedings of the Cape Parliament* (G4, G5 and G6 of '83) [380, 388, 389]
CAPPIERI, M. (1950) 'Population trends among primitive and isolated racial groups and the Bantu', *Proc. 14th Int. Congr. Sociol.*, 4, 1–18, Rome [5]
CARTER, G. (1927) *The Wreck of the Grosvenor*, Cape Town: Van Riebeeck Soc. Publ. No. 8 [129]
CASALIS, J.-E. (1861) *The Basutos*, London: Nisbet [128–30 passim, 297, 320 bis, 329, 359]
CATHCART, SIR G. (1857) *Correspondence Relative to his Military Operations in Kaffraria*, London: Murray [373]
CHADWICK, G. C. (1958) 'Initiation rites among the Basuto', *African World*, February 9–10 [228]
CHALMERS, J. A. (1877) *Tiyo Soga*, Edinburgh: Elliot [412]
CHARLTON, R. W. and T. H. BOTHWELL (1961) 'Primaquine sensitivity of red cells in various races in Southern Africa', *Brit. Med. J.*, 1, 941–4
CHISIZA, D. K. (1962) *Africa. What Lies Ahead*, Occasional Paper No. 1, African American Institute [406]
CILLIERS, S. P. (1969) 'Border Industries' *Optima*, 19, 3, 164–73
CLARK, J. D. (1950) 'A note on the pre-Bantu inhabitants of Northern Rhodesia and Nyasaland', *S. Afr. J. Sci.*, 47, 3, 80–5 [45]
—— (1962) 'The spread of food production in sub-Saharan Africa', *J. Afr. History*, 3, 2, 211–28 [39]
—— (1964) 'The prehistoric origins of African culture', *J. Afr. History*, 5, 2, 161–83 [37, 39–40 passim, 45]
CLARK, J. D. and B. M. FAGAN (1965) 'Charcoals, sands, and channel decorated pottery from Northern Rhodesia', *Amer. Anthrop.*, 67, 354–71 [45]
CLERC, A. (1938), 'The marriage laws of the Ronga tribe', *Bantu Studies*, 12, 75–104
COERTZE, P. J. (1931) 'Dolosgooiery in Suid-Afrika', *Annale Univ. Stellenbosch*, 9, B, 2
—— (1933) 'Huweliksgewoontes en erfreg by die Batlokwa van Basoetoland', *Bantu Studies*, 7, 257–73
COHEN, Y. A. (1964) *The Transition from Childhood to Adolescence: Crosscultural studies in initiation ceremonies, legal systems and incest taboos*, Chicago: Aldine [239, 244]
COLSON, E. (1958) 'The role of bureaucratic norms in African political structure' in V. F. Ray (ed.), *Systems of Political Control and Bureaucracy*, Proceedings of the American Ethnological Society, Seattle: American Ethnological Society [265 bis]
—— (1960) *Social Organization of the Gwembe Tonga*, Manchester University Press
—— (1970) 'Family and kinship' in J. Middleton (ed.), *Black Africa: Its peoples and their cultures today*, London: Collier-Macmillan
COOK, G. C. (1969) 'Lactase deficiency: a probable ethnological marker in East Africa', *Man*, 4, 2, 265–7 [83]
COOK, P. A. W. (1927) 'Customs relating to twins among the Bomvana of the Transkei', *S. Afr. J. Sci.*, 24, 516–20 [214]
—— (1931) *The Social Organization and Ceremonial Institutions of the Bomvana*, Cape Town: Juta [128, 229–30 passim, 243, 244, 357]
—— (1934) *The Education of a South African Tribe*, Cape Town: Juta
COON, C. S. (1962) *The Origin of Human Races*, New York: Knopf [45]
COON, C. S., S. M. GARN and J. B. BIRDSELL (1950) *Races: A Study of the Problems of Race Formation in Man*, Springfield, Illinois: Thomas [22]
CORY, SIR G. (1913) *The Rise of South Africa*, 2 vols, London: Longmans [370]
CRAGG, D. (1959) 'The Relations of the Amapondo and the Colonial Authorities, 1830–1886', unpublished D.Phil. thesis, Oxford University [387]

CRANKSHAW, G. B. (1960) 'The Diary of C. L. Stretch', unpublished M.A. thesis, Rhodes University, Grahamstown [371 *bis*]
CRAVIOTO, J. and B. ROBLES (1965) 'Evolution of adaptive and motor behaviour during rehabilitation from kwashiorkor', *Amer. J. Orthopsychiat.*, 35, 449–64 [45]
CRUZ, A. F. and R. R. GALVAN (1966) 'Influence of nutrition on pubertal growth of male adolescents from Mexico city', *Boletin Med. Hosp. Infantil de Mexico*, 23, 7–9
DART, R. A. (1937) 'Racial origins' in I. Schapera (ed.) (1937a), pp. 1–31 [5, 14, 45]
—— (1951) 'African serological patterns and human migration', *S. Afr. Archaeol. Bull.*, 6, 1–39 [83]
DART, R. A. and P. B. BEAUMONT (1967) 'Amazing antiquity of mining in Southern Africa', *Nature*, London, 216, 5113, 407–8 [40]
—— (1968) 'Ratification and retrocession of earlier Swaziland iron ore mining radiocarbon datings', *S. Afr. J. Sci.*, 64, 6, 241–6 [40]
DE ALMEIDA, A. (1956) 'La macronymphie chez les femmes indigènes de l'Angola', *C. R. Assoc. Anat.* (Lisbon), 43ᵉ Réunion, 26 March, 131–50 [22–3]
DE ALMEIDA, M. E. DE C. (1956) 'Da estatura, peso e sua correlaçao em gentes nativas de Angola', *Garcia de Orto*, 4, 3, 349–58
—— (1957a) 'Subsidio para o estudo antropológico dos Mussoccos e Cuangares (Angola)', *Estudos Ultramarinos*, 6, 2, 1–14
—— (1957b) 'Cânones de mulheres indígenas de Angola', *Communicaçao apresentada á 4ª Seccao do 23rd Congresso Luso-Espanhol-Coimbra 1956*, 5–16
DE JAGER, E. J. (1963) 'Notes on the magical charms of the Cape Nguni tribes', *Fort Hare Papers*, 2, 293–302
—— (1964a) 'Settlement types of the Nguni and Sotho tribes', *Fort Hare Papers*, 3, 19–30
—— (1964b) 'Die geskiedenis van die Ama-Xhosa en Ama-Thembu', *Historia*, 9, 215–27
—— (1964c) 'Die tradisionele seksuele sedelikheid van die Suid-Afrikaanse Bantoe: 'n kruis-kulturele ondersoek', *Nederduits Gereformeerde Teologiese Tyds.*, 5, 4, 226–41
DE JAGER, E. J. and V. Z. GITYWA (1963) 'A Xhosa *umhlwayelelo* ceremony in the Ciskei', *African Studies*, 22, 3, 109–16 [322]
DE JAGER, E. J. and M. O. M. SEBONI (1964) 'Bone divination amongst the Kwenda of the Molopolole district Bechuanaland Protectorate', *Afrika und Uebersee*, 48, 2–16
DE KIEWIET, C. W. (1941) *A History of South Africa—Social and Economic*, London: Oxford University Press
DE KOCK, M. H. (1924) *Economic History of South Africa*, Cape Town: Juta
DE LANGE, M. (1961) 'Dolls for the promotion of fertility as used by some of the Nguni tribes and the Basotho', *Annals Cape Prov. Mus.*, 1, 86–101 [213]
—— (1963) 'Some cosmetic practices of the Xhosa', *Annals Cape Prov. Mus.*, 3, 85–95 [103, 130]
—— (1967) 'Catalogue of the Musical Instruments in the Collection of Prof. P. R. Kirby' (roneod), Africana Museum, Johannesburg
DE VILLIERS, H. (1961) 'The tablier and steatopygia in Kalahari Bushwomen', *S. Afr. J. Sci.*, 57, 8, 223–7 [45]
—— (1968) *The Skull of the South African Negro: A biometrical and morphological study*, Johannesburg: Witwatersrand University Press [10–14 *passim*]
—— (1969) 'The morphology and incidence of the tablier in Bushman, Griqua and Negro females', *Proc. 8th Int. Congr. Anthrop. Ethnol. Sci.*, Tokyo and Kyoto, 48–51 [22 *bis*, 23, 33, 45]
DE VILLIERS, W. J. (1962) 'Key to Native wage increases', *Optima*, 12, 4, 202–12
DIETERLEN, H. (1930) *La Médécine et les Médécins au Lessouto*, Paris: Soc. Miss. évangeliques [333]
DOHNE, J. L. (1843) *Das Kaffernland und Seine Bewohner*, Berlin [129–30 *passim*]
DORNAN, S. S. (1932) 'Some beliefs and ceremonies connected with birth and death of twins among South African Natives', *S. Afr. J. Sci.*, 29, 690–700

DOXEY, G. V. (1961) *The Industrial Colour Bar in South Africa*, Cape Town: Oxford University Press [403, 404, 406, 413]
DRENNAN, M. R. (1929) 'The dentition of a Bushman tribe', *Annals S. Afr. Mus.*, 24, 1, 61–87 [14]
DRURY, J. and M. R. DRENNAN (1926) 'The pudendal parts of the South African Bush race', *Med. J. S. Afr.*, 22, 113–17 [45]
DUBB, A. A. (1961) 'The Role of the Church in an Urban African Society', unpublished M.A. thesis, Rhodes University, Grahamstown [439, 466, 467 *bis*, 472 *bis*]
—— (1962) 'Tribalism in the African Church' in A. A. Dubb (ed.), 'The Multitribal Society' (mim.), Proceedings of the Sixteenth Conference of the Rhodes–Livingstone Institute, Lusaka [465]
—— (1966) 'Red and School: A quantitative approach', *Africa*, 36, 292–302 [427, 470 471]
DUBB, A. A., L. MELAMED and M. MAJODINA (1973) 'African attitudes in town: the search for precision', *African Studies*, 32, 2, 85–97 [465]
DUGMORE, H. H. (1858) 'Papers' in J. Maclean (ed.) (1858a), ch. 4, pp. 1–36 [288, 291, 297–8, 300]
DUMBRELL, H. J. E. (1952) 'Pyre burning in Swaziland', *African Studies*, 11, 4, 190–1 [84]
DU PLESSIS, H. (1945) 'Die territoriale organisasie van die Venda', *African Studies*, 4, 3, 122–7
DU PLESSIS, J. (1911) *A History of Christian Missions in South Africa*, London: Longmans [415]
DU TOIT, A. E. (1954) 'The Cape Frontier, 1847–1866', *Archives Yearbook for South African History*, 1, Pretoria: Government Printer [373–5 *passim*, 395, 412]
DU TOIT, B. M. (1960) 'Some aspects of the soul-concept among the Bantu-speaking Nguni tribes of South Africa', *Anthrop. Quarterly*, 33, 3, 134–42
DU TOIT, S. J. (1959) 'African farm labour', *Race Rel. J.*, 26, 2 [xix]
DUTTON, E. A. T. (1923) *The Basuto of Basutoland*, London: Cape
EARTHY, E. D. (1933) *ValLenge Women: The social and economic life of the ValLenge women of Portuguese East Africa*, London: Oxford University Press
EATON, J. W. and G. J. BREWER (1969) 'Red cell ATP and malaria infection', *Nature*, 222, 5191, 389–90
EATON, J. W. and J. I. MUCHA (1971) 'Increased fertility in males with the sickle cell trait?', *Nature*, 231, 456–7 [27]
EBERHARDT, J. (1958) 'The mythical python among the Venda and Fulani: a comparative note', *Arch. f. Völkerkunde*, 13, 15–24
EDELSTEIN, M. L. (1972) *What do Young Africans Think?*, Johannesburg: SAIRR
EDWARDS, E. A. and S. Q. DUNTLEY (1939) 'The pigments and colour of living human skin', *Amer. J. Anat.*, 65, 1–33 [17]
EICHENWALD, H. F. and P. C. FRY (1969) 'Nutrition and learning', *Science*, 163, 644–8
EISELEN, W. M. (1928a) 'Nuwe Sesoeto tekste van volkekundige belang', *Annale Univ. Stellenbosch*, 6, B 3
—— (1928b) 'Die eintlike reëndiens van die BaPedi', *S. Afr. J. Sci.*, 25, 387–92
—— (1928c) 'Preferential marriage: correlation of the various modes among the Bantu tribes of the Union of South Africa', *Africa*, 1, 413–28
—— (1929) *Stamskole in Suid-Afrika*, Pretoria: Van Schaik
—— (1932a) 'Ueber die Häuptlingswürde bei den BaPedi', *Africa*, 5, 297–306
—— (1932b) 'The art of divination as practised by the BaMasemola', *Bantu Studies*, 6, 1–29, 251–63
—— (1932c) 'Initiation rites of the BaMasemola', *Annale Univ. Stellenbosch*, 10, B 2
—— (1934) 'Christianity and the religious life of the Bantu' in I. Schapera (ed.) (1934a), pp. 65–82

EISELEN, W. M. and I. SCHAPERA (1937) 'Religious beliefs and practices' in I. Schapera (ed.) (1937a), pp. 247–70
ELLENBERGER, D. and J. MACGREGOR (1912) *History of the Basuto, Ancient and Modern*, London: Caxton [73 *bis*, 202–3, 264, 379]
ELLENBERGER, V. (1939) 'History of the BaTlôkwa of Gaberones', *Bantu Studies*, 13, 166–97
ELSDON-DEW, R. (1936) 'The blood-groups of the Bantu of Southern Africa', *S.A. Inst. Med. Res.*, 39, 7, 217–300, Johannesburg [83]
ENGEL, R. (1956) 'Abnormal brain-wave patterns in kwashiorkor', *Electroenceph. & Clin. Neurophysiol.*, 8, 489–500 [45]
ENGELBRECHT, J. A. (1930) 'Swazi customs relating to marriage', *Annale Univ. Stellenbosch*, 8, B 3
EPSTEIN, A. L. (1958) *Politics in an Urban African Community*, Manchester University Press [449]
—— (1961) 'The network and urban social organization', *Rhodes–Livingstone Journal*, 29, 29–62 [450]
EVANS-PRITCHARD, E. (1937) *Witchcraft, Oracles and Magic Among the Azande*, London: Oxford University Press
—— (1940) *The Nuer*, London: Oxford University Press [xv, 196]
—— (1951) *Kinship and Marriage Among the Nuer*, London: Oxford University Press [190]
—— (1956) *Nuer Religion*, London: Oxford University Press [354]
EYBERS, G. W. (1918) *Select Constitutional Documents illustrating South African History 1795–1910*, London: Routledge [379–80 *passim*, 385, 391]
FAGAN, B. M. (1961) 'Pre-European ironworking in central Africa with special reference to Northern Rhodesia', *J. Afr. History*, 2, 2, 199–210 [45]
—— (1963) 'The Iron Age sequence in the Southern Province of Northern Rhodesia', *J. Afr. History*, 4, 2, 157–77 [45]
—— (1965) 'Radiocarbon dates for sub-Saharan Africa (from c. 1000 B.C.)—III' *J. Afr. History*, 6, 1, 107–16 [40]
—— (1969) 'The later Iron Age in S. Africa' in L. Thompson (ed.), pp. 50–70 [412]
FAGAN, H. A. (Chairman) (1948) *Native Laws Commission of Enquiry*, Pretoria: Government Printer, Union Government, 28 [405, 416]
FAIR, T. J. D. and L. P. GREEN (1962) 'Development of the "Bantu Homelands"', *Optima*, 12, 1, 7–22
FEDDEMA, J. P. (1966) 'Tswana ritual concerning rain', *African Studies*, 25, 4, 181–95
FERNANDEZ, J. W. (1967) *Divinations, Confessions, Testimonies: Zulu Confrontations with the Social Superstructure*, Inst. Social Research, University of Natal, Occasional Paper No. 9
FISCHER, E. (1955) 'Über die sogenannte Hottentotschürze, nebst Bemerkungen über der Descensus Testiculorum', *Z. Morph. Anthrop.*, 47, 1, 58–66 [45]
FODOR, I. (1966) 'The problems in the classification of the African languages', *Publ. No. 5, Center for Afro-Asian Research of Hungarian Academy of Sciences*, Budapest, 1–158 [38]
FORTES, M. (1945) *The Dynamics of Clanship among the Tallensi*, London: Oxford University Press [196]
—— (1949) *The Web of Kinship among the Tallensi*, London: Oxford University Press [183 *bis*]
—— (1953) 'The structure of unilineal descent groups', *Amer. Anthrop.*, 55, 17–41
—— (1958) 'The developmental cycle in domestic groups' in J. Goody (1958)
—— (1965) 'Some reflections on ancestor worship in Africa' in M. Fortes and G. Dieterlen (eds.), *African Systems of Thought*, London: Oxford University Press [330]
FORTES, M. and E. EVANS-PRITCHARD (eds.) (1940) *African Political Systems*, London: Oxford University Press [260, 363]

FOUCHÉ, L. (1933) *Mapungubwe*, London: Cambridge University Press
FOURIE, H. C. M. (1921) *Amandebele van Fene Mahlangu en hun religieus-sociaal leven*, Zwolle: La Rivière en Voorhoeve [84, 290, 291 *bis*, 294, 297, 299, 316]
FOX, F. W. (1936) 'Diet and health in South Africa', *S. Afr. Med. J.*, 10, 25-36 [45]
FOX, R. (1967) *Kinship and Marriage*, Harmondsworth: Penguin
FOY, H., A. KONDI, A. REBELLO and F. MARTINS (1952) 'The distribution of sickle-cell trait and the incidence of sickle-cell anaemia in the negro tribes of Portuguese East Africa', *E. Afr. Med. J.*, 29, 7, 247-51 [28]
FRANKEL, S. H. (1938) *Capital Investment in Africa: Its course and effects*, London: Oxford University Press [413]
FRANKLIN, N. N. (n.d.) *Natives and the Administration of Justice*, Consultative Committee of Joint Councils, Lovedale
—— (1942) 'Industrial expansion and native policy in South Africa', *African Studies*, 1, 201-6
FRANZ, H. M. (1929) 'Mädchenbeschneidung in Nord-West Transvaal', *Die Brücke*, 6, Wiss. Beilage No. 2
FRASSETTO, F. (1909-18) *Lezioni di Antropologia*, Bologna: Corp. Tipografia-Libreria Mareggiana [14]
FREEMAN, J. J. (1851) *A Tour in South Africa*
FRIED, M. H. (1957) 'The classification of corporate unilineal descent groups', *J. Roy. Anthrop. Inst.*, 87, 1-29
FRITSCH, G. (1872) *Die Eingeborenen Süd-Afrikas ethnographisch und anatomisch beschrieben*, Breslau: Hirt
FULLER, C. E. (1953) 'The early Portuguese in Southern Africa', *African Studies*, 12:1, 31-7
GALBRAITH, J. S. (1959) 'The turbulent frontier as a factor in British expansion', *Comparative Studies in Society and History*, 2, 1959-60 [368, 370, 371 *bis*]
—— (1963) *Reluctant Empire*, Berkeley: University of California Press
GALLOWAY, A. (1937) 'A contribution to the physical anthropology of the Ovambo', *S. Afr. J. Sci.*, 34, 351-64 [10]
GARDINER, A. F. (1836) *Narrative of a Journey to the Zoolu Country in South Africa*, London: Crofts
GARN, S. M. (1961) *Human Races*, Springfield, Illinois: Thomas [45]
GARSON, N. G. (1957) 'The Swaziland Question and a Road to the Sea, 1887-1895', *Archives Year Book for South African History 1957*, vol. II, Pretoria: Government Printer [384]
GARVIN, J. L. (1935) *Life of Joseph Chamberlain*, I, London: Macmillan [382]
GATES, R. R. (1957) 'Forms of hair in South African races', *Man*, Contrib. No. 98, 1-4 [45]
GEAR, J. H. (1929) 'Cranial form in the native races of South Africa', *S. Afr. J. Sci.*, 26, 684-97 [14]
GERDENER, G. B. A. (1958) *Recent Developments in the South African Mission Field*, Cape Town: N. G. Kerk-uitgewers [415]
GIESEKKE, E. D. (1930) 'Die Eisenindustrie der Bawenda', *Die Brücke*, 7, 4, 5-9 [130, 363]
—— (1930-1) 'Wahrsagerei bei den Venda', *Zeitschrift für Eingeborenen Sprache*, 21, 257-310
GIESS, W. and K. L. TINLEY (1968) 'South West Africa' in I. and O. Hedberg (eds.), *Conservation of Vegetation in Africa South of the Sahara*, Uppsala
GILLMAN, J. and T. GILLMAN (1951) *Perspectives in Human Malnutrition*, New York: Grune & Stratton, pp. 1-584
GLANVILLE, E. V. (1969) 'Nasal shape, prognathism and adaptation in man', *Amer. J. Physi. Anthrop.*, 30, 1, 29-38 [13]
GLASS, S. (1968) *The Matabele War*, London: Longmans [384]

GLASS, Y. (1963) 'The industrialization of an indigenous people', *S. Afr. J. Sci.*, 58, 8, 386–94
GLUCKMAN, M. (1935) 'Zulu women in hoe cultural ritual', *Bantu Studies*, 9 [355–6]
—— (1937) 'Mortuary customs and the belief in the survival after death among the S.-E. Bantu', *Bantu Studies*, 11, 117–34
—— (1940) 'The kingdom of the Zulu of South Africa' in M. Fortes and E. Evans-Pritchard (eds.) (1940), pp. 25–55 [140–1, 249, 263, 279–80 *passim*]
—— (1942) 'Some processes of social change illustrated from Zululand', *African Studies*, 1, 4, 243–61
—— (1943) *Essays on Lozi Land and Royal Property*, Manchester University Press [146]
—— (1950) 'Kinship and marriage among the Lozi of Northern Rhodesia and the Zulu of Natal' in A. R. Radcliffe-Brown and Daryll Forde (eds.), *African Systems of Kinship and Marriage*, London: Oxford University Press, pp. 166–206 [163, 179–81 *passim*, 188–91 *passim*, 194 *bis*, 196]
—— (1954) *Rituals of Rebellion in South-East Africa*, Manchester University Press [323, 342, 363]
—— (1955a) *The Judicial Process Among the Barotse*, Manchester University Press [362]
—— (1955b) *Custom and Conflict in Africa*, Oxford: Blackwell [267, 280]
—— (1960) 'Tribalism in modern British Central Africa', *Cahiers d'Etudes Africaines*, 6 Sections, 55–70 [448]
—— (1961) 'Anthropological problems arising from the industrial revolution' in A. Southall (ed.), *Social Change in Modern Africa*, London: Oxford University Press for the International African Institute [169]
—— (1962) 'Les rites de passage' in M. Gluckman (ed.), *Essays on the Ritual of Social Relations*, Manchester University Press, pp. 1–52 [243]
—— (1965) *Politics, Law and Ritual in Tribal Societies*, Oxford: Blackwell [xv, 146, 255]
GODEE-MOLSBERGEN, E. C. (1922–32) *Reizen in Zuid-Afrika in de Hollandse Tijd*, 3, 4, Hague: Nijhoff (Linschoten Werken 20, 36)
GOODFELLOW, D. M. (1931) *Economic History of South Africa*, London: Routledge
GOODWIN, A. J. H. (1937) 'Habitat' in I. Schapera (ed.) (1937a), pp. 33–41 [47, 138]
GOODY, J. (ed.) (1958) *The Developmental Cycle in Domestic Groups*, Cambridge Papers in Social Anthropology No. 1., London: Cambridge University Press
—— (1959) 'The mother's brother and sister's son in West Africa', in *J. Roy. Anthrop. Inst.*, 89, 61 ff. [347]
GORDON, R. E. (1968) *Shepstone*, Cape Town: Balkema [376–7]
GOTTLIEB, D., J. REEVES and W. D. TEN HOUTEN (1966) *The Emergence of Youth Societies: a cross-cultural approach*, New York: Free Press [238]
GOTTSCHLING, E. (1905) 'The Bawenda: a sketch of their history and customs', *J. Roy. Anthrop. Inst.*, 35, 365–86
GRANDE, N. R. (1968) 'Zonas de drenagem venosa em rins de Portugueses Africanos', *Arquivo Ant. Antrop.*, 34, 165–74
GRANT, G. V. (1969) 'The Organization of Mental Abilities of an African Ethnic Group in Cultural Transition', Ph.D. thesis submitted to University of the Witwatersrand [472]
GREENBERG, H. (1955) *Studies in African Linguistic Classification*, New Haven, Connecticut: Compass Publishing [38 *bis*]
—— (1963) *Languages of Africa*, The Hague: Mouton [38 *bis*]
GROUT, L. (1862) *Zulu-Land; or Life among the Zulu-Kaffirs of Natal and Zululand*, London: Trübner
GULLIVER, P. H. (ed.) (1969a) *Tradition and Transition in East Africa*, London: Routledge & Kegan Paul [xix]
—— (1969b) 'Introduction' in P. H. Gulliver (ed.) (1969a), pp. 5–38 [xix]
GUMA, S. M. (1965) 'Some aspects of circumcision in Basutoland', *African Studies*, 24, 3–4, 241–51 [243]
GUSINDE, M. (1954) 'Twins in South Africa', *Anthropos*, 49, 685–7

GUTHRIE, M. (1962) 'Some developments in the pre-history of the Bantu languages', *J. Afr. History*, 3, 273–82 [38–9 *passim*]
HAILEY, BARON (1953) *Native Administration in the British African Territories*, V, London: HMSO [384 *bis*, 395]
HALLBECK, H. P. and J. G. FRITSCH (1826) 'Account of the Tambookies, (June 1827)', *Periodical Accounts . . . of the . . . United Brethren*, 10, 298–300, London [129]
HAMILTON, G. N. G. (1935) 'Ancient workings in Southern Swaziland', *S. Afr. J. Sci.*, 32, 582–6 [130]
HAMMOND-TOOKE, W. D. (1953) 'The function of annual first fruit festivals in Baca social structure', *African Studies*, 12, 2, 75–87
—— (1954) 'Baca, Hlubi and Xesibe' in A. M. Duggan-Cronin, *The Bantu Tribes of South Africa*, Vol. III, Sec. 5, London: Cambridge University Press
—— (1955) 'The initiation of a Baca *isangoma* diviner', *African Studies*, 14, 1, 16–22 [349]
—— (1956a) *The Tribes of the Mount Frere District*, Ethnological Publication No. 33, Pretoria: Government Printer
—— (1956b) *The Tribes of Umtata District*, Ethnological Publication No. 35, Pretoria: Government Printer
—— (1957) *The Tribes of Willowvale District*, Ethnological Publication No. 36, Pretoria: Government Printer [351]
—— (1958a) *The Tribes of King William's Town District*, Ethnological Publication No. 41, Pretoria: Government Printer
—— (1958b) 'The attainment of adult status among the East Griqualand Bhaca', *African Studies*, 17, 1, 16–20
—— (1960) 'Some Bhaca religious categories', *African Studies*, 19, 1, 1–13
—— (1962) *Bhaca Society: A People of the Transkeian Uplands, South Africa*, Cape Town: Oxford University Press [128–9 *passim*, 141–3 *passim*, 169, 173, 178–81 *passim*,, 183, 195–6, 198, 200–1, 204–5 *passim*, 214, 216, 218, 228–9 *passim*, 242, 245, 261, 288–9, 291, 304, 307, 311, 316, 317, 330, 333, 335, 337–8, 341 *bis*, 345, 349, 354–6 *passim*, 363, 425, 427–8, 440, 470]
—— (1963) 'Kinship, neighbourhood and association: hospitality groups among the Cape Nguni', *Ethnology*, 2, 3, 302–19 [152, 199–200 *passim*]
—— (1964) 'Chieftainship in Transkeian political development', *J. Modern African Studies*, 2, 4, 513–29
—— (1965a) 'Segmentation and fission in Cape Nguni political units', *Africa*, 35, 2, 143–67 [xv, 290, 368–9]
—— (1965b) 'In Search of the Sacred; a problem in the anthropological study of religion', Inaugural Lecture, Rhodes University, Grahamstown
—— (1968a) 'The morphology of Mpondomise descent groups', *Africa*, 38, 1, 26–45 [185, 195–7 *passim*, 200–2 *passim*, 210, 325–6, 329–30 *passim*, 347, 471]
—— (1968b) 'Descent group scatter in a Mpondomise ward', *African Studies*, 27, 2, 83–94 [471]
—— (1968c) 'The Transkeian council system, 1895–1955: an appraisal', *J. Afr. History*, 9, 3, 455–77 [389, 390, 395]
—— (1969a) 'The present state of Cape Nguni ethnographic studies' in *Ethnological and Linguistic Studies*, Pretoria: Government Printer, 81–97
—— (1969b) 'The "other side" of frontier history: a model of Cape Nguni political process' in L. M. Thompson (ed.) (1969)
—— (1970a) 'Urbanization and the interpretation of misfortune: a quantitative analysis', *Africa*, 40, 1, 25–38 [359]
—— (1970b) 'Tribal cohesion and the incorporative process in the Transkei, South Africa' in R. Cohen and J. Middleton (eds.), *From Tribe to Nation in Africa*, Scranton: Chandler
HANEKOM, C. (1967) 'Tradisionele geneeskunde by enkele Noord-Sothostamme', *African Studies*, 26, 37–42

HARINCK, G. (1969) 'Interaction between Xhosa and Khoi: emphasis on the period 1620-1750' in L. M. Thompson (ed.) (1969) [368]
HARRIES, C. H. L. (1906) *Handbook of Sepedi Law and Custom*, Pretoria: Government Printer
—— (1929) *The Laws and Customs of the Bapedi and Cognate Tribes of the Transvaal*, Johannesburg: Hortors [147, 269, 270, 297-300 *passim*, 309 *bis*, 316 *bis*]
HARRISON, G. A. (1957) 'The measurement and inheritance of skin colour in "man"', *Eugenics Rev.*, 49, 73-6 [17]
—— (1961) 'Pigmentation' in G. A. Harrison (ed.), *Genetical Variation in Human Populations*, London, New York: Pergamon, pp. 99-115 [20]
HARRISON, G. A. and J. J. T. OWEN (1956) 'The application of spectrophotometry to the study of skin colour inheritance', *Acta. Genet.*, 6, 481-4 [17, 18 *bis*]
HAYWARD, V. E. W. (ed.) (1963) *African Independent Church Movements*, I.M.C. Research pamphlets, No. 11, London: Edinburgh House [418]
HELLMANN, ELLEN (1934) 'The importance of beer-brewing in an urban Native yard', *Bantu Studies*, 8, 39-60
—— (1935a) 'Native life in a Johannesburg slum yard', *Africa*, 8, 34-62
—— (1935b) 'Methods of urban field work', *Bantu Studies*, 9, 185-202
—— (1936) 'Urban native food in Johannesburg', *Africa*, 9, 277-90
—— (1937) 'The native and the towns' in I. Schapera (ed.) (1937a), pp. 405-34 [468]
—— (1948) *Rooiyard: A Sociological Survey of an Urban Native Slum Yard*, Rhodes-Livingstone Papers No. 13, Cape Town: Oxford University Press [443, 447-9 *passim*, 461, 470, 471]
—— (1953) *Sellgoods: A Sociological Survey of an African Commercial Labour Force*, Johannesburg: SAIRR
—— (1967a) 'The African family today', paper delivered to conference on African family life organized by Southern Transvaal Region, South African Institute of Race Relations, and the Witwatersrand Christian Council (mimeographed), Johannesburg [458]
—— (1967b) *Soweto: Johannesburg's African City*, Johannesburg: SAIRR
HELM, J. (ed.) (1968) *Essays on the Problems of Tribe*, Seattle: American Ethnological Society [xix]
HERSKOVITS, M. J. (1926) 'The cattle complex in East Africa', *Amer. Anthrop.*, 28, 230-72, 361-8, 494-528, 633-64
HIERNAUX, J. (1955) 'Physical anthropology and the frequency of genes with a selective value: The sickle cell gene', *Am. J. Phys. Anthrop.*, 13, 3, 455-72 [28-9 *passim*]
—— (1959) 'Recent research at protohistoric sites in Ruanda, in the Belgian Congo (Katanga Province) and in Uganda (Kibiro)', *Uganda Mus. Occ. Pap.*, 4, 26-30 [45]
—— (1968a) *La Diversité humaine en Afrique subsaharienne*, Brussels: Université Libre, pp. 1-261 [34, 36-7, 40]
—— (1968b) 'Variabilité du dimorphisme sexuel de la stature en Afrique subsaharienne et en Europe' in G. Kurth (ed.), *Anthropologie und Humangenetik*, Stuttgart: Fischer, pp. 42-50
—— (1968c) 'Bantu expansion: the evidence from physical anthropology confronted with linguistic and archaeological evidence', *J. Afr. History*, 9, 4, 505-15 [32, 34, 38 *bis*, 40-3, 45]
HOERNLÉ, A. W. (1925) 'The importance of the sib in the marriage ceremonies of the S.E. Bantu', *S. Afr. J. Sci.*, 22, 484-92 [194]
—— (1928) 'Religion in Native life' in M. Stauffer (ed.), *Thinking With Africa*, London: Student Christian Movement
—— (1931) 'An outline of the Native conception of education in Africa', *Africa*, 4, 145-63
—— (1937a) 'Social organization' in I. Schapera (ed.) (1937a), pp. 67-94 [181, 186, 304, 306-7, 309, 314]

—— (1937b) 'Magic and medicine' in I. Schapera (ed.) (1937a), pp. 221–46
HOFFMANN, A. C. (1952) 'Venda dug-out canoe', *Researches of the National Museum*, 1, 23–8 [129]
HOFFMANN, C. (1914–15) 'Die Mannbarkeitsschule der Bassutho im Holzbuschgebirge Transvaals', *Z. Kol. Spr.*, 5, 81–112
HOFMEYR, J. D. J. (1967) 'Racial biology of the Bantu of South Africa' in R. E. Kuttner (ed.), *Race and Modern Science*, New York: Social Science Press, pp. 69–92
HOLLAND ROSE, J. et al. (eds.) (1936) *The Cambridge History of the British Empire*, VIII, London: Cambridge University Press [394]
HOLLEMAN, F. D. (1949) *Het Bantoe-Grondenrecht in die Unie van Zuid-Africa en Omgeving*, Amsterdam
HOLLEMAN, J. F. (1940) 'Die twee-eenheidsbeginsel in die sosiale en politieke samelewing van die Zulu', *Bantu Studies*, 14, 31–75 [141, 147–8 *passim*, 156, 165]
—— (1941) 'Die Zulu *isigodi*', *Bantu Studies*, 15, 91–118, 245–76
—— (1960) 'Bantu marriage at the cross-roads', *J. Rac. Affairs*, 11, 82–117
HOMANS, G. C. (1960) *English Villagers of the Thirteenth Century*, New York: Russell & Russell [176]
HORRELL, M. (1951–) *A Survey of Race Relations in South Africa*, Johannesburg: South African Institute of Race Relations (annual)
—— (1956) *South Africa's Non-White Workers*, Johannesburg: South African Institute of Race Relations
—— (1961) *South African Trade Unionism*, Johannesburg: South African Institute of Race Relations
HORWITZ, R. (1957) *Expand or Explode: Apartheid's Threat to Industry*, Cape Town: Business Bookman
HORWOOD, O. (1962) 'The private budget of the urban Native', *Optima*, Johannesburg
HOUGHTON, D. HOBART (1960a) 'Men of two worlds: some aspects of migratory labour', *S. Afr. J. Econ.*, 28, 3, 177–90 [470]
—— (ed.) (1960b) *Economic Development in a Plural Society*, Cape Town: Oxford University Press
—— (1961) 'Land reform in the Bantu areas and the effect upon urban labour', *S. Afr. J. Econ.*, 29, 3
—— (1967) *The South African Economy* (2nd edn.), Cape Town: Oxford University Press [404, 407, 413 *bis*]
HOUGHTON, D. H. and E. M. WALTON (1952) *The Economy of a Native Reserve: Keiskammahoek Rural Survey*, Vol. II, Pietermaritzburg: Shuter & Shooter [169–70, 173, 174, 444]
HUFFMAN, T. N. (1970) 'The early Iron Age and the spread of the Bantu', *S. Afr. Archaeol. Bull.*, 25, 97, 3–21
HUGHES, A. J. B. (1964) 'Demography: religious affiliation' in J. F. Holleman (ed.), *Experiment in Swaziland*, Cape Town: Oxford University Press, pp. 151–66 [421]
—— (1970) 'Land Tenure, Land Rights and Land Communities on Swazi National Land: A discussion of some inter-relationships between the traditional tenurial system and problems of agrarian development', unpublished Ph.D. thesis, University of Natal
HUGHES, A. J. B. and J. VAN VELSEN (1955) 'The Ndebele' in *The Shona and Ndebele of Southern Rhodesia*, Ethnographic Survey of Africa, Southern Africa, IV, London: International African Institute [129–30 *passim*]
HUNT, D. R. (1931) 'An account of the Bapedi', *Bantu Studies*, 5, 4, 275–326 [84, 268–9]
HUNT, K. S. (1970) 'The Governorships of Sir G. Lowry Cole in Mauritius (1823–8) and the Cape of Good Hope (1828–33): A Study in Colonial Administration', unpublished Ph.D. thesis: London University [370]
HUNTER, MONICA (1932) 'Results of culture contact on the Pondo and Xosa Family', *S. Afr. J. Sci.*, 29, 681–6

—— (1933) 'The effects of contact with Europeans on the status of Pondo women', *Africa*, 6, 259–76
—— (1934) 'Methods of study of culture contact', *Africa*, 7, 335–50
—— (1936) *Reaction to Conquest: effects of contact with Europeans on the Pondo of South Africa*, London: Oxford University Press [xvi, 128–30 *passim*, 141, 151–4 *passim*, 173, 201 *bis*, 204, 214, 219, 223–4 *passim*, 228–9, 241–2 *passim*, 284, 289–91 *passim*, 297, 300, 302 *bis*, 305, 307, 314, 316, 326–42 *passim*, 332 *bis*, 345, 347, 349, 353, 355–8 *passim*, 363, 415, 427, 440, 470]
—— (1937) 'The Bantu on European-owned farms' in I. Schapera (ed.) (1937a), pp. 389–404
—— (1938) 'Contact between Europeans and Natives in S. Africa, I. In Pondoland' in *Methods for the Study of Culture Contact in Africa* Memorandum XV, Int. African Inst.
HUTCHINSON, B. (1957) 'Some social consequences of nineteenth century minority culture among the South African Bantu', *Africa*, 27, 2, 160–1, 175
HUTT, W. H. (1934) 'The economic position of the Bantu in South Africa' in I. Schapera (ed.) (1934a), pp. 195–237
—— (1964) *The Economics of the Colour Bar*, London: Deutsch
HUTTON, C. W. (ed.) (1887) *The Autobiography of Sir Andries Stockenstrom, Bart.*, 2 vols. Cape Town: Juta [394]
ILI (INTER-AFRICAN LABOUR INSTITUTE) (1957) *Human Factors of Productivity in Africa: a Preliminary Survey*, London: CCTA [445, 470]
INSKEEP, R. R. (1960) 'Some Iron Age sites in Northern Rhodesia', *S. Afr. Archaeol. Bull.*, 17, 67, 136–80 [412]
ISAACS, N. (1836) *Travels and Adventures in Eastern Africa; description of the Zulus, their manners, customs, etc.*, 2 vols, London: Churton [129]
JACKSON, A. O. (1969) 'The Langa Ndebele calendar and annual agricultural ceremonies' in *Ethnological and Linguistic Studies in Honour of N. J. van Warmelo*, Pretoria: Government Printer, 233–42 [355]
JACOBSON, A. (1967) 'The Bantu Dentition: A Morphological and Metrical Study of the Teeth, the Jaws and the Bony Palate of Several Large Groups of South African Bantu-Speaking Negroids', thesis accepted for the degree of Doctor of Philosophy in the University of the Witwatersrand, Johannesburg, pp. 1–458 [14, 15]
JACOTTET, E. (1896–7) 'Moeurs, coutumes et superstitions des BaSouto', *Bull. Soc. Géog.*, 9, 107 151, Neuchâtel
JACQUES, A. A. (1929) 'Terms of kinship and corresponding patterns of behaviour among the Thonga', *Bantu Studies*, 3, 327–48
—— (1931) 'Notes on the Lemba tribe of the Northern Transvaal', *Anthropos*, 26, 245–51
—— (1934) 'Genealogy of male and female chiefs of a Sotho tribe', *Bantu Studies*, 8, 377–82
JANISCH, M. (1941) 'Some administrative aspects of native marriage problems in an urban area', *Bantu Studies*, 15, 1–11
JANSEN, G. J. (1966) 'Some observations about ritual mutilation in a Transkei mission hospital, with special reference to the *ingqithi* custom', *African Studies*, 25, 2, 73–81
JASPAN, M. A. (1953), 'A sociological case study: communal hostility to imposed change in South Africa' in P. Duopp (ed.), *Approaches to Community Development*, The Hague: van Hoeve [169]
JEFFREYS, K. (ed.) (1928) *Kaapse argiefstukken, 1780*, Cape Times [367]
JEFFREYS, M. D. W. (1951) 'Lobolo *is* child-price', *African Studies*, 10, 4 [188]
—— (1953) 'Negro birth-sex ratios', *S. Afr. J. Sci.*, 50, 114–15
—— (1956) 'Some rules of directed culture change under Roman Catholicism', *Amer. Anthrop.*, 58, 721–31
JENKINS, T. (1969) 'Haemoglobins and anthropology' (manuscript), presented to Symposium on Sero-Anthropology, *S. Afr. Inst. Med. Res.*, 12 December 1969, pp. 1–7 [28 *bis*]

JENKINS, T., H. C. HARPENDING, H. GORDON, M. M. KERAAN and S. JOHNSTON (1971) 'Red cell enzyme polymorphisms in the Khoisan peoples of Southern Africa', *Am. J., Human Genetics*, 23, 513–32 [45]

JENKINS, T. and A. G. STEINBERG (1966) 'Some serum protein polymorphisms in Kalahari Bushmen and Bantu: gammaglobulins, haptoglobins and transferrins', *Am. J. Hum. Genet.*, 18, 399–407 [23, 26]

JENKINS T., A. ZOUTENDYK and A. G. STEINBERG (1970) 'Gammaglobulin groups (Gm and Inv) of various Southern African populations', *Am. J. Phys. Anthrop.*, 32, 2, 197–218 [26–7, 31, 34–5, 43–4]

JERSKY, J. and R. H. KINSLEY (1967) 'Lactose deficiency in the S. A. Bantu', *S.A. Med. J.*, 41, 1194–6 [83]

JOHNSTON, F. E. (1964) 'Racial taxonomies from an evolutionary perspective', *Amer. Anthrop.*, 66, 822–7 [45]

JONES, G. I. (1966) 'Chiefly succession in Basutoland' in J. Goody (ed.), *Succession to High Office*, London: Cambridge University Press [191, 207]

JONES, J. D. R. (1934) 'Social and economic condition of the urban Native' in I. Schapera (ed.), (1934a), pp. 159–92

JONES, S. M. (1963) 'A study of Swazi nutrition', report of the Swaziland Nutrition Survey 1961–62 for the Swaziland Administration, University of Natal, Durban: Inst. Soc. Res., pp. 1–264 [45]

JUNOD, H. A. (1905–6) 'The theory of witchcraft amongst South African Natives', *S. Afr. J. Sci.*, 3, 230–41

—— (1908) 'The Balemba of the Zoutpansberg', *Folk-Lore*, 19, 276–87

—— (1910) 'Les conceptions physiologiques des Bantous sud-africains et leurs tabous', *Rev. d'Ethnogr. et de Sociologie*, 1, 126–69

—— (1914) 'The condition of the Natives of South East Africa in the 16th century according to the early Portuguese documents', *S. Afr. J. Sci.*, 10, 137–61 [84]

—— (1920) 'Some features of the religion of the BaVenda', *S. Afr. J. Sci.*, 17, 207–20

—— (1924) 'Le totémisme chez les Thongas, les Pèdis et les Vendas', *Le Globe*, 63, 1–22

—— (1925) 'La divination au moyen de tablettes d'ivoire chez les Pèdis', *Bull. Soc. Géog.*, 34, 38–56, Neuchâtel

—— (1927) *The Life of a South African Tribe* (2nd ed., revised and enlarged), 2 vols, London: Macmillan (reprinted 1963) [69 bis, 84, 129–31 passim, 171, 178, 189, 214–15, 217–19 passim, 241, 242 bis, 305, 319, 320, 324, 326–8 passim, 332–4 passim, 345–7 passim, 354, 356, 363 bis]

—— (1929) 'La seconde école de circoncision chez les Ba-Khaha du Nord de Transvaal', *J. Roy. Anthrop. Inst.*, 59, 131–47

—— (1932) 'Le sacrifice dans l'ancêtrolatrie Sud-Africaine', *Archives de Psychologie*, 23, 303–35

KATZEN, L. B. (1961) 'The case for minimum wage legislation in South Africa', *S. Afr. J. Econ.*, 29, 3

KAY, S. (1833) *Travels and Researches in Kaffraria*, London: Mason [128, 129, 130]

KEAY, R. W. et al. (1959) *Vegetation Map of Africa South of the Tropic of Cancer*, London: Oxford University Press

KERR, A. J. (1953) *The Native Common Law of Immovable Property in South Africa*, Durban: Butterworth [288, 304, 310 bis, 311, 315]

—— (1957) 'The application of Native law in the Supreme Court', *S.A. Law J.*, 74, 313–30

—— (1958) 'The reception and codification of systems of law in Southern Africa', *J. African Law*, 2, 89–100

—— (1960) 'Roman-Dutch Law marriages and the *lobola* contract', *Acta Juridica*, 334–8

—— (1961) *The Native Law of Succession in South Africa*, London: Butterworth (African Law Series, No. 3)

—— (1963) *Law and Justice*, Grahamstown

BIBLIOGRAPHICAL INDEX

—— (1964) 'Bantu law in the Republic of South Africa', E/31 in J. Gilissen (ed.), *Bibliographical Institution to Legal History and Ethnology*, Brussels: Université Libre de Bruxelles
KEYTER, C. (n.d.) *Feeding Customs and Food Habits of Urban Africans*, Johannesburg: South African Institute of Race Relations
KIDD, D. (1904) *The Essential Kaffir*, London: Black
—— (1906) *Savage Childhood: a study of Kaffir children*, London: Black
KIRBY, P. R. (1934) *The Musical Instruments of the Native Races of South Africa*, London: Oxford University Press [130 *bis*]
—— (1937) 'The musical practices of the native races of South Africa' in I. Schapera (ed.) (1937a), pp. 274-81 [111]
—— (1943) 'South African native drums', *S. Afr. Museum Assoc. Bull.*, 3, 2, 48 [84, 106]
—— (1954) 'Gquma, Ndepa and the ama Tshomane clan; a by-way of miscegenation in South Africa', *African Studies*, 13, 1, 1-25
KISTNER, W. (1952) 'The anti-slavery agitation against the Transvaal Republic 1852-68', *Archives Year Book for South African History*, vol. II, Pretoria: Government Printer [385]
KOHLER, M. (1931) 'Die Krankengeschichte eines Zulu-Kaffern', *Anthropos*, 26, 585-93
—— (1933) *Marriage Customs in Southern Natal*, Ethnological Publications, Vol. iv, Pretoria: Government Printer [229]
KOKOT, D. F. (1948) 'An investigation into the evidence bearing on recent climatic changes over Southern Africa', *Irrigation Dept. Mem.*, 48 [48]
KRIEL, F. (1960) *Die Aansluiting van die Christelike Sending by die Kultuureie van die Bantoe*, Pretoria
KRIGE, E. J. (1931) 'Agricultural ceremonies and practices of the Balobedu', *Bantu Studies*, 5, 207-40 [261]
—— (1932) 'The social significance of beer among the BaLobedu', *Bantu Studies*, 6, 343-57 [129]
—— (1936a) *The Social System of the Zulus*, London: Longmans [128-31 *passim*, 147-8 *passim*, 156, 164-5, 178-9, 201, 204-5 *passim*, 213-14, 219, 225-6 *passim*, 280, 285-6, 288-91 *passim*, 293-4, 296-8 *passim*, 290 *bis*, 300 *bis*, 301-7 *passim*, 316, 317, 324, 326, 328-9, 332, 340, 346, 349, 353-4, 357 *bis*]
—— (1936b) 'Changing conditions in marital relations and parental duties among urbanized natives', *Africa*, 9, 1-23 [297]
—— (1937a) 'Note on the Phalaborwa and their morula complex', *Bantu Studies*, 11, 357-66
—— (1937b) 'Individual development' in I. Schapera (ed.) (1937a), pp. 95-118 [228-9, 303-8 *passim*, 316]
—— (1938) 'The place of the North-Eastern Transvaal Sotho in the South Bantu complex', *Africa*, 11, 265-93 [266 *bis*, 274, 276-8 *passim*]
—— (1941) 'Economics of exchange in a primitive society', *S. Afr. J. Econ.*, 9, 1
—— (1964) 'Property, cross-cousin marriage, and the family cycle among the Lobedu' in R. F. Gray and P. H. Gulliver (eds) *The Family Estate in Africa*, London: Routledge & Kegan Paul [160, 180-5 *passim*, 191-2 *passim*, 194-5 *passim*, 202-6 *passim*, 274]
—— (1968) 'Girls' puberty songs and their relation to fertility, health, morality and religion among the Zulu', *Africa*, 38, 2, 173-97 [227, 261, 342, 363]
—— (ed.) (1969a) 'Some Zulu concepts important for an understanding of fertility and other rituals' in *Ethnological and Linguistic Studies in Honour of N. J. van Warmelo*, Pretoria: Government Printer, pp. 13-20
—— (1969b) 'Report on an Ecological Study of the Tembe-Thonga of Natal and Mozambique', unpublished MS., University of Natal [184, 196 *bis*]
KRIGE, J. D. (1934) 'Bride-wealth in Balobedu marriage ceremonies', *Bantu Studies*, 8, 135-49 [180]

—— (1937) 'Traditional origins and tribal relationships of the Sotho of the Northern Transvaal', *Bantu Studies*, 11, 321–56 [278]
—— (1939) 'Some aspects of Lovhedu judicial arrangements', *Bantu Studies*, 13, 113–29
—— (1944) 'The magical thought-pattern of the Bantu in relation to health services', *African Studies*, 3, 1, 1–13
KRIGE, E. J. and J. D. KRIGE (1943) *The Realm of a Rain Queen*, London: International African Institute [xvii, 99, 127, 128–30 *passim*, 155 *bis*, 170, 172, 174–5, 178 *bis*, 180, 189–92 *passim*, 195, 202, 204 *bis*, 207, 214, 218, 222–4 *passim*, 227–8, 232–3 *passim*, 238, 240, 242–5 *passim*, 274–5 *passim*, 277–9 *passim*, 321, 325–6, 328, 330–4 *passim*, 337–9 *passim*, 342, 346, 348 *bis*, 350, 352–3, 355, 357–8, 362, 421, 425, 427–9 *passim*, 433]
—— (1954) 'The Lobedu of the Transvaal' in D. Forde (ed.), *African Worlds*, London: Oxford University Press, pp. 55–82 [319]
KROLL, H. (1928) 'Die Haustiere der Bantu', *Z. f. Ethnol.*, 60, 177–290
KROPF, A. (1889) *Das Volk der Xosa-Kaffern im östlichen Südafrika*, Berlin: Evangel. Missionsgesellschaft [129 *bis*, 284, 291]
—— (1915) *A Kafir-English Dictionary* (2nd edn, ed. R. Godfrey), Alice, Cape Province: Lovedale Press [306]
KRUGER, F. (1937) 'Tlôkwa traditions', *Bantu Studies*, 11, 85–115
KUPER, A. (1970) *Kalahari Village Politics: An African Democracy*, Cambridge Studies in Social Anthropology 3, Cambridge
KUPER, H. (1941) 'The development of a primitive nation', *Bantu Studies*, 15, 339–68
—— (1943) 'The uniform of colour in Swaziland', *African Studies*, 2, 97–107
—— (1945) 'Marriage of a Swazi princess', *Africa*, 15, 3, 145–55
—— (1946) 'The Swazi reaction to missions', *African Studies*, 5, 177–88
—— (1947a) *An African Aristocracy*, London: Oxford University Press [xvii, 202, 206, 249, 261, 319, 324 *bis*, 342 *bis*, 363]
—— (1947b) *The Uniform of Colour*, Johannesburg: Witwatersrand University Press [192]
—— (1950) 'Kinship among the Swazi' in A. R. Radcliffe-Brown and Forde, D. (eds) *African Systems of Kinship and Marriage*: London: Oxford University Press, pp. 86–110 [178, 188, 189, 192, 194, 206]
—— (1952) *The Swazi*, Ethnographic Survey of Africa, Daryll Forde (ed.), London: International African Institute [154, 195, 204]
—— (1963) *The Swazi: a South African Kingdom*, New York: Holt, Rinehart & Winston [213, 215, 219, 220]
—— (1965) 'The Swazi of Swaziland' in J. L. Gibbs (ed)., *Peoples of Africa*, New York: Holt, Rinehart & Winston [151 *bis*, 264]
KUPER, H. and S. KAPLAN (1944) 'Voluntary associations in an urban township', *African Studies*, 3, 4, 178–86 [472]
LAGERCRANTZ, S. (1937) 'Ethnographical reflections on Hottentot aprons', *Ethnos*, 4, 145–74 [22, 23]
LAIDLER, P. W. (1931) 'Social survey of an urban Native location', *Annual Report of the M.O.H., East London, 1930–1*, pp. 29–78
LANDELL-MILLS, P. (1970) 'Rural income and urban wage returns', *Botswana Notes and Records*, 2, 79–84 [168]
LANHAM, L. W. (1964) 'The proliferation and extension of Bantu phonetic systems influenced by Bushman and Hottentot', *Proc. Ninth. Int. Congr. Ling.*, Cambridge, Mass. (1962), The Hague
LANGUAGE, F. J. (1942) 'Herkoms en geskiedenis van die Tlhaping', *African Studies*, 1, 115–33
—— (1943a) *Stamregering by die Tlhaping*, Stellenbosch: Pro. Ecclesia [288, 290–1, 293, 294 *bis*, 298–9 *passim*]
—— (1943b) 'Die verkryging en verlies van lidmaatskap tot die stam by die Tlhaping', *African Studies*, 2, 77–92

—— (1943c) 'Die *bogwera* van die Tlhaping', *Tydskrif vir Wetenskap en Kuns*, 4, 110–34
LAREDO, J. E. (1968) *Patterns of Socio-economic Transition: A Study in a Bantu Reserve in the Three Rivers District of Natal*, Inst. for Soc. Res., University of Natal
LARSON, T. (1966) 'Significance of rainmaking for the Mbukushu', *African Studies*, 25 (1), 23–36
LASKER, G. W. (1954) 'Photoelectric measurement of skin colour in a Mexican mestizo population', *Amer. J. Phys. Anthrop.*, 12, 115–22 [18]
LAUBSCHER, B. J. F. (1937) *Sex, Custom and Psychopathology*, London: Routledge
LAUTENSCHLAGER, P. G. M. (1963) *Die Sozialen Ordnungen bei den Zulu und die Mariannhiller Mission 1882–1909*, Reinlingen
LAVANHA, J. B. (1593) (1597) (1898) 'Naufragio da nao *Santo Alberto* no Penedo das fontes no anno de 1593' (Wreck of the ship *Saint Albert* at the rock of the fountains in the year 1593) in G. M. Theal (1898–1902), 2, pp. 225–346 [130]
LAWTON, A. C. (1967) 'Bantu pottery of Southern Africa', *Ann. S. Afr. Mus.*, 49 (1) [72, 84, 130]
LAYDEVANT, F. (1931) 'Étude sur la famille en Basutoland' *J. Soc. Africanistes*, 1, 207–57
—— (1933) 'The praises of the divining bones among the BaSotho', *Bantu Studies*, 7, 341–73
LEACH, E. R. (1951) 'The structural implications of matrilateral cross-cousin marriage', *J. Roy. Anthrop. Inst.*, 81, 23–55 [273–8 *passim*]
LEAKEY, M. D., W. E. OWEN and L. S. B. LEAKEY (1948) 'Dimple-based pottery from Central Kavirondo, Kenya Colony', *Coryndon Mem. Mus. Occ. Pap.*, No. 2, 1–43
LEBZELTER, V. (1933) 'Das Betschuanendorf Epukiro (Südwestafrika)', *Z. f. Ethnol.*, 65, 44–74
—— (1934) *Eingeborenenkulturen in Südwest-und Südafrika*, Leipzig: Hiersemann
LEGASSICK, M. (1969) 'The Sotho-Tswana peoples before 1800' in L. M. Thompson (ed.) (1969), pp. 86–123
LEGUEBE, A. (1961) 'Contribution a l'étude de la pigmentation chez l'homme' (1ère partie) *Inst. Roy. des Sci. Nat. du Belg.*, 37, 1–29 [18]
LEHMANN, H. (1954) 'Distribution of the sickle-cell gene: a new light on the origin of the East Africans', *Eugen. Rev.*, 46, 1–23 [28]
LEHMANN, H. and M. CUTBUSH (1952a) 'Sickle-cell trait in Southern India', *Brit. Med. J.*, 1, 404–5 [28]
—— (1952b) 'Sub-division of some Southern Indian communities according to the incidence of sickle-cell trait and blood groups', *Trans. Roy. Soc. Trop. Med. Hyg.*, 46, 380–3
LEISTNER, G. M. E. (1964) 'Patterns of urban Bantu labour', *S. Afr. J. Econ.*, 32, 4, 253–77
—— (1967) 'Foreign Bantu workers in South Africa: their present position in the economy', *S. Afr. J. Econ.*, 35, 1, 30–56
LESLIE, D. (1875) *Among the Zulus and Amatongas*, London: Macmillan
LESTRADE, G. P. (1926) 'Some notes on the *bogadi* system of the BaHurutshe', *S. Afr. J. Sci.*, 23, 937–42
—— (1928) 'Some notes on the political organization of the BeChwana', *S. Afr. J. Sci.*, 25, 427–32
—— (1930a) 'Some notes on the political organization of the Venda-speaking tribes', *Africa*, 3, 306–22
—— (1930b) 'The *mala* system of the Venda-speaking tribes', *Bantu Studies*, 4, 193–204
—— (1932) 'Some notes on the political organization of the Venda-speaking tribes' in N. J. van Warmelo (ed.) (1932), pp. 1–11 [351]
—— (1934) 'Some aspects of the economic life of the South African Bantu', *S. Afr. J. Econ.*, 2, 426–43
—— (1937a) 'Some notes on the political organization of certain Xhosa-speaking tribes of the Transkeian Territories', *Trans. Roy. Soc. S. Afr.*, 24, 4, 281ff.

—— (1937b) 'Domestic and communal life' in I. Schapera (ed.) (1937a), pp. 119–30
LEUBUSCHER, C. (1931) *Der Südafrikanische Eingeborene als Industriearbeiter und als Stadtbewohner*, Jena: Fischer
LÉVI-STRAUSS, C. (1965) 'The future of kinship studies', *Proc. Roy. Anthrop. Inst.*, 13–22
—— (1969) *The Elementary Structures of Kinship*, London: Eyre & Spottiswoode (English trans. of 1949 French ed.) [205]
LEWIN, J. (1940) 'Native law and its background: the limits of tribal law in modern Bantu life', *Race Rel. J.*, 7, 2
—— (1941) 'A short survey of Native law in South Africa', *Bantu Studies*, 15, 65–90
—— (1947) *Studies in African Native Law*, Cape Town
LICHTENSTEIN, H. (1812) *Reisen im Südlichen Africa*, 2 vols, Berlin: Salfeld, [130 bis]
LIENGME, G. (1901) 'Un potentat africain: Goungounyane et son règne', *Bull. Soc. Géog.*, 13, 99–135, Neuchâtel
LINDBLOM, K. G. (1931) 'The use of oxen as pack and riding animals in Africa', *Riksmuseets Etnografiska Avdelning Smärre Meddelanden*, 10, [129]
LIVINGSTONE, F. B. (1958) 'Anthropological implications of sickle-cell gene distribution in West Africa', *Amer. Anthrop.*, 60, 533–62
—— (1962) 'On the non-existence of human races', *Curr. Anthrop.*, 3, 279 [45]
—— (1969) 'Polygenic models for the evolution of human skin colour differences', *Human Biol.*, 41, 4, 480–93 [20 bis]
LLOYD, H. (n.d.) MS. letter in Cory Library, Rhodes University, Grahamstown
LOEB, E. M. (1948) 'Transition rites of the Kuanyama Ambo' (2 parts), *African Studies*, 7, 16–28, 71–84
LOMBARD, J. A., J. J. STADLER and P. J. VAN DER MERWE (1968) *The Concepts of Economic Co-Operation in Southern Africa*, Pretoria
LONGMORE, L. (1952) 'Death and burial customs of the Bapedi of Sekukuniland', *African Studies*, 11, 2, 83–4
—— (1959) *The Dispossessed: A study of the sex-life of Bantu women in urban areas in and around Johannesburg*, London: Cape [59, 465 bis, 469, 470–1 passim]
LORAM, C. T. (1926) 'The separatist church movement', *Int. Rev. Missions*, 15, 476–82
LOUDON, J. B. (1970) *White Farmers and Black Labour-tenants: a study of a farming community in the South African Province of Natal*, Cambridge: African Studies Centre (Afr. Soc. Res. Doc. 1), pp. 1–135 [xvi]
LUGG, H. C. (1929) 'Agricultural ceremonies in Natal and Zululand', *Bantu Studies*, 3, 357–83
—— (1945) 'The practice of *lobolo* in Natal', *African Studies*, 4, 23–7
LYE, W. F. (1967) 'The *Difaqane*; The *Mfecane* in the Southern Sotho area, 1822–4', *J. Afr. History*, 8, 1, 107–31 [84, 379]
—— (1969a) 'The Ndebele kingdom south of the Limpopo', *J. Afr. History*, 10, 1 (1969), 87–104 [379, 383, 385]
—— (1969b) 'The distribution of the Sotho peoples after the Difaqane' in L. M. Thompson (ed.) (1969), pp. 191–206 [84]
MABILLE, H. E. (1905) 'The Basutos of Basutoland', *J. African Society*, 5, 233–51, 351–76
MACDONALD, J. (1889–90) 'Manners, customs, superstitions, and religions of South African tribes', *J. Roy. Anthrop. Inst.*, 19, 264–96; 20, 113–40
MACKENZIE, J. (1871) *Ten Years North of the Orange River* Edinburgh: Edmondston & Douglas [252–3, 268]
—— (1887) *Austral Africa: Losing it or Ruling it*, 2 vols, London: Sampson Low [254, 381]
MCKNIGHT, J. D. (1967) 'Extra-descent group ancestor cults in African societies', *Africa*, 37, 1, 1–20 [333, 335]

MACLAREN, P. I. R. (1958) 'The fishing devices of Central and Southern Africa', *Occ. Papers Rhodes-Livingstone Mus.*, 12, 1–48 [129]

MACLEAN, J. (1858a) *A Compendium of Kafir Laws and Customs*, Mount Coke: Wesleyan Mission Press; London: Cass, 1968 (reprint) [323, 373]

—— (1858b) 'Queries' in J. Maclean (ed.) (1858a), Ch. 6, pp. 140–8 [290 *bis*]

MACMILLAN, W. M. (1963) *Bantu, Boer and Briton* (rev. ed), London: Oxford University Press [369, 370, 375, 395]

MAFEJE, A. (1964) 'Leadership in the Transkei', unpublished M.A. thesis, University of Cape Town

MAGUBANE, B. (n.d.) 'Sport and politics in an urban African community: A study of African voluntary organizations', unpublished thesis, University of Natal

MAHLOBO, G. W. and E. J. KRIGE (1934) 'Transition from childhood to adulthood amongst the Zulus', *Bantu Studies*, 8, 157–91

MAINGARD, L. E. (1932) 'History and distribution of the bow and arrow in South Africa', *S. Afr. J. Sci.*, 29, 711–23

MALINOWSKI, B. (1929) *The Sexual Life of Savages*, New York: Harcourt, Brace

MANSVELT, P. R. and J. D. SKINNER (1962) *The Cattle of the Bavenda*, Pretoria: Government Printer

MARAIS, J. S. (1937) 'The imposition and nature of European control' in I. Schapera (ed.) (1937a), pp. 333–56

—— (1939) *The Cape Coloured People*, London: Longmans [370, 375]

MARKS, S. (1969) 'The traditions of the Natal "Nguni": a second look at the work of A. T. Bryant' in L. M. Thompson (ed.) (1969), pp. 126–44

—— (1970) *Reluctant Rebellion*, Oxford: Clarendon Press [378]

MARQUARD, L. (1962) *The Peoples and Policies of South Africa* (3rd edn), London: Oxford University Press

MARTIN, M. (1903a) *Basutoland*, London: Nichols [156–7]

—— (1903b) 'Basutoland, its legends and customs', *Folk-Lore*, 14, 414–18

MARTIN, M. L. (1964) *The Biblical Concept of Messianism and Messianism in Southern Africa, etc.* Morija: Morija Sesuto Book Depot

MARTIN, R. and K. SALLER (1959) *Lehrbuch der Anthropologie* Vols 1–4, Stuttgart: Gustav Fischer Verlag [10]

MARTINS, D. DA C. (1968) 'Dinâmica do crescimento e desenvolvimento da crianca em Mocambique', Dissertacao de Doutoramento apresentada à Faculdade de Medicina de Coimbra, Coimbra, pp. 1–197; tables 1–64

MARWICK, B. A. (1940) *The Swazi*, London: Cambridge University Press; London: Cass, 1966 (reprint) [128–30 *passim,* 201, 287, 288 *bis*, 290–1, 297–300 *passim*, 314, 316, 317, 363]

MARWICK. M. G. (1952). 'The social context of Cewa witch beliefs', *Africa*, 22, 120–35, 215–33

—— (1958) 'The modern family in social-anthropological perspective', *African Studies*, 17, 3, 137–58 [xviii]

—— (1965) *Sorcery in its Social Setting*, Manchester University Press

MARX, L. (1903) 'Die Amahlubi' in S. R. Steinmetz (ed) *Rechtsverhältnisse von eingeborenen Völkern in Afrika und Ozeanien*, Berlin: Springer, pp. 346–59 [291, 293, 297–8, 307 *bis*, 309–10, 316, 317 *bis*]

MASSIE, R. H. (1905) *Native Tribes of the Transvaal*, London: HMSO [247]

MATTHEWS, J. W. (1887) *Incwadi Yami or Twenty Years Personal Experience in South Africa*, New York: Rogers & Sherwood

MATTHEWS, Z. K. (1940) 'Marriage customs among the Barolong', *Africa*, 13, 1–24

MAYER, P. (1954) *Witches*, Inaugural Lecture, Rhodes University, Grahamstown

—— (1961) *Townsmen or Tribesmen: Conservatism and the Process of Urbanization in a South African City*, Cape Town: Oxford University Press

—— (1962) 'Migrancy and the study of Africans in town', *Amer. Anthrop.*, 64, 3 (1), 576–92
—— (1963) 'Some forms of religious organization in a South African city' in *Urbanization in African Social Change*, Proceedings of the inaugural seminar held in the Centre of African Studies, University of Edinburgh, 5–7 January 1963, Edinburgh University Press, pp. 113–26
—— (ed.) (1970) *Socialization: The Approach from Social Anthropology*, London: Tavistock, ASA Monographs No. 8
MAYER, P. and I. MAYER (1970) 'Socialization by peers: the youth organization of the Red Xhosa' in P. Mayer (ed.) (1970), pp. 159–89
MAYR, F. (1906–7) 'The Zulu Kaffirs of Natal', *Anthropos*, 1, 453–71; 2, 392–9, 633–45
—— (1907) 'Language of colours amongst the Zulus', *Annals of the Natal Museum*, 1, 159–65
MBATHA, M. B. (1960) 'Migrant Labour and Its Effects on Tribal and Family Life among the Nyuswa of Botha's Hill', unpublished M.A. thesis, University of Natal [187, 197, 198, 201 *bis*]
MEAD, M. (1943) 'Our educational emphases in primitive perspective', *Amer. J. of Soc.*, 48, 6, 633–9 [242]
MEARS, W. G. (1934) 'The educated Native in Bantu communal life' in I. Schapera (ed.) (1934a), pp. 85–101
MEINHOF, C. (1905) 'Hottentotische Laube und Lehnworte im Kafir', *Z. d. Dtsch. Morgenl. Ges.*, 58, 727–69; 59, 36–89 [84]
MEYEROWITZ, H. V. (1936) *Report on the Possibilities of the Development of Village Crafts in Basutoland*, Morija
MIDDLETON, J. and E. H. WINTER (eds) (1963) *Witchcraft and Sorcery in East Africa*, London: Routledge & Kegan Paul
MITCHELL, J. C. (1956a) 'Urbanization, detribalization and stabilization in Southern Africa' in *Social Implications of Industrialization and Urbanization in Africa South of the Sahara*, Paris: UNESCO (prepared by International African Institute) [448]
—— (1956b) *The Kalela Dance*, Rhodes-Livingstone Paper No. 27, Manchester University Press [xvi]
—— (1959) 'Labour migration in Africa South of the Sahara: the causes of labour migration' *Bull. Inter-Afri. Labour Inst.*, 61 [175 *bis*]
—— (1960) *Tribalism and the Plural Society*, Inaugural Lecture given in the University College of Rhodesia and Nyasaland on 2 October 1959, University College of Rhodesia, Salisbury (reprinted 1966) [449]
—— (1966) 'Theoretical orientations in African urban studies' in Michael Banton (ed.); *The Social Anthropology of Complex Societies*, London: Tavistock [446, 471]
—— (1969) *Social Networks in Urban Situations: Analyses of Personal Relationships in Central African Towns*, Manchester University Press [470]
MOFFAT, R. (1842) *Missionary Labours and Scenes in Southern Africa*, London: Snow [130]
MOGEY, J. (ed.) (1963) *Family and Marriage*, International Studies in Sociology and Social Anthropology No. 1, Leiden, Brill
MOLEMA, S. M. (1920) *The Bantu, Past and Present*, Edinburgh: Green
MÖNNIG, H. O. (1961) 'Lobedu kinship terminology', *African Studies*, 20, 4, 226–37
—— (1963a) 'The BaRoka ba Nkwana', *African Studies*, 22, 4, 170–6
—— (1963b) 'The structure of Lobedu social and political organization', *African Studies*, 22, 2, 49–65 [276, 278]
—— (1967) *The Pedi*, Pretoria: van Schaik [128–30 *passim*, 144, 181, 182, 185, 191–4 *passim*, 196–7 *passim*, 200, 202–5 *passim*, 214–16 *passim*, 221–3 *passim*, 226, 232–3 *passim*, 241–4 *passim*, 245, 285, 290–1 *passim*, 299, 310, 316, 317 *bis*, 319–31 *passim*, 349–50, 352, 354–5, 363, 421, 427–9 *passim*]
MONTAGU, M. F. A. (1962) 'The concept of race', *Amer. Anthrop.*, 64, 919–28 [45]

MOORCROFT, E. K. (1967) 'Theories of Millenarianism with reference to certain Southern African Movements', unpublished B. Litt. thesis, Oxford University [374]
MOORE-SMITH, G. C. (ed.) (1902) *The Autobiography of Lieutenant-General Sir Harry Smith*, London: Murray [371]
MORANT, G. M. (1927) 'Studies of Palaeolithic Man. II: A biometric study of Neanderthaloid skulls and of their relationships to modern racial types', *Ann. Eugen.*, 2, 3/4, 318–81 [13]
MORGAN, N. (1833) 'An account of the Amakosae', *S. Afr. Quarterly Journal*, 2nd series, I, 1–12, 33–48, 65–71
MQOTSI, L. and N. MKELE (1946) 'A separatist church: *Ibandla lika Krestu*', *African Studies*, 5, 106–25 [439]
MUDAU, E. (1940) 'Ngoma Lungundu' in N. J. van Warmelo (ed.) (1940), pp. 109–32 [84]
MÜLLER, A. (1906–7) 'Wahrsagerei bei den Kaffern', *Anthropos*, 1, 762–78; 2, 43–58
—— (1917–18) 'Zur materiellen Kultur der Kaffern', *Anthropos*, 12, 13, 852–8 [130]
MÜLLER, C. F. J. (1948) *Die Britse Owerheid en Die Groot Trek*, Cape Town: Juta [370, 385]
MÜLLER, F. (1926) *Die Hlubikaffern: Land und Leben*, Herrnhut; Missionsbuchhandlung
MÜLLER, H. P. N. and J. F. SNELLEMAN (1893) *Industrie des Cafres du Sud-Est de l'Afrique*, Leiden: Brill
MURDOCK, G. P. (1959) *Africa: Its Peoples and their Culture History*, New York and London: McGraw-Hill, pp. 1–456
MYBURGH, A. C. (1944) *EzakwaZulu*, Pretoria [285 bis, 290, 295–6, 302–9 passim, 314 bis, 316 bis]
—— (1959) *Die Posisie en Versorging van Bejaardes onder die Bantoe in die Unie van Suid-Afrika*, Pretoria: Government Printer [287, 299]
—— (1965) 'Perspectives of South African Bantu Law', *Codicillus*, 6, 2, 6–12 [284, 288, 302, 307 bis, 309]
—— (1969) 'Reflections on delict among the South African Bantu' in *Ethnological and Linguistic Studies in Honour of N. J. van Warmelo*, Ethnological Publication No. 52, Pretoria: Government Printer [286, 287 bis, 296, 304 bis, 312–13 passim]
NADEL, S. F. (1942) *A Black Byzantium*, London: Oxford University Press [xv]
—— (1952) 'Witchcraft in four African societies', *Amer. Anthrop.*, 54, 18–29
NAUDE, S. (ed.) (1949) *Kaapse Plakkaatboek 1754–86*, Cape Times [367]
NDAMASE, POTO V. (1925) *Ama-Mpondo; Ibali ne-Ntlala*, Alice, Cape Province: Lovedale Press [130]
N.E.A.D. (City of Johannesburg Non-European Affairs Department) (1965) 'Cultural Change in Soweto. An Urban Bantu Society' (mimeograph), Johannesburg [456, 465 bis]
NEEDHAM, R. (1962) *Structure and Sentiment*, University of Chicago Press
NEEL, J. V. (1956) 'The genetics of human haemoglobin differences: problems and perspectives', *Ann. Hum. Genet.*, 21, 1, 1–30, London [28]
—— (1969) 'Some changing constraints on the human evolutionary process', *Proc. XII Intern. Congr. Genet.*, 3, 389–403 [45]
NELSON, G. K. (1959) 'The electroencephalogram in kwashiorkor', *Electorenceph. Clin. Neurophysiol. J.*, 11, 73–84 [45]
—— (1963) 'Electroencephalographic studies in sequelae of kwashiorkor and other diseases in Africans' in G. J. Snowball (ed.), *Science and Medicine in Central Africa*, Oxford: Pergamon [45]
NENQUIN, J. (1959) 'Dimple-based pots from Kasai, Belgian Congo', *Man*, 48, No. 90
NGCOBO, S. B. (1954) 'The response of Africans to industrial employment', *Race Rel. J.*, 21, 1, 10–17
NIELSEN, P. (1913) *The Matebele at Home*, Bulawayo: Davis
NIEUWENHUYSEN, J. P. (1964a) 'Economic policy in the reserves since the Tomlinson Report', *S. Afr. J. Econ.*, 32, 1, 3–25

—— (1964b) 'Prospects and issues in the development of the reserves', *S. Afr. J. Econ.*, 32, 2, 128–46
NORBECK, E. (1963) 'African rituals of conflict', *Amer. Anthrop.*, 65, 6, 1254–79 [363]
NYEMBEZI, C. L. S. (1948) 'The historical background to the *izibongo* of the Zulu military age', *African Studies*, 7, 4
NYQUIST, T. (n.d. (c. 1971) *African Middle Class Elite*, unpublished research report, Grahamstown: Rhodes University [464 *bis*]
OKOYE, K. N. C. (1969) 'Dingane: a reappraisal', *J. Afr. History*, 1012, 221–35
OLIVER, R. (1966), 'The problem of the Bantu expansion', *J. Afr. History*, 7, 361–76 [38 *bis*]
OLIVIER, N. J. J. (1969) *Die Privaatreg van die Suid-Afrikaanse Bantoe*, Durban: Butterworth [306 *bis*]
OMER-COOPER, J. D. (1966) *The Zulu Aftermath*, London: Longmans [84, 280, 375, 395]
OOSTHUIZEN, G. C. (1966) 'Attitudes towards Christian churches in the Ciskei', *African Studies*, 25, 2, 81–94
—— (1967) *The Theology of a South African Messiah; An Analysis of the Hymnal of 'The Church of the Nazarites'*, Leiden: Brill (Okumenische Studien, 8) [435]
—— (1968) *Post-Christianity in Africa: A Theological and Anthropological Study*, London: Hurst
PASSARGE, S. (1905) 'Das Okawangosumpfland und seine Bewohner', *Z. f. Ethnol.*, 37, 649–716
—— (1908) *Südafrika: Eine Landes-, Volks-, und Wirtschaftskunde*, Leipzig: Quelle & Meyer
PATERSON, W. (1789) *A Narrative of 4 Journeys into the Country of the Hottentots and Caffraria in the years 1777, 1778, 1779*, London: Johnson
PAUW, B. A. (1960a) *Religion in a Tswana Chiefdom*, London: Oxford University Press [418, 422, 423 *bis*, 435 *bis*, 440]
—— (1960b) 'Some changes in the social structure of the Tlhaping of the Taung reserve', *African Studies*, 19, 1–76
—— (1963a) *The Second Generation: A Study of the Family Among Urbanized Bantu in East London*, Cape Town: Oxford University Press [450–4 *passim*, 457, 459–62 *passim*, 468, 470–72 *passim*]
—— (1963b) 'African Christians and their ancestors' in V. E. W. Hayward (ed.) (1963), pp. 33–46 [440]
—— (1965) 'Patterns of christianization among the Tswana and the Xhosa-speaking peoples' in M. Fortes and G. Dieterlen (eds), *African Systems of Thought*, London: Oxford University Press, pp. 242–53 [423, 427, 440]
—— (forthcoming) *Christianity and Xhosa Tradition*
PEARSON, K. and A. DAVIN (1924) 'On the biometric constants of the human skull', *Biometrika*, 16, 328–63 [13]
PERROT, C. H. (1964) 'Un culte messianique chez les Sotho au milieu du XIXE siècle', *Archives de Sociologie des Religions*, 18, 147–52
PHILLIPS, R. E. (1956) 'The Bantu in the city' in *Social Implications of Urbanization and Industrilization South of the Sahara*, UNESCO
PIERCY, M. J. (1960) 'Statutory work reservation in the Union of South Africa', *S. Afr. J. Econ.*, 28, 2
PITJE, G. M. (1950) 'Traditional system of male education among Pedi and cognate tribes', *African Studies*, 9, 53–76; 105–24; 194–201 [243]
POLACK, K. (1963) 'The defence of act of state in relation to protectorates', *Modern Law Review*, March 1963, 138–55 [383]
POSNANSKY, M. (1961) 'Bantu genesis', *Uganda Journal*, 25, 1, 86–93 [37 *bis*, 45]
—— (1968) 'Bantu genesis—archaeological reflections', *J. Afr. History*, 9, 1–11

POST, A. H. (1887) *Afrikanische Jurisprudenz*, 2 vols, Oldenburg and Leipzig: Schulze [288–301 *passim*, 303–9 *passim*, 314, 316 *bis*, 317]
POTGIETER, E. F. (1958) *Enkele Volksverhale van die Ndzundza van Transvaal*, Pretoria: University of South Africa [84]
PURSELL, D. E. (1968) 'Bantu real wages and employment opportunities', *S. Afr. J. Econ.*, 36, 2, 87–103
QUIN, P. J. (1959) *Foods and Feeding Habits of the Pedi*, Johannesburg: Witwatersrand University Press [45, 99, 129–31 *passim*, 154]
RADCLIFFE-BROWN, A. R. (1924) 'The mother's brother in South Africa', *S. Afr. J. Sci.*, 21, 542–55 [178, 347]
—— (1952) *Structure and Function in Primitive Society*, London: Oxford University Press
RAMOLEFE, A. M. R. (1969) 'Sesotho marriage, guardianship, and the customary-law heir' in M. Gluckman (ed.), *Ideas and Procedures in African Customary Law*, London: Oxford University Press, pp. 196–207
RAMSAY, T. D. (1946) 'Tsonga law in the Transvaal', *African Studies*, 5, 143–56
RAMSEYER, P. (1928) 'La circoncision chez les Bassouto', *Rev. d'Ethnog. et Trad. Pop.*, 9, 40–70
RANGER, T. O. (1967) *Revolt in Southern Rhodesia 1896–7*, London: Heinemann [384]
RAUM, O. F. (1953) 'The rolling-target (hoop and pole) game in Africa', *African Studies*, 12, 3 and 4, 104–21; 163–78 [223]
—— (1965) 'Change in culture and social structure among the South African Xhosa', *Sociologus*, 15, 2, 11–27
—— (1965a) 'Von Stammespropheten zu Sektenführern' in E. Benz (ed.) *Messianische Kirchen, Sekten und Bewegungen im Heutigen Afrika*, Leiden: Brill, pp. 47–70 [417]
—— (1965b) 'Wandel in Kultur und Sozialstruktur der sudafrikanischen Xhosa', *Sociologus* 15, 2, 111–27
—— (1969) 'A topological analysis of Xhosa society' in *Work and Religion: Kalima na Dini*, Stuttgart: Evangelischer Missionsverlag, pp. 321–32 [xix]
READER, D. H. (1961a) *The Black Man's Portion*, Cape Town: Oxford University Press [442 *bis*, 443, 468, 470–2 *passim*]
—— (1961b) Unpublished tables available as Appendix C in A. A. Dubb (1961) [467]
—— (1966) *Zulu Tribe in Transition*, Manchester University Press [141, 175, 182, 185, 195, 197–8 *passim*, 200–1 *passim*, 204–5 *passim*, 210, 259, 427, 429, 432]
REAY, M. (1959) 'Two types of ritual conflict', *Oceania*, 29 [363]
RECKNAGEL, R. (1909) 'On some mineral deposits in the Rooiberg district', *Trans. Geol. Soc. S. Afr.*, 11, 89, 90, 94
REYNOLDS, B. (1968) *Kariba Studies. Vol. III, The Material Culture of the Peoples of the Gwembe Valley*, Manchester University Press, pp. 1–262
RICHARDS, A. I. (1932) *Hunger and Work in a Savage Tribe: A functional study of nutrition among the Southern Bantu*, London: Routledge
—— (1939) *Land, Labour and Diet in Northern Rhodesia*, London: Oxford University Press for the International African Institute [171]
RICHTER, M. (1912) *Die Wirtschaft der südafrikanischen Bantuneger*, dissertation, Dresden: Petchke & Gretschel
RIGHTMIRE, G. P. (1970) 'Bushman, Hottentot and South African Negro crania studies by distance and discrimination', *Am. J. Phys. Anthrop.*, 33, 2, 169–96 [14, 33, 45]
RIORDAN, J. (1961) 'The wrath of the ancestral spirits', *African Studies*, 20, 1, 53–61
ROBERTS, M. (1959) *Labour in the Farm Economy*, Johannesburg: SAIRR [xix, 399]
ROBERTS, N. and C. A. T. WINTER (1915) 'The *kgoma*, or initiation rites of the Bapedi of Sekukuniland', *S. Afr. J. Sci.*, 12, 561–78
ROBERTSON, H. M. (1934) 'The economic condition of the rural Native' in I. Schapera (ed.) (1934a), pp. 143–55 [399 *bis*]

—— (1935) '150 years of economic contact between black and white', Parts I and II, *S. Afr. J. Econ.*, 2, 4; 3, 1 [400–3 *passim*]
ROBINS, A. R. (1970) 'A Study of Skin Pigmentation and its Implications in Psychiatric illness, with special reference to schizophrenia and its affective disorders', Ph.D. thesis submitted to the University of the Witwatersrand [18 *bis*, 19]
ROBINSON, K. R. (1970) 'The Iron Age of the southern lake area of Malawi', *Dept. of Antiquities Publ.*, 8, 1–131, Malawi G.
ROBINSON K. R. and B. H. SANDELOWSKY (1969) 'The Iron Age of Northern Malawi: recent work', *Azania*, 3, 1–40 [45]
ROGERS, H. (1933) *Native Administration in the Union of South Africa*, Johannesburg: University of Witwatersrand
—— (1949) *Native Administration in the Union of South Africa* (2nd edn), Pretoria: Government Printer
RUTHERFORD, J. (1961) *Sir George Grey*, London: Cassell [373–5 *passim*, 396]
RUTMAN, G. L. (1968) 'The Transkei: an experiment in economic separation', *S. Afr. J. Econ.*, 36, 1, 24–31
SABRA (South African Bureau for Racial Affairs) (1954) *Die Naturel in die Suid-Afrikaanse Landbou* [xix]
SADIE, J. L. (1970) 'An evaluation of demographic data pertaining to the non-white population of South Africa: Part III. The Bantu Population', *S. Afr. J. Econ.*, 38, 2, 171–91 [442]
SAHLINS, M. D. (1961) 'The segmentary lineage: an organization of predatory expansion', *Amer. Anthrop.*, 63, 322–44 [283]
—— (1968) *Tribesmen*, Englewood Cliffs: Prentice-Hall [136]
SAIRR (South African Institute of Race Relations) (1962) *A Survey of Race Relations in South Africa*, compiled by Muriel Horrell (annual), Johannesburg: S.A. Institute of Race Relations
SAMUELSON, L. H. (1930) *Zululand: its traditions, legends, customs and folklore*, Marianhill: Mission Press
SAMUELSON, R. C. A. (1929) *Long, Long Ago*, Durban: Knox Printing (Zulu) [323, 327]
SANDELOWSKY, B. H. (1971) 'Later Stone Age Assemblages from Malawi and Their Technologies', Ph.D. dissertation submitted to the University of California, Berkeley [45]
SANDERS, P. B. (1969) 'Sekonyela and Moshweshwe; failure and success in the aftermath of the Difaqane' *J. Afr. History*, 10, 3, (1969), 439–55 [379]
SANSOM, B. L. (1966) *Social Change among the Pedi*, research report presented to National Council for Social Research
—— (1970) 'Leadership and Authority in a Pedi Chiefdom', unpublished Ph.D. thesis, University of Manchester [137, 170, 173]
—— (1971) 'When witches are not named', in M. Gluckman (ed.), *The Allocation of Responsibility*, Manchester University Press, pp. 193–226
SANTOS JN., J. N. DOS (1959) 'Table for the general shape of the negroes' hair', *Trab. Anthrop. Etnol.*, 17, 25–33 [45]
SARGANT, W. (1959) *Battle for the Mind*, London: Pan Books (original ed. 1957, London: Heinemann) [236]
SAUNDERS, C. (n.d.) 'The Political Incorporation of the Transkei', unpublished MS. draft of D.Phil. thesis, Oxford University [387, 389]
SAYCE, R. (1924) 'An ethno-geographical essay on Basutoland', *Geog. Teacher*, 12, 266–88
SCHAPERA, I. (1927) 'Customs relating to twins in South Africa', *J. Afr. Soc.*, 26, 117–37 [214]
—— (1930a) *The Khoisan Peoples of South Africa: Bushmen and Hottentots*, London: Routledge [xii, 22–3 *passim*, 45]
—— (1930b) 'The "Little Rain" (*pulanyana*) ceremony of the Bechuanaland BaKxatla', *Bantu Studies*, 4, 211–16

―――― (1933a) 'Premarital pregnancy and Native opinion: a note on social change', *Africa*, 6, 59–89
―――― (1933b) 'Economic conditions in a Bechuanaland Native reserve', *S. Afr. J. Sci.*, 30, 633–55
―――― (1933c) 'Labour migration from a Bechuanaland Native reserve', *J. Afr. Soc.*, 32, 386–97; 33, 49–58
―――― (ed.) (1934a) *Western Civilization and the Natives of South Africa: Studies in Culture Contact*, London: Routledge [xiii, 186]
―――― (1934b) 'Herding rites of the Bechuanaland BaKxatla', *Amer. Anthrop.*, 37, 561–84 [129]
―――― (1934c) 'Oral sorcery among the Natives of Bechuanaland' in *Essays Presented to C. G. Seligman*, London: Routledge, pp. 293–305
―――― (1934d) 'The present state and future development of ethnographical research in South Africa', *Bantu Studies*, 8, 219–342
―――― (1934e) 'Present-day life in the native reserves' in I. Schapera (ed.), (1934a) pp. 37–62 [429]
―――― (1935) 'The social structure of the Tswana ward', *Bantu Studies*, 9, 203–24 [178, 186 *bis*]
―――― (1936) 'Land tenure among the Natives of Bechuanaland Protectorate', *Z. Vergl. Rechtswiss*, 51, 130–59 [207]
―――― (ed.) (1937a) *The Bantu-Speaking Tribes of South Africa*, London: Routledge [30–1, 130]
―――― (1937b) 'Political institutions' in I. Schapera (ed.) (1937a), pp. 173–96 [284, 287–95 *passim*, 301, 304–5 *passim*]
―――― (1937c) 'Law and justice' in I. Schapera (ed.) (1937a), pp. 197–220 [284–6 *passim*, 293–6 *passim*, 297–300 *passim*, 303, 305–6, 308 *bis*, 310, 312, 314 *bis*, 316 *bis*, 317]
―――― (1937d) 'Cultural changes in tribal life' in I. Schapera (ed.) (1937a), pp. 357–88
―――― (1938a) *A Handbook of Tswana Law and Custom* (2nd edn), London, New York, Toronto: Oxford University Press, 1955 [284–310 *passim*, 314, 316 *bis*, 317 *bis*]
―――― (1938b) 'Ethnological texts in the Boloongwe dialect of Sekgalagadi', *Bantu Studies*, 12, 157–87 [311]
―――― (1940a) *Married Life in an African Tribe*, London: Faber & Faber [224, 228, 231–5 *passim*, 244, 346–7]
―――― (1940b) 'The political organization of the Ngwato of Bechuanaland Protectorate' in M. Fortes and E. Evans-Pritchard (eds) (1940), pp. 56–82 [271–3]
―――― (1942) 'A short history of the Bangwaketse', *African Studies*, 1, 1–26
―――― (1943a) *Tribal Legislation Among the Tswana of the Bechuanaland Protectorate*, London: Lund, Humphries
―――― (1943b) 'The work of tribal courts in the Bechuanaland Protectorate', *African Studies*, 2, 27–40
―――― (1943c) *Native Land Tenure in the Bechuanaland Protectorate*, Alice: Lovedale Press [143, 155, 160, 176]
―――― (1945) 'Notes on the history of the Kaa', *African Studies*, 4, 3, 109–21
―――― (1946) 'Some features of the social organization of the Tlokwa', *South-Western J. Anthrop.*, 2, 16–47
―――― (1947) *Migrant Labour and Tribal Life*, London: Oxford University Press
―――― (1949) 'The Tswana conception of incest' in M. Fortes (ed.), *Social Structure*, London: Oxford University Press
―――― (1950) 'Kinship and marriage among the Tswana' in A. R. Radcliffe-Brown and D. Forde (eds), *African Systems of Kinship and Marriage*, London: Oxford University Press, pp. 140–65 [176 *bis*, 178, 189, 193, 197–8, 253–7 *passim*]
―――― (1951) *The Khoisan Peoples of South Africa*, London: Routledge & Kegan Paul
―――― (1952) *The Ethnic Composition of Tswana Tribes*, London School of Economics, Monographs on Social Anthropology, No. 11, London: Athlone Press [202, 263, 265, 272]

—— (1953) *The Tswana*, Ethnographic Survey of Africa: Southern Africa, part III, London: International African Institute [128–30 *passim*, 180–1, 204–5, 440]
—— (1956) *Government and Politics in Tribal Societies*, London: Watts [166–7, 249, 255, 265]
—— (1957) 'Marriage of near kin among the Tswana', *Africa*, 27, 1, 139–60 [193, 207 *bis*, 273 *bis*]
—— (1958) 'Christianity and the Tswana', *J. Roy. Anthrop. Inst.*, 88, 1–9 [421, 423, 427, 429, 440]
—— (1963a) 'Kinship and politics in Tswana history', *J. Roy. Anthrop. Inst.*, 93, 159–73
—— (1963b) 'Agnatic marriage in Tswana royal families' in I. Schapera (ed.), *Studies in Kinship and Marriage*, London: Royal Anthropological Institute
—— (1965) 'Contract in Tswana case law', *J. African Law*, 11, 142–53
—— (1969a) 'Contract in Tswana law', in M. Gluckman (ed.), *Ideas and Procedures in African Customary Law*, London: Oxford University Press, 318–29
—— (1969b) 'Some aspects of Kgatla magic' in *Ethnological and Linguistic Studies in Honour of N. J. van Warmelo*, Pretoria, pp. 157–68
—— (1970) *Tribal Innovators: Tswana Chiefs and Social Change 1795–1940*, London School of Economics
SCHAPERA, I. and A. J. H. GOODWIN (1937) 'Work and wealth' in I. Schapera (ed.), (1937a), pp. 131–72 [126, 127, 129 *bis*, 131, 303–5 *passim*, 310–11, 314 *bis*, 316, 317 *bis*]
SCHLOSSER, K. (1958) *Eingeborenenkirchen in Süd- und Südwestafrika; Ihre Geschichte und Sozialstruktur; Ergebnisse einer völkerkundlichen Studienreise 1953*, Kiel: Mühlau [419, 422 *bis*, 434, 435 *bis*, 439]
SCHMIDT, J. (1967) 'Stamverbondenheid van die stedelike Bantoegemeenskap', *J. Soc. Res.*, 16, 1, 7–18
SCHNEIDER, D. M. (1965) 'Some muddles in the models' in M. Banton (ed.), *The Relevance of Models for Social Anthropology*, ASA Monograph No. 1, London: Tavistock
SCHNEIDER, H. K. (1968) 'Economics in East African aboriginal societies' in M. J. Herskovits and M. Harwitz (eds), *Economic Transition in Africa*, Evanston: Northwestern University Press; reprinted in E. E. Le Clair and H. K. Schneider (eds), *Economic Anthropology: Readings in Theory and Analysis*, New York: Holt, Rinehart and Winston, 1968 (page references are to this source) [152]
SCHOEMAN, H. S. (1968) 'Preliminary report on traditional beadwork in the Mkhwanazi area of the Mtunzini district, Zululand', *African Studies*, 27, 57–81, 107–33 [131]
SCHOFIELD, J. F. (1940) *Primitive Pottery*, Cape Town: South African Archaeological Society Handbook 3 [130]
SCHREUDER, D. M. (1969) *Gladstone and Kruger*, London: Routledge & Kegan Paul [382]
SCHULTZE-JENA, L. (1928) 'Zur Kenntnis des Körpers der Hottentotten und Buschmänner', *Denkschr. Med.-naturw. Ges. Jena*, 17, 145–227 [45]
SCHUMANN, C. G. W. (1938) *Structural Changes and Business Cycles in South Africa 1806–1936*, London: King [399]
SCHWEIGER, A. (1914) 'Der Ritus der Beschneidung unter den AmaXosa und AmaFingo in der Kaffraria, Südafrika', *Anthropos*, 9, 53–65
SCOTCH, N. A. (1961) 'Magic, sorcery and football among urban Zulu: a case of reinterpretation under acculturation', *Journal of Conflict Resolution*, 5, 1, 70–4
SCUDDER, T. (1962) *Kariba Studies Volume II, The Ecology of the Gwembe Tonga*, Manchester University Press, pp. 1–274
SELIGMAN, C. G. (1930) *Races of Africa*, London: Butterworth
—— (1966) *Races of Africa* (4th edn), London: Oxford University Press, pp. 1–170
SERGI, S. (1912) *Crania Habessinica*, Memoria a Rodolfo Virchow, Roma: Oescher, pp. 1–519 [14]
SEYMOUR, S. M. (1970) *Bantu Law in South Africa* (3rd edn), Cape Town: Wynberg; Johannesburg: Juta [300–15 *passim*, 316, 317 *bis*]

SEYMOUR, W. M. (1911) *Native Law and Custom*, Cape Town: Juta

SHAW, E. M. and N. J. VAN WARMELO (n.d.) MS. in three parts, first part only published as *Material Culture of the Cape Nguni*, Vol. 1, Cape Town: South African Museum (1972) [130]

SHAW, J. C. MIDDLETON (1931) *The teeth, the bony palate and the mandible in Bantu races of South Africa*, London: Bale & Danielson, pp. 1–134 [14]

SHAW, M. (1935) 'Some native snuff-boxes in the South African Museum', *Annals S. Afr. Mus.*, 24, 141–62 [130]

—— (1938a) 'Native pipes and smoking in South Africa', *Annals S. Afr. Mus.*, 24, 277–302 [130]

—— (1938b) 'South African native snuff-boxes', *Annals S. Afr. Mus.*, 24, 221–52

SHAW, W. (1860) *The Story of my Mission in South-Eastern Africa*, London: Hamilton, Adams [128, 129, 412]

SHEDDICK, V. G. J. (1948) *The Morphology of Residential Associations as Found Among the Khwakhwa of Basutoland*, Communications from the School of African Studies, New Series No. 19, University of Cape Town [185–6]

—— (1953) *The Southern Sotho*, Ethnographic Survey of Africa: Southern Africa, Part II, London: International African Institute [189 *bis*, 191, 193–5 *passim*, 197–8 *passim*, 202–3 *passim*, 423, 428, 431, 433, 436]

—— (1954) *Land Tenure in Basutoland*, Colonial Research Studies No. 13, London: HMSO [148]

SHEPHERD, R. H. W. (1940) *Lovedale, South Africa*, Alice, Cape Province: Lovedale Press [374]

SHILUBANA, P. M. and H. E. NTSANWISI (1958) *Muhlaba, hosi ya va ka Nkuna*, Nkune tribe of N.E. Transvaal at Morija Press [84]

SHOOTER, J. (1857) *The Kafirs of Natal and the Zulu Country*, London: Stanford

SILBERBAUER, G. B. (1965) *Bushman Survey Report*, Gaberones: Bechuanaland Press, pp. 7–138

SILBERBAUER, G. B. and A. J. KUPER (1966) 'Kgalagari masters and Bushmen serfs: some observations', *African Studies*, 25, 171–9

SILLERY, A. (1952) *The Bechuanaland Protectorate*, Cape Town: Oxford University Press [254, 382]

—— (1965) *Founding a Protectorate*, The Hague: Mouton [382–3 *passim*, 396]

SIMONS, H. J. (1957) 'Tribal medicine: diviners and herbalists', *African Studies*, 16, 2, 85–92

—— (1960) 'Marriage and succession among Africans', *Acta Juridica*, 312–33

—— (1961) 'The status of customary unions' *Acta Juridica*, 17–37

SINGER, R. (1953) 'The sickle cell trait in Africa', *Amer. Anthrop.*, 55, 634–48 [28]

SINGER, R. and J. S. WEINER (1963) 'Biological aspects of some indigenous African populations', *S. West J. Anthrop.*, 19, 168–76 [32, 44, 45]

SMITH, A. (1939–40) *The Diary of Dr. Andrew Smith, 1834–36* (ed. P. R. Kirby), 2 vols, Cape Town: Van Riebeeck Society (Van Riebeeck Publications 30 and 31)

SMITH, E. W. (1956) 'Sebetwane and the Makololo', *African Studies*, 15, 2, 49–75

SMITH, K. W. (1969) 'The fall of the Bapedi of the North-Eastern Transvaal', *J. Afr. History*, 10, 2, 237–52 [386]

SMITH, S. M. (1954) 'Appendix to notes on sickle-cell polymorphism', *Ann. Hum. Genet.*, 19, 51–7, London [28]

SOGA, J. H. (1930) *The South-Eastern Bantu*, Johannesburg: University of the Witwatersrand [61, 62, 351]

—— (1932) *The Ama-Xosa: Life and Customs*, Lovedale: Mission Press [130, 214, 297, 306 *bis*, 310, 316, 349, 357]

SOUSSI, J. (1968) 'The incidence of light eye-colour in South African Bantu-speaking Negroids, with particular emphasis on the Klein-Waardenburg syndrome', thesis ac-

cepted for degree of Ph.D. in the Department of Anatomy, University of the Witwatersrand, Johannesburg [21 *bis*]
SOUTH AFRICA, UNION OF (1913) *Report from the Select Committee on Native Custom and Marriage Laws* (Senate S.C.6, 1913), *Cape Times*
—— (1916) *Beaumont Commission Report* (*U.G. 19 and 22 of 1916*), Pretoria: Government Printer [391]
SOUTH-WEST ADMINISTRATION (1928) *The Native Tribes of South-West Africa*, Pretoria: Government Printer [xii]
—— (1932) *Report of the Native Economic Commission, 1930–1932* (U.G. 22, 1932) Pretoria: Government Printer
—— (1936) *Report of the Interdepartmental Committee on Native Education* (U.G. 29, 1936), Pretoria: Government Printer
—— (1939) *Report of the Native Farm Labour Committee 1937–1939*, Pretoria: Government Printer [xix]
—— (1955) *Tomlinson Commission Report* (U.G. 61 of 1955), Pretoria: Government Printer
SOUTH AFRICA, REPUBLIC OF, BUREAU OF CENSUS AND STATISTICS (1960) *Union Statistics for Fifty Years*, Pretoria: Government Printer [404, 413; see also *Statistical Year Book*]
—— (1963) *Population Census, 1960: sample tabulation, No. 6, Religion: all races*, Pretoria: Government Printer [420, 421 *bis*, 438, 439]
—— DEPT OF STATISTICS (1969) *Statistical News Release*, Pretoria: Government Printer [404, 411, 413 *bis*, 414: see also *Statistical Year Book*]
SOUTH AFRICA, REPUBLIC OF, ECONOMIC DEVELOPMENT PROGRAMME FOR THE REPUBLIC OF SOUTH AFRICA 1964–9, 1965–70, 1967–72, Pretoria: Government Printer [439]
SOUTH AFRICAN NATIVE AFFAIRS COMMISSION (1903–5) *Report and Minutes of Evidence*, 5 vols, *Cape Times*
SOUTH AFRICAN NATIVE RACES COMMITTEE (1901) *The Natives of South Africa; their economic and social condition*, London: Murray
—— (1908) *The South African Natives: their progress and present condition*, London: Murray
SOUTHALL, A. (1965) 'A critique of the typology of states and political systems' in *Political Systems and the Distribution of Power*, A.S.A. Monographs No. 2, London: Tavistock [273–4]
SOUTHWOLD, M. (1969) 'A games model of African tribal politics' in I. R. Buchler and H. G. Nutini, (eds), *Game Theory in the Behavioural Sciences*, University of Pittsburgh Press [252]
SPARRMAN, A. A. (1785) *Voyage to the Cape of Good Hope, towards the Antarctic Polar Circle, and round the world, but chiefly into the country of the Hottentots and Caffers from the year 1772–1776*, 2 vols, trans. from Swedish, Dublin: White, Cash & Byene [129, 130]
SPECKMANN, F. (1876) *Die Hermannsburger Mission in Afrika*, Hermannsburg: Missionshausdruckerei
STACEY, R. D. (1966) 'Some observations on the economic implications of territorial segregation in South Africa', *S. Afr. J. Econ.*, 34, 1, 50–67
STAFFORD, W. G. (1935) *Native Law as Practised in Natal*, Johannesburg: University of the Witwatersrand
STAFFORD, W. G. and E. FRANKLIN (1950) *Principles of Native Law and the Natal Code*, Pietermaritzburg: Shuter & Shooter
Stavenisse (1686) 'Stranding van's compagnie's fluitschip de "Stavenisse"' in E. C. Godée-Molsbergen, *Reizen in Zuid-Afrika in de Hollandse Tijd*, 3, 50, 's Gravenhage: Nijhoff [129]
Statistical Year Book (1964) Republic of South Africa, Pretoria: Government Printer [442 *bis*]

—— (1965) *Republic of South Africa*, Pretoria: Government Printer [404, 413]
—— (1966) *Republic of South Africa*, Pretoria: Government Printer [412, 414]
STAYT, H. A. (1931a) *The BaVenda*, London: Oxford University Press [22–3 *passim*, 128–31 *passim*, 178, 189, 191, 195, 202 *bis*, 214, 226 *bis*, 234, 237, 241, 242 *bis*, 244, 320–6 *passim*, 328, 332–4 *passim*, 343, 347, 350 *bis*, 354, 357, 363]
—— (1931b) 'Notes on the Balemba', *J. Roy. Anthrop. Inst.*, 61, 231–8
STEENKAMP, W. F. J. (1962) 'Bantu wages in South Africa', *S. Afr. J. Econ.*, 30, 2, 93–118 [413]
STENT, G. E. (1948) 'Migrancy and urbanization in the Union of South Africa', *Africa*, 18, 161–83
STERN, C. (1953) 'Model estimates of the frequency of white and near white segregants in the American Negro', *Acta. Genet.*, 4, 281–98 [20]
STERN, C., A. SCHAEFER and O. J. UKPE (1968) 'Hairy pinnae in Nigeria', *J. Hered.*, 59, 3, 174, 178
STEVENSON, R. F. (1968) *Population and Political Systems in Tropical Africa*, New York: Columbia University Press [247, 257]
STEYN, A. (1966) *Die Bantoe in die Stad: Die Bantoegesin*, Pretoria: SABRA
STEYN, H. S. (1964) 'A statistical study of the distribution of income for Bantu workers', *S. Afr. J. Econ.*, 32, 1, 53–67
STOCH, M. B. and P. M. SMYTHE (1963) 'Does undernutrition during infancy inhibit brain growth and subsequent intellectual development?', *Arch. Dis. Child.*, 38, 546–52 [45]
—— (1967) 'The effect of undernutrition during infancy on subsequent brain growth and intellectual development', *S. Afr. Med. J.*, 41, 1027–31 [45]
STOKES, E. and R. BROWN (eds.) (1966) *The Zambesian Past*, Manchester University Press [384]
STOW, G. W. (1905) *The Native Races of South Africa*, London: Sonnenschein
SUMMERS, R. (1969) *Ancient Mining in Rhodesia*, Salisbury: National Museums of Rhodesia, Museum Memoir 3 [130]
SUMMERS, R. and C. W. PAGDEN (1970) *The Warriors*, Cape Town: Books of Africa [129, 130]
SUNDKLER, B. G. M. (1960) *The Christian Minority in Africa*, Uppsala
—— (1961a) *Bantu Prophets in South Africa* (2nd edn; 1st edn 1948), London: Oxford University Press [418, 420, 434 *bis*, 435, 472]
—— (1961b) 'The concept of Christianity in the African independent churches', *African Studies*, 20, 4, 203–13
TAURAT, W. (1910) *Die Zauberei der Basotho* (pamphlet), Berlin: Evangel. Missionsgesellschaft
TEMPELS, P. (1959) *Bantu Philosophy*, Paris: Présence Africaine
THEAL, G. M. (ed.) (1883) *Basutoland Records*, Cape Town: Struik facsimile reproduction (3B), 1964, 3 vols [380]
—— (1898–1902) *Records of South-Eastern Africa*, 1, 2 and 8, London: Government of the Cape Colony
—— (1919) *Ethnography and Condition of South Africa before A.D. 1505*, London: Allen & Unwin
THELEJANE, T. S. (1963) 'Pondo rainmaking ritual: *ukukhonga*', *African Studies*, 22, 1, 33–6 [354]
THERON, J. J. (1961) 'Voedingstatusopnames onder die Suid-Afrikaanse Bantoe', thesis accepted for the degree of Doctor of Science in the University of Pretoria, pp. 1–285
THILENIUS, G. (1915) 'Die Mädchenbeschneidung der Basotho', *Archiv. f. Anthrop.*, N.F. 13, 72–5
THOMPSON, G. (1827) *Travels and Adventures in Southern Africa* II, London: Colburn; appendix, notes by J. Brownlee [130]
THOMPSON, L. C. (1954) 'A native-made tin ingot', *Nada* 31, 41 [45]

THOMPSON, L. M. (ed.) (1969) *African Societies in Southern Africa: Historical Studies*, London: Heinemann [xix, 396, 412]
THOMPSON, B. P. (1954) 'Two studies in African nutrition', *Rhodes–Livingstone Papers*, No. 24, 1–57
TOBIAS, P. V. (1947) 'Studies in Bantu anatomy: Introduction', *Leech*, Johannesburg, 18, 1, 17–18, 30
—— (1949) 'The excavation of Mwulu's cave, Potgietersrust district', *S. Afr. Archaeol. Bull.*, 13, 2–13 [40]
—— (1955a) 'Teeth, jaws and genes', *J. Dent. Assoc. S. Afr.*, 10, 3, 88–104 [36]
—— (1955b) 'Taurodontism in a Bushman skull from Kimberley', *Br. Dent. J.*, 98, 352–5
—— (1955c) 'Physical anthropology and somatic origins of the Hottentots', *African Studies*, 14, 1, 1–15
—— (1955d) 'Les Bochimans auen et naron de Ghanzi: contribution à l'étude des "anciens jaunes" sud-africains', *L'Anthropologie*, 2, 429–61 [23]
—— (1957) 'Bushmen of the Kalahari', *Man*, 57, 33–40 [21–3 *passim*, 45]
—— (1961a) 'Blue eyed Africans', *S. Afr. J. Sci.*, 57, 161 [21]
—— (1961b) 'Studies on skin reflectance in Bushman–European hybrids', *Proc. II Int. Cong. Hum. Genet.*, Rome, pp. 461–71 [17–18 *passim*]
—— (1962) 'On the increasing stature of the Bushman', *Anthropos*, 57, 801–10 [32]
—— (1964) 'Bushman hunter gatherers: a study in human ecology' in D. N. S. Davis (ed.) *Ecological Studies in Southern Africa*, Monographiae Biologicae XIV, The Hague: Dr W. Junk, pp. 67–86 [45]
—— (1966) 'The peoples of Africa south of the Sahara' in P. T. Baker and J. S. Weiner (eds.) *The Biology of Human Adaptability*, Oxford: Clarendon Press, pp. 111–200 [24, 25, 31–4 *passim*, 45 *bis*]
—— (1969) *Human Adaptability in Africa*, Proc. Inaugural Sci. Conf. of Int. Biol. Prog., Malawi Limbe: University of Malawi, pp. 4–21 [5, 6, 8]
—— (1970a) 'Human biological research in the Anatomy Department, University of the Witwatersrand, 1959–1969', *Leech*, Johannesburg, 40, 2, 23–32
—— (1970b) 'Puberty, growth, malnutrition and the weaker sex—and two new measures of environmental betterment', *Leech*, Johannesburg, 40, 4, 101–7
—— (1972a) 'Stature in Bantu-speaking Negroes and Bushmen of Southern Africa' in *Festschrift on 100th anniversary of birth of R. Pöch*, Vienna, pp. 1–18 [40]
—— (1972b) 'Recent human biological studies in Southern Africa, with special reference to Negroes and Khoisans' (presidential address), *Trans. Roy. Soc. S. Afr.*, 40, 3, 109–33
—— (1972c) 'The men who came before Malawian history' in B. Pachai (ed.), *Early History of Malawi*, London: Longmans, pp. 1–16
TOMLINSON COMMISSION (1955) *Commission for the Socio-economic development of the Bantu areas within the Union of South Africa*, Summary of the Report (U.G. 61, 1955), Pretoria: Government Printer [393, 407 *bis*, 413 *bis*, 441, 443 *bis*]
TORDAY, E. (1930) *African Races*, London: Williams & Norgate
TRANSVAAL NATIVE AFFAIRS DEPARTMENT (1905) *Short History of the Native Tribes of the Transvaal*, Pretoria: Government Printer
TREVOR, J. C. (1955) 'Race', *Encyclopedia Hebraica*, Tel-Aviv [32]
TREVOR, T. G. (1912) 'Some observations on ancient mine-workings in the Transvaal', *J. Chem. Metal and Min. Soc. S. Afr.*, 12, 267–75, 370–72, 414–15; 13, 148–9 [130]
TURNER, G. A. (1909) *The Diet of the South African Natives in their Kraals*, Pretoria: Government Printer
—— (1911) 'Some of the tribal marks of the South African Native races', *Transvaal Med. J.*, 6, 141–53
TURNER, V. W. (1955) 'A revival in the study of African ritual', *Rhodes–Livingstone J.*, 17, 51–6 [363]

TWALA, R. G. (1952) *'Umhlanga* (reed) ceremony of the Swazi maidens', *African Studies*, 11, 3, 93–104
TYLDEN, G. (1950) *The Rise of the Basuto*, Cape Town: Juta [381]
TYRRELL, B. (1968) *Tribal Peoples of Southern Africa*, Cape Town: Books of Africa [102, 130 *bis*]
VAN DEN BERG, M. R. (1965) 'Christus en die Amadlozi', *Opbouw*, 9, 31, 250–2, 258–60
VAN DEN BOGAERDE (1966) *Suid-Afrika in die Politiek-Ekonomiese Proses*, Pretoria
VAN DER HORST, S. (1335) 'Some effects of industrial legislation on the market for native labour in South Africa', *S. Afr. J. Econ.*, 3, 4
—— (1942) *Native Labour in South Africa*, London: Oxford University Press [171, 404, 413, 414]
—— (1960) *The Economic Implications of Political Democracy*, issued as a supplement to *Optima*, June [413]
—— (1964) *African Workers in Town: a study of labour in Cape Town*, Cape Town: Oxford University Press
—— (1965a) 'Africans on the land', *S. Afr. J. Econ.*, 33, 3, 237–46
—— (1965b) 'The effects of industrialization on race relations in South Africa' in G. Hunter (ed.), *Industrialization and Race Relations*, London: Oxford University Press
VAN DER MERWE, P. J. (1969) 'The economic influence of the Bantu Labour Bureau system on the Bantu labour market', *S. Afr. J. Econ.*, 37, 1, 42–54
VAN DER KEMP, J. T. (1804) 'An account of the religion, customs . . . of Caffraria', *Transactions of the London Missionary Society*, I, 432–68 [128, 129 *bis*, 417]
VAN DER SLEEN, W. G. N. (1967) *A Handbook on Beads*, Liège: Musée du Verre [131]
VAN DYCK, P. R. (1960) ''n Studie van Lala, sy fonologie, morfologie, en sintaksis' unpublished Ph.D. thesis, University of Stellenbosch [84]
VAN GENNEP, A. (1909) *The Rites of Passage* (English translation 1960), University of Chicago Press [243 *bis*]
VAN NIEKERK, B. J. (1966) 'Notes on the administration of justice among the Kwena', *African Studies*, 25, 37–45 [291, 294–9 *passim*]
VAN REENEN, J. (1961) 'The use of the concept of tooth material as an indication of tooth size in a group of Kalahari Bushmen', *S. Afr. J. Sci.*, 57, 12, 347–52 [14]
VAN TROMP, J. (1948) *Xhosa Law of Persons*, Cape Town: Juta
VAN WARMELO, N. J. (1930) *Transvaal Ndebele Texts*, Ethnological Publication, Vol. I, Pretoria: Government Printer [84]
—— (1931) *Kinship Terminology of the South African Bantu*, Pretoria: Government Printer (Ethnological publications, Vol. II)
—— (1932) *Contributions Towards Venda History, Religion and Tribal Ritual*, Ethnological Publications, Vol. III, [84, 326]
—— (1935) *A Preliminary Survey of the Bantu Tribes of South Africa*, Pretoria: Government Printer [142, 143]
—— (1938) *History of Matiwane and the Amangwane Tribe*, Ethnological Publication No. 7, Pretoria: Government Printer [362]
——(ed.) (1940) *The Copper Miners of Musina and the Early History of the Zoutpansberg*, Ethnological Publication 8), Pretoria: Government Printer [130]
—— (1944a) *The Ba Letswalo or Banarene*, Pretoria: Government Printer
—— (1944b) *The Bathlabine of Moxobôya*, Pretoria: Government Printer
—— (1944c) *The Bakoni BaMaake*, Pretoria: Government Printer
—— (1944d) *The Banarene of Sekôrôrô*, Pretoria: Government Printer
—— (1944e) *The Banarene of Mmutlana*, Pretoria: Government Printer
—— (1944f) *The Bakoni of Mametša*, Pretoria: Government Printer
—— (1944g) *The Batubatse of Mašišimale*, Pretoria: Government Printer
—— (1944h) *The Genealogy of the House of Sekhukhune*, Pretoria: Government Printer
—— (1948a) *Venda Law: Part I: Betrothal*, Ethnological Publication No. 23, Pretoria [191 *bis*, 193 *bis*, 205]

—— (1948b) *Venda Law: Part II: Married Life*, Pretoria: Government Printer
—— (1948c) *Venda Law: Part III: Divorce*, Pretoria: Government Printer
—— (1949) *Venda Law (Part IV: Inheritance)*, Ethnological Publication No. 23, Pretoria: Government Printer [301, 305 *bis*, 308]
—— (1952) *Language Map of South Africa*, Pretoria: Government Printer [59]
—— (1955) 'Wer sind die Basotho', *Afrikanistische Studien*, Veröff. Nr. 26, Inst. f. Orientforschung, Dtsche Akad. d. Wisensch., Berlin [84 *bis*]
—— (1966) 'Zur Sprache und Herkunft der Lemba', *Dtsches Inst. f. Afrika-Forschung.* Bel. 5, 273–83 [84]
—— (1967) *Venda Law (Part V: Property)*, Ethnological Publication No. 50, Pretoria: Government Printer [310]
VAN ZYL, H. J. (1939) 'Some of the commonest games played by the Sotho people of Northern Transvaal', *Bantu Studies*, 13, 293–305
VEDDER, (1923) *Die Bergdama*, Hamburg: Friederichsen [xii]
VERSTER, J. (1965) 'The trend and pattern of fertility in Soweto: An urban Bantu community', *African Studies*, 24, 3–4, 131–98 [470, 471]
—— (1967) 'Social survey of Western Township, 1964', *African Studies*, 4, 175–245
VILAKAZI, A. (1957) 'A reserve from within', *African Studies*, 16, 2, 93–101 [185, 187, 195, 197, 198, 423 *bis*, 425–30 *passim*, 433, 436]
—— (1962) *Zulu Transformations: A study of the Dynamics of Social Change*, Pietermaritzburg: University of Natal Press
VILJOEN, S. P. (1961) 'Higher productivity and higher wages of native labour in South Africa', *S. Afr. J. Econ.*, 29, 1, 35–40
VON FISCHER, E. (1955) 'Über die sogenannte Hottentottenschürze: nebst bemerkungen über den descensus testiculorum', *Z. f. Morphologie und Anthrop.*, 47, 1, 58–66
VON RICHTER, W. (1970) 'Wildlife and rural economy in S.W. Botswana', *Botswana Notes and Records*, 2, 85–94 [171]
VON SICARD, H. (1952) 'Ngoma Lungundu, eine afrikanische Bundeslede', *Studia Ethnogr. Upsal.*, 5, Uppsala [84 *bis*]
—— (1955) 'Shaka and the North', *African Studies*, 14, 4, 145–55
WADE, P. T., T. JENKINS and E. R. HUEHNS (1967) 'Haemoglobin variant in a Bushman', *Nature*, 216, 5116, 688–90, London
WAGNER, G. (1954) 'Some economic aspects of Herero life', *African Studies*, 13, 3–4, 117–31
WAGNER, P. A. (1926) 'Bronze from an ancient smelter in the Waterberg district of the Transvaal', *S. Afr. J. Sci.*, 23, 899–900
WAGNER, P. A. and H. S. GORDON (1929) 'Further notes on ancient bronze smelters in the Waterberg district, Transvaal', *S. Afr. J. Sci.*, 26, 563–74 [130]
WALK, L. (1928a) 'Die ersten Lebensjahre des Kindes in Südafrika', *Anthropos*, 23, 38–109
—— (1928b) 'Initiationszeremonien und Pubertätsriten der südafrikanischen Stämme', *Anthropos*, 23, 861–966
WALKER, A. R. P. (1958) 'Certain biochemical findings in man in relation to diet', *Ann. N.Y. Acad. Sci.*, 69, art. 5, 989–1008 [45]
—— (1966) 'Nutritional, biochemical and other studies on South African populations', *S. Afr. Med. J.*, 40, 814–52 [45]
WALKER, E. A. (1922) *Historical Atlas*, Cape Town: Oxford University Press [394]
—— (1928) *A History of South Africa*, London: Longmans, Green [399]
—— (1948) *The Great Trek* (3rd edn.), London: Black
—— (1957) *History of Southern Africa*, London: Longmans [370, 375]
WALKER, I. L. and B. WEINBREN (1960) *2,000 Casualties*, Pietermaritzburg: Trade Union Council [414]
WALTER, E. V. (1969) *Terror and Resistance*, New York: Oxford University Press [279–83 *passim*]

WALTHER, M. (1968) 'Patterns of Life in Domestic Service', unpublished dissertation submitted for B.A. Hons. degree to Department of Social Anthropology, University of the Witwatersrand, Johannesburg [465]

WALTON, J. (1948) 'South African peasant architecture', *African Studies*, 7, 139–45

—— (1954) 'The forked sledge in Southern Africa', *Ethnos*, 1–4 [129]

—— (1956a) *African Village*, Pretoria: Van Schaik [128, 131]

—— (1956b) 'Early Bafokeng settlement in South Africa', *African Studies*, 15, 1, 37–45

WANGEMANN, T. (1875) *Die Geschichte der Berliner Mission im Zulu-Lande*, Berlin: Evangel. Missionshaus

WANGEMANN, T. (1957) *Maleo en Sekoekoeni*, Cape Town: van Riebeck Society [270–1]

WANGER, W. (ed.) (1911–13) *The Collector*, Marianhill: Mission Press (Zulu)

WARNER, H. W. (1961) *A Digest of South African Native Civil Law 1894–1957*, Cape Town: Juta

WARNER, J. C. (1858) 'Notes' in J. Maclean (ed.) (1858a), Ch. 3, pp. 59–112 [284, 296, 300 *bis*, 316 *bis*]

WASHBURN, S. L. (1949) 'Sex differences in the pubic bone of Bantu and Bushman', *Am. J. Phys. Anthrop.*, 7, 3, 425–32 [15, 16]

—— (1963) 'The study of race', *Amer. Anthrop.*, 65, 521–31 [45]

WASSERMANN, H. P. and T. HEYL (1968) 'Quantitative data on skin pigmentation in South African races', *S. Afr. Med. J.*, 42, 3, 98–101 [17–19 *passim*, 21]

WATT, J. M. and M. G. BREYER-BRANDWIJK (1932) *The Medical and Poisonous Plants of Southern Africa*, Edinburgh: Livingstone [343]

WATT, J. M. and N. J. VAN WARMELO (1930) 'The medicines and practice of a Sotho doctor', *Bantu Studies*, 4, 47–63

WATSON, W. (1958) *Tribal Cohesion in a Money Economy*, Manchester University Press [171]

—— (1959) 'Migrant labour and detribalization', *Bull. Inter-African Labour Inst.*, 6, 1 (report in J. Middleton (ed.), *Black Africa: Its Peoples and Their Cultures Today*, London: Macmillan, 1970, pp. 38–48)

WEBB, C. DE B. (1969) 'Great Britain and the Zulu people 1879–1887' in L. Thompson (ed.), 302–23 [378]

WEINER, J. S. (1952) 'A spectrophotometer for measurement of skin colour', *Man*, 253, 152–3 [17]

—— (1954) 'Nose shape and climate', *Am. J. Phys. Anthrop.*, 12, 1–4 [13]

WEINER, J. S., G. AINSWORTH HARRISON, R. SINGER, R. HARRIS, and W. JOPP (1964) 'Skin colour in Southern Africa', *Human Biology*, 56, 3, 294–307 [17–19 *passim*]

WEINER, J. S. and ZOUTENDYK, A. (1959) 'Blood group investigation on Central Kalahari Bushmen', *Nature*, 183, 843–4, London [32, 45]

WELSH, D. (1971) *The Roots of Segregation: Natal Native Policy (1845–1910)*, Cape Town: Oxford University Press [378]

WENINGER, M. (1965) 'Cimba and Vatwa, bantuide Viehzuchter und nicht-bantuide Wildbeuter', *Mitt. Anthrop. Ges. Wien*, 95, 180–90

WENNER-GREN FOUNDATION (1968) *Research Conference on Bantu Origins in sub-Saharan Africa*, Chicago, March 24–9 (manuscript), pp. 1–4 [37–40 *passim*]

WERBNER, R. (1970) 'Land and chiefship in the Tati Concession', *Botswana Notes and Records* 2, 6–13 [143, 176, 272]

WERNER, A. (1933) *Myths and Legends of the Bantu*, London: Harrap

WESSMANN, R. (1908) *The Bawenda of the Spelonken (Transvaal)*, London: African World

WESTERMANN, D. (1952) 'African linguistic classification', *Africa*, 22, 250–6 [38]

WESTPHAL, E. O. J. (1963) 'The linguistic prehistory of Southern Africa: Bush, Dwadi, Hottentot and Bantu linguistic relationships', *Africa*, 33, 237–65

WHEELWRIGHT, C. A. (1905) 'Native circumcision lodges in the Zoutpansberg', *J. Roy. Anthrop. Inst.*, 55, 251–5

WHITFIELD, G. M. B. (1948) *South African Native Law*, Cape Town: Juta [304, 307' 310 *bis*, 311, 316]
WHITING, J. W. M., R. KLUCKHOHN and A. ANTHONY (1958) 'The function of male initiation ceremonies at puberty' in E. E. Maccoby, T. M. Newcomb and E. L. Hartley (eds.), *Readings in Social Psychology*, New York: Holt, Rinehart [244]
WIESENFELD, S. L. (1967) 'Sickle-cell trait in human biological and cultural evolution', *Science*, 157, 3793, 1134–40
WILLCOX, A. R. (1956) *Rock Paintings of the Drakensberg, Natal and Griqualand East*, London: Parrish, pp. 1–96 [36]
WILLOUGHBY, W. C. (1905) 'Totemism of the Becwana', *J. Roy. Anthrop. Inst.*, 35, 295–314
—— (1909) 'Notes on the initiation ceremonies of the Becwana', *J. Roy. Anthrop. Inst.*, 39, 228–45
—— (1923) *Race Problems in the New Africa*, Oxford: Clarendon Press [319]
—— (1928) *The Soul of the Bantu*, London: Student Christian Movement [353]
—— (1932) *Nature-Worship and Taboo*, Hartford, Conn.: Hartford Seminary Press [323]
WILSON, F. (1972a) *The Economics of Labour in the South African Gold Mines, 1930–1965*, Cambridge University Press [403, 415]
—— (1972b) *Migrant Labour in South Africa*, Johannesburg: South African Council of Churches and SPRO-CAS
WILSON, M. (1949) 'The Pondo and Pondomise' in A. M. Duggan-Cronin (ed.), *The Bantu Tribes of South Africa*, Vol. III, Sect. 2
—— (1951) 'Witch beliefs and social structure', *Amer. J. of Soc.*, 56, 4, 307–13 [338]
—— (1954a) 'Nyakyusa ritual and symbolism', *Amer. Anthrop.*, 56, 2, 228–41 [344]
—— (1954b) 'Conditions in the Ciskei', *Race Rel. J.*, 21, 1, 1–9
—— (1956) 'An urban community' (East London) in *Social Implications of Industrialization and Urbanization in Africa South of the Sahara*, UNESCO, pp. 191–8
—— (1957) *Rituals of Kinship Among the Nyakyusa*, London: Oxford University Press [351]
—— (1959a) *Communal Rituals Among the Nyakyusa*, London: Oxford University Press [363]
—— (1959b) *Divine Kings and the 'Breath of Men'*, Frazer Lecture, London: Cambridge University Press
—— (1959c) 'The early history of the Transkei and Ciskei', *African Studies*, 18, 4, 167–78 [83, 363]
—— (1966) 'The implications of the gospel in South African society', *S. Afr. Outlook*, 96, 193–6
—— (1969) 'Changes in social structure in Southern Africa: the relevance of kinship studies to the historian' in L. M. Thompson (ed.) (1969)
WILSON, M., S. KAPLAN, E. M. WALTON and T. MAKI (1952) *Social Structure*, Vol. 3, Pietermaritzburg: Keiskammahoek Rural Survey [183, 195, 198, 230, 234–5, 239, 241, 243, 245 *bis*, 322, 325, 358–9, 440]
WILSON, M. and A. MAFEJE (1963) *Langa: A Study of Social Groups in an African Township*, Cape Town: Oxford University Press [443, 459–64 *passim*, 467–8 *passim*, 470–2 *passim*]
WILSON, M. and L. THOMPSON (1969) *The Oxford History of South Africa*, Vol. I, London: Oxford University Press [xix, 83, 203, 223, 368–9 *passim*, 374, 396, 412]
—— (1971) *The Oxford History of South Africa*, Vol. II, Oxford: Clarendon Press [382, 384, 386, 396]
WINKELMAN, F. VON (1788–9) 'Account of a journey' in E. C. Godée-Molsbergen, *Reizen in Zuid Afrika in de Hollandse Tijd*, 4, 63–99, 's Gravenhage: Nijhoff [129–31 *passim*]
WOLPOFF, M. H. (1968) 'Climatic influence on the skeletal nasal aperture', *Am. J. Phys. Anthrop.*, 29, 405–24 [13]

WORSLEY, P. M. (1961) 'The analysis of rebellion and revolution in modern British social anthropology', *Science and Society*, 25, 26–7 [363]

YOUNG, F. W. (1962) 'The function of male initiation ceremonies: a cross-cultural test of an alternative hypothesis', *Am. J. of Soc.*, 67, 379–96

—— (1965) *Initiation Ceremonies: A cross-cultural study of status dramatization*, New York: Bobbs-Merrill [236]

ZIERVOGEL, D. (1954) *The Eastern Sotho*, Pretoria: Van Schaik [78]

ZOUTENDYK A., A. C. KOPEC, and A. E. MOURANT (1953) 'The blood groups of the Bushmen', *Am. J. Phys. Anthrop.*, 11, 361–8

—— (1955) 'The blood groups of the Hottentots', *Am. J. Phys. Anthrop.*, 13, 4, 691–8

Subject Index

absolutism, *see* despotism
administration, *see* government
adoption, 308–9
adultery, 187, 188, 284, 361
affines, 204, 205–6, 270, 273, 275, 279, 358–9, 361; *see* marriage
afterbirth, 214
age organization, 232–3, 234, 235, 238, 239, 269, 280; 'age grade', 239; informal, 221ff, 239, 361; in town, 463; *see also* military organization; regimental system
agnation, 178ff, 187, 207; *see also* descent groups; family groups
agriculture, 90ff, 151ff, 168ff; changes in, 93–4, 168ff; crops, 90–4, 135–75 *passim*; implements, 91–2, 154ff, 159, 401; labour in, 122–5, 154ff; ritual in, 93, 147, 322–3, 355; *see also* rainmaking
ancestor cult, 104–6, 214–15, 260, 318–59 *passim*; confession in, 345–6; cult group, 345ff; officiator in, 346–8, 353
ancestor spirits: abode of, 328; attitude to, 332; calling of, 329–30; characteristics of, 324ff, 330–2; 'communicating ancestors', 329–30; and divination, 348ff; and dreams, 332; as lineage dead, 328–30; manifestations, 332–3; in town, 333–5, 433ff, 439–40; as upholders of law, 285
ancestors, extra-descent group, 330, 333–5, 345, 347–8, 349; *see also* matrilineal kin
animal husbandry, 94–7, 144; *see also* cattle; small stock
annexations (of territory), 367–90 *passim*
appeals, 146, 299
Arab influence, 59, 81–3, 127
archaeological evidence, 39–40, 57–9
army, *see* military organization
associations, voluntary, 446–7, 466ff; burial societies, 447, 468; civic associations, 447; church as, 425–6; homeboy groups, 446–7, 450ff, 461, 466–7; mutual aid societies, 447, 466, 468; social clubs, 466, 468; sports clubs, 447, 466, 467–8; *see also* churches
asylum, 300

asymmetrical alliance, *see* preferential marriage
autochthones, 322, 323
avunculate, 347

banishment, 288, 289, 292
Bantu Authorities, 167, 393ff
Bantu Authorities Act (1951), 393–4
'Bantu genesis', 31ff, 36ff
Bantu 'race', concept of, 30–2
Bantu, Southern: classification of (biological), 3–30, 32ff, *see also* physical characteristics; classification of (cultural), 56–81; early history, 32ff, 36ff, 263ff; population, 4–5, 59–60, 441–3; racial affinities, 32ff; recent history, 56–81, 367–90, 398ff
barracks, military, 280
barrenness, 180, 188, 212–13; *see also* sororal polygyny; sororate
barter, 126, 136, 175; *see also* exchange; trade
basketry, 118–19
Basters, 5
Basutoland, *see* Lesotho
batlhanka, 264; *see also* vassals
beadwork, 121
Beaumont Commission, 391
Bechuanaland, *see* Botswana
beer, 100–1; ritual importance of, 104, 346, 352–3; social importance of, 275–6, 451
betrothal, 306; *see also* marriage
bilateral kin group (Lobedu), 195, 200, 205, 325, 334, 345
birth, 212–16; *imbeleko*, 215; medicines, 213; ritual, 105, 213–14; seclusion at, 214; taboos, 213; of twins, 214
bizmus, 172–3
blood groups, *see* physical characteristics
boats, 90
bogadi, *see* bridewealth
bone-carving, 120–1
Botswana, 3, 6, 136, 167, 168, 381; constitutional development of, 292, 393
boundaries, 137–8, 146, 257, 259, 367ff, 385, 386ff

511

SUBJECT INDEX

bride, 204–5
bridewealth, 160ff, 163–4, 165–6, 174, 179ff, 187ff, 194, 204, 212, 284, 311; economic implications, 160–7, 445; implications of, 163–4, 187ff; political implications, 269–70; rights *in genetricem*, 187–8, 190; rights *in uxorem*, 187, 190; in town, 452, 460; transfer of rights, 187–8, 306–7
British Kaffraria, 372ff, 380, 399
Bunqa system, 389–90, 392
burial rites, *see* mortuary rites
burial societies, *see* associations
Bushman (San), *see* Tribal Index
byali, *see* initiation, girls'

calabashes, 120
calendar of work, 93, 122–3, 154–6
Cape Franchise, 375, 390ff
capital, 135, 149, 152ff; cattle as political capital, 398
capital punishment, 286, 288, 299
cash-cropping, 168, 401
cattle, 94–7, 149ff, 160ff; as bridewealth, 160–7; as conservative force, 174; diseases of, 96; economic value of, 152, 153, 163–4, 165ff, 206; as food, 94, 150–1, 152–3; as house property, 160ff, 164–5; husbandry, 94–7, 141ff, 149ff, 163–7, 174; and inheritance, 164; as money, 152, 275; in political system, 259; and power, 163, 166, 259ff; in ritual, 95, 152, 164, *see also* rituals of kinship; social value of, 94ff, 150ff, 152, 165, 259; uses as capital, 149ff, 152ff; *see also* bridewealth; marriage
'Cattle-killing delusion' (1857–8), 373–4, 399, 417
cattle-linkage, 160, 164, 206–7
cattle posts, 87–8, 141, 144, 155, 165
cephalic index, 10–11
ceremonial, 344–5; *see also* rituals
Chequerboard Realm, 251ff
chief, 79–80, 247ff, 251, 254, 259, 265ff, 273, 288ff, 292ff; authority of, 247, 266, 288, 289, 292; and councils, 291; deposition of, 289, 294; economic functions, 137ff, 155, 157, 251ff, 259; graves of, 324, 354; in law, 247, 288ff; insignia of, 103, 112, 288; and land, 137, 155, 251ff, 257, 266, 289; loyalty to, 288, 354, 362; and people (balance of power), 79–80, 247, 251, 253, 259, 267ff, 272, 288–9, 291; prerogatives of, 95, 103, 138, 266, 284, 285, 288ff; present position of, 291–2, 389ff, 423; regency for, 288–9; ritual functions, 147, 248, 260–2, 266, 350–1, 354–6; succession of, 263, 268, 288–9; wealth, 138, 148, 156–7, 259, 290, 295, *see also* tribute; wives of, 183, 266; *see also* government, local; law, administrative; law, constitutional
Chief, paramount, 146, 249, 268ff, 272, 273, 369
Chiefdom, xvi, 246–67 *passim*, 290, 415; cluster, xv, xvi, 316; composition of, 262ff; fission in, 246, 263, 368; *see also* law, constitutional; states
Chiefs, House of (Botswana), 292
child-rearing, 211ff, 217ff; agents, 218; changes in, 211ff; feeding, 218; in infancy, 217–19; toilet-training, 218; weaning, 219; *see also* socialization
Christianity, 318, 359, 415–38 *passim*; and beliefs in traditional world-view, 430–2, 436–8; patterns of acceptance and growth, 417, 420–3, 427ff; and social change, 429; and social structure, 427–30; and traditional beliefs, 436–8; among urban Africans, 438–40, 462; *see also* churches; missions
Christianization, differential, 420ff, 427ff
Christians, 415–38 *passim*; position in social structure, 415, 420ff; proportion of, 420
churches, 415–38 *passim*, 467; associations, 425–6, 432; distribution of, 420–3; statistics, 420ff, 467; in urban areas, 438–9, 467; *see also* Christianity; missions
cicatrization, 103, 215
circumcision, 58, 82, 105, 228–9, 230ff, 243; *see also* initiation, boys'
clan, 82 (Lemba), 178, 201–3, 262–4, 325; changes in, 201; characteristics of, 201, 262–4; name, 201–2, 262; customs, 302; exogamy, 178, 201–2, 203–4, 262; functions, 201, 202; hospitality, 201; political significance of, 264–5; royal, 196, 263–5; *see also* descent groups; totem groups
classes, 272–3; among urban Africans, 462ff; *see also* serfs; vassals
clientship, 127
climate, 46–9; rainfall, 46–8, 138, 144, 274; *see also* ecology
clothing, 101–3
commensalism, 165, 261, 353; *see also* ritual
complementary filiation, *see* matrilineal kin
compound system, 403, 443, 446

512

confession of anger, 345
congenital blue spot, *see* physical characteristics
contract, 311
cooking, 99–100; *see also* diet
copper mining, 47, 114–15
cosmetics, 103–4
costume (ritual), 102–3, 232–4, 242, 243, 434
councillors, 255; *see also* government, local
councils, 247, 255–6, 267, 289; *see also* government, central
courts, 146, 286, 291; discipline, 294; 'military courts', 294; *see also* law of procedure
co-wives, 180, 189, 358; *see also* polygyny
crafts, 113–22
creditors and debtors, 287
crimes, *see* law, criminal
crops, 92, 144, 153ff, 158; grain as 'money', 153–4; present day, 170; production of, 90–4, 153–7; storage of, 87, 153, 274
cross-cousin marriage, *see* marriage, preferential
cross-cousins, *see* marriage, preferential
customary law, recognition of, 371–2, 377; code of, 372, 377
customary unions, 309

dagga (cannabis), 59, 112
damage to property, 313
dancing, 111, 215–16, 217, 236, 275, 350
dead, spirits of, *see* ancestor spirits
death, *see* mortuary rites
debt, 163, 174
delict, 312–13
descent, 178ff
descent groups, 177–203 *passim*, 284–301 *passim*; cohesion of, 330, 345–6, 354; general, 178ff, 194–203, 262–3; and land, 197ff; in law, 302ff; and locality, 184–7, 196–7, 325; segmentation of, 263; in town, 460ff; *see also* clan; lineage
despotism, 247–8, 259–60, 279–82, 288
'detribalization', 447ff; *see also* migrants; urbanization
diet, 92ff, 99, 149ff, 158, 274; *see also* food; nutrition
discipline: of children, 224; tribal, 294
disease, *see* divination; sorcery; witchcraft
disputes, *see* law of procedure
district council system, 389ff
districts, 139ff, 145, 248, 253, 260–1, 273ff, 277, 280, 290–1; *see also* government, local

divination, 348–57; in courts, 301; and interpretation of misfortune, 352, 356ff; methods of, 105–6, 348–50, 356–7; Nguni pattern of, 105, 348ff; Venda pattern of, 105, 357; *see also* diviners
diviners, 348–50, 434, 437; activities of, 348; and ancestors, 348ff; Christians and, 437; initiation of, 322, 348–9; methods, 348–50, 356–7; in town, 449, 454; *see also* divination
division of labour, 123ff, 158–9; in agriculture, 123, 151, 158–9; boys, 220–2; changes in, 457–8; in children's activities, 220ff; girls, 222
divorce, 194; *see also* marriage, dissolution of
dogs, 97, 98
domba, 217, 233, 236, 240; *see also* initiation, girls'
domestic life, 123–5
draught animals, 90, 169–70
dress, *see* clothing
drums, 59, 106–7
'dual descent', 195
dwellings, 88–90; *see also* settlement
dyes, 117–18, 119

ear-piercing ceremonies, 225, 242
ecology, 46–55, 135, 136–7, 138ff, 148–9, 449; ecological zones, 135ff; ecologies of 'East' and 'West', 135ff; and political power, 135ff
economic development, 167ff, 397–412 *passim*
economic organization, 135ff; changes in, 167ff, 171ff, 397–412 *passim*; concept of 'risk', 139, 143ff, 252; dual economy, 135–6, 167ff; markets, 135; 'unit of exploitation', 139ff, 143, 145, 268, 277, *see also* cattle; crops; work parties
education: African education, 374; training of young, 124, 360; *see also* socialization
emigration and immigration, 293
employment: 'civilized labour policy', 135, 391, 409; on farms, 398ff; in mining, 401ff, 405ff; restrictions on, 167, 135–6, 391, 409–10; in secondary industry, 404–5, 408–10
endogamy, 82, 272
environment (geographical), 46–55 *passim*, 135–75 *passim*; rainfall, 138, 144; soil types, 91, 144; *see also* ecology
estates of administration, 145ff, 148
estates of production, 146ff, 152, 160

ethics, *see* morality
ethiopianism, *see* Independent churches
evidence, law of, 300–1
exchange, 126, 136
exogamy rules, 165, 177, 178, 192–3, 203, 205, 306; urban attitudes to, 461
'exploitation, unit of', 139ff, 143, 145, 268, 277
explorers, early, 56
extra-descent group ancestors, *see* ancestors

fakwa, uku, 311
familiars, 338; *see also* witchcraft
family, 179ff; developmental cycle of, 182–4; dissolution of, 184; as economic unit, 159–67, 179–80; extended, 179, 183–4; fission of, 184; matrifocal, 457; nuclear, 179; polynynous, 179–81; urban, 456ff; *see also* family estate; house property; 'houses'
family estate, 135–75 *passim*; *see also* house property
'family group' (Tswana), 159–67, 179ff, 185–6, 187, 197, 200, 209
farm people, xvi, 392
father's sister, 326, 347–8, 358
feasts, *see* hospitality groups; rituals
federations, 248–9, 251, 268ff, 271ff; *see also* states
fertility, 361
fertility dolls, 213
'fields of office', 148
fines, 259, 299; *see also* law, criminal; law of procedure
fire, sacred (of Pedi), 105, 269–70
first fruits ritual, 105, 147, 248, 260–2, 269, 350, 355–6; *see also* rituals, communal
fishing, 98–9
flutes, 106, 108
food, 90–101, 150ff
food taboos: at birth, 213; at boys' initiation, 226, 230; at girls' initiation, 227
Fort Willshire, 370
fowls, 97
frontier, the moving, 367ff, 385, 386ff
frontier wars, *see* wars with whites
fruits, 99, 158; *see also* diet
funeral ceremonies, *see* mortuary rites
Fynn, H. F., 280

games and toys, 111–12, 222–3
gangs: herdboys, 221–2; *tsotsis*, 463–4; youths, 238ff
genetic markers, 24ff, 31, 32ff; *see also* physical characteristics

genital operation of girls, 233
genitor (as pater), 188; *see also* social fatherhood
Glen Grey system, 389, 391
goats and sheep; *see* small stock
gold, 114
gourds, 120
government, central, 249ff, 258, 287–90; changes in system, 367–90 *passim*; and land tenure, 137, 155, 251ff, 253ff, 266, 289; political integration, 246, 248–9, 251, 266, 268ff, 271ff, 273–90, 354; urban African policy, 441ff; *see also* appeals; chiefs; councils; courts; law, constitutional
government, local, 145ff, 249, 251ff, 256–7, 265, 266, 271, 290–5; and economic control, 137ff, 145–9; and land tenure, 137ff, 144, 145–9, 176, 252, 256–8, 289; officials in, 256, 265; and urban housing, 443–4; *see also* headmen
grain, *see* crops
granaries, 58, 85, 87
grave goods, 327
graves, *see* chief, graves of; mortuary rites
grazing, 141, 144, 253; *see also* cattle; cattle posts
Grey, Sir George, 373ff, 399
guardianship, 301, 303, 306, 308–9

hairdressing, 104
harvest, 93, 147, 159
harvest festival, *see* first fruits ritual
headmen, 139ff, 144, 145ff, 148, 176, 198, 252ff, 255, 256, 257, 265, 267, 270, 273, 276–7, 284–301 *passim*, 374; and land tenure, 144, 145ff, 176, 252, 256–8, 289; powers of, 252; and ruler, 253–4, 255, 259; and subjects, 176, 250ff, 254ff, 258, 265; *see also* councillors; courts; government, local
herbalists, 339–42, 351
herding, 220–1; *see also* cattle; cattle posts
history: anthropobiological evidence, 40–4; archaeological evidence, 39–40, 57, *see* Bantu, Southern; genealogies, 57; language as evidence, 37–8, 58ff; method, 57ff; oral tradition, 56–7; sources of, 37ff, 56ff
hlonipha, 204–5
homeboy groups, *see* associations
'Homeland' concept, 18, 390ff, 393ff, 408
homestead, *see* settlement
horn carving, 120–1

horses, 90
hospitality groups, 197, 199–200
Hottentots (Khoikhoi), 3–30 *passim*, 368; see also Tribal Index
house property, 159–67, 179, 180
'houses', 179ff, 187, 188
hunting, 97–8, 122, 123, 136, 158, 159, 203, 253
husband–wife relationship, 162, 179, 180, 204, 205, 361; see also family marriage
hut building, 123
huts, see settlement

imbeleko, see birth
immigrant groups, 56–81 *passim*, 289
immigration and emigration, 293
incest, 177, 192, 193, 205, 276, 286
Independent churches, 418ff, 432ff; Ethiopian type, 418–19, 439; fission in, 467; number, 418; origin of, 418ff; Sabbatarian-Baptist, 419, 431, 433, 436; and traditional beliefs, 425, see also syncretism; Zionist, 420, 425, 431, 432, 433, 434ff
India, possible gene flow between Africa and, 28
Industrial Reconciliation Act, 410
infancy, 217ff
infanticide, 214
influx control, 167
inheritance, 162, 164, 178, 181, 182, 196
initiation, 105, 111, 227ff, 261, 269; abolition of, 285; of boys, 229–31; functions of, 234ff; genital operation (girls), 233; of girls, 232–4; and moral responsibility, 360; 'supplementary', 231–2; taboos at, 230, 233
inkulu, see lineage head
intra-crural intercourse, 236–7, 459
iron-working, 37, 92, 114, 159, 203
Isaacs, Nathaniel, 280
isibongo, see clan, name
isiduko, see clan, name
isithebe, see hospitality groups
Israelites, 419, 433

job reservation, 391, 409–10
joking relationships, 178, 324, 347
judicial process, 362; see also law of procedure

Kgamêlô, 272, 290
kgôrô, 186, 209–10; see also ward
kgotla, 186, 209–10, see also ward

Khoikhoi (Hottentots), see under Tribal Index
Khoisan peoples: biological relationship with South African Negro, 13–14, 16, 32–6, 43–4; physical characteristics, 32ff; see also Tribal Index under Khoikhoi and San
kin, 159ff, 177ff; categories, 177; in court procedure, 200; and residence, 184–5, 195ff; see also affines; clan; descent group; lineage; matrilineal kin
kingdoms, 246, 249, 250, 266, 273–90 (Lobedu) 279–82 (Zulu); see also states
kingship (Zulu), 248, 279–82; sacred, 248, 273ff, 351
kinship, 177ff, 262–3, 460–2; and authority, 262–3; and residence, 184–7; in urban areas, 460–2; see also agnation; descent groups; matrilineal kin
kinship terminology, 208–9; Iroquois system, 208; Omaha system, 208–9
Kommissie Trek, 375

labour, African, 167, 391, 405ff; employment, 135–6, 410ff, 429, 446, see also migration, labour; organizations, 403; vertical mobility of, 408ff; wages of, 136, 410ff
labour, division of, 117, 118, 123f, 158–9, 173–4; see also division of labour
land, 135–75 *passim*; allocation of, 293; changes in allocation of, 295; ownership of, 91; see also land tenure
land tenure, 90f, 137ff, 140–1, 145ff, 160, 162–3, 168–9, 251–2, 253–5, 256–60; changes in, 94, 168ff; see also estates of production
languages, Bantu, 37–9, 72, 403; migration of, 37ff, 72; origins of, 37ff
law, 284–301 *passim*; constitutional, 287–92; and the courts, 286; and justice, 285; legislation, 284–5; and observance, 285–6; of persons, 301–5; promulgation of, 291; public, 287ff; public and private, 287; rights and duties, 287; and sanctions, 286; sources of, 284–5
law, administrative, 292–5; changes in, 295
law, constitutional, 287–92; changes in, 291–2
law, criminal, 295–7
law, customary: codification of, 372, 377; recognition of, 371–2, 377
law of evidence, 300–1
law, family, 306–9; changes in, 309

515

law of obligations, 311ff; delict, 312–13; quasi-contracts, 312
law of persons, 301–5
law, private, 301ff
law of procedure, 297–300; changes in, 300
law of succession, 313–15
law of things, 310–11
Leach, E. R., 273ff, 278
leeningplaats system, 368
Lemba, 81–3, 115–16
Lesotho, 136, 148, 167, 379–80; constitutional changes, 292, 295, 393
levies, 197, 290; *see also* tribute
levirate, 189–91
life-cycle, 211–20 *passim*; *see also* rituals of kinship; socialization
lightning doctor, 342, 355
lineage head, 178, 185, 196, 197, 198, 303–5, 345–8
lineages, 125ff, 178, 195ff, 325, 330–1; and bridewealth, 193–4; as core of hospitality groups, 197, 199–200; as core of local groups, 185, 196–7; court, 187, 200; as cult group, 196, 325, 345–6; depth, 178, 195–6, 325; in dispute settlement, 200; as economic group, 162–3, 166, 197–8; functions of, 195, 196; and land, 185, 197–9; minimal, 178; recruitment to, 196; solidarity of, 196, 330, 360–1
litigation, 285; *see also* law of procedure
livestock and money equivalents, 172–3
lobola, see bridewealth
location system, 376–7
lova, hu, 275

Mackenzie, A., 252ff, 268
mafisa, 145, 163, 166, 311
magic, 319, 339–42, 432, 433; chief's, 276, 350–1, 354–6; field, 93, 147, 322–3, 355; logic of, 340–1; love, 204, 341; magical elements in Separatist theology, 432, 433, 434–5; *see also* sorcery
magicians, *see* diviners; herbalists
magisterial system, 372ff, 374, 380–1, 387, 389
maintenance, 312
malaria, 27, 28, 29, 35, 48, 55
manyano, 425–6, 432, 439
markets, 135, 172ff
marriage, 160, 179ff, 187ff, 193–4, 304ff; as alliance, 163–4; choice, 192–3, 303; dissolution of, 194, 308; as exchange, 206–9, 263–4, 275, 277–8, 306–7; exogamy rules, 178, 192–3, 306; ghost, 190–1; inter-ethnic marriages in town, 465; legal aspects of, 306–9; major difference in systems, 177, 200, 203–9; preferential, 177, 178, 181, 192–3, 204, 205, 206, 207, 208, 273, 278ff; as political alliance, 192, 207–8, 270, 276–8; rights of woman in, 304ff; stability of, 193–4; in town, 456–60; wider implications of, 205, 276–7, 304ff; wifegivers and wife receivers, 206, 269–70, 275–6; woman-to-woman, 191–2, 276; *see also* bridewealth; family; law
material culture, 85–126 *passim*
matrilineal kin, 178, 207, 347
medicines: agricultural, 93, 96; birth, 215; for children, 217; of herbalist, 339–42; for sorcery, 339f; types of, 339–42; *see also* magic; sorcery
messianism, 434, 435
metal-working, 47, 81, 133, 114–16
Mfecane, 372, 375, 376, 379, 385
'middle class', 463, 464
migrants, 461, 462–4; stabilization and urbanization of, 447–50
migration, labour, 167ff, 171ff, 175, 397, 405ff, 408ff, 444–5; commencement of, 171; control of, 135–6, 167; effects of, 171ff, 405–6; incidence of, 175; numbers, 407; phases of, 171ff; rate of, 175; reasons for, 444–5
migrations, 5, 263, 416; Bantu, 5, 38ff; *see also* Bantu, Southern
military organization, 113, 247–8, 251, 254, 259, 265, 267, 268, 281, 289–90; doctoring of army, 354, 356; *see also* barracks, military; first fruit ritual; regimental system
milk, 150–3, 165, 166, 259; *see also* animal husbandry; cattle
milk taboos, 165, 201
millenarianism, 373–4, 417; *see also* 'Cattle-killing delusion'; Independent churches
mining (traditional), 58, 114–16, 401
mining industry, effect of, *see* labour; migration
misfortune, interpretation of, *see* divination; religion; sorcery; witchcraft
mission chiefdom (Natal), 428–9
mission stations, 423–4
missions, 369, 376, 379, 401, 415ff; activities, 426ff; administration of, 424–5; attitude to tradition, 425–6; changes in, 424–6; educational work of, 423; historical survey of, 415–20; and interpretation of Bantu tradition, 430ff; medical

work of, 423; and society, 427–30, 433ff; types of, 423ff
modisa (comptroller of pasture), 145, 256–7
mogolwane, 186, 187; *see also* headmen; ward
money, 135, 172
morality, 224, 236–7, 318, 337, 359–63, 423, 425, 433
mortuary rites, 105, 327; bringing back the dead, 327–8, 352
mother-in-law, *see* affines
mother's brother, 178, 334, 347, 348
music, 106–11
mutual aid societies, *see* associations
myths (of creation), 319–21

nagana (trypanosomiasis), 48, 55
naming, 215–17; communal (Pedi), 215–16
Natal Code of Native Law, 284–301 *passim*, 377
Natalia, Republic of, 375
'nations', 249, 279ff
'Native policy', 367, 371, 374–5, 378, 380, 385–6, 391ff; of Boer Republics, 385–6; Cape, 369ff, 374, 386ff; High Commission Territories, 378–84; Natal, 375–8
naturalization, 244
neighbours, 361–2
networks, 450–3
'Neutral (Ceded) Territory', 369–70
Nomkhubulwana, 147, 322–3
nqoma, 311
Ntsuanatsatsi, 320
nutrition, 8, 29–30; effect on brain, 30; *see also* diet; physical characteristics, stature

ochre, use of, 103–4
officers, tribal, 256, 265, 280
ordeal, poison, 350, 356, 357

pater (as genitor), 188
Pentacostalism, *see* Independent churches
'people of the river', *see* spirits, local and nature
pests, 55, 444
phakathi, ama, *see* councillors
Philip, Dr John, 370
physical characteristics, 3–30; Bantu 'race', concept of, 30–2; blood groups, 24–9, 31ff; bodily measurements and indices, 8ff; congenital blue spot, 20; eye colour, 20–1; eye folds, 23; genitalia, external, 22–3; hair, 21–2; head measurements, 10–12; migration and genetic structure, 5; pigmentation, 16–20, 35; population, 3–5; relationship to Khoisan, 32–6, 43–4; skeletal features, 12–16; soft tissues, 21–4; South African Negro genotype, 24–9; stature, 5–8; *see also* genetic markers
piacular rites, *see* rituals of kinship
pigs, 97
pipes, 112–13
planting, 92–3
plough, 92–4, 155, 169–70; introduction of, 169–70
political system: political expansion of, 249, 251; politics as zero-sum game, 251, 252–3; *see also* chiefdom; federation; government; kingdoms; states
polygyny, 160, 179ff
population, 3–5, 59–60, 168; density, 4–5
population growth, 5, 400, 412; of urban Africans, 441–4
pottery, 37, 39–40, 72, 116–17, 159, 172
praise names, 201; *see also* clan; totem groups
preferential marriage, *see* marriage
preferential secondary marriage (Tsonga), 189
pregnancy, 213–14; *see also* birth
premarital pregnancy: attitudes towards, 237, 361, 459–60; sanctions against, 237, 459–60
'priest', 346–8
property, 'fighting with', 275; *see also* house property; law of things
prophets, 369, 417, 434ff; *see also* Independent churches
puberty, 225ff; boys', 225–6; girls', 226–7
punishments, 296–7; capital, 297, 299; *see also* law, criminal
pyre-burning, 59

quasi-contract, 312
Queen Adelaide, Province of, 370–1, 377

rafts, 90
rainfall, *see* climate
rainmaking, 69, 93, 104, 147, 266, 267, 274, 276–9, 351, 354–6; *see also* rituals, communal
'raising seed', *see* levirate
Rand Rebellion (1922), 409
rank, 262–4; *see also* status
rattles, 106
reciprocity, 125, 154–7, 274, 275, 360–2; *see also* exchange
reconciliation rite, 345–6, 362

SUBJECT INDEX

'Red and School', xvi, 168, 175, 216, 235, 237, 427ff, 428–9, 431, 462
regency, 288–9
regimental system, 113, 232ff, 234, 235, 252–3, 259, 270–1, 280, 289–90
religion (traditional), 318–59 *passim*; concept of soul, 326; functions of, 318; influence of Christianity on, 430ff; as interpretation of the world, 318ff, 344–5; *see also* ancestor cult; ancestor spirits; morality; ritual
representation, African, 367, 377, 390ff
reserves, 167ff, 376, 377, 415; establishment of, 399
respect for seniors, 360–2; *see also* morality
revenue, 295
Rhodesian affinities of Bantu, 77–9, 81, 321, 348
rights and duties (in law), 287
rights *in geneticem*, *see* bridewealth
rights *in uxorem*, *see* bridewealth
rinderpest, 274, 378
risk, concept of, 139ff, 143ff, 252
ritual objects, *see* shrines
rituals, 104–6, 334–5, 344–59 *passim*; and ceremonial, 344; nature of, 344–5, 351ff; and social roles, 344f
rituals, communal, 105, 227ff, 248, 260–2, 269, 274, 280, 345, 350, 354–6; blessing the seed, 355; against insect pests, 323, 355; against lightning, 355; Nomkhubulwana, 147, 322–3; rainmaking, 266–7, 274, 276, 351, 354–6; *see also* first fruit rituals; rainmaking
rituals of kinship, 351–4; blood sacrifice, 352; commensalism, 165, 261, 353–4; libations, 104, 352ff; life cycle, 104–6, 351–4; piacular, 329, 352f; *see also* ancestor cult; birth; mortuary rites
rituals of rebellion, 355–6, 363ff
rivers, 47–8
role reversal, 323, 356
'rolling target' game, 111

sacred fire (Pedi), 269–70
sacrifice, meaning of, 353–4; *see also* ritual
San (Bushmen), *see under* Tribal Index
sanctions, 224, 237, 286, 324
scarification, 215
'School' people, xvi; *see also* 'Red and School'
secondary unions, 189, 209; *see also* levirate; sororate
segregation, policy of, 392ff, 441ff

self-help, 312–13
separatism, 417ff; *see also* Independent churches
serfs, 272; *see also* classes
settlement patterns, 85–90, 139ff, 140ff, 145ff, 185ff, 260–1
Shangana-Tsonga, 12, 278
share-cropping, 401
shaving rite, 215, 229, 231
sheep and goats, *see* small stock
Shepstone, Sir Theopholis, 376–8, 380, 386
Shepstone's Native Policy, 376ff, 392, 401
shields, 113
shrines, 104, 195, 333
sickle-cell trait, 27–9, 31, 35
sisa, uku (*ho fisa*), 127, 311; *see also* clientship
situational selection, 448ff, 453ff
skin working, 117–18
Sky God, *see* Supreme Being
sleeping sickness, 55; *see also* nagana
small stock, 96–7, 157–8
smelting, 115–16, 203
Smith, Sir Harry, 370–3
smoking, 112–13
snuff-taking, 112
social fatherhood, 188, 189–91, 191–2; *see also* pater
social network, 450ff
socialization, 111–12, 211ff, 234ff, 360; changes in child-rearing techniques, 212; compared with West, 211–12, 220; sanctions, 221, 224
soil types, 48, 144
sorcery, 331, 335ff, 337, 338–9; as interpretation of misfortune, 335ff
sororal polygyny, 189
sororate, 188–9, 213
sowing, 92–3, 154
sound shifts, 57ff, 61, 72
South African Negro, 3–30 *passim*; affinities with Khoisan, 32–6; affinities with other Negro, 31–2, 36ff; concept of, 31–2
spirits, 'free', *see* spirits, local and nature
spirits, local and nature, 321–2; Nomkhubulwana, 322–3; 'people of the river', 322; sacred woods, etc., 324
Spoor Law, 370, 371
sports clubs, *see* associations
stabilization, 448
states, 246–67 *passim*; and ecology, 250, 251ff; expansion of, 249, 251; genesis of, 246; types of, 247ff, 250; *see also* chiefdom; federations; kingdoms

status, 262, 263, 264, 265, 269, 270, 271, 275, 305, 360; *see also* stratification
stick fighting, 223, 235
'stock groups', 262ff
Stockenström, Treaty System, 371
stonework, 121–2
storage, *see* crops
strangers, 289, 363
stratification, 145–6, 264, 270, 272, 360; in town, 462ff; *see also* status
stringed instruments, 109–11
succession, law of, 313–15
suicide, ritual, 276, 351
Supreme Being, 319–20, 350, 354, 431, 432; and ancestors, 319; and Christian God, 431; and nature, 320–1
Swaziland, 3, 136, 167, 384, 421; constitutional development, 292, 295, 393
symbolism, 204, 318, 320, 324, 340–1, 345, 352, 353, 354, 356, 360
syncretism, 418ff, 430ff, 434f, 436ff; in Orthodox churches, 436–8; in Zionist churches, 434–6; *see also* Independent churches

tablier, 22–3
tatooing, 103
taxation, 171
taxonomy, problems of, 3–4
terror, as a political weapon, 280ff
Texas fever, 274
theleka, uku, 309
thikoloshe, 224, 338; *see also* familiars
thomba, see initiation
thondo, see initiation
tick-born diseases, 55–6
tilling, 91–2, 138, 147, 154–6
tin working, 114–15
tobacco, 112, 158
toilet-training, 218
Tomlinson Commission, 393, 404
tools, 113–14
topography, 46ff
totem groups, 178, 202–3, 263; origin of, 202–3; political functions of, 202
townships, urban, 441ff
toys and games, 111–12, 222–3
trade, 109, 114, 116, 118, 121, 126–8, 136, 159, 172, 278; with whites, 171ff, 370
trade fairs, 370
trading stores, 128, 170–1, 173
Transkein Territories, 292, 389ff
transport, 90
Treaty System, 370ff

trespass, law of, 147–8
'Tribal Estates', 251ff
tribalism, xvi, 447–8, 465
tribe: concept discussed, xv–xvi, 262, 354; nature of, 262–3, *see also* chiefdom; states
tribesman, concept of, xvi
tribute, 148, 159, 259–60, 270, 276, 279, 289, 290
trumpets, 107
tsotsis, 444, 463–4
twins, 214, 296, 321

umlaza, 97, 213–14
umndeni, see lineage head
umnumzana, see lineage head
urban Africans, 441–68 *passim*; Christianity among, 438–40; housing of, 441ff, 446; legal position of, 443–4
urban areas, xvi, xviii, 441–68 *passim*; housing in, 441ff; population of, 441–3; *see also* townships, urban
Urban Areas Act, 409
Urban Bantu Council, 465
urban life, 446–7, 456ff; kinship in town, 460ff; marriage and family in, 456ff; social structures and, 462ff
urbanization; concept of, 447ff; cultural aspects of, 453ff; legislation against, 398; 443–4; official policy towards, 441, 443–4; process of, 397–8, 401–8, 441–3, 444ff; reasons for, 444ff; structural aspect of, 450ff; *see also* labour migration
utensils, 100–1

vassals, 156, 249, 264, 272–3
vegetation, 49ff, 142, 158; changes in, 54; regions, 49ff
veld lore, 158, 222, 339f
voluntary associations, *see* associations; churches; missions
vust, uku, see marriage, ghost

wages, mine, 171, 403
War of Mlanjeni, 374; Bambatha Rebellion (1906–7), 378; Basuto-Free State War, 379ff; Cape-Xhosa War (1877–8), 387; Gun War (1880–1), 381; Mpondomise-Thembu Rebellion(1880), 387–8; Zulu War (1879), 377–8
ward, 86, 144–5, 186–7, 252, 255–6, 290–1; *see also* government, local; settlement patterns
wardhead, 186, 197, 291; *see also* headmen; government, local

wars, intertribal, 113, 255, 369, 387
wars with whites, 368ff; frontier wars, 367–75, 386ff, 398ff; War of 1834–5, 370, 372; War of the Axe, 371, 372
weaning, 219, 241
weapons, 113, 159
westernization, 367–468 *passim*; *see also* situational selection; urbanization
widows, 189–91; *see also* levirate
wiremaking, 116
witchcraft, 156, 157, 224, 259, 281, 318, 331, 335ff, 344, 437; accusations, 156, 357ff, 362; beliefs, 335ff, 337ff; Christian belief in, 437; familiars, 338; as interpretation of misfortune, 335ff; sociology of, 357–9
'witchdoctor', *see* diviners; herbalists
wives, 177–203 *passim*; co-wives, 180, 189, 358; death of, 188–9; ranking of, 160, 179–82, 305; *see also* family estate, house property; rights of, 304; status of, 180, 457; as targets of witchcraft accusations, 358–9
Wolseley, Sir Garnet, 268, 377, 386
women: in churches, 422–3; as district heads, 191–2; legal position of, 301ff; political use of, 270, 273ff, 276; rights of, 301ff; status of, 180; *see also* family; family estate; marriage; polygyny; wives
wood carving, 119–20
work parties, 91, 125, 151, 154ff, 163, 170

xylophones, 59, 107

youth groups, 220–2, 238–9

Zebu cattle, 111
Zionism, *see* Independent churches
Zululand Delimitation Commission (1902–4), 378

Tribal Index

Badyaranke (Senegal-Guinea), 41
Basa (Southern Cameroon), 41
Bemba, 171
Bhaca, 44, 63, 101, 104, 141, 173, 181, 183, 200, 213, 214, 218, 227, 228, 229, 239, 241, 263, 326, 327–8, 335, 337, 339, 341, 342, 345, 348, 353, 354, 355–6, 422
Bhala, 62
Bhele, 62, 63
Bila, 69
Birwa, 77
Bomvana, 62, 95, 214, 229, 230, 231, 241, 354, 355, 356, 357
Bomvini, 64
Bunja, 44
Bushmen, *see* San
Bushong, 41
Buthelezi, 65

Cele, 64
Chopi, 68, 205, 208, 229
Cunu, 64

Digôja (Lihoya), 76
Dikgale, 77
Diriko, 44
Djonga, 69
Dlamini, 64, 66, 384
Dumisa, 64
Dushane, 61, 358, 359
Dyola (Senegal), 41

Ewondo (Cameroon), 41, 43

Fakudze, 66
Fingo, *see* Mfengu
Fokeng, 73, 74, 75

Gaika, *see* Ngqika
Gamedze, 66
Ganda, 16
Gazini, 65
Gcaleka, 61, 374, 386
Gcumisa, 64
Gingqi, 62

Govera, 83
Gqunukhwebe, 61, 368
Griqua, 19, 382, 386
Gubevu, 63

Ha-Tshivhasa, 81
Hala, 62
Hananwa, 77, 116
Haya (Western Tanzania), 41
Herero, 47
Himba, 44
Hlakwana, 74
Hlanganu, 69
Hlatjwako, 66
Hlengwe, 69, 70
Hlubi, 44, 62, 63, 64, 65, 73, 213, 228, 239, 422
Hlutshini, 65
Hottentot, *see* Khoikhoi
Huruthse, 75, 76
Hwaduba, 67, 75

Ila, 44

Jumba, 62

Kaa, 75
Kalanga, 12
Karanga, 77, 78, 83, 348
Kasena (Haute Volta-Ghana), 41
Kgaga, 71, 77, 78, 185, 229
Kgalakgadi, 72, 76, 126, 171
Kgatla, 23, 75, 76, 173, 193, 225, 263, 429
Kgolokwe, 73, 74
Kgwakgwa, 73, 74
Khabeleni, 65
Khakhu, 81
Khoikhoi (Hottentot), 3, 4, 14, 19, 22, 23, 26, 27, 32, 33, 34, 35, 36, 37, 42, 59, 60, 61, 108, 368, 370, 398
Kholwa, 64
Khonjwayo, 62
Khosa, 69
Khumalo, 65, 66, 68
Khuruthse, 75

521

TRIBAL INDEX

Khuze, 63, 64
Kolobe, 79
Kolobeng, 75
Kololo, 74, 79
Koni, 77, 78
Koniagi (Senegal-Guinea), 41
Kôpa, 75
Kuambi, 44
Kuangari, 44
Kuanyama, 27, 41, 43, 44
Kubung, 75
Kunene, 63
Kutswe, 78
Kwalo, 62
Kwena, 73, 74, 75, 76, 256, 263, 383
Kwetshube, 62
Kxaxa, see Kgaga

Lala, 60, 61, 64
Lemba, 57, 81, 82, 114, 115, 116, 117, 229, 239
Lembethu, 81
Lenje, 44
Letswalo, 78, 229, 231
Letwaba (Maune), 67
Lobedu, 71, 77, 78, 79, 81, 87, 89, 99, 100, 116, 119, 120, 127, 148, 149, 155, 160, 163, 172, 174, 180, 182, 185, 189, 191, 192, 193, 195, 201, 202, 204, 205, 207, 208, 209, 217, 218, 219, 221–7, 229, 231–3, 235, 236, 240–1, 247–8, 250–1, 266–7, 273–6, 277–9, 281–2, 288, 319, 321, 325, 328, 330, 331–4, 337, 338–40, 342, 345–6, 348–50, 352, 354, 356–9, 362, 427
Logo (Congo), 41
Loswi, 348
Lwamondo, 81

Mabaso, 64
Maduna, 63
Mafunze, 64
Magagula, 66
Magwambane (Mokôpane), 67
Makhanya, 64, 141, 175, 182, 197, 198, 200, 201, 259
Makuya, 81
Malawi, 12, 44
Malete, 75
Maluleke, 69
Mametsa, 78
Manala, 67
Mangwato, 75, 284
Manhisa, 69
Maputa, 69

Maquba, 66
Maravi, 9
Maroteng (Pedi), 76
Masakona, 80
Masarwa, 44; see also San
Masemola, 229
Mashamba, 80
Mashau, 80
Mathabatha, 77
Mathenjwa, 65
Matlala, 77, 229, 231
Matlhako, 75
Matshavha (Matshaba), 81
Matswapong, 75
Maune, 67
Mavunda, 69
Mayogo (N. Congo), 41
Mbangala (Angola), 27
Mbatheni, 65
Mbo, 64, 65
Mbukushu, 27, 44, 47
Mbuthweni, 63
Mdlalose, 65
Mfengu (Fingo), 61, 62, 63, 102, 114, 214, 215, 229, 230, 231, 235, 239, 325, 358, 359, 372, 386, 387, 399, 417
Mhinga, 71
Miya, 63
Mkhize, 64
Mlozi, 44
Mmamabolo, 78, 229, 231
Mmanamela, 75
Mmatau, 75
Mndzebele, 66
Mngomezulu, 65
Modimosana, 75
Mokôpane (Magwambane), 67
Moletlane (Sebitiela), 67
Motsha, 75
Mpfumo, 69
Mphaphuli, 80, 81
Mphatlhele, 77
Mpondo (Pondo), 44, 62, 93, 95, 98, 99, 100, 111, 116, 120, 126, 141, 173, 201, 213, 214, 216, 219, 223, 224, 226, 228, 229, 237, 241, 250, 284, 289, 320, 324, 326, 327, 328–9, 330–1, 337, 338–9, 340, 345, 347, 348–9, 353–4, 355–6, 358, 386, 387, 388
Mpondomise, 62, 102, 185, 187, 197, 199, 200, 201, 202, 231, 238, 319, 325, 327, 329, 330, 333, 346, 355, 357, 361, 386, 388
Mpukunyoni, 65

TRIBAL INDEX

Mthethwa, 65, 66
Mugivhi, 81
Myeni, 65

Narene, 78
Nci, 62
Ndebele, Rhodesian, 67, 68, 102, 383–4, 385, 417
Ndebele, Transvaal, 12, 44, 59, 67, 75, 85, 86, 290; Northern, 59, 60, 61, 67, 70, 229; Southern, 67, 74, 77, 252, 253, 271
Ndlambe, 61, 325, 353, 358, 359
Ndungwana, 62
Ndzundza (Mapoch, Mapôrs), 67, 86
Ngoni, 61, 68, 70
Ngqika, 61
Nguni (general), 4, 22, 23, 59, 60, 61, 65, 66, 68, 71–4, 77, 85, 87–90, 92–4, 100, 101, 103, 106, 107, 109, 112, 121–3, 125, 127, 139–41, 143, 145, 147, 148, 150–3, 157, 159, 164, 165, 177–82, 185, 192–203, 205, 206, 208, 209, 213–15, 230, 239, 250, 251, 259, 262, 263, 264, 273, 280, 293, 300, 306, 308, 325, 328, 329, 330, 332, 333–4, 337, 338–9, 340, 349, 351–2, 355–8
Nguni (Cape), 10, 12, 14, 57, 58, 61, 63, 85, 88, 95, 98, 99, 100–5, 112, 113, 116–19, 121, 151, 167, 181, 190, 195, 196, 198, 201, 223, 226, 229, 230, 231, 235, 236, 284, 289, 296, 297, 299, 300, 308, 314, 322, 325–6, 328, 330, 332, 339, 341, 345, 353, 368, 386–90, 421, 423, 427–8
Nguni (Natal), 12, 14, 85, 88, 100–2, 111, 116, 181, 197, 416, 422, 427–8
Ngutyana, 62
Ngwaketse, 75
Ngwane, 62, 64, 65, 362
Ngwato, 75, 173, 250, 268, 271, 284, 285, 295
Ngwe (Ngweni), 64
Nhlanganu, 69, 70, 71
Nhlangwini, 63, 229
Nibele, 65
Nkosi, 65, 66
Nkuna, 69, 71
Nogeng, 75
Nqabe, 62
Nthabalala, 80
Ntinde, 61
Ntombela, 65
Ntuli, 65
Ntungwa, 64, 65
Ntwane, 75
Nwalungu, 69

Nxamalala, 64
Nxumalo, 65
Nyai, 348
Nyambaan (Inhambane), 44; *see also* Tsonga
Nyamwezi (Tanzania), 41
Nyawo, 65
Nyawuza, 62
Nyoro, 41
Nyuswa, 64, 197, 198, 200, 201
Nzimakwe, 63

Pai, 65, 72, 78
Pedi, 44, 76–8, 86, 98–100, 104, 106, 113, 137, 147, 154, 158, 172, 173, 181, 182, 186, 187, 191, 193, 194, 201, 202, 203, 205, 213–15, 220–1, 223, 226, 227, 229, 230–4, 238–9, 241, 249, 263, 268–71, 276, 285, 297, 300, 308–9, 320–1, 323, 324, 326, 327, 328–9, 330, 331, 333–4, 337, 338, 339, 347–9, 351, 354–5, 385, 387, 417, 427–8
Phalane (Tlase), 75
Phaleng, 75
Phetla, 73
Phiring, 75
Phuthi, 73, 74
Phuthing, 73, 387
Pô, 75
Polane, 73
Pondo, *see* Mpondo
Pulana, 65, 66, 78

Qadi, 197, 198, 200
Qadini, 65
Qanyini, 64
Qhayi, 61
Qwabe, 65
Qwathi, 62

Rambuka, 81
Rapulane, 75
Rathsidi-Rolong, 75, 382
Ratlou-Rolong, 75
Rolong, 75, 76, 193, 416
Ronga, 15, 69, 356
Rozwi, 83

Sambio, 44
San (Bushmen), 3, 4, 13, 14, 15, 16, 17, 19, 21–2, 26–7, 32–4, 36, 37, 43, 126, 138, 215
Sarwa, *see* San
Sebitiêla (Moletlane), 67

TRIBAL INDEX

Seleka-Rolong, 67, 75
Shangana, 15, 68, 71
Shangana-Tsonga, 10, 12, 44, 229, 278
Shiba, 66
Shona, 61, 75, 384
Shongwe, 66
Sia, 73, 74
Singo, 80
Sithole, 65
Sotho (general), 4, 10, 12, 14, 22, 23, 44, 57, 65–9, 72, 73, 76, 79, 80–2, 86–7, 92, 100, 101, 104–10, 114, 120, 121, 123, 125, 127, 136, 142, 145, 147, 148, 153, 166, 178, 179, 181, 184, 185, 187, 192, 193, 195, 197, 198, 200–6, 208–9, 214, 250–2, 254, 255, 257, 263, 288, 290, 297, 319, 325, 327–8, 334, 337, 338–9, 342, 345, 348, 350–2, 355–7
Sotho (North), 57, 59, 70, 71, 74–8, 100–2, 106, 109–12, 116, 117, 119, 137, 148, 185, 231, 250, 264, 296, 416, 421
Sotho (South), 57–9, 72–4, 76, 77, 86–9, 92, 101–4, 110, 112, 113, 116–17, 119, 121, 122, 148, 156, 185, 186, 189, 191, 193, 194, 201–2, 213–16, 219, 221, 224, 229, 230, 232–5, 239, 241, 247, 266, 292, 296, 319–20, 323, 327, 328, 330–1, 332, 333, 334, 338, 347, 348–9, 350, 357, 379–81, 416, 421, 423
Sukati, 66
Swazi, 3, 4, 44, 59, 65, 66, 73, 78, 85, 87, 88, 91, 101, 104, 106–11, 115–16, 137, 151, 188, 189, 192, 201, 202, 205, 213, 215, 216, 219, 220, 225, 250, 264, 288, 291–2, 320, 324, 342, 355–6, 358, 384, 386, 416, 417, 428

Tau, 77
Taung, 73, 74, 75, 76
Tawana, 75, 295
Tembe-Tsonga, 65, 69, 70, 184, 196
Thembu, 62, 64, 65, 88, 101–3, 114, 116, 121, 189, 215, 228, 229, 231, 355, 387, 418
Thengwe, 81
Thenjini, 65
Thulini, 65
Tilharo, 75
Tlhabine (Bedi), 78
Tlhaping, 75, 76, 382, 418
Tlôkwa, 73, 74, 75, 77, 79, 81, 193, 229, 379, 428
Tolo, 62, 63
Tonga, 8, 9, 15, 21, 23, 24, 28, 44

Tonga (Plateau), 8, 9, 10, 28, 44
Tshakhuma, 81
Tshangase, 62
Tshwawa, 62
Tshwene, 77
Tsianka, 81
Tsonga, 52, 57, 59–61, 65, 68–71, 77–9, 81, 85, 87–90, 92–4, 98–111, 113, 114, 116, 119, 123, 126, 171, 189, 201, 208, 209, 214, 215, 217–19, 221, 223, 225–7, 229, 230, 231, 241, 306, 308, 320, 321, 327, 328, 332–4, 337, 342, 345, 346, 347, 348, 349, 350–2, 354–7, 416, 421
Tswa, 69
Tswana, 4, 43, 47, 52, 57, 58, 59, 70–7, 86–90, 92, 95, 96, 100, 102, 106, 108, 110, 112, 113, 114, 116, 118, 119, 126, 142, 144, 147, 148, 153, 160, 165, 173, 181, 185–7, 189, 192, 193, 197, 198, 200–2, 204, 205, 207, 208, 213, 218, 224, 228, 229, 231–5, 247, 250, 253, 254, 257, 258, 263, 264, 268, 272, 273, 288, 290–1, 293, 297, 300, 320, 323, 328, 330, 334, 345–7, 352–3, 381–2, 415, 421, 423, 426, 427

Valoyi, 69
Venda, 8, 9, 10, 12, 23, 44, 57–60, 69, 71, 73, 77–82, 86–90, 92, 94, 97, 99, 100–1, 104–14, 116–21, 123, 126, 148, 149, 159, 189, 191, 192, 193, 195, 202, 208, 213, 214, 216–23, 225, 226, 229–36, 239, 241, 250–1, 306, 319, 320–3, 325–6, 328, 330, 332–4, 337, 338, 342, 345–8, 350–2, 354, 356–7, 386, 416, 421
Vundla, 74

Wushe, 63

Xesibe, 63, 101, 215, 229
Xhosa, 3, 19, 27, 43, 58, 59–62, 75, 87, 88, 90, 101–8, 110–14, 116, 118, 120, 121, 148, 181, 189, 192, 214, 215, 221, 228–31, 235, 237–9, 308, 319, 320, 322, 326–9, 337–9, 342, 348–9, 351–2, 357, 359, 360, 363, 368–75, 399, 415, 417, 422, 429, 436–7, 447
Xigalo, 71
Xikundu, 71
Ximba, 65
Xolo, 63

Zikhali, 65
Zizi, 62, 63, 324
Zondi, 64

Zotsho, 63
Zulu, 3, 44, 57–9, 61, 63–6, 68, 70, 71, 73, 75, 85, 87, 89, 90, 98, 100–2, 104, 106–13, 118, 119, 141, 147, 150, 151, 156, 159, 163, 164, 181, 185, 187–91, 194, 197, 201, 204, 205, 213–16, 219, 223, 225–7, 229, 237, 241, 247–50, 252, 253, 258, 261, 279–82, 285, 290–1, 294, 303, 305–6, 314, 319, 321, 322–4, 326, 327, 328–9, 332, 337–9, 340, 342, 346, 348, 349–50, 352–7, 375, 377–9, 417, 429–30, 434–6
Zwane, 66